Wonders

Mc
Graw
Hill

Also Available from McGraw Hill

studysync®

TIME for KiDS

mheducation.com/prek-12

Mc Graw Hill

Send all inquiries to:
McGraw Hill
1325 Avenue of the Americas.
New York, NY 10019

ISBN: 978-1-26-574587-5
MHID: 1-26-574587-0

Printed in China

6 7 8 9 10 DSS 27 26 25 24 23

B

Welcome to *Wonders*

Designed to support teachers and empower students.

You want all your students to build knowledge while fostering exploration of our world through literacy. Literacy is the key to understanding — across time, across borders, across cultures — and will help students realize the role they play in the world they are creating.

The result: an evidence-based K–5 ELA program, aligned with standards and based on the Science of Reading, that empowers students to take an active role in learning and exploration. Your students will enjoy unparalleled opportunities for student-friendly self-assessments and self-expression through reading, writing, and speaking. By experiencing diverse perspectives and sharing their own, students will expand their learning. Best-in-class differentiation ensures that all your students have opportunities to become strong readers, writers, and critical thinkers.

We're excited for you to get to know *Wonders* and honored to join you and your students on your pathways to success!

Authors
and Consultants

With unmatched expertise in English Language Arts, supporting English language learners, intervention, and more, the *Wonders* team of authors is composed of scholars, researchers, and teachers from across the country. From managing ELA research centers, to creating evidence-based classroom practices for teachers, this highly qualified team of professionals is fully invested in improving student and district outcomes.

Authors

Dr. Douglas Fisher
Close Reading and Writing,
Writing to Sources,
Text Complexity

Dr. Diane August
English Language Learners,
Dual Language

Kathy Bumgardner
Instructional Best Practices,
Multi-Sensory Teaching,
Student Engagement

Dr. Vicki Gibson
Small Group Instruction,
Social Emotional Learning,
Foundational Skills

Dr. Josefina V. Tinajero
English Language Learners,
Dual Language

Dr. Timothy Shanahan
Text Complexity,
Reading and Writing,
Oral Reading Fluency,
Close Reading,
Disciplinary Literacy

Dr. Donald Bear
Word Study, Vocabulary,
Foundational Skills

Dr. Jana Echevarria
English Language Learners,
Oral Language Development

Dr. Jan Hasbrouck
Oral Reading Fluency,
Foundational Skills,
Response to Intervention

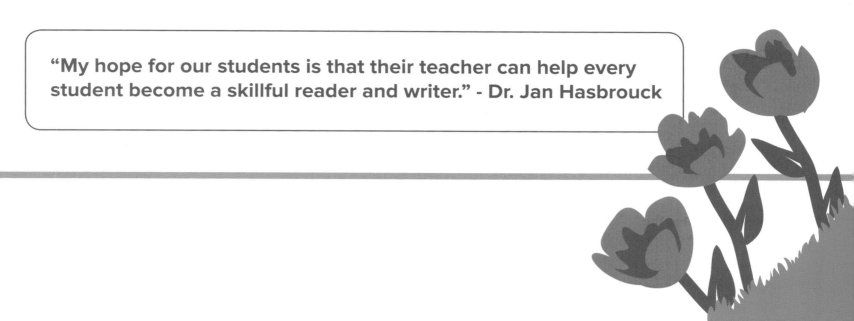

"My hope for our students is that their teacher can help every student become a skillful reader and writer." - Dr. Jan Hasbrouck

Consultants

Dr. Doris Walker-Dalhouse
Multicultural Literature

Dr. David J. Francis
Assessment, English Language
Learners Research

Jay McTighe
Understanding by Design

Dr. Tracy Spinrad
Social Emotional Learning

Dinah Zike
Professional Development,
Multi-Sensory Teaching

"My hope for our students including English Learners, is that they will receive outstanding English language arts and reading instruction to allow them to reach their full academic potential and excel in school and in life." - Dr. Josefina V. Tinajero

Developing **Student Ownership** of Learning

| Reflect on What You Know | Monitor Learning | Choose Learning Resources | Reflect on Progress | Set Learning Goals |

The instructional routines in *Wonders* guide students to understand the importance of taking ownership of their own learning. The **Reading/Writing Companion** Welcome pages introduce students to routines they will be using throughout the year.

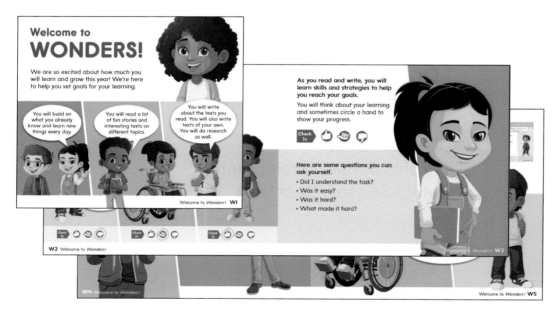

AUTHOR INSIGHT

Learning how to identify what they are learning, talk about what they know, figure out what they need more help with, and figure out next steps are all important aspects of taking ownership of learning that students develop in *Wonders*.

- Dr. Douglas Fisher

Reflect on What You Know

Text Set Goals

Students are introduced to three overarching goals for each text set. Students first evaluate what they know before instruction begins.

Reading and Writing

Students evaluate what they know about reading in a particular genre and writing in response to texts using text evidence.

Build Knowledge Goals

Each text set is focused on building knowledge through investigation of an Essential Question. After an introduction to the Essential Question, students self-evaluate how much they already know about the topic.

Extended Writing Goals

Students also think about their ability to write in a particular genre before instruction begins.

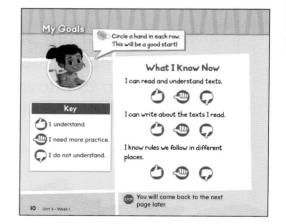

Courtesy of Douglas Fisher

Monitor Learning

Lesson Learning Goals

The journey through a text set and extended writing is made up of a sequence of lessons. The learning goals of these lessons build toward achieving the overarching goals. At the start of each lesson, a targeted learning goal, presented as a "We Can" statement, is introduced to students.

The learning goals are shared with students and parents so that they can track their learning as they work through the lessons.

Check-In Routine

At the end of each lesson, students are asked to self-assess how well they understood the lesson learning goal.

At the end of the lesson, students conference with a partner. They review the lesson learning goal "We Can" statement.

Review

CHECK-IN ROUTINE

Review the lesson learning goal.
Reflect on the activity.
Self-Assess by
- circling the hands in the Reading/Writing Companion
- showing thumbs up, sideways, or down.

Share with your teacher.

Share

Students share their self-assessments with you by showing thumbs up, sideways, or down and sharing the circled hands. This lets you know how students think they are doing.

TEACHING TIP

Valuing students' self-assessments is important to enabling students to take ownership of their learning. As students progress throughout the year, they become more adept at self-assessing what they know and what help they need moving forward.

Reflect

Students take turns self-reflecting on how well they understood the learning goal.

TEACHING TIP

As students develop their ability to reflect on their work, provide sentence frames to support them.

Ask yourself:

Can I _____?

Respond:

I can almost _____.

I am having trouble_____.

I need to work on _____.

Self Assess

Students show thumbs up, sideways, or down to self-assess how well they understood the learning goal. When appropriate, they will circle the hands in the Reading/Writing Companion as well. At the start of the year, review the ratings with students emphasizing that we all learn differently and at a different pace. It is okay to score a thumbs down or a sideways thumb. Understanding what they do not know will help students figure out what to do next.

TEACHING TIP

👍 I understand the learning goal.

✊ I understand how to do the lesson, but I need more practice.

👎 I did not understand the learning goal.

Developing Student Ownership of Learning

Reflect on What You Know	Monitor Learning	Choose Learning Resources	Reflect on Progress	Set Learning Goals

Choose Learning Resources

Student-Teacher Conferencing

As students evaluate what they understand, the next step is to think about whether they need more teaching or more practice. The **Reading/Writing Companion** can serve as a powerful conferencing tool. Reviewing their circled hands while conferring with each student provides you the opportunity to guide students into identifying what they should do next to improve their understanding.

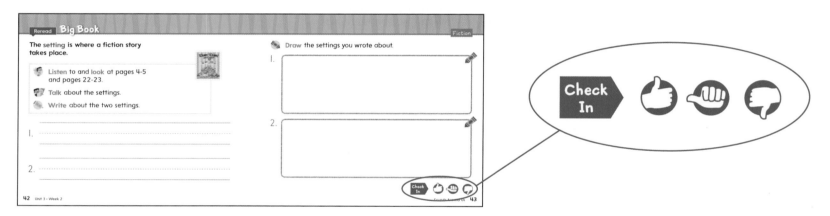

Small Group Teacher-Led Instruction

You and the student may decide that they need more teaching. Student Check-Ins and your observations at the end of each lesson provide timely data that informs the focus for teacher-led small group instruction. Teachers can choose from the small group differentiated lessons provided.

Small Group Independent/Collaborative Work

While you are meeting with small groups, other students can practice the skills and concepts they have determined they need practice with.

My Weekly Work lists options for collaborative and independent practice. Based on student input and your informal observations, you identify "Must Do" activities to be completed. Students then choose activities focused on areas of need and interests they have identified—promoting student choice and voice.

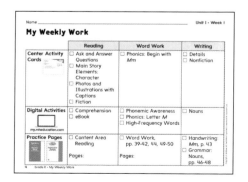

Reflect on Progress

After completing the lessons in the text set and extended writing, students reflect on their overall progress. They share this information during teacher conferences. The focus of the conversations is on progress made and figuring out next steps to continued progress.

TEACHING TIP

As students discuss their progress, ask them to reflect on the following:

- In what areas did you feel that you made a lot of progress?
- What are some examples?
- What areas do you still need to work on?
- What things can you do to make more progress in these areas?

Set Learning Goals

At the end of the unit, students continue to reflect on their learning. They are also asked to set their own learning goals as they move into the next unit of instruction.

See additional guidance online for supporting students in evaluating work, working toward meeting learning goals, and reflecting on progress.

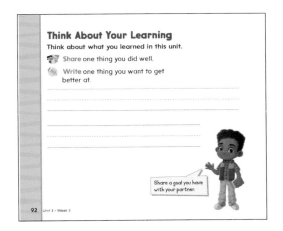

Equity and Access

Differentiated Resources

Every student deserves high-quality instruction. *Wonders* provides high-quality, rigorous instruction that supports access to grade-level content and ELA skills through equitable, differentiated instruction and resources.

Scaffolded Instruction

Gradual Release Model of Instruction Explicit skills lessons start with teacher explanation and modeling, then move to guided and collaborative practice, then culminate with independent practice with the Your Turn activities.

Access Complex Text The complex features of texts students are asked to read are highlighted. Point-of-use scaffolds are provided to help students to attend to those complex aspects of the text.

Data Informed Instruction *Wonders* offers frequent opportunities for informal and formative assessment. The student Check-Ins and teacher Check for Success features provide daily input allowing adjustments for instruction and student practice. The Data Dashboard collects data from online games and activities and the Progress Monitoring assessments.

Differentiated Small Group Time

Teacher-Led Instruction Key skills and concepts are supported with explicit differentiated lessons. The Differentiated Genre Passages and Leveled Readers provide a variety of differentiated texts. Literature Small group lessons guide teachers in scaffolding support so all students have access to the same text.

Tier 2 instruction is incorporated into the Approaching level lessons. Additional Tier 2 instruction is available online.

Gifted and Talented activities are also provided for those students who are ready to extend their learning.

Independent/Collaborative Work

A range of choices for practice and extension are provided to support the key skills and concepts taught. Students use this time to work on their independent reading and writing. Resources include the Center Activity Cards, online games, Practice Book, and Content Area Reading blackline masters.

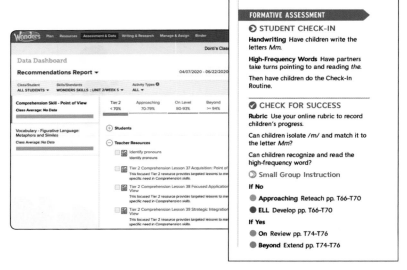

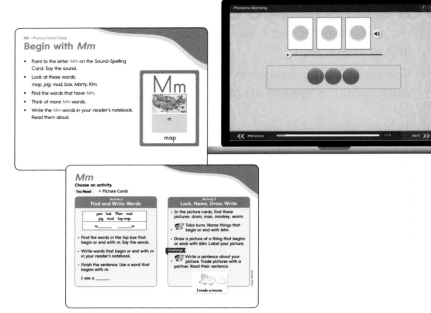

ELL English Language Learners

Access to Grade Level Lessons

English Language Proficiency Levels Targeted support addressing the different English Language Proficiency Levels allows all students to participate.

Spotlight on Language

Point-of-use support that highlights English phrases and vocabulary that may be particularly difficult for English Language Learners.

Multilingual Resources

Home Language Support

The following features are available in Spanish, Haitian-Creole, Portuguese, Vietnamese, French, Arabic, Chinese, Russian, Tagalog, and Urdu:

- Summaries of the Shared Read and Anchor Texts.
- School–to-Home Letters that help families support students in their learning goals.
- Multilingual Glossary of key content words with definitions from grade-level texts.
- Spanish and Haitian-Creole Leveled Readers available online.

> **ELL ENGLISH LANGUAGE LEARNERS**
>
> Use the following scaffolds with **Respond to the Text**.
>
> **Beginning**
> Point to the photos. Ask: *What can the boy see?* Help partners name items in the image and help them answer using a sentence frame.
>
> **Intermediate**
> Provide a model: The boy can see the mop. Have partners point to the image and describe using: The boy can see the mop.
>
> **Advanced**
> Have partners name all the things the boy can see. Have them use complete sentences while speaking and point to the rebuses to show evidence.

Strategic Support

A separate resource is available for small group instruction focused specifically on English Language Learners. The lessons are carefully designed to support the language development, grade level skills, and content. The instruction and resources are differentiated to address all levels of English Language Proficiency and carefully align with the instruction in Reading and Writing.

Additional Resources for Differentiation

Newcomer Kit Instructional cards and practice focused on access to basic, high-utility vocabulary.

Language Development Kit Differentiated instruction and practice for key English grammar concepts.

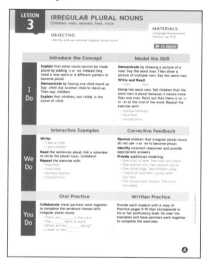

Collection of Diverse Literature

The literature in *Wonders* provides a diverse representation of various individuals and cultures. The texts give students the opportunity to see themselves and others within and outside of their communities. As students read, listen to, discuss, and write about texts, they are able to make real-life connections to themselves and the world around them.

Culturally Responsive Teaching

Drawing from the research, there are a number of factors that support classroom equity and enable the underpinnings of culturally responsive teaching: high academic expectations for all students; a socially and emotionally positive classroom; a safe school climate; authentic and rigorous tasks; inclusive, relevant, and meaningful content; open and accepting communication; drawing from students' strengths, knowledge, culture, and competence; critically and socially aware inquiry practices; strong teaching; and school staff professional support and learning about equity and inclusion (Aronson & Laughter, 2016; Gay, 2010; Krasnoff, 2016; Ladson-Billings, 2006; Morrison, Robbins, & Rose, 2008; NYSED, 2019; Saphier, 2017; Snyder, Trowery & McGrath, 2019; Waddell, 2014). It is important to note the emphasis on developing classrooms and instructional practices that support all students, rather than focusing solely on who the students are and what they bring to school.

Through the high-quality content and research-based best practices of the instructional routines embedded in the program, the *Wonders* curriculum supports all important aspects of culturally responsive teaching.

The Learning Community: providing avenues for the development of a classroom community grounded in collaboration, risk-taking, responsibility, perseverance, and communication. This allows all learners to find a pathway to deep learning and academic success.

Wonders promotes classroom practices that best support meaningful learning and collaboration among peers. Valuing students' voices on what they think about the world around them and what they know allows teachers to build on students' funds of knowledge and adapt instruction and application opportunities. Starting in Kindergarten and progressing through the grades, students develop their ability to engage in focused academic discussions, assisting each other in deep understanding of the texts they read and building knowledge on various topics.

Authentic and Rigorous Learning Tasks: providing multiple methods to learn new material, challenging content for all levels of learners, opportunities to discuss, grapple with, and critique ideas, and space to personally connect to the content. This allows all learners to develop enthusiasm and dedication in their academic endeavors.

In *Wonders*, many of the texts center on relevant issues, examples, and real-world problems, along with prompts and questions that encourage students to engage and think critically about how they would address a similar problem or issue. The Essential Question for each text set introduces the topic that will be explored, culminating in a Show Your Knowledge activity. This allows students to synthesize information they learned analyzing all the texts. Extended writing tasks allow additional opportunities for flexible connections, elaboration of student thinking, and original expression.

Differentiation Opportunities: providing instructional pathways to meet the individual needs of all learners, which creates a more equitable learning experience.

In *Wonders*, clarity around differentiation of instruction, flexibility, adaptability, and choice are some of the key guiding principles on which the resources have been built. In addition to providing a range of differentiated leveled texts, *Wonders* is designed to ensure all students have access to rich, authentic grade-level informational and literary texts. A variety of print and digital resources are provided as options for differentiating practice opportunities.

FatCamera/E+/Getty Images

Evidence of Learning: providing continuous opportunities to gather information about each learner's academic progress through a variety of assessment methods. This allows for timely feedback to learners and supports differentiation for meeting the needs of all learners.

In *Wonders*, students' self-evaluation of their own learning and progress over time is integral to student success. Student Check-In Routines assist students in documenting how well they understand leaning goals and encourage them to reflect on what may have been difficult to understand. Resources such as the Learning Goals Blackline Masters and features in the Reading/Writing Companion assist students in monitoring their progress. Teachers use the results of the Student Check-Ins and their informal observations of students with the Check for Success features in the Teacher's Edition to inform decisions about small group differentiated instruction. A range of innovative tools equip the teacher for assessment-informed instructional decision making, and ensure students are equipped to fully participate in responsive, engaging instruction. This Data Dashboard uses student results from assessments and activities to provide instructional recommendations tailored to the individual needs.

Relevant, Respectful, and Meaningful Content: providing content that represents the lives and experiences of a range of individuals who belong to different racial, ethnic, religious, age, gender, linguistic, socio-economic, and ability groups in equitable, positive, and non-stereotypical ways. This allows all learners to see themselves reflected in the content they are learning.

In *Wonders*, resources have been created and curated to promote literacy and deepen understanding for every student. A commitment to multicultural education and our nation's diverse population is evident in the literature selections and themes found throughout every grade. *Wonders* depicts people from various ethnic backgrounds in all types of environments, avoiding stereotypes. Students of all backgrounds will be able to relate to the texts. The authors of the texts in *Wonders* are also diverse and represent a rich range of backgrounds and cultures, which they bring to their writing.

Supporting Family Communication: providing open communication avenues for families by developing regular and varied interactions about program content. This provides opportunities for all families to be involved in the academic progress of their learner.

In *Wonders*, the School to Home tab on the ConnectEd Student Workspace provides information to families about what students are learning. The letters introduce the Essential Questions that the students will be investigating in each text set, as well as the key skills and skills. Activities that families can complete with students at home are provided. Access to texts that students are reading is also available through the Student Workspace. Home-to-school letters and audio summaries of student texts are available in multiple languages, including English, Spanish, Haitian-Creole, Portuguese, Vietnamese, French, Arabic, Chinese (Cantonese and Mandarin), Russian, Tagalog, and Urdu.

Professional Learning: providing instructional guidance for administrators and teachers that supports enacting culturally responsive and sustaining pedagogical practices and focuses on asset-based approaches, bias surfacing, cultural awareness, and connections to learner communities, cultures, and resources.

In *Wonders*, a comprehensive set of resources assists administrators and teachers in a successful implementation of the program to ensure teacher and student success. Information embedded in the Teacher's Edition, and targeted components such as the Instructional Routines Handbook, as well as online Professional Learning videos and resources, provide a wide range of support. Resources focused on helping teachers reflect on their understanding of the different cultures of their students, as well as assisting teachers in facilitating meaningful conversations about texts, are also provided.

Teaching the
Whole Child

Your students are learning so much more than reading from you. They're learning how to learn, how to master new content areas, and how to handle themselves in and out of the classroom. Research shows that this leads to increased academic success. *Wonders* resources have been developed to support you in teaching the whole child, for success this year and throughout your students' lives.

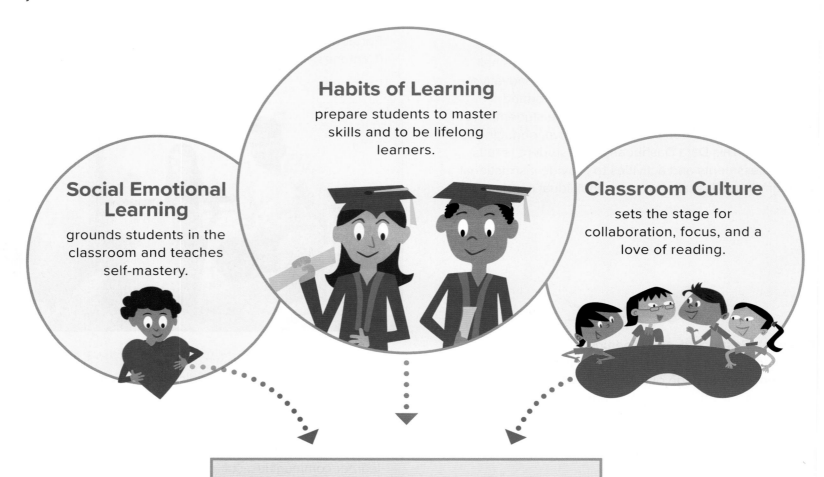

Habits of Learning prepare students to master skills and to be lifelong learners.

Social Emotional Learning grounds students in the classroom and teaches self-mastery.

Classroom Culture sets the stage for collaboration, focus, and a love of reading.

DEVELOPING CRITICAL THINKERS

- Mastery of reading, writing, speaking, and listening
- Knowledge that spans content areas
- College and career readiness
- Strong results this year and beyond

Habits of Learning

I am part of a community of learners.

☐ I listen actively to others to learn new ideas.
☐ I build upon others' ideas in a conversation.
☐ I work with others to understand my learning goals.
☐ I stay on topic during discussion.
☐ I use words that will make my ideas clear.
☐ I share what I know.
☐ I gather information to support my thinking.

I use a variety of strategies when I read.

☐ I make predictions.
☐ I take notes.
☐ I think about how a text is organized.
☐ I visualize what I'm reading.
☐ I think about the author's purpose.

I think critically about what I read.

☐ I ask questions.
☐ I look for text evidence.
☐ I make inferences based on evidence.
☐ I connect new ideas to what I already know.

I write to communicate.

☐ I think about what I read as models for my writing.
☐ I talk with my peers to help make my writing better.
☐ I use rubrics to analyze my own writing.
☐ I use different tools when I write and present.

I believe I can succeed.

☐ I try different ways to learn things that are difficult for me.
☐ I ask for help when I need it.
☐ I challenge myself to do better.
☐ I work to complete my tasks.
☐ I read independently.

I am a problem solver.

☐ I analyze the problem.
☐ I try different ways.

Classroom Culture

We respect and value each other's experiences.

☐ We value what each of us brings from home.
☐ We work together to understand each other's perspectives.
☐ We work with our peers in pairs and in small groups.
☐ We use new academic vocabulary we learn when we speak and write.
☐ We share our work and learn from others.

We promote student ownership of learning.

☐ We understand what our learning goals are.
☐ We evaluate how well we understand each learning goal.
☐ We find different ways to learn what is difficult.

We learn through modeling and practice.

☐ We practice together to make sure we understand.
☐ We access many different resources to get information.
☐ We use many different tools when we share what we learn.

We foster a love of reading.

☐ We create inviting places to sit and read.
☐ We read for enjoyment.
☐ We read to understand ourselves and our world.

We build knowledge.

☐ We investigate what we want to know more about.
☐ We read many different types of texts to gain information.
☐ We build on what we know.

We inspire confident writers.

☐ We analyze the connection between reading and writing.
☐ We understand the purpose and audience for our writing.
☐ We revise our writing to make it stronger.

Social EMOTIONAL Learning

Positive social emotional learning **(SEL) gives young learners the critical foundation to experience success in school and life** with understanding, flexibility, support, and resiliency. Research shows that children's ability to regulate their own emotions and behaviors affects their ability to build and maintain relationships with others, which in turn has a direct impact on their academic success.

The SEL Curriculum

We are proud to partner with Sesame Workshop to provide an integrated approach to SEL skills within the *Wonders* curriculum. Key SEL foundations are sequenced through three interrelated strands:

- **Approaches to learning:** The skills and behaviors that children use to engage in learning.
- **Social and emotional development:** The experiences, expressions, and management of emotions, as well as the ability to establish positive and rewarding relationships with others.
- **Executive function and self-regulation skills:** Cognitive processes that enable us to plan, focus attention, remember instructions, and attend to tasks successfully. Self-regulation and executive function skills help children learn how to learn!

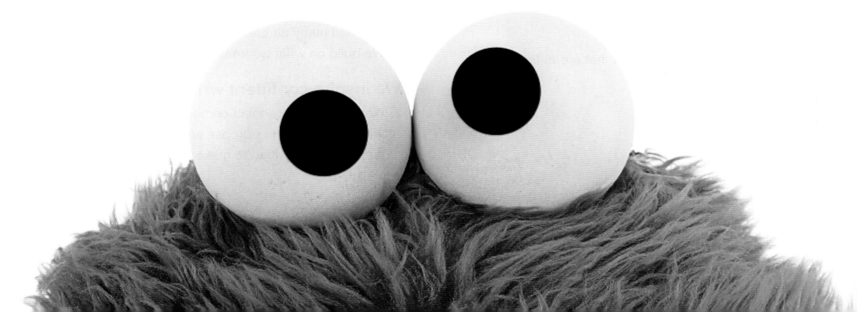

The SEL Lesson Plan

Each SEL lesson is built on active engagement, carefully **crafted to bolster each week's targeted literacy skills.** Through the research-based Sesame Workshop media and engaging learning experiences, we offer strategies for rich teacher/child interactions that are developmentally appropriate and, of course, joyful!

Child-Centered Media
Each resource has been carefully selected to support a specific SEL competency. Additional instruction helps guide learning before and after viewing.

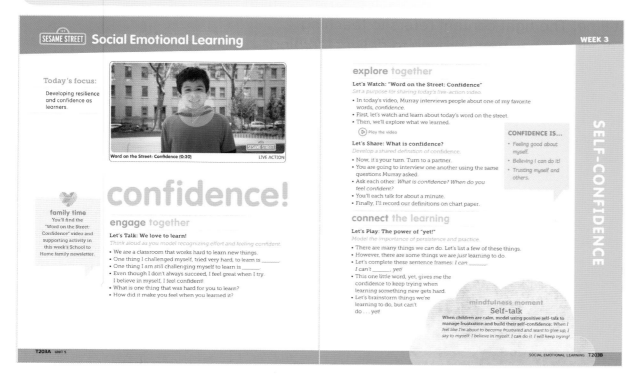

Engage Together
Active learning that bridges children's prior knowledge and skills to the new concept.

Explore Together
A "view and do" experience that combines a media-based investigation with collaborative learning.

Connect the Learning
Language-rich interactions that transfer children's developing understandings to everyday moments and learning at home.

Family Time

Research highlights a consistent relationship between family engagement and student achievement. We engage families in their children's education and development through a powerful home-school partnership that strengthens SEL skills through enriching media and hands-on learning experiences each week.

About Sesame Workshop

Sesame Workshop is the nonprofit media and educational organization behind *Sesame Street*, *The Electric Company*, and much more. Since 1969, our programs have helped kids everywhere grow smarter, stronger, and kinder. Today, Sesame Workshop is an innovative force for change, serving vulnerable children in 150+ countries with media, philanthropically-funded social impact initiatives, and formal education programs, all grounded in rigorous research. Visit www.sesameworkshop.org to learn more.

Wonders and the Science of Reading

Dr. Timothy Shanahan

Wonders supports the delivery of high-quality literacy instruction aligned to the science of reading. It provides a comprehensive, integrated plan for meeting the needs of all students. Carefully monitoring advances in literacy research, the program is developed to ensure that lessons focus on teaching the right content at the right time. The right content refers to teaching sufficient amounts of the content that has been proven to deliver learning advantages to students. The right time refers to a carefully structured scope and sequence within a grade and across grades. This ensures that teaching is presented in the most effective and efficient manner, with sound guidance to better support diverse learners.

Foundational Skills

English is an alphabetic language; developing readers must learn to translate letters and spelling patterns to sounds and pronunciations, and to read text accurately, automatically, and with proper expression. When students learn to manage these foundational skills with a minimum of conscious attention, they will have the cognitive resources available to comprehend what they read.

Research shows that the explicit teaching of phonemic awareness, phonics, and text reading fluency are the most successful ways to succeed in foundational skills. *Wonders* presents a sequence of research-aligned learning activities in its grade-level placements, sequences of instruction, and instructional guidance across the following areas:

- Phonemic Awareness
- Phonics/Decoding
- Text Reading Fluency

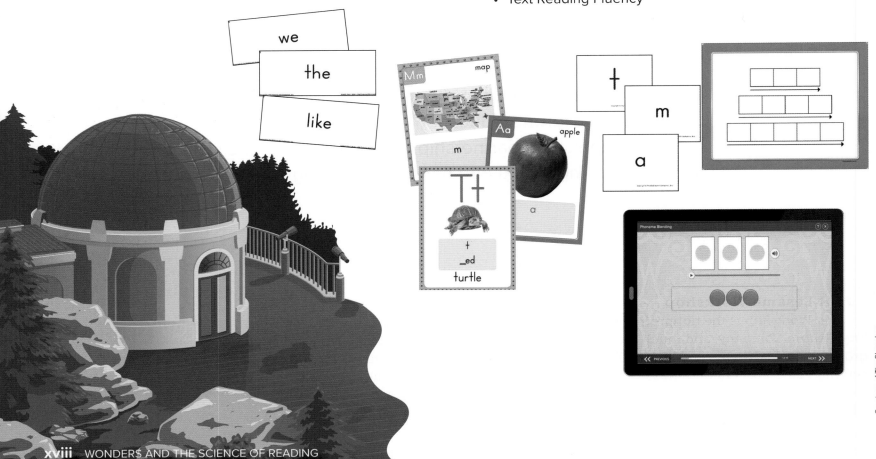

Reading Comprehension

Reading comprehension requires that students extract and construct meaning from text. To comprehend, students must learn to apply the prior knowledge they bring to the text to the information expressed through written language in the text. To accomplish this successfully, readers must do three things. They must:

- expand their knowledge through the reading of high-quality informative texts;
- learn to negotiate increasingly sophisticated and complex written language;
- develop the cognitive abilities to manage and monitor these processes.

Wonders provides lessons built around a high-quality collection of complex literary and informational texts, focused on both the natural and social worlds. Teachers using *Wonders* will find explicit, research-based lessons in vocabulary and other language skills, guidance for high-level, high-quality discussions, and well-designed lessons aimed at building the executive processes that can shift reading comprehension into high gear, including:

- Building Knowledge/Using Knowledge
- Vocabulary and other aspects of written language
- Text complexity
- Executive processes and comprehension strategies

Writing

In the 21st century, it is not enough to be able to read, understand, and learn from the writing of others. Being able to communicate one's own ideas logically and effectively is necessary, too. As with reading, writing includes foundational skills (like spelling and handwriting), as well as higher-order abilities (composition and communication) and the executive processes required to manage the accomplishment of successful writing. Research shows that reading and writing strengthen one another. Focusing writing instruction in the following areas will help students improve their reading:

- Writing foundations
- Quality writing for multiple purposes
- The writing processes
- Writing to enhance reading

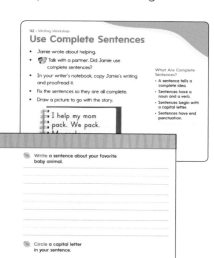

Quality of Instruction

The science of reading is dependent upon the sciences of teaching and learning, as well as on reading research. Reading research has identified specific best practices for teaching particular aspects of literacy. However, research has also revealed other important features of quality instruction that have implications for all learners and that may better support certain student populations. *Wonders* lessons reflect these quality issues in teaching:

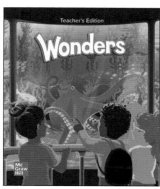

- Lessons with explicit and appropriate purposes
- High-challenge levels
- Appropriate opportunities for review
- Quality discussions promoted by high DOK-level questions
- Ongoing monitoring of learning
- Supports for English language learners
- Connections to social emotional learning

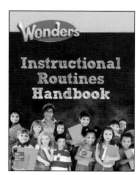

Build Critical Readers, Writers, Communicators, and Thinkers

READING

Build Knowledge Through a Text Set

- **Investigate** an Essential Question.
- **Read** a variety of texts.
- **Closely read** texts for deeper meaning.
- **Respond** to texts using text evidence.
- **Conduct** research.
- **Share** your knowledge.
- **Inspire** action.

WRITING

Communicate Effectively Through Writing

- **Analyze** mentor texts and student models.
- **Understand** purpose and audience.
- **Plan** writing, using sources as needed.
- **Conference** with peers and teachers.
- **Evaluate** work against a rubric.
- **Improve** writing continuously.
- **Share** your writing.

LISTENING

SPEAKING

COLLABORATING

SMALL GROUP

EXTEND   CONNECT

ASSESS

Instruction Aligned to the **Science of Reading**

Reading

Explicit instruction supports students in building knowledge.

- Foundational Reading Skills
  - Phonics/Word Analysis
  - Fluency
- Reading Literature
- Reading Informational Texts
- Comparing Texts
- Vocabulary
- Researching

Writing

Skills-based minilessons support students in developing their writing.

- Writing
  - Narrative
  - Argumentative
  - Expository
- Handwriting
- Speaking and Listening
- Conventions
- Creating and Collaborating

Differentiation

Differentiate resources, instruction, and level of scaffolds.

Small Group Teacher-Led Instruction

- Choose from small group skills lesson options to target instruction to meet students' needs.
- Read texts with scaffolded support.

Independent/Collaborative Work

- Students transfer knowledge of skills to independent reading and practice.
- Students transfer skills to their writing.

Extend, Connect, and Assess

At the end of the unit, students transfer and apply knowledge gained to new contexts.

Demonstrate Understanding

- Extend knowledge through online reading.
- Connect ELA skills to content area reading with science and social studies texts.
- Assess learning with program assessments.

Grade K
Resources

The resources in *Wonders* support skills mastery, differentiated instruction, and the transfer and application of knowledge to new contexts. Teachers will find ways to enhance student learning and ownership through multimodal supports, a strong focus on foundational skills, opportunities to build knowledge, and fostering of expression through writing. All of your *Wonders*-created print resources are available digitally to support a variety of learning environments. The resources shown represent the key instructional elements of your *Wonders* classroom and are a portion of the supports available to you and your students. Login to your **Teacher Workspace** to explore multimedia resources, professional learning, and thousands of resources to meet your students where they are.

Component		Differentiate	Extend, Connect, Assess	Available Digitally
Teacher's Edition		●	●	●
Reading/Writing Companion			●	●
Literature Big Books				●
Classroom Library		●		
Classroom Library Lessons		●		●

TRUCK by Donald Crews. Used by permission of HarperCollins Publishers.

Component	Differentiate	Extend, Connect, Assess	Available Digitally
Leveled Readers & Lesson Cards	●	●	●
Center Activity Cards	●	●	●
ELL Small Group Guide	●		●
Data Dashboard	●	●	●
Unit Assessment		●	●
Benchmark Assessments		●	●
Practice Book Blackline Masters		●	●
Foundational Skills Resources: multimodal manipulatives, cards, activities, and games to build key skills	●	●	●
Skills-Based Online Games	●	●	●
Content Area Reading Blackline Masters		●	●

Professional Learning
Every Step of the Way

Get Started Using *Wonders*. Every day of instruction is based on evidence-based classroom best practices, which are embedded into the daily routines to strengthen your teaching and enhance students' learning. Throughout *Wonders*, you'll find support for employing these new routines and making the most of your literacy block.

Use this checklist to access support resources to help you get started with *Wonders* during the first weeks of school. Then refer to this list during the year for ongoing implementation support and to get the most from *Wonders*.

Beginning the Year

We encourage you to review these resources before the first day of school and then use them to support your first weeks of instruction.

In Your Teacher's Edition: Support pages for planning and teaching are embedded throughout your Teacher's Edition to support your big-picture understanding and help you teach effectively.

- ☐ **StartSmart:** In Unit 1 of your Teacher's Edition, the first three weeks of instruction are the StartSmart weeks. They will introduce you to your instructional routines with on-page supports and guide you through placement testing to get ready for small group lessons.
- ☐ **Text Set Support:** Each text set is accompanied by an introduction that supports your understanding of the content and simplifies instructional planning. These pages include a daily planner, differentiated learning support, guidance for developing student ownership and building knowledge, and more.
- ☐ **Progress Monitoring and Assessment:** Use data to track progress toward mastery of skills-based content, lesson objectives, and student goals.
  The **My Goals Routine** supports continuous self-monitoring and student feedback.

Online Resources: The digital Teacher Dashboard is your access point for key resources to get you up and running with *Wonders*. From the Teacher Dashboard, select *Resources > Professional Development > Overview*

- ☐ ***Wonders* Basics Module:** Set up your classroom, get to know your materials, learn about the structure of *Wonders*, and receive support for placement testing and grouping students for small group learning.
  - ▶ Select *Learn to Use Wonders*
- ☐ **Placement and Diagnostic Assessment:** Access assessments, testing instructions, and placement charts that can be used at the beginning of the year to assess and place students in small groups.
  - ▶ Select *Assessment & Data*

Ongoing Support

Your online **Teacher Workspace** also includes a wide range of additional resources. Use them throughout the year for ongoing support and professional learning. From the Teacher Dashboard, select *Resources > Professional Development*

☐ **Instructional Routines Handbook:** Reference this handbook throughout the year for support implementing the *Wonders* evidence-based routines and understanding the research behind them, and for guidance on what student success looks like.
  ▶ Select *Overview > Instructional Routines*

☐ **Small Group Differentiated Learning Guide:** Use the first few weeks of small group time to teach and model routines and establish small group rules and procedures.
  ▶ Select *Overview > Instructional Routines > Managing Small Groups: A How-to Guide PDF*

☐ **Suggested Lesson Plans and Pacing Guides:** Adjust your instruction to your literacy block and meet the needs of your classroom with flexible lesson plans and pacing.
  ▶ Select *Overview > Instructional Routines*

☐ **Classroom Videos:** Watch *Wonders* teachers model classroom lessons in reading, writing, collaboration, and teaching English language learners.
  ▶ Select *Classroom Videos*

☐ **Small Group Classroom Videos:** Watch *Wonders* teachers model small group instruction and share tips and strategies for effective differentiated lessons.
  ▶ Select *Classroom Videos > Small Group Instruction*

☐ **Author & Coach Videos:** Watch Dr. Douglas Fisher, Dr. Timothy Shanahan, and other *Wonders* authors as they provide short explanations of best practices and classroom coaching. Also provided are videos from Dr. Sheldon Eakins, founder of the Leading Equity Center, that focus on important aspects of educational equity and cultural responsive teaching.
  ▶ Select *Author & Coach Videos*

☐ **Assessment Handbook:** Review your assessment options and find support for managing multiple assessments, interpreting their results, and using data to inform your instructional planning.
  ▶ Select *Overview > Assessment & Data*

☐ **Assessment & Data Guides:** Review your assessment resources and get to know your reporting tools.
  ▶ Select *Overview > Assessment & Data*

☐ **Digital Help:** Access video tutorials and printable PDFs to support planning, assessment, writing and research, assignments, and connecting school to home.
  ▶ Select *Digital Help*

Explore the Professional Development section in your Teacher Workspace for more videos, resources, and printable guides. Select *Resources > Professional Development*

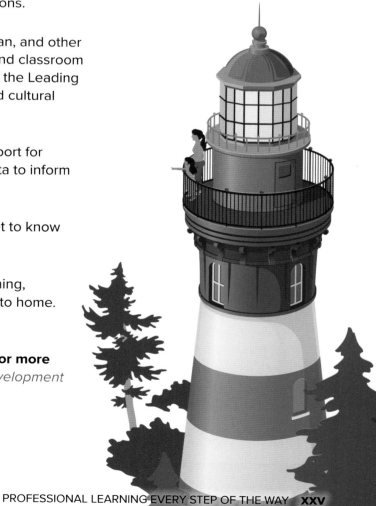

Notes

UNIT 5
READING/WRITING

WEEK 1

Essential Question

What do living things need to grow?

WEEK 2

Essential Question

How do living things change as they grow?

WEEK 3

Essential Question

What kinds of things grow on a farm?

Classroom Library Books

UNIT 5

Contents

UNIT 5

Unit Overview

English Language Arts is not a discrete set of skills. Skills work together to help children analyze the meaningful texts. In *Wonders*, skills are not taught in isolation, rather they are purposefully combined to support student learning of texts they read.

Week 1	Week 2	Week 3
Essential Question: What do living things need to grow?	**Essential Question:** How do living things change as they grow?	**Essential Question:** What kinds of things grow on a farm?

Reading

Week 1

Print Concepts
Locate Printed Word
Parts of a Book

Phonological Awareness
✓ Count and Blend Syllables
✓ Phoneme Blending/Categorization
Phoneme Isolation

Phonics and Word Analysis
/h/h

Fluency
✓ High-Frequency Words

Reading Literature
✓ Character, Setting, Events
Retell

Reading Poetry
Rhyme and Repetition

Vocabulary
Academic Vocabulary
Category Words

Researching
Parts of a Plant

Week 2

Print Concepts
Parts of a Book
Left to Right/Top to Bottom

Phonological Awareness
Onset Rime and Blending
✓ Phoneme Blending
Phoneme Segmentation
Phoneme Isolation

Phonics and Word Analysis
✓ Short e

Fluency
✓ High-Frequency Words

Reading Informational Text
✓ Topic and Details
Retell
Text Feature: Diagrams

Vocabulary
Academic Vocabulary
Category Words

Researching
How a Tree Changes as It Grows

Week 3

Print Concepts
Match Speech to Print
Parts of a Book

Phonological Awareness
Identify Rhyme
Phoneme Isolation
Phoneme Addition
✓ Phoneme Blending

Phonics and Word Analysis
✓ /f/f, /r/r

Fluency
✓ High-Frequency Words

Reading Informational Text
✓ Topic and Details
Retell
Text Feature: Lists

Vocabulary
Academic Vocabulary
✓ Category Words

Researching
A Fruit or Vegetable Grown on a Farm

Writing

Writing
Handwriting
Opinion Writing
Improving Writing: Writing Process

Conventions
Grammar: Subjective Pronouns

Writing
Handwriting
Opinion Writing
Improving Writing: Writing Process

Conventions
Grammar: Subjective Pronouns

Writing
Handwriting
Expository Writing
Improving Writing: Writing Process

Conventions
Grammar: Subjective Pronouns

Key

Key Skills Trace

Print Concepts/Phonological Awareness

The Print Concepts and Phonological Awareness standards are taught throughout the text sets of each unit.

Phonics and Word Analysis

Consonants

Introduce: Unit 1 Week 1, Week 3; Unit 2 Week 1, Week 2; Unit 3 Week 1, Week 2, Week 3; Unit 4 Week 2; Unit 5 Week 1, Week 3; Unit 6 Week 1, Week 2; Unit 7 Week 2, Week 3; Unit 8 Week 1, Week 2

Review: Unit 2 Week 3; Unit 4 Week 3; Unit 6 Week 3; Unit 8 Week 3

Assess: Unit 1, Unit 2, Unit 3, Unit 4, Unit 5, Unit 6, Unit 7, Unit 8

Short Vowels

Introduce: Unit 1 Week 2

Review: Unit 2 Week 3; Unit 3 Week 1; Unit 4 Week 1, Week 3; Unit 5 Week 2; Unit 6 Week 3; Unit 7 Week 1; Unit 8 Week 3

Assess: Unit 1, Unit 2, Unit 3, Unit 4, Unit 5, Unit 6, Unit 7, Unit 8

Reading Literature

Character, Setting, Events

Introduce: Character: Unit 1 Week 1; Setting: Unit 3 Week 2; Events: Unit 5 Week 1

Review: Unit 1 Week 2; Unit 3 Week 1, Week 3; Unit 4 Week 2; Unit 5 Week 1; Unit 6 Week 1, Week 2, Week 3; Unit 7 Week 2, Week 3; Unit 8 Week 1, Week 3; Unit 9 Week 1, Week 2; Unit 10 Week 1

Assess: Unit 1, Unit 2, Unit 3, Unit 4, Unit 5, Unit 6, Unit 7, Unit 8, Unit 9, Unit 10

Reading Poetry

Rhyme and Repetition

Introduce: Unit 2 Week 3

Review: Unit 5 Week 1; Unit 6 Week 1; Unit 10 Week 2

Assess: Unit 2, Unit 10

Reading Informational Text

Text Features

Introduce: Unit 1 Week 1

Review: Unit 1 Week 2; Unit 2 Week 1, Week 2, Week 3; Unit 3 Week 1, Week 2, Week 3; Unit 4 Week 1, Week 2, Week 3; Unit 5 Week 2, Week 3; Unit 6 Week 2, Week 3; Unit 7 Week 2, Week 3; Unit 8 Week 1, Week 2, Week 3; Unit 9 Week 2, Week 3; Unit 10 Week 1, Week 2, Week 3

Topic and Details

Introduce: Unit 1 Week 3

Review: Unit 2 Week 1, Week 2; Unit 4 Week 1, Week 3; Unit 5 Week 2, Week 3; Unit 10 Week 3

Assess: Unit 2, Unit 4, Unit 6, Unit 10

Grammar

Subjective Pronouns

Introduce: Unit 5 Week 1

Review: Unit 5 Week 2, Week 3; Unit 10 Week 1

Extended Writing

Unit 2: Expository/Informative Text
Unit 4: Personal Narrative
Unit 6: Narrative: Realistic Fiction
Unit 8: Narrative: Fantasy
Unit 10: Opinion

Additional Reading Options

Classroom Library Read Alouds

Online Lessons Available

Have You Seen My Duckling?
By Nancy Tafuri
Fiction
Lexile 20L

A Tree Is a Plant
By Clyde Robert Bulla
Informational Text
Lexile 290L

Genre Read-Aloud Anthology

More Leveled Readers to Explore

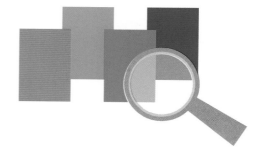

🔊 Search the **Online Leveled Reader Library** to provide children with texts at various levels to apply skills or to learn about various topics.

Unit Bibliography

Choose titles from the online **Unit Bibliography** to read aloud to children.

Richards, Jean. *A Fruit Is a Suitcase for Seeds*. First Avenue Editions, 2006.

Shannon, George. *White Is for Blueberry*. Greenwillow Books, 2005.

Ayres, Katherine. *Up, Down, & Around*. Candlewick, 2008.

Arnosky, Jim. *Babies in the Bayou*. Puffin, 2010.

Goodman, Emily and Tildes, Phyllis Limbacher. *Plant Secrets*. Charlesbridge, 2009.

Henkes, Kevin. *Birds*. Greenwillow Books, 2009.

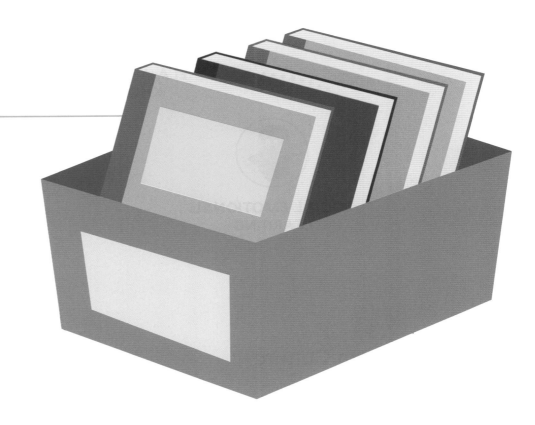

UNIT 5

Teach the Whole Child

Foster student academic success in English Language Arts and Content Knowledge by creating a Classroom Culture that supports children in growing their Social Emotional Learning and developing strong Habits of Learning.

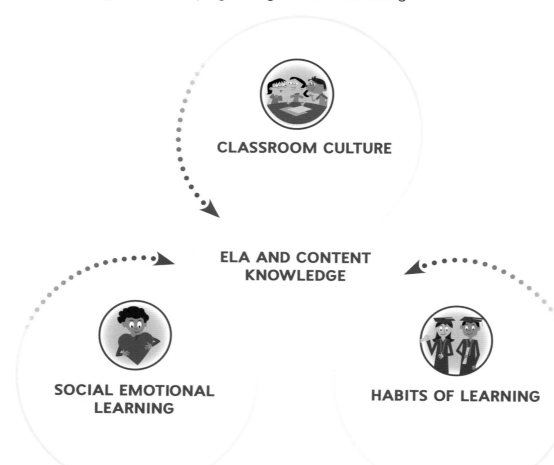

CLASSROOM CULTURE

ELA AND CONTENT KNOWLEDGE

SOCIAL EMOTIONAL LEARNING

HABITS OF LEARNING

 ## Classroom Culture

Focus: We build knowledge.

Explain to children that the routines and activities they do every day are designed to help them build knowledge. Point out that reading, making connections, synthesizing information, writing, collaborating with peers, and conducting research are ways that they will build their knowledge. Remind children that they have ownership of their learning; they can also ask questions to find new information as a way to build knowledge. Discuss the following statements:

• We investigate what we want to know more about.

• We read many different types of texts.

 ## Habits of Learning

Focus: I think critically about what I am reading.

As children grow in their learning and reflect on what they have learned, help them understand that they should continue to think critically about everything they read, both in school and out. Share the "I" statements below and discuss with children how these help them become careful and critical readers.

• I make inferences based on evidence.

• I synthesize and evaluate information throughout the text.

Social Emotional Learning

A Classroom of Confidence!

The Social Emotional Learning (SEL) competencies of this unit help children develop key skills, knowledge, and dispositions. **As children collaborate, self-confidence strengthens their abilities to share ideas and navigate challenges.**

Each weekly SEL lesson helps deepen the skills children need to take academic risks:

Week 1 • Demonstrates Curiosity
Showing an inquisitiveness about learning, others, and the world around them. Video: "Asking Questions"

Week 2 • Working Memory
Learning to hold information in mind while completing a task. Video: "I Can Remember"

Week 3 • Self-Confidence
Deepening resilience and confidence as learners.
Video: "Word on the Street: Confidence"

family time!

At this mid-year point, engage families by supporting their efforts to **acknowledge and celebrate the process of learning, not just the end results.** It's effort, hard work, and practice, practice, practice that allow children to achieve their potential and build the confidence and joy that fuel learning.

Invite families to celebrate the different ways they engage with their children around the weekly Social Emotional Learning video and activity found in the **School to Home** newsletter.

Half-Day Kindergarten

As you plan for your half-day Kindergarten, focus on the following areas important to building children's literacy. Use the Planner for each week in the unit to plan for the whole class and small group lessons.

Oral Language

- Introduce/Build the Concept
- Oral Vocabulary
- Category Words
- Integrate Ideas

Video

Visual Vocabulary Cards

Word Work

- Phonological/Phonemic Awareness
- Phonics: /h/h, /e/e, /f/f, /r/r
- High-Frequency Words: *my, are, with, he*
- Letter and Word Automaticity

Sound-Spelling Cards

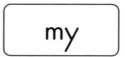
High-Frequency Word Cards

Reading/Writing

- **Literature Big Books** *My Garden; A Grand Old Tree; An Orange in January*
- **Shared Reads** "Hop Can Hop!"; "Ed and Ned"; "Ron with Red"
- **Interactive Read Aloud Cards** "Growing Plants"; "The Pine Tree"; "Farms Around the World"
- Writing Skill and Trait
- Write About the Text
- Grammar

Literature Big Book

Interactive Read Aloud Cards

Independent Practice

- Practice Book pages
- Center Activity Cards
- Online Games and Activities

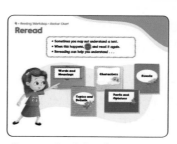
Center Activity Cards

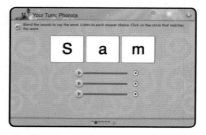
Online Games and Activities

Introduce the Unit

The Big Idea: *What kinds of things can you find growing in nature?*

Talk About It

Read aloud the Big Idea to children. Then ask them to think of places where they see plants growing (e.g., lawns and landscaping, farms and gardens, uncultivated, natural areas, and indoor areas). Encourage children to think of the wide variety of plants they see in these places. Have children discuss what all the plants have in common, for example, what they all need to survive and grow. As children discuss, encourage them to look at and listen to the speaker. Guide students to respect others by not interrupting them but, as appropriate, to repeat classmates' ideas to check understanding.

Ask: *What kinds of things can you find growing in nature?* Have partners or groups discuss, then share their ideas with the class. Let children know that they will discuss the Big Idea throughout the unit. Each week they will talk, read, and write about an Essential Question related to the Big Idea.

Guide children to complete the activities on **Reading/Writing Companion** page 6.

Talk Have partners talk about what they see in the picture. Remind them to speak in a loud, clear voice and use complete sentences to help their partner understand them.

Circle Children can circle things that are growing.

Sing the Song

Introduce the unit song: "The Green Grass Grew All Around." Read aloud the lyrics of the song. Then ask children questions about the song:

- *What is special about the tree?*
- *Where is the tree growing in nature?*
- *How does the tree help other things in nature survive?*

Play the song. After listening to the song a few times, ask children to join in. Audio and print files of the song can be found in the Teacher Resources on **my.mheducation.com**.

Student Outcomes

✓ Tested in *Wonders* Assessments

FOUNDATIONAL SKILLS

Print Concepts
- Locate a printed word on a page
- Identify parts of a book

Phonological Awareness
- ✓ Count and Blend Syllables
- Phoneme Isolation
- ✓ Phoneme Categorization
- ✓ Phoneme Blending

Phonics and Word Analysis
- ✓ /h/h

Fluency
- ✓ High-Frequency Word
  my

READING

Reading Literature
- ✓ Identify and describe characters, settings, and events in a story
- Identify rhyme in a poem
- Retell familiar stories
- Actively engage in group reading activities

COMMUNICATION

Writing
- Handwriting: *Hh*
- Use prompts to write about the text
- Respond to suggestions from peers and add details to strengthen writing

Speaking and Listening
- Present writing and research
- Engage in collaborative conversations
- Ask and answer questions to get information or to clarify something that is not understood

Conventions
- **Grammar:** Recognize subjective pronouns

Researching
- Recall or gather information to answer a question
- Conduct research about different parts of plants

Creating and Collaborating
- Add drawings and visual displays to descriptions
- Use digital tools to produce and publish writing

VOCABULARY

Academic Vocabulary
- Acquire and use grade-appropriate academic vocabulary

Vocabulary Strategy
- Identify and sort common words and objects into categories
- Use the most frequently occurring inflections

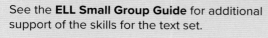 

ELL Scaffolded supports for English Language Learners are embedded throughout the lessons, enabling children to communicate information, ideas, and concepts in English Language Arts and for social and instructional purposes within the school setting.

See the **ELL Small Group Guide** for additional support of the skills for the text set.

FORMATIVE ASSESSMENT

For assessment throughout the text set, use children's self-assessments and your observations.

Use the Data Dashboard to filter class, group, or individual student data to guide group placement decisions. It provides recommendations to enhance learning for gifted and talented children and offers extra support for children needing remediation.

Develop Student Ownership

To build student ownership, children need to know what they are learning, why they are learning it, and determine how well they understood it.

Students Discuss Their Goals

TEXT SET GOALS

- I can read and understand texts.
- I can write about the texts I read.
- I know what living things need to grow.

Have children think about what they know and circle a hand in each row on **Reading/Writing Companion** page 10.

Students Monitor Their Learning

LEARNING GOALS

Specific learning goals identified in every lesson make clear what children will be learning and why. These smaller goals provide stepping stones to help children meet their Text Set Goals.

CHECK-IN ROUTINE

The Check-In Routine at the close of each lesson guides children to self-reflect on how well they understood each learning goal.

Review the lesson learning goal.
Reflect on the activity.
Self Assess by
- circling the hands in the **Reading/Writing Companion.**
- showing thumbs up, sideways, or down.

Share with your teacher.

Students Reflect on Their Progress

TEXT SET GOALS

After completing the Show Your Knowledge task for the text set, children reflect on their understanding of the Text Set Goals by circling a hand in each row on **Reading/Writing Companion** page 11.

Build Knowledge

Literature Big Book

Shared Read
Reading/Writing Companion, p.18

Paired Selection
Literature Big Book

Essential Question
What do living things need to grow?

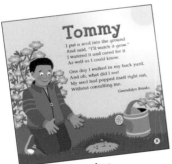 **Video** All living things need some help to grow. Plants need soil, water, and sunlight to grow. They use sunlight to make food.

Literature Big Book A girl helps in her mother's garden. She waters and weeds plants and chases rabbits away. Then she imagines her own special garden, where there are no weeds, flowers always bloom, and unusual things grow.

Shared Read While a girl named Dot takes care of her garden, she takes care of her rabbit named Hop.

 Interactive Read Aloud All plants need soil, food, water, air, sunlight, and space to survive and grow. Plant roots soak up food and water from soil. Sunlight, air, and water help plants make some food on their own. Plants need help from humans to give them space to grow.

Paired Selection Poems describe how seeds need a little hole in the earth, some water, and some sun to grow; little seeds might grow into flowers or weeds or even trees; some seeds grow into red or white carnations.

Poem Mary has a garden that she tends to. She waters her flowers to help them grow.

Differentiated Sources

Leveled Readers 🔊

🔴 A raccoon uses things like a wheelbarrow, hoe, seeds, and a hose to plant and grow corn.

🔴🔴 A fox's garden has seeds, sun, and water, but also weeds and animals that eat the seeds and plants. The garden still grows nicely.

🔴 A girl and her uncle plant mystery seeds. They water them and pull weeds. The seeds grow into fruits and vegetables.

Build Knowledge Routine

After reading each text, ask children to document what facts and details that they learned to help answer the Essential Question of the text set.

 Talk about the source.

 Write about the source.

 Add to the class Anchor Chart.

• Add to the Word Bank.

Show Your Knowledge

Draw What a Plant Needs

Have children think about what living things need to grow. Guide them to draw and label a picture of a plant and what it needs to grow. Encourage children to include vocabulary words in their labels.

Social Emotional Learning

Demonstrates Curiosity

SEL Focus: Model curiosity by asking open-ended questions as you follow children's areas of interest.

Introduce the lesson titled "Asking Questions," on pp. T4–T5, and invite children to ask questions about it before beginning.

Asking Questions (2:19)

Family Time • Share the video and the activity in the **School to Home** newsletter.

WEEK 1

Explore the Texts

Essential Question: What do living things need to grow?

Literature Big Book	Literature Big Book	Interactive Read-Aloud	Reading/Writing Companion
	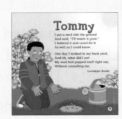		
My Garden Anchor Text Realistic Fiction	"Tommy," "Maytime Magic," "The Seed," "Garden" Paired Text Poetry	"Growing Plants" Interactive Read Aloud Informational Text	"Hop Can Hop!" Shared Read pp. 18–25 Fiction

Qualitative

Meaning/Purpose: High Complexity **Structure:** High Complexity **Language:** High Complexity **Knowledge Demands:** Moderate Complexity	**Meaning/Purpose:** Moderate Complexity **Structure:** Moderate Complexity **Language:** Moderate Complexity **Knowledge Demands:** Moderate Complexity	**Meaning/Purpose:** Moderate Complexity **Structure:** Low Complexity **Language:** Moderate Complexity **Knowledge Demands:** Moderate Complexity	**Meaning/Purpose:** Low Complexity **Structure:** Low Complexity **Language:** Low Complexity **Knowledge Demands:** Low Complexity

Quantitative

Lexile 570L	Lexile NP	Lexile 740L	Lexile 110L

Reader and Task Considerations

Reader Familiarity with a garden and how things grow in a garden will be helpful to children who may live in a city or a place without easy access to gardens.	**Reader** Hands-on activities like sprouting seeds or growing flower bulbs in the classroom may build more engagement for children.	**Reader** The text shares a lot of scientific information. Teachers should ask questions to check for understanding before progressing to new sections of the text.	**Reader** Children will need to use their knowledge of sound-spelling correspondences and high-frequency words to read the text.

Task The questions for the Interactive Read Aloud are supported by teacher modeling. The tasks provide a variety of ways for students to build knowledge and vocabulary about the text set topic. The questions and tasks provided for the other texts are at various levels of complexity, ensuring that all students can interact with the text in meaningful ways.

Additional Read-Aloud Texts

Classroom Library
Have You Seen My Duckling?
Genre: Fiction
Lexile: 20L

A Tree Is a Plant
Genre: Informational Text
Lexile: 290L

See Classroom Library Lessons.

Content Area Reading BLMs
Additional online texts related to grade-level Science, Social Studies, and Arts content.

Access Complex Text (ACT) boxes provide scaffolded instruction for seven different elements that may make the **Literature Big Book** complex.

Leveled Readers 🔊 (All Leveled Readers are provided in eBook format with audio support.)

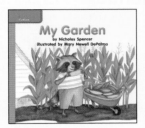   

Approaching	On	Beyond	ELL
My Garden Leveled Reader Fiction	*My Garden Grows* Leveled Reader Fiction	*The Mystery Seeds* Leveled Reader Fiction	*My Garden Grows* Leveled Reader Fiction

Qualitative

Meaning/Purpose: Low Complexity	**Meaning/Purpose:** Moderate Complexity	**Meaning/Purpose:** Moderate Complexity	**Meaning/Purpose:** Moderate Complexity
Structure: Low Complexity	**Structure:** Low Complexity	**Structure:** Low Complexity	**Structure:** Low Complexity
Language: Low Complexity	**Language:** Low Complexity	**Language:** Moderate Complexity	**Language:** Low Complexity
Knowledge Demands: Low Complexity	**Knowledge Demands:** Low Complexity	**Knowledge Demands:** Moderate Complexity	**Knowledge Demands:** Low Complexity

Quantitative

Lexile BR	Lexile 100L	Lexile 240L	Lexile BR

Reader and Task Considerations

Reader Readers will need a basic understanding of gardening and the tools required.	**Reader** Children need to have a basic understanding of gardening and some problems that can occur with gardens.	**Reader** Readers will need a basic understanding of how to grow plants in a garden.	**Reader** Children need to have a basic understanding of gardening and some problems that can occur with gardens.

Task The questions and tasks provided for the Leveled Readers are at various levels of complexity, ensuring that all students can interact with the text in meaningful ways.

WEEK 1

Focus on Word Work

Build Foundational Skills with Multimodal Learning MULTIMODAL

Photo Cards

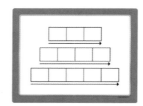

Response Board

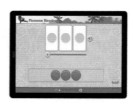

Phonemic Awareness Activities

Phonological/Phonemic Awareness

- Count and blend syllables
- Isolate, blend, and categorize phonemes

Sound-Spelling Cards

Word-Building Cards online

Phonics Practice Activities

Phonics: /h/*h*

- Introduce/review sound-spellings
- Blend/build words with sound-spellings
- Practice handwriting
- Decode and encode in connected texts

Practice Book

Word-Building Cards online

Response Board

Spelling: /h/*h*

- Spell words with /h/*h*

my

High-Frequency Word Cards

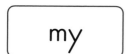

High-Frequency Word Activities

Visual Vocabulary Cards

High-Frequency Words

- Read/Spell/Write routine
- Optional: Build Your Word Bank

See Word Work, pages T14–T17, T26–T29, T34–T39, T48–T49, T54–T55.

Shared Read

Decodable Readers

Take-Home Story

Apply Skills to Read

- Children apply foundational skills as they read decodable texts.
- Children practice fluency to develop word automaticity.

Letter Identification > Consonants > Short Vowels > Blends > Long Vowels

Explicit Systematic Instruction

Word Work instruction expands foundational skills to enable children to become proficient readers.

Daily Routine

- Use the In a Flash: Sound-Spelling routine and the In a Flash: High-Frequency Word routine to build fluency.
- Set Learning Goal.

Explicit Minilessons and Practice

Use daily instruction in both whole and small groups to model, practice, and apply key foundational skills. Opportunities include:

- Multimodal engagement.
- Corrective feedback.
- Supports for English Language Learners in each lesson.
- Peer collaboration.

Formative Assessment

Check-In

- Children reflect on their learning.
- Children show their progress by indicating thumbs down, thumbs sideways, or thumbs up in a Check-In routine.

Check for Success

- Teacher monitors children's achievement and differentiates for Small Group instruction.

Differentiated Instruction

To strengthen skills, provide targeted review and reteaching lessons and multimodal activities to meet children's diverse needs.

- ● ● **Approaching Level, ELL**
  - Includes Tier 2 ②
- ● **On Level**
- ● **Beyond Level**
  - Includes Gifted and Talented ⭐GIFTED and TALENTED

OPTIONAL EXPRESS TRACK

Teachers can choose to introduce long vowel sound-spellings and/or additional high-frequency words.

- Build Your Word Bank

Independent Practice

Provide additional practice as needed. Have children work individually or with partners.

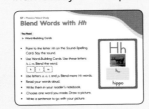

Center Activity Cards

Digital Activities

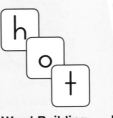

Word-Building Cards online

Decodable Readers

Practice Book

Inspire Early Writers

Build Writing Skills and Conventions

Practice Book

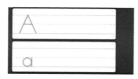

Handwriting Video

Reading/Writing Companion

Write Letter *Hh*

- Learn to write the letters
- Practice writing

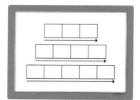

Response Board

Practice Book

High-Frequency Word Activities

Write Words

- Write words with *Hh*
- Write high-frequency words

Reading/Writing Companion

Practice Book

Write Sentences

- Write sentences with high-frequency words
- Write sentences to respond to text

Follow Conventions

- Appropriately use pronouns

My Garden
Literature Big Book

Writing Fluency

To increase children's writing fluency, have them write as much as they can in response to the **Literature Big Book** for four minutes. Tell children to write about all the things in the girl's make-believe garden.

For lessons, see pages T14–T19, T30–T31, T34–T37, T40–T41, T50–T51, T54–T57.

T3G UNIT 5 WEEK 1

Write About Texts

Literature Big Book, pp. 3–30

Modeled Writing

Write about the **Literature Big Book** *My Garden*

- Prompt: What make-believe things would you have in your imaginary garden?

Interactive Writing

- Prompt: What is the girl in the story good at doing?

Reading/Writing Companion, pp. 18–25

Independent Writing

Write to the Shared Read "Hop Can Hop!"

Reading/Writing Companion, pp. 18–25

- Prompt: What do Dot and Hop like to do together?
- Have children follow the steps of the writing process: draft, revise, edit/proofread, share.

Additional Lessons

Writing Skills Minilessons To provide differentiated support for writing skills, see pages T494–T499.

Extended Writing Lessons For a full set of lessons that support the writing process and writing in a specific genre, see pages T476–T485.

Self-Selected Writing

Children can explore different writing modes.

 Picture Spark

 Squiggle Writing

Planner

Customize your own lesson plans at
my.mheducation.com

 Select from your Social Emotional Learning resources.

 LESSON 1

 LESSON 2

TEXT SET GOALS

- I can read and understand texts.
- I can write about the texts I read.
- I know what living things need to grow.

 90+ mins Reading Suggested Daily Time Includes Small Group

SMALL GROUP OPTIONS
The designated lessons can be taught in small groups. To determine how to differentiate instruction for small groups, use Formative Assessment and Data Dashboard.

30+ mins Writing Suggested Daily Time

Reading

Introduce the Concept, T6–T7
Build Knowledge: How Does Your Garden Grow?

Listening Comprehension, T8–T13
My Garden

▶ **Word Work, T14–T17**
Phonemic Awareness: Phoneme Isolation
Phonics/Spelling: Introduce /h/*h*
Handwriting: Write *Hh*
High-Frequency Word: *my*

Build the Concept, T20–T21
Phonological Awareness: Count and Blend Syllables
Category Words: Size Words
Vocabulary: Plurals with -*s*

Listening Comprehension, T22–T25
My Garden

▶ **Word Work, T26–T27**
Phonemic Awareness: Phoneme Blending
Phonics/Spelling: Review /h/*h*
High-Frequency Word: *my*

Shared Read, T28–T29
Read "Hop Can Hop!"

Writing

Modeled Writing, T18
Model Writing About the Big Book
Grammar, T19
Subjective Pronouns

Interactive Writing, T30
Write About the Big Book
Grammar, T31
Subjective Pronouns

Teacher-Led Instruction

 SMALL GROUP

Differentiated Reading
Leveled Readers
- *My Garden,* T60–T61
- *My Garden Grows,* T68–T69
- *The Mystery Seeds,* T74–T75

Differentiated Skills Practice, T62–T77
● **Approaching Level, T62–T67**
Phonological/Phonemic Awareness
- Count and Blend Syllables, T62 ②
- Phoneme Isolation, T62 ②
- Phoneme Blending, T63
- Phoneme Categorization, T63

Phonics
- Sound-Spelling Review, T64 ②
- Connect *h* to /h/, T64 ②
- Blend Words with /h/*h*, T64
- Build Words with /h/*h*, T65
- Reread the Decodable Reader, T65
- Build Fluency with Phonics, T65

High-Frequency Words
- Reteach Words, T66 ②
- Cumulative Review, T66

Oral Vocabulary
- Review Words, T67

Independent/Collaborative Work See pages T3K–T3L

Reading
Comprehension
- Realistic Fiction
- Reread
- Main Story Elements: Character, Setting, Events

Word Work
Phonics
- /h/*h*
High-Frequency Word
- *my*

Writing
Self-Selected Writing
Grammar
- Subjective Pronouns
Handwriting
- Upper and Lowercase *Hh*

LESSON **3**

 LESSON **4**

 LESSON **5**

Reading

Build the Concept, T32
Oral Language

Listening Comprehension, T33
"Growing Plants"

Word Work, T34–T37
Phonemic Awareness: Phoneme Blending
Phonics: Review /h/h, Blend Words, Spell Words
High-Frequency Word: *my*

Shared Read, T38–T39
Reread "Hop Can Hop!"

Extend the Concept, T42–T43
Phonological Awareness: Count and Blend Syllables
Category Words: Size Words

Paired Selection, T44–T47
"Tommy," "Maytime Magic," "The Seed," "Garden"

Word Work, T48–T49
Phonemic Awareness: Phoneme Categorization
Phonics: Build and Read Words, Spell Words
High-Frequency Word: *my*

Research and Inquiry, T52–T53
Parts of a Plant (Research)

Word Work, T54–T55
Phonemic Awareness: Phoneme Categorization
Phonics: Read Words, Spell Words
High-Frequency Word: *my*

Integrate Ideas, T58
Make Connections

Show Your Knowledge, T59

Writing

Independent Writing, T40
Write About the Shared Read
Grammar, T41
Subjective Pronouns

Independent Writing, T50
Write About the Shared Read
Grammar, T51
Subjective Pronouns

Self-Selected Writing, T56
Grammar, T57
Subjective Pronouns

Comprehension
• Self-Selected Reading, T67
● **On Level, T70–T73**
Phonological/Phonemic Awareness
• Phoneme Isolation, T70
• Phoneme Blending, T70
• Phoneme Categorization, T70
Phonics
• Review, T71
• Picture Sort with /h/h, /p/p, T71
• Blend Words with /h/h, T72
• Reread the Decodable Reader, T72

High-Frequency Words
• Review, T73
Comprehension
• Self-Selected Reading, T73
● **Beyond Level, T76–T77**
Phonics
• Review, T76
High-Frequency Words
• Review, T76

Vocabulary
• Oral Vocabulary: Synonyms, T77
Comprehension
• Self-Selected Reading, T77 ⭐GIFTED and TALENTED

 ● **English Language Learners**
See ELL Small Group Guide, pp. 106–113

Content Area Connections
Content Area Reading
• Science, Social Studies, and the Arts
Research and Inquiry
• Parts of a Plant (Research)

 ● **English Language Learners**
See ELL Small Group Guide, pp. 107, 109

Independent and Collaborative Work

As you meet with small groups, have the rest of the class complete activities and projects to practice and apply the skills they have been working on.

Student Choice and Student Voice

- Review the Contract with children and identify the "Must Do" activities.
- Have children choose some additional activities that provide the practice they need.
- Remind children to reflect on their learning each day.

My Weekly Work BLMs

Reading

Text Options

Children can choose a **Center Activity Card** to use while they listen to a text or read independently.

Classroom Library
Read Aloud
Have You Seen My Duckling?
Genre: Fiction
Lexile: 20L

A Tree Is a Plant
Genre: Informational Text
Lexile: 290L

Unit Bibliography
See the online bibliography. Children can select independent reading texts about what living things need to grow.

Leveled Texts Online
🔊 All **Leveled Readers** are provided in eBook format with audio support.
- **Differentiated Texts** provide English Language Learners with passages at different proficiency levels.

Literature Big Book e-Book
🔊 *My Garden*
Genre: Realistic Fiction

Center Activity Cards

Reread Card 4

Realistic Fiction Card 23

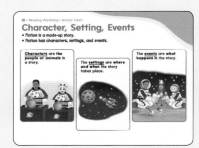

Character, Setting, Events Card 10

Poetry: Rhyme Card 22

Digital Activities

Comprehension

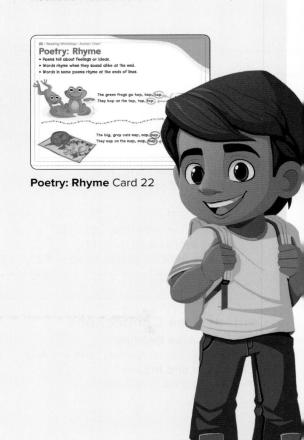

Word Work

Center Activity Cards

/h/h Card 57

Word-Building Cards

Practice Book BLMs

Phonological Awareness: pp. 197, 198, 199

Phonics: pp. 200, 202

Phonics/Spelling: p. 201

High-Frequency Words: p. 204

Category Words: p. 205

Take-Home Story: pp. 209–210

Decodable Readers

Unit 5, pp. 1–12

Digital Activities

Word Work

Phonemic Awareness

Phonics

High-Frequency Words

Writing

Center Activity Cards

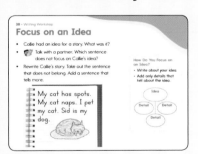

Focus on One Idea Card 38

Practice Book BLMs

Handwriting: p. 203

Grammar: pp. 206–208

Self-Selected Writing

- What do you know about what living things need to grow?
- Write or draw about taking care of living things in a garden.
- Draw and label a picture of a plant and show what it needs to grow.

Digital Activities

Grammar

Content Area Connections

Content Area Reading BLMs
- Additional texts related to Science, Social Studies, Health, and the Arts.

Research and Inquiry
- Complete Parts of a Plant project

WEEK 1

Progress Monitoring
Moving Toward Mastery

Practice Book

Reading/Writing Companion

Online Rubric

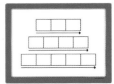

Response Board

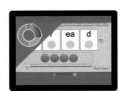

Digital Activities

FORMATIVE ASSESSMENT

> **STUDENT CHECK-IN**

✓ **CHECK FOR SUCCESS**

For ongoing formative assessment, use children's self-assessments at the end of each lesson along with your own observations.

Assessing skills along the way . . .

SKILLS	HOW ASSESSED
Phonological Awareness • Count and Blend Syllables	Practice Book
Phonemic Awareness • Phoneme Isolation • Phoneme Blending • Phoneme Categorization	Practice Book, Response Board, Digital Activities
Phonics • /h/h	Practice Book, Response Board, Digital Activities
High-Frequency Words • my	Practice Book, Response Board, Digital Activities
Category Words • Size Words	Practice Book
Grammar • Subjective Pronouns	Practice Book
Comprehension • Main Story Elements: Character, Setting, Events • Literary Element: Rhyme and Repetition	Reading/Writing Companion
Listening/Presenting/Research	Checklists

Making the Most of Assessment Results

Make data-based grouping decisions by using the following reports to verify assessment results. For additional support options for children, refer to the reteaching and enrichment opportunities.

ONLINE ASSESSMENT CENTER
- *Gradebook*

DATA DASHBOARD
- *Recommendations Report*
- *Activity Report*
- *Skills Report*
- *Progress Report*
- *Grade Card Report*

Reteaching Opportunities with Intervention Online PDFs

TIER 2

ASSESSED SKILLS	✓ CHECK FOR SUCCESS	RETEACH . . .
PHONOLOGICAL AND PHONEMIC AWARENESS	Can children count and blend syllables? Can children isolate, blend, and categorize phonemes? If not . . .	using lessons 34–37; 20–21, 27–29, 62–66 in the **Phonemic Awareness PDF.**
PHONICS	Can children match /h/ to the letter *h*? If not . . .	using lesson 21 in the **Phonics/Word Study PDF.**
HIGH-FREQUENCY WORDS	Can children recognize and read the high-frequency word? If not . . .	by using the **High-Frequency Word Cards** and asking children to read and spell the word. Point out any irregularities in sound-spellings.
COMPREHENSION	Can children describe the main character, setting, and events in a story? Can children identify rhyme and repetition in a poem? If not . . .	using lessons 10–12 and 16–21; 116 and 123 in the **Comprehension PDF.**
CATEGORY WORDS	Can children identify and sort size words? If not . . .	using lesson 15 in the **Vocabulary PDF.**

GIFTED and TALENTED

Enrichment Opportunities

Beyond Level small group lessons and resources include suggestions for additional activities in these areas to extend learning opportunities for gifted and talented children:

- *Leveled Reader*
- *Vocabulary*
- *Comprehension*

- *Leveled Reader Library Online*
- *Center Activity Cards*

 **Social Emotional Learning**

Today's focus:

Showing an inquisitiveness about learning, others, and the world around them.

Asking Questions (2:19) · SONG

asking questions

family time

You'll find the "Asking Questions" video and supporting activity in this week's School to Home family newsletter.

engage together

Let's Be Curious: Mystery item

Spark children's curiosity with a guessing game.

- We are very curious!
- *Curious* means being eager to learn more about something.
- I have a mystery item that I found at the hardware store. What do you think it's used for? To find out, you can each ask me a question about it.
- I'll write down your questions.
- Do you think you know what it is? I'll tell you after we watch a video.

explore together

Let's Watch: "Asking Questions"
Set a purpose for sharing today's song video.

- You asked some great questions!
- Let's watch singer Tracy Chapman sing about asking questions. *What* kind of song do you think it will be? *Who* might be in the video with her? Let's find out!

 **Play the video**

Let's Ask: Who, What, When, Where, Why, and How?
Reinforce the relationship between curiosity and asking questions.

- A *question* is a sentence that asks for information or an opinion. What words can we use to ask a question? I'll write them down.
- Let's go back to our list of questions about the mystery item. Are there any questions we want to add?
- Now that we know what this is, what other questions could we ask about it? There's always more to be curious about.

CURIOSITY IS...

- Wondering about something.
- Asking questions.
- Exploring.
- Discovering.
- Food for a hungry brain!

connect the learning

Let's Share: Curiosity cards
Guide children to explore what they're curious about.

- I'll give you a blank card. Think of something (person, place, thing, activity) you're curious about. Draw a picture of it.
- What do you want to know about it?
- Turn to a neighbor and exchange cards.
- Talk about what you each drew. Share questions about your drawings.

mindfulness moment
Body Scan
Lead children in a whole-body scan: *Gently close your eyes. Lift your shoulders up and let them drop down. Breathe in . . . and out. . . . Continue, guiding children to relax each part of the body from feet to head. End with another deep breath and eyes open; ask children how they now feel.*

DEMONSTRATES CURIOSITY

LESSON 1

OBJECTIVES

Confirm understanding of a text read aloud or information presented orally or through other media by asking and answering questions about key details and requesting clarification if something is not understood.

Use words and phrases acquired through conversations, reading and being read to, and responding to texts.

Identify real-life connections between words and their use.

Follow agreed-upon rules for discussions (e.g., listening to others and taking turns speaking about the topics and texts under discussion).

ELA ACADEMIC LANGUAGE
• opinions
• Cognate: *opinión*

DIGITAL TOOLS

Watch Video

Visual Vocabulary Cards

Collaborative Conversations

LESSON FOCUS

READING
Introduce Essential Question
Read Literature Big Book
My Garden
• Introduce Genre: Realistic Fiction
• Introduce Strategy/Skill
Word Work
• Introduce /h/h

WRITING
Writing/Grammar
• Shared Writing
• Introduce Grammar

Literature Big Book, pp. 3–30

 10 mins ## Build Knowledge MULTIMODAL

 ### Essential Question
What do living things need to grow?

Read the Essential Question aloud. Explain that living things are alive. Examples of living things are plants, animals, and people. Tell children that this week, we will learn about what living things need to grow. Have partners discuss what they know about what plants need to grow.

• **Video Routine** Play the Weekly Opener Video, "How Does Your Garden Grow?" without sound and have partners narrate what they watch. Then replay the video with sound and have children listen.

• **Talk About the Video** Have partners share one thing they learned about what plants need to grow.

 • **Anchor Chart** Create a Build Knowledge anchor chart and have volunteers share what they learned about the theme "How Does Your Garden Grow?" Record their ideas on the chart.

Oral Vocabulary Words

Use the Define/Example/Ask routine on the print or digital **Visual Vocabulary Cards** to introduce oral vocabulary words *require* and *plant*.

Oral Vocabulary Routine

<u>Define</u>: If you **require** something, you need it.

<u>Example</u>: Plants require water to grow.

<u>Ask</u>: What do you require to grow?

<u>Define</u>: A **plant** has roots, stems, and leaves and grows in the ground.

<u>Example</u>: A seed can grow into a plant.

<u>Ask</u>: What is a plant that you can eat?

Visual Vocabulary Cards

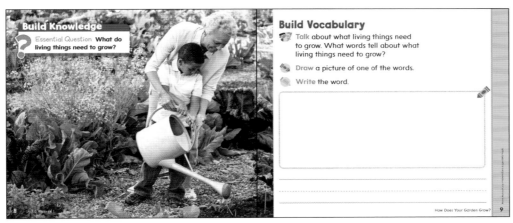

Reading/Writing Companion, pp. 8–9

 Build Knowledge

Have children turn to pages 8–9 of their **Reading/Writing Companion**. Guide a discussion about how the people in the photo are helping plants to grow.

- **Talk** *What do living things need to grow? What words tell about what living things need?* List the words. Have children choose one word and think about how to illustrate what the word represents.

- **Draw and Write** Have children draw a picture that illustrates the word. Then have them write the word. Guide children on how to print letters that have not been taught yet.

Build Vocabulary

Have children share new words they learned about what things need to grow. Add words to a separate section of the Word Bank. Use the words during the week and encourage children to do the same.

 # English Language Learners

Use the following scaffolds with **Build Knowledge**.

Beginning

Point to the garden. Say *garden* and have children repeat. Provide a sentence frame: This is a garden. Repeat with *watering can*.

Intermediate

Help children describe what they see in the photo. Provide sentence frames: This is a garden. I see plants.

Advanced/Advanced High

Encourage partners to talk about what they see in the picture. *What do plants need to grow?* Plants needs water to grow.

 **COLLABORATIVE CONVERSATIONS**

Take Turns Talking As children engage in partner, small group, and whole group discussions, encourage them to:

- Take turns talking.
- Listen carefully to the speaker.
- Ask others to share their ideas and opinions.

ELL NEWCOMERS

To help children develop oral language and build vocabulary, use **Newcomer Cards** 10–14 and the accompanying lessons in the **Newcomer Teacher's Guide**. For thematic connections, use **Newcomer Cards** 16 and 22. For additional practice, have children complete the online **Newcomer Activities**.

MY GOALS ROUTINE

What I Know Now

Read Goals Read aloud the goals and the key on **Reading/Writing Companion** page 10.

Reflect Ask children to reflect on each goal and complete page 10 to show what they know now. Explain that they will complete page 11 at the end of the text set to show their progress.

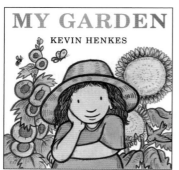

Literature Big Book

LEARNING GOALS

We can understand important ideas and details in a story.

OBJECTIVES

Recognize common types of texts.

Understand that words are separated by spaces in print.

With prompting and support, identify characters, settings, and major events in a story.

With prompting and support, retell familiar stories, including key details.

Actively engage in group reading activities with purpose and understanding.

ELA ACADEMIC LANGUAGE

• realistic fiction, reread
• Cognate: *ficción realista*

 DIFFERENTIATED READING

Celebratory Read You may wish to read the full selection aloud once with minimal stopping before reading with the prompts.

⬤ ⬤ **Approaching Level** and **English Language Learners** After reading, have children listen to the selection to develop comprehension.

 Read

20 mins

Literature Big Book

Connect to Concept

Tell children that you will now read how a make-believe garden grows.

Genre: Realistic Fiction Tell children that the **Big Book** is realistic fiction. Remind them that realistic fiction is a made-up story about things that could happen in real life. *Characters in realistic fiction are like real people.*

 Anchor Chart Display and review the Realistic Fiction anchor chart. Ask: *What new information could be added to the chart?*

Reread Remind children that if something is not clear, they should read it again. Rereading can help to better understand a part of the story.

Main Story Elements: Character, Setting, Events Remind children that the main character is who the story is mostly about and the setting is where and when the story happens. Explain that important events are what happens in the story. Guide children to identify the main character and setting and look for details about important events as they read.

Read the Selection

Concepts of Print Open the Big Book to pages 4–5. Point to the word *I* as you explain that this word is always a capital letter. Then point out the space between each word on the page. Explain that these spaces make the words easier to read.

Set Purpose *Let's read to find out about a special garden.*

Close Reading Routine

Read DOK 1–2

• Identify key ideas and details.
• Take notes and retell.
• Use **A C T** prompts as needed.

Reread DOK 2–3

• Analyze the text, craft, and structure.

Integrate DOK 3–4

• Integrate knowledge and ideas.
• Make text-to-text connections.
• Complete the Show Your Knowledge task.
• Inspire action.

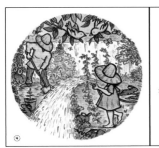

Pages 4–5

Pages 6–7

Pages 8–9

REALISTIC FICTION DOK 2

Think Aloud I know that realistic fiction is a made-up story about things that could happen in real life. The girl helping her mother in the garden is something that could happen in real life. When the girl says, "If *I* had a garden . . ." The dots tell me that the girl is going to imagine a make-believe garden.

CHARACTER DOK 2

Who is the main character? (the girl) *What can you tell about the girl from the picture?* (Her smiling face and open arms tells me that she is happy in her garden.)

BUILD ORAL VOCABULARY

blooming: making flowers

DETAILS DOK 2

Which flowers are real? (The yellow sunflowers on the left.) *Which flowers are in the girl's imaginary garden?* (The sunflowers on the right.) *How do you know?* (They have patterns and swirls and are not the colors of real sunflowers.)

 Spotlight On Language

pp. 4–5

weed: Weeds are plants we do not want to grow. People weed when they pull out weeds from the ground. Invite children to pantomime pulling weeds with you as they say: *I weed.*

pp. 6–7

keep: Explain that the phrase *keep blooming* means the flowers would "continue to make flowers." *Why does the girl imagine the flowers would keep blooming?* (Possible response: She likes flowers.)

pp. 8–9

pattern: Help explain the meaning of *pattern* by contrasting a solid color in children's clothing with clothing that is flowered, checked, striped, dotted, or another pattern. Point out the dotted and plaid sunflowers on page 9.

A C T   Access Complex Text

Use this ACT prompt when the complexity of the text makes it hard for children to understand the story.

Purpose

Young readers that are used to reading informational text may get confused by the approach of this story. Guide children to understand that this book is mostly about a make-believe garden versus facts about a topic.

• Read page 5 aloud. Explain that this real garden needs water and weeding. Point out the final phrase: *but if I had a garden . . . .* Tell children this phrase helps them understand that the girl is thinking of her own make-believe garden.

• Read pages 8 and 10 aloud. Explain that these pages show that this story is about a make-believe garden, so that children don't try to find facts.

LISTENING COMPREHENSION **T9**

 ELL Spotlight On Language

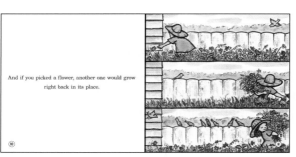

Pages 10–11

EVENTS DOK 1

What is happening on this page?
(The girl is imagining she is picking flowers in her garden.) *What happens when she picks flowers in her imaginary garden?* (The flowers grow back.)

pp. 10–11

in its place: Use two objects to help explain this phrase. Put a book on a table. *I put the book here.* Remove the book, and put an eraser in the same spot as you say: *Now the eraser is in the book's place. The eraser is in its place.*

Pages 12–13

CHARACTER DOK 2

What can you tell about the girl from her appearance? (She likes to walk around the garden barefoot. She wears a hat to keep the sun out of her eyes.)

pp. 12–13

wouldn't: Point out the contraction for *would not.* Explain that *wouldn't* is a shorter way of saying *would not.* Model correct pronunciation, and have children repeat.

Pages 14–15

REALISTIC FICTION DOK 2

What is realistic fiction? (A make-believe story that could happen in real life.) *What is real on page 15?* (shells) *What is make-believe?* (Shells growing in a garden.)

BUILD ORAL VOCABULARY

planted: put in the ground to grow

pp. 14–15

seashell: Some children might not be familiar with seashells. Use real seashells, illustrations in the **Big Book**, or other illustrations to help explain seashells. Say *seashells,* and have children echo you.

Pages 16–17

EVENTS DOK 1

How do you know the girl is still in her imaginary garden? (She is picking jelly beans from a jelly bean bush.)

pp. 16–17

jelly beans: Explain that jelly beans are chewy candies shaped like beans. Have children point to the jelly beans in the illustration. Provide a sentence frame: The girl picks jelly beans.

Pages 18–19

Pages 20–21

Pages 22–23

Pages 24–25

HIGH-FREQUENCY WORDS

Have children identify the high-frequency word *and. How many times does the word* and *appear in this sentence?* (two times)

BUILD ORAL VOCABULARY

unusual: not normal, strange

PHONICS

Reread page 20 and have children identify the words with the short /i/ sound. (In, with, wings) *What letter makes the /i/ sound?* (i)

REREAD DOK 2

What does it mean when something is invisible? (You cannot see it.) *Listen while I reread page 22. Listen to hear why the girl wants the carrots to be invisible.* Reread the page. *What did you learn?* (The girl does not like carrots.)

VISUALIZE DOK 2

Morning glories are a kind of flower. Have a volunteer point them out on page 25. *Can you make a picture in your mind of flowers shining like stars? Tell what you imagine.*

BUILD ORAL VOCABULARY

glow: shine with low light
lantern: a source of light that usually can be carried by a handle

pp. 18–19

pop up: Explain that if something *pops up,* it grows unexpectedly, suddenly, and quickly. *What pops up in the picture?* (umbrellas, rusty keys)

pp. 20–21

humming: Make a humming sound, and have children echo you. Point to the wings on page 21, explaining that when wings flap quickly, they can make a humming sound.

pp. 22–23

as big as: Guide children in understanding that *as big as* means "the same size as." Point to pairs of items in the classroom, and have partners ask and answer the following question: Is the window as big as the door?

pp. 24–25

Make sure children understand what a lantern is. Show a photo of a lit lantern. Say *lantern,* and have children repeat. Have children look at the illustration. *What glows like a lantern?* Provide a sentence frame: The strawberries glow like a lantern.

 Spotlight On Language

Pages 26–27

It's night now. Only the fireflies and the porch light are glowing. Before bed, I take one seashell from the shelf in my room and go to the garden. I poke the seashell into the ground. Who knows what might happen? I cover it up with dirt and pat down the dirt with my foot.

SETTING DOK 2

The girl is not imagining anymore. How do you know? (The girl is in her mother's garden.) *Why is she holding a seashell?* (She is thinking about her imaginary garden and wants to plant the seashell.)

pp. 26–27

poke: Use your hands to act out poking something down. As you act it out, say: *I poke.* Then have children echo and mimic the action.

Pages 28–29

"What are you doing?" asks my mother. "Oh, nothing," I say. "Just working in the garden."

CHARACTER DOK 2

What does the mother ask the girl? (What are you doing?) *Why do you think she asks that question?* (The mother cannot understand why the girl is working in the garden at night.)

pp. 28–29

Point to the quotation marks on page 29, and explain that they show us the words that a character speaks. Then point to the question mark, and remind children that questions end with this mark.

Page 30

EVENTS DOK 2

What is happening in the picture? (The seashell that the girl planted is growing.) *Is that something that is real or make-believe?* (Seashells don't grow in the ground so that is make-believe.)

p. 30

Encourage children to look at the illustration and describe it as much as they can. What do they see? Provide the words *growing, roots, seashell,* and *underground* if necessary.

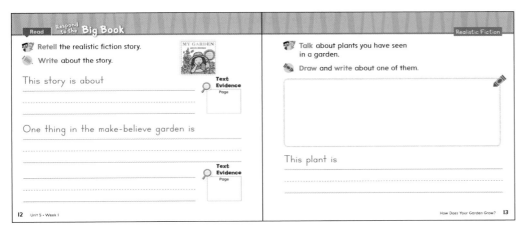

Reading/Writing Companion, pp. 12-13

Respond to the Text

Return to Purpose Remind children of their purpose for reading. Review what they learned about what makes the garden in the story special.

- **Retell** Have children turn to page 12 of the **Reading/Writing Companion**. Guide them to retell the story. Have children use the **Retelling Cards** and the routine as needed.

- **Write** Have children write about the story on the first line. Then have them write about one thing from the garden that is make-believe on the second line. Remind children to find text evidence in the **Literature Big Book** to support their response and to record the page number in the text evidence box. Share the Big Book with children, if needed.

- **Talk** Have children talk with a partner about plants they have seen in a garden. (Possible responses: tomatoes, cucumbers, squash)

- **Draw and Write** Then on page 13 of the Reading/Writing Companion, have children draw and write about a plant they have seen in a garden..

Model Fluency

Reread page 22 of *My Garden*. Remind children that we should read words aloud the way a character would say them. Explain: *I can tell from the words and illustration that the girl is thinking about how wonderful it is to grow a big tomato. I think she would sound happy when she talks about making carrots invisible.* In a happy voice, read aloud the sentence and have children repeat it and mimic your tone.

Writing Fluency

To help children increase writing fluency, have them write as much as they can for four minutes. Tell them to write about all the things in the girl's make-believe garden.

RETELLING ROUTINE

Say: *You will use the Retelling Cards to retell the story.*

- Display **Retelling Card** 1. Based on children's needs, use either the Modeled, Guided, or ELL retelling prompts. Repeat with the rest of the cards. Encourage children to include details.

- Discuss the story. After retelling, have children tell what they would grow in a garden.

- Have children act out an event from the story with a partner.

Retelling Cards

❯ STUDENT CHECK-IN

Have partners tell each other an important detail from the story. Then have children reflect on their learning using the Check-in routine.

In a Flash: Sound-Spellings   sn

Display the Word-Building Cards for *s* and *n*.
1. Teacher: What are the letters?   Children: sn
2. Teacher: What are the sounds?   Children: /sn/
Continue the routine for previously taught sounds.

LEARNING GOALS

- **We can hear the sound /h/ in words.**
- **We can connect the sound /h/ to the letter *h*.**

OBJECTIVES

Isolate and pronounce the initial sounds in three-phoneme words.

Demonstrate basic knowledge of one-to-one letter-sound correspondences by producing the primary sound or many of the most frequent sounds for each consonant.

ELA ACADEMIC LANGUAGE

- *connect, letter*
- Cognates: *conectar, letra*

TEACH IN SMALL GROUP

You may wish to teach the Word Work lessons in small groups.

ELL ENGLISH LANGUAGE LEARNERS

Phonemic Awareness, Guided Practice/Practice Encourage children to say the phoneme /h/ several times. Point to a card, and ask children to name it. Help them self-correct by modeling pronunciation. Then help children identify the initial sound using a sentence frame. For example: Hair begins with /h/.

Wonders   Grade K
Practice Book
Blackline Masters
- Phonological Awareness
- Phonemic Awareness
- Phonics
- Spelling
- Handwriting
- High-Frequency Words
- Grammar
- Vocabulary
- Take-Home Stories
Includes Differentiated Spelling Practice

Phonemic Awareness: p. 198
Phonics: p. 200

Phonemic Awareness
5 mins   MULTIMODAL

Phoneme Isolation

1 **Model** Display the **Photo Card** for *hippo*. Say: *Today we are going to learn a new sound. Listen for the sound at the beginning of* hippo. Hippo *has the /h/ sound at the beginning. Say the sound with me: /h/.* Say *had, hot, heat* and have children repeat. Emphasize /h/.

Photo Card

♪ *Let's play a song. Listen for the words with /h/ at the beginning.* Play "A Hippo in the House," and have children listen for the /h/ sound. *Let's listen to the song again and clap when we hear words that begin with /h/.* Play and/or sing the letter song again, encouraging children to join in. Have children clap when they hear a word that begins with /h/.

2 **Guided Practice/Practice** Display and name each Photo Card: *hair, hat, hook. Say each picture name with me. Tell me the sound at the beginning of the word.* Guide practice and provide corrective feedback as needed. If children need additional practice identifying the /h/ sound, have them use **Practice Book** page 198.

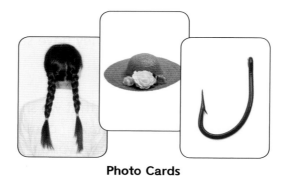
Photo Cards

Articulation Support

Demonstrate the way to say /h/ by opening your mouth. Keep your tongue on the bottom of your mouth. Breathe out a puff of air. Hold your hand in front of your mouth. Can you feel the air? Say *hop, hat, him* and have children repeat.

Phonics

(10 mins)

MULTIMODAL

Introduce /h/h

1 **Model** Display the *hippo* **Sound-Spelling Card**. Say: *This is the hippo card. The sound is /h/. The /h/ sound is spelled with the letter h. Say it with me: /h/. This is the sound at the beginning of the word* hippo. *Listen: /h/ /h/ /h/,* hippo.

Sound-Spelling Card

Display the song "A Hippo in the House." (See **Spelling Song** online.) Read or sing the song with children. Reread the title and point out that the word *hippo* begins with the letter *h*. Model placing a self-stick note below the *h* in *hippo*.

2 **Guided Practice/Practice** Read each line of the song. Stop after each line and ask children to place self-stick notes below words that begin with *H* or *h* and say the letter name and the sound it stands for. If children need additional practice connecting letter *h* with the sound /h/, have them use **Practice Book** page 200.

Corrective Feedback

Sound Error Say /h/ and have children repeat the sound. *My turn. Hippo, /h/ /h/ /h/. Now it's your turn.* Have children say the words *horse* and *his* and isolate the initial sound.

A Hippo in the House

There's a hippo in the house.

There's a hippo in the house.

Not a kitten or a whale, not a

hamster or a snail,

but a hippo in the house.

There's a hippo in the house.

There's a hippo in the house.

Not a penguin or a puppy,

not a hedgehog or a guppy,

but a hippo in the house.

ELL ENGLISH LANGUAGE LEARNERS

Phonics Transfers Use the chart on pages 10–13 in the **Language Transfers Handbook** to check for sound-spelling transfers from a child's native language into English. You can use the Sound-Spelling Cards to support teaching transferable and nontransferable skills.

DIGITAL TOOLS

 **Phonemic Awareness Phonics**

 **Phonics: Spelling Song**

 **Phonics Video**

To differentiate instruction, use these results.

 **Phonics: Data-Generating**

FORMATIVE ASSESSMENT

⊙ **STUDENT CHECK-IN**

Have partners name the letter that stands for /h/. Then have children reflect using the Check-In routine.

LESSON 1

LEARNING GOALS

- We can print the letter *h*.
- We can learn to read the word *my*.

OBJECTIVES

Print many upper- and lowercase letters.

Read common high-frequency words by sight.

ELA ACADEMIC LANGUAGE

- *print, uppercase, lowercase, dotted line, across*

DIGITAL TOOLS

Handwriting

High-Frequency Words

To differentiate instruction, use these results.

High-Frequency Words: Data-Generating

Handwriting: p. 203

⏱ 5 mins

Handwriting: Write *Hh*

1 Model Say the handwriting cues below as you write and then identify the uppercase and lowercase forms of *Hh*. Then trace the letters as you say /h/.

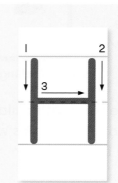

Straight down. Go back to the top. Straight down. Straight across the dotted line.

Straight down. Go to the dotted line. Around and down.

2 Guided Practice

- Say the cues together as children trace both forms of the letter with their index finger. Have children identify the uppercase and lowercase forms of the letter.
- Have children use their index finger to write *H and h* on the rug or a table as they say /h/ multiple times.

3 Practice

- Distribute **Response Boards**. Have children write *H* and *h* on their Response Boards as they say /h/ each time they write the letter.
- Observe children's pencil grip and paper position, and correct as necessary. Guide practice and provide corrective feedback as needed.

Center Idea Have children use pencils or wooden sticks to make an uppercase H. Emphasize the three lines used to form the letter. Have children wave their hands back and forth as though they are hot as the say /h/.

Daily Handwriting

Throughout the week, teach uppercase and lowercase letters *Hh* using the Handwriting models. At the end of the week, have children use the **Practice Book** page 203 to practice handwriting using appropriate directionality.

In a Flash: High-Frequency Words

1. **Teacher:** Read the word.   **Children:** and
2. **Teacher:** Spell the word.   **Children:** a-n-d
3. **Teacher:** Write the word.   **Children write the word.**

Repeat routine with *you* and *do* from previous weeks.

5 mins MULTIMODAL

High-Frequency Words

> my

1 **Model** Display the **Big Book** *My Garden*. Read the title. Point to the high-frequency word *my*. Use the Read/Spell/Write routine to teach the word.

- **Read** Point to the word *my* and say the word. *This is the word* my. *Say it with me:* my. My *mother has a garden.*

- **Spell** *The word* my *is spelled m-y. Spell it with me.*

- **Write** *Let's write* my *on our* **Response Boards** *as we say each letter: m-y.* Guide children on how to print the letter *y*.

- Point out to children that the letter *m* has the same /m/ sound as in the word *mad*.

- Have partners say sentences using the word.

2 **Guided Practice/Practice** Build sentences using the **High-Frequency Word Cards, Photo Cards,** and teacher-made punctuation cards. Have children point to the high-frequency word *my*. Guide practice and provide corrective feedback as needed. Use these sentences.

ENGLISH LANGUAGE LEARNERS

Use the scaffolds with **High-Frequency Words, Model.**

Beginning

Model the meaning of *my* for children. Hold up a pencil. *This is my pencil.* Point to yourself as you say *my*. Have children pick up their pencils and repeat.

Intermediate

Provide sentence frames to help partners create sentences using *my:* This is my desk. That is my friend.

Advanced/Advanced High

Encourage partners to talk about their families using the word *my*. Have them share their sentences with the class.

FORMATIVE ASSESSMENT

❯ STUDENT CHECK-IN

Handwriting Have children print *Hh*.

High-Frequency Words Have partners take turns pointing to and reading the word *my*.

Then have children reflect using the Check-In routine.

✓ CHECK FOR SUCCESS

Rubric Use your online rubric to record children's progress.

Can children isolate /h/ and match it to the letter *Hh*?

Can children recognize and read the high-frequency word?

❯ Small Group Instruction

If No

● **Approaching** Reteach pp. T62–T66

● **ELL** Develop pp. T62–T66

If Yes

● **On** Review pp. T70–T72

● **Beyond** Extend p. T76

LESSON 1

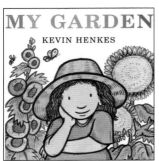

Literature Big Book

LEARNING GOALS

- We can write about make-believe things we would have in our imaginary garden.
- We can learn about words that can take the place of nouns (pronouns).

OBJECTIVES

Use a combination of drawing, dictating, and writing to narrate a single event or several loosely linked events, tell about the events in the order in which they occurred, and provide a reaction to what happened.

Follow agreed-upon rules for discussions.

Continue a conversation through multiple exchanges.

Appropriately use pronouns.

ELA ACADEMIC LANGUAGE

- *pronoun, replace*
- Cognate: *pronombre*

COLLABORATIVE CONVERSATIONS

Turn and Talk Review this routine with children.

Child 1: plants with toys

Child 2: *Can you tell me more?*

Child 1: I would have plants that grow my favorite toys.

Display the speech bubble "Can you tell me more?" Have partners use it to practice collaborating.

---

 10 mins

Modeled Writing

Model Writing About the Literature Big Book

 COLLABORATE

Build Oral Language Talk about what children remember from listening to the **Literature Big Book**. Review what the girl grows in her garden. Ask: *What make-believe things would you have in your imaginary garden?* Have partners use the Turn and Talk routine to talk about what they would have in their imaginary garden. When children are done, encourage them to share out what they talked about with their partner.

Model Writing a Sentence Write and display the following sentence: **I would have candy bushes in my garden**. Then point out the following elements of writing using the Sample Teacher Talk.

- *I wrote the word* have. *I wrote the letter* h *because I hear the /h/ sound at the beginning of* have.   PHONICS

- *This is the word* my. *I used the Word Bank to help me spell it.* My *is spelled with the letters* m-y.   HIGH-FREQUENCY WORDS

- *Every sentence must have an end mark. I put a period at the end of my sentence.*   WRITING SKILL

Writing Practice

Explain to children that they will write a sentence that describes what they would have in their imaginary garden. Have children continue to talk with their partners about their imaginary garden.

Draw/Write Tell children to draw a picture of their imaginary garden. Encourage them to write a sentence about their drawing. As children write, remind them to use the Word Bank, listen for sounds they know, and use an end mark at the end of their sentences.

If needed, provide the following sentence starter: **I would grow _____.**

What make-believe things would you have in your imaginary garden?

I would have candy bushes in my garden.

Grammar

5 mins

Subjective Pronouns

1 **Model** Remind children that a noun names a person, place, or thing. Explain that a pronoun is a word that takes the place of a noun. *Nouns that name people, such as* girl, boy, man, *or* woman, *can be replaced with the pronouns* she *or* he. *Nouns that name things can be replaced with the pronoun* it. Display the *girl, boy,* and *bridge* **Photo Cards**. Read and write: **The girl jumps. The boy smiles. The bridge is red.**

Point to *girl.* Girl *is a noun that names a person. You can replace* girl *with the pronoun* she. Erase *The girl* and write *She.* Read the new sentence. Repeat for the next two sentences.

2 **Guided Practice** Write and read this sentence aloud: **The girl is smart**. Rewrite the sentence: **She is smart**. Chorally read it with children. Underline *girl* and *she* in each sentence. Guide children to identify that the pronoun *she* replaces the noun *girl.*

3 **Practice** Write and read these sentences aloud: **Dan is playing ball. The bridge is long**. Have children copy one of the sentences and replace the noun with the pronoun *He* or *It.* Have volunteers share their new sentences.

Talk About It Have partners work together to orally create sentences with the pronouns *he, she,* or *it.*

Link to Writing Guide children to review the Shared Writing sentences and identify a way to use the pronouns *he, she,* or *it.*

English Language Learners

Use the following scaffolds with **Grammar, Practice**.

Beginning

Display the *bridge* Photo Card. *The bridge is long. It is long.* Have children repeat. *Which pronoun do I use to replace* bridge? You use <u>it</u>.

Intermediate

Display the *bridge* Photo Card. *Is a bridge a person or a thing?* (thing) *Which pronoun do you use to replace a thing:* he, she, *or* it? (it) Repeat for the *boy* Photo Card.

Advanced/Advanced High

Help partners use subjective pronouns by asking and answering questions. *Which pronoun replaces* bridge? <u>It</u> replaces *bridge.*

DIGITAL TOOLS

Grammar Activity

Grammar Song

Grammar Video

DIFFERENTIATED WRITING

● **English Language Learners** For more writing support, see the **ELL Small Group Guide,** p. 112.

FORMATIVE ASSESSMENT

❯ **STUDENT CHECK-IN**

Have partners share a pronoun they learned. Have children reflect using the Check-In routine.

LESSON 2

LEARNING GOALS

- We can clap for each word part and then blend the parts.
- We can use new words.
- We can learn words that tell about size.
- We can add *s* to words to show that it is more than one.

OBJECTIVES

Count, pronounce, blend, and segment syllables in spoken words.

Use words and phrases acquired through conversations, reading and being read to, and responding to texts.

Form regular plural nouns orally by adding /s/ or /es/.

Identify words about size.

ELA ACADEMIC LANGUAGE

- *syllable, plural, noun*
- Cognates: *sílaba, plural*

DIGITAL TOOLS

Weekly Poem

Visual Vocabulary Cards

Category Words Activity

LESSON FOCUS

READING
Review Essential Question
Reread Literature Big Book
My Garden
• Study Genre/Skill
Word Work
• Practice /h/*h*

Read Shared Read
"Hop Can Hop!"
• Practice Strategy
WRITING
Writing/Grammar
• Interactive Writing
• Practice Grammar

Literature Big Book, pp. 3–30

Reading/Writing Companion, pp. 18–25

(10 mins)

Oral Language

MULTIMODAL

 Essential Question

What do living things need to grow?

Remind children that this week we are learning about things that plants need to grow. Have children share some of those things. (water, sunshine, warm weather, soil, no weeds) *Let's read a poem about a girl's garden.* Read aloud "Mary, Mary Quite Contrary." Then use the Build Knowledge anchor chart, the **Big Book,** and the **Weekly Poem** to guide children in discussing the Essential Question.

Phonological Awareness: Count and Blend Syllables

1 Model *We can count the parts of a word. The word* garden *has two parts. Listen: /gär/ /den/.* Clap each syllable as you again say: /gär/ /den/. Have children clap with you as you again segment the word. *We can put the parts of the word together. Listen: /gär/ /den/,* garden. Model segmenting and blending syllables in *silver.*

2 Guided Practice/Practice Guide children to practice segmenting and blending syllables in the following words: *Mary, water, sunshine,* and *weather.* Provide corrective feedback as needed. If children need additional practice segmenting and blending syllables, have them use **Practice Book** page 197.

Review Oral Vocabulary Words

Use the Define/Example/Ask routine to review the oral vocabulary words *require* and *plant.* Prompt children to use the words in sentences.

Visual Vocabulary Cards

Category Words: Size Words

1 Model Use *My Garden* to teach the size words *big, small, short,* and *tall.* Explain to children that *big, small, short,* and *tall* tell the size of something or someone. Display pages 22 and 23 of *My Garden* and reread the text. *The word* big *is a size word. How big is the girl's tomato?* (as big as a beach ball) Point out other illustrations to discuss size words. For example: *On page 4, compare the girl with her mother. Who is short?* (the girl) *Who is tall?* (her mother)

2 Guided Practice/Practice Describe different objects in the classroom by using a different size word in each description. For example: *See the* big *desk. See the* small *block.* Have children name the size word in each sentence and point to the object. (big, small)

Vocabulary: Plurals with -*s*

1 Model Explain to children that words can be broken into parts. Adding the letter -*s* to the end of a noun makes the noun plural. Plural nouns end in -*s* and mean more than one. Use *My Garden* to model how to identify plural nouns.

Think Aloud In *My Garden,* the word *rabbits* is a plural noun because it ends with -*s.* The word *rabbit* means "one rabbit." When you add the -*s* ending to the word *rabbit,* you get the plural noun *rabbits,* which means "more than one rabbit."

2 Guided Practice Point out and discuss other plural nouns in the story that end with -*s.* Discuss what the singular form of each noun is and how it was made plural by adding -*s.*

There would be no **weeds**, *and the* **flowers** *would keep blooming.*

3 Practice Use the word *plants* to discuss and practice plurals. Have children identify the singular form of the word (*plant*) and then practice adding the word part -*s* to form a plural noun. Continue with *seashell/seashells, button/buttons, bean/beans, key/keys.*

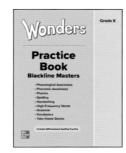

KIDS ON THE MOVE!

Have children follow simple directions that include size words. Have children pretend they are the object and its size. For example: *Be a big tree! Be a small mouse. Be a tall building. Be a short penguin.*

Phonological Awareness: p. 197

ENGLISH LANGUAGE LEARNERS

Use the following scaffolds with **Category Words, Guided Practice/Practice.**

Beginning
Write *big, small, tall,* and *short* on the board. Say and act out each word by making yourself *bigger, smaller, taller,* and *shorter.* Have children act out and repeat the words.

Intermediate
Point to classroom objects of different sizes. *Is it big or small? Is it tall or short?* Provide a sentence frame: It is big.

Advanced/Advanced High
Have partners use size words to describe classroom objects in sentences. Challenge them to use all the size words on the board.

FORMATIVE ASSESSMENT

❯ STUDENT CHECK-IN

Oral Vocabulary Words Have partners ask each other questions using one of the oral vocabulary words.

Category Words Have partners name a word that tells about size.

Vocabulary Have partners name a plural noun.

Have children reflect using the Check-In routine.

Literature Big Book

LEARNING GOALS

- We can tell what makes a story nonfiction.
- We can name character, setting, and events.

OBJECTIVES

Recognize common types of texts.

With prompting and support, identify characters, settings, and major events in a story.

ELA ACADEMIC LANGUAGE

- *character, setting, events*
- Cognate: *eventos*

Reread

Literature Big Book

Genre: Realistic Fiction

1 Model Tell children that you will now reread the **Literature Big Book** *My Garden*. Remind children that this story is realistic fiction.

 Anchor Chart Display and review the characteristics of realistic fiction that you have listed on the Realistic Fiction anchor chart. Add details as needed.

Think Aloud I know that *My Garden* is fiction because it is a made-up story that has characters, a setting, and events. It is realistic fiction, a special kind of fiction that tells about things that could happen in real life. The main character in *My Garden* is just like a real little girl. She helps her mother in the garden and likes to use her imagination. For example, she imagines that she has her own garden with chocolate bunnies and jelly bean bushes.

2 Guided Practice/Practice Read pages 4–9 of *My Garden*. Turn to pages 4–5. *What is happening here that could happen in real life?* (The girl is watering the garden. The mom is digging in the garden. There are birds and bunnies in the garden.) **Now turn to pages 6–9.** *What garden is the girl talking about on these pages?* (She is talking about a garden in her imagination.) *How do you know the garden is make-believe?* (She says the flowers would keep blooming and blooming and never die and that they could change colors. That doesn't happen in real life.) *What changes do you see in the words and pictures that help you know that the girl goes from talking about her mother's garden to talking about her own imaginary garden?* (On page 5, the words say, "if I had a garden . . ." On page 8, the girl says, "In my garden, . . .")

English Language Learners

Genre: Realistic Fiction, Guided Practice/Practice Provide children with sentence frames they can use to contribute to the class discussion about the story and genre: I see bunnies in the garden. The girl is watering the garden. The mom is digging in the garden. On page 5, the girl says, "If I had a garden." The girl says the flowers would keep blooming. That could not happen in real life.

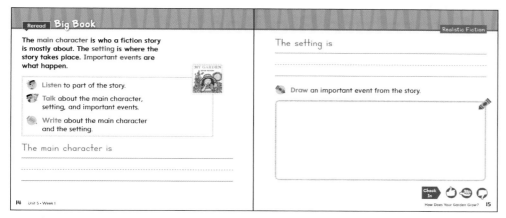

Reading/Writing Companion, pp. 14-15

Main Story Elements: Character, Setting, Events

1 **Model** Remind children that fiction stories have characters, a setting, and events. Children may recall that the main character is who the story is mostly about. The setting is where and when the story takes place. Important events are the important things that happen in a story.

 Anchor Chart Create a Main Story Elements: Events anchor chart and display and review the Main Story Elements: Character and Main Story Elements: Setting anchor charts, adding new information and details as needed.

Think Aloud Most of this story takes place in a make-believe garden. The make-believe garden is the setting. The characters are the people in the story. In *My Garden*, the characters are the girl and her mother. Since the story is mostly about the girl, she is the main character. Events are the things that happen in the story. The important events in this story are the ideas the girl has for what she would grow in her imaginary garden.

2 **Guided Practice/Practice** Direct children to pages 14-15 of the **Reading/Writing Companion**. Have them listen as you read pages 4-13 of *My Garden*. Ask: *Who is the main character?* (the girl) Have children point to the girl in the art. *Where does the story take place?* (in the girl's make-believe garden) *What does the girl's imaginary garden look like?* Have children use clues from the text and illustrations to describe the setting. *What happens in the girl's make-believe garden?* (Possible response: No weeds grow, but flowers that change colors and chocolate bunnies do grow.) Have children write about the main character and the setting on pages 14-15. Then ask them to draw a picture of an important event that the girl imagines happening in her make-believe garden on page 15.

ENGLISH LANGUAGE LEARNERS

Main Story Elements, Guided Practice/ Practice Help children learn and use academic vocabulary. For example, point to an illustration of the girl and say, *I see a character. Who is this character?* The character is the girl. Point to the garden and ask, *Where is the girl? What is the setting?* The setting is the garden. As children draw an event, help them use the language in the book to answer, *What event are you drawing?* I am drawing chocolate bunnies growing in the garden.

For additional support, see the **ELL Small Group Guide,** pp. 110-111.

FORMATIVE ASSESSMENT

❯ STUDENT CHECK-IN

Genre Have children share what makes the story realistic fiction.

Main Story Elements Have partners take turns identify the main character, setting, and an important event.

Have children reflect on their learning using the Check-In routine.

✓ CHECK FOR SUCCESS

Can children identify characteristics of realistic fiction?

Can children identify the main character, setting, and important events?

❯ **Small Group Instruction**

If No

● **Approaching** Reteach pp. T60-61

If Yes

● **On** Review pp. T68-69

● **Beyond** Extend pp. T74-75

LESSON
2

MY GARDEN
KEVIN HENKES

Literature Big Book

LEARNING GOALS

We can name the choices an author made when writing a story.

OBJECTIVES

With prompting and support, describe the relationship between illustrations and the story in which they appear.

Analyze the author's craft.

ELA ACADEMIC LANGUAGE

• *realistic fiction, imaginary*
• Cognates: *ficción realista, imaginario*

Reread

10 mins

Literature Big Book

Once children have reread *My Garden* to study the characteristics of the genre and practice the comprehension skill, guide them to analyze the author's craft. Reread the passages specified below and use the scaffolded instruction in the prompts to help children answer the questions on pages 16-17 of the **Reading/Writing Companion.**

GENRE: REALISTIC FICTION DOK 2

Reread pages 4–5 of the **Big Book**. *In what ways is the main character like a real little girl?* (She helps her mom in the garden. She waters the plants, weeds, and chases away rabbits.) *In what ways is the garden like a real garden?* (It has flowers and lettuce growing. Rabbits are running around.)

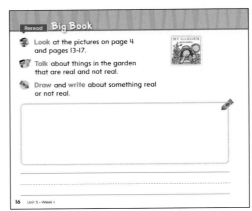

Reread Big Book

Look at the pictures on page 4 and pages 13-17.

Talk about things in the garden that are real and not real.

Draw and write about something real or not real.

16 Unit 5 • Week 1

Reading/Writing Companion, p. 16

AUTHOR'S CRAFT DOK 2

Display pages 4 and 13–17. *What things on page 4 could be found in a real garden?* (flowers, lettuce, rabbits) *What things in the girl's garden could not be found in a real garden?* (chocolate rabbits, seashells, a jelly bean bush) Have children draw and label something real or not real.

ELL

English Language Learners

Author's Craft Help children recognize the objects in the girl's imaginary garden. Have them point to the objects and say the words. Provide the words if necessary. Explain that *unusual* means "not usual" or "not normal." Ask *yes/no* questions to confirm understanding, for example: *Is it normal to see buttons in a garden?* (no) *No, we don't usually see buttons in a garden. It's unusual.*

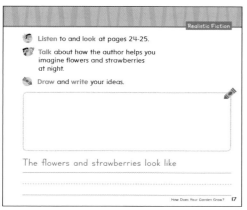

Reading/Writing Companion, p. 17

AUTHOR'S CRAFT DOK 3

Reread page 24 of the **Big Book**. *The text says that the morning glories would stay open and shine. What would they shine like?* (stars) *The text says that the strawberries would glow at night. What would they glow like?* (lanterns) *What do you think the author wants us to understand about the girl's imaginary garden at night?* (It is a bright and happy place.)

 MAKE INFERENCES

Remind children that we make an inference by using clues in the story to figure out something that the author doesn't say.

Think Aloud I think the girl grows things that she likes in her garden. She grows chocolate bunnies and jelly bean bushes. Carrots would be invisible because she doesn't like them. This clue tells me that she grows only things she likes.

 # Spotlight on Language

Author's Craft Review how authors compare two things to help readers make a picture in their minds. Help children use a simile to describe something familiar, such as a person running. Have them use a sentence frame, such as: She runs like a rabbit.

ORGANIZATION DOK 2

Reread pages 26–27 of the Big Book. *How do the illustrations help you know that the girl is no longer in her imaginary garden?* (The illustration shows plants and flowers that you would find in a real garden.) Point out that the illustration is also in a circle. Flip through the book so that children can see that the only other time the illustration is in a circle is on page 4, when the girl is in her mother's garden. Help children notice that when the girl is in her make-believe garden, the illustrations are in a square.

Talk About It

Guide children to use their responses on the **Reading/Writing Companion** pages to answer the following: *What make-believe animals would you have on a class farm?* If necessary, use the sentence starters to focus the discussion: **On our farm _____. If we had a farm_____.**

Integrate

 ## Build Knowledge: Make Connections

Talk About the Text Have partners discuss the living things in the mother's garden. *What does the girl do to take care of them?*

Add to the Anchor Chart Record any new ideas on the Build Knowledge Anchor Chart.

FORMATIVE ASSESSMENT

> **STUDENT CHECK-IN**

Have partners share some things the author/illustrator do with the text and images to help understand the story. Then have them reflect using the Check-In routine.

 LISTENING COMPREHENSION **T25**

LESSON 2

LEARNING GOALS

- We can blend sounds to say words.
- We can connect letters to sounds to read words.
- We can read the word *my*.

OBJECTIVES

Demonstrate understanding of spoken words, syllables, and sounds (phonemes).

Demonstrate basic knowledge of one-to-one letter-sound correspondences by producing the primary sound or many of the most frequent sounds for each consonant.

Read common high-frequency words by sight.

Blend phonemes to form words.

ELA ACADEMIC LANGUAGE

- blend, connect, words
- Cognate: *conectar*

▷ TEACH IN SMALL GROUP

You may wish to teach the Word Work lesson in small groups.

DIGITAL TOOLS

Word Work

Phonemic Awareness

To differentiate instruction for key skills, use the results of these activities.

Phonics: Data-Generating

High-Frequency Words: Data-Generating

In a Flash: Sound-Spellings

Display the Sound-Spelling Card for *h*.
1. **Teacher:** What's the letter?   **Children:** h
2. **Teacher:** What's the sound?   **Children:** /h/
3. **Teacher:** What's the word?   **Children:** hippo

Continue the routine for previously taught sounds.

OPTIONAL · 5 mins

Phonemic Awareness

Phoneme Blending

1 **Model** Say: *I am going to say the sounds in the word hippo:* /h/ /i/ /p/ /ō/. *I can blend those sounds to make the word:* /hiiipōōō/, *hippo. Listen as I say more sounds and blend them to make words.* Model phoneme blending with the following.

/h/ /i/ /p/ hip	/s/ /n/ /i/ /p/ snip
/h/ /a/ /d/ had	/h/ /ou/ how

2 **Guided Practice/Practice** *Listen to the sounds in a different word:* /s/ /t/ /a/ /k/. *Let's blend the sounds and say the word together:* /s/ /t/ /a/ /k/, /staaak/ *stack.* Tell children to listen to the sounds in words, repeat the sounds, and then blend them to say the word. Guide practice and provide corrective feedback as needed.

/h/ /a/ /t/ hat	/h/ /o/ /t/ hot	/h/ /e/ /n/ hen
/h/ /i/ /m/ him	/h/ /e/ /d/ head	/h/ /a/ /z/ has

5 mins

Phonics

MULTIMODAL

Review /h/*h*

1 **Model** Display the *hippo* Sound-Spelling Card. *This is the letter* h. *The letter* h *stands for the sound /h/ as in the word* hippo.

2 **Guided Practice/Practice** Display the *hippo* Sound-Spelling Card and point to the letter *Hh*. Have children say the letter name and sound with you. Have children listen as you say some words. Ask them to write the letter *h* on their **Response Boards** if the word begins with /h/. Do the first two words with children.

Sound-Spelling Card

hand	his	gate	high	hill	end	hope
jump	into	horse	hero	ball	sad	house

Blend Words

1 **Model** Place **Word-Building Cards** *h, i* and *m* in a pocket chart. Point to the *h. This is the letter* h. *The letter* h *stands for /h/. Say /h/. This is the letter* i. *The letter* i *stands for /i/. Say /i/. This is the letter* m. *The letter* m *stands for /m/. Say /m/. Listen as I blend the three sounds together: /hiiimmm/. Blend the sounds with me to read the word.*

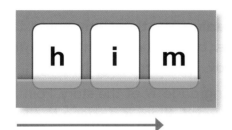

2 **Guided Practice/Practice** Change Word-Building Cards to *h, a, t*. Point to the letter *h* and have children say the sound. Point to the letter *a* and have children say the sound. Point to the letter *t* and have children say the sound. Then move your hand from left to right under the word and have children blend and read *hat*. Repeat with *hip* and *hot*. Guide practice and provide corrective feedback as needed.

OPTIONAL 5 mins

High-Frequency Words

MULTIMODAL

my

1 **Guided Practice** Display the **High-Frequency Word Card** *my*. Use the Read/Spell/Write routine to review the word. Then ask children to write *my* without looking at the word card. If needed, guide children on how to form the letter *y* because it has not been taught yet. Then have children self-correct by checking the High-Frequency Word Card.

2 **Practice** Add the word *my* to the cumulative word bank.

• Have partners say sentences using the word.

Cumulative Review Review the high-frequency words *to, and, go, you,* and *do* by displaying each word and having children read it with automaticity.

Have children practice high-frequency words using **Practice Book** page 204.

ELL ENGLISH LANGUAGE LEARNERS

High-Frequency Words, Practice Remind children of the meaning of the word *my*. To help partners create sentences, provide sentence frames, such as: This is my _____. My _____ is _____.

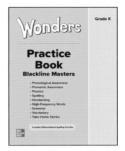

High-Frequency Words: p. 204

FORMATIVE ASSESSMENT

◆ STUDENT CHECK-IN

Phonics Have partners blend and read *him*.

High-Frequency Words Have partners take turns pointing to and reading *my*.

Then have children reflect using the Check-In routine.

✔ CHECK FOR SUCCESS

Rubric Use your online rubric to record children's progress.

Can children blend phonemes to make words and match /h/ to *Hh*?

Can children recognize and read the high-frequency word?

▷ Small Group Instruction

If No

● **Approaching** Reteach pp. T62–T66

● **ELL** Develop pp. T62–T66

If Yes

● **On** Review pp. T70–T72

● **Beyond** Extend p. T76

LEARNING GOALS

We can read and understand a story.

OBJECTIVES

Understand that words are separated by spaces in print.

Know and apply grade-level phonics and word analysis skills in decoding words.

Demonstrate basic knowledge of one-to-one letter-sound correspondences by producing the primary sound or many of the most frequent sounds for each consonant.

Read common high-frequency words by sight.

Read emergent-reader texts with purpose and understanding.

ELA ACADEMIC LANGUAGE

• *rhyme*
• Cognate: *rima*

DIFFERENTIATED READING

● **English Language Learners** Have children listen to a summary of the selection, available in multiple languages.

 10 mins

Read "Hop Can Hop!"

Connect to Concept

As children read this story, have them look for details that will help them answer the Essential Question: *What do living things need to grow?*

Foundational Skills

Book Handling Hold up the **Reading/Writing Companion**. Display the front cover. *This is the front cover of the book.* Then display the back cover. *This is the back cover of the book.* Model turning the pages.

Concepts of Print Model reading page 19 of the story. Point to the spaces between each word. *After each word, there is a space to show where one word ends and the next word begins.* Point to the period at the end of each sentence and explain that a period tells where a sentence ends.

Phonics Have children review the letter *h* and the /h/ sound.

High-Frequency Words Have children review the word *my*.

Read the Shared Read

Reread Remind children that they can reread a word or sentence to help them better understand what they are reading.

 Anchor Chart Create a Reread anchor chart. Tell children they will be using this strategy with the story they are about to read.

Choral Read Before reading, invite children to share any questions they have about the story. Then have children chorally read the story with you.

Read Tell children that now they will read the story, and you will pause to ask them the questions in the blue column. Have children use the box on the right-hand pages to do the following:

• Draw a picture about the text or the art.

• Draw something whose name begins with the /h/ sound.

• Write the letter *h*.

Reading/Writing Companion, pp. 18–19

SET PURPOSE

Tell children that they will read to find out what Hop can do.

PHONICS

Have children underline the uppercase letters in the title of the story on page 18.

Reading/Writing Companion, pp. 20–21

Reading/Writing Companion, pp. 22-23

Reading/Writing Companion, pp. 24-25

HIGH-FREQUENCY WORDS

Have children circle and read the word *my*.

PHONICS

Tell children to underline two words that rhyme on page 21.

CONCEPTS OF PRINT

Have children point to each word on page 22, as they read. *How many words are in this sentence?* (five)

PHONICS

Have children circle the words that begin with the same sound as *had*. (hop, hop, hop)

COMPREHENSION

Have children circle who can sip. (*Pop, Hop,* and *I* or the images of these characters.) Then have partners use the images and text to retell the story. Guide them to point out an important event in the story as part of their retelling.

ELL ENGLISH LANGUAGE LEARNERS

Use the following scaffolds with **Respond to the Text**.

Beginning
Point to the illustration on page 24 and say: *Hop can sit. Dot can sit.* Have children point to the picture and repeat the sentences.

Intermediate
Direct children to page 25. Have them look at the illustration and the text. *What can Dot do? What can Hop do?* Have them use the sentence frames to answer: Dot can sip. Hop can sip.

Advanced/Advanced High
Have partners use the illustrations to name things Hop, Dot, and Pop can do. Have them use complete sentences while speaking and pointing to the text.

Focus on Fluency: Accuracy

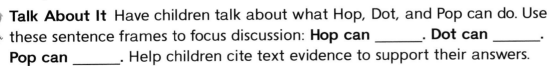

Model reading with accuracy for children. Remind them of the importance of recognizing high-frequency words as well as decoding words in the text correctly. Encourage children to practice reading for accuracy with a partner. Listen in and offer support and corrective feedback as needed.

Respond to the Text

Talk About It Have children talk about what Hop, Dot, and Pop can do. Use these sentence frames to focus discussion: **Hop can** _____. **Dot can** _____. **Pop can** _____. Help children cite text evidence to support their answers.

FORMATIVE ASSESSMENT

▶ STUDENT CHECK-IN

Have partners take turns sharing their retelling of the story to one another. Then have them reflect on their learning using the Check-In routine.

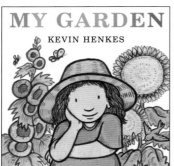

MY GARDEN
KEVIN HENKES

Literature Big Book

LEARNING GOALS

- We can write what the girl in the story is good at doing.
- We can learn about words that can take the place of nouns (pronouns).

OBJECTIVES

Use a combination of drawing, dictating, and writing to compose opinion pieces in which they tell a reader the topic or the name of the book they are writing about and state an opinion or preference about the topic or book.

Write a letter or letters for most consonant and short-vowel sounds.

Write in response to a text.

Appropriately use pronouns.

ELA ACADEMIC LANGUAGE

- *pronoun*
- Cognate: *pronombre*

COLLABORATIVE CONVERSATIONS

Circulate as partners talk about the prompt. Notice who needs to provide more information. Remind them to use the speech bubbles. As you listen in to conversations, you may choose to make observations on children's language development.

10 mins

Interactive Writing

Write About the Literature Big Book

Analyze the Prompt Tell children that today they will write about the **Literature Big Book,** *My Garden.* Ask: *What is the girl in the story good at doing?* Point out some things the girl does. Have partners turn and talk about what they think the girl is good at doing. Encourage them to use clues in the text and illustrations to support their ideas.

Find Text Evidence Turn to pages 5–6. Ask children what the girl does in the garden. Encourage children to use the text and illustration to tell what they think the girl is good at.

Write a Response: Share the Pen Have children provide a response to the prompt and encourage them to share the pen to help you write a response. Alternatively, use the following sentence: **The girl is good at pretending.** Then point out the following elements of writing using the Sample Teacher Talk below.

- *We can look at the Word Bank to help us spell the word* the. *Who can point to the word* The? *Let's spell it:* T-h-e. Write the word as children dictate it to you. HIGH-FREQUENCY WORDS

- *Say the word* good. *What is the last sound we hear? /d/ Who can write the letter that stands for the /d/ sound?* d. PHONICS

- *When we write we focus on one idea. We are writing about what the girl is good at doing.* TRAIT: ORGANIZATION

- *What do we always put at the end of a sentence?* Have a volunteer add a period to the end of the sentence. WRITING SKILL

What is the girl in the story good at doing?

The girl is good at pretending.

Writing Practice

Write Provide children with the following sentence frames and have them complete them in their writer's notebook.

The girl pretends _____.   **The girl can _____.**

As children write, encourage them to:

- Use the Word Bank to help spell high-frequency words.
- Stretch the sounds in words as they write.
- Remember to use end punctuation.
- Focus on one idea.

Stephen Coburn/Shutterstock

Grammar

Subjective Pronouns

1 **Model** Remind children that a pronoun can take the place of a noun. *The pronouns* he *or* she *can take the place of a person's name. The pronoun* it *can take the place of a thing. We don't have to use the name over and over again when we use a pronoun.* Write and read aloud the following sentences: **Jim is at home. He is at home.** Underline *Jim* and *He*. Explain that the pronoun *He* can take the place of the name *Jim*. Repeat with: **Mia is at school. She is at school.**

2 **Guided Practice** Write the following words in two columns and read them aloud: (Column 1) *hat, Mike, mom;* (Column 2) *he, she, it.* Guide volunteers to draw a line to match each noun with the pronoun that can replace it. (mom/she, Mike/he, hat/it) *How do you know that* it *can replace* hat? (*It* is a pronoun that is used for things.) Repeat the routine with the words *Mike* and *mom.* Continue guiding practice as necessary.

3 **Practice** Have partners draw pictures of an object and a person that they see in the classroom. They can use nouns to label each picture and then write the corresponding pronoun under each label. Circulate and provide feedback and support as needed. Have partners share their drawings and read the labels aloud to the class. If children need additional practice with subjective pronouns, have them use **Practice Book** page 206.

Talk About It

Have partners work together to think of sentences using the pronouns *he, she,* and *it.*

English Language Learners

Grammar, Practice Review *he, she,* and *it* before children label their drawings. Write each pronoun on the board, point to it, say it aloud, and have children repeat. Then name a familiar person or object, and demonstrate how the appropriate pronoun is used to replace that noun.

Keep in mind that different languages treat pronouns differently. In Chinese, for example, the words for *he, she,* and *it* all sound the same. Children might need extra practice using and recognizing pronouns correctly in English.

DIGITAL TOOLS

Grammar Activity

DIFFERENTIATED WRITING

● **English Language Learners** For more writing support, see the **ELL Small Group Guide,** p. 112.

Grammar: p. 206

FORMATIVE ASSESSMENT

STUDENT CHECK-IN

Have partners share a pronoun they learned. Have children reflect using the Check-In routine.

LEARNING GOALS

We can learn new words.

OBJECTIVES

Use words and phrases acquired through conversations, reading and being read to, and responding to texts.

Identify real-life connections between words and their use.

Develop oral vocabulary.

ELA ACADEMIC LANGUAGE

• *nonfiction, text, important*
• Cognates: *no ficción, texto, importante*

DIGITAL TOOLS

Weekly Poem

Visual Vocabulary Cards

Interactive Read Aloud

FORMATIVE ASSESSMENT

◐ STUDENT CHECK-IN

Have partners tell each other the meaning of one vocabulary word. Then have children reflect using the Check-In routine.

LESSON FOCUS

READING
Review Essential Question
Read Interactive Read Aloud
"Growing Plants"
• Practice Strategy
Word Work
• Review /h/*h*

Reread Shared Read
"Hop Can Hop!"
WRITING
Writing/Grammar
• Independent Writing
• Practice Grammar

Interactive Read-Aloud Cards

Reading/Writing Companion, pp. 18–25

⏱ 5 mins

Oral Language

? Essential Question
What do living things need to grow?

This week we are learning about what living things need to grow. What have we learned so far about what living things need to help them grow? Remind children to actively listen when their classmates are speaking. Then read the **Weekly Poem** aloud.

Oral Vocabulary Words

Remind children that on Lesson 1 they learned the vocabulary words *require* and *plant.* Ask: *Which word means that you need something?* (require) *What kinds of* plants *do you know about?* Then use the Define/Example/Ask routine on the print or digital **Visual Vocabulary Cards** to introduce *harmful, soak,* and *crowd.*

Oral Vocabulary Routine

Define: Something **harmful** can hurt you.

Example: Pollution is harmful to air and water.

Ask: Why is it important to keep harmful materials out of our oceans?

Define: **Soak** up means "to take in."

Example: You can use a towel to soak up the spilled water.

Ask: What would you use to soak up spilled milk?

Define: When you **crowd** something, you push it into a small space.

Example: I can't crowd another pencil into my pencil box.

Ask: How many coats can we crowd into the closet?

Visual Vocabulary Cards

Read the Interactive Read Aloud

Connect to Concept

Tell children that they will listen to a nonfiction text. Remind children that we are learning about what living things need to grow. Use the print or digital **Interactive Read-Aloud Cards**. Read the title.

"Growing Plants"

Set Purpose *Let's find out how plants grow. Why are they important?*

Oral Vocabulary Use the Oral Vocabulary prompts as you read to provide more practice with the words in context.

Unfamiliar Words Read "Growing Plants." Ask children to listen for words they do not understand and to think about what the words mean. Pause after Card 1 to model.

Teacher Think Aloud Where have I heard the word *familiar?* We learned it in Unit 3. When something or someplace is *familiar,* it means that I know about it. I'll reread the text, "... plants require the same things to survive and to grow. Those things are soil, food, water, air, sunlight, and space. Does all this sound *familiar*?" Yes, it is familiar because I know that living things need those things to grow.

Student Think Along After Card 3: The text says: "Roots grow in many *directions*--downward and out to the sides." At first, I thought the word *directions* meant instructions, but that doesn't make sense. The rest of the sentence says that roots grow down and to the sides. *Directions* must mean how roots grow pointing in different ways.

Build Knowledge: Make Connections

Talk About the Text Have partners share details about why plants are important to people and animals.

Add to the Anchor Chart Record new ideas on the Build Knowledge anchor chart.

Add to the Word Bank Add new words children learned to a separate section of the Word Bank.

Compare Texts

Guide children to make connections between "Growing Plants" and *My Garden*. How are the selections alike and how are they different?

LEARNING GOALS

We can actively listen to a text to understand how plants grow.

OBJECTIVES

Ask and answer questions about unknown words in a text.

Determine or clarify the meaning of unknown and multiple-meaning words and phrases based on *kindergarten reading and content.*

With prompting and support, identify basic similarities in and differences between two texts on the same topic.

⏚ SPOTLIGHT ON LANGUAGE

Card 1 Explain that *plants* is a word that names many different types of growing things. *A tree, bush, flower, and cactus are all plants.* Have children think of types of plants they know and then name different plants in your classroom, outside, and on the cards.

For additional support, see the **ELL Small Group Guide,** pp. 108-109.

FORMATIVE ASSESSMENT

❯ STUDENT CHECK-IN

Have partners share what they learned about the things plants need in order to grow. Then have children reflect using the Check-In routine.

LESSON 3

Display the Sound-Spelling Card for *h*.

1. **Teacher:** What's the letter?   **Children:** h
2. **Teacher:** What's the sound?   **Children:** /h/
3. **Teacher:** What's the word?   **Children:** hippo

Continue the routine for previously taught sounds.

LEARNING GOALS

- **We can blend sounds to say words.**
- **We can blend and read words.**

OBJECTIVES

Demonstrate understanding of spoken words, syllables, and sounds (phonemes).

Know and apply grade-level phonics and word analysis skills in decoding words.

Demonstrate basic knowledge of one-to-one letter-sound correspondences by producing the primary sound or many of the most frequent sounds for each consonant.

Spell simple words phonetically, drawing on knowledge of sound-letter relationships.

Blend phonemes to form words.

ELA ACADEMIC LANGUAGE

- *blend, beginning, spell*

 TEACH IN SMALL GROUP

You may wish to teach the Word Work lesson in small groups.

DIGITAL TOOLS

 **Phonemic Awareness Phonics**

 **Phonics: Spelling Song**

⏱ 5 mins

Phonemic Awareness

MULTIMODAL

Phoneme Blending

1 **Model** Say: *Listen to the sounds in a word: /h/ /a/ /z/. I can blend those sounds to make the word: /haaazzz/, has. Listen as I say more sounds and blend them to make words.* Tell children to listen for /h/ at the beginning of the word. Model phoneme blending with the following.

/h/ /a/ /d/ had   **/h/ /o/ /p/ hop**   **/h/ /i/ /z/ his**

2 **Guided Practice/Practice** Say: *Listen to the sounds in a different word: /h/ /o/ /t/. Let's blend the sounds and say the word together: /h/ /o/ /t/, /hooot/ hot.* Tell children to listen to the sounds in words, repeat the sounds, and then blend them to say the word. Guide practice and provide corrective feedback as needed.

/h/ /a/ /d/ had   **/h/ /ō/ /p/ hope**   **/h/ /i/ /m/ him**

/h/ /a/ /t/ hat   **/h/ /i/ /z/ his**   **/h/ /o/ /p/ hop**

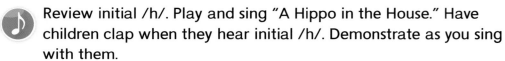 Review initial /h/. Play and sing "A Hippo in the House." Have children clap when they hear initial /h/. Demonstrate as you sing with them.

Phonics
MULTIMODAL

Review /h/h

1 **Model** Display **Word-Building Card** h. *This is the letter* h. *The letter* h *stands for /h/, the sound you hear in the beginning of* hippo. *Say the sound with me: /h/. I will write the letter* h *because* hippo *has /h/ at the beginning.*

2 **Guided Practice/Practice** Tell children that you will say some words that begin with /h/ and some words that do not. Have children say /h/ and write the letter *h* on their **Response Boards** when they hear /h/ at the beginning of the word. Guide practice and provide corrective feedback as needed.

had   him   gym   hat   lot   hold   told   have

Blend Words

1 **Model** Display Word-Building Cards h, i, t. *This is the letter* h. *It stands for /h/. This is the letter* i. *It stands for /i/. This is the letter* t. *It stands for /t/. Let's blend the three sounds together: /hiiit/. The word is* hit. Continue with: *hip, him, hop.*

2 **Guided Practice/Practice** Write the words: *hop, him, had, hit, hot.* Have children read each word. Guide practice with the first word. Have children read the connected text, sounding out the decodable words: *I like the hat. Dan hid my hat. We like to hop.*

Spell Words

Dictation Say *at* and have children repeat. Have them say *at* again, stretching the sounds. Children can use **Sound Boxes** before they write the word. Then write *at* as you say the letters, and have children check their work. Repeat the routine for *hat, hot, hit,* and *hip.* For additional practice, use **Practice Book** page 201.

 # English Language Learners

Use with **Phonemic Awareness, Guided Practice/Practice.**

Beginning

Model each sound in *had, him* and *hat.* Blend the sounds with children.

Intermediate

Model blending all the words. Guide children to blend all the sounds.

Advanced/Advanced High

Help children self-correct by modeling pronunciation.

EXTEND THE LESSON

You may wish to use this lesson to teach the final *s* sound /z/. Remind children that the letter *s* usually stands for /s/. Have children give examples of words with /s/ spelled *s* such as *sun, same,* and *Sam.* Tell children that sometimes when the letter *s* is at the end of a word, it can sound like /z/. Place the Word-Building Cards *h, i, s* in the pocket chart and model blending and reading the word. Emphasize the /z/ sound at the end. Blend the word *is* with children. Then continue with the words *as* and *has.*

CORRECTIVE FEEDBACK

Sound Error Model the sound that children missed when blending words, and then have them repeat. Tap under the letter *h* in the word *hop* and ask: *What's the sound?* (/h/) Return to the beginning of the word. *Let's start over. Blend the word again.*

Phonics/Spelling: p. 201

FORMATIVE ASSESSMENT

> **STUDENT CHECK-IN**

Have partners read *hat.* Then have children reflect using the Check-In routine.

LESSON 3

LEARNING GOALS

- We can sort words that begin with the letter *h* or the letter *d*.
- We can read sentences with the word *my*.

OBJECTIVES

Demonstrate basic knowledge of one-to-one letter-sound correspondences by producing the primary sound or many of the most frequent sounds for each consonant.

Read common high-frequency words by sight.

Sort words by initial letter.

ELA ACADEMIC LANGUAGE

- *sort*

DIGITAL TOOLS

To differentiate instruction for key skills, use the results of these activities.

Phonics: Data-Generating

High-Frequency Words: Data-Generating

OPTIONAL 5 mins

Phonics

MULTIMODAL

Picture Sort

1 **Model** Remind children that the letter *h* can stand for /h/. Place **Word-Building Card** *h* on the left side of the pocket chart.

Hold up the **Photo Card** for *hat*. *Here is the picture for* hat. *Hat* begins with /h/. *Listen, /h/ /h/,* hat. *I will place* hat *under the letter* h *because the letter* h *stands for /h/.*

Use the same routine for the letter *d* and the *dog* Photo Card.

Photo Cards

2 **Guided Practice/Practice** Have children sort the Photo Cards *hand, doll, hippo, door, hair, dime, hammer, dolphin.* Have them say the sound at the beginning of the word and tell which letter the Photo Card should be placed under. Guide practice and provide feedback.

Photo Cards

ELL English Language Learners

Phonics, Guided Practice/Practice Confirm children's understanding that *h* and *d* Photo Cards stand for /h/ and /d/. *Is the beginning sound in* had *the sound /h/ or /d/?* (/h/) Use sentence frames to help children tell how they sorted the cards: Hippo begins with the sound /h/. We place the card for hippo below the letter h.

High-Frequency Words

5 mins

MULTIMODAL

my

1 **Guided Practice** Display the **High-Frequency Word Card** *my*. Review the word using the Read/Spell/Write routine.

2 **Practice** Point to the High-Frequency Word Card *my* and have children read it. Repeat with previous words *to, and, go, you, do.*

Build Fluency

Word Automaticity Write the following sentences. Have children chorally read as you track the print. Have them reread the sentences until they can read the words automatically and fluently.

Do you *see my* hat?   I like *my* top.
My cat can hop.   You sat on *my* hat.

Read for Fluency Distribute **Practice Book** pages 209–210 and help children make their Take-Home Books. Chorally read the book. Distinguish letters from words for children using the letter *m* and the word *my*. Have children do the same using the letter *c* and the word *cat*. Have children reread the book to review high-frequency words and to build automaticity.

BUILD YOUR WORD BANK

Use this lesson to teach additional high-frequency words.

1 **Model** Display the **Build Your Word Bank Cards** for *than, his,* and *three* from the **Practice Book High-Frequency Word Cards**. Use the Read/Spell/Write routine to teach each word.

- **Read** Point to the word *than* and say the word. *This is the word* than. *Say it with me:* than. *I wrote more* than *Nat.*

- **Spell** *The word* than *is spelled* t-h-a-n. *Spell it with me.*

- **Write** *Let's write the word* than *on our **Response Boards** as we spell it:* t-h-a-n.
  Repeat the Read/Spell/Write routine with *his* and *three*.

2 **Guided Practice** Display *than, his,* and *three*. Point to each of the words and have children chorally read each word. Then have children take turns using the words in a sentence. Guide practice and provide corrective feedback as needed.

ELL **ENGLISH LANGUAGE LEARNERS**

High-Frequency Words, Practice Reinforce the use of the word *my* by having children use the word in sentences. Provide sentence frames, such as: My ___ is ___. I like my ___. Where is my ___? My ___ can ___.

Take-Home Story: pp. 209–210

FORMATIVE ASSESSMENT

❯ STUDENT CHECK-IN

Phonics Have partners think of words that they would add to the word sort.

High-Frequency Words Have partners take turns reading a sentence from the Take-Home Book.

Then have children reflect using the Check-In routine.

✓ CHECK FOR SUCCESS

Rubric Use your online rubric to record children's progress.

Can children blend phonemes to make words and sort words by initial /h/ *h* and /d/ *d*?

Can children recognize and read the high-frequency word?

❯❯ **Small Group Instruction**

If No

- **Approaching** Reteach pp. T62–66

- **ELL** Develop pp. T62–66

If Yes

- **On** Review pp. T70–72

- **Beyond** Extend p. T76

OBJECTIVES

Understand that words are separated by spaces in print.

With prompting and support, describe the relationship between illustrations and the story in which they appear.

Demonstrate basic knowledge of one-to-one letter-sound correspondences by producing the primary sound or many of the most frequent sounds for each consonant.

Read common high-frequency words by sight.

Read emergent-reader texts with purpose and understanding.

ELA ACADEMIC LANGUAGE

• *pronoun, exclamation point*
• Cognate: *pronombre*

ENGLISH LANGUAGE LEARNERS

Reread "Hop Can Hop!"
Concepts of Print Remind children that people's names begin with a capital letter. In this story, *Dot* and *Hop* are characters' names. Point out the difference between *Hop* as a name and *hop* as an action word, and *Dot* as a name and *dot* as a noun.

10 mins Reread "Hop Can Hop!"

Focus on Foundational Skills

Book Handling Demonstrate book handling. Hold up the **Reading/Writing Companion** and point to the front cover. *This is the front cover of the book.* Point to the back cover. *This is the back cover.* Open to the title page. *This is the title page.* Model turning the pages of the book.

Concepts of Print Read the sentences on page 20. Ask a volunteer to point to a single word on the page. Then have the child point to the spaces that separate the words. Point out the period at the end of the first sentence and the exclamation mark at the end of the second sentence. Tell children to point to the pronoun *I.* Say: *I refers to the little girl, Dot. She is telling the story.*

Reread Guide children to reread the story. Children should sound out the decodable words and read the high-frequency words with automaticity. Encourage them to look for details that they did not notice the first time they read the story.

Have children use the box on the right-hand pages to do the following:

• Draw a picture about the text or the art.
• Draw something whose name begins with the /h/ sound.
• Write the letter *h.*

Reading/Writing Companion, pp. 18–19

COMPREHENSION

Who is Dot? (a girl) *Who is Hop?* (Hop is a bunny.) *How do you know?* Encourage children to use picture clues to support their responses.

Reading/Writing Companion, pp. 20–21

COMPREHENSION

What does Dot do when she gets hot? (Dot wears a hat when she gets hot.) *What does Hop do when he gets hot?* (Hop jumps on the flowers.)

Reading/Writing Companion, pp. 22-23

Reading/Writing Companion, pp. 24-25

COMPREHENSION

Have children point to the exclamation point. Ask: *What is this?* (an exclamation point) Model reading the sentence with excitement. Have children repeat. *What is Dot excited about?* (hopping)

COMPREHENSION

What does the word sip *mean?* (to drink) Guide children to use the illustration to learn the meaning of the word *sip. How are Dot and Pop sipping?* (with a straw) *How is Hop sipping?* (with his tongue)

Focus on Fluency: Accuracy and Rate

Have partners practice reading the story "Hop Can Hop!" accurately. Encourage children to track the print as they sound out decodable words and read high-frequency words with automaticity. Remind children to pay attention to punctuation marks so they read sentences with the correct tone. Then have partners read the story again, this time focusing on rate—reading a bit more quickly and making the text sound like speech.

Listen in: If children struggle with accuracy, have them start again at the beginning of the sentence and correct any errors. If they struggle with rate, model an appropriate rate as you read and have children repeat.

Build Knowledge: Make Connections

Talk About the Text Have partners discuss the living things in the story. *What do they need to grow?*

Write About the Text Have children add their ideas to their reader's notebook.

DECODABLE READERS

Have children read "Hap Hid the Ham" (pp. 1-6) to practice decoding words in connected text.

Unit 5 Decodable Reader

❯ STUDENT CHECK-IN

Have partners share something they learned from the text. Then have children reflect using the Check-In routine.

LEARNING GOALS

- **We can write about the texts we read.**
- **We can learn about words that can take the place of nouns (pronouns).**

OBJECTIVES

Use a combination of drawing, dictating, and writing to compose opinion pieces in which they state an opinion or preference about the topic or book.

Write a letter or letters for most consonant and short-vowel sounds.

Write in response to a text.

Appropriately use pronouns.

ELA ACADEMIC LANGUAGE

- *clue, idea, pronoun*
- Cognates: *idea, pronombre*

 TEACH IN SMALL GROUP

Choose from these options to enable all children to complete the writing activity:

- draw a picture
- complete sentence starters
- write a caption
- write one sentence

For differentiated support, see Writing Skills minilessons on pages T494–T499. These can be used throughout the year.

 5 mins # Independent Writing

Write About the Shared Read

 Analyze the Prompt Have children turn to page 18 of their **Reading/Writing Companion.** Tell them they are going to write a response to a prompt about the story "Hop Can Hop!" Read the prompt aloud: *What do Dot and Hop like to do together?*

Talk Have partners turn and talk about things they think Dot and Hop like to do together. Encourage them to use clues in the text and the illustrations to support their opinions.

Find Text Evidence *We need to find text evidence, or clues, in the text and illustrations to help us answer the prompt.*

- *Let's look at page 22. We read that Hop can hop. The words on page 23 tell us that Dot can hop, too. Look at the illustration. What are Dot and Hop doing together?* (Dot and Hop both hop.) *Now look at page 24. What do Dot and Hop do together?* (They sit.)

- Continue guiding children to look for text evidence to use in their writing.

 Write to the Prompt Guide children to review the text evidence they found and plan their writing in their writer's notebook. Encourage them to think about which clues they would like to include in their writing.

Draft Have children write a response to the prompt in their writer's notebook. If children need additional support, you may choose to have them dictate their ideas to an adult or use the following sentence frames:

Dot and Hop can _____ together.

They _____.

As children add sentences to their drafts, have them do the following:

- Use an end mark, such as a period, at the end of your sentence. WRITING SKILL

- Focus on one idea as you write. TRAIT: ORGANIZATION

- Use **pronouns**, such as *he, she,* and *it,* to replace nouns. GRAMMAR

Tell children they will continue to work on their writing on Lesson 4.

Grammar

OPTIONAL 5 mins

Subjective Pronouns

1 **Review** Remind children that a subjective pronoun takes the place of a noun. Display the **Big Book**, *My Garden*. Show page 7 and point to one sunflower. Write and read aloud: **The sunflower is large. It is large.** Remind children that *it* is a pronoun because it can take the place of a noun in a sentence. The pronoun *it* replaces the noun *sunflower* in the second sentence.

2 **Guided Practice/Practice** Display page 13. Point to a bunny. Write and read aloud: **The bunny is cute. It is cute.** Circle *bunny*. Guide children to identify *it* as the pronoun that replaces *bunny* in the second sentence.

Then write sentences about the bunny using children's names such as: **Lin sees a bunny. Andre likes the bunny.** Underline the names. Have partners work together to rewrite the sentences using the pronoun *he* or *she*. Have volunteers share their completed sentences.

Talk About It

Have partners work together to orally generate sentences with pronouns. Have them use pronouns to describe a game they like to play with their friends.

English Language Learners

Independent Writing, Analyze the Prompt Check children's understanding of the prompt by reviewing the meaning of the word *together*. Clap your hands, and ask two volunteers to clap theirs. *We are clapping our hands together, or at the same time.* Then use the illustrations to help children respond to the prompt. Display page 18. *Are Dot and Hop together on this page of the story?* (no) Turn to page 21. *Are Dot and Hop together on this page?* (yes) Point to the illustration. *What do Dot and Hop do together?* Have children respond: Hop and Dot hop together.

For additional support, refer to the **ELL Small Group Guide,** p. 113.

DIGITAL TOOLS

Grammar Activity

Grammar Song

Grammar Video

FORMATIVE ASSESSMENT

❯ STUDENT CHECK-IN

Have partners share a pronoun they learned. Have children reflect using the Check-In routine.

- We can clap for each word part and then blend the parts.
- We can understand new words.
- We can use words that tell about size.
- We can add *s* to words to show that it is more than one.

OBJECTIVES

Count, pronounce, and segment syllables in spoken words.

Use words and phrases acquired through conversations, reading and being read to, and responding to texts.

Form regular plural nouns orally by adding /s/ or /es/.

Develop oral vocabulary.

Identify words about size.

ELA ACADEMIC LANGUAGE

- *blend, syllables, plural*
- Cognates: *sílabas, plural*

DIGITAL TOOLS

Weekly Poem

Visual Vocabulary Cards

Category Words Activity

LESSON FOCUS

READING
Review Essential Question
Read/Reread Paired Selection
"Tommy," "Maytime Magic," "The Seed," "Garden"
Word Work
- Build words with short *a, i, o* and *h, t, p*

WRITING
Writing/Grammar
- Independent Writing
- Practice Grammar
Research and Inquiry
- Create Presentation

Literature Big Book, pp. 31–36

⏱ 10 mins Oral Language

MULTIMODAL

❓ Essential Question

What do living things need to grow?

Have children discuss what they have learned about what living things need to grow. Add new ideas to the Build Knowledge anchor chart.

Phonological Awareness: Count and Blend Syllables

1 Model Read the **Weekly Poem** aloud. Then have children say: *With silver bells and cockle-shells.* Say: *We can count the parts of the word* silver. *Listen:* sil-ver. *The word* silver *has two parts.* Clap out each syllable and say: *sil-ver.* Have children repeat. Then say: *We can blend the word parts together. Listen:* silver. Have children repeat.

2 Guided Practice/Practice Invite a volunteer to clap out the parts of the word *garden.* (gar-den) *How many parts does the word* garden *have?* (two) Then have the volunteer blend the syllables to form the word. (garden) Repeat with the words: *flower, purple, shovel, ivy,* and *digging.* Guide practice and provide corrective feedback as needed.

Review Oral Vocabulary Words

Use the Define/Example/Ask routine on print or digital **Visual Vocabulary Cards** to review the oral vocabulary words *require, soak, plant, crowd,* and *harmful.* Then have children use the words in sentences.

Visual Vocabulary Cards

Category Words: Size Words

1 **Explain/Model** Read aloud the story below. Ask children to listen for size words such as *big, small, short,* or *tall.* Say: *When you hear a size word, use your hands to show what the size looks like. For example, if you hear the size word tall, lift both of your hands over your head and stand on your tippy toes.* Demonstrate as you read.

Mom and I went for a hike in the woods. We stopped next to a tall tree to have a picnic. Mom brought two apples for us to eat. One apple was big, and the other was small. I wanted the big apple because I had a small breakfast. Then Mom saw a small bird in the tall tree. I was too short to see it, so Mom lifted me up on her shoulders. I felt so tall!

2 **Guided Practice** Display the **Photo Cards** for *alligator* and *dinosaur.* Read each sentence as you display the Photo Card. Ask children to name the size words in each sentence.

The **big** alligator ate a **small** fish.
The **tall** dinosaur chased the **short** dinosaur.

Work with children to identify other size words to describe the animals. (Possible responses: little, huge, giant, great) Then rewrite the sentences. Use the suggested size words to make new sentences. Chorally read the new sentences.

The _____ alligator ate a _____ fish.
The _____ dinosaur chased the _____ dinosaur.

For additional practice, use **Practice Book** page 205.

Vocabulary: Plurals with -s

1 **Model** Remind children that the word ending *-s* can make a singular noun into a plural noun. Review that plural nouns ending with *-s* mean "more than one."

Think Aloud In *My Garden,* I can read this phrase: *In my garden, there would be birds.* I see two nouns: *garden* and *birds. Garden* does not end with *-s.* The word *garden* means "one garden." *Birds* ends with *-s. Birds* means "more than one bird."

2 **Guided Practice/Practice** Work with children to create plural nouns. Point to singular items in the classroom, such as a desk, a pen, and a book. Have children say the name of each item and then add *-s* to the end of each word to create a plural noun.

KIDS ON THE MOVE!

Play Simon Says using size words. Have children move around the room as you give them directions. *Simon says, move to the big table. Simon says, stand by the tall flag. Move to the short stool.*

Wonders Grade K

Practice Book
Blackline Masters

• Phonological Awareness
• Phonemic Awareness
• Phonics
• Spelling
• Handwriting
• High-Frequency Words
• Grammar
• Vocabulary
• Take-Home Stories

Includes Differentiated Spelling Practice

Category Words: p. 205

ELL ENGLISH LANGUAGE LEARNERS

Category Words, Guided Practice
Review the meaning of size words, and use them in context with familiar examples. *This is a big school. That is a small toy.* Then provide children with a word bank of other descriptive size words they can use.

ELL NEWCOMERS

Use the **Newcomer Online Visuals** and their accompanying prompts to help children expand vocabulary and language about family (Unit 2), the park (Unit 3, #16), and growth and change (Unit 4, #22). Use the Conversation Starters, Speech Balloons, and Games in the **Newcomer Teacher's Guide** to continue building vocabulary and developing oral and written language.

FORMATIVE ASSESSMENT

◉ STUDENT CHECK-IN

Oral Vocabulary Words Have partners name what they *require* before school.

Category Words Have partners act out a size word then tell the word.

Vocabulary Have partners point to objects that are more than one and name it, such as pencils, tables, etc.

Then have children reflect using the Check-In routine.

LESSON
4

MY GARDEN
KEVIN HENKES

Literature Big Book

Read

10 mins

Poetry

Rhyme

1 Explain/Model Tell children that they will be reading poems. Explain that many poems include words that rhyme, or words that have the same ending sounds. Display page 31 of the **Big Book** and read the first stanza of "Tommy" aloud. Point out that the words *grow* and *know* rhyme. Say *grow* and *know* and ask: *What sound do you hear at the end of* grow *and* know*?* (/ō/) Then have a volunteer point to the words and notice where they are located. *Where are the rhyming words?* (the end of the line)

Online Teaching Chart 22

Now display **Online Teaching Chart 22**. *This chart includes a poem titled "I Am Min."* Read the poem aloud. Point out and say the words in yellow. Draw children's attention to the hen and the numbers. *Say with me:* hen, ten. *What do you notice about these words?* (The words *hen* and *ten* rhyme. The rhyming words are at the end of the line.)

2 Guided Practice/Practice Draw children's attention to the pictures of the pig and Min. Then ask these questions:

• *What is the pig doing?* (dancing a jig) *What word rhymes with* pig? (jig) *In what part of the line are the words?* (the end)

• *What is Min doing?* (spinning) *What rhymes with* Min? (spin) Have a volunteer point to and say where the words are located.

Read the Paired Selection

Set Purpose *Let's listen for rhyming words in poems about plants.*

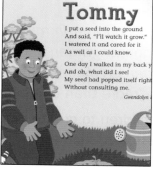

Literature Big Book, p. 31

RHYME DOK 2

Reread the second stanza of the poem aloud. *What rhyming words do you hear?* (see, me) *What sound do you hear at the end of* see *and* me? (/ē/) *Where are the rhyming words?* (the end of the line)

Literature Big Book, pp. 32–33

REREAD DOK 1

Reread the last stanza of the poem aloud. *What does the flower need to grow?* (a little sun, a little shower) *What does a little shower mean?* (a little rain)

Literature Big Book, pp. 34–35

RHYME DOK 2

Which words rhyme? (seed/weed; shoot/root; small/all) Guide children to identify the location of the rhyming words and tell the sounds that are the same for each pair of words.

Literature Big Book, p. 36

REREAD DOK 2

Reread the last two lines of the poem. *What does the word* they *refer to?* (the carnations)

BUILD ORAL VOCABULARY

Explain that the prefix *re-* means *again. Replanting* in line 6 means "planting again."

Return to Purpose

Remind children of their purpose for reading. (to listen for words that rhyme as they hear poems about growing plants) Prompt them to tell what new information they learned from reading the poems.

Retell

Guide children to use the pictures to retell the details of the different poems. Encourage them to use the vocabulary words they have been learning. You may also wish to invite children to retell the poems by sharing their favorite part(s) of the poem.

Close Reading Routine

Read DOK 1–2

- Identify key ideas and details.
- Take notes and retell.
- Use **A C T** prompts as needed.

Reread DOK 2–3

- Analyze the text, craft, and structure.

Integrate DOK 3–4

- Integrate knowledge and ideas.
- Make text-to-text connections.
- Complete the Show Your Knowledge task.
- Inspire action.

ELL SPOTLIGHT ON LANGUAGE

Page 34 *seed/tree/deep:* Children might think *tree* or *deep* rhyme with *seed* because they all contain the /ē/ sound. Review the concept of rhyming words and that the final sounds of the words need to be the same. Seed *ends with* /d/. *What sound does* tree *end with?* (/ē/) *What sound does* deep *end with?* (/p/)

> **STUDENT CHECK-IN**

Have partners take turns identifying rhyming words from the poems. Then have children reflect on their learning using the Check-In routine.

LESSON 4

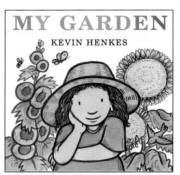

MY GARDEN
KEVIN HENKES

Literature Big Book

LEARNING GOALS

We can think about how an author uses a picture to share information about a poem.

OBJECTIVES

Recognize and produce rhyming words.

Use words and phrases acquired through conversations, reading and being read to, and responding to texts.

Demonstrate command of the conventions of standard English grammar and usage when writing or speaking.

Analyze the author's craft.

ELA ACADEMIC LANGUAGE

• *poem*
• Cognate: *poema*

Reread

"The Seed"

Analyze the Text

After children read "The Seed," reread it with them. Use the instructions in the prompts below to help children answer the questions on pages 26-27 in the **Reading/Writing Companion**.

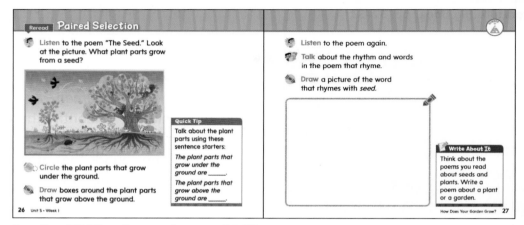

Reading/Writing Companion, pp. 26-27

AUTHOR'S CRAFT DOK 2

• Have children turn to page 26 and look at the picture. Ask: *What grows from a seed?* (roots, branches, leaves) As you speak, model using the new vocabulary words and encourage children to respond in that way.

• Have children circle the parts of the tree that grow under the ground. (roots) Then have them draw a box around the parts that grow above the ground. (trunk, branches, leaves)

• Read the poem this time clapping out the rhythm. Have children listen for words that rhyme. (weed/seed, be/tree, shoot/root, small/all, suppose/knows) Then have them draw a picture that rhymes with *seed.* (weed)

Write About It

Tell children that they will write a poem about a plant or a garden.

Review the Paired Selection Reread "The Seed." Have children listen for details about seeds and plants. Then have volunteers retell the poem, using their newly acquired vocabulary.

Plan Have children talk with a partner about growing a plant or a garden. Ask them to choose one of these things and draw a picture of it.

Draft Have partners begin writing their poem. Share these sentence frames to get them started: **My plant is _____. My garden has _____.** Remind them to include rhyming words in their poem.

Revise and Edit Have children read their poems and ask themselves the following questions:

- Did I choose interesting words?
- Do I need to add important details?
- Do I want to include words that rhyme?

Tell children to revise and edit their poems as appropriate.

Share Have children take turns reading their poems aloud.

Integrate

Build Knowledge: Make Connections

Talk About the Text Have partners discuss the living things that they see and hear about in the poem, "The Seed." *What do these living things need to grow?*

Add to the Anchor Chart Record any new ideas on the Build Knowledge Anchor Chart.

Add to the Word Bank Record any new words on the Word Bank.

English Language Learners

Use the following scaffolds with **Analyze the Text, Author's Craft.**

Beginning

Say and point: *I see branches. I see roots. I see a trunk.* Have children repeat the sentences as they point to each item in the picture.

Intermediate

Help children point to and name details they see in the picture. Provide children with a word bank. Then have children use sentence frames, such as: The tree has branches and roots.

Advanced/Advanced High

Have children point to the picture and describe what they see. Encourage children to use complete sentences. Model, if necessary: *A tree is growing. I see branches and leaves.*

 CONNECT TO CONTENT

How Flowers Are Alike and Different Discuss the illustration on pages 32–33. Ask children to describe what the picture shows. (The picture shows flowers growing.) Have volunteers point to the things in the picture that help a flower to grow. (sun, rain, soil) Explain to children that most flowers are alike because they need soil, sunlight, and water to grow. Have children discuss how flowers are different. (color, size, shape)

STEM

 **FORMATIVE ASSESSMENT**

❯ STUDENT CHECK-IN

Have partners share something they learned from the picture. Then have children reflect using the Check-in routine.

In a Flash: Sound-Spellings

Display the Sound-Spelling Card for *h*.
1. **Teacher:** What's the letter?   **Children:** h
2. **Teacher:** What's the sound?   **Children:** /h/
3. **Teacher:** What's the word?   **Children:** hippo

Continue the routine for previously taught sounds.

LEARNING GOALS

- We can name the word that does not begin with the same sound.
- We can read and spell words with the letter *h*.
- We can read sentences with the word *my*.

OBJECTIVES

Isolate the initial sounds (phonemes) in words.

Distinguish between similarly spelled words by identifying the sounds of the letters that differ.

Spell simple words phonetically, drawing on knowledge of sound-letter relationships.

Read common high-frequency words by sight.

ELA ACADEMIC LANGUAGE

- *belong, middle*

TEACH IN SMALL GROUP

You may wish to teach the Word Work lesson in small groups.

DIGITAL TOOLS

Visual Vocabulary Cards

Wonders Practice Book Blackline Masters

Phonemic Awareness: p. 199
Phonics: p. 202

Phonemic Awareness

(5 mins)

Phoneme Categorization

1 Model Display the **Photo Cards** for *hand, hammer,* and *jacket. Which picture names begin with the same sound?* Say the picture names. Hand *and* hammer *both begin with /h/.* Jacket *does not begin with /h/.* Jacket *does not belong.*

Photo Cards

2 Guided Practice/Practice Show children sets of Photo Cards. Name the pictures with children and have them identify the picture in each set that does not begin with the same sound. Guide practice and provide corrective feedback as needed.

hair, hat, night	snack, snap, helicopter	hippo, hook, nut
horse, light, house	seal, hair, hammer	door, dog, hay

If children need additional practice categorizing words by phoneme, have them use **Practice Book** page 199.

Phonics

(5 mins)

MULTIMODAL

Build and Read Words

Provide children with **Word Building Cards** a–z. Have them put the letters in alphabetic order as quickly as possible.

1 Guided Practice Use the Word-Building Cards *h, i, p* to form the word *hip.* Have children use their word cards to build the word *hip.* Then say: *I will change the middle letter in* hip *to make the word* hop. Change the *i* to *o,* and read aloud the word *hop* together.

2 Practice Write *hat* and *hit.* Have children say the sounds for each letter and blend and read the words. Have children say both words and tell which sounds are different. /a/, /i/ Ask children to tell which letters are different. (*a, i*) Discuss the sounds each letter stands for and how it changes the word. Repeat with *hot* and *pot.* If children need additional practice in identifying the sounds for letters, have them use **Practice Book** page 202.

Spell Words

Dictation Dictate these sounds for children to spell. Have them repeat the sound and then write the appropriate letter. Repeat.

/h/   /i/   /n/   /k/   /o/   /d/   /a/   /t/   /p/

Dictate the following words for children to spell: *hit, hat, hot, hop, hip.* Model for children how to segment each word to scaffold the spelling. Say: *When I say the word* hit *I hear three sounds: /h/ /i/ /t/. I know the letter* h *stands for /h/, the letter* i *stands for /i/, and the letter* t *stands for /t/. I will write the letters* h, i, t *to spell the word* hit. Then, write the letters and words for children to self-correct.

OPTIONAL 5 mins

High-Frequency Words

MULTIMODAL

Practice Say the word *my* and have children write it. Display the print or digital **Visual Vocabulary Card** *my.* Follow the Teacher Talk routine on the back.

Build Fluency Build sentences in the pocket chart using the **High-Frequency Word Cards, Photo Cards** and teacher-made punctuation cards. Have children chorally read the sentences as you track the print.

I like my kitten.   **Do you see my bike?**

 Word Activity Tape several High-Frequency Word Cards to a wall or sheet. Have children take turns using a pointer to tap a word and read it. This can be done as a small group or center activity.

Have partners say sentences using the word *my.*

EXTEND THE LESSON

You may wish to use this lesson to teach final /z/ *s.* Write the word *his.* Underline *s.* Point out that when *s* appears at the end of a word, it sometimes stands for /z/. Blend *his* with children, emphasizing the /z/ sound at the end. Write *is, as, has.* Blend each word with children.

DECODABLE READERS

Have children read "Hip Hop" (pages 7–12), to practice decoding words in connected text.

Unit 5 Decodable Reader

FORMATIVE ASSESSMENT

⊙ STUDENT CHECK-IN

Phonics Have partners use Word-Building Cards to spell and read *him.*

High-Frequency Words Have partners point to and read a sentence from the lesson.

Then have children reflect using the Check-In routine.

⊘ CHECK FOR SUCCESS

Rubric Use your online rubric to record children's progress.

Can children categorize words with the same initial phoneme and blend words with /h/ and match it to the letter *Hh*?

Can children read and recognize high-frequency words?

⊙ Small Group Instruction

If No

● **Approaching** Reteach pp. T62–66

● **ELL** Develop pp. T62–66

If Yes

● **On** Review pp. T70–72

● **Beyond** Extend p. T76

LEARNING GOALS

- We can revise our writing.
- We can learn about words that can take the place of nouns (pronouns).

OBJECTIVES

With guidance and support from adults, respond to questions and suggestions from peers and add details to strengthen writing as needed.

Produce and expand complete sentences in shared language activities.

Appropriately use pronouns.

ELA ACADEMIC LANGUAGE

- *pronoun*
- Cognate: *pronombre*

 Independent Writing

5 mins

Write About the Shared Read

 Revise

Reread the prompt about "Hop Can Hop!": *What do Dot and Hop like to do together?* Have children read their drafts to see if they responded to the prompt by focusing on one idea, by using pronouns, and by using end punctuation.

Peer Review Have partners review each other's writing. Children should share what they like most about the writing, questions they have for the author, and additional ideas they think the author could include. Provide time for children to make revisions and add details to strengthen their writing.

Edit/Proofread

After children have revised their work, have them edit it carefully, checking for the following:

- Each sentence begins with a capital letter.
- Each sentence tells a complete thought.

If children need additional practice with editing and proofreading, have them use **Practice Book** page 208.

 Write Final Draft

After children have edited their writing and finished their peer review, have them write their final draft in their writer's notebook. Tell children to write neatly so that others can read their writing, or guide them to explore a variety of digital tools they can use to publish their work.

Teacher Conference As children review their drafts, confer with them to provide guidance. Suggest places in their writing where they might add details or replace a noun with a pronoun.

 Share and Evaluate

After children have finalized their draft, have them work with a partner to practice presenting their writing to one another. Remind children to speak in complete sentences. If possible, record children as they share so that they can see themselves presenting, or you can use as a topic of discussion for a teacher conference.

Have children add their work to their writing folder. Invite children to look at their previous writing and discuss with a partner how it has improved.

Grammar

5 mins

Grammar Activity

Grammar: p. 207
Edit/Proofread: p. 208

Subjective Pronouns

1 **Review** Explain to children that different pronouns are used to replace different kinds of nouns. Write and read aloud these sentences: **Dad is funny**. **He tells jokes**. Circle *Dad* and *He*. *The pronoun* He *replaces* Dad *in the second sentence.*

2 **Guided Practice/Practice** Display the *camel, cow, boy, farm,* and *girl* **Photo Cards**. Read aloud the label on each card. Write the pronouns *it, she,* and *he* on self-stick notes. *We can match each noun in the picture with a pronoun that can replace it in a sentence.* Guide children to match each photo card to the appropriate pronoun card.

Write sentence strips for each Photo Card, such as: **The camel is brown**. Underline the noun. Have partners place a self-stick note with the appropriate pronoun over the underlined word. Ask partners to share their sentences. If children need additional practice with subjective pronouns, have them use **Practice Book** page 207.

Talk About It

Have partners orally generate sentences using *he, she,* and *it*. Have them describe how they work with a partner to do an activity.

English Language Learners

Use the following scaffolds with **Independent Writing, Revise.**

Beginning

Review subjective pronouns. Write *Dot/She* on the board. Help children identify and/or add subjective pronouns in their drafts.

Intermediate

Have children identify a noun in their draft. Discuss the pronoun they can use to replace the noun. Help them rewrite the sentence using the pronoun.

Advanced/Advanced High

Have partners circle the subjective pronouns in each other's draft. If there are no subjective pronouns, have partners suggest a place where one could be added. Provide guidance as needed.

For additional support, see the **ELL Small Group Guide**, p. 113.

❯ STUDENT CHECK-IN

Have partners share a pronoun they used in their writing. Have children reflect using the Check-In routine.

LESSON
4

READING · RESEARCH AND INQUIRY

LEARNING GOALS

We can research different parts of a plant.

OBJECTIVES

With guidance and support from adults, recall information from experiences or gather information from provided sources to answer a question.

Add drawings or other visual displays to descriptions as desired to provide additional detail.

Produce and expand complete sentences in shared language activities.

Follow agreed-upon rules for discussions.

Participate in shared research and writing projects.

ELA ACADEMIC LANGUAGE

• *research*

 COLLABORATIVE CONVERSATIONS

Listen Carefully As children engage in partner, small group, and whole class discussions, encourage them to do the following:

• Look at the person who is speaking.

• Listen to what the speaker is saying.

• Respect others by not interrupting them.

• Repeat classmates' ideas to check understanding.

Integrate

⏱ 10 mins

Parts of a Plant

Model

Tell children that they will research different parts of a plant. Display pages 28-29 of the **Reading/Writing Companion**. Model completing each step in the research process.

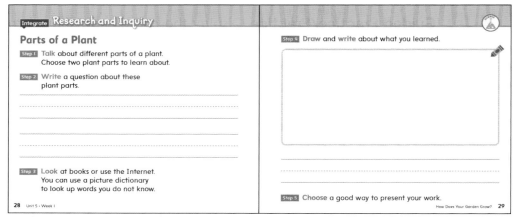

Reading/Writing Companion, pp. 28-29

STEP 1 Choose a Topic

The project is to choose two plant parts to learn about. First, I will to talk to my partner about plants and the different parts of a plant.

STEP 2 Write Your Question

I need to decide what plant parts to learn more about. I know that roots and leaves help plants. How do roots and leaves help a plant make food?

STEP 3 Find Information

To find the answer to my question, I need to do some research. I can do research by looking at the books my teacher has on plants.

STEP 4 Draw and Write What You Learned

Now that I have read and looked at the pictures in the books, I will draw my own picture of a plant and label its parts. I will also write something that I learned about how roots and leaves help plants make food.

STEP 5 Choose a Way to Present Your Work

I am going to create a poster with labels so that everyone can see the different parts of a plant and how they help the plant make food.

Apply

Have children turn to page 28 in their **Reading/Writing Companion**. Guide them through the steps of the research process.

If children are unsure about how to do their research, model for them how to identify the best way to gather the information.

Choose the Presentation Format

Have children turn to pages 28-29 in their Reading/Writing Companion to review their research, their drawings, and what they learned about the different parts of a plant. Tell them that today they are going to take the next step by creating their finished product, which they will present tomorrow. Work with children to select a good way to present their findings. Options may include drawing and labeling a picture, creating a poster, making a model or putting on a dramatic presentation.

Create the Presentation

Guide children to develop their presentation individually, in teams, or as a class. Remind them of the rules of working with others.

Gather Materials Gather together the materials children will need to create their finished product. Most of the materials should be available in the classroom or can be brought from home.

Make the Finished Product Once children have gathered the materials they need, provide time for them to create their finished product. You can dedicate an area in the classroom for project work and store all the materials there. Remind children will be presenting their work to their classmates the next day.

English Language Learners

Apply, Step 2 Brainstorm with children the different parts of plants they have learned about. Create a word bank on the board with words, such as *seed, roots, trunk, branches,* and *leaves.* Provide sentence frames to help children write their questions: How do leaves help a plant? What does a seed do?

TEACH IN SMALL GROUP

You may wish to have children create their presentation during Small Group time. Group children of varying abilities together, or group children together if they are doing similar projects.

CONNECT TO CONTENT

Diagrams Explain to children that a diagram is a way to show the parts of a plant. Diagrams include labels that name the different plant parts. Share some plant diagrams with children so they can use them as a model for their presentation. Tell children that when they present a diagram, the labels can be used as a way to walk through the presentation.

STEM

RESEARCH AND INQUIRY: SHARING FINAL PROJECTS

As children get ready to wrap up the week, have them share their Research and Inquiry projects. Then have children self-evaluate.

Prepare Have children gather any materials they need to present their Research and Inquiry projects. Have partners practice their presentations.

Share Guide children to present their Research and Inquiry projects. Encourage children to speak in complete sentences.

Evaluate Have children discuss and evaluate their own presentations. You may wish to have them complete the online Student Checklist.

FORMATIVE ASSESSMENT

STUDENT CHECK-IN

Have partners share one part of a plant that they researched. Have children reflect using the Check-In routine.

LESSON 5

LEARNING GOALS

- We can name the word that does not begin with the same sound.
- We can spell words with the letter *h*.
- We can spell the word *my*.

OBJECTIVES

Isolate the initial sounds (phonemes) in words.

Demonstrate basic knowledge of one-to-one letter-sound correspondences by producing the primary sound or many of the most frequent sounds for each consonant.

Spell simple words phonetically, drawing on knowledge of sound-letter relationships.

Read common high-frequency words by sight.

ELA ACADEMIC LANGUAGE

- *begin, same*

 TEACH IN SMALL GROUP

You may wish to teach this lesson in small groups.

DIGITAL TOOLS

 Word Work — Phonemic Awareness

 Visual Vocabulary Cards

 Phonics: Spelling Song

LESSON FOCUS

READING
Wrap Up
Word Work
- Read Words

WRITING
Writing/Grammar
- Self-Selected Writing
- Review Grammar

Research and Inquiry
- Share and Evaluate Presentation

Text Connections
- Connect Essential Question to a poem
- Show Your Knowledge

Reading/Writing Companion, pp. 30–31

---

 5 mins

Phonemic Awareness

Phoneme Categorization

1. **Model** Display the **Photo Cards** for *hook, hippo,* and *kitten. Listen for which picture names begin with the same sound.* Say the picture names. Hook *and* hippo *both begin with /h/.* Kitten *does not begin with /h/.* Kitten *does not belong.*

2. **Guided Practice/Practice** Show children sets of Photo Cards. Name the pictures with children and have them identify the pictures in each set that begin with the same sound and the one that does not. Guide practice and provide corrective feedback as needed.

inch, house, hat	horse, insect, hay	dog, hay, helicopter
hand, house, jump	egg, hair, hat	hook, cowboy, comb

 5 mins

Phonics

 MULTIMODAL

Read Words

1. **Guided Practice** Display **Word-Building Cards** *a, t.* Point to the letter *a. The letter a stands for the sound /a/. Say /aaa/. The letter* t *stands for /t/. Say /t/. Let's blend the sounds to make the word: /aaat/ at. Now let's add* h *to the beginning.* Blend and read *hat.*

2. **Practice** Write these words and sentences for children to read:

hop	hit	hot	ham	hid	hip	him

I like ham.   Pam can hop.

Pam and Pat like the hat.   Tim can hit.

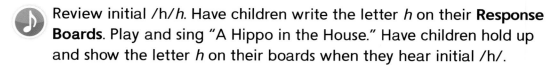 Review initial /h/*h.* Have children write the letter *h* on their **Response Boards**. Play and sing "A Hippo in the House." Have children hold up and show the letter *h* on their boards when they hear initial /h/.

In a Flash: Sound-Spellings

Display the Sound-Spelling Card for *h*.
1. **Teacher:** What's the letter?   **Children:** h
2. **Teacher:** What's the sound?   **Children:** /h/
3. **Teacher:** What's the word?   **Children:** hippo

Continue the routine for previously taught sounds.

Spell Words

Dictation Dictate the following sounds for children to spell. As you say each sound, have children repeat it and then write the letter on their **Response Boards** that stands for the sound.

/h/   /i/   /n/   /k/   /o/   /d/   /sn/

Dictate the following words for children to spell. Model for children how to segment words to scaffold the spelling. *I will say a word. You will repeat the word, then think about how many sounds are in the word. Use your Sound Boxes to count the sounds. Then write one letter for each sound you hear.*

hip   snip   hat   hop   pin   hot   hit   ham

Then write the letters and word for children to self-correct.

 5 mins

High-Frequency Words

 MULTIMODAL

Review Display the print or digital **Visual Vocabulary Card** *my*. Have children Read/ Spell/Write the word. Then choose a Partner Talk activity.

Visual Vocabulary Card

Distribute the following **High-Frequency Word Cards** to children: *I, can, go, to, my, you*. Tell children that you will say some sentences. *When you hear the word that is on your card, stand and hold up the word card.*

I can go to my house.
Sam can ride my horse.
My garden is beautiful.
Nat will go in my car.
Would you like to share my lunch?
I like to go fishing in my boat.

Build Fluency: Word Automaticity Display High-Frequency Word Cards *to, and, go, you, do, my*. Point to each card, at random, and have children read as quickly as they can to build automaticity.

MULTIMODAL LEARNING

Color Coding After each dictation, reveal the secret color-coding-letter(s) for children to find on their **Response Boards**. Have them say the sound(s) as they trace each letter in color. Use one or two of the phonics skills of the week for color-coding.

FORMATIVE ASSESSMENT

STUDENT CHECK-IN
Phonics Have partners spell *had*.

High-Frequency Words Have partners spell the word *my*.

Then have children reflect using the Check-In routine.

CHECK FOR SUCCESS
Rubric Use your online rubric to record children's progress.

Can children categorize initial phonemes and read words with /h/*h*?

Can children read and recognize high-frequency words?

Small Group Instruction

If No
● **Approaching** Reteach pp. T62–66
● **ELL** Develop pp. T62–66

If Yes
● **On** Review pp. T70–72
● **Beyond** Extend p. T76

LEARNING GOALS

- **We can choose a writing activity and share it.**
- **We can learn about words that can take the place of nouns (pronouns).**

OBJECTIVES

With guidance and support from adults, explore a variety of digital tools to produce and publish writing, including in collaboration with peers.

Ask and answer questions in order to seek help, get information, or clarify something that is not understood.

Speak audibly and express thoughts, feelings, and ideas clearly.

Produce and expand complete sentences in shared language activities.

Appropriately use pronouns.

ELA ACADEMIC LANGUAGE
- *topic, detail, pronoun*
- Cognates: *detalle, pronombre*

DIFFERENTIATED WRITING

You may wish to conference with children to provide additional support for the writing activities below.

- **Picture Spark:** Point out a detail in the picture and have children find another detail.
- **Squiggle Writing:** Brainstorm a list of living things that children learned about or are interested in.

 5 mins

Self-Selected Writing

Talk About the Topic

Have children continue the conversation about living things. Remind them of the Essential Question: *What do living things need to grow?* Encourage partners to share what they learned this week and encourage them to ask one another questions.

Choose A Writing Activity

Tell children they will select a type of writing to share their ideas. They may choose to write about what living things need to grow or a different topic. Encourage them to draw first as a way to get their ideas down on paper. Children may choose from the following modes of writing:

 Picture Spark Display pictures of living things. Explain that pictures can "spark" ideas for writing. Have children choose a picture. Guide them to identify details in the picture that they may want to write about. Then have them write about the picture they chose or another picture in their writer's notebook.

 Squiggle Writing Draw a squiggle on the board and have children copy the squiggle in their writer's notebook. Explain to children that they should turn the squiggle into a drawing of a living thing or another type of picture they are interested in. Model as needed. When children are done with their drawing, have them write about it.

Use Digital Tools You may wish to work with children to explore a variety of digital tools to produce or publish their work.

Share Your Writing

 COLLABORATE

Invite volunteers to share their writing with the class or have partners share their writing with each other. Remind children to use the strategies below as they share out. After children share their work, you may wish to display it on a bulletin board or in a classroom writing area.

SPEAKING STRATEGIES	LISTENING STRATEGIES
✔ Wait until it is your turn to speak.	✔ Listen actively and quietly.
✔ Speak loud enough so that everyone can hear you.	✔ Wait until the speaker has finished to ask questions.

Grammar

10 mins

Subjective Pronouns

1 **Review** Write and read aloud this sentence: **The girl went skating**. Circle *girl*. Remind children that *girl* can be replaced with the pronoun *she*. Rewrite the sentence with the pronoun *she* and read it aloud.

2 **Guided Practice/Practice** Write and read aloud these sentences: **The car is fast. Dad likes to drive. Mom likes to drive**. Guide children to identify the noun in each sentence. Tell children they will rewrite the sentences with pronouns in the place of the nouns. List the pronouns *She, He,* and *It*. Then write these sentence frames on the board:

_____ **is fast.**   _____ **likes to drive.**

_____ **likes to drive.**

Complete the first sentence frame together. (It is fast.) Then have partners copy the two remaining sentence frames and complete each, using the correct pronoun. (He likes to drive. She likes to drive.) Have children circle the pronouns in their sentences.

English Language Learners

Self-Selected Writing, Choose a Writing Activity Present the writing activities, and tell children that they will vote on one of the activities. Then, you will work on the writing as a group. Make sure to do the activity on chart paper as you will revise and publish it during small group time. Provide sentence frames and starters as you talk through the writing together. For example, if children have selected squiggle writing, make a squiggle on the board, and have children talk about what living thing you could turn it into. After choosing a living thing, finish the drawing. Then, talk about it. Possible sentence frames are: My living thing is ___. It has/is ___. One thing I know about it is ___.

For additional support, see the **ELL Small Group Guide,** p. 113.

DIGITAL TOOLS

Grammar Activity

How to Give a Presentation

⟩ TEACH IN SMALL GROUP

You may wish to review the grammar skill during Small Group time.

● **Approaching** Provide more opportunities for children to practice identifying pronouns before they write sentences.

● ● **On-Level** and **Beyond** Children can do the Practice sections only.

● **ELL** Use the chart in the **Language Transfers Handbook** to identify grammatical forms that may cause difficulty.

FORMATIVE ASSESSMENT

❯ STUDENT CHECK-IN

Have partners share which activity they chose and tell why. Then have children reflect using the Check-In routine.

LESSON 5

LEARNING GOALS

We can compare texts we have read.

OBJECTIVES

Confirm understanding of a text read aloud or information presented orally or through other media by asking and answering questions about key details and requesting clarification if something is not understood.

ELA ACADEMIC LANGUAGE

• *compare, nursery rhyme, experience*

• Cognate: *comparar*

Close Reading Routine

Read   DOK 1–2

• Identify key ideas and details.
• Take notes and retell.
• Use prompts as needed.

Reread   DOK 2–3

• Analyze the text, craft, and structure.

Integrate   DOK 3–4

• Integrate knowledge and ideas.
• Make text-to-text connections.
• Use the Integrate lesson.
• Complete the Show Your Knowledge task.

FORMATIVE ASSESSMENT

❯ STUDENT CHECK-IN

Have partners share what they learned from comparing texts.

Have children reflect using the Check-in routine.

T58 UNIT 5 WEEK 1

Integrate

🕙 10 mins

Make Connections

Connect to the Essential Question

Review the Essential Question. Turn to page 30 of the **Reading/Writing Companion**. Have children listen to the nursery rhyme. *What things does Mary grow?*

Find Text Evidence Have children answer the following questions about this page and the **Big Book**: *What grows in Mary's garden?* (different kinds of flowers) *What does the girl in* My Garden *want to grow in her garden?* (flowers that never die and change color) Use the Quick Tip box for support.

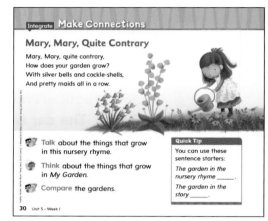

Reading/Writing Companion, p. 30

Record Ideas Guide partners to compare the nursery rhyme on page 30 of the Reading/Writing Companion with *My Garden. How are the gardens alike? How are they different? How do they help you answer the Essential Question?* Help children use a Two-Tab Foldable® to record their ideas. Have children support their ideas with evidence from the texts.

Dinah Zike's
FOLDABLES
Study Organizer

Build Knowledge: Make Connections DOK 4

Talk About the Text Have partners compare the text with experiences from their own lives.

Add to the Anchor Chart Record any new ideas on the Build Knowledge anchor chart.

Integrate

Show Your Knowledge

15 mins

Draw What a Plant Needs DOK 4

Display the texts for the week along with the Build Knowledge anchor chart and Word Bank. Turn to page 31 of the **Reading/ Writing Companion** and guide children through the steps below.

1. Think Ask: *What did you learn about what living things need to grow?* Encourage partners to refer to their reader's notebook and the resources on display as they discuss their response.

2. Draw Have partners talk about what plants need to grow and then show their ideas in a drawing (e.g. sun, water).

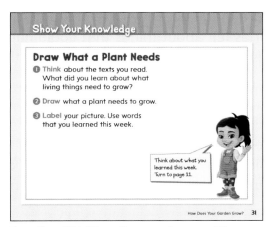

Reading/Writing Companion, p. 31

3. Label Have children label their drawings. Encourage them to use words they learned this week as they write.

Inspire Action

Grow a Plant Have children plant seeds in cup. Teach them to provide the seeds with what they need to grow. Once seeds start to grow, you may wish to transplant them to a class garden.

How Do Plants Help? Explain that plants help the earth by cleaning the air. Encourage children to research other ways that plants help, such as by providing food or happiness.

Choose Your Own Action Have children talk about the texts they read this week. *What do the texts inspire or make you want to do?*

LEARNING GOALS

We can show what we learned about what living things need to grow.

OBJECTIVES

With guidance and support from adults, recall information from experiences or gather information from provided sources to answer a question.

Use words and phrases acquired through conversations, reading, and being read to, and responding to texts.

ELA ACADEMIC LANGUAGE

• *label, inspire*

ELL ENGLISH LANGUAGE LEARNERS

Show Your Knowledge, Write Have children point to different parts of their picture, and ensure that they can name each part. Point to the appropriate words in the Word Bank, as needed.

Draw Provide and model sentence starters or frames to talk about how plants grow. For example, Plants need____. Plants should be ____ to ____.

DIGITAL TOOLS

To enhance the class discussion, use these additional components.

Visual Vocabulary Cards

RUBRIC

Show Your Knowledge Rubric

MY GOALS ROUTINE

Review Have children turn to page 11 of the **Reading/Writing Companion**. Read the goals aloud.

Reflect Have children think about the progress they've made toward the goals. Review the Key, if needed. Then have children complete page 11.

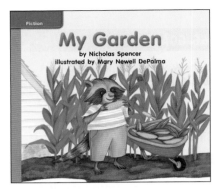

Lexile BR

OBJECTIVES

Understand that words are separated by spaces in print.

Demonstrate understanding of the organization and basic features of print.

With prompting and support, identify characters, settings, and major events in a story.

Read emergent-reader texts with purpose and understanding.

ELA ACADEMIC LANGUAGE

• *characters, setting, events*
• Cognate: *eventos*

● Approaching Level

Leveled Reader: *My Garden*

Preview and Predict

Read aloud the title and the names of the author and the illustrator. Turn to the title page and read it aloud. Ask children what is happening in the picture. Preview the rest of the illustrations and identify the rebus pictures. Ask: *Who is this story about? Where does this story take place? What do you think will happen?*

Review Genre: Fiction

Remind children that fiction stories are made up. They have characters, events, and a setting. Explain that some stories tell about things that could happen in real life. Tell children that this story is about a raccoon and the things that he likes in his garden.

Set Purpose

Remind children of the Essential Question: *What do living things need to grow?* Help children set a purpose for reading: *Let's read to find out more about the raccoon and his garden.* Review rebuses with children to help them name the words.

Foundational Skills

Model Concepts of Print Demonstrate concepts of print. Open the book to page 3 and point to the spaces between words. Say: *In a sentence there is a space between each word. At the end of the sentence there is a period.*

Review High-Frequency Words Point to the high-frequency word *my* on page 2 of the story. Have them find the word *my* on pages 3, 4, and 5.

Guided Comprehension

As children read *My Garden*, monitor and provide guidance by offering support and corrective feedback as needed. Model rereading and identifying story elements, such as character, setting, and events, where applicable.

Rereading

Remind children that if they come to a part of the story that is confusing, they can reread the text to make sure they understand it.

Main Story Elements: Character, Setting, Events

Tell children that they can learn a lot about the characters, the setting, and the events in a story by looking at the pictures. After reading, ask: *Who is this story about? Where does this story take place?*

Think Aloud The words on page 4 tell me that Raccoon likes his gloves. I can see in the picture that his wheelbarrow is full of other things he uses in his garden. I can see a garden tool—a hoe—and a hose. And I can see his garden in the background, too.

Guide children to identify the character and the setting in the illustrations on the rest of the pages. Ask them to tell what is happening on pages 6 and 7.

Respond to the Text

Have children respond to the text by discussing these questions:

- *Where does the story take place?* (a garden) *How can you tell?* (Raccoon's garden is shown in the illustrations.)

- *Whose garden is this? How do you know?* (The illustrations show Raccoon.)

- *What happens at the end of the story?* (Raccoon has grown corn.)

- *In this story, what do plants need to grow?* (soil, water)

Retell Have children take turns retelling the story, using characters, the setting, and events. Help them make a personal connection. Ask: *What would you grow in a garden?*

Focus on Fluency

Practice fluency with children. Remember that children need to read with accuracy first.

Once children have read the text with accuracy, have them read the story again, focusing on rate. Have them practice reading with partners. Provide corrective feedback as necessary.

Build Knowledge: Make Connections

- **Talk About the Texts** Have partners discuss what plants need to grow.

- **Write About the Texts** Then have children add their ideas to their Build Knowledge page of their Reader's Notebook.

LITERACY ACTIVITIES

Have children complete the Collaborate and Write About It activities on the inside back cover of the book.

LEVEL UP

IF Children read *My Garden* Approaching Level with fluency and correctly answer the Respond to the Text questions,

THEN Tell children that they will read another story about a garden.

- Have children page through *My Garden Grows* On Level as you introduce the story and characters. Preview the illustration on page 7.

- Have children read the story, monitoring their comprehension and providing assistance as necessary.

●Approaching Level

Phonological/Phonemic Awareness

COUNT AND BLEND SYLLABLES

OBJECTIVES
Count, pronounce, blend, and segment syllables in spoken words.

I Do Say: *I'll count the parts of the word* contrary. *Listen: /kon/ /tre/ /rē/. The word* contrary *has three parts*. Clap out each syllable as you say the word. Then blend the syllables to say the word: /kon/ /tre/ /rē/, *contrary*.

We Do *Listen to this word:* pretty. *Clap out with me as we say the parts together: /prit/ /ē/. Say the word parts, then say the word with me: /prit/ /ē/,* pretty. Repeat with *Mary. How many word parts do you hear?* (2)

You Do Say *pretty* and *garden*. Have children say the words, clapping once for each syllable. *How many word parts do you hear?* (2) Then have children blend the syllables to say the words. Continue the routine with the words *flower, silver,* and *Mary*.

PHONEME ISOLATION

OBJECTIVES
Isolate and pronounce the initial sounds in words.

I Do Display the *hat* **Photo Card**. *This is a* hat. *The first sound in* hat *is /h/.* Have children repeat the word with you, emphasizing the initial sound. Then have children say the first sound with you: /h/.

We Do Display the *hand* Photo Card. Name the photo and have children say the name. *What is the first sound in* hand? (/h/) Say the sound together. Repeat with the *horse* Photo Card.

You Do Show the *house* Photo Card. Have children name it and say the initial sound of the picture name. Repeat with the *hippo* and *hook* Photo Cards.

ELL You may wish to review phonological awareness, phonics, decoding, and fluency using this section. Use scaffolding methods as necessary to ensure children understand the meanings of the words. Refer to the **Language Transfers Handbook** for phonics elements that may not transfer in children's native languages.

PHONEME BLENDING

OBJECTIVES

Demonstrate understanding of spoken words, syllables, and sounds (phonemes).

Blend phonemes to make words.

I Do *I am going to say the sounds in a word: /h/ /ō/ /m/. I can blend these sounds together: /hōōōmmm/,* home. Repeat with *hit.*

We Do *Now I am going to say the sounds in another word. Say the sounds with me: /h/ /o/ /t/. Let's blend the sounds together: /hooot/,* hot. Repeat with *hip* and *ham.*

You Do Have children blend sounds to form words. Practice together: /h/ /o/ /p/, /hooop/, *hop.* Have children blend the following sounds to say the words: /h/ /a/ /d/, had; /h/ /o/ /g/, hog; /h/ /i/ /l/, hill; /h/ /e/ /m/, hem.

You may wish to use a puppet, if one is available in the classroom, for the *I Do* and *We Do* parts of this lesson.

PHONEME CATEGORIZATION

OBJECTIVES

Isolate and pronounce the initial sounds in words.

I Do Display the *hammer, hippo,* and *dinosaur* **Photo Cards**. Say each picture name, emphasizing the initial sound. Hammer *and* hippo *begin with /h/.* Dinosaur *does not begin with /h/.* Dinosaur *does not belong.*

We Do Display the *corn, hand,* and *cow* Photo Cards. Have children name each picture with you, emphasizing the initial sound. *Which word does not have the same beginning sound?* (hand) Repeat the routine with the *rake, horse,* and *rock* Photo Cards.

You Do Display and name the *mouse, moon,* and *house* Photo Cards. Have children name each picture and tell which pictures have the same initial sound and which picture does not have the same initial sound. Repeat the routine with these sets of Photo Cards: *helicopter, hat, net; pizza, pumpkin, house.*

● Approaching Level

Phonics

SOUND-SPELLING REVIEW

OBJECTIVES
Demonstrate basic knowledge of one-to-one letter-sound correspondences by producing the primary or many of the most frequent sounds for each consonant.

I Do Display **Word-Building Card** *n*. Say the letter name and the sound it stands for: *n, /n/.* Repeat for *c, o, d,* the initial blend *sn,* and *i.*

We Do Display Word-Building Cards one at a time and together say the letter name and the sound that each letter stands for.

You Do Display Word-Building Cards one at a time and have children say the letter name and the sound that each letter stands for.

CONNECT *h* TO /h/

OBJECTIVES
Demonstrate basic knowledge of one-to-one letter-sound correspondences by producing the primary or many of the most frequent sounds for each consonant.

I Do Display the *hippo* **Sound-Spelling Card**. *The letter* h *stands for /h/, the sound at the beginning of* hippo. *I will write* h *when I hear /h/ in these words.* Say: *happy, cow, heart, heat, open.*

We Do *The word* head *begins with /h/. Let's write* h. Guide children to write *h* when they hear a word that begins with /h/. Say: *hope, sink, candle, horse, hide.*

You Do Say the following words and have children write the letter *h* if the word begins with /h/: *ink, high, core, happy, deep, hello, hop.*

BLEND WORDS WITH /h/h

OBJECTIVES
Know and apply grade-level phonics and word analysis skills in decoding words.

Build words with *h.*

I Do Display Word-Building Cards *h, a,* and *t. This is the letter* h. *It stands for /h/. This is the letter* a. *It stands for /a/. This is the letter* t. *It stands for /t/. Listen as I blend all the sounds: /haaat/,* hat. *The word is* hat. Repeat for *has.*

We Do *Now let's blend more sounds to make words.* Display the word *ham. Let's blend: /haaammm/,* ham. Have children blend to read the words. Repeat with the word *him. Let's blend and read the new word: /hiiimmm/,* him.

You Do Distribute sets of Word-Building Cards with *h, a, i, t,* and *m.* Write: *hit, hat, ham, him.* Have children form the words and then blend and read the words.

BUILD WORDS WITH /h/h

OBJECTIVES

Know and apply grade-level phonics and word analysis skills in decoding words.

Build words with *h*.

I Do Display **Word-Building Cards** *h, o,* and *t. These letters stand for /h/, /o/, /t/. I will blend the sounds together to read the word: /hooot/,* hot.

We Do Distribute Word-Building Cards with *h, o, t, i,* and *p.* Make the word *hot* and replace the letter *t* with a *p. Let's blend /hoooppp/,* hop. *Now we have read a new word,* hop.

You Do Have children change the medial *o* in *hop* to an *i* and read the new word.

REREAD THE DECODABLE READER

OBJECTIVES

Know and apply grade-level phonics and word analysis skills in decoding words.

Read emergent-reader texts with purpose and understanding.

Unit 5 Decodable Reader

Focus on Foundational Skills

Review the high-frequency word *my* with children. Review the letter *h* and the sound /h/. Guide children to blend sounds to read *hat* and *him*.

Read the Decodable Reader

Have children read "Hap Hid the Ham" and "Hip Hop." Point out the high-frequency word *my* as well as words with /h/ at the beginning. If children struggle sounding out words, model blending.

Focus on Fluency

Have partners read "Hap Hid the Ham" and "Hip Hop." Guide them to focus on their accuracy and reading with automaticity and at an appropriate rate. You may wish to have them reread "Hop Can Hop!" (pages 18-25) in the **Reading/Writing Companion**.

BUILD FLUENCY WITH PHONICS

Sound/Spelling Fluency

Display the following Word-Building Cards: *i, n, c, o, d, s, n,* and *h.* Have children chorally say each sound. Repeat and vary the pace.

Approaching Level

High-Frequency Words

RETEACH WORDS

OBJECTIVES
Read common high-frequency words by sight.

I Do Display **High-Frequency Word Card** *my* and use the Read/Spell/Write routine to reteach the word.

We Do Write this sentence and read it aloud: *Do you like my hat?* Have children point to the word *my* in the sentence. Then distribute index cards with the word *my* written on them. Have children match their word cards with the word *my* in the sentence. Use the same routine for the sentence: *It is hot in my garden.*

You Do Write the sentence frame: *I can see my _____.* Have children copy the sentence frame on their **Response Boards**. Then have partners work together to read and orally complete the frame by talking about what they can see in or on their desk.

CUMULATIVE REVIEW

OBJECTIVES
Read common high-frequency words by sight.

I Do Display the High-Frequency Word Cards *I, can, the, we, see, a, like, to, and, go, you, do,* and *my.* Use the Read/Spell/Write routine to review words. Have children practice reading the words until they can read them accurately and with automaticity. Use the High-Frequency Word Cards and **Word-Building Cards** to create sentences, such as *I can go to see him. Do you like to go?*

We Do Use the High-Frequency Word Cards and Word-Building Cards to create sentences, such as *I can go to the house. You and I like my cats.* Have children identify the high-frequency words that are used in each sentence.

You Do Have partners use the High-Frequency Word Cards and Word-Building Cards to create short sentences. Have partners take turns reading the sentences to each other.

Oral Vocabulary

REVIEW WORDS

OBJECTIVES

Use words and phrases acquired through conversations, reading and being read to, and responding to texts.

Identify real-life connections between words and their use.

I Do Use the Define/Example/Ask routine on the print or digital **Visual Vocabulary Cards** to review *plant, require, harmful, soak,* and *crowd.*

We Do Ask questions to build understanding. *What kind of plant could we grow in our classroom? What do you require to draw a picture? What is something that is harmful to us? What can you use to soak up water? Why might it be hard to crowd a lot of toys into a shoe box?*

You Do Have children complete these sentence frames:
One thing a plant needs to grow is _____.
Children require a coat and hat in the _____.
Running down the stairs can be harmful because you could _____.
The dirty clothes soak in the water before _____.
People sometimes have to crowd into a _____.

Comprehension

SELF-SELECTED READING

OBJECTIVES

With prompting and support, identify characters, settings, and major events in a story.

Read emergent-reader texts with purpose and understanding.

Independent Reading

Help children select an illustrated fiction story for independent reading. Encourage them to read for twelve minutes. Remind children that the main character is who a fiction story is mostly about. The setting is where a story takes place. Important events are what happen. Remind children that if they come to a part of the story that is confusing, they can reread the text to make sure they understand it.

If children need practice with concepts of print, use **Practice Book, page 507.**

After reading, guide children to participate in a group discussion about the story they read. In addition, children can choose activities from the **Reading Center Activity Cards** to help them apply skills to the text as they read. Offer assistance and guidance with self-selected assignments.

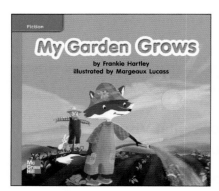

Lexile 100L.

OBJECTIVES

Follow words from left to right, top to bottom, and page by page.

With prompting and support, identify characters, settings, and major events in a story.

Read emergent-reader texts with purpose and understanding.

ELA ACADEMIC LANGUAGE

• *fiction, skill*

• Cognate: *ficción*

●On Level

Leveled Reader: *My Garden Grows*

Preview and Predict

Read the title and the names of the author and illustrator. Ask children to identify the animal on the cover. Preview the illustrations. Explain that the fox is the main character in the story. Ask: *What is the fox doing?* (working in her garden) *What do you think this book is about?*

Review Genre: Fiction

Remind children that fiction stories are made up. They have characters, events, and a setting. Explain that some stories tell about things that could happen in real life. Tell children that this story is about a fox and the things she has in her garden.

Set Purpose

Remind children of the Essential Question: *What do living things need to grow?* Help children set a purpose for reading: *Let's read to find out about the fox's garden.* Remind children to use the illustrations to help them understand the text.

Model Concepts of Print Have children open their books to page 2 and point to the sentence. Say: *I read each sentence from left to right. The sentence begins with a capital letter and ends with a period.* Model tracking the print from left to right as you read the sentence.

Review High-Frequency Words Point out the word *my* on page 2. Ask children to use the word in a sentence of their own.

Guided Comprehension

As children read *My Garden Grows*, monitor and provide guidance by offering support and corrective feedback as needed. Model rereading and identifying story elements, such as character, setting, and events, where applicable.

Reread

Remind children that if they are confused about what is happening in the story, they can reread the text to better understand it.

Main Story Elements: Character, Setting, Events

Help children understand that they can learn about the character, setting, and events by reading the words and looking at the pictures.

Think Aloud On page 6, the words and pictures tell me about a problem Fox has. I read that the garden has rabbits. The picture shows me that they are eating the lettuce in the garden. On page 7, I see that Fox has built a fence to keep the rabbits out. The pictures give me details about the events in the story.

Guide children to use the words and pictures on pages 3, 4, and 5 to find details about Fox and what happens in her garden. Have children point to evidence in the text or pictures to support their statements.

Respond to the Text

Have children respond to the text by discussing these questions:

- *What do the birds do to Fox's garden?* (They eat the seeds.)

- *How does Fox solve this problem?* (She puts up a scarecrow.)

- *What does Fox grow in her garden?* (berries) *How do you know?* (from the words and pictures)

Retell Have children make a paper bag puppet of Fox to help them retell the story. Remind children to use characters, the setting, and events. Help them make personal connections. Ask: *Do you think Fox did a good job solving problems in her garden? Tell why or why not.*

Focus on Fluency

Practice fluency with children. Remember that children need to read with accuracy first.

Once children have read the text with accuracy, have them read the story again, focusing on rate. Have them practice reading with partners. Provide corrective feedback as necessary.

Build Knowledge: Make Connections

- **Talk About the Texts** Have partners discuss what plants need to grow.

- **Write About the Texts** Then have children add their ideas to their Build Knowledge page of their reader's notebook.

LITERACY ACTIVITIES

Have children complete the Collaborate and Write About It activities on the inside back cover of the book.

LEVEL UP

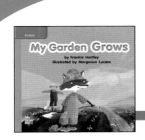

IF Children read *My Garden Grows* On Level with fluency and correctly answer the Respond to the Text questions,

THEN Tell children that they will read another story about someone who has a garden.

- Have children page through *The Mystery Seeds* Beyond Level. Point out the dialogue in the story, and remind children that words characters say to each other are in quotation marks.

- Have children read the story, monitoring their comprehension and providing assistance as necessary.

●On Level

Phonological/Phonemic Awareness

PHONEME ISOLATION

OBJECTIVES

Isolate and pronounce the initial sounds in words.

I Do Display the *hair* **Photo Card**. *This is* hair. *The first sound is /h/. Say it with me. Say* hope. *The first sound in* hope *is /h/. Say the sound with me.*

We Do Say *hike* and have children repeat it. *What is the first sound in* hike? (/h/) Say the sound together. Repeat with *hat, net,* and *can.*

You Do Say *had, mud, pin, hip,* and *new* and have children tell the initial sound in each word.

PHONEME BLENDING

OBJECTIVES

Demonstrate understanding of spoken words, syllables, and sounds (phonemes).

I Do Place the *hair, hand, hat, hay,* and *hook* Photo Cards facedown. Choose a card. Do not show the card. *The sounds in the word are: /h/ /a/ /t/. I'll blend the sounds: /haaat/,* hat. *The word is* hat. Show the picture.

We Do Choose another picture and say the sounds in the word. Together, say and blend the sounds to say the word. Then show the picture.

You Do Continue choosing Photo Cards. Say the sounds and have children blend the sounds and say the words. Show the pictures.

PHONEME CATEGORIZATION

OBJECTIVES

Isolate and pronounce the initial sounds in words.

I Do Display the *hook, house,* and *sock* Photo Cards. Say each picture name. Hook *and* house *begin with /h/.* Sock *does not.* Sock *does not belong.*

We Do Display the *pea, pig,* and *hand* Photo Cards. Have children name each picture with you. Ask: *Which two words begin with the same sound?* (pea, pig) *Which word does not have the same beginning sound?* (hand)

You Do Display and name the *hat, moon,* and *hair* Photo Cards. Have children name each picture and tell which pictures have the same initial sound and which picture does not have the same initial sound. Repeat with *table, hair, tie; dog, fish, dolphin.*

Phonics

REVIEW PHONICS

OBJECTIVES

Demonstrate basic knowledge of one-to-one letter-sound correspondences by producing the primary or many of the most frequent sounds for each consonant.

I Do Display the *hippo* **Sound-Spelling Card**. Say: *The letter* h *stands for the /h/ sound you hear at the beginning of* hippo. Say *hippo,* emphasizing the /h/.

We Do Display the *hat, hammer, hay, hand, horse,* and *house* **Photo Cards**. Have children say the name of each picture together with you.

You Do Write the words *hop, ham, hip, hot, hid,* and *him* and have children read each one. Provide corrective feedback as needed.

PICTURE SORT WITH /h/h, /p/p

OBJECTIVES

Demonstrate basic knowledge of one-to-one letter-sound correspondences by producing the primary sound or many of the most frequent sounds for each consonant.

I Do Display **Word-Building Cards** *h* and *p* in a pocket chart. Then show the *house* Photo Card. Say *house*. Tell children that the sound at the beginning is /h/. *The letter* h *stands for /h/. I will put the* house *Photo Card under the letter* h. Show the *pie* Photo Card. Say *pie*. Tell children that the sound at the beginning is /p/. *The letter* p *stands for /p/. I will put the* pie *Photo Card under the letter* p.

We Do Show the *hook* Photo Card and say *hook*. Have children repeat. Then have them tell the sound they hear at the beginning of *hook*. Ask them if they should place the photo under the *h* or the *p*.

You Do Continue the activity using the *hammer, helicopter, hippo, house, hat, horse, paint, penguin, penny, piano,* and *pitcher* Photo Cards. Have children say the picture name and the initial sound. Then have them place the card under the letter *h* or *p*.

●On Level

Phonics

BLEND WORDS WITH /h/h

MULTIMODAL

OBJECTIVES

Know and apply grade-level phonics and word analysis skills in decoding words.

Build words with *h*.

I Do   Display **Word-Building Cards** *h, o, p. This is the letter* h. *It stands for /h/. Say it with me: /h/. This is the letter* o. *It stands for /o/. Say it with me: /ooo/. This is the letter* p. *It stands for /p/. Say it with me: /p/. I'll blend the sounds together to read the word: /hooop/,* hop.

We Do   Use Word-Building Cards to form the words *hit* and *him*. Guide children to form the words and then to blend the words, sound by sound, to read each of the words.

You Do   Use the following words and have children blend the words, sound by sound, to read each word: *hip, hat, hot, hid, had*.

REREAD THE DECODABLE READER

OBJECTIVES

Know and apply grade-level phonics and word analysis skills in decoding words.

Read emergent-reader texts with purpose and understanding.

Unit 5 Decodable Reader

Focus on Foundational Skills

Review the high-frequency word *my* with children. Review the letter *h* and the sound /h/. Guide children to blend sounds to read *hat* and *him*.

Read the Decodable Reader

Have children read "Hap Hid the Ham" and "Hip Hop." Point out the high-frequency word *my* as well as words with /h/ at the beginning. If children struggle sounding out words, model blending.

Focus on Fluency

Have partners read "Hap Hid the Ham" and "Hip Hop." Guide them to focus on their accuracy. Children can give feedback on their accuracy to their partners. Then have them focus on reading with automaticity and at an appropriate rate. You may wish to have them reread "Hop Can Hop!" (pages 18–25) in the **Reading/Writing Companion**.

High-Frequency Words

REVIEW WORDS

MULTIMODAL

OBJECTIVES

Read common high-frequency words by sight.

I Do Display the **High-Frequency Word Card** *my* and use the Read/Spell/Write routine to review the word.

We Do Write these sentences and read them aloud: *Do you like my hat? It is hot in my garden.* Point to the word *my* and have children read it. Then chorally read the sentences. Have children frame the word *my* in the sentences and read the word.

You Do Say the word *my*. Ask children to close their eyes, picture the word, and write it as they see it. Have children self-correct.

Reteach previously introduced high-frequency words, including the **Build Your Word Bank** high-frequency words, using the Read/Spell/Write routine.

Fluency Use the **Practice Book Word Cards** to review the previously introduced High-Frequency and Build Your Word Bank words. In random order, point to the words. Have children practice reading the words until they can read accurately and with automaticity.

Comprehension

SELF-SELECTED READING

OBJECTIVES

With prompting and support, identify characters and settings in a story.

Read emergent-reader texts with purpose and understanding.

Independent Reading

Help children select an illustrated fiction story for independent reading. Encourage them to read for twelve minutes. Guide children to transfer what they have learned this week as they read. Remind children that the main character is who a fiction story is mostly about. The setting is where a story takes place. Important events are what happen. Remind children that if they come to a part of the story that is confusing, they can reread the text to make sure they understand it.

After reading, guide children to participate in a group discussion about the story they read. In addition, children can choose activities from the **Reading Center Activity Cards** to help them apply skills to the text as they read. Offer assistance and guidance with self-selected assignments.

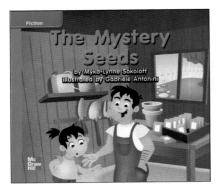

Lexile 240L

OBJECTIVES

With prompting and support, name the author and illustrator of a story and define the role of each in telling the story.

With prompting and support, identify characters, settings, and major events in a story.

With prompting and support, retell familiar stories, including key details.

Read emergent-reader texts with purpose and understanding.

ELA ACADEMIC LANGUAGE

• title, author

• Cognates: *título, autor*

● Beyond Level

Leveled Reader: *The Mystery Seeds*

Preview and Predict

Ask children to point to the title on their books while you read it aloud. Read the author and illustrator's names aloud. Ask children to explain what the author does and what the illustrator does. Have children describe the picture on the front cover. Ask: *What do you think this story will be about? What do you think the "mystery seeds" are?* Have children page through the book and look at the illustrations. Ask: *Do you have any more ideas about what this story is about?*

Review Genre: Fiction

Remind children that fiction stories are made up. They have characters, a setting, and events. Say: *The events in this story are about a girl growing a garden. A girl growing a garden could happen in real life. Why is that fiction?* (The girl is not a real girl, but a character the author made up.)

Set Purpose

Remind children of the Essential Question: *What do living things need to grow?* Say: *Let's read to find out about the girl and the mystery seeds.* Remind children to use the illustrations to help them understand the text.

Guided Comprehension

As children read *The Mystery Seeds*, monitor and provide guidance by offering support and corrective feedback as needed. Model rereading and identifying story elements, such as character, setting, and events, where applicable. Remind them that, when they come to a word they don't know, they can look at the first letter of the word and the illustration on the page for clues.

Reread

Remind children that they can reread the text to help them better understand the story.

Main Story Elements: Character, Setting, Events

Remind children that the people in a story are the characters, the place where the characters are is the setting, and the things that happen in the story are the events. Model how to use illustrations to learn more about the characters, setting, and events in the story.

Think Aloud After reading page 2, I learned that the two characters are the girl and her Uncle Hank. On page 3, I see that the girl and her uncle are in his shed. I see lots of tools for gardening. The girl's uncle is giving her some seeds. I'll keep reading and looking at the pictures to find out what happens next.

Guide children to read the rest of the story. Have them use the text and the details in the illustrations to explain what is happening on each page.

Respond to the Text

Have children respond to the text by discussing these questions:

- *Who are the main characters in this story?* (Uncle Hank and the little girl) *What is the setting?* (Uncle Hank's garden)

- *What happens after the girl tells her uncle she wants a garden?* (He gives her some seeds.)

- *What does the girl do to help her seeds grow?* (plants them, waters them, picks weeds)

- *How can you tell the girl enjoys working in the garden?* (Possible answer: She looks happy in the pictures.)

Retell Have partners take turns retelling the story, using characters, the setting, and events. To retell, have children take turns playing the parts of Uncle Hank and the little girl.

Focus on Fluency

Practice fluency with children. Remember that children need to read with accuracy first.

Once children have read the text with accuracy, have them read the story again, focusing on rate. Have them practice reading with partners. Provide corrective feedback as necessary.

Build Knowledge: Make Connections

- **Talk About the Texts** Have partners discuss what plants need to grow.

- **Write About the Texts** Then have children add their ideas to their Build Knowledge page of their reader's notebook.

LITERACY ACTIVITIES

Have children complete the Collaborate and Write About It activities on the inside back cover of the book.

⭐ GIFTED AND TALENTED

Evaluate Have children recall how the little girl and Uncle Hank helped their gardens grow. Challenge children to talk about what plants need to grow big and strong.

Extend Have children draw a picture of their favorite fruit or vegetable. Ask them to write on the stem, the leaves, the fruit, and/or the vegetable all the things a plant needs to grow. For example, sun, water, and room to grow.

Beyond Level

Phonics

OBJECTIVES Demonstrate basic knowledge of one-to-one letter-sound correspondences by producing the primary or many of the most frequent sounds for each consonant.	**I Do** Display the *hippo* **Sound-Spelling Card**. Say: *The letter* h *stands for the /h/ sound you hear at the beginning of* hippo. Say *hippo*, emphasizing the /h/.
	We Do Display the *hat, hammer, hay, hand, horse,* and *house* **Photo Cards**. Have children say the name of each picture together with you. Then ask children to share other words they know that begin with /h/.
	You Do Write the words *hop, ham, hip, hot, hid,* and *him* and have children read each one. Provide corrective feedback as needed. Have partners read each word. Ask them to write the words on their **Response Boards**, and underline the letter in each word that stands for /h/.
	Fluency Have children reread the story "Hop Can Hop!" for fluency.
	Innovate Have children create a new page for "Hop Can Hop!" using the sentence frame *Dot can see a _____.* Have children suggest other things that Dot sees near the garden.

High-Frequency Words

OBJECTIVES Read common high-frequency words by sight.	**I Do** Use the **Practice Book Build Your Word Bank High-Frequency Word Cards** for *than, his,* and *three*. Introduce the words using the Read/Spell/Write routine.
	We Do Display the **Practice Book High-Frequency Word Cards** for *my, we, can, go, the, I,* and *to*. Have children help you create sentence frames using both sets of word cards.
	You Do Have partners write sentences using the **Build Your Word Bank High-Frequency** words *than, his,* and *three* on their Response Boards. Have them read their sentences.

Vocabulary

ORAL VOCABULARY: SYNONYMS

OBJECTIVES

With guidance and support from adults, explore word relationships and nuances in word meanings.

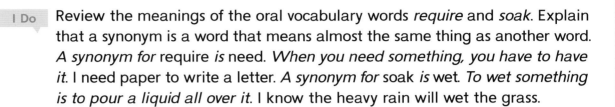

I Do Review the meanings of the oral vocabulary words *require* and *soak*. Explain that a synonym is a word that means almost the same thing as another word. *A synonym for* require *is* need. *When you need something, you have to have it.* I need paper to write a letter. *A synonym for* soak *is* wet. *To wet something is to pour a liquid all over it.* I know the heavy rain will wet the grass.

We Do With children, think of a few sentences using the new words *need* and *wet*.

You Do Have partners think of two or three sentences to give directions for planting and caring for a garden. Tell them to use *need* and *wet*. Ask them to share.

GIFTED and TALENTED **Extend** Have partners act out different jobs two people can do together that need lots of water (e.g., washing a car, watering flowers). Encourage them to use the words *need* and *wet* in their dialogue.

Comprehension

SELF-SELECTED READING

OBJECTIVES

With prompting and support, identify characters, settings, and major events in a story.

Read emergent-reader texts with purpose and understanding.

Independent Reading

Help children select an illustrated fiction story for independent reading. Encourage them to read for twelve minutes. Guide children to transfer what they have learned this week as they read by identifying character, setting, and events. Remind children that if they come to a part of the story that is confusing, they can reread the text to make sure they understand it.

After reading, guide children to participate in a group discussion about the story they read. In addition, children can choose activities from the **Reading Center Activity Cards** to help them apply skills to the text as they read. Offer assistance and guidance with self-selected assignments.

GIFTED and TALENTED **Independent Study** Have children use the stories they read this week to think about how plants grow. Challenge them to write a story or a poem about a garden.

Student Outcomes

✓ Tested in *Wonders* Assessments

FOUNDATIONAL SKILLS

Print Concepts
- Identify parts of a book
- Understand reading moves from left to right and top to bottom

Phonological Awareness
- Onset and Rime Blending
- Phoneme Isolation
- Phoneme Segmentation
- ✓ Phoneme Blending

Phonics and Word Analysis
- ✓ /e/e

Fluency
- ✓ High-Frequency Word
  are

READING

Reading Informational Text
- ✓ Identify the main topic and key details in a text
- Describe the relationship between illustrations and the text
- Retell familiar stories
- Actively engage in group reading activities

COMMUNICATION

Writing
- Handwriting: *Ee*
- Use prompts to write about the text
- Respond to suggestions from peers and add details to strengthen writing

Speaking and Listening
- Present writing and research
- Engage in collaborative conversations
- Ask and answer questions to get information or to clarify something that is not understood

Conventions
Grammar: Recognize subjective pronouns

Researching
- Recall or gather information to answer a question
- Conduct research about how a tree changes as it grows

Creating and Collaborating
- Add drawings and visual displays to descriptions
- Use digital tools to produce and publish writing

VOCABULARY

Academic Vocabulary
- Acquire and use grade-appropriate academic vocabulary

Vocabulary Strategy
- Identify and sort common words and objects into categories
- Use the most frequently occurring inflections

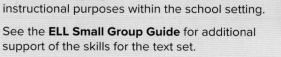

ELL Scaffolded supports for English Language Learners are embedded throughout the lessons, enabling children to communicate information, ideas, and concepts in English Language Arts and for social and instructional purposes within the school setting.

See the **ELL Small Group Guide** for additional support of the skills for the text set.

FORMATIVE ASSESSMENT

For assessment throughout the text set, use children's self-assessments and your observations.

Use the Data Dashboard to filter class, group, or individual student data to guide group placement decisions. It provides recommendations to enhance learning for gifted and talented children and offers extra support for children needing remediation.

DATA DASHBOARD

Develop Student Ownership

To build student ownership, children need to know what they are learning, why they are learning it, and determine how well they understood it.

Students Discuss Their Goals

TEXT SET GOALS

- I can read and understand texts.
- I can write about the texts I read.
- I know how living things change as they grow.

Have children think about what they know and circle a hand in each row on **Reading/Writing Companion** page 34.

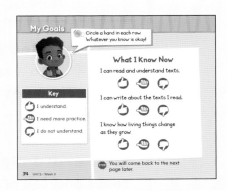

Students Monitor Their Learning

LEARNING GOALS

Specific learning goals identified in every lesson make clear what children will be learning and why. These smaller goals provide stepping stones to help children meet their Text Set Goals.

CHECK-IN ROUTINE

The Check-In Routine at the close of each lesson guides children to self-reflect on how well they understood each learning goal.

Review the lesson learning goal.
Reflect on the activity.
Self Assess by
- circling the hands in the **Reading/Writing Companion.**
- showing thumbs up, sideways, or down.

Share with your teacher.

Students Reflect on Their Progress

TEXT SET GOALS

After completing the Show Your Knowledge task for the text set, children reflect on their understanding of the Text Set Goals by circling a hand in each row on **Reading/Writing Companion** page 35.

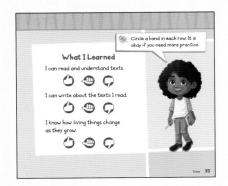

Build Knowledge

Literature Big Book

Shared Read
Reading/Writing Companion, p.42

Paired Selection
Literature Big Book

Essential Question
How do living things change as they grow?

Video A tree begins as a tiny seed. The seed grows into a sapling. Buds grow on the branches as the tree grows. The buds grow into flowers. Trees change during each season.

Literature Big Book A grand old tree once had deep roots and tall branches. It flowered, bore fruit, sowed seeds, and shed leaves. Eventually it crumbled and became part of the earth.

Shared Read Two young bears, Ed and Ned, play while learning to do tasks they need to do when they grow up.

Interactive Read Aloud A young pine tree wonders what happens to larger pine trees that are cut down. Over the years he grows much taller. He develops long needles and thick, brown cones and seeds. He is glad he was not cut down.

Paired Selection An apple seed develops under ground. With water and sunlight, it sprouts, becomes a seedling, then a sapling, then a big tree. It grows flowers and apples.

Photograph Rings in a tree stump can show how a tree grew and help tell us the tree's age. Some trees grow one ring each year.

Differentiated Sources

Leveled Readers 🔊

● As a tree gets bigger, so does its trunk, roots, branches, buds, flowers, leaves, and cherries.

●● A girl looks at trees that are small, big, wet, dry, full of green leaves, and full of red leaves.

● A girl tells how her family's apple tree grew—from a small seed that grew roots into a small tree then a big tree. Flowers grew on the tree and became apples.

Build Knowledge Routine

After reading each text, ask children to document what facts and details that they learned to help answer the Essential Question of the text set.

 Talk about the source.

 Write about the source.

 Add to the class Anchor Chart.

• Add to the Word Bank.

Show Your Knowledge

Draw How a Plant Grows

Have children think about how living things change as they grow. Guide them to draw and label a picture of how a plant grows. Encourage children to use numbered steps and vocabulary words in their labels.

Social Emotional Learning

I Can Remember (1:08)

Working Memory

SEL Focus: Encourage children to practice strategies for developing their working memories throughout the day.

Talk with children about the question: how do our memories help us? Then begin the "Remembering Time!" lesson on pp. T82–T83.

SESAME STREET

Family Time • Share the video and the activity in the **School to Home** newsletter.

Explore the Texts

Essential Question: How do living things change as they grow?

Literature Big Book	Literature Big Book	Interactive Read-Aloud	Reading/Writing Companion

A Grand Old Tree Anchor Text Informational Text	**"From a Seed to a Tree"** Paired Text Informational Text	**"The Pine Tree"** Interactive Read Aloud Fairy Tale	**"Ed and Ned"** Shared Read pp. 42–49 Informational Text

Qualitative

Meaning/Purpose: Moderate Complexity **Structure:** High Complexity **Language:** High Complexity **Knowledge Demands:** Moderate Complexity	**Meaning/Purpose:** Low Complexity **Structure:** Low Complexity **Language:** Moderate Complexity **Knowledge Demands:** Low Complexity	**Meaning/Purpose:** Moderate Complexity **Structure:** Moderate Complexity **Language:** Moderate Complexity **Knowledge Demands:** Moderate Complexity	**Meaning/Purpose:** Low Complexity **Structure:** Moderate Complexity **Language:** Low Complexity **Knowledge Demands:** Low Complexity

Quantitative

Lexile 530L	Lexile 400L	Lexile 650L	Lexile 230L

Reader and Task Considerations

Reader Teachers may need to be sensitive of the fact that the tree dies in the end. This could be discussed in a positive way as the tree lives on in all of her "grandchildren" and becomes a home for animals.	**Reader** Some of the words many be unfamiliar to children. Previewing new vocabulary may support deeper understanding of this text.	**Reader** Because the main pine tree is given human characteristics, it may be jarring that some of the adult trees are chopped down. Children may need to be reassured that real trees don't think and feel like humans.	**Reader** Children will need to use their knowledge of sound-spelling correspondences and high-frequency words to read the text.

Task The questions for the Interactive Read Aloud are supported by teacher modeling. The tasks provide a variety of ways for students to build knowledge and vocabulary about the text set topic. The questions and tasks provided for the other texts are at various levels of complexity, ensuring that all students can interact with the text in meaningful ways.

Additional Read-Aloud Texts

Content Area Reading BLMs

Additional online texts related to grade-level Science, Social Studies, and Arts content.

Access Complex Text (ACT) boxes provide scaffolded instruction for seven different elements that may make the **Literature Big Book** complex.

A C T

Leveled Readers 🔊 (All Leveled Readers are provided in eBook format with audio support.)

Approaching	On	Beyond	ELL
The Tree Leveled Reader Informational Text	**Many Trees** Leveled Reader Informational Text	**Our Apple Tree** Leveled Reader Informational Text	**Many Trees** Leveled Reader Informational Text

Qualitative

Meaning/Purpose: Low Complexity	**Meaning/Purpose:** Low Complexity	**Meaning/Purpose:** Low Complexity	**Meaning/Purpose:** Low Complexity
Structure: Low Complexity	**Structure:** Low Complexity	**Structure:** Low Complexity	**Structure:** Low Complexity
Language: Low Complexity	**Language:** Low Complexity	**Language:** Moderate Complexity	**Language:** Low Complexity
Knowledge Demands: Low Complexity	**Knowledge Demands:** Low Complexity	**Knowledge Demands:** Low Complexity	**Knowledge Demands:** Low Complexity

Quantitative

Lexile BR	Lexile 70L	Lexile 250L	Lexile BR

Reader and Task Considerations

Reader Children may be unfamiliar with the names of tree parts. Previewing these words will help children understand the text.	**Reader** Children should be familiar with trees, but may need some support understanding the adjectives in the text.	**Reader** Readers will need a basic understanding of apple trees and how they grow.	**Reader** Children should be familiar with trees, but may need some support understanding the adjectives in the text.

Task The questions and tasks provided for the Leveled Readers are at various levels of complexity, ensuring that all students can interact with the text in meaningful ways.

Focus on Word Work

WEEK 2

Build Foundational Skills with Multimodal Learning

Photo Cards

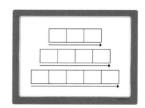
Response Board

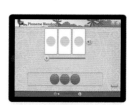
Phonemic Awareness Activities

Phonological/Phonemic Awareness
- Blend onset and rime to form words
- Isolate and blend phonemes
- Segment words into individual sounds

Sound-Spelling Cards

Word-Building Cards online

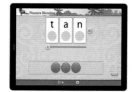
Phonics Practice Activities

Phonics: /e/e
- Introduce/review sound-spellings
- Blend/build words with sound-spellings
- Practice handwriting
- Decode and encode in connected texts

Practice Book

Word-Building Cards online

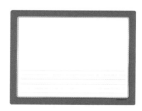
Response Board

Spelling: /e/e
- Spell words with /e/e

High-Frequency Word Cards

High-Frequency Word Activities

Visual Vocabulary Cards

High-Frequency Words
- Read/Spell/Write routine
- Optional: Build Your Word Bank

See Word Work, pages T92–T95, T104–T107, T112–T117, T126–T127, T132–T133.

Shared Read

Decodable Readers

Take-Home Story

Apply Skills to Read
- Children apply foundational skills as they read decodable texts.
- Children practice fluency to develop word automaticity.

Explicit Systematic Instruction

Word Work instruction expands foundational skills to enable children to become proficient readers.

Daily Routine

- Use the In a Flash: Sound-Spelling routine and the In a Flash: High-Frequency Word routine to build fluency.
- Set Learning Goal.

Explicit Minilessons and Practice

Use daily instruction in both whole and small groups to model, practice, and apply key foundational skills. Opportunities include:

- Multimodal engagement.
- Corrective feedback.
- Supports for English Language Learners in each lesson.
- Peer collaboration.

Formative Assessment

Check-In

- Children reflect on their learning.
- Children show their progress by indicating thumbs down, thumbs sideways, or thumbs up in a Check-In routine.

Check for Success

- Teacher monitors children's achievement and differentiates for Small Group instruction.

Differentiated Instruction

To strengthen skills, provide targeted review and reteaching lessons and multimodal activities to meet children's diverse needs.

● ● **Approaching Level, ELL**
- Includes Tier 2 **2**

● **On Level**

● **Beyond Level**
- Includes Gifted and Talented **GIFTED and TALENTED**

OPTIONAL EXPRESS TRACK

Teachers can choose to introduce long vowel sound-spellings and/or additional high-frequency words.

- **Long Vowel Express:** Long *a* (*a_e*)
- Build Your Word Bank

Independent Practice

Provide additional practice as needed. Have children work individually or with partners.

Center Activity Cards

Digital Activities

Word-Building Cards online

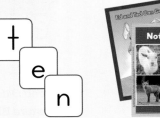

Decodable Readers

Practice Book

Inspire Early Writers

Build Writing Skills and Conventions

Practice Book

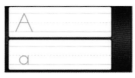
Handwriting Video

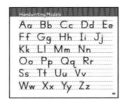
Reading/Writing Companion

Write Letter *Ee*

- Learn to write the letters
- Practice writing

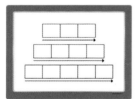
Response Board

Practice Book

High-Frequency Word Activities

Write Words

- Write words with *Ee*
- Write high-frequency words

Reading/Writing Companion

Practice Book

Write Sentences

- Write sentences with high-frequency words
- Write sentences to respond to text

Follow Conventions

- Appropriately use pronouns
- Capitalize the pronoun *I*

A Grand Old Tree
Literature Big Book

Writing Fluency

To increase children's writing fluency, have them write as much as they can in response to the **Literature Big Book** for four minutes. Tell children to write about how the grand old tree changed as she grew.

For lessons, see pages T92–T97, T108–T109, T112–T115, T118–T119, T128–T129, T132–T135.

Write About Texts

WRITING ROUTINE

Analyze the Prompt → Find Text Evidence → Write to the Prompt

Literature Big Book, pp. 4–32

Modeled Writing

Write about the **Literature Big Book** *A Grand Old Tree*

- Prompt: How can you play in a tree?

Interactive Writing

- Prompt: What did the tree provide for the animals?

Reading/Writing Companion, pp. 42–49

Independent Writing

Write to the Shared Read "Ed and Ned"

Reading/Writing Companion, pp. 42–49

- Prompt: What do Ed and Ned like to do together?

- Have children follow the steps of the writing process: draft, revise, edit/proofread, share.

Additional Lessons

Writing Skills Minilessons To provide differentiated support for writing skills, see pages T494–T499.

Extended Writing Lessons For a full set of lessons that support the writing process and writing in a specific genre, see pages T476–T485.

Self-Selected Writing

Children can explore different writing modes.

 Storyboard

 Build and Write

Planner

Customize your own lesson plans at
my.mheducation.com

Select from your Social Emotional
Learning resources.

 LESSON 1

 LESSON 2

TEXT SET GOALS

- **I can read and understand texts.**
- **I can write about the texts I read.**
- **I know how living things change as they grow.**

90+ mins Reading
Suggested Daily Time
Includes Small Group

 **SMALL GROUP OPTIONS**
The designated lessons can be taught in small groups. To determine how to differentiate instruction for small groups, use Formative Assessment and Data Dashboard.

30+ mins Writing
Suggested Daily Time

Reading

LESSON 1

Introduce the Concept, T84–T85
Build Knowledge: Trees

Listening Comprehension, T86–T91
A Grand Old Tree

 Word Work, T92–T95
Phonemic Awareness: Phoneme Isolation
Phonics/Spelling: Introduce /e/e
Handwriting: Write *Ee*
High-Frequency Word: *are*

LESSON 2

Build the Concept, T98–T99
Phonological Awareness: Onset and Rime Blending
Category Words: Tree Parts
Vocabulary: Inflectional Ending -*ed*

Listening Comprehension, T100–T103
A Grand Old Tree

Word Work, T104–T105
Phonemic Awareness: Phoneme Blending
Phonics: Review Short *e*
High-Frequency Word: *are*

Shared Read, T106–T107
Read "Ed and Ned"

Writing

LESSON 1

Modeled Writing, T96
Model Writing About the Literature Big Book
Grammar, T97
Subjective Pronouns

LESSON 2

Interactive Writing, T108
Write About the Big Book
Grammar, T109
Subjective Pronouns

Teacher-Led Instruction

SMALL GROUP

Differentiated Reading
Leveled Readers
- *The Tree*, T138–T139
- *Many Trees*, T146–T147
- *Our Apple Tree*, T152–T153

Differentiated Skills Practice, T140–T155
Approaching Level, T140–T145
Phonological/Phonemic Awareness
- Onset and Rime Blending, T140 ②
- Phoneme Isolation, T140 ②
- Phoneme Blending, T141
- Phoneme Segmentation, T141

Phonics
- Sound-Spelling Review, T142 ②
- Connect *e* to /e/, T142 ②
- Blend Words with Short *e*, T142
- Build Words with Short *e*, T143
- Reread the Decodable Reader, T143
- Build Fluency with Phonics, T143
High-Frequency Words
- Reteach Words, T144 ②
- Cumulative Review, T144
Oral Vocabulary
- Review Words, T145

Independent/Collaborative Work See pages T81I–T81J

Reading
Comprehension
- Informational Text
- Reread
- Topic and Details

Word Work
Phonics
- /e/e
High-Frequency Word
- *are*

Writing
Self-Selected Writing
Grammar
- Subjective Pronouns
Handwriting
- Upper and Lowercase *Ee*

ORAL VOCABULARY
develop, amazing, enormous, imagine, content

 LESSON 3

 LESSON 4

 LESSON 5

Reading

Build the Concept, T110
Oral Language

Listening Comprehension, T111
"The Pine Tree"

Word Work, T112–T115
Phonemic Awareness: Phoneme Blending
Phonics: Review Short *e,* Blend Words, Spell Words
High-Frequency Word: *are*

Shared Read, T116–T117
Reread "Ed and Ned"

Extend the Concept, T120–T121
Phonological Awareness: Onset and Rime Blending
Category Words: Tree Parts
Vocabulary: Inflectional Ending *-ed*

Paired Selection, T122–T125
"From a Seed to a Tree"

Word Work, T126–T127
Phonemic Awareness: Phoneme Segmentation
Phonics: Build and Read Words, Spell Words
High-Frequency Word: *are*

Research and Inquiry, T130–T131
How a Tree Grows (Research)

Word Work, T132–T133
Phonemic Awareness: Phoneme Segmentation
Phonics: Read Words, Spell Words
High-Frequency Word: *are*

Integrate Ideas, T136
Make Connections

Show Your Knowledge, T137

Writing

Independent Writing, T118
Write About the Shared Read
Grammar, T119
Subjective Pronouns

Independent Writing, T128
Write About the Shared Read
Grammar, T129
Subjective Pronouns

Self-Selected Writing, T134
Grammar, T135
Subjective Pronouns

Comprehension
• Self-Selected Reading, T145
● **On Level, T148–T151**
Phonological/Phonemic Awareness
• Phoneme Isolation, T148
• Phoneme Blending, T148
• Phoneme Segmentation, T148
Phonics
• Review, T149
• Picture Sort with Medial /e/e, /o/o, T149
• Blend Words with Short *e,* T150
• Reread the Decodable Reader, T150

High-Frequency Words
• Review, T151
Comprehension
• Self-Selected Reading, T151
● **Beyond Level, T154–T155**
Phonics
• Review, T154
High-Frequency Words
• Review, T154

Vocabulary
• Oral Vocabulary: Synonyms, T155
Comprehension
• Self-Selected Reading, T155

 GIFTED and TALENTED

 ● **English Language Learners**
See ELL Small Group Guide,
pp. 114–121

Content Area Connections
Content Area Reading
• Science, Social Studies, and the Arts
Research and Inquiry
• How a Tree Grows (Research)

 ● **English Language Learners**
See ELL Small Group Guide,
pp. 115, 117

WEEK 2
Independent and Collaborative Work

As you meet with small groups, have the rest of the class complete activities and projects to practice and apply the skills they have been working on.

Student Choice and Student Voice

- Review the My Weekly Work blackline masters with children and identify the "Must Do" activities.
- Have children choose some additional activities that provide the practice they need.
- Remind children to reflect on their learning each day.

My Weekly Work BLMs

Reading

Text Options

Children can choose a **Center Activity Card** to use while they listen to a text or read independently.

Classroom Library Read Aloud
Have You Seen My Duckling?
Genre: Fiction
Lexile: 20L

A Tree Is a Plant
Genre: Informational Text
Lexile: 290L

Unit Bibliography
See the online bibliography. Children can select independent reading texts about how living things change as they grow.

Leveled Texts Online
All **Leveled Readers** are provided in eBook format with audio support.
- **Differentiated Texts** provide English Language Learners with passages at different proficiency levels.

Literature Big Book e-Book
A Grand Old Tree
Genre: Informational Text

Center Activity Cards

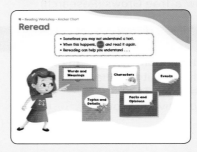

Reread Card 4

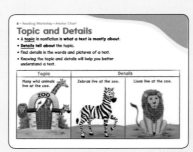

Nonfiction Card 21

Topic and Details Card 6

Diagrams with Labels Card 18

Digital Activities

Comprehension

Word Work

Center Activity Cards

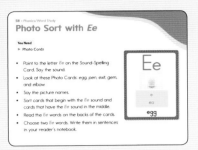

58 · Phonics/Word Study
Photo Sort with *Ee*

You Need
▶ Photo Cards

- Point to the letter *Ee* on the Sound-Spelling Card. Say the sound.
- Look at these Photo Cards: egg, pen, exit, gem, and elbow.
- Say the picture names.
- Sort cards that begin with the *Ee* sound and cards that have the *Ee* sound in the middle.
- Read the *Ee* words on the backs of the cards.
- Choose two *Ee* words. Write them in sentences in your reader's notebook.

/e/e Card 58

Word-Building Cards

Practice Book BLMs

Phonological Awareness: pp. 211, 212, 213
Phonics: pp. 214, 216
Phonics/Spelling: p. 215
High-Frequency Words: p. 218
Category Words: p. 219
Take-Home Story: pp. 223–224

Decodable Readers

Unit 5, pp. 13–24

Digital Activities

Word Work

Phonemic Awareness
Phonics
High-Frequency Words

Writing

Center Activity Cards

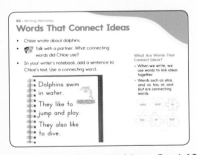

140 · Writing Workshop
Words That Connect Ideas

- Chloe wrote about dolphins.
- 🗨 Talk with a partner. What connecting words did Chloe use?
- In your writer's notebook, add a sentence to Chloe's text. Use a connecting word.

Dolphins swim in water.
They like to jump and play.
They also like to dive.

What Are Words That Connect Ideas?
- When we write, we use words to link ideas together.
- Words such as *also, and, so, too, or,* and *but* are connecting words.

Words That Connect Ideas Card 40

Practice Book BLMs

Handwriting: p. 217
Grammar: pp. 220–222

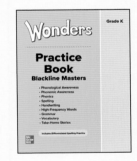

Self-Selected Writing

- What do you know about how living things grow?
- Write about a person taking care of a tree or plant to help it grow.
- Draw and label three pictures in sequence that show a plant growing.

Digital Activities

Grammar

Content Area Connections

Content Area Reading BLMs
- Additional texts related to Science, Social Studies, Health, and the Arts.

Research and Inquiry
- Complete How a Tree Grows project

Progress Monitoring
Moving Toward Mastery

Practice Book

Reading/Writing Companion

Online Rubric

Response Board

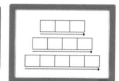

Digital Activities

FORMATIVE ASSESSMENT

➤ STUDENT CHECK-IN

✔ CHECK FOR SUCCESS

For ongoing formative assessment, use children's self-assessments at the end of each lesson along with your own observations.

Assessing skills along the way . . .

SKILLS	HOW ASSESSED
Phonological Awareness • Onset and Rime Blending	Practice Book
Phonemic Awareness • Phoneme Isolation • Phoneme Blending • Phoneme Segmentation	Practice Book, Response Board, Digital Activities
Phonics • /e/e	Practice Book, Response Board, Digital Activities
High-Frequency Words • *are*	Practice Book, Response Board, Digital Activities
Category Words • Tree Words	Practice Book
Grammar • Subjective Pronouns	Practice Book
Comprehension • Topic and Details • Text Feature: Diagram	Reading/Writing Companion
Listening/Presenting/Research	Checklists

Making the Most of Assessment Results

Make data-based grouping decisions by using the following reports to verify assessment results. For additional support options for children, refer to the reteaching and enrichment opportunities.

ONLINE ASSESSMENT CENTER
- *Gradebook*

DATA DASHBOARD
- *Recommendations Report*
- *Activity Report*
- *Skills Report*
- *Progress Report*
- *Grade Card Report*

TIER 2

Reteaching Opportunities with Intervention Online PDFs

ASSESSED SKILLS	✓ CHECK FOR SUCCESS	RETEACH . . .
PHONOLOGICAL AND PHONEMIC AWARENESS	Can children blend onsets and rimes? Can children isolate, blend, and segment phonemes? If not . . .	using lessons 38–40; 27–29, and 62–71 in the **Phonemic Awareness PDF.**
PHONICS	Can children match /e/ to the letter e? If not . . .	using lesson 23 in the **Phonics/Word Study PDF.**
HIGH-FREQUENCY WORDS	Can children recognize and read the high-frequency word? If not . . .	by using the **High-Frequency Word Cards** and asking children to read and spell the word. Point out any irregularities in sound-spellings.
COMPREHENSION	Can children identify the topic and details in a text? Can children use text features including diagrams? If not . . .	using lesson 76–78 and 135 in the **Comprehension PDF.**
CATEGORY WORDS	Can children identify and sort tree words? If not . . .	using lesson 16 in the **Vocabulary PDF.**

GIFTED and TALENTED

Enrichment Opportunities

Beyond Level small group lessons and resources include suggestions for additional activities in these areas to extend learning opportunities for gifted and talented children:

- *Leveled Reader*
- *Vocabulary*
- *Comprehension*
- *Leveled Reader Library Online*
- *Center Activity Cards*

Today's focus:

Learning to hold information in mind while completing a task.

I Can Remember (1:08)

REALISTIC FICTION

family time

You'll find the "I Can Remember" video and supporting activity in this week's School to Home family newsletter.

remembering time!

engage together

Let's Remember: What's missing?

Invite children to play a memory game.

- Today we're going to use our memories to exercise our brains.
- First, let's write three things we need to do today on separate sticky notes. Close your eyes, and picture those activities in your mind.
- Now let's play a memory game. Look at this set of five objects. Think about their shapes, sizes, and colors.
- I'm going to take one away without you seeing which one.
- Now look. Which object is missing? What do you remember about it?

explore together

Let's Watch: "I Can Remember"

Set a purpose for sharing today's realistic fiction video.

- The girl in today's video has to remember what to buy at the store.
- Let's see what strategies she uses to remember.

(▷) **Play the video**

Let's Try It: Self-talk.

Discuss the working memory strategy of self-talk.

- What did the girl's mother ask her to buy?
- How did she remember? She used a strategy called "self-talk." *Self-talk* is what we say to ourselves quietly or in our heads. It helps us remember.
- Let's try out the self-talk strategy and repeat the grocery list together.

REMEMBERING STRATEGIES

- Self-talk: *I say what I have to remember to myself.*
- Sticky Notes: *I visualize pictures in my mind.*

connect the learning

Let's Remember: Sticky notes in your brain.

Put children's working memories to work!

- The girl also uses a strategy called "sticky notes." She visualized what she needed to remember.
- Earlier, I asked you to picture three class activities. It's remembering time! Close your eyes and picture them. These pictures act like sticky notes in *your brain*.
- Whenever I say "It's remembering time," picture your sticky notes. It will strengthen our brains and keep our day on track!

mindfulness moment
Musical Belly Breathing

Calming strategies like belly breathing can involve upbeat music. Try playing a song that children like to dance or move to. Then, pause it. Invite children to focus and belly breathe to practice slowing down.

WORKING MEMORY

OBJECTIVES

Confirm understanding of a text read aloud or information presented orally or through other media by asking and answering questions about key details and requesting clarification if something is not understood.

Use words and phrases acquired through conversations, reading and being read to, and responding to texts.

Identify real-life connections between words and their use.

Follow agreed-upon rules for discussions (e.g., listening to others and taking turns speaking about the topics and texts under discussion).

ELA ACADEMIC LANGUAGE

• *change, speaker, respect, interrupting*

• Cognate: *respeto*

DIGITAL TOOLS

Watch Video

Build Background Images

Visual Vocabulary Cards

LESSON FOCUS

READING
Introduce Essential Question
Read Literature Big Book
A Grand Old Tree
• Introduce Genre: Informational Text
• Introduce Strategy/Skill
Word Work
• Introduce short /e/e

WRITING
Writing/Grammar
• Shared Writing
• Introduce Grammar

Literature Big Book, pp. 3–32

---

10 mins # Build Knowledge

 MULTIMODAL

 ## Essential Question

How do living things change as they grow?

Read the Essential Question aloud. Explain that children will learn about how living things, such as trees, change as they grow. Have partners discuss what they know about how trees change as they grow.

• **Video Routine** Play the Weekly Opener Video, "Trees," without sound and have partners narrate what they watch. Then replay the video with sound and have children listen.

• **Talk About the Video** Have partners share one thing they learned about how trees change.

 • **Anchor Chart** Create a Build Knowledge anchor chart and have volunteers share what they learned about the theme "Trees." Record their ideas on the chart.

Oral Vocabulary Words

Use the Define/Example/Ask routine on the print or digital **Visual Vocabulary Cards** to introduce the oral vocabulary words *develop* and *amazing*.

 ### Oral Vocabulary Routine

<u>Define</u>: To **develop** is to grow.

<u>Example</u>: Trees develop into big plants.

<u>Ask</u>: What is one way a person develops?

<u>Define</u>: To be **amazing** is to be surprising and wonderful.

<u>Example</u>: The fruit that grows on trees is amazing.

<u>Ask</u>: What is an amazing animal you have seen?

Visual Vocabulary Cards

Reading/Writing Companion, pp. 32–33

 ## Build Knowledge

Use pages 32–33 of the **Reading/Writing Companion** to guide a discussion about how the tree in the photo will change as it grows.

- **Talk** *How do living things change as they grow? What words tell about how living things change?* List the words. Have children choose one word and think about how to illustrate it.

- **Draw and Write** Have children draw a picture that illustrates the word. Then have them write the word. Guide children on how to print letters that have not been taught yet.

Build Vocabulary

Have children share new words they learned about how living things change. Add words to a separate section of the Word Bank. Use the words during the week and encourage children to do the same.

 # English Language Learners

Use the following scaffolds with **Build Knowledge.**

Beginning

Point to the trees in the photo. Have children repeat: *This is a small tree. These are big trees.*

Intermediate

Have partners point to the photo. Provide sentence frames: The tree will grow bigger. The tree grows branches and leaves.

Advanced/Advanced High

Encourage children to use complete sentences as they describe the life cycle of trees. Provide models: *A tree grows larger. The trunk grows wider and taller. The branches become full of leaves.*

 ## COLLABORATIVE CONVERSATIONS

Take Turns Talking As children engage in partner and group discussions, encourage them to do the following:

- Look at the person who is speaking.
- Listen to the words the speaker is saying.
- Respect others by not interrupting them.
- Repeat classmates' ideas to confirm understanding.

ELL NEWCOMERS

To help children develop oral language and build vocabulary, use **Newcomer Cards** 10–14 and the accompanying lessons in the **Newcomer Teacher's Guide**. For thematic connections, use **Newcomer Cards** 21 and 22. For additional practice, have children complete the online **Newcomer Activities**.

MY GOALS ROUTINE

What I Know Now

Read Goals Read aloud the goals and the key on **Reading/Writing Companion** page 34.

Reflect Ask children to reflect on each goal and complete page 34 to show what they know now. Explain that they will complete page 35 at the end of the text set to show their progress.

LESSON 1

Literature Big Book

We can understand important ideas and details in a text.

OBJECTIVES

Recognize common types of texts.

Follow words from left to right and top to bottom.

With prompting and support, identify the main topic and retell key details of a text.

Actively engage in group reading activities with purpose and understanding.

Reread for understanding.

ELA ACADEMIC LANGUAGE

• *nonfiction, reread,*
• Cognate: *no ficción*

 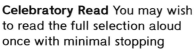 **DIFFERENTIATED READING**

Celebratory Read You may wish to read the full selection aloud once with minimal stopping before reading with the prompts.

⬤⬤ **Approaching Level** and **English Language Learners** After reading, have children listen to the selection to develop comprehension.

 Read

A Grand Old Tree

20 mins

Connect to Concept

Tell children that you will read a selection about the ways one amazing tree develops as the years pass.

Genre: Informational Text: Nonfiction *This book is a nonfiction text. Nonfiction text gives information about a topic. Nonfiction text can include specific details to give us a deeper understanding of the topic.*

 Anchor Chart Display the Nonfiction anchor chart. Add: *Nonfiction text can include specific details that describe things and help us understand the topic on a deeper level.*

Reread Remind children that if they don't understand an idea or a fact while they are reading, they can go back and reread the text. Explain that rereading can help them understand what they read.

Topic and Details Remind children that the topic is what a text is mostly about. *Details in the words and photos of a nonfiction text tell about the topic. Knowing the topic of a selection helps readers understand it better.*

Read the Selection

Display the Big Book. Read the title and look at the image. *What do you predict this text will be about?* Write and display children's predictions.

Concepts of Print Display the title page of the Big Book. Track the print from left to right as you read the title and the name of the author.

Set Purpose *Let's read to find out about the life of a tree.*

Close Reading Routine

Read DOK 1–2

• Identify key ideas and details.
• Take notes and retell.
• Use ⒶⒸⓉ prompts as needed.

Reread DOK 2–3

• Analyze the text, craft, and structure.

Integrate DOK 3–4

• Integrate knowledge and ideas.
• Make text-to-text connections.
• Complete the Show Your Knowledge task.
• Inspire action.

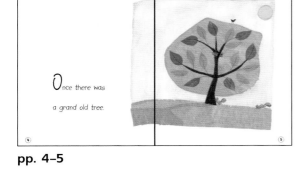

pp. 4–5

TOPIC AND DETAILS DOK 2

Think Aloud I know that the topic is what the text is mostly about. I can tell from what we discussed about the title of the book and these first pages that the topic of this book is a grand old tree and what happens to it.

BUILD ORAL VOCABULARY

grand: big and wonderful

 Spotlight On Language

pp. 4–5

once: Review pronunciation of the word and then explain that *once* has the same meaning as *once upon a time*, which might be a familiar phrase. Explain that *once* talks about things that happened in the past.

pp. 6–7

REREAD DOK 2

Think Aloud I can reread these pages to make sure I understand what the illustrations show. Oh, I see now. The picture on the left shows the tree's roots under the ground. The picture on the right shows the tree's branches against the sky.

pp. 6–7

arms reached high into the sky: Reach your arms high into the air. *My arms reach high into the sky.* Have children repeat the words and motions. Explain that the tree's branches are like our arms.

pp.8–9

NONFICTION DOK 1

Think Aloud Nonfiction text can include specific details to give me a deeper understanding of the topic. On these pages, the details tell about the creatures that live in the tree: birds, squirrels, caterpillars, and ladybugs.

BUILD ORAL VOCABULARY

creatures: living beings, animals

pp. 8–9

scurried: Point to the squirrels scurrying. *The squirrels are scurrying.* Scurrying *is when animals or people move quickly from place to place.* Say *scurried* and have children repeat.

 Access Complex Text

Use this ACT prompt when the complexity of the text makes it hard for children to understand the selection.

Organization

This book is set up cyclically. To help children see the sequence of events, draw a large circle. Starting at the top and moving clockwise around the circle, draw these events: 1) The tree grows leaves. 2) Then the tree grows fruit with seeds. 3) The seeds land on the ground and sprout. 4) The seeds grow and become new trees. 5) The tree dies and becomes part of the earth. 6) The new trees grow fruit. Explain to children that this cycle repeats.

pp. 10–11

TOPIC AND DETAILS DOK 1

What is happening to the tree on these pages? (It is flowering.)

BUILD ORAL VOCABULARY

flowered: grew flowers

pp. 10–11

flowered: Children might be confused by the use of *flower(ed)* as a verb. Point to the tree on page 11 as you say: *Flowers grew. The tree flowered.* Have children repeat as they point to the tree.

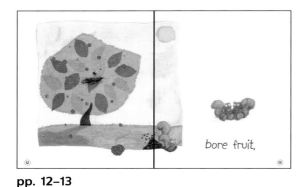

pp. 12–13

TOPIC AND DETAILS DOK 1

What is growing on the tree now? (fruit)

BUILD ORAL VOCABULARY

bore: made or grew

pp. 12–13

bore fruit: Point to the fruit on the tree. *The tree bore fruit. This is another way to say that the tree had fruit.* Have children repeat *bore fruit* after you.

pp. 14–15

REREAD DOK 2

Who are the tree's children? Let's reread these pages to make sure we understand. Listen as I reread. (The tree's children are tiny trees. The text says that the tree "sowed seeds," and we know that seeds grow into trees.)

BUILD ORAL VOCABULARY

sowed: spread

pp. 14–15

sowed seeds: Children might hear the word *sowed* and think of *sewed.* To clarify, point to the seeds floating in the picture and show a photo of sewing. Explain that sewing with thread is different from a tree sowing, or spreading, seeds.

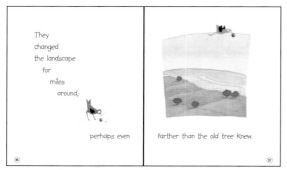

pp. 16–17

NONFICTION DOK 1

These pages tell us specific details about how seeds travel. Look at this illustration. Where does the bird take the seed? (All the way to the ocean.)

pp. 16–17

landscape: With your hand, sweep the landscape in the illustration as you have children repeat: *landscape.* Then provide additional illustrations of landscapes from classroom books and repeat the routine.

ELL Spotlight On Language

pp. 18–19

TOPIC AND DETAILS DOK 2

What do the details in the words and pictures on these pages help us understand about the tree? (The tree lived a long time. As she grew and got older, she experienced the seasons and changed again and again.)

BUILD ORAL VOCABULARY

shed: lost or had something fall off

pp. 18–19

shed: Put on a sweater, cap, or other piece of outerwear. Take it off as you say: *I shed my [name of item].* Have children echo and mimic. Then point to the illustrations and say: *When a tree sheds its leaves, the leaves fall off.*

pp. 20–21

NONFICTION DOK 1

These pages tell us specific details about what the tree looks and feels like when she gets old. Her branches no longer sway and dance. What do they do instead? (crack and snap in the wind)

pp. 20–21

millions: Say: *A million is a very large number.* Compare it to more familiar number words: *hundred* and *thousand*. In this story, the phrase *many millions* means "so many leaves that we can't count them."

pp. 22–23

VISUALIZE DOK 2

Picture in your mind the grand old tree falling. What do you think it would sound like? The picture shows her animal friends all around her. Why do you think they are there?

BUILD ORAL VOCABULARY

gently: in a soft way

pp. 22–23

finally: Review words that indicate order and remind children that *finally* describes the very last thing that happens. Explain that the event on this page is the last thing the tree does while she is alive.

pp. 24–25

TOPIC AND DETAILS DOK 2

Think Aloud The detail on these pages is that the old tree died. This is the end of the tree's life cycle, or the stages it goes through during its life. The tree starts as a seed. Then it becomes a young tree. It continues to grow until it becomes a mature tree. Finally, the tree gets old and dies.

pp. 24–25

no longer: Guide children in understanding that *no longer* means that something is not happening anymore. Put a pencil on the table and say, *The pencil is on the table.* Pick up the pencil and say, *The pencil is no longer on the table.*

Spotlight On Language

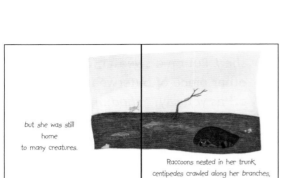

pp. 26–27

REREAD DOK 1

What things live in the grand old tree now? Let's reread the pages to make sure we understand. Listen as I reread. (raccoons, centipedes, lichen) *What other things do you see in the picture?* (mice and mushrooms)

pp. 26–27

raccoons, centipedes, lichen: Point to the living things in the illustration—*raccoons, centipedes, lichen*—as you name them. Have children repeat the name of each living thing as you point to it.

pp. 28–29

CONCEPTS OF PRINT

As you read these pages aloud, track the print with your finger. Point out that you are reading the text from left to right and from top to bottom. Demonstrate return sweep. Invite volunteers to come up and follow the print with their finger as you read certain pages.

pp. 28–29

crumbled: Explain that when something crumbles, it breaks into many little pieces. If possible, demonstrate an object crumbling. After you crumble the item, say *crumbled.* Have children repeat after you.

pp. 30–31

HIGH-FREQUENCY WORD

Have children identify and read the high-frequency word *to* on page 31.

pp. 30–31

creatures: Remind children that *creatures* are animals that are alive. Guide children to point to the different creatures shown on these pages and name them if they are able.

p. 32

REREAD DOK 1

How are the grand old tree's grandchildren just like her? Let's reread pages 29–31 to make sure we understand. (They have roots and branches, and they are home to many creatures.)

p. 32

Encourage children to look at the illustration and describe as much as they can. What colors do they see? What does the picture show?

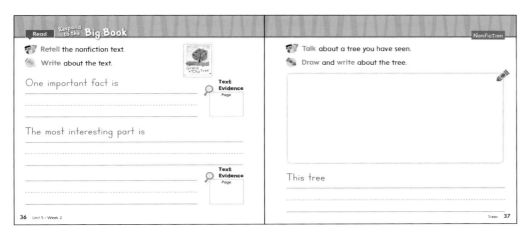

Reading/Writing Companion, pp. 36-37

Respond to the Text

Read children's predictions. Ask: *Were the predictions correct?*

Return to Purpose Remind children of their purpose for reading. Review what they learned about the life of a tree.

- **Retell** Have children turn to page 36 of the **Reading/Writing Companion**. Guide them to retell the text using the **Retelling Cards** and the routine.

- **Write** Have children write an important fact they learned. Model how to find text evidence in the **Big Book** to support their response and how to record the page number in the text evidence box. Share the book with each group of children to give them an opportunity to look at the pages. Then have children write the page number in the text evidence box. Repeat this routine as children complete the page. For the second sentence starter, encourage children to tell about the part they found the most interesting.

- **Talk** Have partners talk about a tree that they have seen or know about.

- **Draw and Write** Then have children draw the tree. Remind them that some trees look different at different times of year. Finally, have children describe the tree they drew by completing the sentence starter at the bottom of page 37.

Model Fluency

Turn to pages 6–7. Tell children that the words in a selection should be read in a way that shows the feelings the author wants to convey. *I think the author wants to show a happy feeling on these pages.* Then read pages 6–7 aloud, using a positive, upbeat voice. Have children echo.

Writing Fluency

To help children increase their writing fluency, have them write as much as they can for four minutes. Tell them to write about how the grand old tree changed as she grew.

RETELLING ROUTINE

Tell children that they will use the Retelling Cards to retell the selection.

- Display Retelling Card 1. Based on children's needs, use either the Modeled, Guided, or ELL retelling prompts. The ELL prompts provide support for children based on levels of language acquisition. Repeat with the rest of the cards, using the prompts as a guide. Tell children to include details from the selection.

- Choose an event from the text and explain why it is a necessary part of a tree's life cycle. Offer support as needed.

- Invite children to choose a favorite part of the selection and act it out.

Retelling Cards

● STUDENT CHECK-IN

Have partners share an important detail from the text. Then have children reflect on their learning using the Check-In routine.

LESSON 1

In a Flash: Sound-Spellings

Display the Sound-Spelling Card for *h*.

1. **Teacher:** What's the letter?   **Children:** h
2. **Teacher:** What's the sound?   **Children:** /h/
3. **Teacher:** What's the word?   **Children:** hippo

Continue the routine for previously taught sounds.

LEARNING GOALS

- We can hear the sound /e/ in words.
- We can connect the sound /e/ to the letter *e*.

OBJECTIVES

Isolate and pronounce the initial sounds in words.

Associate the short sounds with common spellings (graphemes) for the five major vowels.

ELA ACADEMIC LANGUAGE

- *connect, letter, vowel*
- Cognates: *conectar, letra*

▶ TEACH IN SMALL GROUP

You may wish to teach the Word Work lesson in small groups.

ELL ENGLISH LANGUAGE LEARNERS

Phonemic Awareness, Guided Practice/Practice Encourage children to say the phoneme /e/ several times. Point to a card and ask children to name it. Help them self-correct by modeling pronunciation. Then help children identify the initial sound using a sentence frame. For example: *Egg* begins with the sound /e/.

Phonemic Awareness: p. 212
Phonics: p. 214

(5 mins) # Phonemic Awareness

MULTIMODAL

Phoneme Isolation

1 **Model** Display the **Photo Card** for *egg*. *Listen for the sound at the beginning of* egg. *Egg has the /e/ sound at the beginning.* Say *end, Ed, enter* and have children repeat. Emphasize /e/.

Let's play a song. Listen for the words with /e/ at the beginning. Play "Scrambled Egg, Fried Egg" and have children listen for the /e/ sound. *Let's listen to the song again and signal thumbs up when we hear words that begin with /e/.* Play and/or sing the letter song again, encouraging children to join in. Have children signal thumbs up when they hear a word that begins with /e/.

Photo Card

2 **Guided Practice/Practice** Display and name each Photo Card: *elevator, elbow, exit, envelope. Say each picture name with me. Tell me the sound at the beginning of the word.* Guide practice and provide corrective feedback as needed. If children need more practice identifying the /e/ sound, have them use **Practice Book** page 212.

Photo Cards

Articulation Support

Demonstrate the way to say /e/. Open your mouth a little. Start with your tongue in the middle of your mouth. Now use your voice and just let your jaw move down a bit as you say /e/. Say *egg, enter, elbow* and have children repeat. Stretch initial /e/.

Phonics

10 mins

Introduce /e/e

1 **Model** Display the *egg* **Sound-Spelling Card**. Say: *This is the egg card. The sound is /e/. The /e/ sound is spelled with the letter* e. *Say it with me: /e/. The letter* e *is a vowel. This is the sound at the beginning of the word* egg. *Listen: /eeeg/,* egg.

Sound-Spelling Card

Display the song "Scrambled Egg, Fried Egg." (See **Spelling Song** online.) Read or sing the song with children. Reread the title and point out that the word *egg* begins with the letter *e*, which can stand for /e/. Model placing a self-stick note below the *e* in *egg*.

2 **Guided Practice/Practice** Read each line of the song. Stop after each line and ask children to place self-stick notes below words that begin with *E* or *e* and say the letter name and the sound it stands for. If children need additional practice connecting the letter *e* with the sound /e/, use **Practice Book** page 214.

Corrective Feedback

Sound Error Say /e/, then have children repeat the sound. *My turn. Egg, /e/ /e/ /e/. Now it's your turn.* Have children say the words *egg* and *exit* and isolate the initial sound.

Scrambled Egg, Fried Egg

Scrambled egg, fried egg, egg on a plate,

boiled egg, egg on toast, hurry, don't be late!

Eggs are good for breakfast or in a salad, too.

No matter how you cook them, they are good for you.

Scrambled egg, fried egg, egg on a plate,

boiled egg, egg on toast, hurry, don't be late!

But no matter where you go, and no matter what you do, never, ever put an egg in your shoe!

ELL ENGLISH LANGUAGE LEARNERS

Phonics Transfers Use the chart on pages 10–13 in the **Language Transfers Handbook** to check for sound-spelling transfers from a child's native language into English. You can use the Sound-Spelling Cards to support teaching transferable and nontransferable skills.

DIGITAL TOOLS

Word Work

Phonemic Awareness Phonics

Phonics: Spelling Song

PHONICS video

Phonics Video

To differentiate instruction, use these results.

Phonics: Data-Generating

FORMATIVE ASSESSMENT

❯ STUDENT CHECK-IN

Have partners name the letter that stands for /e/. Then have children reflect using the Check-In routine.

LESSON 1

LEARNING GOALS

- We can print the letter *e*.
- We can learn to read *are*.

OBJECTIVES

Print many upper- and lowercase letters.

Read common high-frequency words by sight.

ELA ACADEMIC LANGUAGE

- *uppercase, lowercase, capital*

DIGITAL TOOLS

Handwriting

To differentiate instruction, use these results.

High-Frequency Words: Data-Generating

MULTIMODAL LEARNING

Center Idea Have children use pencils or wooden sticks to make the capital letter *E*. Emphasize the four lines used to form the letter. Use chenille stems to make lowercase *e*. Have children run their fingers over it beginning with the line that goes straight across. Have children practice saying /e/, as they pretend to be an engine slowly going up a hill.

Handwriting: p. 217

Handwriting: Write *Ee*

⏱ 5 mins

1 **Model** Say the handwriting cues below as you write and then identify the upper- and lowercase forms of *Ee*. Then trace the letters as you say /e/.

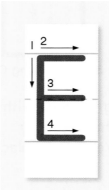

Straight down.
Straight across.
Straight across.
Straight across.

Straight across. Circle back and around, then stop.

2 **Guided Practice**

- Say the cues together as children trace both forms of the letter with their index finger. Have children identify the upper- and lowercase forms of the letter.

- Have children use their index finger to write *E* and *e* on the rug or a table as they say /e/ multiple times.

3 **Practice**

- Distribute **Response Boards**. Have children write *E* and *e* on their Response Boards as they say /e/ each time they write the letter.

- Observe children's pencil grip and paper position and correct as necessary. Guide practice and provide corrective feedback.

 Daily Handwriting

Throughout the week, teach upper- and lowercase letters *Ee*, using the Handwriting models. At the end of the week, have children use **Practice Book** page 217 to practice handwriting, using appropriate directionality.

In a Flash: High-Frequency Words

1. **Teacher:** Read the word.   **Children:** my
2. **Teacher:** Spell the word.   **Children:** m-y
3. **Teacher:** Write the word.   **Children write the word.**

Repeat routine with *do, you,* and *go* from last week.

High-Frequency Words

MULTIMODAL

5 mins

are

1 **Model** Display **Big Book** *A Grand Old Tree*. Read the sentence "They are home to many creatures, just like the grand old tree." Point to the high-frequency word *are*. Use the Read/Spell/Write routine to teach the word.

- **Read** Point to the word *are* and say the word. *This is the word* are. *Say it with me:* are. *The branches are home to many creatures.*

- **Spell** *The word* are *is spelled* a-r-e. *Spell it with me.*

- **Write** *Let's write* are *on our* ***Response Boards*** *as we say each letter:* a-r-e. Guide children on how to print the letter *r*.

- Point out to children that the letter *a* followed by *r* has a different sound from the /a/ sound in *am*.

- Have partners say sentences using *are*.

2 **Guided Practice/Practice** Build sentences using the **High-Frequency Word Cards, Photo Cards,** and teacher-made punctuation cards. Have children point to the high-frequency word *are*. Guide practice and provide corrective feedback as needed. Use these sentences.

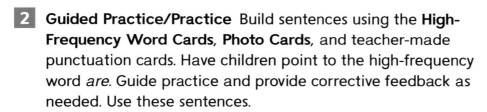

We *are* at my house.	Are you at my house?
You *are* like a kitten.	Are you like a kitten?

ELL ENGLISH LANGUAGE LEARNERS

Use the scaffolds with **High-Frequency Words.**

Beginning
Tell children that we can use the word *are* to talk about groups of people. *What are they doing?* They are sitting.

Intermediate
Point to each card as you read. Have children repeat. Ask a volunteer to point to *are*. Repeat with the second sentence.

Advanced/Advanced High
Challenge partners to say sentences using *are*.

FORMATIVE ASSESSMENT

STUDENT CHECK-IN

Handwriting Have children print *Ee*.

High-Frequency Words Have partners take turns pointing to and reading the word *are*.

Then have children reflect using the Check-In routine.

CHECK FOR SUCCESS

Rubric Use your online rubric to record children's progress.

Can children isolate /e/ and match it to the letter *Ee*?

Can children recognize and read the high-frequency word?

Small Group Instruction

If No

- **Approaching** Reteach pp. T140–144
- **ELL** Develop pp. T140–144

If Yes

- **On** Review pp. T148–150
- **Beyond** Extend p. T154

Literature Big Book

LEARNING GOALS

- We can write about how we can play in a tree.
- We can learn about words that can take the place of nouns (pronouns).

OBJECTIVES

Using a combination of drawing, dictating, and writing to compose informative/ explanatory texts in which they name what they are writing about and supply some information about the topic.

Continue a conversation through multiple exchanges.

Capitalize the pronoun *I*.

Appropriately use pronouns.

ELA ACADEMIC LANGUAGE

- *pronoun*
- Cognate: *pronombre*

 COLLABORATIVE CONVERSATIONS

Turn and Talk Review this routine.

Child 1: I can climb.

Child 2: Can you tell me more?

Child 1: I can climb a tree.

Display the speech bubble "Can you tell me more?" Have partners use it to practice collaborating.

---

 10 mins # Modeled Writing

Model Writing About the Literature Big Book

Build Oral Language Talk about what children learned from listening to the **Literature Big Book**. Review how trees are useful. Ask: *How can you play in a tree?* Have partners use the Turn and Talk routine to talk about different ways they might play in a tree. When children are done, encourage them to share what they talked about with their partner.

Model Writing a Sentence Write and display the following sentence on two lines: **I can climb a tree and sit**. Then point out the following elements of writing, using the Sample Teacher Talk.

- *This is the word* can. *I used the Word Bank to help me spell the word.* Can *is spelled with the letters* c-a-n. HIGH-FREQUENCY WORD

- *I wrote the word* climb. *I wrote the letter* c *because I heard the /k/ sound at the beginning of* climb. PHONICS SKILL

- *When I got to the end of the line, I returned to the beginning of the next line to continue writing my sentence.* Model by tracking the sentence with your finger, pointing out how the sentence continues on the next line. WRITING SKILL

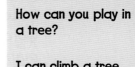

How can you play in a tree?

I can climb a tree and sit.

Writing Practice

Explain to children that they will write a sentence that tells how they play in a tree. Have children turn and talk with a partner to decide one way they might play in a tree.

Draw/Write Tell children to draw a picture of themselves playing in or around a tree. Encourage them to write a sentence about their drawing. As children write, remind them to use the Word Bank and to write letters for the sounds they know. Tell them that if they come to the end of the line as they write, they should continue writing on the next line beginning on the left side of the page.

If needed, provide the following sentence starter: **I _____ in a tree.**

Grammar

5 mins

Subjective Pronouns

1 **Model** Say these sentences: **Brianna likes apples. She eats an apple every day.** *The pronoun* she *replaces the girl's name.* Review *he* and *it* by modeling these sentences: **Lucas is happy. He rides a bike. This book is great. It is about a mouse.**

Introduce the pronouns *you, I,* and *we* as you point to yourself and to the children. *I like cookies. You like cookies. We like cookies.* I, you, *and* we *are pronouns.* Write and read: **Can I have a cookie?** Circle *I* and explain that it is always a capital.

2 **Guided Practice** Write and read the following sentences. Read each pair and guide children to identify and circle the pronoun in the second sentence. Then help them identify the word or words in the first sentence that the pronoun replaced.

Sarah wakes up early. She walks her dog at 6:00 a.m. My sister and I play a game. We like to play after school.

3 **Practice** Write and read these sentence pairs aloud: **That tree is tall. It is taller than the building. My friend and I are neighbors. We live on the same block.**

Ask partners to circle the pronoun in the second sentences and identify the noun it replaces.

 Talk About It Have partners create sentences using *I, you,* and *we.*

Link to Writing Guide children to review the Shared Writing sentences and identify any pronouns they may have used.

 # English Language Learners

Use the following scaffolds with **Grammar, Practice.**

Beginning
Draw a tree. Say, *The tree is big. It is big.* Have children echo, saying both sentences.

Intermediate
Read the first sentence and ask children to repeat. Guide them to replace *tree* with *it* and ask them to repeat the new sentence.

Advanced/Advanced High
Help children use subjective pronouns by describing objects in the room. Provide an example: *The board is white. It is a white board.*

DIGITAL TOOLS

 Grammar Activity

 Weekly Song

 Grammar Video

DIFFERENTIATED WRITING
● **English Language Learners** For more writing support, see the **ELL Small Group Guide,** p. 120.

FORMATIVE ASSESSMENT

STUDENT CHECK-IN
Have each partner share two pronouns. Have children reflect using the Check-In routine.

LEARNING GOALS

- We can blend word parts to say a word.
- We can use new words.
- We can learn words that tell about tree parts.
- We can add *-ed* to words to tell about something that already happened.

OBJECTIVES

Blend and segment onsets and rimes of single-syllable spoken words.

Use words and phrases acquired through conversations, reading and being read to, and responding to texts.

Use the most frequently occurring inflections and affixes (e.g., -ed, -s, re-, un-, pre-, -ful, -less) as a clue to the meaning of an unknown word.

Identify words about tree parts.

ELA ACADEMIC LANGUAGE

- *verb, past*
- Cognate: *verbo*

DIGITAL TOOLS

 Weekly Song

 Visual Vocabulary Cards

 **Category Words Activity**

LESSON FOCUS

READING
Review Essential Question
Reread Literature Big Book
A Grand Old Tree
- Study Genre/Skill

Word Work
- Practice /e/*e*

Read Shared Read
"Ed and Ned"
- Practice Strategy

WRITING
Writing/Grammar
- Interactive Writing
- Practice Grammar

Literature Big Book, pp. 3–32

Reading/Writing Companion, pp. 42–49

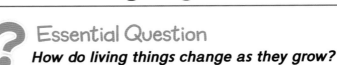 **Oral Language** MULTIMODAL

10 mins

Essential Question

How do living things change as they grow?

Remind children that this week they are learning how a tree changes as it grows. *What have we learned so far about how trees change as they grow? Let's sing a song about a tree.* Sing "My Oak Tree" with children. Then use the Build Knowledge anchor chart, the **Big Book,** and the **Weekly Song** to guide children in discussing the Essential Question.

Phonological Awareness: Onset/Rime Blending

1 **Model** Say the word *ground*. Repeat the word, segmenting and blending the onset and rime: ground, */gr/ /ound/*. Explain that the beginning sounds in *ground* are /gr/ and the ending sounds in the word are /ound/. Then segment and blend the onset and rime in additional words, such as *little* and *plant*.

2 **Guided Practice/Practice** Guide children to practice segmenting and blending the onset and rime in other words from the song, such as *saw, tree, helped,* and *Daddy*. Provide corrective feedback as needed. If children need additional practice segmenting and blending onset and rime, have them use **Practice Book** page 211.

Review Oral Vocabulary Words

Use the Define/Example/Ask routine to review the oral vocabulary words *amazing* and *develop*. Prompt children to use the words in sentences.

Visual Vocabulary Cards

Category Words: Tree Parts

1 **Model** Use *A Grand Old Tree* to introduce words that name tree parts: *roots* (page 6), *branches* (page 8), *leaves* (page 9), *trunk* (page 27), and *bark* (page 27). Point out each tree part in the illustrations. Then display different pages of the book and ask questions about each tree part. For example, on page 6: *What sank deep into the earth?* (the tree's roots) Then on page 7: *Where is the little blue bird?* (on a branch)

2 **Guided Practice/Practice** Display an illustration of the tree from the **Big Book**. Ask children to describe the picture and point to the different tree parts. Ask children to identify each part. *Which tree part is this?*

Have children discuss what they know about trees. Encourage them to use words that name tree parts in their answers. (Possible response: We rake leaves every fall.)

Vocabulary: Inflectional Ending *-ed*

1 **Model** Explain to children that adding the word part *-ed* to the end of a present-tense verb (a verb that tells what is happening now) changes the verb into a past-tense verb (a verb that tells what happened earlier). Use *A Grand Old Tree* to show how the *-ed* ending can change word meanings.

Think Aloud In *A Grand Old Tree*, I can read part of this sentence on page 9: . . . *caterpillars and ladybugs crawled about*. I see *-ed* at the end of the word *crawl*, which tells me that the action happened in the past. I can also read this sentence on page 29: *Their arms reach high into the sky*. I don't see *-ed* at the end of the word *reach*. This tells me that the action is happening now.

2 **Guided Practice** Point out and discuss other verbs in the Big Book that end with *-ed*. Cover the *-ed* ending and read the present tense form of the verb. Then reveal the *-ed* ending and read the past-tense form.

The grand old tree *flowered*, bore fruit, and *sowed* seeds.

3 **Practice** Talk about the verb *develop* and use it in context to help children understand its meaning. Have children add the ending *-ed* to *develop* to form a past-tense verb. Point out that sometimes *-ed* stands for /t/. Continue with the verbs *sway, nest,* and *crawl*.

KIDS ON THE MOVE!

Have children stand up straight and tall like a tree. Call out tree parts *(trunk, branches, leaves, roots)* and have children move the body part that most closely corresponds to that tree part *(waist, arms, fingers, feet)*.

Phonological Awareness: p. 211

ENGLISH LANGUAGE LEARNERS

Category Words, Guided Practice/Practice Display an illustration of the tree from the **Big Book**. Model for children how to talk about the parts of the tree that are already developed, stressing the *-ed* ending. *The branch developed*. Then have children work with a partner to discuss additional examples.

❯ STUDENT CHECK-IN

Oral Vocabulary Words Have partners say a sentence using a vocabulary word.

Category Words Have partners name a word that tells a tree part.

Vocabulary Have partners name a past-tense word with *-ed*.

Then have children reflect using the Check-In routine.

Literature Big Book

Literature Big Book

LEARNING GOALS

- **We can tell what makes a text nonfiction.**
- **We can identify topic and details.**

OBJECTIVES

Recognize common types of texts.

With prompting and support, identify the main topic and retell key details of a text.

ELA ACADEMIC LANGUAGE

- *nonfiction, details, topic*
- Cognates: *no ficción, detalles*

Reread

Literature Big Book

Genre: Informational Text: Nonfiction

1 **Model** Tell children that you will now reread the **Big Book** *A Grand Old Tree.* Remind children that this story is a nonfiction text.

 Anchor Chart Display and review the characteristics of nonfiction text that you have listed on the Nonfiction anchor chart. Add details as needed.

Think Aloud I know that *A Grand Old Tree* is nonfiction because it gives facts and information about a topic—in this case, trees. This book tells about the long life of one tree. The author includes details about what happens to the tree to give us a deeper understanding of a tree's life cycle.

2 **Guided Practice/Practice** Turn to page 18 of *A Grand Old Tree* and read pages 18–19 aloud. *What is happening to the tree on these pages?* (The tree is growing and changing with each season.) *How does the tree change as time passes?* (The tree flowers, bears fruit, and loses its leaves many times. The tree gets bigger.) *What different kinds of weather does the tree live through?* (sunshine, rain, snow, wind) Encourage children to tell what they learn about the tree's life from the text and the illustrations on these pages.

ELL English Language Learners

Genre: Informational Text, Guided Practice/Practice Point to the illustrations on pages 18-19. *The tree starts very small. It gets bigger and bigger.* Ask guiding questions about individual pictures, such as: *What is on this tree?* Green leaves are on this tree. *Where are the leaves?* The leaves are on the tree. *What happens after the snow?* After the snow, flowers grow. Then provide children with sentence frames they can use to contribute to the class discussion about the story and genre. This text is about trees. The text is an informational text. This text has facts/information. I learned that trees change.

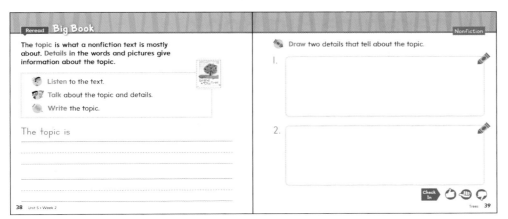

Reading/Writing Companion, pp. 38-39

Topic and Details

1 **Model** Remind children that knowing the topic of a text can help you understand it better. Turn to page 38 in the **Reading/Writing Companion**. Read the definitions aloud.

 Anchor Chart Display the Topic and Details anchor chart. Review the anchor chart and add new information as needed.

Think Aloud I know that this book is about what happens to a tree during its life. That is the topic. Let's find details that tell about the topic. On page 10, it says that the tree flowered. This is a detail about the topic. On page 13, it says that the tree bore fruit. These are changes that the tree goes through. These details help me understand more about what happens to the tree during its life.

2 **Guided Practice/Practice** Have children turn to pages 38-39 of the Reading/Writing Companion. Display pages 18–19 of *A Grand Old Tree*. Talk about how the tree changes in the illustrations. Ask children to listen for details about the tree as you read pages 19-21 aloud. Remind them about the topic discussed during the think aloud. Then have children write the topic on page 38 and draw two details on page 39.

 English Language Learners

Topic and Details, Guided Practice/Practice Point to the illustrations and model saying: *The topic is the life of a tree*. Have children repeat. Have partners look at the illustrations and discuss a detail about the topic. Provide sentence frames: A key shows the tree in winter. The tree has no leaves. Have partners repeat the routine for several of the illustrations.

For additional support, see the **ELL Small Group Guide**, pp. 118–119.

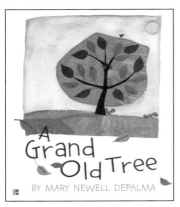

A Grand Old Tree
BY MARY NEWELL DEPALMA

Literature Big Book

Reread

Literature Big Book

10 mins

Analyze the Text

Once children have reread *A Grand Old Tree* to study the characteristics of the genre and practice the comprehension skill, guide them to analyze author's craft. Reread the passages specified below and use the scaffolded instruction in the prompts to help children answer the questions on pages 40-41 of the **Reading/Writing Companion**.

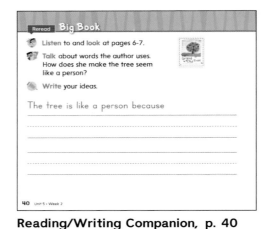

Reread Big Book

Listen to and look at pages 6-7.

Talk about words the author uses. How does she make the tree seem like a person?

Write your ideas.

The tree is like a person because

40 Unit 5 · Week 2

Reading/Writing Companion, p. 40

AUTHOR'S CRAFT DOK 2

Reread pages 6-7 of the **Big Book**. *What words does the author use to make the tree seem like a person?* (The author talks about the tree's roots, using the words *her roots* and calls the tree's branches *her arms*. Trees do not have arms—people do.)

ELL English Language Learners

Remind children that the pronouns *she* and *her* refer to a girl or woman. Explain that the author writes about the tree as a character. *The tree in the story is a woman. This helps you picture in your mind what is happening in the story.*

ORGANIZATION DOK 1

Display and reread pages 10–15 of the Big Book. *The author tells the story of the tree's life in time order. First the tree flowered. Then it bore, or had, fruit. What happens after that?* (The tree sowed seeds and had many children.)

USE ILLUSTRATIONS DOK 1

Display and reread pages 18–19 of the Big Book. *How do the pictures teach you more about the life of the tree?* (The pictures show the tree during each season of the year. They show how the tree is always changing.)

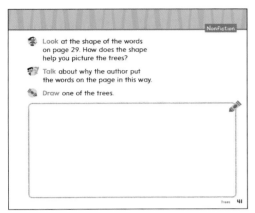

Reading/Writing Companion, p. 41

AUTHOR'S CRAFT DOK 3

Display and reread page 29 of the **Big Book**. Look closely at the shape of the words. *How does the shape of the words help you picture the trees?* (The words make the shape of a tree.) *Why do you think the author placed the words this way?* (The text is about the tree's grandchildren, who are just like the old tree. The words about the grandchildren make the shape of the old tree.)

Spotlight on Language

Author's Craft Point to page 28. *The shape of these words is curvy.* Point to page 29. *These words go down the page. How are the shapes of the words like a tree?* Provide sentence frames. The words curve like a tree. The words go down the page like a tree trunk and roots. Help children understand that the words are like the tree's grandchildren.

AUTHOR'S PURPOSE DOK 3

Why do you think the author wrote this book? (Possible response: The author wanted to teach children about the life cycle of a tree.)

Talk About It

Guide children to use their responses on the **Reading/Writing Companion** pages to answer the question: *How does the Big Book help you understand how a tree changes as it grows?* If necessary, use these sentence starters to focus the discussion: **First, the tree _____. Next, the tree _____. Then the tree _____. Finally, the tree _____.**

Integrate

Build Knowledge: Make Connections

Talk About the Text Have partners discuss the changes the tree went through in its life. *How did the tree change as it grew older?*

Add to the Anchor Chart Record new ideas on the Build Knowledge anchor chart.

FORMATIVE ASSESSMENT

⊘ STUDENT CHECK-IN

Have children share something the author/illustrator does with the text and images to help them understand the selection. Then have children reflect on their learning using the Check-In routine.

Ee

Display the Sound-Spelling Card for *e*.

1. **Teacher:** What's the letter?	**Children:** e
2. **Teacher:** What's the sound?	**Children:** /e/
3. **Teacher:** What's the word?	**Children:** egg

Continue the routine for previously taught sounds.

LEARNING GOALS

- **We can blend sounds to say words.**
- **We can connect letters to sounds to read words.**
- **We can read the word *are*.**

OBJECTIVES

Demonstrate understanding of spoken words, syllables, and sounds (phonemes).

Associate the short sounds with the common spellings (graphemes) for the five major vowels.

Read common high-frequency words by sight.

Blend phonemes to form words.

ELA ACADEMIC LANGUAGE

- *middle, vowel*

 TEACH IN SMALL GROUP

You may wish to teach the Word Work lesson in small groups.

DIGITAL TOOLS

Word Work — Phonemic Awareness / Phonics

To differentiate instruction for key skills, use the results of these activities.

Phonics: Data-Generating

High-Frequency Words: Data-Generating

OPTIONAL 5 mins

Phonemic Awareness

Phoneme Blending

1 **Model** Demonstrate how to blend phonemes to make words. *Let's listen for /e/ in the middle of a word:* pet. *I am going to say the sounds in* pet: /p/ /e/ /t/. *I can blend those sounds to make the word:* /peeet/, pet. *Listen as I say the sounds and blend them to make words.* Tell children to listen for /e/ in the middle of the word. Model phoneme blending with the following.

/s/ /e/ /t/ set	/m/ /e/ /t/ met	/m/ /e/ /n/ men

2 **Guided Practice/Practice** *Listen to the sounds in a different word:* /g/ /e/ /t/. *Let's blend the sounds and say the word together:* /g/ /e/ /t/, /geeet/ get. Tell children to listen to the sounds in words, repeat the sounds, and then blend them to say the word. Guide practice and provide corrective feedback as needed.

/b/ /e/ /g/ beg	/t/ /e/ /n/ ten	/h/ /e/ /n/ hen
/sp/ /i/ /n/ spin	/d/ /e/ /n/ den	/j/ /e/ /t/ jet
/p/ /e/ /t/ pet	/st/ /a/ /k/ stack	

---

5 mins

Phonics

 MULTIMODAL

Review Short *e*

1 **Model** Display the *egg* Sound-Spelling Card. *This is the letter e. This letter is a special letter. It is a vowel. The letter e stands for the sound /e/ as in the word egg.*

2 **Guided Practice/Practice** Display the *egg* Sound-Spelling Card and point to the letter *Ee*. Have children say the letter name and sound with you. Have children listen as you say some words. Ask them to write the letter *e* on their **Response Boards** if the word has the sound /e/ at the beginning of the word. Guide children with the first word.

echo	snow	Ed	have	end	elf

Have children listen for /e/ in the middle of the word.

door	ten	five	speck	get	pen

Blend Words

1 **Model** Place **Word-Building Cards** *m, e,* and *t* in a pocket chart. Point to the *m. This is the letter* m. *The letter* m *stands for* /m/. *Say* /m/. *This is the letter* e. *The letter* e *stands for* /e/. *Say* /e/. *This is the letter* t. *The letter* t *stands for* /t/. *Say* /t/. *Listen as I blend the three sounds together:* /mmmeeet/. *Met. Now blend the sounds with me to read the word.*

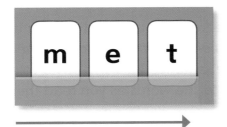

2 **Guided Practice/Practice** Change Word-Building Cards to *n, e, t.* Point to the letter *n* and have children say /n/. Point to the letter *e* and have children say /e/. Point to the letter *t* and have children say /t/. Move your hand from left to right under the word and have children blend and read *net.* Repeat with *ten, hen, men.* Guide practice and provide corrective feedback as needed.

OPTIONAL
5 mins

High-Frequency Words

MULTIMODAL

are

1 **Guided Practice** Display the **High-Frequency Word Card** *are.* Use the Read/Spell/Write routine to teach the word. Ask children to write *are* without looking at the word card. If needed, guide children on how to form the letter *r* because it has not been taught yet. Then have children self-correct by checking the High-Frequency Word Card.

2 **Practice** Add the high-frequency word *are* to the cumulative word bank.

• Have partners say sentences using the word.

Cumulative Review Review the high-frequency words *my, do, you, go,* and *and* by displaying each word and having children read it with automaticity.

For additional practice with high-frequency words, see **Practice Book** page 218.

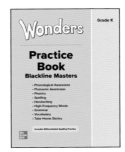
FORMATIVE ASSESSMENT

❯ STUDENT CHECK-IN

Phonics Have partners blend and read *men.*

High-Frequency Words Have partners take turns pointing to and reading *are.*

Then have children reflect using the Check-In routine.

✓ CHECK FOR SUCCESS

Rubric Use your online rubric to record children's progress.

Can the children identify initial and medial /e/ and match /e/ to the letter *Ee*?

Can children recognize and read the high-frequency word?

❯ **Small Group Instruction**

If No

● **Approaching** Reteach pp. T140–144

● **ELL** Develop pp. T140–144

If Yes

● **On** Review pp. T148–150

● **Beyond** Extend p. T154

LESSON 2

LEARNING GOALS

We can read and understand a text.

OBJECTIVES

Follow words from left to right, top to bottom, and page by page.

Know and apply grade-level phonics and word analysis skills in decoding words.

Associate the short sounds with the common spellings (graphemes) for the five major vowels.

Read common high-frequency words by sight.

With prompting and support, identify the main topic and retell key details of a text.

Read emergent-reader texts with purpose and understanding.

ELA ACADEMIC LANGUAGE
• *reread, underline*

 DIFFERENTIATED READING

● **English Language Learners** Have children listen to a summary of the selection, available in multiple languages.

Read "Ed and Ned"

⏱ 10 mins

Connect to Concept

As children read this selection, have them look for details to help them answer the Essential Question: *How do living things change as they grow?*

Foundational Skills

Concepts of Print Read a page from "Ed and Ned" as you track the print with your finger. *I begin reading on the left and move to the right. As soon as I finish a sentence, I read the sentence below it.* Invite volunteers to come up to the book and point to the words as you read them.

Phonics Have children review the letter *e* and the /e/ sound.

High-Frequency Words Have children review the words *can, see,* and *are*.

Read the Shared Read

Reread Remind children that they can go back and reread the text whenever they have trouble understanding what is happening. *If something is not clear to you, go back and reread all or part of the text. Look closely at the photos. This will help you understand the text better.*

Anchor Chart Display and review the Reread anchor chart. Remind children to use this strategy as they read "Ed and Ned." Explain that good readers ask and answer questions before, during, and after they read to help them understand what they are reading.

Choral Read Before reading, invite children to share any questions they have about what they are about to read. Then have children chorally read the story with you.

Read Tell children that now they will read the text and you will pause to ask them the questions in the blue column.

Have children use the box on the right-hand pages to do the following:

• Draw a picture about the text or the photos.

• Draw something whose name includes the /e/ sound.

• Write the letter *e*.

Reading/Writing Companion, pp. 42–43

SET PURPOSE

Have children read to find out about Ed and Ned.

PHONICS

Have children underline words that begin with the /e/ sound. (Ed)

Reading/Writing Companion, pp. 44-45

Reading/Writing Companion, pp. 46-47

Reading/Writing Companion, pp. 48-49

COMPREHENSION

Have children circle the words that tell where Ned is. (up, up, up)

PHONICS

Tell children to underline words that have the same middle sound as *hen*. (Ned x5, met x2)

PHONICS

Have children underline words that begin with /e/. (Ed x3)

HIGH-FREQUENCY WORDS

Tell children to circle the word *are*. (*Are* appears twice on page 47.)

COMPREHENSION

Have children circle who can "nap, nap, nap." (Circle the name *Ned*, the photo or both.)

COMPREHENSION

Have partners use the photos to retell the text. Guide them to identify the topic as part of their retelling.

ENGLISH LANGUAGE LEARNERS

Use the following scaffolds with **Respond to the Text**.

Beginning
Display page 46. *What do bear cubs do?* (drink/sip water) Ask children to point to the word that tells them the answer. (sip)

Intermediate
Display page 46. Ask children to describe what baby cubs do. Provide the sentence frame: Baby cubs sip water.

Advanced/Advanced High
Have partners talk about what baby cubs do. Have them use complete sentences while speaking and pointing to the text to show evidence.

Focus on Fluency: Accuracy

Model reading with accuracy for children. Remind them of the importance of recognizing high-frequency words as well as decoding words in the text correctly. Encourage children to practice reading for accuracy with a partner. Listen in and offer support and corrective feedback.

Respond to the Text

Talk About It Have children talk about what they learned about Ed and Ned from the text. Use the sentence starters to focus the discussion. **Ed and Ned are _____. Ed and Ned can _____.** Help children cite text evidence to support their answers.

FORMATIVE ASSESSMENT

❯ STUDENT CHECK-IN

Have partners take turns sharing their retelling of the text with one another. Then have children reflect on their learning using the Check-In routine.

LESSON 2

Literature Big Book

- We can write what we think the tree provided for the animals.
- We can learn about words that can take the place of nouns (pronouns).

OBJECTIVES

Use a combination of drawing, dictating, and writing to compose opinion pieces in which they state an opinion or preference about the topic or book.

Write a letter or letters for most consonant and short-vowel sounds.

Follow agreed-upon rules for discussions.

Capitalize the pronoun *I*.

Appropriately use pronouns.

ELA ACADEMIC LANGUAGE
- *provide, idea, pronoun*
- Cognates: *idea, pronombre*

COLLABORATIVE CONVERSATIONS

Circulate as children talk with a partner. Notice who needs to provide more information. Remind them to use the speech bubbles to help them.

---

10 mins

Interactive Writing

Write About the Literature Big Book

Analyze the Prompt Tell children that today they will write about the **Literature Big Book**, *A Grand Old Tree*. Ask: *What did the tree provide for the animals?* Explain that *provide* means "to give." Point to the birds and nest on pages 8 and 9. Have partners use clues in the text and illustrations to discuss how they think the tree provides for the animals.

Find Text Evidence Reread pages 12 and 13. Point to the fruit on the tree and the fruit being eaten by the bird and squirrels. Have children use the text and illustration to tell what the tree provided for the animals.

Write a Response: Share the Pen Have children provide a response to the prompt. Encourage them to share the pen. Alternatively, use the sentence: *The tree gave birds and squirrels food to eat.* Point out elements of writing, using the Sample Teacher Talk below.

- *Say* tree. *What is the first sound? /t/ I know that /t/ is a sound the letter* t *can make. Who can write the letter that stands for /t/?* PHONICS

- *We can look at the Word Bank to help us spell the word* to. *Who can point to the word* to? *Let's spell it:* t-o. *Write the word as children dictate it to you.* HIGH-FREQUENCY WORDS

- *When we write, we use words to connect ideas. The word* and *lets the reader know that both birds and squirrels eat food from the tree.* TRAIT: ORGANIZATION

- *What do we do when we come to the end of a line while we're writing? That's right. We move down to the next line.* WRITING SKILL

What did the tree provide for the animals?

The tree gave birds and squirrels food to eat.

Writing Practice

Write Provide children with the following sentence starters and have them complete them in their writer's notebook.

The tree gave the animals _____.   Animals can _____ in the tree.

As children write, encourage them to:

- Use the Word Bank to help spell high-frequency words.
- Identify phonics skills. Stretch the sounds they hear in words as they write.
- When they've written to the end of a line, move down to the next line.
- Use words such as *and* to organize ideas.

5 mins

Grammar

Subjective Pronouns

1 **Model** Remind children that a pronoun can take the place of a noun. Write these sentences and read them: **Paulo is my friend. He goes to my school. The rose looks pretty. It smells good.**

Circle the pronoun in each sentence and point to the noun it replaces. *(Paulo/he, rose, It)* Say: *I use the pronoun I to talk about myself.* Write this sentence and read it aloud: **I am a teacher.** *I use the pronoun we to talk about myself and other people.* **My students and I like to read. We read every day.**

2 **Guided Practice** Display the paragraph below and read it aloud. Guide children to identify the pronouns. Circle the pronouns as children identify them. Invite volunteers to help circle the pronouns.

We will make a salad. (We) **She can cut up some carrots.** (She) **He can slice tomatoes.** (He) **You can wash the lettuce.** (You) **I can make the dressing.** (I) **It will be delicious!** (It)

3 **Practice** Display the paragraph below and read it. Have partners work together to identify the pronouns.
We went to the park. (We) **I went down the slide.** (I) **He went down the slide, too.** (He) **She played on the swings.** (She) **It was fun.** (It)
Have volunteers share their answers with the class. If children need more practice with pronouns, have them use **Practice Book** page 220.

Talk About It

Pair children and have partners make up sentences about something they do at school using *I, you,* and *we.* As children share their sentences, ask them to identify the pronoun, and if appropriate, the word or words it replaces.

English Language Learners

Grammar, Model Write and read: *I play at the park. We play at the park. You play at the park.* Have children identify the pronoun in each sentence. *What is the pronoun?* Have children respond: *I is the pronoun.* Point out how the verb stays the same when using *I, you,* and *we.*

DIGITAL TOOLS

 I see a fish. Grammar Activity

DIFFERENTIATED WRITING

● **English Language Learners** For more writing support, see the **ELL Small Group Guide**, p. 120.

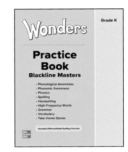

Grammar: p. 220

FORMATIVE ASSESSMENT

❯ STUDENT CHECK-IN

Have each partner share two pronouns. Have children reflect using the Check-In routine.

LESSON 3

LESSON FOCUS

READING
Review Essential Question
Read Interactive Read Aloud
"The Pine Tree"
• Practice Strategy
Word Work
• Practice /e/e

Reread Shared Read
"Ed and Ned"
WRITING
Writing/Grammar
• Independent Writing
• Practice Grammar

Interactive Read-Aloud Cards

Reading/Writing Companion, pp. 42–49

Oral Language

5 mins

MULTIMODAL

? Essential Question

How do living things change as they grow?

This week we are learning about how living things change as they grow. Have children discuss what they have learned about how trees change as they grow. Then sing the **Weekly Song** together.

Oral Vocabulary Words

Remind children that in Lesson 1 they learned the words *develop* and *amazing*. Ask: *What is something that will* develop*? What do you find* amazing*?* Then use the Define/Example/Ask routine on the print or digital **Visual Vocabulary Cards** to introduce *enormous, imagine,* and *content*.

Oral Vocabulary Routine

Define: Something that is **enormous** is very large.

Example: The mall is an enormous building with many shops.

Ask: An elephant is enormous. What other animal is enormous?

Define: When you **imagine** something, you see it in your mind.

Example: I can imagine what happens at a carnival.

Ask: What do you imagine it would be like to fly an airplane?

Define: When you are **content**, you feel happy and satisfied.

Example: I am content when I spend time with my family.

Ask: What does a content person look like?

Visual Vocabulary Cards

Read the Interactive Read Aloud

Connect to Concept

Tell children that they will listen to a fairy tale about a pine tree. Explain that a fairy tale is a story about magical characters and make believe places. Then remind children that this week we are learning about how living things, such as trees, change as they grow.

"The Pine Tree"

Set Purpose *Let's read to find out how the pine tree changes as it grows.*

Oral Vocabulary Use the Oral Vocabulary prompts as you read to provide more practice with the words in context.

Unfamiliar Words As you read "The Pine Tree," ask children to listen for words they do not understand and to think about what the words mean. Pause after Card 1 to model.

Teacher Think Aloud What is a logger? The text says that the logger cut down trees with his ax and then put them in a truck and drove away. A logger must be a person who cuts logs for wood.

Student Think Along After Card 1: I'm not sure what sparrows are. The text says that there were three of them and they were sitting on a branch. Then it says that they flew away. A sparrow must be a bird. There are three birds in the picture. Those must be the sparrows.

Build Knowledge: Make Connections

Talk About the Text Have partners share important details about how the cut-down trees changed. *How did the pine tree change?*

Add to the Anchor Chart Record new ideas on the Build Knowledge anchor chart.

Add to the Word Bank Add new words children learned to a separate section of the Word Bank.

Compare Texts

Guide children to make connections between "The Pine Tree" and *A Grand Old Tree. How are the texts alike and how are they different?*

Display the Sound-Spelling Card for *e*.
1. **Teacher:** What's the letter?   **Children:** e
2. **Teacher:** What's the sound?   **Children:** /e/
3. **Teacher:** What's the word?   **Children:** egg
Continue the routine for previously taught sounds.

LEARNING GOALS

• **We can blend sounds to say words.**

• **We can blend and read words.**

OBJECTIVES

Demonstrate understanding of spoken words, syllables, and sounds (phonemes).

Know and apply grade-level phonics and word analysis skills in decoding words.

Associate the short sounds with the common spellings (graphemes) for the five major vowels.

Spell simple words phonetically, drawing on knowledge of sound-letter relationships.

Blend phonemes to form words.

ELA ACADEMIC LANGUAGE

• *blend, middle, vowel*

TEACH IN SMALL GROUP

You may choose to teach the Word Work lesson in small groups.

DIGITAL TOOLS

Word Work   **Phonemic Awareness Phonics**

Phonics: Spelling Song

---

5 mins

Phonemic Awareness

MULTIMODAL
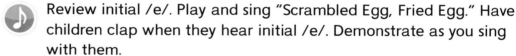

Phoneme Blending

1 **Model** Demonstrate how to blend phonemes to make words. *Listen to the sounds in the word* set: */s/ /e/ /t/. I can blend those sounds to make the word: /ssseeet/,* set. *Listen as I say more sounds and blend them to make words.* Tell children to listen for /e/ in the middle of the word. Model phoneme blending with the following.

   /n/ /e/ /t/ net   /s/ /t/ /e/ /m/ stem   /r/ /e/ /d/ red

2 **Guided Practice/Practice** *Listen to the sounds in a different word:* /s/ /t/ /e/ /p/. *Let's blend the sounds and say the word together:* /s/ /t/ /e/ /p/, /steeep/ step. Tell children to listen to the sounds in words, repeat the sounds, and then blend them to say the word. Guide practice and provide corrective feedback as needed.

   /e/ /d/ Ed   /t/ /e/ /n/ ten   /e/ /g/ egg

   /e/ /d/ /j/ edge   /b/ /e/ /d/ bed   /g/ /e/ /t/ get

♪ Review initial /e/. Play and sing "Scrambled Egg, Fried Egg." Have children clap when they hear initial /e/. Demonstrate as you sing with them.

Phonics

e

Review Short *e*

1 **Model** Display **Word-Building Card** *e*. *This is the letter* e. *It is a vowel. The letter* e *can stand for /e/, the sound you hear at the beginning of* egg. *Say the sound with me: /e/. I will write the letter* e *because* egg *has /e/ at the beginning.* Repeat with *bed*.

2 **Guided Practice/Practice** Tell children that you will say some words that have the /e/ sound in the middle and some words that do not. Have children say /e/ and write the letter *e* on their **Response Boards** when they hear /e/ in the middle. Guide practice and provide corrective feedback as needed.

jet	ride	man	set	could
wet	bed	two	hot	pen

Blend Words

1 **Model** Display **Word-Building Cards** *s, e, t. This is the letter* s. *It stands for /s/. This is the letter* e. *It stands for /e/. This is the letter* t. *It stands for /t/. Let's blend the three sounds together: /ssseeet/, /set/. The word is* set. Continue with *ten, Ted, men*.

2 **Guided Practice/Practice** Write the following words and sentences. Have children read each word, blending the sounds. Then have them read the sentences.

met	Ed	den	stem	hen	net	set	pet

Prompt children to read the following sentences: *We are in the den. I like the hen. Ed can see the net.*

Spell Words

Dictation Say *pet* and have children repeat. Ask children to say *pet* again, stretching the sounds. Say: *I hear three sounds in the word* pet: /p/ /e/ /t/. *I will write a letter for each sound: p, e, t. I know the spelling rule that every word has at least one vowel. I wrote the letter* e *for the middle vowel sound /e/ in* pet. *Let's read the word.* Then dictate these words for children to spell: *Ed, Ted, ten, sit, spin*. If children need additional spelling practice, have them use **Practice Book** page 215.

LONG VOWEL EXPRESS TRACK

Review Remind children that a vowel is a special letter. It can have a short sound and a long sound. Write the following words on the board. Have children read them and point out the differences in the words in each set: *can/cane; tap/tape; cap/cape; pan/pane; hat/hate; nap/nape.*

ENGLISH LANGUAGE LEARNERS

Phonics, Guided Practice/Practice Point to the letters in *jet* and say their sounds. Have children repeat each one. Then have children blend the sounds along with you. If needed, stretch out the /e/ and have students repeat.

CORRECTIVE FEEDBACK

Sound Error Model the sound that children missed when blending words, then have them repeat. Tap under the letter *e* in the word *met* and ask: *What's the sound?* (/e/) Return to the beginning of the word. *Let's start over.* Blend the sounds in the word again.

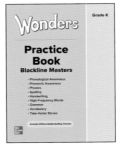

Phonics/Spelling: p. 215

FORMATIVE ASSESSMENT

◊ STUDENT CHECK-IN

Have partners read *set*. Then have children reflect using the Check-In routine.

LESSON 3

LEARNING GOALS

- We can sort words with *e* at the beginning from those with *e* in the middle.
- We can read sentences with the word *are*.

OBJECTIVES

Associate the short sounds with the common spellings (graphemes) for the five major vowels.

Read common high-frequency words by sight.

Sort words by initial and medial phonemes.

ELA ACADEMIC LANGUAGE

- *beginning, middle*
- Cognate: *medio*

DIGITAL TOOLS

Word Work

Phonics Activity

To differentiate instruction for key skills, use the results of this activity.

Phonics: Data-Generating

High-Frequency Words: Data-Generating

OPTIONAL 5 mins

Phonics

MULTIMODAL

Picture Sort

1 **Model** Remind children that the letter *e* can stand for /e/. Place **Word-Building Card** *e* at the top center of the pocket chart. Hold up the **Photo Card** for *egg*. *Here is the picture for* egg. Egg *has the /e/ sound at the beginning. Listen, /eeeg/.* Place the *egg* Photo Card on one side of the pocket chart.

Photo Cards

Use the same routine for medial /e/ and the Photo Card for *jet*. Place *jet* on the other side of the pocket chart.

Hold up the Photo Card for *elevator*. Elevator *begins with /e/. I will place it under the egg because they both begin with /e/.*

2 **Guided Practice/Practice** Have children sort the Photo Cards *elbow, envelope, exit, gem, net, pen, web*. Have them identify if /e/ is at the beginning or in the middle of the word. Then have them tell which Photo Card each should be placed under: *egg* or *jet*. Guide practice and provide corrective feedback as needed.

Photo Cards

English Language Learners

Phonics, Guided Practice/Practice Confirm children's understanding that *e* stands for the initial sound in *egg* and the medial sound in *jet*. Guide children to identify if /e/ is at the beginning or end of the names of the Photo Cards. *Is /e/ a beginning or middle sound in the word* net? (middle sound) Provide sentence frames to help children tell how they sorted the cards: Net *has the sound /e/* in the middle *of the word. We place* net *below the* jet.

High-Frequency Words

5 mins

MULTIMODAL

are

1 **Guided Practice** Display the **High-Frequency Word Card** *are*. Review the word using the Read/Spell/Write routine.

2 **Practice** Point to the High-Frequency Word Card *are* and have children read it. Repeat with last week's word *my*.

Build Fluency

Word Automaticity Write the following sentences. Have children chorally read as you track the print. Have them reread the sentences until they can read the words automatically and fluently.

We *are* in the den.

Pam and Tim *are* in.

Ted and Sam *are* like you.

You *are* in the pen.

Read for Fluency Distribute **Practice Book** pages 223–224 and help children assemble their Take-Home Books. Chorally read the Take-Home Book with children. Then have children reread the book to review high-frequency words and to build automaticity.

BUILD YOUR WORD BANK

You may wish to use this lesson and the Read/Spell/Write routine to teach additional high-frequency words.

1 **Model** Display the **Build Your Word Bank Cards** for *when, which,* and *soon* from the **Practice Book High-Frequency Word Cards**. Use the Read/Spell/Write routine to teach words.

- **Read** Point to the word *when* and say the word. *This is the word* when. *Say it with me:* when. *I use a pen* when *I write.*
- **Spell** *The word* when *is spelled w-h-e-n. Spell it with me.*
- **Write** *Let's write the word* when *on our **Response Boards** as we say each letter: w-h-e-n.*

Repeat the Read/Spell/Write routine with *which* and *soon.*

2 **Guided Practice** Display the Build Your Word Bank Cards for *when, which,* and *soon.* Point to each word and have children chorally read it. Then have children take turns using the Build Your Word Bank words in a sentence. Guide practice and provide corrective feedback as needed.

ELL **ENGLISH LANGUAGE LEARNERS**

High-Frequency Words, Practice Have children read *are* and *my* aloud with you and then independently. For additional practice, model the words in simple sentences or phrases for children to repeat.

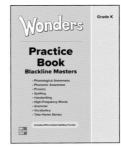

Wonders
Grade K

Practice Book
Blackline Masters

- Phonological Awareness
- Phonemic Awareness
- Phonics
- Spelling
- Handwriting
- High-Frequency Words
- Grammar
- Vocabulary
- Take-Home Stories

Includes Differentiated Spelling Practice

Take-Home Story: pp. 223–224

FORMATIVE ASSESSMENT

❯ STUDENT CHECK-IN

Phonics Have partners think of words that they would add to the word sort.

High-Frequency Words Have partners take turns reading a sentence from the Take-Home Book.

Then have children reflect using the Check-In routine.

✔ CHECK FOR SUCCESS

Rubric Use your online rubric to record children's progress.

Can children sort words by initial and medial /e/*e*?

Can children recognize and read the high-frequency word?

❯❯ Small Group Instruction

If No

● **Approaching** Reteach pp. T140–144

● **ELL** Develop pp. T140–144

If Yes

● **On** Review pp. T48–150

● **Beyond** Extend p. T154

LEARNING GOALS

We can read and understand a text.

OBJECTIVES

Follow words from left to right, top to bottom, and page by page.

Associate the short sounds with the common spellings (graphemes) for the five major vowels.

Read common high-frequency words by sight.

Read emergent-reader texts with purpose and understanding.

ELA ACADEMIC LANGUAGE

- *front cover, back cover, title page*

10 mins

Reread "Ed and Ned"

Focus on Foundational Skills

Book Handling Demonstrate book handling. Hold up a picture book and point to the front cover. *This is the front cover of the book.* Point to the back cover. *This is the back cover.* Open to the title page. *This is the title page.* Model turning the pages of the book.

Concepts of Print Have children turn to page 43 of the **Reading/Writing Companion** and model reading from left to right and from top to bottom, using your finger to track the print. *When I read, I start on the left side of the page and move to the right. I begin at the top of the page and move to the bottom.* Then invite a volunteer to come up and demonstrate reading from left to right and top to bottom, tracking the print with his or her finger and doing a return sweep in between lines.

Focus on Comprehension

Reread Have children reread the story. Guide them to sound out decodable words and read high-frequency words with automaticity. Have them look for details that they did not notice in the first reading.

Have children use the box on the right-hand pages to do the following:

- Draw a picture about the text or the photos.
- Draw something whose name includes /e/.
- Write the letter *e*.

Reading/Writing Companion, pp. 42-43

COMPREHENSION

Who is this story about? (Ed and Ned) *What kind of animals are Ed and Ned?* (bears) *Are they pets?* (No. They are wild animals.) *How old are Ed and Ned?* (They are young cubs.)

HIGH-FREQUENCY WORDS

Have children identify the word *a* on page 43. *How many times does the word* a *appear?* (twice)

Reading/Writing Companion, pp. 44-45

Reading/Writing Companion, pp. 46-47

Reading/Writing Companion, pp. 48-49

COMPREHENSION

Which bear is higher on page 44? (Ned) *What are the bears doing on page 44?* (climbing a tree)

PHONICS

Which word begins with the same sound as map*?* (met)

COMPREHENSION

Where are the bear cubs on page 46? What are they doing? (They are at a river. They are sipping water.) *Why are Ed and Ned wet on page 47?* (They went swimming.)

COMPREHENSION

What is Ed doing on page 48? (He is hopping.)

DECODABLE READERS

Have children read "Ed and Ted Can Go On" (pp. 13–18) to practice decoding words in connected text.

Unit 5 Decodable Reader

ⓔⓛⓛ ENGLISH LANGUAGE LEARNERS

Comprehension Point to the word *met* on page 45 as you read it aloud. Stress the correct pronunciation of the vowel sound. Then have children repeat the word. *The two bears met.* Met *means that they saw each other. They started to get to know each other.* With a volunteer, demonstrate shaking hands and say, *I am happy we met.* Have children repeat with a partner.

Focus on Fluency: Accuracy and Rate

Have partners practice reading the text "Ed and Ned" accurately. Encourage them to track the print as they sound out decodable words and read high-frequency words with automaticity. Remind children to pay attention to punctuation marks so they read sentences with the correct tone. Then have partners read the text again, this time focusing on rate—reading a bit more quickly and making the text sound more like speech. Listen in: If children struggle with accuracy, have them start again at the beginning of the sentence and correct any errors. If they struggle with rate, model an appropriate rate and have them repeat.

 ## Build Knowledge: Make Connections

Talk About the Text Have partners discuss Ed and Ned. *How do they change and grow in the text?*

Write About the Text Have children add their ideas to their reader's notebook.

❯ STUDENT CHECK-IN

Have partners share one thing they learned from the text. Then have children reflect on their learning using the Check-In routine.

LESSON
3

LEARNING GOALS

- **We can write about the texts we read.**
- **We can learn about words that can take the place of nouns (pronouns).**

OBJECTIVES

Use a combination of drawing, dictating, and writing to compose opinion pieces in which they state an opinion or preference about the topic or book.

Write a letter or letters for most consonant and short-vowel sounds.

Write in response to a text.

Appropriately use pronouns.

ELA ACADEMIC LANGUAGE

- *clue, pronoun*
- Cognate: *pronombre*

 TEACH IN SMALL GROUP

Choose from these options to enable all children to complete the writing activity:

- draw a picture
- complete sentence starters
- write a caption
- write one sentence

For differentiated support, see Writing Skills minilessons on pages T494–T499. These can be used throughout the year.

---

15 mins

Independent Writing

Write About the Shared Read

Analyze the Prompt Have children turn to page 42 of their **Reading/Writing Companion**. Tell them they are going to write a response to a prompt about the story "Ed and Ned." Read the prompt aloud: *What do Ed and Ned like to do together?*

Talk Have partners turn and talk about things they think Ed and Ned like to do together. Encourage them to use clues in the text and the illustrations to support their opinions.

Find Text Evidence *We need to find text evidence, or clues, in the text and illustrations to help us answer the prompt.*

- *Let's look at pages 44-45. What are Ed and Ned doing?* (climbing a tree, playing) *Let's look at pages 46-47. What are they doing now?* (drinking, getting wet)

- Continue guiding children to look for text evidence to use in their writing.

Write to the Prompt Guide children to review the text evidence they found and plan their writing in their writer's notebook. Encourage them to think about which clues they would like to include in their writing.

Draft Remind children they are writing about what Ed and Ned do together. If children need additional support, you may choose to have them dictate their ideas to an adult or use the following sentence frames:

Ed and Ned like to _____.
They also _____.
Then they _____.

As children write their drafts, have them do the following:

- When they get to the end of a line, return to the beginning of the next line. WRITING SKILL

- Use words to connect ideas. TRAIT: ORGANIZATION

- Use **pronouns** in their writing. GRAMMAR

Tell children they will continue to work on their writing in Lesson 4.

Grammar

Subjective Pronouns

1 **Review** Remind children that a pronoun is a word that can take the place of a noun. Write the following sentences:

Maya sees an alligator.　　　**Ben sees a bear.**

Circle the names. Point out that the pronoun *She* can replace *Maya* and the pronoun *He* can replace *Ben.* Rewrite the sentences with pronouns and read them aloud.

2 **Guided Practice/Practice** Write the sentences below and read them aloud. Guide children to complete the first two sentence frames with the pronoun that correctly replaces the name in the sentence. For the remaining sentences, have children tell you which pronoun should replace the name. **Maria can climb a tree. _____ can climb a tree.** (She) **Adam likes to swim. _____ likes to swim.** (He) **Nicholas has a new bike. _____ has a new bike.** (He) **Darren walks the dog. _____ walks the dog.** (He) **Christina can run fast. _____ can run fast.** (She)

Read the new sentences aloud with children.

Talk About It

Have partners look out the window or think about something they see outside on their way to school each morning. Encourage children to use these sentence frames to talk about what they see and about what their partner sees. **I see _____. He/She sees _____.**

English Language Learners

Independent Writing, Analyze the Prompt Check children's understanding of the prompt before writing. Display page 41 of the Shared Read. *Who are Ed and Ned?* (the bears) *The prompt is asking us to tell what Ed and Ned like to do together.* Turn to page 42. *What are Ed and Ned doing together on this page?* Have children respond: Ed and Ned are drinking water. Display page 43 and guide children to make an inference based on the photo. *Look at the photo. Why do you think Ed and Ned are wet?* Ed and Ned were swimming/in a river. Continue this routine with the remaining pages of the selection. Provide vocabulary support as children complete the writing sentence frames from page T118.

For additional support, refer to the **ELL Small Group Guide**, p. 121.

DIGITAL TOOLS

Grammar Activity

Grammar Song

Grammar Video

FORMATIVE ASSESSMENT

> **STUDENT CHECK-IN**

Have each partner share two pronouns. Have children reflect using the Check-In routine.

LEARNING GOALS

- We can blend word parts to say a word.
- We can understand new words.
- We can use words that tell about tree parts.
- We can understand that words with -ed tell that the action happened in the past.

OBJECTIVES

Blend and segment onsets and rimes of spoken words.

Use words and phrases acquired through conversations, reading and being read to, and responding to texts.

Use the most frequently occurring inflections and affixes as a clue to the meaning of an unknown word.

Develop oral vocabulary.

Identify words about tree parts.

ELA ACADEMIC LANGUAGE

- category, verb, past
- Cognates: categoría, verbo

DIGITAL TOOLS

Weekly Song

Visual Vocabulary Cards

Category Words Activity

LESSON FOCUS

READING
Review Essential Question
Read/Reread Paired Selection
"From a Seed to a Tree"
Word Work
- Build Words with Short *e*

WRITING
Writing/Grammar
- Independent Writing
- Practice Grammar
Research and Inquiry
- Create Presentation

Literature Big Book, pp. 33–36

---

10 mins

Oral Language

MULTIMODAL

? Essential Question

How do living things change as they grow?

Have children discuss what they have learned about how living things change as they grow. Add new ideas to the Build Knowledge anchor chart.

Phonological Awareness: Onset and Rime Blending

1 **Model** Have children sing "My Oak Tree" with you. Say the word *found*. Have children repeat the word *found*. Say the word again, segmenting and blending the onset and rime: /f/ /ound/. Say: *We can blend these sounds to make the word* found.

2 **Guided Practice/Practice** *Now let's blend the sounds together!* Guide children to practice segmenting and blending the onset and rime in other words from the song, such as *put, pocket, came,* and *grown.* Provide corrective feedback as needed.

Review Oral Vocabulary Words

Use the Define/Example/Ask routine on print or digital **Visual Vocabulary Cards** to review the oral vocabulary words *develop, amazing, enormous, imagine,* and *content.* Then have children use the words in sentences.

Visual Vocabulary Cards

Category Words: Tree Parts

1 **Explain/Model** Arrange children in groups. Assign each group the name of a tree part: *seed, roots, stem, trunk, branches, leaves,* and *bark.* Have children draw their tree part. Then read the passage below aloud. Have children hold up their pictures when they hear the name of their tree part.

A tree begins as a tiny seed. The seed breaks open, and roots begin to grow. Soon a stem pops out of the ground. This is the beginning of the tree's trunk. Over time, the tree grows bigger. Soon it has branches, which look like arms. Leaves grow from the branches. The trunk and the branches are covered with bark. The bark protects the tree.

2 **Guided Practice** Display the **Photo Card** for *tree*. Read these sentences aloud and have children point to each tree part on the Photo Card.

A squirrel climbs up the trunk. A bird builds a nest on a branch. Roots soak up water from the ground. (Roots are not shown on the Photo Card. Children will point to the ground underneath the tree trunk.) **Tree bark is brown and rough. Leaves change color and fall to the ground.**

For additional practice, use **Practice Book** page 219.

Vocabulary: Inflectional Ending *-ed*

1 **Model** Remind children that the *-ed* ending can be added to many present-tense verbs to make past-tense verbs. Review that past-tense verbs tell what happened before now.

Think Aloud Most of the text in *A Grand Old Tree* tells us about what happened to the tree long ago. Most of the verbs end with *-ed* because we are reading about the past. We can look for the *-ed* ending to tell when the action happened in a story.

2 **Guided Practice/Practice** Write and say *talk*. Have children repeat. Add *-ed* to *talk* and read *talked*. Explain that the word *talk* is a present-tense verb that tells an action happening now. The word *talked* is a past-tense verb that tells the action has already happened. Have children change the following words to past-tense verbs: *jump, walk, smile, share, plant, change.*

KIDS ON THE MOVE

Place children in groups. Assign each group the name of a tree part. Then give directions such as: *Branches, sway in the wind. Leaves, rustle and shake. The trunk stands strong.* Have children follow the directions.

Wonders — Grade K
Practice Book
Blackline Masters
• Phonological Awareness
• Phonemic Awareness
• Phonics
• Spelling
• Handwriting
• High-Frequency Words
• Grammar
• Vocabulary
• Take-Home Stories
Includes Differentiated Spelling Practice

Category Words: p. 219

ELL ENGLISH LANGUAGE LEARNERS

Category Words, Guided Practice
Say the main parts of the tree--*trunk, branch, roots, leaves*--and have children repeat. Point to the roots on the Photo Card and say *roots*. Have children point and repeat. Continue the routine with the other words.

ELL NEWCOMERS

Use the **Newcomer Online Visuals** and their accompanying prompts to help children expand vocabulary and language about living things (Unit 5). Use the Conversation Starters, Speech Balloons, and Games in the **Newcomer Teacher's Guide** to continue building vocabulary and developing oral and written language.

FORMATIVE ASSESSMENT

❯ STUDENT CHECK-IN

Oral Vocabulary Words Have partners use body language to show *enormous*.

Category Words Have partners use tree parts to describe a tree they've seen.

Vocabulary Have partners use a word with *-ed* in a sentence.

Then have children reflect using the Check-In routine.

Literature Big Book

OBJECTIVES

Recognize common types of texts.

With prompting and support, identify the main topic and retell key details of a text.

With prompting and support, describe the relationship between illustrations and the text in which they appear.

Actively engage in group reading activities with purpose and understanding.

Use a diagram to understand information.

ELA ACADEMIC LANGUAGE

• *diagram*

• Cognate: *diagrama*

Read

10 mins

"From a Seed to a Tree"

Text Feature: Diagrams

1 **Explain/Model** Tell children that the selection you are about to read is a nonfiction text about how a seed grows into a tree. Explain that this text has a diagram. Display page 34 of the **Big Book** and point to the diagram. *This is a diagram. It is a labeled picture that shows the steps a seed goes through as it becomes a sapling. The picture and the labels in the diagram tell about the steps.*

Display **Online Teaching Chart 16**. *This is a diagram that shows the different parts of a wasp's body.*

What can you learn from this diagram? (I can learn the names of the different parts of a wasp. I can also see what each part looks like.)

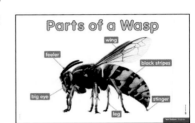

Online Teaching Chart 16

2 **Guided Practice/Practice** Draw children's attention to the chart. Call out the different parts of a wasp and have volunteers come up and point to the corresponding part on the diagram.

Read the Paired Selection

Display the Big Book. Read the title and look at the photo. *What do you predict this book will be about?* Write and display children's predictions.

Set Purpose *Let's read to find out about how a seed grows into a tree.*

Literature Big Book, p. 33

TOPIC AND DETAILS DOK 2

What details do you see in the photos? (an apple cut in half to show its seeds; an apple tree) *What might those details tell about the topic?* (Possible response: An apple seed like the one shown can grow into an apple tree.)

Literature Big Book, pp. 34–35

TEXT FEATURE:
DIAGRAMS DOK 1

Look at the pictures in the diagram. *Which picture shows the plant with the most leaves?* (The picture of the sapling has the most leaves.) Explain that we can learn about how plants grow by observing them.

BUILD ORAL VOCABULARY

sprout: start to grow

Literature Big Book, p. 36

TOPIC AND DETAILS DOK 1

This page tells the four stages that a seed goes through as it becomes a tree. Let's see if we can name them in order. (1. seed, 2. sprout, 3. seedling, 4. sapling)

Return to Purpose

Read children's predictions. Ask: *Were our predictions correct?* Remind children of their purpose for reading. (to find out about how a seed grows into a tree) Prompt them to share what they learned from the selection.

Retell

Help children use the text and the photos to retell details from the selection. Encourage them to use the vocabulary words they have been learning this week. You might also have children retell the selection by using the diagram on page 34.

Close Reading Routine

Read DOK 1–2

- Identify key ideas and details.
- Take notes and retell.
- Use **ACT** prompts as needed.

Reread DOK 2–3

- Analyze the text, craft, and structure.

Integrate DOK 3–4

- Integrate knowledge and ideas.
- Make text-to-text connections.
- Complete the Show Your Knowledge task
- Inspire action.

ELL SPOTLIGHT ON LANGUAGE

Page 34 *sprout:* Explain that *sprout* refers to the time when a seed breaks open and the tiny stem of the plant begins to grow out of the seed.

FORMATIVE ASSESSMENT

⊘ STUDENT CHECK-IN

Have partners share one thing that they learned from a diagram. Then have children reflect on their learning using the Check-In routine.

Literature Big Book

LEARNING GOALS

We can think about how the author uses a diagram to share information about the text.

OBJECTIVES

With prompting and support, describe the relationship between illustrations and the text in which they appear.

Use words and phrases acquired through conversations, reading and being read to, and responding to texts.

Analyze the author's craft.

Use a diagram to understand information.

ELA ACADEMIC LANGUAGE

• *diagram, stages*
• Cognate: *diagrama*

---

10 mins

Reread

"From a Seed to a Tree"

SCIENCE

Analyze the Text

After children read and retell "From a Seed to a Tree," reread it with them. Use the instructions in the prompts below to help children answer the questions on pages 50-51 in the **Reading/Writing Companion**.

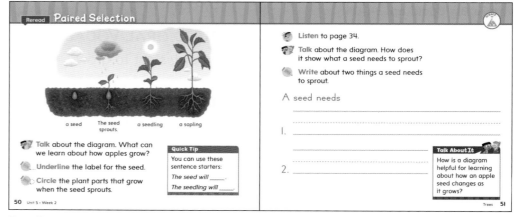

Reading/Writing Companion, pp. 50-51

AUTHOR'S CRAFT DOK 3

• Have children look at page 50. Say: *A diagram is a drawing that explains something. What can we learn about how apples grow?* Encourage children to use the sentence starters in the Quick Tip box. Help them understand that the diagram shows the different stages a seed goes through to becomes a tree. (First, a seed is planted. Then it sprouts. It grows roots and leaves to become a seedling. The seedling grows more roots and leaves and gets taller to become a sapling.)

• Have children underline the label for the seed. Then have them circle the parts of the plant that grow when the seed sprouts.

• Guide children to look closely at the diagram on page 50 as you reread page 34 of the **Big Book**. Talk about the diagram. Have children point to the sun and the rain clouds in the diagram. *Why do you think the author included this in the diagram?* (It shows that the seed needs sun and water to grow.) Then have children complete the sentence starter on page 51.

COLLABORATE

Talk About It

Review page 50. *How does the diagram help us understand how an apple seed changes as it becomes a tree?* Remind children that the diagram uses pictures to explain the process the seed goes through as it becomes a tree. The labels tell what is happening in each picture. Have volunteers use the diagram to tell the stages of how a seed becomes a tree.

Integrate

Build Knowledge: Make Connections

Talk About the Text Have partners discuss how an apple seed changes as it grows. *What does the apple seed need to grow?*

Add to the Anchor Chart Record any new ideas on the Build Knowledge Anchor Chart.

Add to the Word Bank Record new words in the Word Bank.

English Language Learners

Use the following with **Build Knowledge: Make Connections.**

Beginning

Review vocabulary related to the Essential Question: *living things, change, grow.* Guide children to point to examples in the text and say the appropriate word or phrase.

Intermediate

Provide children with sentence frames they can use to contribute: A seedling is a living thing. A living thing changes/grows.

Advanced/Advanced High

Encourage children to use more complex sentences. Prompt them by asking guiding questions: *How does a living thing change? What happens when a plant or animal grows?*

CONNECT TO CONTENT

Observing Trees Review the life stages of a young apple tree (seed, sprout, seedling, sapling). Have partners discuss the trees they have seen growing in their neighborhood. Have them describe the changes they have observed as the trees go though different stages.

STEM

FORMATIVE ASSESSMENT

❯ STUDENT CHECK-IN

Have partners share something they learned from the diagram. Then have children reflect on their learning using the Check-In routine.

LESSON 4

Display the Sound-Spelling Card for *e*.
1. **Teacher:** What's the letter?   **Children:** e
2. **Teacher:** What's the sound?   **Children:** /e/
3. **Teacher:** What's the word?   **Children:** egg
Continue the routine for previously taught sounds.

LEARNING GOALS

- We can say and count each sound in a word.
- We can build and spell words with the letter *e*.
- We can read sentences with the word *are*.

OBJECTIVES

Isolate and pronounce the initial, medial vowel, and final sounds in three-phoneme words.

Distinguish between similarly spelled words by identifying the sounds of the letters that differ.

Spell simple words phonetically, drawing on knowledge of sound-letter relationships.

Read common high-frequency words by sight.

ELA ACADEMIC LANGUAGE

- *belong, middle*

▶ TEACH IN SMALL GROUP

You may wish to teach the Word Work lesson in small groups.

DIGITAL TOOLS

Word Work
Phonemic Awareness
Phonics
High-Frequency Words

Visual Vocabulary Cards

Phonemic Awareness: p. 213
Phonics: p. 216

Phonemic Awareness

(5 mins)

MULTIMODAL

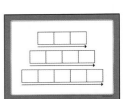

Phoneme Segmentation

1 **Model** Display the **Photo Cards** for *egg* and *gem*. *Let's say the sounds in the word* egg *together: /e/ /g/. For each sound, let's put a marker in a box: /e/ /g/. We'll count the sounds as we say them: /e/ /g/. There are two sounds.* Place markers in **Sound Boxes** for each sound. *Say the sounds in* egg: */e/ /g/. Now say the word:* egg. Repeat the routine for *gem*.

Sound Boxes

2 **Guided Practice/Practice** Distribute **Response Boards** for children to use the Sound Boxes on the reverse side. *I will say a word. Repeat the word, then say the sounds in the word. Place a marker in the Sound Box for each sound you hear.* Guide practice with the first word.

den (/d/ /e/ /n/)	**bed** (/b/ /e/ /d/)	**echo** (/e/ /k/ /ō/)
edge (/e/ /d/ /j/)	**led** (/l/ /e/ /d/)	**fed** (/f/ /e/ /d/)
bell (/b/ /e/ /l/)	**else** (/e/ /l/ /s/)	**snake** (/sn/ /ā/ /k/)

If additional practice is needed, use **Practice Book** page 213.

Phonics

(5 mins)

Build and Read Words

Provide children with **Word-Building Cards** a–z. Have children put the letters in alphabetical order as quickly as possible.

1 **Guided Practice** Use the Word-Building Cards *t, e, n* to form the word *ten*. Have children use their word cards to build the word *ten*. Then say: *I will change the middle letter in* ten *to make the word* tin. Change the *e* to *i* and read *tin* aloud. Repeat, asking children to read the word with you.

2 **Practice** Have children continue changing letters using Word-Building Cards to form the words *pin, pit, pet, pat, pot, pop, stop, step, stem*. Once children have finished using the word cards to build each word, have them write each word in the list on a sheet of paper. Children can work with a partner to correct any errors they make when encoding.

If additional practice is needed, use **Practice Book** page 216.

Spell Words

Dictation Distribute **Response Boards.** Dictate these sounds for children to spell. Have them repeat each sound and then write the appropriate letter. Repeat several times.

/h/   /n/   /e/   /d/   /t/   /p/   /sn/   /sp/   /st/

Dictate the following words for children to spell: *ten, men, hen, pen, pet, set,* and *step.* Model for children how to segment each word to scaffold the spelling. Say: *When I say the word* ten, *I hear three sounds: /t/ /e/ /n/. I know the letter* t *stands for /t/, the letter* e *stands for /e/, and the letter* n *stands for /n/. I will write the letters* t, e, n *to spell the word* ten.

When children finish, write the letters and words for them to self-correct.

High-Frequency Words

OPTIONAL 5 mins

Practice Say the word *are* and have children write it. Then display the print or digital **Visual Vocabulary Card** for *are* and follow the Teacher Talk routine on the back.

Visual Vocabulary Card

Build Fluency Build sentences in the pocket chart using the **High-Frequency Word Cards** and **Photo Cards.** Use an index card to create a punctuation card for a period. Have children chorally read the sentences as you track the print. Then have them identify the word *are*.

You and I are upside down.

You are a girl.

You are a boy.

Are you a doctor?

Have partners say sentences using the word *are*.

Pass the Plate Activity Write the high-frequency words on paper plates. Have children stand or sit in a circle. Play music and have children pass the plate, facedown. When the music stops, the child holding the plate turns it over and reads the word. Another way to play is to give each child a plate, facedown. Then pass the plates and, when the music stops, have each child turn the plate over and read the word.

DECODABLE READERS

Have children read "Not a Pet!" (pages 19–24) to practice decoding words in connected text.

Not a Pet!

Unit 5 Decodable Reader

FORMATIVE ASSESSMENT

STUDENT CHECK-IN

Phonics Have partners use Word-Building Cards to spell and read *met*.

High-Frequency Words Have partners point to and read a sentence from the lesson.

Then have children reflect using the Check-In routine.

CHECK FOR SUCCESS

Rubric Use your online rubric to record children's progress.

Can children segment words with /e/ and distinguish between initial and medial /e/e/?

Can children read and recognize high-frequency words?

Small Group Instruction

If No

● **Approaching** Reteach pp. T140–144

● **ELL** Develop pp. T140–144

If Yes

● **On** Review pp. T148–150

● **Beyond** Extend p. T154

Independent Writing

5 mins

Write About the Shared Read

Revise

Reread the prompt about "Ed and Ned": *What do Ed and Ned like to do together?* Have children read their draft to check whether they responded to the prompt by using words to connect ideas, using pronouns, and returning to the beginning of the next line when they write to the end of a line.

Peer Review Have partners review each other's writing. Children should share things they like most about the writing, questions they have for the author, and additional ideas they think the author could include. Provide time for children to make revisions and add details to strengthen their writing.

Edit/Proofread

After children have revised their work, have them edit it carefully, checking for the following:

• Each sentence begins with a capital letter.

• Each sentence tells a complete thought.

If children need additional practice with editing and proofreading, have them use **Practice Book** page 222.

Write Final Draft

After children have edited their writing and finished their peer review, have them write their final draft in their writer's notebook. Remind them to write neatly so that others can read their writing, or guide them to explore a variety of digital tools they can use to publish their work.

Teacher Conference As children review their draft, confer with them to provide guidance. Suggest places in their writing where they might add details or replace a noun with a pronoun.

Share and Evaluate

After children have finalized their draft, have them work with a partner to practice presenting their writing to one another. Remind children to speak in complete sentences. If possible, record children as they share so that they can see themselves presenting or you can use as a topic of discussion during a teacher conference.

Have children add their work to their writing folder. Invite them to look at their previous writing and discuss with a partner how it has improved.

5 mins

Grammar

Subjective Pronouns

1 **Review** Remind children that a pronoun takes the place of a noun. Write and read aloud: **Ned is taking a nap.** Circle *Ned*. Say: *The pronoun* he *can be used to replace the name* Ned.

2 **Guided Practice/Practice** Write the sentence pairs below and read them aloud. Guide children through the first sentence. Have them identify a pronoun that correctly replaces the name in the sentence. Then allow partners to work together to name the pronoun that replaces the noun in the remaining sentences. Have volunteers share their answers.

Tom reads a book. _____ reads a book. (He)
Pam eats her lunch. _____ eats her lunch. (She)
The car is fast. _____ is fast. (It)
Zack and I sing songs. _____ sing songs. (We)

If children need additional practice with subjective pronouns, have them use page 221 of the **Practice Book**.

 ## Talk About It

Have children work with partners to tell about the things they do at school using pronouns. Encourage them to use complete sentences.

 # English Language Learners

Use the following scaffolds with **Independent Writing, Peer Review**.

Beginning
Provide sentence frames to express opinions: I like how you used a pronoun. Could you add a detail about Ed and Ned?

Intermediate
Provide partners with question and answer frames: What did you like? I liked how you used a capital letter. Could you add a detail? I could add a detail about Ed and Ned swimming.

Advanced/Advanced High
Encourage children to provide their classmates with positive reinforcement during peer review after telling what could be improved. Provide model sentences they can use: I like your draft. Could you tell another thing Ed and Ned do together?

For additional support, see the **ELL Small Group Guide** p. 121.

DIGITAL TOOLS

 **I see a fish.** Grammar Activity

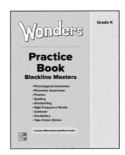 **Wonders** Grade K
Practice Book
Blackline Masters
- Phonological Awareness
- Phonemic Awareness
- Phonics
- Spelling
- Handwriting
- High-Frequency Words
- Grammar
- Vocabulary
- Take-Home Stories

Includes Differentiated Spelling Practice

Grammar: p. 221
Edit/Proofread: p. 222

FORMATIVE ASSESSMENT

⊘ STUDENT CHECK-IN

Have each partner share two pronouns. Have children reflect using the Check-In routine.

LESSON 4

How a Tree Grows

LEARNING GOALS

We can research about how trees grow.

OBJECTIVES

With guidance and support from adults, recall information from experiences or gather information from provided sources to answer a question.

Add drawings or other visual displays to descriptions as desired to provide additional detail.

Produce and expand complete sentences in shared language activities.

Follow agreed-upon rules for discussions.

Participate in shared research and writing projects.

ELA ACADEMIC LANGUAGE

• *research, presentation*
• Cognate: *presentación*

COLLABORATIVE CONVERSATIONS

Take Turns Talking As children engage in partner and group discussions, have them do the following:

• Take turns speaking.
• Speak clearly.
• Speak loud enough so that everyone can hear.
• Share their ideas and opinions with others.

Model

Tell children that they will research how trees grow. Display pages 52-53 of the **Reading/Writing Companion**. Model completing each step in the research process.

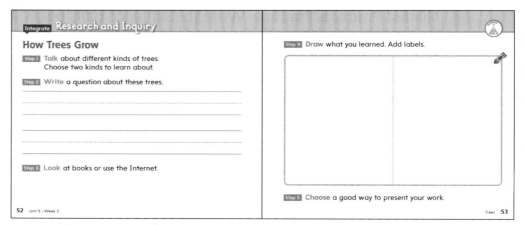

Reading/Writing Companion, pp. 52–53

STEP 1 Choose a Topic

I like peaches and pears, so my research topic will be about those trees.

STEP 2 Write Your Question

I need to write questions to guide my research. My questions will be: Does a peach tree grow from a seed? Does a pear tree grow from a seed?

STEP 3 Find Information

To find the answer to my question, I need to do formal research. I can do this by looking at books or using the Internet.

STEP 4 Draw and Write What You Learned

I can draw a picture showing a peach pit and pear seeds. I will add labels with the tree name under my drawing.

STEP 5 Choose a Way to Present Your Work

I will make a poster showing the differences between a peach tree and a pear tree. It will show how the trees begin from a pit and a seed.

Apply

Have children turn to page 52 in their Reading/Writing Companion. Guide them through the steps of the research process.

Choose the Presentation Format

Have children turn to pages 52-53 in their **Reading/Writing Companion** to review their research, their drawing, and what they learned about how different trees grow. Tell them that today they are going to take the next step by creating their finished product, which they will present tomorrow. Work with children to select a good way to present their findings. Options may include drawing and labeling a picture, creating a poster, making a model, or putting on a dramatic presentation.

Create the Presentation

Guide children to develop their presentation individually, in teams, or as a class. Remind them of the rules of working with others.

Gather Materials Gather together the materials children will need to create their finished product. Most of the materials should be available in the classroom or can be brought from home.

Make the Finished Product Once children have gathered the materials they need, provide time for them to create their finished product. You can dedicate an area in the classroom for project work and store all the materials there. Remind children that they will be presenting their work to their classmates the next day.

English Language Learners

Apply, Step 2 Help children write their question. Remind them of question words such as: *who, what, when, where, how,* and *why.* Ask children to form their questions independently or with a partner and then support them in writing the question correctly.

TEACH IN SMALL GROUP

You may choose to have children create their presentation during Small Group time. Group children of varying abilities together, or group children doing similar projects.

CONNECT TO CONTENT

Growing Plants Tell children that many plants start out as seeds that sprout and then go through different stages to become fully grown. Work with children to plant seeds and grow the plants in the classroom. Teach children how to take care of the plants. Encourage them to observe and record the different ways the plants change as they grow.

STEM

RESEARCH AND INQUIRY: SHARING FINAL PROJECTS

As children get ready to wrap up the week, have them share their Research and Inquiry projects. Then have children self-evaluate.

Prepare Have children gather any materials they need to present their Research and Inquiry project. Have partners practice their presentations.

Share Guide children to present their Research and Inquiry projects. Encourage children to speak in complete sentences.

Evaluate Have children discuss and evaluate their own presentation. You may wish to have them complete the online Student Checklist.

FORMATIVE ASSESSMENT

❯ STUDENT CHECK-IN

Have partners share one way that trees change as they grow. Have children reflect using the Check-In routine.

LEARNING GOALS

- We can say and count each sound in a word.
- We can spell words with the letter *e*.
- We can spell the word *are*.

OBJECTIVES

Isolate and pronounce the initial, medial vowel, and final sounds in three-phoneme words.

Associate the short sounds with common spellings (graphemes) for the five major vowels.

Spell simple words phonetically, drawing on knowledge of sound-letter relationships.

Read common high-frequency words by sight.

ELA ACADEMIC LANGUAGE

- *count, marker*

 **TEACH IN SMALL GROUP**

You may wish to teach this lesson in small groups.

DIGITAL TOOLS

 Word Work
Phonemic Awareness

 Visual Vocabulary Cards

 Spelling Song

---

LESSON FOCUS

READING
Wrap Up
Word Work
- Read Words
WRITING
Writing/Grammar
- Self-Selected Writing
- Review Grammar

Research and Inquiry
- Share and Evaluate Presentation
Text Connections
- Connect Essential Question to a photo
- Show Your Knowledge

Reading/Writing Companion, pp. 54–55

---

 5 mins

Phonemic Awareness

 MULTIMODAL

Phoneme Segmentation

1 **Model** Display the **Photo Card** for *net*. *This is a net. I'll say the sounds in the word* net. */n/ /e/ /t/. For each sound, I'll put a marker in a box: /n/ /e/ /t/. I'll count the sounds after I say them: /n/ /e/ /t/. There are three sounds.* Repeat the routine for *jet*.

2 **Guided Practice/Practice** Distribute **Response Boards**. Have children put a marker in a box for each sound and say the word. *I will say a word. Say each sound in the word. Place a marker in the* **Sound Box** *for each sound.* Guide practice and provide corrective feedback as needed, using the following words:

pen (/p/ /e/ /n/)	**led** (/l/ /e/ /d/)	**ten** (/t/ /e/ /n/)
Ed (/e/ /d/)	**den** (/d/ /e/ /n/)	**men** (/m/ /e/ /n/)
bet (/b/ /e/ /t/)	**egg** (/e/ /g/)	**peck** (/p/ /e/ /k/)

---

 5 mins

Phonics

 MULTIMODAL

Read Words

1 **Guided Practice** Remind children that the letter *e* can stand for the sound /e/. Display **Word-Building Cards** *n, e, t*. Point to the letter *n*. *The letter* n *stands for /n/. The letter* e *stands for /e/. Say /eee/. The letter* t *stands for /t/. Say /t/. Let's blend the sound: /nnneeet/* net. *Let's change the* n *to an* s. Repeat routine with *set*.

2 **Practice** Write these words and sentences for children to read:

ten	den	pen	pet	met	step	hen

I like my pet Stan.   Sam met Pam in the den.
We are in the den.   Ted has a pen.

Remove words from view before dictation.

In a Flash: Sound-Spellings

Ee

Display the Sound-Spelling Card for e.

1. **Teacher:** What's the letter?   **Children:** e
2. **Teacher:** What's the sound?   **Children:** /e/
3. **Teacher:** What's the word?   **Children:** egg

Continue the routine for previously taught sounds.

MULTIMODAL LEARNING

Color Coding After each dictation, reveal the secret color-coding-letter(s) for children to find on their response boards. Have them say the sound(s) as they trace each letter in color. Use one or two of the phonics skills of the week for color coding.

 Review initial /e/e. Have children write the letter e on their **Response Boards.** Play and sing "Scrambled Egg, Fried Egg." Have children hold up and show the letter e on their board when they hear initial /e/. Demonstrate as you sing with children.

Spell Words

Dictation Dictate the following sounds for children to spell. As you say each sound, have children repeat it and then write the letter that stands for the sound on their Response Board.

/h/   /i/   /n/   /k/   /o/   /d/   /e/   /sp/

Dictate the following words for children to spell. Use the first word to model how to segment words to scaffold the spelling. *I will say a word. You will repeat the word, then think about how many sounds are in the word. Use your* **Sound Boxes** *to count the sounds. Then write one letter for each sound you hear.*

net   pen   set   met   pit   pat   pin   step

Then write the letters and words for children to self-correct.

High-Frequency Words

MULTIMODAL

5 mins

1 **Review** Display the print and digital **Visual Vocabulary Card** *are.* Have children Read/Spell/Write the word. Then choose a Partner Talk activity.

Visual Vocabulary Card

Distribute **High-Frequency Word Cards** to children: *and, my, are, the, to, you, I.* Tell children that you will say some sentences. *When you hear the word that is on your card, stand and hold up the word card.*

Emily and Pat like my tree house.
They are at my school.
The peaches are amazing.
Fruits and vegetables are good things to eat.
Are you planting flower seeds?
I think you are nice.

2 **Build Fluency: Word Automaticity** Display High-Frequency Word Cards *and, my, are, the, to, you, I.* Point to each card and have children read as quickly as they can to build automaticity.

FORMATIVE ASSESSMENT

STUDENT CHECK-IN

Phonics Have partners spell *net.*

High-Frequency Words Have partners spell the word *are.*

Then have children reflect using the Check-In routine.

CHECK FOR SUCCESS

Rubric Use your online rubric to record children's progress.

Can children segment words into phonemes and match /e/ to *Ee*?

Can children read and recognize high-frequency words?

Small Group Instruction

If No

● **Approaching** Reteach pp. T140–144

● **ELL** Develop pp. T140–144

If Yes

● **On** Review pp. T148–150

● **Beyond** Extend p. T154

LESSON 5

- We can choose a writing activity and share it.
- We can learn about words that take the place of nouns (pronouns).

OBJECTIVES

With guidance and support from adults, explore a variety of digital tools to produce and publish writing, including in collaboration with peers.

Speak audibly and express thoughts, feelings, and ideas clearly.

Produce and expand complete sentences in shared language activities.

Appropriately use pronouns.

ELA ACADEMIC LANGUAGE

- *topic, detail*
- Cognate: *detalle*

DIFFERENTIATED WRITING

You may wish to conference with children to provide additional support for the writing activities below.

- Storyboard: Have partners talk about how living things change, using the words *first, next,* and *then* before they begin drawing their storyboard.
- Build and Write: Provide sentence frames: First, the _____ was a little _____. Then, it grew into a big _____.

5 mins

Self-Selected Writing

Talk About the Topic

Have children continue the conversation about things that grow in nature. Remind children of the Essential Question: *How do living things change as they grow?* Encourage partners to share what they learned this week about how living things change as they grow.

Choose A Writing Activity

Tell children they will choose a type of writing to share their ideas. They may choose to write about how living things change as they grow or about a different topic that is important to them. Encourage them to draw first as a way to get their ideas down on paper and to give more details to their writing. Children may choose from the following modes of writing:

Storyboard Explain that a storyboard is a series of three pictures with labels or sentences that tell a story. Have children create a storyboard to show how a living thing changes as it grows. Remind them that they need to show the progression in order from left to right. Children write a sentence for each picture.

Build and Write Explain to children that they will build an example of a living thing, such as a plant or an animal, out of clay. Provide any of the following building materials: clay, building blocks, cubes, etc. Remind children to write about their plant or animal when they are done building.

Use Digital Tools You may wish to work with children to explore a variety of digital tools to produce or publish their work.

Share Your Writing

COLLABORATE

Invite volunteers to share their writing with the class or have partners share with each other. Remind children to think about what they want their audience to know as they share. After children share, you may wish to display their work on a bulletin board or in a classroom writing area.

SPEAKING STRATEGIES	LISTENING STRATEGIES
✔ Wait patiently until it is your turn to speak.	✔ Listen actively and politely.
✔ Speak in a loud voice so that everyone can hear you.	✔ Ask questions if you don't understand something.

Grammar

Subjective Pronouns

1 **Review** Remind children that a pronoun is a word that takes the place of a noun. List pronouns: *he, she, it, we, you,* and *I.* Then write this sentence and read it aloud: **Anne and I will plant a tree.** Circle *Anne and I.* Explain: *These words can be replaced with the pronoun* we. Rewrite the sentence with *We* and read it aloud.

2 **Guided Practice/Practice** Write the sentences below and read them aloud. Guide children to identify the subject in the first sentence and tell which pronoun should replace it. Then have partners identify a pronoun to replace the subject in the remaining sentences. Have volunteers share their work.

June and I go to the park. _____ go to the park. (We)
Sergio goes on the swings. _____ goes on the swings. (He)
Lucy goes down the slide. _____ goes down the slide. (She)
The roller coaster will be fun. _____ will be fun. (It)

 # English Language Learners

Self-Selected Writing, Choose a Writing Activity Present the writing activities and tell children that they will vote to select one of them and then you will work on the writing as a group. Make sure to do the activity on chart paper as you will revise and publish it during small group time. Provide sentence frames and starters as you talk through the writing together. For example, if children have selected making a storyboard, choose a living thing together. Then create the storyboard on chart paper. Possible sentence frames are: First, the ___ is a/an ___. Then it grows into ___. Finally, the ___ becomes a ___.

For additional support, see the **ELL Small Group Guide** p. 121.

DIGITAL TOOLS

 **Grammar Activity**

⊙ TEACH IN SMALL GROUP

You may choose to review the grammar skill during Small Group time.

● **Approaching** Provide more opportunities for children to practice identifying pronouns before they write sentences.

●● **On-Level** and **Beyond** Children can do the Practice sections only.

● **ELL** Use the chart in the **Language Transfers Handbook** to identify grammatical forms that may cause difficulty.

FORMATIVE ASSESSMENT

❯ STUDENT CHECK-IN

Have partners share which activity they chose and tell why. Have children reflect using the Check-In routine.

MULTIMODAL

We can compare texts we have read.

OBJECTIVES

Confirm understanding of a text read aloud or information presented orally or through other media by asking and answering questions about key details and requesting clarification if something is not understood.

ELA ACADEMIC LANGUAGE

• *compare, experience*
• Cognate: *comparar*

Close Reading Routine

Read DOK 1–2

• Identify key ideas and details.
• Take notes and retell.
• Use **ACT** prompts as needed.

Reread DOK 2–3

• Analyze the text, craft, and structure.

Integrate DOK 3–4

• Integrate knowledge and ideas.
• Make text-to-text connections.
• Use the Integrate lesson.
• Complete the Show Your Knowledge task.

❯ STUDENT CHECK-IN

Have partners share what they learned from comparing texts.

Have children reflect using the Check-In routine.

(10 mins)

Make Connections

Connect to the Essential Question

Review the Essential Question. Turn to page 54 of the **Reading/Writing Companion**. Have children look at the picture and listen to the caption. *What does the photo show?*

Find Text Evidence Have children answer the following questions about this page and about the **Big Book**: *How old do you think this tree is? How old do you think the grand old tree is?* Use the Quick Tip box for support.

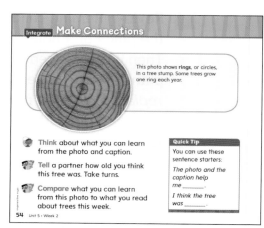

Reading/Writing Companion, p. 54

Record Ideas Guide partners to compare the tree on page 54 of the Reading/Writing Companion with the tree in "A Grand Old Tree." *How are the trees alike? How are they different? How do they help you answer the Essential Question?* Prompt children to use a Two-Tab Foldable® to record their ideas. Have them support their ideas with evidence from the photo and text.

Dinah Zike's
FOLDABLES
Study Organizer

 Build Knowledge: Make Connections DOK 4

Talk About the Text Have partners compare the text with their own experience.

Add to the Anchor Chart Record any new ideas on the Build Knowledge anchor chart.

Integrate

Show Your Knowledge

15 mins

Draw How a Plant Grows DOK 4

Display the texts for the week along with the Build Knowledge anchor chart and Word Bank. Turn to page 55 of the **Reading/ Writing Companion** and guide children through the steps below.

1. Think Ask: *What did you learn about how living things change as they grow?* Encourage partners to refer to their reader's notebook and the resources on display as they discuss their response.

2. Draw Have children divide a piece of paper into three sections. Prompt them to draw three stages of plant growth, in order, in the sections. For example, a seedling, a sapling, and a mature tree.

Show Your Knowledge

Draw How a Plant Grows
1 Think about the texts you read. What did you learn about how living things change as they grow?
2 Draw how a plant changes as it grows. What part grows first? What part grows next? Draw the steps in order.
3 Label the steps. Use words that you learned this week.

Think about what you learned this week. Turn to page 35.

Trees 55

Reading/Writing Companion, p. 55

3. Label Encourage children to use the Word Bank as they label the steps of growth. Post the finished drawings on the wall.

Inspire Action

Plant Observations Invite children to plant seeds in the classroom. As the plants grow, have children add any new observations to their drawings.

Our Class Garden Work with school personnel to find an area around the school for a class garden. Encourage children to observe the plants as they grow.

Choose Your Own Action Have children talk about the texts they read this week. *What do the texts inspire or make you want to do?*

OBJECTIVES

With guidance and support from adults, recall information from experiences or gather information from provided sources to answer a question.

Add drawings or other visual displays to descriptions as desired to provide additional detail.

Describe familiar people, places, things, and events and, with prompting and support, provide additional detail.

ELA ACADEMIC LANGUAGE

• *section, grow, inspire, observe*

ELL ENGLISH LANGUAGE LEARNERS

Show Your Knowledge, Draw Provide and model sentence frames or starters to talk about how a plant grows. For example, First, _____ becomes _____. Next, the seedling _____. Then the small _____ starts to _____.

DIGITAL TOOLS

To enhance the class discussion, use these additional components.

Visual Vocabulary Cards

RUBRIC

Show Your Knowledge Rubric

MY GOALS ROUTINE

Review Have children turn to page 35 of the **Reading/Writing Companion**. Read the goals aloud.

Reflect Have children think about the progress they've made toward the goals. Review the Key, if needed. Then have children complete page 35.

Lexile BR

OBJECTIVES

Follow words from left to right, top to bottom, and page by page.

With prompting and support, identify the main topic and retell key details of a text.

Read emergent-reader texts with purpose and understanding.

ELA ACADEMIC LANGUAGE

• *nonfiction, preview*
• Cognate: *no ficción*

● Approaching Level

Leveled Reader *The Tree*

Preview and Predict

Read the title and the names of the author and illustrator as children follow along in their books. Ask children to describe what they see on the cover. Turn to the title page, point to the title, and say: *Let's read the title together.* Preview the pictures and identify the rebuses. Ask: *What do you think this book is about?*

Review Genre: Informational Text: Nonfiction

Remind children that nonfiction texts give facts and information about real topics. Ask: *What information might we learn in this text?* (how a tree changes and grows during the seasons) Have children point to evidence in the pictures to support their answers.

Set Purpose

Remind children of the Essential Question: *How do living things change as they grow?* Help children set a purpose for reading: *Let's read to find out how a tree changes as it grows through each season.* Review rebuses with children to help them name the words.

Foundational Skills

Model Concepts of Print Hold up your copy of the book and model how you read it. Say: *I begin reading on page 2. I read the words from left to right. I read page 3. When I am finished, I turn the page. I keep reading from left to right.*

Review High-Frequency Words Point to the high-frequency word *are* on page 2. Then ask children to look at pages 4 and 5 to find the word *are*. Have children say a sentence that has the word *are* in it.

Guided Comprehension

As children read *The Tree*, monitor and provide guidance by offering support and corrective feedback as needed. Model rereading and identifying the topic and details where applicable.

Reread

Remind children that if they find a part of the book confusing, they can reread the text to help them better understand what is happening.

Topic and Details

Review with children that reading the words and looking at the pictures will help them learn about the topic and details in this selection about a tree.

Think Aloud The words on page 4 tell me "the branches are big." I can see snow, so it must be winter. The words on page 5 tell me "the buds are big." It looks warmer outside. It must be spring. These details in the words and the pictures tell me about the topic—how a tree grows and changes through the year.

Guide children to identify details about the tree in the words and pictures on pages 6 and 7 and have them explain how each detail supports the topic.

Respond to the Text

Have children respond to the text by discussing these questions:

- *What do you learn about the roots of the tree?* (The roots are big.) *What other parts of the tree are big?* (The trunk, branches, buds, flowers, leaves, and cherries are also big.)
- *When does the tree grow leaves?* (in the summer)
- *What is the topic of this book?* (how a tree grows and changes)
- *What happens at the end of the selection?* (The tree has cherries, and a boy and girl eat the cherries.)

Retell Have partners take turns retelling the selection, focusing on the topic and details. Help them make a personal connection by asking: *What do you like about trees?*

Focus on Fluency

Practice fluency with children. Remember that children need to read with accuracy first.

Once children have read the text with accuracy, have them read the selection again, focusing on rate. Have them practice reading with partners. Provide corrective feedback as necessary.

Build Knowledge: Make Connections

- **Talk About the Texts** Have partners discuss how plants change as they grow.
- **Write About the Texts** Then have children add their ideas to the Build Knowledge page of their Reader's Notebook.

LITERACY ACTIVITIES

Have children complete the Collaborate and Write About It activities on the inside back cover of the book.

 **LEVEL UP**

IF Children read *The Tree* Approaching Level with fluency and correctly answer the Respond to the Text questions,

THEN Tell children that they will read another book about trees and how they change through the seasons.

- Have children page through *Many Trees* On Level as you talk about how trees change and grow through the seasons.
- Have children read the book, monitoring their comprehension and providing assistance as necessary.

● Approaching Level

Phonological/Phonemic Awareness

ONSET AND RIME BLENDING

OBJECTIVES
Blend and segment onsets and rimes of spoken words.

| I Do | Say *found* from the song "My Oak Tree." Repeat the word, segmenting and then blending the onset and rime, /f/ /ound/, *found*. |

| We Do | Segment and blend the onset and rime in *found*. Have children repeat after you. Together segment and blend *saw: /s/ /aw/,* saw; and *just /j/ /ust/,* just. |

| You Do | Ask children to segment and blend onsets and rimes in other words from the song, such as *ground, told, little, pocket,* and *tree*.

You may want to use a puppet, if one is available, for the *I Do* and *We Do* parts of this lesson. |

PHONEME ISOLATION

OBJECTIVES
Isolate and pronounce the initial sounds in words.

| I Do | Display the *egg* **Photo Card**. *This is an* egg. *The first sound in* egg *is /e/.* Have children repeat the word with you, emphasizing the initial sound. Then have children say the first sound with you: */e/.* |

| We Do | Display the *exit* Photo Card. Name the photo and have children say the name. *What is the first sound in* exit? (/e/) Say the sound together. Repeat with the *elbow* Photo Card. |

| You Do | Show the *egg* Photo Card. Have children name it and say the initial sound of the picture name. Repeat with the *envelope* Photo Card. |

ELL You may wish to review phonological awareness, phonics, decoding, and fluency using this section. Use scaffolding methods as necessary to ensure children understand the meanings of the words. Refer to the **Language Transfers Handbook** for phonics elements that may not transfer in children's native languages.

PHONEME BLENDING

OBJECTIVES

Demonstrate understanding of spoken words, syllables, and sounds (phonemes).

Blend phonemes to make words.

I Do *I am going to say the sounds in a word. Listen: /mmm/ /eee/ /t/. I can blend these sounds together: /mmmeeet/,* met. *Repeat with the three sounds in* pet.

We Do *Now I am going to say the sounds in the word* web. *Say the sounds with me: /w/ /eee/ /b/. Let's blend the sounds together: /weeeb/,* web. *Repeat with* let *and* ten.

You Do Have children blend sounds to form words. Practice together: */sss/ /eee/ /t/,* set. Then have children practice blending the following sounds to say the words.

/t/ /e/ /d/ Ted   /p/ /e/ /t/ pet   /d/ /e/ /n/ den   /s/ /p/ /e/ /d/ sped

You may wish to use a puppet, if one is available, for the *I Do* and *We Do* parts of this lesson.

PHONEME SEGMENTATION

OBJECTIVES

Demonstrate understanding of spoken words, syllables, and sounds (phonemes).

I Do Use **Sound Boxes** and markers. *Listen as I say a word:* let. *There are three sounds in the word* let: */l/ /e/ /t/. I'll place a marker in one box for each sound.* Repeat with the word *well.*

We Do Distribute Sound Boxes and markers. *Let's listen for the number of sounds in more words. Listen as I say a word:* web. *Say the word with me:* web. *Say the sounds with me: /w/ /e/ /b/. Let's place a marker in one box for each sound. There are three sounds in* web. *Repeat with* exit.

You Do Say the following words. Have children repeat the word, segment it into sounds, and place a marker in a box for each sound.

net /n/ /e/ /t/   hen /h/ /e/ /n/   egg /e/ /g/   end /e/ /n/ /d/

Approaching Level

Phonics

SOUND-SPELLING REVIEW

OBJECTIVES

Demonstrate basic knowledge of one-to-one letter-sound correspondences by producing the primary sound or many of the most frequent sounds for each consonant.

I Do Display **Word-Building Card** *h*. Say the letter name and the sound it stands for: *h*, /h/. Repeat for *d, o, c, n, i,* and the initial blend *sp*.

We Do Display Word-Building Cards one at a time and, together, say the letter name and the sound that each letter stands for.

You Do Display Word-Building Cards one at a time and have children say the letter name and the sound that each letter stands for.

CONNECT *e* TO /e/

OBJECTIVES

Associate the long and short sounds with the common spellings (graphemes) for the five major vowels.

I Do Display the *egg* **Sound-Spelling Card**. *The letter* e *can stand for /e/, the sound in* egg. *I'll write* e *when I hear /e/:* empty, horse, end, ever, pin.

We Do *The word* elephant *begins with /e/. Let's write* e. Guide children to write *e* when they hear a word that begins with /e/. Say: *every, find, elf, elk, camp.*

You Do Say the following words and have children write the letter *e* if a word begins with /e/: *match, extra, part, egg, end, actor, enjoy.*

BLEND WORDS WITH SHORT *e*

OBJECTIVES

Know and apply grade-level phonics and word analysis skills in decoding words.

Build words with short *e*.

I Do Display Word-Building Cards *p, e, t*. *These are the letters* p, e, t. *They stand for /p/, /e/, /t/. Listen as I blend: /peeet/,* pet. Repeat for *set*.

We Do *Now let's blend more sounds to make words.* Display the word *hen*. *Let's blend: /heeennn/,* hen. Have children blend to read the word. *I am going to change the letter* h *in* hen *to the letter* m. Change *h* to *m. Let's blend and read the new word: /mmm/ /eee/ /nnn/, /mmmeeennn/,* men.

You Do Distribute Word-Building Cards with *s, e, t, p,* and *n*. Write: *set, pet, ten, pen*. Have children form the words and then blend and read the words.

BUILD WORDS WITH SHORT e

OBJECTIVES

Know and apply grade-level phonics and word analysis skills in decoding words.

Build words with short e.

| I Do | Display **Word-Building Cards** m, e, t and blend the sounds: /mmmeeet/, met. *The word is* met.

| We Do | Distribute sets of Word-Building Cards with m, e, t, and n. Make the word *met*. Replace the letter m at the beginning of *met* with an n. *Let's blend* /nnneeet/, net. *Now we have read a new word,* net.

| You Do | Have children change the initial n in *net* to p and read the new word, *pet*. Point out that by changing one letter we make a new word.

REREAD THE DECODABLE READER

OBJECTIVES

Know and apply grade-level phonics and word analysis skills in decoding words.

Read emergent-reader texts with purpose and understanding.

Unit 5 Decodable Reader

Focus on Foundational Skills

Review the high-frequency word *are* with children. Review the letter e and the short sound /e/. Guide children to blend sounds to read *pen* and *men*.

Read the Decodable Reader

Have children read "Ed and Ted Can Go On" and "Not a Pet!" Point out the high-frequency word *are* as well as words with /e/ at the beginning or in the middle. If children struggle sounding out words, model blending.

Focus on Fluency

Have partners read "Ed and Ted Can Go On" and "Not a Pet!" Guide them to focus on their accuracy. Children can give feedback on their accuracy to their partners. Then have them focus on reading with automaticity and at an appropriate rate. You may wish to have them reread "Ed and Ned" (pages 42-49) in the **Reading/Writing Companion**.

BUILD FLUENCY WITH PHONICS

Sound/Spelling Fluency

Display the following Word-Building Cards: i, n, c, o, d, h, sp, and e. Have children chorally say each sound. Repeat and vary the pace.

● Approaching Level

High-Frequency Words

RETEACH WORDS

OBJECTIVES
Read common high-frequency words by sight.

I Do Display the **High-Frequency Word Card** *are* and use the Read/Spell/Write routine to reteach the word.

We Do Write this sentence and read it aloud: *Ted and Ed are friends.* Have children point to the word *are* in the sentence. Then distribute index cards with the word *are* written on them. Have children match their word card with the word *are* in the sentence. Use the same routine for the sentence: *The branches are bare.*

You Do Write the sentence frame: *We are _____.* Have children copy the sentence frame on their **Response Boards**. Then have partners work together to read and orally complete the frame by talking about how they are feeling today.

CUMULATIVE REVIEW

OBJECTIVES
Read common high-frequency words by sight.

I Do Display the High-Frequency Word Cards *I, can, the, we, see, a, like, to, and, go, you, do, my,* and *are.* Use the Read/Spell/Write routine to review words. Have children practice reading the words until they can read them accurately and with automaticity. Use the High-Frequency Word Cards and **Word-Building Cards** to create sentences, such as *You are in the car.*

We Do Use the High-Frequency Word Cards and Word-Building Cards to create sentences, such as *Do you like my map? We are in the cab.* Have children identify the high-frequency words that are used in each sentence. Read the sentences together.

You Do Have partners use the High-Frequency Word Cards and Word-Building Cards to create short sentences. Have partners take turns reading the sentences to each other.

Oral Vocabulary

REVIEW WORDS

OBJECTIVES
Use words and phrases acquired through conversations, reading and being read to, and responding to texts.

Identify real-life connections between words and their use.

I Do Use the Define/Example/Ask routine on the print or digital **Visual Vocabulary Cards** to review *develop, amazing, enormous, imagine,* and *content.*

We Do Ask questions to build understanding. *How can you help a plant develop into a flower? What is the most amazing flower you have seen? What type of tree is enormous? What details can you imagine about a tree in the spring season? How do you show you are content?*

You Do Have children complete these sentence frames: **I know a plant develops over time because _____. Flowers are amazing because _____. A type of tree that is enormous is _____. When I think of a tree in the spring season, I imagine _____. I feel content when I am _____.**

Comprehension

SELF-SELECTED READING

OBJECTIVES
With prompting and support, identify the main topic and retell key details of a text.

Read emergent-reader texts with purpose and understanding.

Independent Reading

Help children select an informational text with photographs or illustrations for independent reading. Encourage them to read for ten minutes. Remind children that the topic is what a nonfiction text is mostly about. Details help readers understand the topic. Review with children that readers ask themselves questions before, during, and after they read and look for answers in the photographs and the text.

If children need practice with concepts of print, use **Practice Book** page 507.

After reading, guide children to participate in a group discussion about the selection they read. In addition, children can choose activities from the Reading **Center Activity Cards** to help them apply skills to the text as they read. Offer assistance and guidance with self-selected assignments.

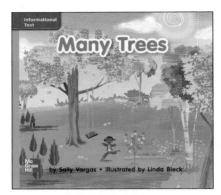

Lexile 70L

OBJECTIVES

Follow words from left to right, top to bottom, and page by page.

With prompting and support, identify the main topic and retell key details of a text.

Read emergent-reader texts with purpose and understanding.

ELA ACADEMIC LANGUAGE

• *purpose, illustration*

• Cognate: *ilustración*

● On Level

Leveled Reader *Many Trees*

Preview and Predict

After reading the title, ask: *What do you see on the cover?* Then read the author and illustrator's names aloud. Preview the illustrations, pointing out how the trees change. Ask: *What do you think this book will be about?*

Review Genre: Informational Text: Nonfiction

Remind children that nonfiction texts gives details about a topic. Ask: *What information might we learn in this selection?* (that there are many kinds of trees)

Set Purpose

Remind children of the Essential Question: *How do living things change as they grow?* Help children set a purpose for reading: *Let's read the book to find out how trees change as they grow through the seasons of the year.* Remind children to use the illustrations to help them understand the text.

Foundational Skills

Model Concepts of Print Have children follow along in their own books as you track the print on pages 2 and 3. Say: *I start reading on page 2. I always read from left to right.*

Review High-Frequency Words Point out the high-frequency word *are* on page 3 and read it with children. Have children find *are* on page 5. Ask them to use the word in a sentence.

Guided Comprehension

As children read *Many Trees,* monitor and provide guidance by offering support and corrective feedback as needed. Model rereading and identifying the topic and details where applicable.

Reread

Remind children that if they find a part of the book confusing, they can reread the text to help them better understand what is happening.

Topic and Details

Tell children that both words and pictures give details about a selection and its topic. Explain that identifying the details will help them figure out what the topic is.

Think Aloud On page 4, I read, "There are wet trees." In the picture on page 4, I see that it is raining. The tree leaves are dripping with rain. Reading the words *and* looking at the pictures helps me understand key details—such as why the trees are wet. It also gives me information about the main topic—that trees grow and change.

Guide children to read the words and use the pictures on pages 5 and 6 to find details about the topic.

Respond to the Text

Have children respond to the text by discussing these questions:

- *What is the first thing you read about trees?* (There are small trees.)

- *Why are there red trees?* (It is fall. The leaves have turned red.)

- *What is the main topic of this book?* (Trees grow and change with the seasons.)

- *What kind of changes do trees go through during the year?* (Possible answers: They grow. They get wet. Their leaves change color.)

Retell Have children retell the selection to a partner, focusing on the topic and details. Help them make personal connections. Ask: *What do you know about how trees change?*

Focus on Fluency

Practice fluency with children. Remember that children need to read with accuracy first.

Once children have read the text with accuracy, have them read the selection again, focusing on rate. Have children practice reading in pairs. Provide corrective feedback as necessary.

Build Knowledge: Make Connections

- **Talk About the Texts** Have partners discuss how plants change as they grow.

- **Write About the Texts** Then have children add their ideas to the Build Knowledge page of their Reader's Notebook.

LITERACY ACTIVITIES

Have children complete the Collaborate and Write About It activities on the inside back cover of the book.

LEVEL UP

IF Children read *Many Trees* On Level with fluency and correctly answer the Respond to the Text questions,

THEN Tell children that they will read another book about trees and how they grow and change.

- Have children page through *Our Apple Tree* Beyond Level as you talk about how a tree grows from a seed.

- Have children read the book, monitoring their comprehension and providing assistance as necessary.

●On Level

Phonological/Phonemic Awareness

PHONEME ISOLATION

OBJECTIVES

Isolate and pronounce the initial sounds in words.

| I Do | Display the *elbow* **Photo Card**. *This is an* elbow. *The first sound is /e/. Say it with me. Say* end. *The first sound in* end *is /e/. Say the sound with me.* |

| We Do | Say *exit* and have children repeat it. *What is the first sound in* exit? (/e/) Say the sound together. Repeat with *ever, egg, edge.* |

| You Do | Say *egg, empty, dot, tip, enter,* and *ox* and have children tell the initial sound. |

PHONEME BLENDING

OBJECTIVES

Demonstrate understanding of spoken words, syllables, and sounds (phonemes).

| I Do | Place the *jet, nest, net, vest,* and *web* Photo Cards facedown. Choose a card. Do not show the card. *These are the sounds in the word: /n/ /e/ /t/. I will blend the sounds: /nnneeet/,* net. *The word is* net. Show the picture. |

| We Do | Choose another picture and say the sounds in the word. Together, say and blend the sounds to say the word. Then show the picture. |

| You Do | Continue choosing Photo Cards. Say the sounds and have children blend the sounds and say the words. |

PHONEME SEGMENTATION

OBJECTIVES

Isolate and pronounce the initial, medial vowel, and final sounds in words.

| I Do | Distribute **Sound Boxes** and markers. *How many sounds are in the word* set? /s/ /e/ /t/. *I'll place a marker in one box for each sound. There are three sounds.* |

| We Do | *Let's listen for the number of sounds in more words. Listen:* ten. *Let's place a marker in one box for each sound. There are three sounds in* ten. |

| You Do | Repeat with the following words: test /t/ /e/ /s/ /t/; pet /p/ /e/ /t/; egg /e/ /g/; hat /h/ /a/ /t/; cap /k/ /a/ /p/; so /s/ /ō/. |

Phonics

REVIEW PHONICS

OBJECTIVES
Associate the long and short sounds with the common spellings (graphemes) for the five major vowels.

I Do Display the *egg* **Sound-Spelling Card**. Say: *The letter* e *stands for the /e/ sound you hear at the beginning of* egg. Say *egg*, emphasizing the /e/.

We Do Display the *elbow, envelope, exit, jet, net,* and *pen* **Photo Cards**. Have children say the name of each picture with you. Then ask them to identify the words with initial /e/ and the words with medial /e/.

You Do Write and display the words *Ed, pet, ten, den, net,* and *met*. Repeat, asking children to raise their hand when they hear /e/ in the middle of the word and lower their hand when they hear /e/ in the beginning of the word. Provide corrective feedback as needed.

PICTURE SORT WITH MEDIAL /e/e, /o/o

OBJECTIVES
Associate the long and short sounds with the common spellings (graphemes) for the five major vowels.

I Do Display **Word-Building Cards** *e* and *o* in a pocket chart. Then show the *pen* Photo Card. Say *pen*. Tell children that the sound in the middle is /e/. *The letter* e *stands for /e/. I will put the* pen *under the letter* e. Show the *mop* Photo Card. Say *mop*. Tell children that the sound in the middle is /o/. *The letter* o *stands for /o/. I will put the* mop *Photo Card under the* o.

We Do Display and name the *lock* Photo Card. Have children repeat and say the sound in the middle of lock. Ask if the photo should be placed under the *e* or the *o*.

You Do Continue the activity using the *jet, net, vest, web, rock, doll,* and *top* Photo Cards. Have children say the picture name and the sounds in the name. Then have them place the card under *e* or *o*.

On Level

Phonics

BLEND WORDS WITH SHORT *e*

MULTIMODAL

OBJECTIVES

Know and apply grade-level phonics and word analysis skills in decoding words.

Build words with short *e*.

I Do Display **Word-Building Cards** n, e, t. *This is the letter* n. *It stands for /n/. Say it with me: /nnn/. This is the letter* e. *It stands for /e/. Say it with me: /eee/. This is the letter* t. *It stands for /t/. Say it with me: /t/. I'll blend the sounds together to read the word: /nnneeet/,* net.

We Do Use Word-Building Cards to form the words *ten* and *tin*. Guide children to blend the words, sound by sound, to read each word. Point out that the letters *t* and *n* are the same and the middle letter changed from *e* to *i* to make a new word.

You Do Distribute sets of Word-Building Cards and ask children to form and then blend and read the following words:

set   sit   Ed   pen   spin   pet   pit   hen   met

REREAD THE DECODABLE READER

OBJECTIVES

Know and apply grade-level phonics and word analysis skills in decoding words.

Read emergent-reader texts with purpose and understanding.

Unit 5 Decodable Reader

Focus on Foundational Skills

Review the high-frequency word *are* with children. Review the letter *e* and the short sound /e/. Guide children to blend sounds to read *pen* and *men*.

Read the Decodable Reader

Have children read "Ed and Ted Can Go On" and "Not a Pet!" Point out the high-frequency word *are* as well as words with /e/ at the beginning or in the middle. If children struggle sounding out words, model blending.

Focus on Fluency

Have partners read "Ed and Ted Can Go On" and "Not a Pet!" Guide them to focus on their accuracy. Children can give feedback on their accuracy to their partners. Then have them focus on reading with automaticity and at an appropriate rate. You may wish to have them reread "Ed and Ned" (pages 42–49) in the **Reading/Writing Companion**.

High-Frequency Words

OBJECTIVES

Read common high-frequency words by sight.

I Do Display the **High-Frequency Word Card** *are* and use the Read/Spell/Write routine to review the word.

We Do Write these sentences and read them aloud: *Ted and Ed are friends. The branches are bare.* Point to the word *are* and have children read it. Chorally read the sentences. Have them frame *are* in the page and read it.

You Do Say the word *are.* Ask children to close their eyes, picture the word, and write it as they see it. Have children self-correct.

Reteach previously introduced high-frequency words, including the **Build Your Word Bank High-Frequency Words**, using the Read/Spell/Write routine.

Fluency Use the **Practice Book Word Cards** to review the High-Frequency and Build Your Word Bank words. Point to the words. Have children practice reading the words until they can read accurately and with automaticity.

Comprehension

OBJECTIVES

With prompting and support, identify the main topic and retell key details of a text.

Read emergent-reader texts with purpose and understanding.

Independent Reading

Help children select an informational text with photographs or illustrations for independent reading. Encourage them to read for ten minutes. Guide children to transfer what they have learned this week as they read. Remind children that the topic is what a nonfiction text is mostly about. Details help readers understand the topic. Review with children that as they read, they can ask questions about things they do not understand and look for answers in the text and photographs.

After reading, guide children to participate in a group discussion about the selection they read. In addition, children can choose activities from the Reading **Center Activity Cards** to help them apply skills to the text as they read. Offer assistance and guidance with self-selected assignments.

Lexile 250L

OBJECTIVES

With prompting and support, describe the relationship between illustrations and the text in which they appear.

With prompting and support, identify the main topic and retell key details of a text.

Read emergent-reader texts with purpose and understanding.

ELA ACADEMIC LANGUAGE

• *selection, predict*
• Cognate: *predecir*

●Beyond Level

Leveled Reader *Our Apple Tree*

Preview and Predict

Have children point to and read the title; then read to them the names of the author and illustrator. Ask children to describe the pictures on the front and back covers. Ask: *What do you think this book is about?* Have children page through the book and look at the illustrations.

Review Genre: Informational Text: Nonfiction

Remind children that nonfiction texts give details about a topic. Ask: *What information might we learn in this selection?* (How an apple tree grows.)

Set Purpose

Remind children of the Essential Question: *How do living things change as they grow?* Help children set a purpose for reading. Say: *Let's find out how an apple tree changes as it grows.* Remind children to use the illustrations to help them understand the text.

Guided Comprehension

As children read *Our Apple Tree*, monitor and provide guidance by correcting blending. Model rereading and identifying the topic and details where applicable. As children read, stop periodically to ask questions, such as *How has the apple tree changed?* Build on children's responses to help them develop a deeper understanding of the text.

Reread

Remind children that as they read they can ask questions about things they don't understand, look for answers in the text and pictures, and reread to clarify what is happening in the selection.

Topic and Details

Review with children that reading the words and looking at the illustrations will help them identify the topic and details in a selection. After reading ask: *What is this selection mainly about?*

Think Aloud On page 4, I learn from the text and the illustration that roots grow from an apple seed and that the roots grow down into the soil. These details give me information about the topic—how an apple tree grows from a seed into a tree that bears apples.

Guide children to read the words and use the pictures on pages 5 and 6 to find details about the topic. Have children point to evidence in the text and pictures to support their answers.

Respond to the Text

Have children respond to the text by discussing these questions:

- How does the apple tree change? (It begins as a seed, grows roots, a stem, leaves, flowers, and, finally, apples.)

- How did the apple tree change in the spring? (It grew flowers.)

- How does the little girl change during the selection? (She is little when they plant the seed and grows up alongside the tree.)

Retell Have children draw a series of pictures showing an apple tree growing from a seed into a tree. Have them use the pictures as they take turns retelling the selection, focusing on the topic and details. Help them make a personal connection by asking: *What kind of tree would you like to plant? Explain your choice.*

Focus on Fluency

Practice fluency with children. Remember that children need to read with accuracy first.

Once children have read the text with accuracy, have them read the selection again, focusing on rate. Have children practice reading with partners. Provide corrective feedback as necessary.

Build Knowledge: Make Connections

- **Talk About the Texts** Have partners discuss how plants change as they grow.

- **Write About the Texts** Then have children add their ideas to the Build Knowledge page of their Reader's Notebook.

LITERACY ACTIVITIES

Have children complete the Collaborate and Write About It activities on the inside back cover of the book.

⭐ GIFTED AND TALENTED

Evaluate Ask children to recall how the tree in *Our Apple Tree* changed as it grew. Challenge children to compare how trees grow and change to how children grow and change.

Extend Have children make a scrapbook about themselves with photographs or drawings to show how they've grown and changed through the years.

Beyond Level

Phonics

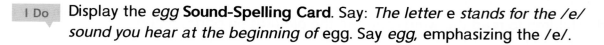

OBJECTIVES

Associate the long and short sounds with the common spellings (graphemes) for the five major vowels.

I Do Display the *egg* **Sound-Spelling Card.** Say: *The letter* e *stands for the /e/ sound you hear at the beginning of* egg. Say *egg,* emphasizing the /e/.

We Do Display the *elbow, envelope, exit, jet, net,* and *pen* **Photo Cards.** Have children say the name of each picture. Repeat the names, emphasizing /e/. Then ask children to share other words they know with /e/.

You Do Write and display the words *Ed, pet, ten, den, net,* and *met.* Have partners read each word. Ask them to write the words on their **Response Boards** and underline the letter in each word that stands for /e/.

Fluency Have children reread the story "Ed and Ned" for fluency.

Innovate Have children create a new page for "Ed and Ned," using the sentence frame: *Ed and Ned* _____.

High-Frequency Words

OBJECTIVES

Read common high-frequency words by sight.

I Do Use the **Practice Book Build Your Word Bank High-Frequency Word Cards** for *when, which,* and *soon.* Review the words using the Read/Spell/Write routine.

We Do Display the **Practice Book High-Frequency Word Cards** for *are, to, see, do,* and *you.* Have children help you create sentence frames using both sets of word cards.

You Do Have partners write sentences using the Build Your Word Bank High-Frequency words *when, which,* and *soon* on their **Response Boards.** Have them read their sentences.

Vocabulary

ORAL VOCABULARY: SYNONYMS

OBJECTIVES
With guidance and support from adults, explore word relationships and nuances in word meanings.

I Do Review the meanings of the oral vocabulary words *develop* and *amazing*. Explain that a synonym is a word that means almost the same thing as another word. *A synonym for* develop *is* grow. *When something grows, it changes.* I will grow taller as I get older. *A synonym for* amazing *is* fantastic. *Something that is fantastic is very good or excellent.* My lunch was fantastic.

We Do Together, make sentences with *grow* and *fantastic* and read them aloud.

You Do Have partners draw a picture of a place that would be fun to visit and then think of two or three sentences to describe it. Tell them to use *grow* and *fantastic*. Ask them to share their picture and description with the class.

GIFTED and TALENTED **Extend** Challenge partners to find more synonyms for *grow* and *fantastic*. Have them tell a story using some of their synonyms.

Comprehension

SELF-SELECTED READING

OBJECTIVES
With prompting and support, identify the main topic and retell key details of a text.

Read emergent-reader texts with purpose and understanding.

Independent Reading

Help children select an informational text with photographs or illustrations for independent reading. Encourage them to read for ten minutes. Guide children to transfer what they have learned this week as they read by identifying the topic and details. Remind children that readers ask questions as they read to help understand the text.

After reading, guide children to participate in a group discussion about the selection they read. In addition, children can choose activities from the Reading **Center Activity Cards** to help them apply skills to the text as they read. Offer assistance and guidance with self-selected assignments.

 Have children draw the life cycle of a living thing. Have them write captions for the drawings and share with a partner.

Student Outcomes

✓ Tested in *Wonders* Assessments

FOUNDATIONAL SKILLS

Print Concepts

- Match speech to print
- Identify parts of a book

Phonological Awareness

- Identify Rhyme
- Phoneme Isolation
- Phoneme Addition
- ✓ Phoneme Blending

Phonics and Word Analysis

- ✓ /f/f, /r/r

Fluency

- ✓ High-Frequency Words
  with   he

READING

Reading Informational Text

- ✓ Identify the main topic and key details in a text
- Describe the relationship between illustrations and the text
- Retell familiar stories
- Actively engage in group reading activities

COMMUNICATION

Writing

- Handwriting: *Ff*
- Use prompts to write about the text
- Respond to suggestions from peers and add details to strengthen writing

Speaking and Listening

- Present writing and research
- Engage in collaborative conversations
- Ask and answer questions to get information or to clarify something that is not understood

Conventions

- **Grammar:** Recognize subjective pronouns

Researching

- Recall or gather information to answer a question
- Conduct research about a plant that grows on a farm

Creating and Collaborating

- Add drawings and visual displays to descriptions
- Use digital tools to produce and publish writing

VOCABULARY

Academic Vocabulary

- Acquire and use grade-appropriate academic vocabulary

Vocabulary Strategy

- ✓ Identify and sort common words and objects into categories
- Use sentence-level context clues

ELL Scaffolded supports for English Language Learners are embedded throughout the lessons, enabling children to communicate information, ideas, and concepts in English Language Arts and for social and instructional purposes within the school setting.

See the **ELL Small Group Guide** for additional support of the skills for the text set.

FORMATIVE ASSESSMENT

For assessment throughout the text set, use children's self-assessments and your observations.

Use the Data Dashboard to filter class, group, or individual student data to guide group placement decisions. It provides recommendations to enhance learning for gifted and talented children and offers extra support for children needing remediation.

DATA DASHBOARD

Develop Student Ownership

To build student ownership, children need to know what they are learning, why they are learning it, and determine how well they understood it.

Students Discuss Their Goals

TEXT SET GOALS

- I can read and understand texts.
- I can write about the texts I read.
- I know the kinds of things that grow on a farm.

Have children think about what they know and circle a hand in each row on **Reading/Writing Companion** page 58.

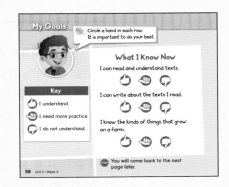

Students Monitor Their Learning

LEARNING GOALS

Specific learning goals identified in every lesson make clear what children will be learning and why. These smaller goals provide stepping stones to help children meet their Text Set Goals.

CHECK-IN ROUTINE

The Check-In Routine at the close of each lesson guides children to self-reflect on how well they understood each learning goal.

Review the lesson learning goal.
Reflect on the activity.
Self Assess by
- circling the hands in the **Reading/Writing Companion.**
- showing thumbs up, sideways, or down.

Share with your teacher.

Students Reflect on Their Progress

TEXT SET GOALS

After completing the Show Your Knowledge task for the text set, children reflect on their understanding of the Text Set Goals by circling a hand in each row on **Reading/Writing Companion** page 59.

Build Knowledge

Literature Big Book

Shared Read
Reading/Writing Companion, p.66

Look at the farmers' stands.
They are filled with fresh foods.
Who grows the vegetables and fruits?
How did they get here?

Paired Selection
Literature Big Book

Essential Question
What kinds of things grow on a farm?

 Video Some of our favorite foods might grow on a farm. Strawberries, green beans, tomatoes, and other fruits and vegetables grow on farms. When they are ripe, some are sold to grocery stores.

Literature Big Book An orange grows slowly in an orchard, fed by the earth's soil, rain, and sunlight. It is picked and loaded from one truck to another, delivered to a grocery store, and chosen by a young boy.

Shared Read Ron, his family, and his pet dog, Red, pick oranges in an orchard and tomatoes in a field.

Interactive Read Aloud Farms all around the world grow different foods. Potatoes grow on vines in places like Idaho, Washington, and Wisconsin. Rice grows on plants under water in China and other countries in Asia. Bananas grow on trees in places with warm temperatures.

Paired Selection Farmers grow fruits and vegetables, such as squash, peas, and blueberries. Some sell their foods at local markets. Other sell their foods far away, sending their crops on trains, planes, or boats.

Photograph Many things grow on a rooftop farm in a city, including carrots and tomatoes.

Differentiated Sources

Leveled Readers 🔊

🔴 A farmer sells apples, peppers, grapes, potatoes, tomatoes, berries, and flowers (all red).

🔴🔴 On a picnic table at a farm, a man prepares lettuce, carrots, tomatoes, peppers and radishes for a salad.

🔴 Finn does not want to eat his carrots or corn. Then he visits Grandpa's farm and helps pick vegetables. He and Grandpa cook with red peppers, corn, and tomatoes. Finn enjoys eating them.

Build Knowledge Routine

After reading each text, ask children to document what facts and details that they learned to help answer the Essential Question of the text set.

 Talk about the source.

 Write about the source.

 Add to the class Anchor Chart.

• Add to the Word Bank.

Show Your Knowledge

Make a Shopping List

Have children think about the kinds of foods that grow on a farm. Guide them to draw a shopping list of items they could buy at a farmers' market. Have children label their drawings using vocabulary words they learned during the week.

Social Emotional Learning

Self Confidence

SEL Focus: Deepen children's self-confidence by acknowledging and celebrating attempts and the process of learning.

Invite children to think about something that helps them feel confident, in preparation for the lesson titled "Confidence!" on pp. T160-T161.

Word on the Street: Confidence (0:34)

Family Time • Share the video and the activity in the **School to Home** newsletter.

Explore the Texts

Essential Question: What kinds of things grow on a farm?

Literature Big Book	Literature Big Book	Interactive Read-Aloud	Reading/Writing Companion

An Orange in January Anchor Text Informational Text	**"Farmers' Market"** Paired Text Informational Text	**"Farms Around the World"** Interactive Read Aloud Informational Text	**"Ron With Red"** Shared Read pp. 66–73 Fiction

Qualitative

Meaning/Purpose: Moderate Complexity **Structure:** Moderate Complexity **Language:** High Complexity **Knowledge Demands:** Moderate Complexity	**Meaning/Purpose:** Low Complexity **Structure:** Moderate Complexity **Language:** Moderate Complexity **Knowledge Demands:** Low Complexity	**Meaning/Purpose:** Low Complexity **Structure:** Moderate Complexity **Language:** High Complexity **Knowledge Demands:** Low Complexity	**Meaning/Purpose:** Low Complexity **Structure:** Low Complexity **Language:** Low Complexity **Knowledge Demands:** Low Complexity

Quantitative

Lexile 610L	Lexile 340L	Lexile 840L	Lexile 170L

Reader and Task Considerations

Reader The informational words and complex phrases might be unfamiliar to children. Readers may need to hear this story several times.	**Reader** Before reading this text, encourage children to discuss their understanding of where some favorite fruits and vegetables come from.	**Reader** Many children are likely to be unfamiliar with the concept of commercial farming, so the packaging and distribution of crops mentioned in the text may need to be carefully explained.	**Reader** Children will need to use their knowledge of sound-spelling correspondences and high-frequency words to read the text.

Task The questions for the Interactive Read Aloud are supported by teacher modeling. The tasks provide a variety of ways for students to build knowledge and vocabulary about the text set topic. The questions and tasks provided for the other texts are at various levels of complexity, ensuring that all students can interact with the text in meaningful ways.

Additional Read-Aloud Texts

Classroom Library
Have You Seen My Duckling?
Genre: Fiction
Lexile: 20L

A Tree Is a Plant
Genre: Informational Text
Lexile: 290L

See Classroom Library Lessons.

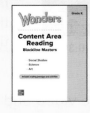

Content Area Reading BLMs
Additional online texts related to grade-level Science, Social Studies, and Arts content.

Access Complex Text (ACT) boxes provide scaffolded instruction for seven different elements that may make the **Literature Big Book** complex.

A C T

Leveled Readers 🔊 (All Leveled Readers are provided in eBook format with audio support.)

Approaching

The Farmer
Leveled Reader
Informational Text

On

Let's Make a Salad!
Leveled Reader
Informational Text

Beyond

Farm Fresh Finn
Leveled Reader
Informational Text

ELL

Let's Make a Salad!
Leveled Reader
Informational Text

Qualitative

Meaning/Purpose: Low Complexity
Structure: Low Complexity
Language: Low Complexity
Knowledge Demands: Low Complexity

Meaning/Purpose: Low Complexity
Structure: Low Complexity
Language: Low Complexity
Knowledge Demands: Low Complexity

Meaning/Purpose: Moderate Complexity
Structure: Low Complexity
Language: Moderate Complexity
Knowledge Demands: Low Complexity

Meaning/Purpose: Low Complexity
Structure: Low Complexity
Language: Low Complexity
Knowledge Demands: Low Complexity

Quantitative

Lexile BR

Lexile BR

Lexile 260L

Lexile BR

Reader and Task Considerations

Reader Children will likely be familiar with the food and color words in this story.

Reader Children should be familiar with the food mentioned in the text. Discuss with children what they like to put in their salad.

Reader Discussing how the main character's attitude about vegetables shifted in this story will support children's understanding of the text.

Reader Children should be familiar with the food mentioned in the text. Discuss with children what they like to put in their salad.

Task The questions and tasks provided for the Leveled Readers are at various levels of complexity, ensuring that all students can interact with the text in meaningful ways.

Focus on Word Work

WEEK 3

Build Foundational Skills with Multimodal Learning

Photo Cards

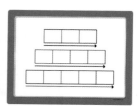

Response Board

Phonemic Awareness Activities

Phonological/Phonemic Awareness

- Identify rhyming words
- Isolate and blend phonemes
- Add sounds to words to make new words

Sound-Spelling Cards

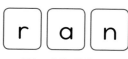

Word-Building Cards online

Phonics Practice Activities

Phonics: /f/f, /r/r

- Introduce/review sound-spellings
- Blend/build words with sound-spellings
- Practice handwriting
- Decode and encode in connected texts

Practice Book

Word-Building Cards online

Response Board

Spelling: /f/f, /r/r

- Spell words with /f/f, /r/r

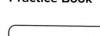
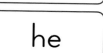

High-Frequency Word Cards

High-Frequency Word Activities

Visual Vocabulary Cards

High-Frequency Words

- Read/Spell/Write routine
- Optional: Build Your Word Bank

See Word Work, pages T170–T173, T182–T185, T190–T195, T204–T205, T210–T211.

Shared Reads

Decodable Readers

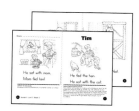

Take-Home Story

Apply Skills to Read

- Children apply foundational skills as they read decodable texts.
- Children practice fluency to develop word automaticity.

Explicit Systematic Instruction

Word Work instruction expands foundational skills to enable children to become proficient readers.

Daily Routine

- Use the In a Flash: Sound-Spelling routine and the In a Flash: High-Frequency Word routine to build fluency.
- Set Learning Goal.

Explicit Minilessons and Practice

Use daily instruction in both whole and small groups to model, practice, and apply key foundational skills. Opportunities include:

- Multimodal engagement.
- Corrective feedback.
- Supports for English Language Learners in each lesson.
- Peer collaboration.

Formative Assessment

Check-In

- Children reflect on their learning.
- Children show their progress by indicating thumbs down, thumbs sideways, or thumbs up in a Check-In routine.

Check for Success

- Teacher monitors children's achievement and differentiates for Small Group instruction.

Differentiated Instruction

To strengthen skills, provide targeted review and reteaching lessons and multimodal activities to meet children's diverse needs.

- ● **Approaching Level, ELL**
- Includes Tier 2 **②**

● **On Level**

● **Beyond Level**
- Includes Gifted and Talented 🌟 GIFTED and TALENTED

OPTIONAL EXPRESS TRACK

Teachers can choose to introduce long vowel sound-spellings and/or additional high-frequency words.

- Build Your Word Bank

Independent Practice

Provide additional practice as needed. Have children work individually or with partners.

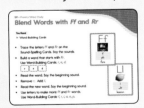

Center Activity Cards

Digital Activities

Word-Building Cards online

Decodable Readers

Practice Book

Inspire Early Writers

Build Writing Skills and Conventions

Practice Book

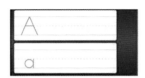

Handwriting Video

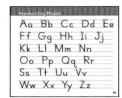

Reading/Writing Companion

Write Letters *Ff, Rr*

- Learn to write the letters
- Practice writing

Response Board

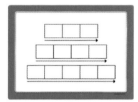

Practice Book

High-Frequency Word Activities

Write Words

- Write words with *Ff, Rr*
- Write high-frequency words

Reading/Writing Companion

Practice Book

Write Sentences

- Write sentences with high-frequency words
- Write sentences to respond to text

Follow Conventions

- Appropriately use pronouns

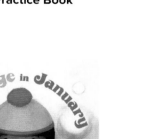

An Orange in January
Literature Big Book

Writing Fluency

To increase children's writing fluency, have them write as much as they can in response to the **Literature Big Book** for four minutes. Tell children to write about what they learned about the orange.

For lessons, see pages **T170–T175, T186–T187, T190–T193, T196–T197, T206–T207, T210–T213.**

Write About Texts

WRITING ROUTINE

Analyze the Prompt > Find Text Evidence > Write to the Prompt

Literature Big Book, pp. 3–33

Modeled Writing

Write about the **Literature Big Book** *An Orange in January*

- Prompt: What is your favorite fruit?

Interactive Writing

- Prompt: Where did the orange begin and end its journey?

**Reading/Writing
Companion, pp. 66–73**

Independent Writing

Write to the Shared Read "Ron With Red"

Reading/Writing Companion, pp. 66–73

- Prompt: What does Ron do at the park?

- Have children follow the steps of the writing process: draft, revise, edit/proofread, share.

Additional Lessons

Writing Skills Minilessons To provide differentiated support for writing skills, see pages T494–T499.

Extended Writing Lessons For a full set of lessons that support the writing process and writing in a specific genre, see pages T476–T485.

Self-Selected Writing

Children can explore different writing modes.

Journal Writing

Make a Book

Planner

Customize your own lesson plans at
my.mheducation.com

 LESSON 1

 LESSON 2

Select from your Social Emotional Learning resources.

TEXT SET GOALS

- **I can read and understand texts.**
- **I can write about the texts I read.**
- **I know the kinds of things that grow on a farm.**

90+ mins Reading Suggested Daily Time Includes Small Group

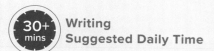 **SMALL GROUP OPTIONS** The designated lessons can be taught in small groups. To determine how to differentiate instruction for small groups, use Formative Assessment and Data Dashboard.

30+ mins Writing Suggested Daily Time

Reading

LESSON 1

Introduce the Concept, T162–T163
Build Knowledge: Fresh from the Farm

Listening Comprehension, T164–T169
An Orange in January

⏩ **Word Work, T170–T173**
Phonemic Awareness: Phoneme Isolation
Phonics/Spelling: Introduce /f/f and /r/r
Handwriting: Write *Ff* and *Rr*
High-Frequency Words: *with, he*

LESSON 2

Build the Concept, T176–T177
Phonological Awareness: Identify Rhyme
Category Words: Food Words
Vocabulary: Sentence Clues

Listening Comprehension, T178–T181
An Orange in January

⏩ **Word Work, T182–T183**
Phonemic Awareness: Phoneme Blending
Phonics: Review *f* and *r*, Blend Words with *f* and *r*
High-Frequency Words: *with, he*

Shared Read, T184–T185
Read "Ron With Red"

Writing

Modeled Writing, T174
Model Writing About the Literature Big Book
Grammar, T175
Subjective Pronouns

Interactive Writing, T186
Write About the Literature Big Book
Grammar, T187
Subjective Pronouns

Teacher-Led Instruction

 SMALL GROUP

Differentiated Reading
Leveled Readers
- *The Farmer*, T216–T217
- *Let's Make a Salad!*, T224–T225
- *Farm Fresh Finn*, T230–T231

Differentiated Skills Practice, T218–T233
Approaching Level, T218–T223
Phonological/Phonemic Awareness
- Recognize Rhyme, T218 🔵2
- Phoneme Isolation, T218 🔵2
- Phoneme Blending, T219
- Phoneme Addition, T219

Phonics
- Sound-Spelling Review, T220 🔵2
- Connect *f* to /f/ and *r* to /r/, T220 🔵2
- Blend Words with /f/f and /r/r, T220
- Build Words with /f/f and /r/r, T221
- Reread the Decodable Reader, T221
- Build Fluency with Phonics, T221
High-Frequency Words
- Reteach Words, T222 🔵2
- Cumulative Review, T222
Oral Vocabulary
- Review, T223

Independent/Collaborative Work See pages T159I–T159J

Reading
Comprehension
- Informational Text
- Reread
- Topic and Details

Word Work
Phonics
- /f/f, /r/r
High-Frequency Words
- *with, he*

Writing
Self-Selected Writing
Grammar
- Subjective Pronouns
Handwriting
- Upper and Lowercase *Ff, Rr*

LESSON 3

LESSON 4

LESSON 5

Reading

Build the Concept, T188
Oral Language

Listening Comprehension, T189
"Farms Around the World"

Word Work, T190–T193
Phonemic Awareness: Phoneme Blending, Long Vowel Awareness
Phonics: Review *f, r*; Blend Words; Spell Words
High-Frequency Words: *with, he*

Shared Read, T194–T195
Reread "Ron With Red"

Extend the Concept, T198–T199
Phonological Awareness: Identify Rhyme
Category Words: Food Words
Vocabulary: Sentence Clues

Paired Selection, T200–T203
"Farmers Market"

Word Work, T204–T205
Phonemic Awareness: Phoneme Addition, Long Vowel Awareness
Phonics: Build and Read Words with /f/f, /r/r
High-Frequency Words: *with, he*

Research and Inquiry, T208–T209
Plants (Research)

Word Work, T210–T211
Phonemic Awareness: Phoneme Addition, Long Vowel Awareness
Phonics: Read Words, Spell Words
High-Frequency Words: *with, he*

Integrate Ideas, T214
Make Connections

Show Your Knowledge, T215

Writing

Independent Writing, T196
Write About the Shared Read
Grammar, T197
Subjective Pronouns

Independent Writing, T206
Write About the Shared Read
Grammar, T207
Subjective Pronouns

Self-Selected Writing, T212
Grammar, T213
Subjective Pronouns

Comprehension
• Self-Selected Reading, T223
● **On Level, T226–T229**
Phonological/Phonemic Awareness
• Phoneme Isolation, T226
• Phoneme Blending, T226
• Phoneme Addition, T226
Phonics
• Review Phonics, T227
• Picture Sort, T227
• Blend Words with /f/f and /r/r, T228
• Reread the Decodable Reader, T228

High-Frequency Words
• Review Words, T229
Comprehension
• Self-Selected Reading, T229
● **Beyond Level, T232–T233**
Phonics
• Review, T232
High-Frequency Words
• Review, T232

Vocabulary
• Oral Vocabulary: Synonyms, T233
Comprehension
• Self-Selected Reading, T233

GIFTED and TALENTED

● **English Language Learners**
See ELL Small Group Guide, pp. 122–129

Content Area Connections
Content Area Reading
• Science, Social Studies, and the Arts
Research and Inquiry
• Plants (Research)

● **English Language Learners**
See ELL Small Group Guide, pp. 123, 125

WEEK 3

Independent and Collaborative Work

As you meet with small groups, have the rest of the class complete activities and projects to practice and apply the skills they have been working on.

Student Choice and Student Voice

- Review the My Weekly Work blackline masters with children and identify the "Must Do" activities.
- Have children choose some additional activities that provide the practice they need.
- Remind children to reflect on their learning each day.

My Weekly Work BLMs

Reading

Text Options

Children can choose a **Center Activity Card** to use while they listen to a text or read independently.

Classroom Library Read Aloud
Have You Seen My Duckling?
Genre: Fiction
Lexile: 20L

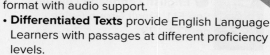

A Tree Is a Plant
Genre: Informational Text
Lexile: 290L

Unit Bibliography
See the online bibliography. Children can select independent reading texts about what kinds of things grow on a farm.

Leveled Texts Online
All **Leveled Readers** are provided in eBook format with audio support.
- **Differentiated Texts** provide English Language Learners with passages at different proficiency levels.

Literature Big Book e-Book
An Orange in January
Genre: Informational Text

Center Activity Cards

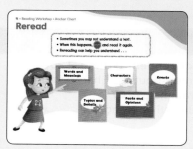

Reread Card 4

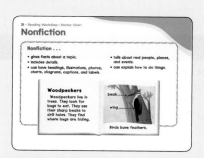

Nonfiction Card 21

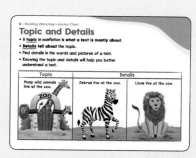

Topic and Details Card 6

Digital Activities

Comprehension

Word Work

Center Activity Cards

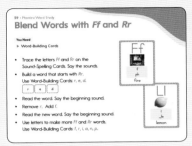

Blend Words with *Ff* and *Rr*

You Need
▶ Word-Building Cards

- Trace the letters *Ff* and *Rr* on the Sound-Spelling Cards. Say the sounds.
- Build a word that starts with *Rr*. Use Word-Building Cards: *r, e, d*.
- Read the word. Say the beginning sound.
- Remove *r*. Add *f*.
- Read the new word. Say the beginning sound.
- Use letters to make more *Ff* and *Rr* words. Use Word-Building Cards: *f, r, i, a, n, p*.

/f/f, /r/r Card 59

Word-Building Cards

Practice Book BLMs

Phonological Awareness: p. 225, 226–227, 228
Phonics: pp. 229–230, 232
Phonics/Spelling: p. 231
High-Frequency Words: p. 234
Category Words: p. 235
Take-Home Story: pp. 239–240

Decodable Readers

Unit 5, pp. 25–36

Digital Activities

Word Work

Phonemic Awareness
Phonics
High-Frequency Words

Writing

Center Activity Cards

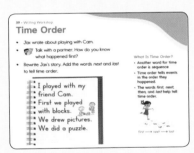

Time Order

- Jax wrote about playing with Cam.
- Talk with a partner. How do you know what happened first?
- Rewrite Jax's story. Add the words *next* and *last* to tell time order.

  I played with my friend Cam. First we played with blocks. We drew pictures. We did a puzzle.

What Is Time Order?
- Another word for time order is sequence
- Time order tells events in the order they happened.
- The words *first, next, then,* and *last* help tell time order.

Time Order Card 39

Self-Selected Writing

- What do you know about things that grown on a farm?
- Write about you or someone you know visiting a farm.
- Draw and label a picture of foods that grow on a farm.

Practice Book BLMs

Handwriting: p. 233
Grammar: pp. 236–238

Digital Activities

I see a fish.

Grammar

Content Area Connections

Content Area Reading BLMs
- Additional texts related to Science, Social Studies, Health, and the Arts.

Research and Inquiry
- Complete Research a Plant project

Progress Monitoring
Moving Toward Mastery

Practice Book

Reading/Writing Companion

Online Rubric

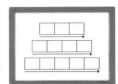

Response Board

Digital Activities

> **FORMATIVE ASSESSMENT**
> ❯ STUDENT CHECK-IN
> ✓ CHECK FOR SUCCESS

For ongoing formative assessment, use children's self-assessments at the end of each lesson along with your own observations.

Assessing skills along the way . . .

SKILLS	HOW ASSESSED
Phonological Awareness • Identify Rhyme	Practice Book
Phonemic Awareness • Phoneme Isolation • Phoneme Blending • Phoneme Addition	Practice Book, Response Board, Digital Activities
Phonics • /f/f, /r/r	Practice Book, Response Board, Digital Activities
High-Frequency Words • *with, he*	Practice Book, Response Board, Digital Activities
Category Words • Food Words	Practice Book
Grammar • Subjective Pronouns	Practice Book
Comprehension • Topic and Details • Text Feature: Lists	Reading/Writing Companion
Listening/Presenting/Research	Checklists

Making the Most of Assessment Results

Make data-based grouping decisions by using the following reports to verify assessment results. For additional support options for children, refer to the reteaching and enrichment opportunities.

ONLINE ASSESSMENT CENTER
- *Gradebook*

DATA DASHBOARD
- *Recommendations Report*
- *Activity Report*
- *Skills Report*
- *Progress Report*
- *Grade Card Report*

TIER 2

Reteaching Opportunities with Intervention Online PDFs

ASSESSED SKILLS	✓ CHECK FOR SUCCESS	RETEACH . . .
PHONOLOGICAL AND PHONEMIC AWARENESS	Can children identify rhyme? Can children isolate, blend, and add phonemes? If not . . .	using lessons 6–8; 27–29, 62–66, and 98–99 in the **Phonemic Awareness PDF.**
PHONICS	Can children match /f/ to the letter *f* and /r/ to the letter *r*? If not . . .	using lessons 25–26 in the **Phonics/Word Study PDF.**
HIGH-FREQUENCY WORDS	Can children recognize and read the high-frequency words? If not . . .	by using the **High-Frequency Word Cards** and asking children to read and spell the word. Point out any irregularities in sound-spellings.
COMPREHENSION	Can children identify the topic and details in a text? Can children use text features including lists? If not . . .	using lessons 76–78 and 133 in the **Comprehension PDF.**
CATEGORY WORDS	Can children identify and sort food words? If not . . .	using lesson 17 in the **Vocabulary PDF.**

GIFTED and TALENTED

Enrichment Opportunities

Beyond Level small group lessons and resources include suggestions for additional activities in these areas to extend learning opportunities for gifted and talented children:

- *Leveled Reader*
- *Vocabulary*
- *Comprehension*
- *Leveled Reader Library Online*
- *Center Activity Cards*

Today's focus:

Developing confidence and resilience as learners.

Word on the Street: Confidence (0:34)   LIVE ACTION

family time

You'll find the "Word on the Street: Confidence" video and supporting activity in this week's School to Home family newsletter.

confidence!

engage together

Let's Talk: We love to learn!

Think aloud as you model recognizing effort and feeling confident.

- We are a classroom that works hard to learn new things.
- One thing I challenged myself, or tried very hard, to learn is _____.
- One thing I am *still* challenging myself to learn is _____.
- Even though I don't always succeed, I feel great when I try. I believe in myself! I feel confident!
- What is one thing that was hard for you to learn?
- How did it make you feel when you learned it?

explore together

Let's Watch: "Word on the Street: Confidence"
Set a purpose for sharing today's live-action video.

- In today's video, Murray interviews people about one of my favorite words, *confidence*.
- First, let's watch and learn about today's word on the street.
- Then, we'll explore what we learned.

  (▷) **Play the video**

Let's Share: What is confidence?
Develop a shared definition of confidence.

- Now, it's your turn. Turn to a partner.
- You are going to interview one another using the same questions Murray asked.
- Ask each other: *What is confidence? When do you feel confident?*
- You'll each talk for about a minute.
- Finally, I'll record our definitions on chart paper.

CONFIDENCE IS...

- Feeling good about myself.
- Believing I can do it!
- Trusting myself and others.

connect the learning

Let's Play: The power of *yet*!
Model the importance of persistence and practice.

- There are many things we *can* do. Let's list a few of these things.
- However, there are some things we are *just* learning to do.
- Let's complete these sentence frames: *I can _____.
  I can't _____, yet!*
- This one little word, *yet*, gives me the confidence to keep trying when learning something new gets hard.
- Let's brainstorm things we're learning to do, but can't do . . . yet!

mindfulness moment
Self-Talk
When children are calm, model using positive self-talk to manage frustration and build their self-confidence: *When I feel like I'm about to become frustrated and want to give up, I say to myself: I believe in myself. I **can** do it. I will keep trying!*

SELF-CONFIDENCE

LESSON 1

OBJECTIVES

Confirm understanding of a text read aloud or information presented orally or through other media by asking and answering questions about key details and requesting clarification if something is not understood.

Use words and phrases acquired through conversations, reading and being read to, and responding to texts.

Identify real-life connections between words and their use.

Follow agreed-upon rules for discussions (e.g., listening to others and taking turns speaking about the topics and texts under discussion).

ELA ACADEMIC LANGUAGE

• *discuss, fresh, topic, ideas*
• Cognates: *discutir, fresco*

DIGITAL TOOLS

Watch Video

Build Background Images

Visual Vocabulary Cards

LESSON FOCUS

READING
Introduce Essential Question
Read Literature Big Book
An Orange in January
• Introduce Genre: Informational Text
• Introduce Strategy/Skill
Word Work
• Introduce /f/f, /r/r

WRITING
Writing/Grammar
• Shared Writing
• Introduce Grammar

Literature Big Book pp. 3–33

---

10 mins

Build Knowledge

MULTIMODAL

 Essential Question

What kinds of things grow on a farm?

Read aloud the essential question. Explain that this week we will read and learn about things that grow on farms. Have partners discuss foods that farmers grow. (Possible responses: corn, potatoes, tomatoes)

• **Video Routine** Play the Weekly Opener Video, "Fresh from the Farm" without sound and have partners narrate what they watch Then replay the video with sound and have children listen.

• **Talk About the Video** Have partners share one thing they learned about what grows on farms.

 • **Anchor Chart** Create a Build Knowledge anchor chart and have volunteers share what they learned about the theme "Fresh from the Farm." Record their ideas on the chart.

Oral Vocabulary Words

Use the Define/Example/Ask routine on the print or digital **Visual Vocabulary Cards** to introduce the oral vocabulary words *fresh* and *delicious*.

 Oral Vocabulary Routine

<u>Define</u>: Food that is **fresh** has just been grown or made.

<u>Example</u>: We picked the apple from the tree and ate the fresh fruit.

<u>Ask</u>: What fresh food have you eaten?

<u>Define</u>: Something that is **delicious** tastes very good.

<u>Example</u>: The juicy strawberry was delicious.

<u>Ask</u>: What delicious food have you eaten?

Visual Vocabulary Cards

Reading/Writing Companion, pp. 56–57

 Build Knowledge

Have children turn to pages 56-57 of their **Reading/Writing Companion**. Guide a discussion about foods that grow on farms.

- **Talk** *What kinds of foods are grown on farms? What are some words that name these foods?* List the words. Have children choose a word and think about how to illustrate it.

- **Draw** and **Write** Have children draw a picture that illustrates the word. Then have them write the word. Guide children on how to print letters that have not been taught yet.

Build Vocabulary

Have children share new words they learned about foods that grow on farms. Add words to a separate section of the Word Bank. Use the words during the week and encourage children to do the same.

 # English Language Learners

Use the following scaffolds with **Build Knowledge.**

Beginning

Point to the carrots in the photo. *Carrots are vegetables.* Have children repeat the words. Repeat with other items in the photo.

Intermediate

Help children describe the photo. Provide sentence frames for children to use: The girl has carrots. Carrots are vegetables.

Advanced/Advanced High

Have partners discuss the photo. Encourage them to use complete sentences, such as: *Carrots and broccoli are vegetables. They are fresh and delicious.*

COLLABORATIVE CONVERSATIONS

Add New Ideas As children engage in partner, small group, and whole group discussions, encourage them to:

- Stay on topic.
- Connect their own ideas to the ideas of others.
- Connect their personal experiences to the conversation.

ELL NEWCOMERS

To help children develop oral language and build vocabulary, use **Newcomer Cards** 15-19 and the accompanying lessons in the **Newcomer Teacher's Guide.** For thematic connections, use **Newcomer Cards** 9 (Weather), 18 (Food and meals), and 19 (Shopping). For additional practice, have children complete the online **Newcomer Activities.**

MY GOALS ROUTINE

What I Know Now

Read Goals Read aloud the goals and the key on **Reading/Writing Companion** page 58.

Reflect Ask children to reflect on each goal and complete page 58 to show what they know now. Explain that they will complete page 59 at the end of the text set to show their progress.

Literature Big Book

LEARNING GOALS

We can understand important ideas and details in a text.

OBJECTIVES

Recognize common types of texts.

With prompting and support, name the author and illustrator of a story and define the role of each in telling the story.

With prompting and support, identify the main topic and retell key details of a text.

Actively engage in group reading activities with purpose and understanding.

Reread for understanding.

ELA ACADEMIC LANGUAGE

• *details, reread*
• Cognate: *detalles*

DIFFERENTIATED READING

Celebratory Read You may wish to read the full selection aloud once with minimal stopping before reading with the prompts.

⬤⬤ **Approaching Level** and **English Language Learners** After reading, have children listen to the selection to develop comprehension.

Read

Literature Big Book

Connect to Concept

Explain you are going to read about a fruit that grows on a tree. *What does fruit need to grow? How does fruit get from the farm to our homes?*

Genre: Informational Text: Nonfiction Tell children that *An Orange in January* is nonfiction. *Nonfiction text gives information in a certain order.*

 Anchor Chart Display and review the Nonfiction anchor chart. Ask children what new information should be added to the chart.

Reread Remind children that rereading or reading a text again, can help them understand the information in a text better.

Topic and Details Help children recall that nonfiction text has a topic and details. *What is a topic? What are details?* Then summarize by reminding children that the topic is what a selection is about and details in the words and images can give information about a topic.

Read the Selection

Display the Big Book. Read the title and look at the photo. *What do you predict this text will be about?* Write and display children's predictions.

Concepts of Print Display the front cover. Read the title. Have volunteers point to the names of the author and illustrator and tell what each does.

Set Purpose *Let's read to find out about an orange in January.* Remind children to read nonfiction texts at a slower rate.

Close Reading Routine

Read DOK 1–2

• Identify key ideas and details.
• Take notes and retell.
• Use ⒶⒸⓉ prompts as needed.

Reread DOK 2–3

• Analyze the text, craft, and structure.

Integrate DOK 3–4

• Integrate knowledge and ideas.
• Make text-to-text connections.
• Complete the Show Your Knowledge task.
• Inspire action

Spotlight On Language

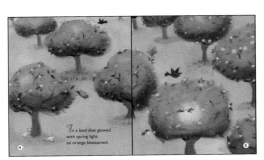

Pages 4–5

CONCEPTS OF PRINT

Point to the last word in the sentence on page 4. (blossomed) *How do you know this is the last word in the sentence?* (There is an end mark after the word. The end mark is a period.)

BUILD ORAL VOCABULARY

blossomed: a flower appeared

pp. 4–5

glowed with spring light: Explain that *spring light* is sunlight in the springtime. Remind children that spring is one of the four seasons. Point to the sun or illustrations of the sun to help explain.

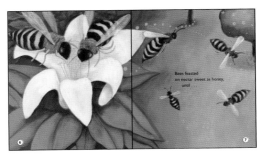

Pages 6–7

CONCEPTS OF PRINT

Think Aloud I know that the three dots after the last word on the page *(until)* means that the sentence continues on the next page. I will turn the page and keep reading to find out what happens.

BUILD ORAL VOCABULARY

feasted: ate a large amount of food

pp. 6–7

feasted: Point to the illustration on page 6. *What are the bees doing?* They are eating. Feasted *means "ate a lot of food."* Pantomime eating. *I feasted on delicious food.* Have children repeat the words as they mimic your actions.

Pages 8–9

NONFICTION DOK 2

Think Aloud I know that nonfiction text can give information in a certain order. First, the orange blossomed, which means that a flower appeared. Then the petals from the flower fell off, and the orange began to grow. These details tell about the order in which things happen as an orange grows.

pp. 8–9

meant to be: Explain that every living thing has a life cycle. A thing starts small and then grows up. Help children connect to the concept by asking: *What were you like when you were small?* Then point to the illustration on page 8. *The orange starts as a blossom. Then it grows into what it's meant to be, a fruit.*

A C T **Access Complex Text**

Use this ACT prompt when the complexity of the text makes it hard for children to understand the selection.

Sentence Structure

Many sentences in this book include ellipses. This sentence structure can confuse young readers. Make sure the words flow smoothly as you read aloud.

Point out that three dots mean that the sentence keeps going.

- Point out the word *until* on page 7. Then read aloud pages 7–9, allowing your intonation to indicate that the sentence continues. Point out that the sentence continues on the next page.

- Repeat the routine with pages 13–15 and 20–24, having children echo.

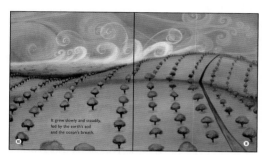

Pages 10–11

REREAD DOK 2

Think Aloud I'm not sure I understand what *It* is. I will go back and reread page 9. Now I understand that *It* is a pronoun that stands for *the orange*. The orange is what grew slowly and steadily.

BUILD ORAL VOCABULARY

steadily: a little bit at a time

pp. 10–11

fed by the earth's soil and the ocean's breath: Explain that people need food and water to live. Point to the soil in the illustration. Say *soil,* and have children repeat. *Plants need soil and water to live, just like people need food and water.*

Pages 12–13

REREAD DOK 2

Think Aloud *Soaked* and *drenched* both mean "very wet." How can something be "drenched in sunshine?" Sunshine does not make things wet. Let me reread the text. Oh, I know. Maybe *drenched in sunshine* means that the orange got lots of sunshine. The orange grew plump and bright from so much rain and sunshine.

pp. 12–13

plump: Explain that *plump* fruit is big and juicy. Say *plump.* Have children echo.

Pages 14–15

TOPIC AND DETAILS DOK 2

Think Aloud We have been reading details about how an orange grows. On this page, we learn that the orange's days of growing are over, but it still has far to go. I think the topic of the text is an orange's journey.

BUILD ORAL VOCABULARY

plucked: picked

pp. 14–15

plucked: Pretend to pick the orange on page 14. *I picked the orange. I plucked it.* Have children echo and mimic.

Pages 16–17

TOPIC AND DETAILS DOK 2

Look at the illustration. Turn to a partner and discuss: *What happens to the baskets after they are full?* (They are put onto a small truck.) *How do the illustrations help you understand the text?* (The illustrations show details that are not in the text.)

pp. 16–17

from and *to:* Explain that the words *from* and *to* can tell us where something starts and where something ends. Walk across the classroom. *I walked* from *my desk* to *the door.*

Spotlight On Language

Pages 18–19

NONFICTION DOK 1

What has happened to the orange so far? (First, the orange grew on a tree. Next, it was plucked from the tree. Then it went from a bag to a basket. Now it's on a truck.)

pp. 18–19

to: Point to one truck and then the other truck as you say *truck to truck.* To *is a direction word.* Hand a child a pen. *I give the pen to you.* Have the child repeat the phrase as he or she hands the pen to another child. Repeat until every child passes the pen and says the phrase.

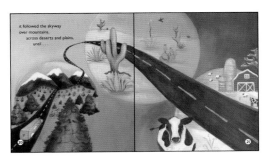

Pages 20–21

TOPIC AND DETAILS DOK 1

What followed the skyway? (the orange)
Where did the orange travel? (over mountains and across deserts and plains)

BUILD ORAL VOCABULARY

skyway: a raised highway

pp. 20–21

over; across: To guide children's understanding of these prepositions, walk your fingers over the mountains on page 20 as you say *over.* Have children echo and mimic. Then slide a finger across the plains as you say *across.* Have children repeat.

Pages 22–23

TOPIC AND DETAILS DOK 2

Where did the truck bring the oranges? (a grocery store) *How do you know?* (The text says that the orange arrived "at a grocery store." The illustration shows oranges and other types of fruits.)

BUILD ORAL VOCABULARY

aglow: glowing, or shining brightly

pp. 22–23

aglow with the goodness inside it: Point to an orange in the illustration. *Is the orange glowing?* Explain that the orange is not glowing. *"Glowing with the goodness inside it"* means the orange is really delicious on the inside.

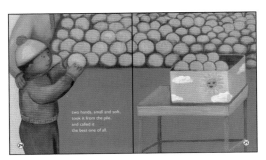

Pages 24–25

TOPIC AND DETAILS DOK 1

What detail of the orange's journey do these pages tell about? (The illustration shows that a boy came and picked out the orange. The text says that his hands "took it from the pile, and called it the best one of all.")

pp. 24–25

it: Point to an orange in the illustration. *This is an orange. It is delicious.* It *is a word we can use instead of orange.* Read the text aloud, emphasizing the pronoun *it.* Then point to the orange in the boy's hand to make it clear that *it* refers to the orange.

ELL Spotlight On Language

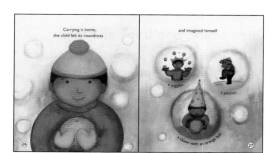

Pages 26–27

REREAD DOK 2

Think Aloud I'm not sure I understand this part of the story. I'll reread these pages to help me understand. Oh, I see. The boy imagined ways he could use his orange. He could be a juggler, or a pitcher, or a clown.

pp. 26–27

roundness: Use your finger to track the shape of the orange as you say the word *roundness.* Have children echo and mimic. Repeat the routine with other round objects in the classroom.

Pages 28–29

PHONICS

Read aloud page 28 and invite a volunteer to point to a word that begins with the /s/ sound at the beginning. (summer) Have children say the word with you. *Which letter stands for the /s/ sound?* (s)

pp. 28–29

gleamed: Explain that *gleamed* means "shined." Ask children to describe how ice looks. Guide them to recognize that it *sparkles* and *shines.* Point out that *gleamed* and *dreamed* rhyme.

Pages 30–31

TOPIC AND DETAILS DOK 1

Where does the orange's journey end? (the boy's lunch box) *What details in the illustration tell you?* (The illustration shows the boy and his mom in the kitchen. She is in her robe, so it must be morning. The boy is putting the orange in his lunch box. He must be helping to pack his lunch for school.)

pp. 30–31

bursting with the seasons inside it: Explain that oranges grow throughout the spring and summer. *What might spring and summer taste like?* Allow children to share ideas. *"Bursting with the seasons inside it"* is a way for the author to say that the orange tastes juicy and delicious.

Pages 32–33

TOPIC AND DETAILS DOK 1

What happens to the orange in the end? (It gets eaten.) *What details in the text and illustrations let you know?* (The words say that the boy's hands "shared its segments." The illustration shows the boy giving a piece of the orange to the girl next to him. The other two children are each eating a piece of orange.)

pp. 32–33

segments: A segment *is a piece.* If possible, show children the inside of an orange, pointing out the segments. Have them repeat the word *segments.* You might also use an object such as a math manipulative that contains segments.

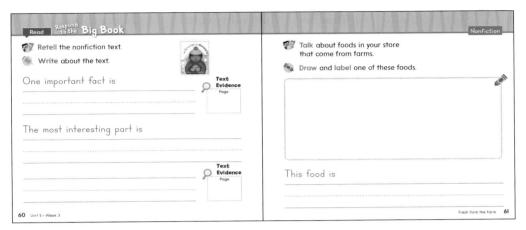

Reading/Writing Companion, pp. 60-61

Respond to the Text

Read children's predictions. Ask: *Were the predictions correct?*

Return to Purpose Remind children of their purpose for reading. Review what they learned about what happens to the orange on its journey.

- **Retell** Open the **Reading/Writing Companion** to page 60. Model for children how to retell the story in order using the text and images. You may also wish to use the **Retelling Cards** and the Retelling Routine as needed.

- **Write** Have children complete the sentence starters. First ask them to write an important fact they learned from the selection. Then ask them to write about an interesting part of the selection. Model how to find text evidence in the **Literature Big Book** to support their writing and how to record the page number in the text evidence box. You may wish to share the Big Book with each table or group of children.

- **Talk** Help children make connections between the text and their community by talking with a partner about foods found in their neighborhood store that come from farms.

- **Draw and Label** Then have them draw one of these foods on page 61. Encourage children to add labels to their drawings.

Model Fluency

Model reading sentences with ellipses. Turn to pages 6–7 of *An Orange in January*. Read aloud: *Bees feasted on nectar sweet as honey,* (pause) *until* (voice indicates that the sentence continues). Have children echo. Repeat the routine with pages 13 and 20. Then read page 22, tracking the words as you say them, and invite children to say *until* with you.

Writing Fluency

To help increase writing fluency, have children write for four minutes. Tell them to write about what they learned about the orange.

RETELLING ROUTINE

Tell children that they will use the **Retelling Cards** to retell the selection.

- Display Retelling Card 1. Based on children's needs use either the Modeled, Guided, or ELL retelling prompts. The ELL prompts include support for children based on levels of language acquisition.

- Repeat with the rest of the cards, using the prompts as a guide.

- Invite children to retell the story in order by acting out different parts of the story.

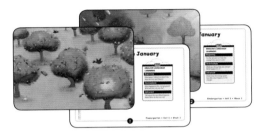

Retelling Cards

❯ STUDENT CHECK-IN

Have partners share an important detail from the text. Then have children reflect using the Check-In routine.

In a Flash: Sound-Spellings

Display the Sound-Spelling Card for *e*.

1. **Teacher:** What's the letter?   **Children:** e
2. **Teacher:** What's the sound?   **Children:** /e/
3. **Teacher:** What's the word?   **Children:** egg

Continue the routine for previously taught sounds.

LEARNING GOALS

- We can hear the sound /f/ in words.
- We can hear the sound /r/ in words.
- We can connect the sound /f/ to the letter *f*.
- We can connect the sound /r/ to the letter *r*.

OBJECTIVES

Isolate and pronounce the initial sounds in three-phoneme words.

Demonstrate basic knowledge of one-to-one letter-sound correspondences by producing the primary sound or many of the most frequent sounds for each consonant.

ELA ACADEMIC LANGUAGE

- *connect, letter*
- Cognates: *conectar, letra*

▷ TEACH IN SMALL GROUP

You may wish to teach the Word Work lessons in small groups.

ELL ENGLISH LANGUAGE LEARNERS

Phonemic Awareness, Guided Practice/Practice Encourage children to say the phoneme /f/ several times. Point to a card, and ask children to name it. Help them self-correct by modeling pronunciation. Then help children identify the initial sound using a sentence frame: Feet begins with the sound /f/. Repeat the routine with the Photo Cards for /r/.

Phonemic Awareness: p. 226–227
Phonics: p. 229–230

5 mins Phonemic Awareness

MULTIMODAL

Phoneme Isolation

1 **Model** Display the **Photo Card** for *fire*. *Listen for the sound at the beginning of* fire. Fire *has the /f/ sound at the beginning.* Say these words and have children repeat: *fast, fish.* Emphasize the phoneme /f/. Repeat with /r/ using the *rose* Photo Card and the words *red, right.*

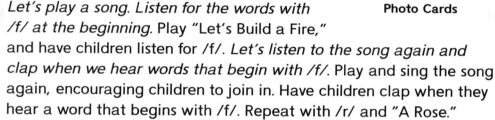

Photo Cards

♪ *Let's play a song. Listen for the words with /f/ at the beginning.* Play "Let's Build a Fire," and have children listen for /f/. *Let's listen to the song again and clap when we hear words that begin with /f/.* Play and sing the song again, encouraging children to join in. Have children clap when they hear a word that begins with /f/. Repeat with /r/ and "A Rose."

2 **Guided Practice/Practice** Display and name the following Photo Cards: *feet, five, fan. Say each picture name with me. Tell me the sound at the beginning of the word.* Guide practice and provide corrective feedback as needed. If children need additional practice identifying the /f/ and /r/ sounds, use **Practice Book** pages 226–227. Repeat with /r/ and the *rock, rabbit,* and *rope* Photo Cards.

Articulation Support

Demonstrate the way to say /f/. Put your top front teeth on your lower lip. Don't use your voice. Push air through your teeth. Hold your hand in front of your mouth as you practice. Can you feel the air? Say *fish, fan, fed* and have children repeat. Stretch /f/.

Demonstrate the way to say /r/. Open your mouth a little. Move your tongue to the back of your mouth. Put the tip of your tongue close to, but not touching, the top of your mouth. Use your voice, and let air move over the top of your tongue. Say *run, rat, rip* and have children repeat. Stretch initial /r/.

Phonics

10 mins

MULTIMODAL

Introduce /f/f and /r/r

1 Model Display the *fire* **Sound-Spelling Card**. *This is the* fire *card. The sound is /f/. The /f/ sound is spelled with the letter* f. *Say it with me: /f/. This is the sound at the beginning of* fire. *Listen: /fff/ /ire/,* fire.

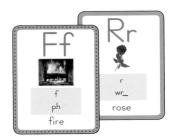

Sound-Spelling Cards

Display "Let's Build a Fire." (See **Spelling Song** online.) Read or sing the song with children. Reread the title and point out that *fire* begins with the letter *f*. Model placing a self-stick note below the *f* in *fire*.

2 Guided Practice/Practice Read each line of the song. Stop after each line and ask children to place self-stick notes below words that begin with *F* or *f* and say the letter name and the sound it stands for. If children need additional practice connecting letter *f* with the sound /f/ or the letter *r* with the sound /r/, use **Practice Book** pages 229–230. Repeat Steps 1–2 with /r/ *r* and the song "A Rose."

Corrective Feedback

Sound Error Say /f/, then have children repeat the sound. *My turn.* Fire. */fff/. Now it's your turn.* Have children say the words *food* and *fine* and isolate /f/. Repeat for /r/r with *rose, rabbit, run.*

Let's Build a Fire

"Let's build a fire," Fiona said to Farley.

"Let's build a fire and invite all our friends.

You bring the hot dogs. I'll bring the buns.

Let's build a fire and we'll have a lot of fun."

A Rose

A rose is nice.

A rose is sweet.

It's the loveliest flower that you will meet.

But here is a warning and a word to the wise:

Be careful or you're in for a sharp surprise!

ELL ENGLISH LANGUAGE LEARNERS

Phonics Transfers Use the chart on pages 10–13 in the **Language Transfers Handbook** to check for sound-spelling transfers from a child's native language into English. You can use the **Sound-Spelling Cards** to support teaching transferable and nontransferable skills.

DIGITAL TOOLS

Word Work — **Phonemic Awareness Phonics**

Phonics: Spelling Song

PHONICS video — **Phonics Video**

To differentiate instruction, use these results.

Phonics: Data-Generating

FORMATIVE ASSESSMENT

⊙ STUDENT CHECK-IN

Have partners name the letter that stands for /f/ and the letter that stands for /r/. Then have children reflect using the Check-In routine.

WORD WORK **T171**

READING • WORD WORK

- We can print the letters *f* and *r*.
- We can learn to read the words *with* and *he*.

OBJECTIVES

Print many upper- and lowercase letters.

Read common high-frequency words by sight.

ELA ACADEMIC LANGUAGE

- uppercase, lowercase

DIGITAL TOOLS

Handwriting

High-Frequency Words

To differentiate instruction, use these results.

High-Frequency Words: Data-Generating

MULTIMODAL LEARNING

Center Idea Have children move their hands like they are using a fan and say /f/. Have them pretend to race a car as they say /r/.

Handwriting: p. 233

T172   UNIT 5 WEEK 3

MULTIMODAL

Handwriting: Write *Ff* and *Rr*

⏱ 5 mins

1   **Model** Say the cues as you write and identify both forms of *Ff*. Then trace the letters as you say the sounds.

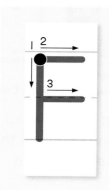

Straight down.
Straight across.
Straight across.

Circle back a little, then straight down. Go to the dotted line. Straight across.

2   **Guided Practice**

- Say the cues together as children trace both forms of the letter with their index finger. Have children identify the uppercase and lowercase forms of the letter.
- Have children use their index finger to write *F and f* on the rug or a table as they say /f/ multiple times.

3   **Practice**

- Distribute **Response Boards**. Have children write *F* and *f* on their Response Boards as they say /f/ each time they write the letter.
- Observe children's pencil grip and paper position, and correct as necessary. Guide practice and provide corrective feedback.

Repeat steps with *Rr*.

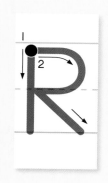

Straight down. Go back to the top. Around and in at the dotted line. Slant down.

Straight down. Curl forward.

🖉 Daily Handwriting

Throughout the week, teach upper- and lowercase *Ff* and *Rr* using the Handwriting models. At the end of the week, have children use **Practice Book** page 233.

In a Flash: High-Frequency Words

1. **Teacher:** Read the word.   **Children:** are
2. **Teacher:** Spell the word.   **Children:** a-r-e
3. **Teacher:** Write the word.   **Children write the word.**

Repeat routine with *to, and, go, you, do,* and *my* from previous weeks.

High-Frequency Words

MULTIMODAL

with	he

1 **Model** Display the **High-Frequency Word Cards** for *with* and *he*. Use the Read/Spell/Write routine to teach the words.

- **Read** Point to the word *with* and say the word. *This is the word* with. *Say it with me:* with. *He came* with *me to pick oranges.*

- **Spell** *The word* with *is spelled* w-i-t-h. *Spell it with me.*

- **Write** *Let's write* with *on our **Response Boards** as we say each letter:* w-i-t-h. Guide children on how to print *w.*

- Point out to children that the letter *i* in *with* has the same /i/ sound as in *sit.* Explain that the letters *t* and *h* do not have the same sounds as the /t/ in *tip* or the /h/ in *hot.*

- Have partners say sentences using the word.

Repeat the routine to introduce *he.* Use the sentence on page 28 of the Big Book. "That night, as ice gleamed on the branches, *he* dreamed of a land that shone in summer light."

- Point out that the letter *h* in *he* has the same /h/ as in *hat* but the letter *e* in *he* does not have the same /e/ sound in *egg.*

2 **Guided Practice/Practice** Build sentences using the High-Frequency Word Cards, **Photo Cards**, and teacher-made punctuation cards. Have children point to the high-frequency words *with* and *he.* Use these sentences.

He can jump with you.
Can he go with you?

Guide practice and provide corrective feedback as needed.

ELL ENGLISH LANGUAGE LEARNERS

Use with **High-Frequency Words, Guided Practice/Practice** and the **High-Frequency Word Routine.**

Beginning
We can use with *to show that things go together. Who are you sitting with?* Have children repeat. Repeat with *he.*

Intermediate
Point to each card as you read the first sentence. Ask children to repeat. Have a volunteer point to *with.* Repeat for *he.*

Advanced/Advanced High
Have partners create sentences with the words.

FORMATIVE ASSESSMENT

❯ STUDENT CHECK-IN

Handwriting Have children print *Ff* and *Rr.*

High-Frequency Words Have partners take turns pointing to and reading the words *with* and *he.*

Then have children reflect using the Check-In routine.

✓ CHECK FOR SUCCESS

Rubric Use your online rubric to record children's progress.

Can children isolate /f/ and /r/ and match the sounds to the letters *Ff* and *Rr*? Can children recognize and read the high-frequency words?

❯ Small Group Instruction

If No
- **Approaching** Reteach pp. T218–222
- **ELL** Develop pp. T218–222

If Yes
- **On** Review pp. T226–228
- **Beyond** Extend pp. T232

LESSON 1

Literature Big Book

LEARNING GOALS

- We can write about our favorite fruit.
- We can learn about words that can take the place of nouns (pronouns).

OBJECTIVES

Use a combination of drawing, dictating, and writing to compose opinion pieces in which they state an opinion or preference about the topic.

Spell simple words phonetically, drawing on knowledge of sound-letter relationships.

Appropriately use pronouns.

ELA ACADEMIC LANGUAGE

- *noun, pronoun*
- Cognates: *nombre, pronombre*

 COLLABORATIVE CONVERSATIONS

Turn and Talk Review this routine.

Child 1: I like melon.

Child 2: Can you tell me more?

Child 1: I like melon because it is sweet.

Display the speech bubble, "Can you tell me more?" Have partners use it to practice collaborating.

---

 10 mins

Modeled Writing

Model Writing About the Literature Big Book

 Build Oral Language Talk about what children learned from listening to the **Literature Big Book**. Review what they learned about oranges. Ask: *What is your favorite fruit?* Have partners use the Turn and Talk routine to talk about why they like their favorite fruit. When children are done, encourage them to share out what they talked about with their partner.

Model Writing a Sentence Write and display the following sentence: **Grapes are my favorite fruit**. Then point out the following elements of writing using the Sample Teacher Talk.

- *This is the word* grapes. *I stretched the sounds in the word* grapes *to help me write the beginning, middle, and end sounds.* **WRITING SKILL**

- *This is the word* are. *I used the Word Bank to help me spell the word.* Are *is spelled with the letters:* a-r-e. **HIGH-FREQUENCY WORD**

- *I wrote the words* favorite *and* fruit. *I hear the /f/ sound at the beginning of both words. I know the letter* f *stands for the sound /f/, so I know* favorite *and* fruit *start with* f. **PHONICS SKILL**

> What is your favorite fruit?
>
> Grapes are my favorite fruit.

 ## Writing Practice

Explain to children that they will write a sentence that tells about their favorite fruit. Have children turn and talk with a partner about the fruit they plan to write about.

Draw/Write Tell children to draw a picture of their favorite fruit. Encourage them to write a sentence about their drawing. As children write, remind them to use the Word Bank, to listen for sounds they know, and to stretch words to write the beginning, middle, and end sounds.

If needed, provide the following sentence starter: **I like _____.**

Grammar

5 mins

Subjective Pronouns

1 **Model** Remind children that a pronoun can take the place of a noun in a sentence. Review the pronouns children have learned: *he, she, it, we, you,* and *I.* Write and read aloud: **they.** They *is a pronoun that takes the place of the names of two or more people.* Write and read aloud: **Jane and Mike eat corn. They eat corn.** Point out that *they* takes the place of *Jane and Mike.*

2 **Guided Practice** Write and read the sentences below. Guide children to identify the nouns that the pronoun *they* can replace.

Emma and Eli read a book. (Emma and Eli)
Kate and Spot play fetch. (Kate and Spot)

3 **Practice** Write the sentences below on sentence strips and read them aloud. Group children in pairs and provide each with one set of sentence strips. Ask partners to circle the nouns on their sentence strips that the pronoun *they* could replace.

Mom and Dad pick apples. (Mom and Dad)
Maya and Max plant flower seeds. (Maya and Max)

Talk About It Have partners generate sentences, using the pronoun *they.* Challenge children to tell who *they* refers to in their sentences.

Link to Writing Review the sentences from the Shared Writing activity. Have children identify any pronouns they may have used.

English Language Learners

Use the following scaffolds with **Grammar, Practice.**

Beginning

Mom and Dad pick apples. Who picks apples? They *pick apples.* Have children repeat. Repeat for the other sentence.

Intermediate

Have pairs point to nouns, or names, in the first sentence. Then have them use a pronoun with the sentence frame: They *pick pumpkins.* Repeat with the second sentence.

Advanced/Advanced High

Have partners read aloud the sentences with the nouns and the pronoun *they.* Challenge them to make new sentences using *they.*

DIGITAL TOOLS

Grammar
Activity

Grammar
Song

Grammar
Video

DIFFERENTIATED WRITING

● **English Language Learners** For more writing support, see the **ELL Small Group Guide,** p. 128.

FORMATIVE ASSESSMENT

◗ STUDENT CHECK-IN

Have partners share one thing they know about pronouns. Then have children reflect using the Check-In routine.

LEARNING GOALS

- We can tell if words rhyme.
- We can use new words.
- We can learn words that tell about food.
- We can use clues to find the meaning of a word.

OBJECTIVES

Recognize rhyming words.

Use words and phrases acquired through conversations, reading and being read to, and responding to texts.

Sort common objects into categories to gain a sense of the concepts the categories represent.

Use context clues.

ELA ACADEMIC LANGUAGE

- clues, sort

DIGITAL TOOLS

Weekly Song

Visual Vocabulary Cards

Category Words Activity

LESSON FOCUS

READING
Review Essential Question
Reread Literature Big Book
An Orange in January
• Study Genre/Skill
Read Shared Read
"Ron With Red"
• Practice Strategy

Word Work
• Practice /f/f, /r/r
WRITING
Writing/Grammar
• Interactive Writing
• Practice Grammar

Literature Big Book, pp. 3–33

Reading/Writing Companion, pp. 66–73

Oral Language

10 mins

MULTIMODAL

? Essential Question

What kinds of things grow on a farm?

Remind children that this week we are learning about things that grow on farms. *What foods grow on the farms? Let's sing a song about foods that grow on farms.* Sing "Oats Peas, Beans, and Barley Grow" with children. Then use the Build Knowledge anchor chart, the **Big Book,** and the **Weekly Song** to guide children in discussing the Essential Question.

Phonological Awareness: Identify Rhyme

1 **Model** Tell children that these words from the song rhyme: *grow* and *know*. Remind them that words that rhyme have the same end sounds. Have children repeat *grow* and *know* after you, stressing the end sounds.

2 **Guided Practice/Practice** Say each of the following sets of words. Have children raise their hands if they hear words that rhyme: cub/tub, wall/wish, lag/tag, rake/take, ball/bat, hot/tab. Guide practice and provide feedback as needed. If children need additional practice identifying rhyming words, have them use **Practice Book** page 225.

Review Oral Vocabulary Words

Use the Define/Example/Ask routine to review the oral vocabulary words *fresh* and *delicious*. Prompt children to use the words in sentences.

Visual Vocabulary Cards

Category Words: Food Words

1 **Model** Use the **Big Book** *An Orange in January* to talk about food words. Turn to the title page and point to each piece of fruit, saying its name with children. Display the **Photo Card** for *cherry* and say: *A cherry is another kind of fruit.* Then hold up the Photo Card of the *carrots* and say: *Carrots are vegetables. Fruits and vegetables are two kinds of food.*

Now display the Photo Cards for *apple, grapes, carrots,* and *peas* and recite the rhyme below. Have children think about which of these foods are fruits and which are vegetables.

Apples grow on trees, and grapes come from a vine. Carrots grow underground, and peas form in a line.

Which foods are fruits? Which are vegetables? Guide children as they sort the cards appropriately.

2 **Guided Practice/Practice** Display the Photo Cards for *banana, cherry, peach, lemon, corn, celery, peas,* and *zucchini* in random order. Have groups of children take turns sorting the cards into the categories "fruits" and "vegetables." Guide practice as needed.

Vocabulary: Sentence Clues

1 **Model** Remind children that they can ask questions about words they do not know. Explain that they can also use clues from other words in the sentence or in nearby sentences to figure out the meaning of unknown words. Use *An Orange in January* to model sentence clues.

Think Aloud What does *nectar* mean in this sentence? "Bees feasted on nectar, sweet as honey, until the petals fell away and the orange began to grow." The sentence tells me that nectar is sweet. I know that bees like to eat sweet things. The sentence talks about flower petals, and I know that bees feed on flowers. The clues tell me that nectar is something sweet that bees drink from flowers.

2 **Guided Practice/Practice** Have children figure out the meaning of *glowed* in this sentence from the selection: *In a land that glowed with spring light, an orange blossomed.* Tell children that the word *light* is a clue. Guide practice as needed to help them understand that *glowed* means "shiny" or "bright."

KIDS ON THE MOVE!

Have children stand up. Tell them that you are going to name different fruits and vegetables. If you name a fruit, children should raise both hands high in the air. If you name a vegetable, they should put their hands on their knees.

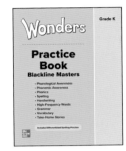

Phonological Awareness: p. 225

ELL ENGLISH LANGUAGE LEARNERS

Context Clues: Sentence Clues, Guided Practice/Practice Read aloud the sentence in **Think Aloud**. Point to and say the word *nectar* and have children repeat. *How does the nectar taste?* Then point to the sentence clue. The nectar tastes as sweet as honey. *What is nectar?* Nectar is something sweet to eat.

FORMATIVE ASSESSMENT

STUDENT CHECK-IN

Oral Vocabulary Words Have partners say a sentence using a vocabulary word.

Category Words Have partners name a fruit or vegetable.

Vocabulary Have partners explain how to use clues to find the meaning of a word.

Then have children reflect using the Check-In routine.

LESSON 2

Literature Big Book

OBJECTIVES

Recognize common types of texts.

With prompting and support, identify the main topic and retell key details of a text.

Actively engage in group reading activities with purpose and understanding.

ELA ACADEMIC LANGUAGE

• *reread, nonfiction*

• Cognate: *no ficción*

Reread

10 mins

Literature Big Book

Genre: Nonfiction

1 **Model** Tell children that you will now reread the **Literature Big Book** *An Orange in January*. Remind them that this selection is a nonfiction text.

Anchor Chart Display and review the characteristics of nonfiction text that you have listed on the Nonfiction anchor chart. Add details as needed.

Think Aloud I know that the selection *An Orange in January* is a nonfiction text because it gives information in a certain order. The first few pages of the selection tell us how the orange grows. First, it blossoms, then the petals from the flower fall off, and last, the orange begins to grow. These details tell about the order in which things happen as the orange grows.

2 **Guided Practice/Practice** Read pages 15–23 of *An Orange in January*. Ask children about the sequence of events. *What happens first?* (The orange is plucked from a tree.) *Then what happens?* (The orange goes from a bag to a basket. Once the basket is full, it is placed on a truck.) *What happens next?* (The truck brings the orange to a grocery store.)

ELL English Language Learners

Genre: Informational Text, Guided Practice/Practice Review the words *first, next, then,* and *last*. Have children repeat. Read page 15. *What happens first to the orange?* Help children discuss with a partner by providing a sentence frame: First, the orange is plucked from the tree. Repeat the routine for pages 16–23 using the words *next, then,* and *last*. Provide sentence frames to help children tell the story events in order.

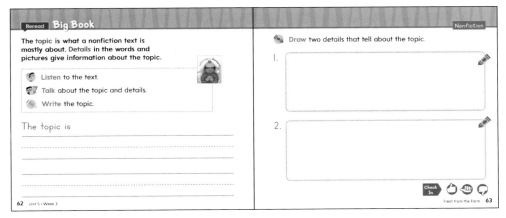

Reading/Writing Companion, pp. 62-63

Topic and Details

1 **Model** Explain that identifying the topic and details of a selection can help readers understand it better. Have children turn to page 62 in the **Reading/Writing Companion**. Read the definitions of topic and details aloud and discuss with children.

 Anchor Chart Display the Topic and Details anchor chart. Remind children to look for the topic and details as they read.

Think Aloud I know that this book is about what happens to an orange. That is the topic of the text. Let's find a detail that supports the topic, or gives more information about it. On page 24 the boy chooses the orange from a pile of oranges in a grocery store. This detail tells me more about what happens to the orange on its journey from the tree to the boy's home.

2 **Guided Practice/Practice** Have children talk about the topic and then write it on page 62 of the Reading/Writing Companion. Then tell them to listen for details as you reread pages 22–23 of *An Orange in January* aloud. Guide children to draw two details in the boxes on page 63. Have children point to the details they drew and tell how they support the topic. Say: *Think about the details you drew. What do they tell about what happens to the orange?*

ENGLISH LANGUAGE LEARNERS

Topic and Details, Guided Practice/Practice Have partners discuss the topic. Provide a sentence frame: The topic is about oranges. Reread pages 22–25. *What details about the topic do you learn in these pages?* Have partners discuss the detail. Provide a sentence frame to help them respond: A detail is a boy picks an orange from the grocery store. Repeat the routine with pages 26–33. Then have children draw one of the details they discussed.

For additional support, see the **ELL Small Group Guide**, pp. 126-127.

FORMATIVE ASSESSMENT

STUDENT CHECK-IN

Genre Have partners identify one way they know the text is nonfiction.

Topic and Details Have children take turns identifying the topic and multiple details.

Then have children reflect on their learning using the Check-In routine.

CHECK FOR SUCCESS

Can children identify characteristics of nonfiction text?

Can children identify topic and details?

Small Group Instruction

If No

● **Approaching** Reteach pp. T216–217

If Yes

● **On** Review pp. T224–225

● **Beyond** Extend pp. T230–231

LESSON 2

Literature Big Book

LEARNING GOALS

We can name the choices an author/illustrator made when writing a text.

OBJECTIVES

With prompting and support, describe the relationship between illustrations and the text in which they appear.

With guidance and support from adults, explore word relationships and nuances in word meanings.

Identify new meanings for familiar words and apply them accurately.

Analyze author and illustrator's craft.

Analyze author's purpose.

ELA ACADEMIC LANGUAGE

• *author, illustrator*

• Cognates: *autor, ilustrador*

Reread

 10 mins

Literature Big Book

Analyze the Text

Once children have reread *An Orange in January* to study the characteristics of the genre and practice the comprehension skill, guide them to analyze the author's craft. Reread the passages specified below and use the scaffolded instruction in the prompts to help children answer the questions on pages 64–65 of the **Reading/Writing Companion**.

ORGANIZATION DOK 2

Display and reread pages 12–15 of the **Big Book**. *The author tells the story of the orange in sequence, or time order. What happens to the orange on these pages?* (It has finished growing, and someone picks it.) *What words hint at what will happen next?* ("it still had far to go")

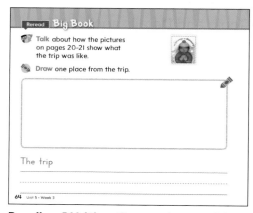

Reading/Writing Companion, p. 64

AUTHOR/ILLUSTRATOR'S CRAFT DOK 2

Display and reread pages 20–21 of the Big Book. *Why did the illustrator draw such a long road on these pages?* (to show that the truck carries the orange a long way) *How does the illustration help you understand the text?* (The illustration shows the truck on a long, curvy road. The road goes through the mountains, across the desert, and past a farm. The text says that the truck "followed the skyway over mountains, across deserts and plains.")

English Language Learners

Have children point to the part of the illustration that matches each description as you say: *These are the mountains. This is the desert.* Have children repeat after you. Then say: *Trace the road with your finger. Is it a long road or a short road? Is it a straight road or a curvy road?* Have partners discuss. Provide sentence frames: The road is long. The road is curvy.

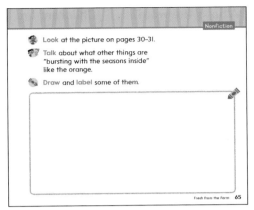

Reading/Writing Companion, p. 65

WORD CHOICE DOK 2

Display and reread pages 30–31 of the **Big Book**. *What does the author mean by saying that the orange was "bursting with the seasons inside it"?* (Possible responses: The author means that the orange had spring, summer, and fall inside it. The orange grew during those seasons in a place where there was sunshine and rain to make it plump and juicy.) *What other things are "bursting with the seasons inside" them?* (bananas, grapes, and apples)

AUTHOR'S PURPOSE DOK 3

Display and reread pages 32–33 of the Big Book. Ask: *Why do you think the author chose "An Orange in January" for the title of this book?* (Possible responses: to show all the things that must happen so that people can eat oranges in the winter; to help us see that oranges don't grow in cold places but have to come from warmer places)

 # Spotlight on Language

Read pages 32–33 and have partners discuss the illustrations. Provide the following sentence frames: I see children swinging. It is snowing outside. *Why did the author title the book* An Orange in January*?* Have children discuss. (It is January. The children are eating oranges. The oranges come from far away.)

Talk About It

Guide children to use their responses on the **Reading/Writing Companion** pages to answer the question: *What does the author want you to understand about oranges?* Use the following sentence starter to focus the discussion and help children cite text evidence: **An orange_____.**

Integrate

 ### Build Knowledge: Make Connections

Talk About the Text Have partners discuss the farm in the text. *What grew on the farm? What helped it grow?*

Add to the Anchor Chart Record any new ideas on the Build Knowledge Anchor Chart.

 **FORMATIVE ASSESSMENT**

❯ STUDENT CHECK-IN

Have partners share something that the author/illustrator does with the text or images. Then have children reflect using the Check-In routine.

In a Flash: Sound-Spellings

Display the Sound-Spelling Card for *f*.
1. **Teacher:** What's the letter?   **Children:** f
2. **Teacher:** What's the sound?   **Children:** /f/
3. **Teacher:** What's the word?   **Children:** fire

Continue the routine for *r* and previously taught sounds.

LEARNING GOALS

- We can blend sounds to say words.
- We can connect letters to sounds to read words.
- We can read the words *with* and *he*.

OBJECTIVES

Demonstrate understanding of spoken words, syllables, and sounds (phonemes).

Demonstrate basic knowledge of one-to-one letter-sound correspondences by producing the primary sound or many of the most frequent sounds for each consonant.

Read common high-frequency words by sight.

Blend phonemes to form words.

ELA ACADEMIC LANGUAGE

- *blend, connect, words*
- Cognate: *conectar*

⊳ TEACH IN SMALL GROUP

You may wish to teach the Word Work lesson in small groups.

DIGITAL TOOLS

Word Work — Phonemic Awareness Phonics

High-Frequency Word

Phonics: Data-Generating

High-Frequency Words: Data-Generating

 OPTIONAL 5 mins

Phonemic Awareness

Phoneme Blending

1 **Model** Say: *I am going to say the sounds in a word: /f/ /a/ /n/. I can blend those sounds to make the word: /fffaaannn/, fan. Listen as I say more sounds and blend them to make words.* Model phoneme blending with the following.

/f/ /i/ /t/ fit	/f/ /ī/ /n/ fine	/f/ /i/ /n/ fin	/i/ /f/ if

2 **Guided Practice/Practice** *Listen to the sounds in a different word: /f/ /e/ /d/. Let's blend the sounds and say the word together: /f/ /e/ /d/, /fffeeed/ fed.* Tell children to listen to the sounds in words, repeat the sounds, and then blend them to say the word. Guide practice and provide corrective feedback as needed.

/f/ /a/ /n/ fan	/f/ /u/ /n/ fun	/f/ /ē/ /t/ feet

Repeat Steps 1–2 with /r/ and the words *red, rug, ran* for Step 1 and *rat, ride, rise* for Step 2.

 5 mins

Phonics

 MULTIMODAL

Review *f* and *r*

1 **Model** Display the *fire* **Sound-Spelling Card**. *This is the letter* f. *The letter* f *stands for the sound /f/ as in the word* fire. Repeat for /r/ *r* with the *rose* Sound-Spelling Card.

2 **Guided Practice/Practice** Display the *fire* Sound-Spelling Card and point to the letter *Ff*. Have children say the letter name and sound with you. Then repeat, pointing to the *Rr* on the *rose* Sound-Spelling Card and asking children to say the letter name and sound. Have children listen as you say some words. Ask them to write the letter *f* on their **Response Boards** if the word begins with /f/ or the letter *r* if the word begins with /r/.

four	rest	follow	five	read	foot
rip	fun	red	ripe	fix	row

Blend Words with *f* and *r*

1 **Model** Place **Word-Building Cards** *r*, *e*, and *d* in a pocket chart. Point to *r*. *This is the letter* r. *The letter* r *stands for /r/. Say /r/. This is the letter* e. *The letter* e *stands for /e/. Say /e/. This is the letter* d. *The letter* d *stands for /d/. Say /d/. Listen as I blend the three sounds together: /rrreeed/ red. Let's blend the sounds to read the word.*

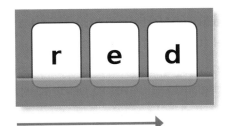

2 **Guided Practice/Practice** Change Word-Building Cards to *r*, *i*, *p*. Point to the letter *r* and have children say /r/. Point to the letter *i* and have children say /i/. Point to the letter *p* and have children say /p/. Then move your hand from left to right under the word and have children blend and read the word *rip*. Repeat with *rat*. Guide practice and provide corrective feedback as needed.

Repeat Steps 1–2 with *f* using the words *fat, fin, fit.*

OPTIONAL
5 mins

High-Frequency Words

 MULTIMODAL

with	he

1 **Guided Practice** Display the **High-Frequency Word Cards** *with* and *he*. Use the Read/Spell/Write routine to teach each word. Then ask children to write the words without looking at the word cards. If needed, guide children on how to form the letter *w* because it has not been taught yet. Then have children self-correct by checking the High-Frequency Word Cards.

COLLABORATE

2 **Practice** Add the words *he* and *with* to the cumulative word bank.

• Have partners say sentences using the words.

Cumulative Review Review the high-frequency words *are, my, do, you,* and *go* by displaying each word and having children read it with automaticity.

• For additional practice with high-frequency words, see **Practice Book** page 234.

ELL ENGLISH LANGUAGE LEARNERS

Blend Words with *f* and *r*, Guided Practice/Practice Remind children of the sounds that each letter stands for. Then have children repeat saying /r/, /i/, and /p/ as you point to the respective cards. Move your hand from left to right, and blend the sounds in *rip*. Then have children blend the new word with you.

High-Frequency Words: p. 234

FORMATIVE ASSESSMENT

STUDENT CHECK-IN

Phonics Have partners blend and read *red* and *fed*.

High-Frequency Words Have partners take turns pointing to and reading *with* and *he*.

Then have children reflect using the Check-In routine.

CHECK FOR SUCCESS

Rubric Use your online rubric to record children's progress.

Can children blend phonemes with /f/ and /r/ to make words and match /f/ to *Ff* and /r/ to *Rr*? Can children recognize and read the high-frequency words?

Small Group Instruction

If No

● **Approaching** Reteach pp. T218–222

● **ELL** Develop pp. T218–222

If Yes

● **On** Review pp. T226–228

● **Beyond** Extend p. T232

LESSON 2

LEARNING GOALS

We can read and understand a story.

OBJECTIVES

Recognize that spoken words are represented in written language by specific sequences of letters.

Know and apply grade-level phonics and word analysis skills in decoding words.

Demonstrate basic knowledge of one-to-one letter-sound correspondences by producing the primary sound or many of the most frequent sounds for each consonant.

Read common high-frequency words by sight.

Read emergent-reader texts with purpose and understanding.

With prompting and support, retell familiar stories, including key details.

ELA ACADEMIC LANGUAGE
• retell

DIFFERENTIATED READING

● **English Language Learners**
Have children listen to a summary of the selection, available in multiple languages.

(10 mins) # Read "Ron With Red"

Connect to Concept

As children read this story, have them look for details that will help them answer the Essential Question: *What kinds of things grow on a farm?*

Foundational Skills

Book Handling Hold up the **Reading/Writing Companion** and identify the front and back covers. Model turning the pages.

Concepts of Print Turn to page 67 and read the first sentence, tracking the print with your finger to help children develop print-to-speech match.

Phonics Have children review the letters *f* and *r* and the sound each letter stands for.

High-Frequency Words Have children review the words *he* and *with*.

Read the Shared Read

Reread Remind children that they can stop and reread parts of the text as they read if they have trouble understanding the story.

 Anchor Chart Review the Reread anchor chart with children. Keep it displayed as they read to remind them to apply the strategy as needed.

Choral Read Before reading, review each rebus and discuss what it stands for. Then have children chorally read the selection with you.

Read Tell children that now they will read the story, and you will pause to ask the questions in the blue column. Explain that they can circle the image, the rebus, or both.

Have children use the box on the right-hand pages to do the following:

• Draw a picture about the text or the art.

• Draw something whose name begins with the /f/ or /r/ sounds.

• Write the letters *f* or *r*.

Reading/Writing Companion, pp. 66–67

SET PURPOSE

Have children read to find out what Ron and Red do.

HIGH-FREQUENCY WORDS

Have children circle and read the high-frequency word *with*.

Reading/Writing Companion, pp. 68–69

Reading/Writing Companion, pp. 70–71

Reading/Writing Companion, pp. 72–73

HIGH-FREQUENCY WORDS

Ask children to underline and read the high-frequency word *He.*

PHONICS

Have children circle the word that begins with the same sound as *fed.* (fit) Guide them to blend the sounds to read the word.

PHONICS

Have children circle the words that begin with he same sound as *rat.* (Red, Ron) Guide them to blend the sounds to read the words.

COMPREHENSION

Have children find words that tell where the bird is. (on top)

CONCEPTS OF PRINT

Read and point to each word in the sentences on page 73.

COMPREHENSION

Have children use the pictures to retell the story in order. Tell them to identify the setting as part of their retelling.

Focus on Fluency: Accuracy

Model reading with accuracy for children. Remind them of the importance of recognizing high-frequency words as well as decoding words in the text correctly. Encourage children to practice reading for accuracy with a partner. Listen in and offer support and corrective feedback as needed.

Respond to the Text

Talk About It Have children talk about what Ron and Red do at the farm. Use the sentence frame to focus the discussion: **Ron and Red**_____. Help children cite text evidence to support their answers.

ENGLISH LANGUAGE LEARNERS

Use these scaffolds with **Respond to the Text.**

Beginning
Point to page 68. Say *bird,* and have children repeat. *What do Ron and Red see?* Provide the sentence frame: Ron and Red see a bird.

Intermediate
Reread pages 68–71. Have pairs use sentence frames to tell what the family sees: Dad sees oranges. Ron and Red see a bird. Mom sees tomatoes.

Advanced/Advanced High
Have pairs discuss what happens at the farm. Ask them to use complete sentences, such as: *Ron and Red see a bird at the farm.*

FORMATIVE ASSESSMENT

◉ STUDENT CHECK-IN

Have partners take turns sharing their retelling of the story with one another. Then have children reflect using the Check-In routine.

Literature Big Book

⏱ 10 mins

Interactive Writing

Write About the Literature Big Book

 COLLABORATE

Analyze the Prompt Tell children that today they will write about the **Literature Big Book,** *An Orange in January.* Ask: *Where did the orange begin and end its journey?* Turn to page 4 of the Big Book. Reread the text and have children look at the picture. Have partners turn and talk about where this orange began its journey.

Find Text Evidence Turn to and reread pages 8 and 9. Ask children what else they can tell about the orange's beginning. Encourage children to use the text and illustrations to find evidence, or clues, about the orange's journey.

Write a Response: Share the Pen Have children provide a response to the prompt and encourage them to share the pen to help you write a response. Alternatively, use the following sentence: **It began on a tree and ended with a boy.** Then point out the following elements of writing using the Sample Teacher Talk below.

- *What sounds do you hear when I say the word it? Stretch the word to write the sounds for each letter: /iiit/,* it. **WRITING SKILL**

- Say *began. What is the last sound we hear? /n/ Who can come up to the board and write the letter that stands for the /n/ sound?* **PHONICS**

- *We can look at the Word Bank to help us spell the word* and. *Who can point to the word* and? *Let's spell it:* a-n-d. Have volunteers write the word as they are able. **HIGH-FREQUENCY WORDS**

- *When we write, we tell the events in the order that they happened. First, we wrote first that the orange began on a tree.* **TRAIT: ORGANIZATION**

> Where did the orange begin and end its journey?
>
> It began on a tree and ended with a boy.

Writing Practice

Write Provide children with the following sentence starters and have them complete them in their writer's notebook.

First, the orange began _____.   **Last, the orange ended _____.**

As children write, encourage them to:

- Use the Word Bank to help spell high-frequency words.
- Stretch the sounds they hear in words as they write.
- Stretch words to write the beginning, middle, and end sounds.
- Write the events in order, or sequence.

Stephen Coburn/Shutterstock

Grammar

Subjective Pronouns

1 **Model** Remind children that a pronoun can take the place of a noun. Write on index cards and read aloud: *he, she, it, they, we, you,* and *I.* Point out that *I* is always written with a capital letter.

Write the following sentences and sentence frames. Place the appropriate pronoun index card in the correct blank.

Grace is my friend. _____ **likes corn.** *(She)*
An orange is a fruit. _____ **is round.** *(It)*
My parents eat vegetables. _____ **like peas.** *(They)*

2 **Guided Practice** Write and read aloud: **Dana and Olivia are friends.** _____ **pick strawberries every summer.** Guide children to identify the pronoun index card to fill in the blank. (They) They *is the best pronoun for this sentence because* they *can be used in place of the names of two or more people.* Repeat the activity with: **My dog and I go for walks.** _____ **go twice a day.** (We)

3 **Practice** Write and read: _____ **like to eat peaches.** Have children work with a partner to choose a pronoun index card that will correctly complete the sentence. Have them place that pronoun index card in the blank. Then, give each pair a sentence strip and have them write the completed sentence on it. If children need additional practice with pronouns, have them use **Practice Book** page 236 or online activities.

 ## Talk About It

Have partners think of sentences, using the pronouns *I, they,* and *we.* Encourage them to share their sentences with the class.

 # English Language Learners

Grammar, Practice Write and read: *Dana and Olivia like to eat peaches.* Replace the names with pronouns (i.e., *He and she, We, They*) and ask children if it is correct. Guide them to respond with a thumbs up for correct pronouns. Repeat with other variations of the sentence: *Olivia likes to eat peaches; My friend and I like to eat peaches.* As partners choose a pronoun to complete the frame from the Practice activity, draw children's attention to the plural verb *like.* Ask them to identify pronouns that can correctly be used with the verb. (I, we, they, you)

DIGITAL TOOLS

 Grammar Activity

⟩⟩ **DIFFERENTIATED WRITING**

● **English Language Learners** For more writing support, see the **ELL Small Group Guide,** p. 128.

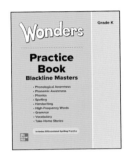

Grammar: p. 236

FORMATIVE ASSESSMENT

⊘ **STUDENT CHECK-IN**

Have partners share one thing they know about pronouns. Then have children reflect using the Check-In routine.

LESSON FOCUS

READING
Review Essential Question
Read Interactive Read Aloud
"Farms Around the World"
- Practice Strategy

Word Work
- Practice /f/f, /r/r

Reread Shared Read
"Ron With Red"

WRITING
Writing/Grammar
- Independent Writing
- Practice Grammar

Interactive Read-Aloud Cards

Reading/Writing Companion pp. 66–73

LEARNING GOALS

We can learn new words.

OBJECTIVES

Use words and phrases acquired through conversations, reading and being read to, and responding to texts.

Identify real-life connections between words and their use.

Develop oral vocabulary.

ELA ACADEMIC LANGUAGE

- *concept*
- Cognate: *concepto*

DIGITAL TOOLS

MULTIMODAL

Weekly Song

Visual Vocabulary Cards

Interactive Read Aloud

FORMATIVE ASSESSMENT

STUDENT CHECK-IN

Have partners tell each other the meaning of one vocabulary word. Then have children reflect using the Check-In routine.

Oral Language

5 mins

MULTIMODAL

Essential Question

What kinds of things grow on a farm?

Remind children that this week we are learning about things that grow on farms. Ask them to name foods that grow on farms. Then sing the **Weekly Song** together.

Oral Vocabulary Words

Remind children that on Lesson 1 we learned the vocabulary words *fresh* and *delicious*. *What is a* fresh *food that you like? Name a* delicious *food.* Then use the Define/Example/Ask routine on the print or digital **Visual Vocabulary Cards** to introduce the words *beneath, raise,* and *special*.

Oral Vocabulary Routine

Visual Vocabulary Cards

Define: If you are **beneath** something, you are under it.

Example: The sidewalk is beneath our feet as we walk.

Ask: What is beneath a desk or table in the classroom?

Define: When you **raise** something or someone, you take care of it to make sure it grows.

Example: People who raise horses give them plenty of exercise.

Ask: How can you care for a puppy as you raise it?

Define: When something is **special**, it is different in a good way.

Example: The coconut is a special food because every part of it can be used in some way.

Ask: Do you have a special food you like to eat? What is it? Why do you think it is special?

Read the Interactive Read Aloud

Connect to Concept

Tell children they will listen to an informational text about farms. Remind them that we are learning about food that grows on farms. Use the print or digital **Interactive Read-Aloud Cards**. Read the title aloud.

"Farms Around the World"

Set Purpose *Let's find out about what food grows on farms in different parts of the world.*

Oral Vocabulary Use the Oral Vocabulary prompts as you read the selection to provide more practice with the words in context.

Unfamiliar Words As you read "Farms Around the World," ask children to listen for words they do not understand or for new words they have learned and to think about what the words mean. Pause after Card 1 to model.

Teacher Think Aloud I remember that we learned the word *world* in Unit 2. It is the planet earth. The text says that people all around the *world* work on farms. That is a lot of farms!

Student Think Along After Card 1: I heard the word *crops*. What is a *crop*? The text says that farmers send their crops to stores and then people buy them. *Crops* must be the food that farmers grow and sell.

Build Knowledge: Make Connections

Talk About the Text Have partners share important details about the kinds of food that grows on farms.

Add to the Anchor Chart Record new ideas on the Build Knowledge anchor chart.

Add to the Word Bank Add new words children learned to a separate section of the Word Bank.

Compare Texts

Guide children to make connections between "Farms Around the World" and *An Orange in January*. How are the texts alike and how are they different?

LEARNING GOALS

We can listen actively to understand how food grows on farms.

OBJECTIVES

Ask and answer questions about unknown words in a text.

Determine or clarify the meaning of unknown and multiple-meaning words and phrases based on kindergarten reading and content.

With prompting and support, identify basic similarities in and differences between two texts on the same topic.

 SPOTLIGHT ON LANGUAGE

Card 1 Point to the fields of corn in the photo. *Corn is a crop. It grows on a farm.* Have children repeat. Explain that crops are different kinds of plants that people and animals eat as food. *Corn, rice, and bananas are all crops. They grow on a farm.*

For additional support, see the **ELL Small Group Guide**, pp. 124-125.

FORMATIVE ASSESSMENT

> **STUDENT CHECK-IN**

Have partners share which farm they liked the most and why. Then have children reflect using the Check-In routine.

In a Flash: Sound-Spellings

Display the Sound-Spelling Card for *f*.

1. **Teacher:** What's the letter?	**Children:** f
2. **Teacher:** What's the sound?	**Children:** /f/
3. **Teacher:** What's the word?	**Children:** fire

Continue the routine for *r* and previously taught sounds.

LEARNING GOALS

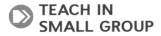

- We can blend sounds to say words.
- We can tell /ē/ from /e/.
- We can blend and read words.

OBJECTIVES

Demonstrate understanding of spoken words, syllables, and sounds (phonemes).

Know and apply grade-level phonics and word analysis skills in decoding words.

Demonstrate basic knowledge of one-to-one letter-sound correspondences by producing the primary sound or many of the most frequent sounds for each consonant.

Spell simple words phonetically, drawing on knowledge of sound-letter relationships.

Blend phonemes to form words.

ELA ACADEMIC LANGUAGE
- *blend, middle, different, vowel*

TEACH IN SMALL GROUP

You may wish to teach the Word Work lesson in small groups.

DIGITAL TOOLS

Word Work — Phonemic Awareness, Phonics

Phonics: Spelling Song

5 mins

Phonemic Awareness

Phoneme Blending

1 **Model** Say: *I am going to say the sounds in a word: /r/ /i/ /p/. I can blend those sounds to make the word: /rrriiip/, rip. Listen as I say more sounds and blend them to make words.* Continue to model phoneme blending with the following.

/r/ /a/ /p/ rap	/f/ /e/ /d/ fed	/f/ /i/ /sh/ fish
/r/ /e/ /d/ red	/f/ /i/ /t/ fit	/i/ /f/ if

2 **Guided Practice/Practice** *Listen to the sounds in a different word: /f/ /e/ /d/. Let's blend the sounds and say the word together: /f/ /e/ /d/, /fffeeed/ fed.* Tell children to listen to the sounds in words, repeat the sounds, and then blend them to say the word. Guide practice and provide corrective feedback as needed.

Place the following **Photo Cards** facedown: *fan, fox, five, rope, rake, rock.* Choose a card but do not display it. Tell children that you will say the sounds in the word. *Listen as I says each sound. You will repeat the sounds, then blend them to say the word.* After children have said the word, show the Photo Card.

/f/ /a/ /n/ fan	/f/ /o/ /ks/ fox	/f/ /ī/ /v/ five
/r/ /ō/ /p/ rope	/r/ /ā/ /k/ rake	/r/ /o/ /k/ rock

Long Vowel Awareness

1 **Model** Display the *green, key,* and *jet* **Photo Cards**. Say: *green, key, jet.* Green *and* key *both have the /ē/ sound.* Jet *has the /e/ sound.* Jet *has a different sound in the middle. It does not belong.*

2 **Guided Practice/Practice** Display the following sets of Photo Cards one set at a time: *leaf, gem pea; web, teeth, tree, cheese, gem, knee; net, wheel, pen.* Say the picture name for each set and have children repeat. Then have children tell which picture name has a different middle sound. Guide practice with the first set.

Review Say each set of words and have children identify which word has the /ā/, /ī/, or /ō/ sound: *cap/cape; bite/bit; rob/robe; kite/kit.*

Sound-Spelling Connection You may wish to introduce the sound spelling for long e, *ee* using the *tree* **Sound-Spelling Card**. Point to the letters *ee* and explain that these letters stand for the /ē/ sound they hear in *tree.*

Phonics

10 mins

MULTIMODAL

| f | r |

Review *f, r*

1 **Model** Display **Word-Building Card** r. *This is the letter* r. *The letter* r *stands for* /r/, *the sound you hear in the beginning of* rose. *Say the sound with me:* /r/. *I will write the letter* r *because* rose *has* /r/ *at the beginning.* Repeat for /f/ f using the word *fire*.

2 **Guided Practice/Practice** Tell children that you will say words that begin with /f/ or /r/. Have them say /f/ and write the letter *f* on their **Response Boards** when they hear words beginning with /f/. Tell them to say /r/ and write the letter *r* when they hear words beginning with /r/. Guide practice and provide corrective feedback as needed.

| ride | fact | rope | run | fine |
| fun | rip | face | find | rat |

Blend Words

1 **Model** Display Word-Building Cards *i, f*. *This is the letter* i. *It stands for* /i/. *This is the letter* f. *It stands for* /f/. *Let's blend the two sounds together:* /iiifff/, /if/. *The word is* if. Continue with the following words: *fed, ran, red*.

2 **Guided Practice/Practice** Write the following words and sentences: *fat, rip, fit, red, fan, rat, if. We fed the pet. The red hat fit. He ran with you.* Have children read the words and sentences, blending the sounds. Guide practice and provide corrective feedback as needed.

Spell Words

Dictation Say the word *pen* and have children repeat. Ask children to say *pen* again, stretching the sounds. Then write the word as you say the letter names. Have children read the word and say the letter names. Then say the words: *ten, men, den*, and *hen* and have children write them. For more spelling practice, use **Practice Book** page 231.

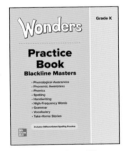

Phonics/Spelling: p. 231

FORMATIVE ASSESSMENT

▸ STUDENT CHECK-IN

Have partners read *fan* and *ran*. Then have children reflect using the Check-In routine.

LESSON 3

Take-Home Story: pp. 239–240

---

5 mins

Phonics

MULTIMODAL

Picture Sort

1 **Model** Remind children that the letter *f* stands for /f/ and the letter *r* stands for /r/. Place **Word-Building Card** *f* on the left side of the pocket chart. Continue the routine for letter *r* placing the letter on the right side of the pocket chart.

Hold up the **Photo Card** for *fan*. *Here is the picture for* fan. *Fan* has the /f/ sound at the beginning. I will place fan under the letter f because the letter f stands for /f/. Continue the same routine for *rose*.

Photo Cards

2 **Guided Practice/Practice** Have children sort the Photo Cards for *feather, feet, fork, rabbit, ring,* and *ruby.* Have them say the initial sound and decide which letter the Photo Card should be placed under. Guide practice and provide corrective feedback as needed.

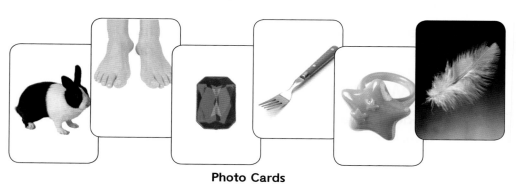

Photo Cards

ELL English Language Learners

Phonics, Guided Practice/Practice Confirm children's understanding that *f* and *r* stand for /f/ and /r/. Guide children to identify the initial sounds for the Photo Cards. *Is the beginning sound in* feather /f/ *or* /r/? (/f/) Use sentence frames to help children tell how they sorted the cards: Feather begins with the sound /f/. We place feather below the letter f.

High-Frequency Words

| with | he |

1 **Guided Practice** Display the **High-Frequency Word Cards** *with* and *he*. Review the words using the Read/Spell/Write routine.

2 **Practice** Point to the High-Frequency Word Card *with* and have children read it. Repeat with *he* and last week's word *are*.

Build Fluency

Word Automaticity Write the following sentences. Have children chorally read as you track the print. Have them reread the sentences until they can read the words automatically and fluently.

Sam and Tim are *with* him.   **Pat ran *with* him.**
He ran *with* you.   **He and I are *with* Pam.**

Read for Fluency Distribute **Practice Book** pages 239–240 and help children assemble their Take-Home Books. Chorally read the Take-Home Book. Explain that words are made up of letters. Point out the letter *w* and the word *with* on page 1. Then ask children to point to the letter *H* and the word *He* on page 2. Have children reread the book to review high-frequency words and to build automaticity.

BUILD YOUR WORD BANK

Use this lesson to teach additional high-frequency words.

1 **Model** Display the **Build Your Word Bank Cards** for *many, them,* and *eat* from the **Practice Book High-Frequency Word Cards**. Use the Read/Spell/Write routine to teach each word.

- **Read** Point to the word *many* and say the word. *This is the word* many. *Say it with me:* many. *Bob has* many *pens.*
- **Spell** *The word* many *is spelled* m-a-n-y. *Spell it with me.*
- **Write** *Let's write* many *on our **Response Boards** as we spell the word:* m-a-n-y.
  Repeat the Read/Spell/Write routine with *them* and *eat*.

2 **Guided Practice** Display the Build Your Word Bank Cards for *many, them,* and *eat*. Point to each of the words and have children chorally read each word. Then have children take turns using the Build Your Word Bank words in a sentence. Guide practice and provide corrective feedback as needed.

ELL ENGLISH LANGUAGE LEARNERS

High-Frequency Words, Practice Have children read *with* and *he* aloud with you and then independently. For additional practice, ask questions, and have children answer them using the words. For example: Who are you with? What is he doing with the pencil? (I am with a friend; He is drawing.)

FORMATIVE ASSESSMENT

STUDENT CHECK-IN

Phonics Have partners think of words that they would add to the word sort.

High-Frequency Words Have partners take turns reading a sentence from the Take-Home Book.

Then have children reflect using the Check-in routine.

CHECK FOR SUCCESS

Rubric Use your online rubric to record children's progress.

Can children blend phonemes to make words and sort words by initial /f/f and /r/r?

Can children recognize and read the high-frequency word?

Small Group Instruction

If No
- **Approaching** Reteach pp. T218–222
- **ELL** Develop pp. T218–222

If Yes
- **On** Review pp. T226–228
- **Beyond** Extend p. T232

LESSON 3

LEARNING GOALS

We can read and understand a story.

OBJECTIVES

Follow words from left to right, top to bottom, and page by page.

Demonstrate basic knowledge of one-to-one letter-sound correspondences by producing the primary sound or many of the most frequent sounds for each consonant.

Read common high-frequency words by sight.

Read emergent-reader texts with purpose and understanding.

ELA ACADEMIC LANGUAGE

• reread

10 mins

Reread "Ron With Red"

Focus on Foundational Skills

Book Handling Have volunteers point to the front and back covers of the book and model turning the pages.

Concepts of Print Remind children that we read from left to right and from top to bottom. Develop print-to-speech match as you read aloud. *As I read this sentence, I will point to each word I say as I move from left to right and from top to bottom, like this.* Now read a sentence from the story and point to the last word. *This is the last word in the sentence. I will pause for a moment before I read the next sentence.* Finally, have volunteers take turns following the words with their finger, moving from left to right and top to bottom.

Focus on Comprehension

Reread Review each rebus and discuss what it stands for. Guide children to reread the story. Children should sound out the decodable words and read the high-frequency words with automaticity. Offer support and corrective feedback as needed. Ask questions to monitor comprehension.

You may wish to have children use the box on the right-hand pages to:

- Draw a picture about the text or the art.
- Draw something whose name begins with the /f/ or /r/ sound.
- Write the letter *f* or *r*.

Reading/Writing Companion, pp. 66–67

COMPREHENSION

Who is Red? (Red is Ron's dog.) *Where are Ron and Red going?* (They are going to a place where oranges grow.)

Reading/Writing Companion, pp. 70–71

COMPREHENSION

How do tomatoes grow? (Tomatoes grow on plants called vines.) *In what way is this different from how oranges grow?* (Oranges grow on trees.)

Reading/Writing Companion, pp. 72-73

COMPREHENSION

What did Red do at the farm? (He chased a bird.) *What did Ron do at the farm?* (He sipped a drink.)

Focus on Fluency: Accuracy and Rate

Have partners practice reading the story "Ron With Red" accurately. Encourage them to track the print as they sound out decodable words and read high-frequency words with automaticity. Remind children to pay attention to punctuation marks so they read sentences with the correct tone. Then have partners read the story again this time focusing on rate—reading a bit more quickly and making the text sound more like speech.

Listen in: If children struggle with accuracy, have them start again at the beginning of the sentence and correct any errors they make. If they struggle with rate, model an appropriate rate and have them repeat.

 ## Build Knowledge: Make Connections

Talk About the Text Have partners discuss the farm that Ron and Red visited. *What food was growing on the farm?*

Write About the Text Have children add their ideas to their reader's notebook.

DECODABLE READERS

Have children read "Ron Ram" (pages 25–30) to practice decoding words in connected text.

Unit 5 Decodable Reader

ELL ENGLISH LANGUAGE LEARNERS

Seek Clarification Remind children that if they are confused or unsure about what is being said, they should seek clarification. *If you don't understand what someone is saying, ask them to explain.* Give the following examples, having children repeat after each one: *Could you say that again? I am not sure what you mean. Could you please explain?*

❯ STUDENT CHECK-IN

Have partners share something they learned from the story. Then have children reflect using the Check-In routine.

LESSON 3

- **We can write about the texts we read.**
- **We can learn about words that can take the place of nouns (pronouns).**

OBJECTIVES

Use a combination of drawing, dictating, and writing to compose informative/ explanatory texts in which they name what they are writing about and supply some information about the topic.

Write a letter or letters for most consonant and short-vowel sounds.

Write in response to a text.

Appropriately use pronouns.

ELA ACADEMIC LANGUAGE

- *clue, event, pronoun*
- Cognates: *evento, pronombre*

 TEACH IN SMALL GROUP

Choose from these options to enable all children to complete the writing activity:

- draw a picture
- complete sentence starters
- write a caption
- write one sentence

For differentiated support, see Writing Skills minilessons on pages T494–T499. These can be used throughout the year.

---

5 mins

Independent Writing

Write About the Shared Read

Analyze the Prompt Have children turn to page 66 of their **Reading/ Writing Companion**. Tell them they are going to write a response to a prompt about the story "Ron With Red." Read the prompt aloud: *What does Ron do at the park?*

Talk Have partners turn and talk about the different things Ron does at the park.

Find Text Evidence *We need to find text evidence, or clues, in the text and illustrations to help us answer the prompt.*

- *Let's look at page 68. What is Ron doing?* (walking Red; looking for a bird in a tree) *On page 70, what is Ron doing with Red here?* (walking next to the tomatoes, looking for a bird) *Let's look at page 72. What is Ron doing now?* (He is sitting and sipping a drink.)

- Continue guiding children to look for text evidence to use in their writing.

 Write to the Prompt Guide children to review the text evidence they found and plan their writing in their writer's notebook. Encourage them to think about which clues they would like to include in their writing.

Draft Have children draw a response to the prompt in their writer's notebook. Then, remind them that they are writing about what Ron does at the park. If children need additional support, you may choose to have them dictate their ideas to an adult or use the following sentence frames:

First, Ron _____.
Next, he and Red _____.
Then, Ron _____.

As children draw and add sentences to their drafts, have them do the following:

- Stretch words to write the beginning, middle, and end sounds in them. WRITING SKILL

- Write about events in the order in which they happen. TRAIT: ORGANIZATION

- Use **pronouns** in their writing. GRAMMAR

Tell children they will continue to work on their writing on Lesson 4.

Grammar

OPTIONAL 5 mins

Subjective Pronouns

1 **Review** Display the *man* **Photo Card**. Write and read: **The man is tall. He is tall**. Point out that the pronoun *he* replaces *the man* in the second sentence.

2 **Guided Practice/Practice** Display the *mix* Photo Card. Write sentence strips that tell what the boy is doing. For example: *The boy puts in flour. The boy puts in water. The boy adds eggs. The boy mixes it up.* Then cut each sentence strip into two parts, dividing subject and verb. Provide four short sentence strips with the word *He*. Guide children to take out the words *The boy* and replace them with *He* in one of the sentences. Read the new sentence together with children. Guide practice as needed.

Have partners work together using the sentence strips to replace *The boy* with the pronoun *He* in the remaining sentences. Have them read their new sentences and point to the pronoun. Ask volunteers to share out their sentences. Have all children in the class read the new sentences together.

Talk About It

Have partners work together to choose a game they like to play at school. Then have them tell how to play the game, step by step. Have children use pronouns in their descriptions.

English Language Learners

Independent Writing, Analyze the Prompt Check children's understanding of the prompt before writing. Display page 67 of the Shared Read and ask: *Who is Ron?* (the boy) *Who is Red?* (the dog) *The prompt is asking us to tell what Ron does at the park. We will tell what Ron does in time order using the words* first, next, *and* then. *What does Ron do first?* First, Ron walks with Red. Turn to page 68. Demonstrate with your hand over your eyes how Ron looks for a bird. *What does Ron do next?* Next, he looks for a bird. Continue this routine with the remaining pages of the story using the sequence words *then* and *last*.

For additional support, see the **ELL Small Group Guide**, p. 129.

DIGITAL TOOLS

Grammar Activity

Grammar Song

Grammar Video

FORMATIVE ASSESSMENT

STUDENT CHECK-IN

Have partners share one thing they know about pronouns. Have children reflect using the Check-In routine.

LEARNING GOALS

- We can tell if words rhyme.
- We can understand new words.
- We can sort words about food into groups.
- We can use clues to find out the meaning of a word.

OBJECTIVES

Recognize and produce rhyming words.

Use words and phrases acquired through conversations, reading and being read to, and responding to texts.

Determine or clarify the meaning of unknown and multiple-meaning words and phrases based on *kindergarten reading and content*.

Sort common objects into categories to gain a sense of the concepts the categories represent.

Develop oral vocabulary.

ELA ACADEMIC LANGUAGE

- *clues, sort, category, strategy*
- Cognates: *categoría, estrategia*

DIGITAL TOOLS

Weekly Song

Visual Vocabulary Cards

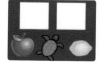
Category Words Activity

LESSON FOCUS

READING
Review Essential Question
Read/Reread Paired Selection
"Farmers' Market"
Word Work
• Build Words with /f/f, /r/r

WRITING
Writing/Grammar
• Independent Writing
• Practice Grammar
Research and Inquiry
• Create Presentation

Literature Big Book, pp. 34–40

---

10 mins

Oral Language

MULTIMODAL

 Essential Question

What kinds of things grow on a farm?

Remind children that this week they are learning about things that grow on farms. *What have you learned about things that grow on farms?* Add to the Build Knowledge anchor chart.

Phonological Awareness: Identify Rhyme

1 **Model** Sing the Weekly Song and have the children listen closely. Point out the words *grow* and *know*. Remind children: *Words that rhyme have the same end sounds. Listen:* grow, know. *I can say more words with this end sound:* snow, blow, low, show.

2 **Guided Practice/Practice** Say the following word pairs and have children clap if the words rhyme: *bone/lone, take/tell, eat/even, sit/bit, race/face, go/toe.* Ask children to say another word that rhymes with each pair. Guide practice and provide corrective feedback.

Review Oral Vocabulary Words

Use the Define/Example/Ask routine on the print or digital **Visual Vocabulary Cards** to review the oral vocabulary words *fresh, raise, delicious, beneath,* and *special.* Then have children use the words in sentences.

Visual Vocabulary Cards

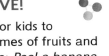

Category Words: Food Words

1 **Explain/Model** *Let's sort the different kinds of foods that come from farms.* Use the **Photo Cards** for *berries, grapes, cheese,* and *yogurt.* Display the card for *grapes. Grapes are fruit. I will put them in the fruit group.* Display the card for *cheese. Cheese is made from milk. I will put cheese in the milk, or dairy, group.* Continue in the same way to sort the remaining cards.

2 **Guided Practice/Practice** Tell children that they will sort different types of food into the following categories: *Fruits, Vegetables, Dairy.* Say the following words in random order for children to sort into the three categories:

banana, watermelon, peach, strawberry (Fruit);

carrots, corn, celery, peas (Vegetables);

cheese, butter, yogurt (Dairy).

Have children sort the words by food type. Ask them to explain how they decided which food belongs in each category. Guide practice as needed.

For additional practice, use **Practice Book** page 235.

Vocabulary: Sentence Clues

1 **Model** Remind children that they can ask questions about words that they do not know. They can also use clues from the sentences and pictures to figure out the meaning. Model using sentence clues with an example from *An Orange in January.*

Think Aloud Listen to this sentence and think about the word *segments:* "And two hands, pink with cold, shared its *segments,* so that everyone could taste the sweetness of an orange in January. " I have eaten an orange, and I know that the fruit can be separated into small pieces. The sentence talks about sharing, and I see the boy hand a girl a small piece of orange in the picture. A *segment* must be "one small part of the orange."

2 **Guided Practice/Practice** Read the following sentence from pages 16–22 of *An Orange in January.*

From bag to basket, truck to truck, it followed the skyway over mountains, across deserts and plains, until the orange arrived at a grocery store.

Have children use sentence and picture clues to figure out the meaning of *skyway* and *plains.* Guide children as needed.

KIDS ON THE MOVE!

Give simple directions for kids to act out that include names of fruits and vegetables. For example: *Peel a banana. Pull a carrot from the ground. Bite into a piece of celery.*

Category Words: p. 235

ENGLISH LANGUAGE LEARNERS

Category Words, Guided Practice/ Practice Display Photo Cards for *banana, carrot,* and *cheese.* Say the words, and have children repeat the words. Put cards in separate piles. *A banana is a fruit. A carrot is a vegetable. Cheese is a dairy food.* Have children repeat. Repeat with other cards.

NEWCOMERS

Use the **Newcomer Online Visuals** and accompanying prompts to help children expand vocabulary and language about Community (Unit 3) and Weather (Unit 4). Use the Conversation Starters, Speech Balloons, and Games in **the Newcomer Teacher's Guide** to continue building vocabulary and developing oral and written language.

FORMATIVE ASSESSMENT

❯ STUDENT CHECK-IN

Oral Vocabulary Words Have partners name something that is *special.*

Category Words Have partners name a fruit or vegetable and tell which group it belongs in.

Vocabulary Have partners tell how they figured out the meaning of *plains* from the lesson.

Then have children reflect using the Check-in routine.

LESSON 4

Literature Big Book

OBJECTIVES

Recognize common types of texts.

With prompting and support, identify the main topic and retell key details of a text.

With prompting and support, describe the relationship between illustrations and the text in which they appear.

Actively engage in group reading activities with purpose and understanding.

Use lists to gather information about a text.

ELA ACADEMIC LANGUAGE

• lists, photograph
• Cognates: *listas, fotografía*

Read

⏱ 10 mins "Farmers' Market"

Text Feature: Lists

1 **Explain/Model** Tell children that nonfiction text can sometimes include a list, or a series of words or sentences. Display page 40 in the **Big Book** and point to the list. *This list shows what a shopper needs to buy at the market. Sometimes lists are numbered. This list has a check box next to each word.*

Display **Online Teaching Chart 14** and read the list aloud. Point out the numbers. *This is a numbered list of things to do.* Read the first item on the list aloud. *The first thing this person has to do is feed the dog.*

Online Teaching Chart 14

2 **Guided Practice/Practice** Read items 2–4 on the poster aloud. Guide children to discuss the things on the list. Point out the pictures on the list. *What game do you think the person has to play in?* (soccer) *How do you think he or she will help Miss Trent?* (by raking leaves)

Read the Paired Selection

Display the Big Book. Read the title and look at the photo. *What do you predict this text will be about?* Write and display children's predictions.

Set Purpose *Let's read to find out about a farmer's market.*

Literature Big Book, pp. 34–35

TOPIC AND DETAILS DOK 2

What is the topic of this text? (how food goes from farm to market) *What details in the photos give information about the topic?* (farmers grow different types of fruit and vegetables; farmers use tools and baskets to pick the fruit and vegetables.)

Literature Big Book, pp. 36–37

TEXT FEATURE:
PHOTOGRAPHS DOK 1

What information do the photographs show that is not described in the text? (The photographs show what the fruits and vegetables look like and how they grow.)

Literature Big Book, pp. 38–39

REREAD DOK 2

Reread the pages aloud. Point out the words *Some farmers* on page 38 and *Other farmers* on page 39. *How are these farmers different?* (Some farmers sell their food nearby, and other farmers sell their food far away.)

Literature Big Book, p. 40

TEXT FEATURE: LISTS DOK 2

Why are there check marks next to some of the things on the list? (Shoppers put a check mark next to each item on the list as they collect it.)

Return to Purpose

Read children's predictions. Ask: *Were the predictions correct?* Remind children of their purpose for reading. (to find out about a farmer's market) Prompt children to share any new information they learned from the selection.

Retell

Help children use the photographs to retell details in the selection in order. Remind them to use some of the new words they have learned.

Close Reading Routine

Read   DOK 1–2
- Identify key ideas and details.
- Take notes and retell.
- Use **ACT** prompts as needed.

Reread   DOK 2–3
- Analyze the text, craft, and structure.

Integrate   DOK 3–4
- Integrate knowledge and ideas.
- Make text-to-text connections.
- Complete the Show Your Knowledge task.
- Inspire action.

ELL **SPOTLIGHT ON LANGUAGE**

Pages 38–39 Explain that *nearby* and *far away* describe location, or where things are. Gesture to a child close to you, and say *nearby*, then gesture with your arm stretched out, and say *far away*. Have children repeat each phrase. Then, ask children to name examples of objects in the room that are nearby and far away.

FORMATIVE ASSESSMENT

❯ **STUDENT CHECK-IN**

Have partners share something they learned from the list in the text. Then have children reflect using the Check-In routine.

LESSON 4

Literature Big Book

OBJECTIVES

With prompting and support, describe the relationship between illustrations and the text in which they appear.

Use words and phrases acquired through conversations, reading and being read to, and responding to texts.

Analyze the author's craft.

ELA ACADEMIC LANGUAGE

• *photos, connections*
• Cognates: *fotos, conexiones*

Reread

"Farmers' Market"

10 mins

Analyze the Text

After children read and retell "Farmers' Market," reread it with them. Use the instructions in the prompt below to help children answer the questions on pages 74-75 in the **Reading/Writing Companion**.

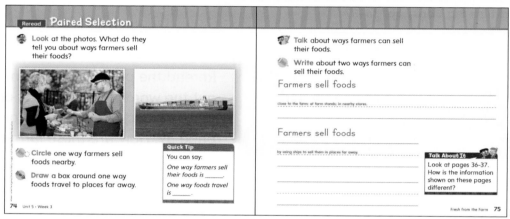

Reading/Writing Companion, pp. 74-75

AUTHOR'S CRAFT DOK 2

• Have children look at the photographs on page 74. *What do they tell you about the ways that farmers sell their foods?* Tell children to circle one way that farmers sell foods nearby and draw a box around one way that foods travel to places far away.

• Display pages 38–39 of the **Literature Big Book**. Lead a discussion about the different ways that farmers can sell their foods. Then guide children to complete the sentence starters on page 75.

Talk About It

COLLABORATE

Review pages 38–39 of the selection with children. Remind them that these pages show the different ways that farmers sell their foods. Then have them compare the information. *How is the information on page 38 different from the information on page 39?* (Page 38 shows a farmer selling his food at a local market. Page 39 shows food being shipped to faraway places by airplanes, boats and trains.) Invite children to come up and point to pictures in the Big Book as they contribute to the conversation.

Integrate

Build Knowledge: Make Connections

Talk About the Text Have children discuss what they learned about farms from the text. *What types of fruits and vegetables were grown on the farms in the text?* Encourage children to identify the different fruits and vegetables they see in the photographs.

Add to the Anchor Chart Record any new ideas on the Build Knowledge Anchor Chart.

Add to the Word Bank Record any new words on the Word Bank.

English Language Learners

Use the following scaffolds with **Analyze the Text, Author's Craft.**

Beginning

Point to the peas on page 36. Model saying the word *peas* and have children repeat. Model the sentence and have children repeat: *Peas are a vegetable.* Repeat routine with other vegetables and fruits on pages 36–37.

Intermediate

Display pages 36–37 and describe ways that farmers sell their foods. *Where do farmers sell their foods?* Help partners respond using the sentence frame: Farmers sell foods at a market.

Advanced/Advanced High

Display pages 36–37 and describe ways that farmers sell their foods. *Farmers sell foods at a market.* Then have partners discuss other places that farmers sell their food. Provide a model: Farmers sell foods at a grocery store.

 CONNECT TO CONTENT

Growing Food to Sell Help children understand that farmers can eat some of the foods they grow. But the main reason farmers grow food is to sell it. They use the money they make to buy things that they need to live, such as food, clothing, and shelter. In this way, farmers meet their basic needs by self-producing, trading, and purchasing.

FORMATIVE ASSESSMENT

STUDENT CHECK-IN

Have partners share something they learned from the photographs. Then have children reflect using the Check-In routine.

In a Flash: Sound-Spellings

Display the Sound-Spelling Card for *f*.
1. **Teacher:** What's the letter?   **Children:** f
2. **Teacher:** What's the sound?   **Children:** /f/
3. **Teacher:** What's the word?   **Children:** fire
Continue the routine for *r* and previously taught sounds.

LEARNING GOALS

- We can add sounds to words to make new words.
- We can blend sounds to say words.
- We can read and spell words with *f* and *r*.
- We can read sentences using the words *with* and *he*.

OBJECTIVES

Add or substitute individual sounds (phonemes) in simple, one-syllable words to make new words.

Distinguish between similarly spelled words by identifying the sounds of the letters that differ.

Read common high-frequency words by sight.

⊙ TEACH IN SMALL GROUP

You may wish to teach the Word Work lesson in small groups.

DIGITAL TOOLS

Word Work

Phonemic Awareness

Phonics

High-Frequency Words

Visual Vocabulary Cards

---

5 mins

Phonemic Awareness

Phoneme Addition

1 **Model** *We can add sounds to the beginning of words to make new words. Listen as I say a word:* an. *What word do we have when we add /f/ to the beginning of* an? *When we add /f/ to* an, *we make the word* fan. *Repeat substituting /r/ to make* ran.

2 **Guided Practice/Practice** Say: *Listen carefully to these questions about words. Answer the questions by adding the beginning sound to make a new word.* Allow children ample time to respond. Guide practice and provide corrective feedback as needed.

Say *it*. Add /f/ to the beginning of *it*. What's the new word? (fit)
Say *ed*. Add /r/ to the beginning of *ed*. What's the new word? (red)
Say *in*. Add /f/ to the beginning of *in*. What's the new word? (fin)
Say *at*. Add /r/ to the beginning of *at*. What's the new word? (rat)

If children need additional practice adding sounds to make new words, use **Practice Book** page 228.

Long Vowel Awareness

1 **Model** *I am going to say the sounds in* seed: /s/ /ē/ /d/. *I can blend those sounds to make the word: /sēēēd/,* seed. Tell children to listen for the /ē/ sound. Model phoneme blending with the words below.

/w/ /ē/ /d/, weed   **/m/ /ē/, me**   **/f/ /ē/ /d/, feed**

2 **Guided Practice/Practice** *Listen as I say the sounds in words. You will repeat the sounds and then blend them to say the word.*

/b/ /ē/, bee   **/m/ /ē/ /t/, meet**   **/t/ /ē/ /n/, teen**
/n/ /ē/ /d/, need   **/b/ /ē/ /p/, beep**   **/s/ /ē/, see**

Review Repeat the blending routine for /ā/, /ī/, and /ō/ using the following words: **/m/ /ā/ /k/   /b/ / ī/ /k/   /h/ /ō/ /p/**

Sound-Spelling Connection You may wish to introduce the sound spelling for long e, *ee* using the *tree* **Sound-Spelling Card.** Point to the letters *ee* and explain that these letters stand for the /ē/ sound they hear in *tree*.

Phonics

5 mins

MULTIMODAL

Build and Read Words

1 **Guided Practice** Provide children with **Word-Building Cards** *a–z*. Use the Word-Building Cards *r, e, d* to form the word *red* and ask children to do the same. *I will change the letter* r *to* f *to make* fed. Read *fed* aloud and have children read it with you.

2 **Practice** Have children change the cards for *rap* to form the word *rip*. Ask them which letters are the same and which one is different and how its sound changes the word. Have them change letters to spell *dip, snip, fin, fan, ran, ram,* and *rim.* Then have children list the words and work with a partner to correct any errors they made. If they need more practice in identifying letters that differ in words, see **Practice Book** p. 232.

OPTIONAL
5 mins

High-Frequency Words

MULTIMODAL

Practice Have children write *with* and *he.* Then display the **Visual Vocabulary Cards** *with* and *he.* Follow the Teacher Talk routine on the back.

Visual Vocabulary Cards

Build Fluency Build the following sentences in the pocket chart using the **High-Frequency Word Cards, Photo Cards** and teacher-made punctuation cards. Have children read the sentences as you track the print. Ask them to identify *with* and *he.* **He can go *with* you. *He* can see the map *with* you. *He* and I like to write. I can go to the zoo *with* you.**

Have partners say sentences using the words *with* and *he.*

Build and Write High-Frequency Words Have partners build high-frequency words using letter cubes, magnetic letters, or **Word-Building Cards.** Have children build the words without looking at the Word Cards and then they may use the High-Frequency Word Cards to check their spelling. Then have them write the words on a piece of paper. As a challenge, set a timer and see how many words children can build and write words in that amount of time.

DECODABLE READERS

Have children read "Red and Ron" (pp. 31–36)

Unit 5 Decodable Reader

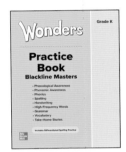

Phonemic Awareness: p. 228
Phonics: p. 232

FORMATIVE ASSESSMENT

❯ STUDENT CHECK-IN

Phonics Have partners use Word-Building Cards to spell and read *rot* and *fat.*

High-Frequency Words Have partners point to and read a sentence from the lesson.

Then have children reflect using the Check-In routine.

✔ CHECK FOR SUCCESS

Rubric Use your online rubric to record progress. Can children add /f/ and /r/ to words, blend words with /f/ and /r/? Can they read high-frequency words?

❯ Small Group Instruction

If No

● **Approaching** Reteach pp. T218–222

● **ELL** Develop pp. T218–222

If Yes

● **On** Review pp. T226–228

● **Beyond** Extend p. T232

LESSON 4

LEARNING GOALS

- We can revise our writing.
- We can learn about words that can take the place of nouns (pronouns).

OBJECTIVES

With guidance and support from adults, respond to questions and suggestions from peers and add details to strengthen writing as needed.

Capitalize the first word in a sentence.

Produce and expand complete sentences in shared language activities.

Appropriately use pronouns.

ELA ACADEMIC LANGUAGE

- *review, edit*
- Cognates: *revisar, editar*

Independent Writing

5 mins

Write About the Shared Read

Revise

Reread the prompt about "Ron With Red": *What does Ron do at the park?* Have children read their drafts to see if they responded to the prompt by organizing events in the order in which they happened, using pronouns, and stretching sounds to write words.

Peer Review Have partners review each other's writing. Children should share what they like most about the writing, questions they have for the author, and additional ideas they think the author could include. Provide time for children to make revisions and add details to strengthen their writing.

Edit/Proofread

After children have revised their work, have them edit it carefully, checking for the following:

- Use a capital letter at the beginning of each sentence.
- Make sure your sentence(s) tells a complete thought..

If children need additional practice with editing and proofreading, have them use **Practice Book** page 238.

Write Final Draft

After children have edited their writing and finished their peer review, have them write their final draft in their writer's notebook. Tell children to write neatly so that others can read their writing, or guide them to explore a variety of digital tools they can use to publish their work.

Teacher Conference As children review their drafts, confer with them to provide guidance. Suggest places in their writing where they might add details, correct the order of events, or replace a noun with a pronoun.

Share and Evaluate

After children have finalized their draft, have them work with a partner to practice presenting their writing to one another. Remind children to speak in complete sentences. If possible, record children as they share so that they can see themselves presenting, or you can use as a topic of discussion for a teacher conference.

Have children add their work to their writing folder. Invite children to look at their previous writing and discuss with a partner how it has improved.

Grammar

5 mins

Subjective Pronouns

1 **Review** Remind children that a pronoun is a word that takes the place of a noun or nouns. Write and read aloud: **Mr. Chang is my neighbor. He grows tomatoes.** Point out that the pronoun *he* takes the place of *Mr. Chang* in the second sentence.

2 **Guided Practice/Practice** Have a girl and a boy stand at the front of the room. Point out what each person is wearing. For example: *Ty is wearing a blue shirt. Eva is wearing red shoes.* Then guide children to repeat the sentences using the pronouns *he* and *she*. Continue by asking children to say something that is true of both children. For example: *Ty and Eva are five.* Guide them to say the same thing using a pronoun. (They are five.)

Invite children to work with a partner. Have one child say a sentence about something the other child is wearing while using the pronoun *he* or *she*. Then have children switch roles. Ask partners to share some of their sentences with the rest of the class. If children need additional practice with pronouns, use **Practice Book** page 237 or online activities.

Talk About It

Have children work with partners to use the pronoun *they* to tell about things they do together in class.

English Language Learners

Use with **Independent Writing, Edit/Proofread.**

Beginning

Help children check that their sentences tell complete thoughts. Then help children check for correct capitalization.

Intermediate

Ask questions to support children: *Did you begin each sentence with a capital letter? Do your sentences tell a complete thought?*

Advanced/Advanced High

Provide models for partners to use as they discuss their drafts: This sentence ends with a period, but it does not start with a capital letter. I will use a capital letter at the beginning of my sentence.

For additional support, see the **ELL Small Group Guide,** p. 129.

DIGITAL TOOLS

Grammar Activity

Grammar: p. 237
Edit/Proofread: p. 238

FORMATIVE ASSESSMENT

▶ STUDENT CHECK-IN

Have each partner share two pronouns. Then have children reflect using the Check-In routine.

LESSON **4**

LEARNING GOALS

We can research about plants that grow on a farm.

OBJECTIVES

Participate in shared research and writing projects.

With guidance and support from adults, recall information from experiences or gather information from provided sources to answer a question.

Add drawings or other visual displays to descriptions as desired to provide additional detail.

Produce and expand complete sentences in shared language activities.

Follow agreed-upon rules for discussions.

ELA ACADEMIC LANGUAGE

• *research, topic*

 COLLABORATIVE CONVERSATIONS

Be Open to All Ideas As children engage in partner, small-group, and whole-class discussions, tell them to:

• Listen carefully because all ideas, questions, or comments are important.

• Ask a question if something is unclear.

• Respect the opinions of others.

• Give their opinions, even if they are different from those of other people.

Integrate

(10 mins)

Plants

Model

Tell children that they will research about plants that grow on a farm. Display pages 76-77 of the **Reading/Writing Companion**. Model completing each step in the research process.

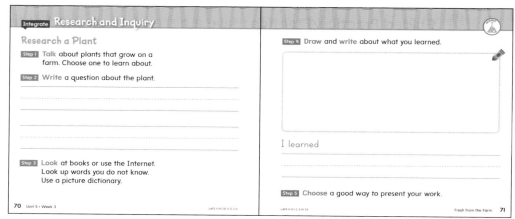

Reading/Writing Companion, pp. 76-77

STEP 1 Choose a Topic

I will research a plant that grows on a farm. First, I need to choose a topic. I like to eat string beans, so my topic will be string beans.

STEP 2 Write Your Question

I need to write a question to guide my research. My question will be: How do string beans grow?

STEP 3 Find Information

To find the answer to my question, I need to do some research. I can do this by looking at books or using the Internet. I can look up words I don't know in a picture dictionary.

STEP 4 Draw/Write What You Learned

I will draw and label a picture showing what I have learned about how string beans grow. I will also write some facts I have learned about how string beans grow.

STEP 5 Choose a Way to Present Your Work

I am going to create a book about how string beans grow. Each page will show a part of the process. I will then present the book to the class.

Apply

Have children turn to page 76 in their **Reading/Writing Companion**. Guide them through the steps of the research process. Remind children that they will draw and write about what they learned and present their work to the class. Provide guidance as needed.

Choose the Presentation Format

Have children turn to pages 76-77 in their Reading/Writing Companion to review their research, their drawing, and what they learned about the plant they chose to research. Tell them that today they are going to take the next step by creating their final product, which they will present tomorrow. Work with children to select a way to present their findings. Options may include drawing and labeling a picture, creating a poster, making a model, or putting on a dramatic presentation.

Create the Presentation

Have children develop their presentations in pairs or in small groups. Remind them of the rules of working with others.

Gather Materials Have children gather the materials they will need to create their finished product. Most of the materials should be available in the classroom or can be brought from home.

Make the Finished Product Once children have gathered their materials, give them time to create their finished product. You can set aside an area in the classroom for project work and store materials there. Remind children that they will be presenting their work to their classmates the next day.

English Language Learners

Apply, Step 2 Model saying the names of plants, such as *peas, carrots, corn, oranges, blueberries,* and *grapes,* and have children repeat. Have partners discuss which plant that they want to do research for. Provide and model sentence frames, such as: I want to learn more about _____. How do _____?

TEACH IN SMALL GROUP

You may wish to have children create their presentation during small group time. Group children of varying abilities together, or group children together if they are doing similar projects.

CONNECT TO CONTENT

Growing Foods Based on Location
Tell children that farmers grow certain foods based on the location of the farm. Remind children in the selection "Farms Around the World," they learned about foods that grow on different farms around the world. Ask children to share some of the foods they have learned about or know of and where they grow in the world. You may wish to write children's responses on chart paper.

RESEARCH AND INQUIRY: SHARING FINAL PROJECTS

As children get ready to wrap up the week, have them share their Research and Inquiry projects. Then have children self-evaluate.

Prepare Have children gather any materials they need to present their Research and Inquiry project. Have partners practice their presentations.

Share Guide children to present their Research and Inquiry project. Encourage children to speak in complete sentences.

Evaluate Have children discuss and evaluate their own presentations. You may wish to have them complete the online Student Checklist.

STUDENT CHECK-IN

Have partners share one plant that grows on a farm. Then have children reflect using the Check-In routine.

LESSON FOCUS

READING
Wrap Up
Word Work
• Read Words
WRITING
Writing/Grammar
• Self-Selected Writing
• Review Grammar

Research and Inquiry
• Share and Evaluate Presentation
Text Connections
• Connect Essential Question to a photo
• Show Your Knowledge

Reading/Writing Companion, pp. 78–79

LEARNING GOALS

• We can add a sound to words to make new words.

• We can tell /ē/ from /e/.

• We can spell words with the letters *f* and *r*.

• We can spell the words *with* and *he*.

OBJECTIVES

Add or substitute individual sounds (phonemes) in simple, one-syllable words to make new words.

Demonstrate basic knowledge of one-to-one letter-sound correspondences by producing the primary sound or many of the most frequent sounds for each consonant.

Spell simple words phonetically, drawing on knowledge of sound-letter relationships.

Read common high-frequency words by sight.

ELA ACADEMIC LANGUAGE
• *add, beginning*

TEACH IN SMALL GROUP

You may wish to teach the Word Work lesson in small groups.

DIGITAL TOOLS

Word Work **Phonemic Awareness**

Visual Vocabulary Cards

Spelling Song

5 mins

Phonemic Awareness

MULTIMODAL

Phoneme Addition

1 **Model** *Listen to this word:* at. *What word do we make if we add /f/ to the beginning of* at? *When we add /f/ to* at, *we make the word* fat. Repeat substituting /r/ to make the word *rat*.

2 **Guided Practice/Practice** *Answer these questions by adding the sound to make a new word.* Guide practice and provide corrective feedback as needed.

Say *an*. Add /f/ to the beginning of *an*. What's the new word? (fan)
Say *an*. Add /r/ to the beginning of *an*. What's the new word? (ran)
Say *it*. Add /f/ to the beginning of *it*. What's the new word? (fit)
Say *am*. Add /r/ to the beginning of *am*. What's the new word? (ram)

Long Vowel Awareness

1 **Model** Hold up the **Photo Card** for *feet*. *This is a picture of feet. Feet has the /ē/ sound in the middle. Listen: /f/ /ēēē/ /t/.* Place the *feet* card on one side of a pocket chart to begin a column for /ē/. Repeat with the Photo Card for *jet* placing it on the other side of the pocket chart to begin a column for /e/.

2 **Guided Practice/Practice** Display and name each of the following Photo Cards: *cheese, gem, green, leaf, net, pen, queen, shell, teeth, web*. Have children say the picture name and sort the picture by the middle sounds /ē/ or /e/. Guide practice and provide corrective feedback as needed.

Review Repeat the sorting routine with /ā/, /ī/, and /ō/ using the following Photo Cards: *bike, goat, rake, nose, dime*.

Sound-Spelling Connection You may wish to introduce the sound spelling for long e, *ee* using the *Tree* **Sound-Spelling Card**. Point to the letters *ee* and explain that these letters stand for the /ē/ sound they hear in *Tree*.

In a Flash: Sound-Spellings

Display the Sound-Spelling Card for *f*.

1. **Teacher:** What's the letter?   **Children:** f
2. **Teacher:** What's the sound?   **Children:** /f/
3. **Teacher:** What's the word?   **Children:** fire

Continue the routine for *r* and previously taught sounds.

Phonics

Read Words

1 **Guided Practice** Display **Word-Building Cards** *f, a, n.* Point to *f. The letter* f *stands for /f/. Say /f/. The letter* a *stands for /a/. Say /a/. The letter* n *stands for /n/. Say /n/. Let's blend the sounds to make the word: /fffaaannn/* fan. *Now let's change the* f *to an* r *at the beginning of the word.* Blend and read *ran.*

2 **Practice** Write these words and sentences for children to read:

rid	red	fit	fat	rod	rip	fad	fin	if

I like the red fan.   **I fit in the hat.**   **We ran to the den.**

Remove words from view before dictation.

Review /f/ *f* and /r/ *r*. Have children write the letter *f* on their **Response Boards**. Play and sing the song "Let's Build a Fire." Have children hold up and show the letter *f* when they hear initial /f/. Repeat with /r/ *r* and the song "A Rose."

Spell Words

Dictation Dictate the following sounds. As you say each sound, have children repeat it and then write the letter/s that stands for it:

/r/   /f/   /e/   /h/   /d/   /o/   /k/   /n/   /i/   /st/

Model how to segment words to scaffold the spelling. *I will say a word. You will repeat the word, then think about how many sounds are in the word. Use your **Sound Boxes** to count the sounds. Then write one letter for each sound you hear:* fan, Stan, fit, ran, red, fin, rod, rid. Write the letters and words for children to self-correct.

High-Frequency Words

1 **Review** Display **Visual Vocabulary Cards** *with* and *he*. Have children Read/Spell/Write each word.

Distribute one of these **High-Frequency Word Cards** to children: *he, with, are, my, do, you.* Say: *I'll say some sentences. When you hear the word on your card, stand and hold up the card.*

He likes fresh peaches.   **Can *he* go *with you*?**
Can *he* go *with you*?   **Apples *are* delicious.**

MULTIMODAL LEARNING

Color Coding After each dictation, reveal the secret color-coding-letter(s) for children to find on their response boards. Have them say the sound(s) as they trace each letter in color. Use one or two of the phonics skills of the week for color coding.

FORMATIVE ASSESSMENT

❯ STUDENT CHECK-IN

Phonics Have partners spell *ram* and *fan*.

High-Frequency Words Have partners spell the words *with* and *he*.

Then have children reflect using the Check-In routine.

✅ CHECK FOR SUCCESS

Rubric Use your online rubric to record children's progress.

Can children add phonemes to words to make new words and read words with /f/ *f* and /r/ *r*?

Can children read and recognize high-frequency words?

❯ **Small Group Instruction**

If No

● **Approaching** Reteach pp. T218–222

● **ELL** Develop pp. T218–222

If Yes

● **On** Review pp. T226–228

● **Beyond** Extend p. T232

LESSON 5

Self-Selected Writing

LEARNING GOALS

- **We can choose a writing activity and share it.**
- **We can learn about words that can take the place of nouns (pronouns).**

OBJECTIVES

With guidance and support from adults, explore a variety of digital tools to produce and publish writing, including in collaboration with peers.

Ask and answer questions in order to seek help, get information, or clarify something that is not understood.

Speak audibly and express thoughts, feelings, and ideas clearly.

Produce and expand complete sentences in shared language activities.

Appropriately use pronouns.

ELA ACADEMIC LANGUAGE

- *topic, order*
- Cognate: *orden*

DIFFERENTIATED WRITING

You may wish to conference with children to provide additional support for the writing activities below.

- Journal Writing: Have partners brainstorm different living things that grow on farms.
- Make a Book: Have children tell their story to a partner using *first, next,* and *last* before drawing and writing.

Talk About the Topic

Have children continue the conversation about different living things that grow in nature. Remind children of the Essential Question: *What kinds of things grow on a farm?* Have partners ask each other questions about living things that grow on farms.

Choose a Writing Activity

Tell children they will choose what type of writing to do today. They may choose to write about things that grow on farms or a different topic. Encourage them to draw first as a way to get their ideas down on paper as well as to give more details to their writing. Children may choose from the following modes of writing:

 Journal Writing Remind children that a journal is a book in which they can draw and write whatever they wish. Have children write in their journals about things that grow on farms or choose another topic to write about. Encourage them to draw their ideas first and then write about them.

 Make a Book Provide children with paper they can use to make a small book about farms or another topic. Model how to fold the paper to make it look like a book. Have children look at classroom library books as models for their hand-made books. Encourage them to include a cover with a title. If their books tell about events, remind children to tell what happens in order.

Use Digital Tools You may wish to work with children to explore a variety of digital tools to produce or publish their work.

Share Your Writing

 COLLABORATE

Invite volunteers to share their writing with the class or have partners share their writing with each other. Remind children to use the strategies below as they share out. After children share their work, you may wish to display it on a bulletin board or in a classroom writing area.

SPEAKING STRATEGIES	LISTENING STRATEGIES
✓ Speak slowly and clearly.	✓ Listen actively and politely.
✓ Speak at an appropriate volume.	✓ Wait until the speaker has finished to ask questions.

Grammar

Subjective Pronouns

1 **Review** Write and read aloud: **Max eats a banana. He likes it**. Point out that *Max* and *banana* are naming words. *The pronoun* he *is used to replace* Max *because* Max *is a boy. The pronoun* it *is used to replace* banana *because a banana is a thing.*

2 **Guided Practice/Practice** *What fruit or vegetable do you like best? What fruit or vegetable do you like least?* Make a list of children's responses on the board. Write sentence pairs using nouns in the first sentence and pronouns in the second sentence. Read the sentences aloud. Guide children to identify the pronoun in the second sentence and the noun that it replaces. For instance: **Mike likes cherries. He likes cherries**. (Mike/he)

Write two more sentence pairs on the board. Have partners identify the nouns and the pronouns that replace them: **Jack read the book. He read the book**. (Jack/He) **The tree is green. It is green**. (tree/It) Then, challenge partners to make up their own sentence pairs with pronouns. Circulate and provide corrective feedback as needed.

🔵 English Language Learners

Self-Selected Writing, Choose a Writing Activity Present the writing activities, and tell the children that they will vote on one of the activities. Then, you will work on the writing as a group. Make sure to do the activity on chart paper as you will revise and publish it during small group time. Provide sentence frames and starters as you talk through the writing together. For example, if children have selected making a book about farms, talk about what children know about farms. Possible sentence frames are: You can see ____ on a farm. ____ live on a farm. Farmers ____ their ____.

For additional support, see the **ELL Small Group Guide,** p. 129.

DIGITAL TOOLS

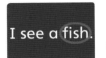

Grammar Activity

⊗ TEACH IN SMALL GROUP

You may wish to have children review the grammar skill during small group time.

● **Approaching** Provide more opportunities for children to replace nouns with pronouns before they write sentences.

●● **On-Level** and **Beyond** Children can do the Practice sections only.

● **ELL** Use the chart in the **Language Transfers Handbook** to identify grammatical forms that may cause difficulty for children.

FORMATIVE ASSESSMENT

❯ STUDENT CHECK-IN

Have partners share which activity they chose and tell why. Then have children reflect using the Check-In routine.

LESSON 5

LEARNING GOALS

We can compare texts we have read.

OBJECTIVES

Confirm understanding of a text read aloud or information presented orally or through other media by asking and answering questions about key details and requesting clarification if something is not understood.

ELA ACADEMIC LANGUAGE

• photo, caption, experience
• Cognate: foto

Close Reading Routine

Read   DOK 1–2

• Identify key ideas and details.
• Take notes and retell.
• Use **ACT** prompts as needed.

Reread   DOK 2–3

• Analyze text, craft and structure.

Integrate   DOK 3–4

• Integrate knowledge and ideas.
• Make text-to-text connections.
• Use the Integrate lesson.
• Complete the Show Your Knowledge task.

FORMATIVE ASSESSMENT

❯ STUDENT CHECK-IN

Have partners share what they learned from comparing texts.

Have children reflect using the Check-In routine.

⏱ 10 mins Make Connections

Connect to the Essential Question

Review the Essential Question. Turn to page 78 of the **Reading/Writing Companion**. Have children look at the photo and listen to the caption. What does the photo show?

Find Text Evidence Have children answer the following questions about this page and the **Big Book**: *What is growing on this farm?* (vegetables) *What is growing on the farm in* An Orange in January? (oranges) Use the Quick Tip box for support.

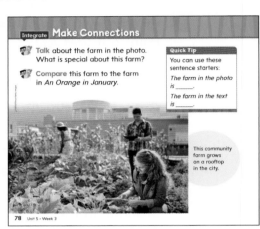

Reading/Writing Companion, p. 78

Record Ideas Guide partners to compare the photo of the farm on page 78 of the Reading/Writing Companion with the farm in the selection *An Orange in January. How are the farms alike? How are they different? How do they help you answer the Essential Question?* Help children use a Two-Tab Foldable® to record their ideas. Have children support their ideas with evidence from the pictures, caption, and text.

Dinah Zike's

FOLDABLES®
Study Organizer

 Build Knowledge: Make Connections DOK 4

Talk About the Text Have partners compare the text with experiences from their own lives.

Add to the Anchor Chart Record any new ideas on the Build Knowledge anchor chart.

Integrate

Show Your Knowledge

15 mins

Make a Shopping List DOK 4

Display the texts for the week along with the Build Knowledge anchor chart and Word Bank. Turn to page 79 of the **Reading/ Writing Companion** and guide children through the steps below.

1. Think Ask: *What did you learn about the kinds of things that grow on a farm?* Encourage partners to refer to their reader's notebook and the resources on display as they discuss their response.

2. Draw Guide children to draw a list of foods that they can buy at a farmers' market.

Reading/Writing Companion, p. 79

3. Label Have children label each food using words they learned this week. Encourage them to use words they learned this week as they write. Have children share their shopping lists with a neighbor or with the class.

Inspire Action

Add to the List Group children according to the foods they drew. Provide each group with picture books about farms and markets. Challenge children to identify new foods to add to their drawings.

To the Market Invite children to set up a pretend farmers' market in the classroom. Encourage them to use their shopping lists for ideas about what to include at the market. Children can refer to their lists when they go "shopping."

Choose Your Own Action Have children talk about the texts they read this week. *What do the texts inspire or make you want to do?*

OBJECTIVES

With guidance and support from adults, recall information from experiences or gather information from provided sources to answer a question.

Add drawings or other visual displays to descriptions as desired to provide additional detail.

Describe familiar people, places, things, and events and, with prompting and support, provide additional detail.

ELA ACADEMIC LANGUAGE

• *list, market, inspire*

ELL ENGLISH LANGUAGE LEARNERS

Show Your Knowledge, Think Provide and model sentence starters or frames to talk about the kinds of things that grow on a farm. For example, _____ grow on a farm. _____ in the fall. You can find _____ growing _____.

DIGITAL TOOLS

To enhance the class discussion, use these additional components.

Visual Vocabulary Cards

 RUBRIC **Show Your Knowledge Rubric**

MY GOALS ROUTINE

Review Goal Have children turn to page 59 of the **Reading/Writing Companion**. Read the goals aloud.

Check for Progress Have children think about the progress they've made toward the goals. Review the Key, if needed. Then have children complete page 59.

Lexile BR

OBJECTIVES

Follow words from left to right, top to bottom, and page by page.

With prompting and support, identify the main topic and retell key details of a text.

Read emergent-reader texts with purpose and understanding.

ELA ACADEMIC LANGUAGE

• *preview, predict*

• Cognate: *predecir*

●Approaching Level

Leveled Reader: *The Farmer*

Preview and Predict

Point to the cover and read the title and the names of the author and illustrator, as children follow along in their books. *What does the author do? What does the illustrator do?* Preview the illustrations and identify the rebus pictures in the book with children. *What do you think the selection will be about?*

Review Genre: Informational Text: Nonfiction

Remind children that nonfiction texts can give information in a certain order or sequence. Ask children: *What kind of information do you think we might learn from this book?* (the things a farmer sells from his farm)

Set Purpose

Remind children of the Essential Question: *What kinds of things grow on a farm?* Set a purpose for reading: *Let's find out what kinds of foods are grown on farms that a farmer might sell.* Review rebuses with children to help them name the words.

Foundational Skills

Model Concepts of Print Model reading a sentence as children follow along with their books. *I begin reading at the left and move to the right. The sentence begins with a capital letter and ends with a period.*

Review High-Frequency Words Point out the word *he* on page 2, and read it with children. Have them find the word on pages 3 and 4. Ask: *Who is "he"?* (the farmer)

Guided Comprehension

As children read *The Farmer,* monitor and provide guidance by correcting blending. Model rereading and identifying the topic and details where applicable.

Reread

Remind children that, if they find a part of the book confusing, they can reread the text to help them better understand what is happening.

Topic and Details

Review with children that reading the text and looking at the illustrations will help them learn about the topic and details in a selection.

Think Aloud The words on page 2 don't tell me who the man is or where he is. The title of the book is *The Farmer*, and the picture shows a man selling red apples to a woman at a market. I can confirm that detail by reading the words on page 2: *He sells red apples.* The title and these details tell me that the topic of this selection is a farmer selling things at a farmers' market.

Guide children to identify details on pages 4 and 5 that support the topic. *Do these things grow on a farm?*

Respond to the Text

Have children respond to the text by discussing these questions:

- *Where does this selection take place?* (at a farmers' market)
- *How do you know?* (from the title and the pictures)
- *What kinds of things does the farmer sell?* (apples, peppers, flowers)
- *What color is everything the farmer sells?* (red)

Retell Have children take turns retelling the text, using the topic and details, while other children act it out. Help them make a personal connection. *What would you like to buy at a farmers' market?*

Focus on Fluency

Practice fluency with children. Remember that children need to read with accuracy first.

Once children have read the text with accuracy, have them read the selection again, focusing on rate. Have them practice reading with partners. Provide corrective feedback as necessary.

Build Knowledge: Make Connections

- **Talk About the Texts** Have partners discuss food that grows on a farm.
- **Write About the Texts** Then have children add their ideas to their Build Knowledge page of their reader's notebook.

LITERACY ACTIVITIES

Have children complete the Collaborate and Write About It activities on the inside back cover of the book.

LEVEL UP

IF Children read *The Farmer* Approaching Level with fluency and correctly answer the Respond to the Text questions,

THEN Tell children that they will read another book about food that's grown on a farm.

- Have children page through *Let's Make a Salad!* On Level as you introduce the topic of a farmer growing food.
- Have children read the book, monitoring their comprehension and providing assistance as necessary.

Approaching Level

Phonological/Phonemic Awareness

RECOGNIZE RHYME

MULTIMODAL

TIER 2

OBJECTIVES
Recognize rhyming words.

I Do Say the words *grow* and *know*, emphasizing the final sound. Tell children that *grow* and *know* both end in /ō/. These words rhyme because they have the same ending sound.

We Do Have children repeat *grow* and *know* after you, emphasizing the ending sound. Then say *cub, tub* and have children repeat. *Do these words rhyme:* cub, tub? *Yes, because they have the same ending sounds:* /ub/.

You Do Say the following word pairs and have children touch their noses if the words rhyme: *feed, need; far, car; fan, fit; roof, room; land, hand.*

PHONEME ISOLATION

TIER 2

OBJECTIVES
Isolate and pronounce the initial, medial vowel, and final sounds in three-phoneme words.

I Do Display the *fan* **Photo Card**. *This is a* fan. *The first sound in* fan *is /fff/.* Have children repeat the word with you, emphasizing the initial sound. Then have children say the first sound with you: /fff/.

We Do Display the *farm* Photo Card. Name the photo and have children say the name. *What is the first sound in* farm? (/f/) Say the sound together. Repeat with the *feather* Photo Card.

You Do Show the *feet* Photo Card. Have children name it and say the initial sound of the picture name. Repeat with the *fire* Photo Card.

Repeat the routine for /r/ using the *rock* Photo Card in *I Do* and the *rabbit, rake, ring,* and *rose* Photo Cards in the rest of the lesson.

ELL You may wish to review phonological awareness, phonics, decoding, and fluency using this section. Use scaffolding methods as necessary to ensure children understand the meaning of the words. Refer to the **Language Transfers Handbook** for phonics elements that may not transfer in children's native languages.

PHONEME BLENDING

OBJECTIVES

Demonstrate understanding of spoken words, syllables, and sounds (phonemes).

Blend phonemes to make words.

I Do *I am going to say the sounds in a word. Listen: /f/ /i/ /t/. I can blend these sounds together: /fffiiit/, fit. Repeat with foot.*

We Do *Now I am going to say the sounds in another word. Say the sounds with me: /f/ /a/ /n/. Let's blend the sounds together: /fffaaannn/, fan. Repeat with fox and fun.*

You Do Have children blend sounds to form words. Practice together: /f/ /ē/ /t/ /fffēēēt/, feet. Then have children blend sounds to say the words.

/f/ /i/ /l/ fill   /f/ /a/ /t/ fat   /f/ /ō/ /n/ phone   /f/ /e/ /d/ fed

Repeat the routine for /r/ and the sounds in the words *red, ripe, rat,* and *rip.*

You may wish to use a puppet, if one is available in the classroom, for the *I Do* and *We Do* parts of this lesson.

PHONEME ADDITION

OBJECTIVES

Add or substitute individual sounds (phonemes) in simple, one-syllable words to make new words.

I Do *Listen as I say a word:* in. *Now I will add /f/ to the beginning of* in: fin. *By adding /f/ to* in, *I made a new word:* fin. Repeat the routine using *an* and /f/.

We Do Say *at.* Now add /f/ to the beginning of *at.* *What is the new word?* (fat) Then add /f/ to *it* to make the new word *fit.* Have children repeat the new word after you.

You Do Say *all* and the sound /f/. Ask children to add the /f/ sound to *all* to make *fall.* Repeat, having them add the /f/ sound to *ed.*

Repeat for /r/. Have children add /r/ to *an* (ran), *am* (ram), and *at* (rat).

You may wish to use a puppet, if one is available, for the *I Do* and *We Do* parts of this lesson.

●Approaching Level

Phonics

SOUND-SPELLING REVIEW

OBJECTIVES
Associate the long and short sounds with the common spellings (graphemes) for the five major vowels.

I Do Display **Word-Building Card** *e*. Say the letter name and the sound it stands for: *e, /e/*. Repeat for *h, d, o, c, n, i*, and the initial blend *st*.

We Do Display Word-Building Cards one at a time and together say the letter name and the sound that each letter stands for.

You Do Display Word-Building Cards one at a time and have children say the letter name and the sound that each letter stands for.

CONNECT *f* TO /*f*/ AND *r* TO /*r*/

OBJECTIVES
Demonstrate basic knowledge of one-to-one letter-sound correspondences by producing the primary sound or many of the most frequent sounds for each consonant.

I Do Display the *fire* **Sound-Spelling Card**. *The letter* f *stands for /f/ at the beginning of* fire. *I will write* f *when I hear /f/ in these words:* fit, feet, neck, fin, peel, food.

We Do *The word* fair *begins with /f/. Let's write* f. Guide children to write *f* when they hear a word that begins with /f/. Say: *find, meet, den, fan, mop, fast.*

You Do Have children write *f* on their **Response Boards** if a word begins with /f/: *face, orange, fish, far, fork.* Repeat for /r/ using the *rose* Sound-Spelling Card and the words *red, run, melt, arm, reach, come, duck, real,* and *rabbit.*

BLEND WORDS WITH /*f*/*f* AND /*r*/*r*

OBJECTIVES
Know and apply grade-level phonics and word analysis skills in decoding words.

Build words with *f* and *r*.

I Do Display Word-Building Cards *f, e,* and *d. This is the letter* f. *It stands for /f/. This is the letter* e. *It stands for /e/. This is the letter* d. *It stands for /d/. Listen as I blend the sounds: /fffeeed/,* fed. *The word is* fed. Repeat for *fit.*

We Do *Now let's blend more sounds to make words.* Show the word *fan. Let's blend: /fffaaannn/,* fan. Have children blend to read the word. *I will change the letter* a *in* fan *to an* i. *Let's blend and read the new word: /fiiinnn/,* fin.

You Do Distribute sets of Word-Building Cards with *f, a, d, e, i, n, t.* Write: *fit, fan, fin, fed.* Have children form the words, blend, and read them. Repeat the routine for /r/ using the words *red, rod, rot, rip, rid, rim, ram.*

BUILD WORDS WITH /f/ f AND /r/ r

OBJECTIVES

Know and apply grade-level phonics and word analysis skills in decoding words.

Build words with f and r.

I Do Display **Word-Building Cards** f, i, and n. *These are letters* f, i, *and* n. *They stand for /f/, /i/, /n/. I will blend /f/, /i/, /n/ together: /fffiiin/,* fin. *The word is* fin. Repeat the routine with /r/ and the word *ram*.

We Do Distribute sets of Word-Building Cards with f, i, n, t, r, a, and m. Show how to make the word *fin* and have children do the same. Replace the letter n at the end with the letter t and have children do the same. *Let's blend /fiiittt/,* fit. *Now we have read a new word,* fit.

You Do Have children change the final m in *ram* to t and read the new word, *rat*. Repeat with the word *fed*. Have them change the initial f to r and read the new word, *red*. Point out that by changing one letter we make a new word.

REREAD THE DECODABLE READER

OBJECTIVES

Know and apply grade-level phonics and word analysis skills in decoding words.

Read emergent-reader texts with purpose and understanding.

Unit 5 Decodable Reader

Focus on Foundational Skills

Review the high-frequency words *with* and *he* with children. Review the letter-sound relationships /f/ f and /r/ r. Guide children to blend sounds to read *fan* and *rot*.

Read the Decodable Reader

Have children read "Ron Ram" and "Red and Ron." Point out the high-frequency words *with* and *he* as well as words with /f/ and /r/. If children struggle sounding out words, model blending.

Focus on Fluency

Have partners read "Ron Ram" and "Red and Ron." Guide them to focus on their accuracy. Children can give feedback on their accuracy to their partners. Then have them focus on reading with automaticity and at an appropriate rate. You may wish to have them reread "Ron With Red" (pages 66–73) in the **Reading/Writing Companion**.

BUILD FLUENCY WITH PHONICS

Sound/Spelling Fluency

Display the following Word-Building Cards: e, h, d, o, c, n, i, f, st, and r. Have children chorally say each sound. Repeat and vary the pace.

Approaching Level

High-Frequency Words

RETEACH WORDS

MULTIMODAL

TIER 2

OBJECTIVES
Read common high-frequency words by sight.

I Do Display the **High-Frequency Word Card** *he* and use the Read/Spell/Write routine to reteach the word. Repeat for the high-frequency word *with*.

We Do Write this sentence and read it aloud: *He picked a red apple.* Have children point to the word *he* in the sentence. Reread the sentence with children. Use the same routine for *with* and the sentence: *I go with Ron to the farm.*

You Do Write the sentence frame: *He can go with you to the* _____. Have children copy the sentence frame on their **Response Boards**. Then have partners work together to read and orally complete the frame by talking about a place that one boy in the class could visit.

CUMULATIVE REVIEW

MULTIMODAL

OBJECTIVES
Read common high-frequency words by sight.

I Do Display the High-Frequency Word Cards *I, can, the, we, see, a, like, to, and, go, you, do, my, are, he,* and *with*. Use the Read/Spell/Write routine to review words. Have children practice reading the words until they can read them accurately and with automaticity.

We Do Use the High-Frequency Word Cards and **Word-Building Cards** to create sentences, such as *We like to go with you. Can the man see the cat?* Have children identify the high-frequency words that are used in each sentence. Read the sentences together.

You Do Have partners use the High-Frequency Word Cards and Word-Building Cards to create short sentences. Have partners take turns reading the sentences to each other.

Oral Vocabulary

OBJECTIVES

Use words and phrases acquired through conversations, reading and being read to, and responding to texts.

Identify real-life connections between words and their use.

I Do Use the Define/Example/Ask routine on the print or digital **Visual Vocabulary Cards** to review *fresh, delicious, beneath, raise,* and *special.*

We Do Ask questions to build understanding. *Which is a fresh food: a can of corn or an ear of corn? Why? What is the most delicious food you have ever tried? What is beneath a boat on a lake? How can you help raise a pet? What is a special activity you do at school?*

You Do Have children complete these sentence frames:

The market sells fresh _____. The lunchroom serves delicious _____. Earthworms live beneath the _____. It would be easy to raise a _____. To make a day special, I like to _____.

Comprehension

OBJECTIVES

With prompting and support, identify the main topic and retell key details of a text.

Read emergent-reader texts with purpose and understanding.

Independent Reading

Help children select a nonfiction text for independent reading. Encourage them to read for twelve minutes. Remind children that details in the words and pictures of a nonfiction text give information about the topic. If they find a part of the book confusing, they can reread the text to help them better understand what is happening.

If children need additional practice with concepts of print, have them use **Practice Book** page 507.

Read Purposefully

After reading, guide children to participate in a group discussion about the selection they read. In addition, children can choose activities from the Reading **Center Activity Cards** to help them apply skills to the text as they read. Offer assistance and guidance with self-selected assignments.

Lexile BR

OBJECTIVES

Follow words from left to right, top to bottom, and page by page.

With prompting and support, identify the main topic and retell key details of a text.

Read emergent-reader texts with purpose and understanding.

ELA ACADEMIC LANGUAGE

• *title, author, illustrator*
• Cognates: *título, autor, ilustrador*

●On Level

Leveled Reader: *Let's Make a Salad!*

Preview and Predict

Show children the cover of the book. Read the title aloud with them. Ask children to point to the names of the author and illustrator on their copies of the book. *What does the author do? What does the illustrator do?* Preview the illustrations in the book. *What do the illustrations show? What do you think this book is about?*

Review Genre: Informational Text: Nonfiction

Remind children that nonfiction texts can give information in a certain order, or sequence. Display the cover of the book. Read the title of the book aloud. Ask: *What information do you think we might learn from this book?* (Children may guess that the book is about how to make a salad.)

Set Purpose

Remind children of the Essential Question: *What kinds of things grow on a farm?* Model setting a purpose for reading: *Let's read the book to find out how a man uses foods that come from a farm.* Remind children to use the illustrations to help them understand the text.

Foundational Skills

Model Concepts of Print Have children follow along in their own books as you model reading from left to right and turning the pages. *When I reach the end of a sentence, I pause before I begin a new sentence.*

Review High-Frequency Words Point to the word *he* on page 2, and read it aloud with children. Have them find the word on pages 3 and 4.

Guided Comprehension

As children read *Let's Make a Salad!* monitor and provide guidance by correcting blending. Model rereading and identifying the topic and details where applicable.

Reread

Remind children that, if they come to a part of the text that they do not fully understand, they can go back and reread. Rereading can often clear up confusion or misunderstanding.

Topic and Details

Remind children that both the text and the illustrations can help them understand details of a selection. Explain that details give information about the topic, or what the selection is about.

Think Aloud The book's title tells me that the topic of the selection is how to make a salad. On page 2, I learn that the man gets the lettuce. I can see lettuce growing in the field. I think the man is the farmer. On page 3, I read that he gets the carrots. Lettuce and carrots are shown near the salad bowl. These details tell me more about the topic. The farmer is getting food that he grows on his farm to make a salad.

Have children use the pictures and words on pages 7 and 8 to find details about what else the farmer gets to make his salad.

Respond to the Text

Have children respond to the text by discussing these questions:

- *What is the topic of the book?* (making a salad at a farm)
- *What does the farmer get first?* (lettuce)
- *What does he get next?* (carrots)
- *What does the farmer get last?* (the family)

Retell Invite children to draw pictures of each vegetable in the book. Have them use their drawings to retell the text, using the topic and details. Help children make personal connections by asking: *What do you like to put in a salad?*

Focus on Fluency

Practice fluency with children. Remember that they need to read with accuracy first.

Once children have read the text with accuracy, have them read the selection again, focusing on rate. Have children practice reading in pairs. Provide corrective feedback as necessary.

Build Knowledge: Make Connections

- **Talk About the Texts** Have partners discuss food that grows on a farm.
- **Write About the Texts** Then have children add their ideas to their Build Knowledge page of their reader's notebook.

LITERACY ACTIVITIES

Have children complete the Collaborate and Write About It activities on the inside back cover of the book.

LEVEL UP

IF Children can read the *Let's Make a Salad!* On Level with fluency and correctly answer the questions,

THEN Tell children that they will read another book about a farm and how vegetables grow.

- Have children page through *Farm Fresh Finn* Beyond Level as you introduce the characters and the premise for the book. Say: *Finn is a boy who lives in the city and doesn't like eating vegetables. This changes, though, when he goes to visit his grandfather's farm.*

- Have children read the book, monitoring their comprehension and providing assistance as necessary.

●On Level

Phonological/Phonemic Awareness

PHONEME ISOLATION

OBJECTIVES

Isolate and pronounce the initial sounds in words.

I Do Display the *fox* **Photo Card**. *This is a* fox. *The first sound is /f/. Say it with me.* Repeat with /r/ and the *rose* Photo Card.

We Do Say *fan* and have children repeat it. *What is the first sound in* fan? (/f/) Say the sound together. Repeat with *face, fun, rat,* and *rope.*

You Do Say *feet, find, felt, fool, ramp, road, rest, rice* and have children tell the initial sound in each word.

PHONEME BLENDING

OBJECTIVES

Demonstrate understanding of spoken words, syllables, and sounds (phonemes).

I Do Place the *fish, five, fox, rake, rock, rope* Photo Cards facedown. Choose a card. Do not show the card. *These are the sounds in the word: /f/ /i/ /sh/. I will blend the sounds: /fffiiish/,* fish. *The word is* fish. Show the picture.

We Do Choose another picture and say the sounds in the word. Together say and blend the sounds to say the word. Then show the picture.

You Do Continue choosing Photo Cards. Say the sounds and have children blend the sounds and say the words.

PHONEME ADDITION

OBJECTIVES

Add or substitute individual sounds (phonemes) in simple, one-syllable words to make new words.

I Do Say: *Listen as I add a sound to the beginning of a word to make a new word. Listen to this word:* an. *When I add /f/ to the beginning of* an, *I make the new word* fan. Repeat with adding /r/ to *an.*

We Do *Listen to this word:* in. *Say the word. Let's add /f/ to* in: fin. *Say the new word with me:* fin. Repeat with *at* and /r/.

You Do Say *all. What word do you have when you add /f/ to the beginning of* all? (fall) Repeat, having children add /m/ to *ask,* and /r/ and /k/ to *an,* to make the words *mask, ran,* and *can.*

Phonics

REVIEW PHONICS

OBJECTIVES

Demonstrate basic knowledge of one-to-one letter-sound correspondences by producing the primary sound or many of the most frequent sounds for each consonant.

I Do Display the *fire* **Sound-Spelling Card**. *The letter* f *stands for the /f/ sound you hear at the beginning of* fire. Say *fire,* emphasizing the /f/. Repeat the routine with the *rose* Sound-Spelling Card.

We Do Display the *fish, fan,* and *five* **Photo Cards**. Have children say the name of each picture together with you. Then ask them to identify the words with /f/ at the beginning. Repeat with the *rope, rabbit,* and *rake* Photo Cards by having children identify words with /r/ at the beginning.

You Do Write the words *fin, fed, fan, rip, rat,* and *rod* and have children read each one. Provide corrective feedback as needed. Repeat, asking them to raise their hands if they hear /f/ at the beginning of the word or touch their heads if they hear /r/ at the beginning of the word.

PICTURE SORT

OBJECTIVES

Demonstrate basic knowledge of one-to-one letter-sound correspondences by producing the primary sound or many of the most frequent sounds for each consonant.

I Do Display **Word-Building Cards** *f* and *p* in a pocket chart. Then show the *fan* Photo Card. Say: /f/ /a/ /n/, fan. Tell children that the beginning sound is /f/. *The letter* f *stands for /f/. I will put the fan under the letter* f. Show the *pig* Photo Card. Say: /p/ /i/ /g/, pig. Tell children that the beginning sound is /p/. *The letter* p *stands for /p/. I will put the Photo Card for* pig *under the* p.

We Do Show the Photo Card for *fork* and say *fork*. Have children repeat. Then have them tell the sound they hear at the beginning of *fork*. Ask them if they should place the photo under the *f* or the *p*.

You Do Continue the activity using Photo Cards for *five, fire, feet, fox, football, pea, pear, pen, pie,* and *pillow*. Have children say the picture name and the initial sound. Then have them place the card under the *f* or *p*.

Repeat the routine for initial /r/*r* and /m/*m* with the Photo Cards for *rabbit, rake, rock, rose, ruby, man, mix, moon, moth,* and *mouse*.

●On Level

Phonics

BLEND WORDS WITH /f/f AND /r/r

OBJECTIVES

Know and apply grade-level phonics and word analysis skills in decoding words.

Build words with short *f* and *r*.

I Do Display **Word-Building Cards** *f, i, t. This is the letter* f. *It stands for /f/. Say it with me: /fff/. This is the letter* i. *It stands for /i/. Say it with me: /iii/. This is the letter* t. *It stands for /t/. Say it with me: /t/. I'll blend the sounds together to read the word: /fffiiit/,* fit. *Repeat the routine with /r/ and the word* ran.

We Do Use Word-Building Cards to form the words *fan* and *rip*. Guide children to blend the words sound by sound to read each word.

You Do Use the following words and have children blend the words sound by sound to read each word.

fat   if   rat   ram   rim   red   Ron   fed

REREAD THE DECODABLE READER

OBJECTIVES

Know and apply grade-level phonics and word analysis skills in decoding words.

Read emergent-reader texts with purpose and understanding.

Unit 5 Decodable Reader

Focus on Foundational Skills

Review the high-frequency words *with* and *he* with children. Review the letter-sound relationships /f/f and /r/r. Guide children to blend sounds to read *fan* and *rot*.

Read the Decodable Reader

Have children read "Ron Ram" and "Red and Ron." Point out the high-frequency words *with* and *he* as well as words with /f/ or /r/. If children struggle sounding out words, model blending.

Focus on Fluency

Have partners read "Ron Ram" and "Red and Ron." Guide them to focus on their accuracy. Children can give feedback on their accuracy to their partners. Then have them focus on reading with automaticity and at an appropriate rate. You may wish to have them reread "Ron With Red" (pages 66–73) in the **Reading/Writing Companion**.

High-Frequency Words

REVIEW WORDS

OBJECTIVES

Read common high-frequency words by sight.

 Display the **High-Frequency Word Card** *he* and use the Read/Spell/Write routine to review the word. Repeat for the high-frequency word *with*.

 Write and read the sentences: *He picked a red apple* and *I go with Ron to the farm.* Point to the word *he* and have children read it. Chorally read the sentence. Have them frame *he* in the sentence and read it. Repeat with the word *with*.

 Say the word *he*. Ask children to close their eyes, picture the word, and write it as they see it. Have them self-correct. Repeat with the word *with*. Reteach previously introduced high-frequency words, including the **Build Your Word Bank** words, using the routine.

Fluency Use the **Practice Book Word Cards** to review all the High-Frequency and Build Your Word Bank words. In random order, point to the words. Have children practice reading the words until they can read accurately and with automaticity.

Comprehension

SELF-SELECTED READING

OBJECTIVES

With prompting and support, identify the main topic and retell key details of a text.

Read emergent-reader texts with purpose and understanding.

Independent Reading

Help children select a nonfiction text with photographs for independent reading. Have them read for twelve minutes. Guide children to transfer what they have learned this week as they read. Remind children that details in the words and pictures of a nonfiction text give information about the topic. If they find a part of the book confusing, they can reread the text to help them better understand what is happening.

After reading, guide children to participate in a group discussion about the selection they read. In addition, children can choose activities from the Reading **Center Activity Cards** to help them apply skills to the text as they read. Offer assistance and guidance with self-selected assignments.

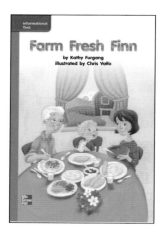

Lexile 260L

OBJECTIVES

Recognize common types of texts.

Ask and answer questions in order to seek help, get information, or clarify something that is not understood.

With prompting and support, identify the main topic and retell key details of a text.

Read emergent-reader texts with purpose and understanding.

ELA ACADEMIC LANGUAGE

• *skill, comprehension*

• Cognate: *comprensión*

● Beyond Level

Leveled Reader: *Farm Fresh Finn*

Preview and Predict

Point to the cover and read aloud the title and the author's and illustrator's names with children. Have them use the picture on the cover to predict what the book is about. Have children page through the book and look at the illustrations. Have children confirm or revise their predictions.

Review Genre: Informational Text: Nonfiction

Remind children that they have been reading nonfiction texts this week. Explain that nonfiction texts give information about real topics. Ask: *How do you know when a book is nonfiction?* (Nonfiction texts give facts and information about a topic.)

Set Purpose

Remind children of the Essential Question: *What kinds of things grow on a farm?* Have children set a purpose for reading. *Let's find out how people use the food they grow on farms.* Remind children to use the illustrations to help them understand the text.

Guided Comprehension

As children read *Farm Fresh Finn,* monitor and provide guidance by correcting blending. Model rereading and identifying the topic and details where applicable.

Stop periodically to ask open-ended questions, such as *What is happening now? How does Finn feel?* Build on children's responses to help them understand the text.

Reread

Remind children that, as they read, they can reread parts of the text to help them better understand what is going on in the selection.

Topic and Details

Remind children that details in the text and illustrations will help them figure out the topic of the selection. Explain that they can find details in the illustrations and the text.

Think Aloud After reading page 2, I learned that Finn does not like carrots or corn. On page 3, Finn's mother is asking him to try his vegetables. This detail tells me that Finn probably does not eat most vegetables. I'll keep reading and looking at the pictures to find out what happens next.

Have children read the rest of the book. Remind them to look for details in the text and the illustrations. Have children explain why these details are important to the text. Ask them to pay attention to how Finn changes when he is at his grandfather's farm.

Respond to the Text

Have children respond to the text by discussing these questions:

- *Where does Finn live?* (in the city) *How can you tell?* (The picture shows the city skyline through the window.)
- *Where did Finn and his mom go?* (to his grandpa's farm)
- *What does Grandpa grow on his farm?* (vegetables)
- *How does Grandpa help Finn like vegetables?* (He invites Finn to help pick and prepare them for dinner.)
- *How does Finn change from the beginning of the selection to the end?* (He goes from not liking vegetables to liking them.)

Retell Have children work in groups of three to retell the text by acting it out. Encourage children to use the topic and details. Help them make a personal connection. *If you were Grandpa, what kinds of food would you grow on your farm?*

Focus on Fluency

Practice Fluency routine with children. Remember that children need to read with accuracy first.

Once children have read the text with accuracy, have them read the selection again, focusing on rate. Have children practice reading with partners. Provide corrective feedback as necessary.

Build Knowledge: Make Connections

- **Talk About the Texts** Have partners discuss food that grows on a farm.
- **Write About the Texts** Then have children add their ideas to their Build Knowledge page of their reader's notebook.

LITERACY ACTIVITIES

Have children complete the Collaborate and Write About It activities on the inside back cover of the book.

⭐ GIFTED AND TALENTED

Evaluate Have children recall the different vegetables Grandpa grows at his farm and how he and Finn used those foods. Challenge children to think about the foods they eat. Ask: *How do you and your family use foods that are grown on a farm?*

Extend Have children draw a picture of a vegetable plot and the vegetables and fruits they would grow there. Have them explain why they chose the foods they did.

● Beyond Level

Phonics

REVIEW

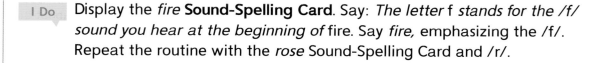

OBJECTIVES

Demonstrate basic knowledge of one-to-one letter-sound correspondences by producing the primary sound or many of the most frequent sounds for each consonant.

I Do Display the *fire* **Sound-Spelling Card**. Say: *The letter* f *stands for the /f/ sound you hear at the beginning of* fire. Say *fire,* emphasizing the /f/. Repeat the routine with the *rose* Sound-Spelling Card and /r/.

We Do Display the *fish, fan, five, rope, rabbit,* and *rake* **Photo Cards**. Have children say the name of each picture together with you. Then ask children to share other words they know that begin with /f/ and /r/.

You Do Write the words *fin, fed, fan, rip, rat,* and *rod* and have partners read each one. Provide corrective feedback as needed. Ask them to write the words on their **Response Boards** and underline the letter in each word that stands for /f/ and /r/.

Fluency Have children reread the story "Ron With Red" for fluency.

Innovate Have children create a new page for "Ron With Red" by writing about another fruit Ron and Red might see at the orchard.

High-Frequency Words

REVIEW

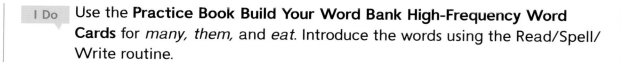

OBJECTIVES

Read common high-frequency words by sight.

I Do Use the **Practice Book Build Your Word Bank High-Frequency Word Cards** for *many, them,* and *eat.* Introduce the words using the Read/Spell/ Write routine.

We Do Display the Practice Book High-Frequency Word Cards for *I, can, the, we, see, a, like, to, and, go, you, do, my, are, he,* and *with.* Have children help you create sentence frames using both sets of word cards.

You Do Have partners write sentences using the Build Your Word Bank High-Frequency words *many, them,* and *eat* on their Response Boards. Have them read their sentences.

Vocabulary

ORAL VOCABULARY: SYNONYMS

OBJECTIVES
With guidance and support from adults, explore word relationships and nuances in word meanings.

I Do Review the meanings of *delicious* and *beneath.* Explain that a synonym is a word that means almost the same thing as another word. *A synonym for* delicious *is* tasty. I like tasty treats. *A synonym for* beneath *is* below. The bottom shelf is below the top shelf.

We Do Create sentences together with *tasty* and *below.* Read the sentences aloud.

You Do Have partners draw a picture and think of two or three sentences about an apple tree. Tell them to use the words *tasty* and *below* in their sentences. Ask them to share their pictures and sentences with the class.

GIFTED and TALENTED **Extend** Challenge children to list two or three opposite words for *tasty* and *below.* Then have them say a sentence using the opposite words.

Comprehension

SELF-SELECTED READING

OBJECTIVES
With prompting and support, identify the main topic and retell key details of a text.

Read emergent-reader texts with purpose and understanding.

Independent Reading

Have children select a nonfiction text for independent reading. Encourage them to read for twelve minutes. Guide children to transfer what they have learned this week as they read by identifying topic and details. Remind children that, as they read, they can reread parts of the text to help them better understand the selection.

After reading, guide children to participate in a group discussion about the selection they read. In addition, children can choose activities from the Reading **Center Activity Cards** to help them apply skills to the text as they read. Offer assistance and guidance with self-selected assignments.

GIFTED and TALENTED **Independent Study** Have children create books by drawing and writing sentences about fruits or vegetables. Have them title their books. Challenge partners to predict what the books are about with the title and pictures.

LEARNING GOALS

We can make connections across texts to gain information.

OBJECTIVES

With prompting and support, identify basic similarities in and differences between two texts on the same topic.

Participate in collaborative conversations with diverse partners about *kindergarten topics and texts* with peers and adults in small and larger groups.

The Big Idea: *What kinds of things can you find growing in nature?*

Connect to the Big Idea

Text to Text Display the **Literature Big Books** *A Grand Old Tree* and *An Orange in January.* Tell children that they will compare the selections using a Two-Tab Foldable®. Say: *We will compare the things in the texts that grow in nature. The Two-Tab Foldable® will help us record and organize our information.*

As a class, create a Two-Tab Foldable® out of poster board. On the left flap, write *A Grand Old Tree.* On the right flap, write *An Orange in January.*

Dinah Zike's
FOLDABLES®
Study Organizer

Display *A Grand Old Tree* and review the selection, focusing on the topic and the details of the text. Say: *We read a lot of details about the tree.* Display pages 10–11 in *A Grand Old Tree* and say: *I noticed that flowers grow on the grand old tree.* Point to the illustration and then to the word *flowered* as you read it. Write *flowered* on the Foldable® as you say it aloud. Ask: *What other details did we read about in the text?* (Possible Answers: the tree sows seeds; the tree grows in the sun and rain; many creatures live in the tree) Write children's responses on the Foldable®. Point to the words as you read them back to the class.

Repeat the routine with *An Orange in January.* Ask: *What details does the text give about the orange tree?* (Possible Answers: the tree has flowers, bees eat the nectar, the tree grows in the sun and rain, the oranges grow, the tree has branches) Write children's responses on the Foldable®.

Use the responses on the Two-Tab Foldable® to compare and contrast the trees in the two texts. Ask: *How are the two trees similar? How are they different?*

Collaborative Conversations Have children turn and talk with a partner about trees and other things they see growing in nature.

Present Ideas and Synthesize Information When children have finished their conversations, have volunteers share their ideas with the class. As children share, help them make connections to the Unit 5 Big Idea. Lead a class discussion and list children's ideas on the board.

Building Knowledge Have children continue to build knowledge about the Unit 5 Big Idea. Display classroom and library resources and have children look through them to find out more information about things that grow in nature. If time permits, have volunteers share something new they learned.

FORMATIVE ASSESSMENT

❯ STUDENT CHECK-IN

Have children reflect on how well they compared information across texts. Have children reflect using the Check-In routine.

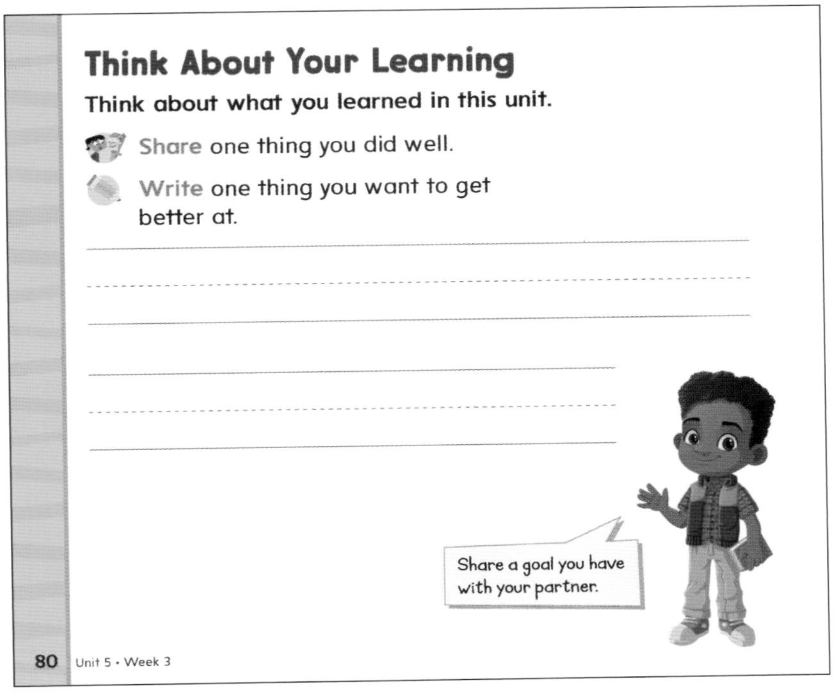

Think About Your Learning

Think about what you learned in this unit.

Share one thing you did well.

Write one thing you want to get better at.

_____

- -

_____

- -

_____

Share a goal you have with your partner.

80 | Unit 5 · Week 3

Reading/Writing Companion, p. 80

LEARNING GOALS

We can reflect on our learning.

OBJECTIVES

Follow agreed-upon rules for discussions.

Reflect on and record skills learned in the unit.

What Did You Learn?

Guide children in thinking about and discussing some of the skills, concepts, and content they learned during this unit. You may also have them recall how they rated themselves in the **Reading/Writing Companion**.

Have children turn to page 80 in the Reading/Writing Companion.

- Have children turn to a partner and share something they think they did well in this unit.

- After partners have finished sharing, have children look at the pencil icon. Tell them to fill in the set of blank lines by writing one thing they want to get better at as the year continues.

Summative Assessment

After every three weeks of instruction, *Wonders* assesses foundational skills taught in the unit. After every six weeks of instruction, *Wonders* provides a more comprehensive assessment of comprehension skills, foundational skills, high-frequency words, and category words.

Online Assessment Center

Unit 5 Tested Skills

PHONOLOGICAL/PHONEMIC AWARENESS	PHONICS	HIGH-FREQUENCY WORDS
• Count and Blend Syllables • Phoneme Blending • Phoneme Categorization	• /e/e (initial/medial) • /h/h (initial) • /f/f (initial) • /r/r (initial)	• *are* • *he* • *my* • *with*

Additional Assessment Options

Fluency

Access fluency using the Letter Naming Fluency (LNF), Phoneme Segmentation Fluency (PSF), and Sight Word Fluency (SWF) assessments in **Fluency Assessment**.

Fluency Assessment

ELL Assessment

Assess English Language Learner proficiency and track children's progress using the **English Language Development Assessment**. This resource provides unit assessments and rubrics to evaluate children's progress in the areas of listening and reading comprehension, vocabulary, grammar, speaking, and writing. These assessments can also be used to determine the language proficiency levels for subsequent set of instructions.

Unit Assessments
English Language Learners

Making the Most of Assessment Results

Make data-based grouping decisions by using the following reports to verify assessment results. For additional support options for children, refer to the reteaching and enrichment opportunities.

ONLINE ASSESSMENT CENTER

- *Gradebook*

DATA DASHBOARD

- *Recommendations Report*
- *Activity Report*
- *Skills Report*
- *Progress Report*
- *Grade Card Report*

TIER 2

Reteaching Opportunities with Intervention Online PDFs

IF CHILDREN . . .	THEN RETEACH . . .
answer 0-3 **phonological/phonemic awareness** items correctly	tested skills using the **Phonological Awareness PDF**
answer 0-1 **phonics** items correctly	tested skills using the **Phonics/Word Study PDF** and Sections 2 and 4 of the **Fluency PDF**
answer 0-3 **high-frequency words** items correctly	tested skills using Section 3 of the **Fluency PDF**

Enrichment Opportunities

Beyond Level small group lessons include suggestions for additional activities in the following areas to extend learning opportunities for gifted and talented children:

- *Leveled Readers*
- *Leveled Reader Library Online*
- *Center Activity Cards*

UNIT 5

Next Steps

NEXT STEPS FOR YOUR CHILDREN'S PROGRESS . . .

Interpret the data you have collected from multiple sources throughout this unit, including formal and informal assessments.

Data Dashboard

Who

Regrouping Decisions

- Check children's progress against your interpretation of the data. Consider whether children are ready to Level Up or accelerate.
- Use the English Learner Benchmark Assessment to determine how English language learners are progressing.

LEVEL UP

What

Target Instruction

- Decide whether to review and reinforce particular skills or concepts or whether you need to reteach them.
- Target instruction to meet children's strengths/needs.
- Use Data Dashboard recommendations to help determine which lessons to provide to different groups of children.

Coach and Classroom Videos

Methodology

How

Modify Instruction

- Vary materials and/or instructional strategies.
- Address children's social and emotional development.
- Provide children with opportunities for self-reflection and self-assessment.

AUTHOR INSIGHT

For young English learners, their comprehension may exceed what they are able to articulate. During instruction, monitor students' comprehension by asking English learners to gesture, or use simple expression.
—Jana Echevarria

Victoria Sanchez, CSULB

PROFESSIONAL DEVELOPMENT

NEXT STEPS FOR YOU . . .

As you prepare your children to move on to the next unit, don't forget to take advantage of the many opportunities available online for self-evaluation and professional development.

Instructional Routines

Manage Assessments

Program Author Whitepapers

Research Base

UNIT 6
READING/ WRITING

WEEK 1

Essential Question

How are the seasons different?

WEEK 2

Essential Question

What happens in different kinds of weather?

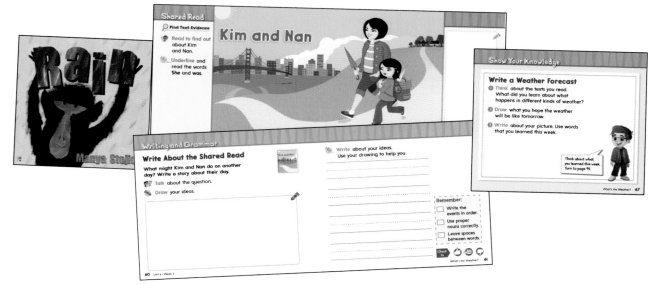

WEEK 3

Essential Question

How can you stay safe in bad weather?

Classroom Library Books

UNIT 6

Contents

Unit Overview

English Language Arts is not a discrete set of skills. Skills work together to help children analyze the meaningful texts. In *Wonders*, skills are not taught in isolation, rather they are purposefully combined to support student learning of texts they read.

Reading

Week 1

Essential Question: How are the seasons different?

Print Concepts
- Parts of a Book
- Left to Right/Top to Bottom

Phonological Awareness
- Onset and Rime Segmentation
- ✓ Phoneme Isolation
- ✓ Phoneme Blending
- ✓ Phoneme Segmentation

Phonics and Word Analysis
- ✓ /b/b, /l/l

Fluency
- ✓ High-Frequency Words

Reading Literature
- ✓ Events: Sequence
- Retell

Reading Poetry
- Rhyme

Vocabulary
- Academic Vocabulary
- Category Words

Researching
- A Season

Week 2

Essential Question: What happens in different kinds of weather?

Print Concepts
- Parts of a Book

Phonological Awareness
- Identify Rhyme
- ✓ Phoneme Isolation
- ✓ Phoneme Blending
- ✓ Phoneme Segmentation

Phonics and Word Analysis
- ✓ /k/k, ck

Fluency
- ✓ High-Frequency Words

Reading Literature
- ✓ Events: Sequence
- Retell

Reading Informational Text
- Text Feature: Speech Bubbles

Vocabulary
- Academic Vocabulary
- ✓ Category Words

Researching
- A Type of Weather

Week 3

Essential Question: How can you stay safe in bad weather?

Print Concepts
- Locate Printed Word
- Parts of a Book

Phonological Awareness
- Identify Alliteration
- Phoneme Identity
- ✓ Phoneme Addition
- ✓ Phoneme Blending

Phonics and Word Analysis
- *l*-blends (*bl, cl, fl, sl*)

Fluency
- ✓ High-Frequency Words

Reading Literature
- ✓ Events: Sequence
- Descriptive Words
- Retell

Reading Informational Text
- Text Feature: Directions

Vocabulary
- Academic Vocabulary
- Category Words

Researching
- Staying Safe in Bad Weather

Writing

Week 1

Writing
- Handwriting
- Opinion Writing
- Improving Writing: Writing Process

Conventions
- Grammar: Singular and Plural Nouns

Week 2

Writing
- Handwriting
- Narrative Writing
- Improving Writing: Writing Process

Conventions
- Grammar: Proper Nouns

Week 3

Writing
- Handwriting
- Narrative Writing
- Improving Writing: Writing Process
- Extended Writing: Realistic Fiction

Conventions
- Grammar: Singular and Plural Nouns

Key

Extend, Connect, and Assess

Extend previously taught skills and connect to new content.

Extend

Reading Informational Text
- Reading Digitally
- Topic and Details
- Retell
- Use a Multimedia Element

Connect

Connect to Social Studies
- Physical System
- Academic Vocabulary
- Read Grade-Level Text
- Collaborate

Assess

Unit Assessment
- Unit 6 Test

Fluency Assessment

Key Skills Trace

Print Concepts/Phonological Awareness

The Print Concepts and Phonological Awareness standards are taught throughout the text sets of each unit.

Phonics and Word Analysis

Consonants

    Introduce: Unit 1 Week 1, Week 3; Unit 2 Week 1, Week 2; Unit 3 Week 1, Week 2, Week 3; Unit 4 Week 2; Unit 5 Week 1, Week 3; Unit 6 Week 1, Week 2; Unit 7 Week 2, Week 3; Unit 8 Week 1, Week 2

    Review: Unit 2 Week 3; Unit 4 Week 3; Unit 6 Week 3; Unit 8 Week 3

    Assess: Unit 1, Unit 2, Unit 3, Unit 4, Unit 5, Unit 6, Unit 7, Unit 8

Blends

    Introduce: Unit 4 Week 3; Unit 6 Week 3; Unit 8 Week 3; Unit 10 Week 3

    Review: Unit 4 Week 3; Unit 6 Week 3; Unit 8 Week 3; Unit 10 Week 3

Reading Literature

Events: Sequence

    Introduce: Unit 6 Week 1

    Review: Unit 6 Week 2, Week 3; Unit 9 Week 1; Unit 10 Week 1

    Assess: Unit 6, Unit 9, Unit 10

Reading Poetry

Rhyme

    Introduce: Unit 2 Week 3

    Review: Unit 5 Week 1; Unit 6 Week 1; Unit 10 Week 2

    Assess: Unit 2, Unit 10

Reading Informational Text

Text Features

    Introduce: Unit 1 Week 1

    Review: Unit 1 Week 2; Unit 2 Week 1, Week 2, Week 3; Unit 3 Week 1, Week 2, Week 3; Unit 4 Week 1, Week 2, Week 3; Unit 5 Week 2, Week 3; Unit 6 Week 2, Week 3; Unit 7 Week 2, Week 3; Unit 8 Week 1, Week 2, Week 3; Unit 9 Week 2, Week 3; Unit 10 Week 1, Week 2, Week 3

Grammar

Nouns

    Introduce: Unit 1 Week 1

    Review: Unit 1 Week 2, Week 3; Unit 6 Week 1, Week 2, Week 3

Extended Writing

    Unit 2: Expository/Informative Text

    Unit 4: Personal Narrative

    Unit 6: Narrative: Realistic Fiction

    Unit 8: Narrative: Fantasy

    Unit 10: Opinion

Read Alouds

Additional Reading Options

Classroom Library Read Alouds

Online Lessons Available

A Kitten Tale

A Kitten Tale
By Eric Rohmann
Fiction
Lexile 590L

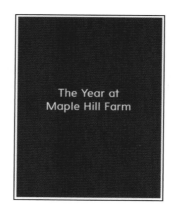

The Year at
Maple Hill Farm

The Year at Maple Hill Farm
By Alice and Martin Provensen
Informational Text
Lexile 560L

Genre Read-Aloud Anthologyy

More Leveled Readers to Explore

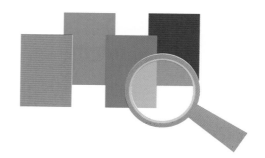

Search the **Online Leveled Reader Library** to provide children with texts at various levels to apply skills or to learn about various topics.

Unit Bibliography

Choose titles from the online **Unit Bibliography** to read aloud to children.

de Roo, Elena. *Rain Train*. Candlewick, 2011.

Rotner, Shelley, and Woodhull, Anne Love. *Every Season*. Roaring Brook Press, 2007.

Branley, Franklyn M. *Sunshine Makes the Seasons*. Collins, 2005.

Saltzberg, Barney. *All Around the Seasons*. Candlewick, 2010.

McClure, Nikki. *To Market, to Market*. Abrams Books for Young Readers, 2011.

Rylant, Cynthia, and McClure, Nikki. *All in a Day*. Abrams Books for Young Readers, 2009.

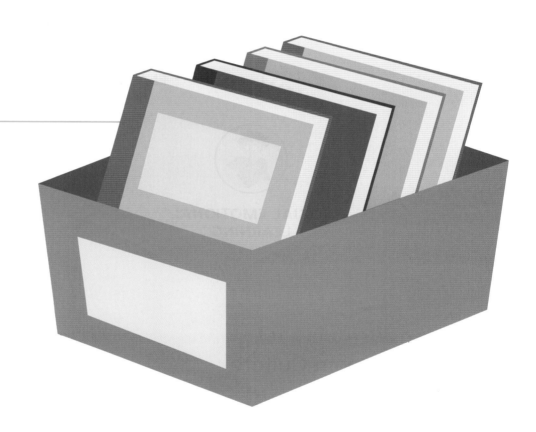

Teach the Whole Child

Foster student academic success in English Language Arts and Content Knowledge by creating a Classroom Culture that supports children in growing their Social Emotional Learning and developing strong Habits of Learning.

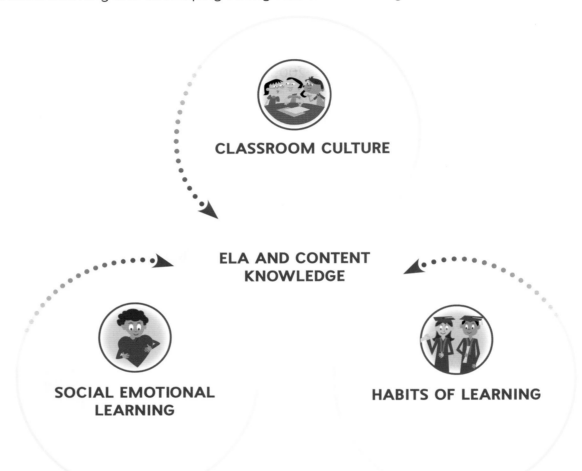

CLASSROOM CULTURE

ELA AND CONTENT KNOWLEDGE

SOCIAL EMOTIONAL LEARNING

HABITS OF LEARNING

 ## Classroom Culture

Focus: We promote ownership of learning.

Every child is ultimately responsible for his or her own learning. Create an environment where children develop a mindfulness about learning. Encourage them to use the anchor charts; to ask questions and dig deeper; to try different ways to learn difficult things; to seek help as needed; to record their efforts using the Track Your Progress pages; to discover strategies to help themselves; and to support each other's learning. The *Wonders* program encourages self-evaluation, as it is essential to the learning process. Getting to know themselves as listeners, speakers, readers, writers, and thinkers will help children take charge of their learning.

 ## Habits of Learning

Focus: I believe I can succeed.

The goal of this Habit of Learning is to help children develop a positive attitude about learning. When children are encouraged to find the learning strategies and tools that work best for them, they develop a sense of agency and see that their actions make a difference. Share the following statements and discuss with children.

- I stay on task until it is completed.
- I read independently.
- I choose the right book.

Social Emotional Learning

We Are Flexible Thinkers!

The Social Emotional Learning (SEL) competencies of this unit support children as they **explore and think critically and flexibly to solve problems.**

Each lesson provides opportunities for children to use their developing SEL competencies to investigate their world and make sense of their findings:

Week I • Logic & Reasoning
Learning to think critically to solve a problem or make decisions. **Video: "Super Grover 2.0: Lemonade Stand"**

Week 2 • Emotional Functioning
Expressing and recognizing a range of emotions.
Video: "Jealous"

Week 3 • Flexible Thinking
Demonstrating flexibility in thinking and behavior.
Video: "Car Experiment"

family time!

Deepen engagement by highlighting how families' efforts are connected to learning objectives. **Share everyday activities that can motivate interest in learning,** such as thinking together about how to dress for the weather, or thinking flexibly about what to have for dinner given a set of ingredients.

Invite families to celebrate the different ways they engage with their children around the weekly Social Emotional Learning video and activity found in the **School to Home** newsletter.

Half-Day Kindergarten

As you plan for your half-day Kindergarten, focus on the following areas important to building children's literacy. Use the Planner for each week in the unit to plan for the whole class and small group lessons.

Oral Language

- Introduce/Build the Concept
- Oral Vocabulary
- Category Words
- Integrate Ideas

Video

Visual Vocabulary Cards

Word Work

- Phonological/Phonemic Awareness
- Phonics: /b/b, /l/l, /k/k, ck; l-Blends bl, cl, fl, sl; Review
- High-Frequency Words: is, little, she, was, are, he, my, with
- Letter and Word Automaticity

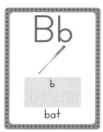

Sound-Spelling Cards

High-Frequency Word Cards

Reading/Writing

- **Literature Big Books** *Mama, Is It Summer Yet?*; *Rain*; *Waiting Out the Storm*
- **Shared Reads** "Is It Hot?"; "Kim and Nan"; "Mack and Ben"
- **Interactive Read Aloud Cards** "A Tour of the Seasons"; "The Battle of Wind and Rain"; "The Storm that Shook the Signs"
- Writing Skill and Trait
- Write About the Text
- Grammar

Literature Big Book

Interactive Read Aloud Cards

Independent Practice

- Practice Book pages
- Center Activity Cards
- Online Games and Activities

Center Activity Cards

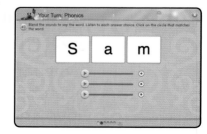

Online Games and Activities

Introduce the Unit

Reading/Writing Companion, pp. 6–7

The Big Idea: *How do weather and seasons affect us?*

 Talk About It

Read aloud the Big Idea to children. Then ask them what the weather is generally like during each of the four seasons where they live. What kinds of things do they do outdoors during each season? How do they dress for the weather? Have children discuss how changes in the weather and the seasons affect both people and the environment. What should people do to stay safe in bad weather? As children discuss, encourage them to ask questions to clarify ideas they do not understand. Prompt them to wait after asking questions to give others a chance to respond.

Ask: *How do weather and seasons affect us?* Have children discuss with partners or in groups, then share their ideas with the class. Let children know that they will discuss the Big Idea throughout the unit. Each week they will talk, read, and write about an Essential Question related to the Big Idea.

Guide children to complete the activities on **Reading/Writing Companion** page 7.

Talk Have partners talk about what the boy and his mother might be saying.

Circle Children can circle clues in the art that tell what the weather is like.

 Sing the Song

Introduce the unit song: "What Shall We Do on a Rainy Day?" Read aloud the lyrics of the song. Then ask children questions about the song:

- *What are some things you like to do outdoors when the weather is sunny and warm?*

- *Are there ways to enjoy those activities outside even when the weather is rainy and cold?*

- *What can you do indoors instead?*

Play the song. After listening to the song a few times, ask children to join in. Audio and print files of the song can be found in the Teacher Resources on **my.mheducation.com.**

Student Outcomes

✓ Tested in *Wonders* Assessments

FOUNDATIONAL SKILLS

Print Concepts
- Identify parts of a book
- Understand reading moves from left to right and top to bottom

Phonological Awareness
- Onset and Rime Segmentation
- ✓ Phoneme Isolation
- ✓ Phoneme Blending
- ✓ Phoneme Segmentation

Phonics and Word Analysis
- ✓ /b/b, /l/l

Fluency
- ✓ High-Frequency Words
  - is   little

READING

Reading Literature
- ✓ Identify and describe the events in a story
- Identify rhyme in a poem
- Retell familiar stories
- Actively engage in group reading activities

COMMUNICATION

Writing
- Handwriting: *Bb, Ll*
- Use prompts to write about the text
- Respond to suggestions from peers and add details to strengthen writing

Speaking and Listening
- Present writing and research
- Engage in collaborative conversations
- Ask and answer questions to get information or to clarify something that is not understood

Conventions
- **Grammar:** Recognize singular and plural nouns

Researching
- Recall or gather information to answer a question
- Conduct research about a season

Creating and Collaborating
- Add drawings and visual displays to descriptions
- Use digital tools to produce and publish writing

VOCABULARY

Academic Vocabulary
- Acquire and use grade-appropriate academic vocabulary

Vocabulary Strategy
- Identify and sort common words and objects into categories
- Use sentence-level context clues

ELL Scaffolded supports for English Language Learners are embedded throughout the lessons, enabling children to communicate information, ideas, and concepts in English Language Arts and for social and instructional purposes within the school setting.

See the **ELL Small Group Guide** for additional support of the skills for the text set.

FORMATIVE ASSESSMENT

For assessment throughout the text set, use children's self-assessments and your observations.

Use the Data Dashboard to filter class, group, or individual student data to guide group placement decisions. It provides recommendations to enhance learning for gifted and talented children and offers extra support for children needing remediation.

Develop Student Ownership

To build student ownership, children need to know what they are learning, why they are learning it, and determine how well they understood it.

Students Discuss Their Goals

TEXT SET GOALS

- I can read and understand texts.
- I can write about the texts I read.
- I know how the seasons are different.

Have children think about what they know and circle a hand in each row on **Reading/Writing Companion** page 10.

Students Monitor Their Learning

LEARNING GOALS

Specific learning goals identified in every lesson make clear what children will be learning and why. These smaller goals provide stepping stones to help children meet their Text Set Goals.

CHECK-IN ROUTINE

The Check-In Routine at the close of each lesson guides children to self-reflect on how well they understood each learning goal.

Review the lesson learning goal.
Reflect on the activity.
Self Assess by
- circling the hands in the **Reading/Writing Companion.**
- showing thumbs up, sideways, or down.

Share with your teacher.

Students Reflect on Their Progress

TEXT SET GOALS

After completing the Show Your Knowledge task for the text set, children reflect on their understanding of the Text Set Goals by circling a hand in each row on **Reading/Writing Companion** page 11.

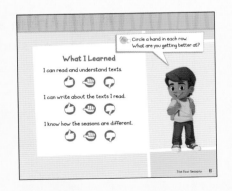

Literature Big Book

Shared Read
Reading/Writing Companion p. 20

Paired Selection
Literature Big Book

Essential Question
How are the seasons different?

Video In winter, we might bundle up in warm clothes. In spring, rain helps the flowers grow. In summer, the sun is hot, and we need to stay cool. In fall, the air is cooler, and leaves drop from trees.

Literature Big Book A mama tells her son about signs that summer is coming, including swelling buds, a squirrel building a nest for her babies, and trees blossoming. Then, it is summer; the sun is warm, and berries are juicy and sweet.

Shared Read A kitten is hot in the spring. Deb plays baseball in the summer. Rob and Lin dress warmly in the fall. Children hop in the snow in the winter.

Interactive Read Aloud In winter, snow falls, and kids might sled. In spring, it gets warmer, animals come out, and farmers plant seeds. In summer, it gets hotter, insects buzz, and crops grow. In autumn, it gets cooler, most birds migrate, and leaves change color.

Paired Selection Poems describe new snow sparkling in the sun; rain in all four seasons; windows keeping the cold away; and playing in a sprinkler in summer.

Art In a snowy, wintry scene, people ice skate and sled.

Differentiated Sources

Leveled Readers 🔊

🔴 Different things are hot in different seasons. The beach is hot in summer, and a mug of cocoa is hot in winter.

🔴🔵 Little Bear likes different things in each season, such as a hat in spring, a berry in summer, and a nap in winter.

🔴 Ant plants beans in spring, picks them in fall, and makes chili with them in winter. Grasshopper plays the whole time, then has no food in winter.

Build Knowledge Routine

After reading each text, ask children to document what facts and details that they learned to help answer the Essential Question of the text set.

 Talk about the source.

 Write about the source.

 Add to the class Anchor Chart

• Add to the Word Bank.

Show Your Knowledge

Write a Poem

Have children think about how the seasons are different. Guide them to draw a picture of one season and write a poem about it. Encourage children to use vocabulary words they learned during the week.

Social Emotional Learning

Super Grover 2.0: Lemonade Stand (5:15)

Logic & Reasoning

SEL Focus: Deepen engagement by asking open-ended questions that support children's critical thinking.

Share a riddle or guessing game with children. Then begin the lesson titled "Think It Through," pp. T244–T245.

Family Time • Share the video and the activity in the **School to Home** newsletter.

Explore the Texts

Essential Question: How are the seasons different?

Literature Big Book	Literature Big Book	Interactive Read-Aloud	Reading/Writing Companion

Mama, Is It Summer Yet? Anchor Text Realistic Fiction	**"New Snow," "Rain Song," "Covers," "Honey, I Love"** Paired Text Poetry	**"A Tour of the Seasons"** Interactive Read Aloud Informational Text	**"Is It Hot?"** Shared Read pp. 20–27 Informational Text

Qualitative

Meaning/Purpose: Moderate Complexity **Structure:** Moderate Complexity **Language:** Moderate Complexity **Knowledge Demands:** Low Complexity	**Meaning/Purpose:** High Complexity **Structure:** High Complexity **Language:** High Complexity **Knowledge Demands:** Moderate Complexity	**Meaning/Purpose:** Low Complexity **Structure:** Low Complexity **Language:** Moderate Complexity **Knowledge Demands:** Moderate Complexity	**Meaning/Purpose:** Low Complexity **Structure:** Moderate Complexity **Language:** Low Complexity **Knowledge Demands:** Low Complexity

Quantitative

Lexile 330L	Lexile NP	Lexile 640L	Lexile 200L

Reader and Task Considerations

Reader Since young children are more familiar with a story format, the question and answer approach might be less confusing if read by different people.	**Reader** As they listen to each poem, encourage children to visualize themselves in the seasons described.	**Reader** Children may not have experience with all the activities mentioned in the text. For example, children that live in warm climates may be less familiar with the experience of building a snowman.	**Reader** Children will need to use their knowledge of sound-spelling correspondences and high-frequency words to read the text.

Task The questions for the Interactive Read Aloud are supported by teacher modeling. The tasks provide a variety of ways for students to build knowledge and vocabulary about the text set topic. The questions and tasks provided for the other texts are at various levels of complexity, ensuring that all students can interact with the text in meaningful ways.

Additional Read-Aloud Texts

Classroom Library
A Kitten Tale
Genre: Fiction
Lexile: 590L

The Year at Maple Hill Farm
Genre: Informational Text
Lexile: 560L

See Classroom Library Lessons.

Content Area Reading BLMs
Additional online texts related to grade-level Science, Social Studies, and Arts content.

Access Complex Text (ACT) boxes provide scaffolded instruction for seven different elements that may make the **Literature Big Book** complex.

ACT

Leveled Readers 🔊 (All Leveled Readers are provided in eBook format with audio support.)

   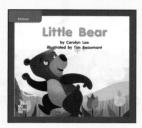

Approaching	On	Beyond	ELL
It Is Hot!	*Little Bear*	*Ant and Grasshopper*	*Little Bear*
Leveled Reader	Leveled Reader	Leveled Reader	Leveled Reader
Fiction	Fiction	Fiction	Fiction

Qualitative

Meaning/Purpose: Low Complexity	**Meaning/Purpose:** Low Complexity	**Meaning/Purpose:** Moderate Complexity	**Meaning/Purpose:** Low Complexity
Structure: Moderate Complexity	**Structure:** Moderate Complexity	**Structure:** Moderate Complexity	**Structure:** Moderate Complexity
Language: Low Complexity	**Language:** Moderate Complexity	**Language:** Moderate Complexity	**Language:** Moderate Complexity
Knowledge Demands: Low Complexity	**Knowledge Demands:** Low Complexity	**Knowledge Demands:** Moderate Complexity	**Knowledge Demands:** Low Complexity

Quantitative

Lexile BR	Lexile 300L	Lexile 280L	Lexile 300L

Reader and Task Considerations

Reader Children should be famlilar with the objects mentioned in the text. Engage children in a discussion about other things that can be hot.	**Reader** Children should be famlilar with the objects mentioned in the text. Encourage children to discuss things that they like.	**Reader** Children may need extra support understanding the moral of the text.	**Reader** Children should be famlilar with the objects mentioned in the text. Encourage children to discuss things that they like.

Task The questions and tasks provided for the Leveled Readers are at various levels of complexity, ensuring that all students can interact with the text in meaningful ways.

WEEK 1

Focus on Word Work

Build Foundational Skills with Multimodal Learning

Photo Cards

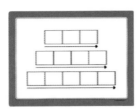

Response Board

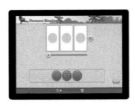

Phonemic Awareness Activities

Sound-Spelling Cards

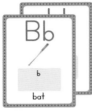

Word-Building Cards online

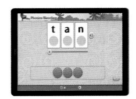

Phonics Practice Activities

Practice Book

Word-Building Cards online

Response Board

 is

 little

High-Frequency Word Cards

High-Frequency Word Activities

Visual Vocabulary Cards

Phonological/Phonemic Awareness

- Segment and blend onset and rime in spoken words
- Isolate, blend, and segment phonemes

Phonics: /b/b, /l/l

- Introduce/review sound-spellings
- Blend/build words with sound-spellings
- Practice handwriting
- Decode and encode in connected texts

Spelling: /b/b, /l/l

- Spell words with /b/b, /l/l

High-Frequency Words

- Read/Spell/Write routine
- Optional: Build Your Word Bank

See Word Work, pages T254–T257, T266–T269, T274–T279, T288–T289, T294–T295.

Shared Read

Decodable Readers

Take-Home Story

Apply Skills to Read

- Children apply foundational skills as they read decodable texts.
- Children practice fluency to develop word automaticity.

Explicit Systematic Instruction

Word Work instruction expands foundational skills to enable children to become proficient readers.

Daily Routine

- Use the In a Flash: Sound-Spelling routine and the In a Flash: High-Frequency Word routine to build fluency.
- Set Learning Goal.

Explicit Minilessons and Practice

Use daily instruction in both whole and small groups to model, practice, and apply key foundational skills. Opportunities include:

- Multimodal engagement.
- Corrective feedback.
- Supports for English Language Learners in each lesson.
- Peer collaboration.

Formative Assessment

Check-In

- Children reflect on their learning.
- Children show their progress by indicating thumbs down, thumbs sideways, or thumbs up in a Check-In routine.

Check for Success

- Teacher monitors children's achievement and differentiates for Small Group instruction.

Differentiated Instruction

To strengthen skills, provide targeted review and reteaching lessons and multimodal activities to meet children's diverse needs.

- ● ● **Approaching Level, ELL**
- Includes Tier 2 **2**
- ● **On Level**
- ● **Beyond Level**
- Includes Gifted and Talented 🌟GIFTED and TALENTED

OPTIONAL EXPRESS TRACK

Teachers can choose to introduce long vowel sound-spellings and/or additional high-frequency words.

- Build Your Word Bank

Independent Practice

Provide additional practice as needed. Have children work individually or with partners.

Center Activity Cards

Digital Activities

Word-Building Cards online

Decodable Readers

Practice Book

Inspire Early Writers

Build Writing Skills and Conventions

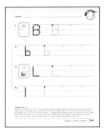

Practice Book

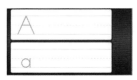

Handwriting Video

Reading/Writing Companion

Write Letters *Bb, Ll*

- Learn to write the letters
- Practice writing

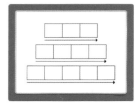

Response Board

Practice Book

High-Frequency Word Activities

Write Words

- Write words with *Bb, Ll*
- Write high-frequency words

Reading/Writing Companion

Practice Book

Write Sentences

- Write sentences with high-frequency words
- Write sentences to respond to text

Follow Conventions

- Recognize singular and plural nouns

Mama, Is It Summer Yet?
Literature Big Book

Writing Fluency

To increase children's writing fluency, have them write as much as they can in response to the **Literature Big Book** for four minutes. Have children write about how the seasons change.

For lessons, see pages T254–T259, T270–T271, T274–T277, T280–T281, T290–T291, T294–T297.

Write About Texts

WRITING ROUTINE

Analyze the Prompt → Find Text Evidence → Write to the Prompt

Literature Big Book

Reading/Writing Companion, pp. 14–15

Modeled Writing

Write about the **Literature Big Book** *Mama, Is It Summer Yet?*

- Prompt: What do you like to do in the summer?

Interactive Writing

- Prompt: Do you think the author did a good job showing that summer is coming? Why or why not?

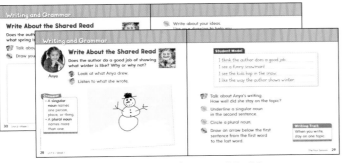

Reading/Writing Companion, pp. 28–31

Independent Writing

Write to the Shared Read "Is It Hot?"

- Prompt: Does the author do a good job of showing what spring is like? Why or why not?

- Have children follow the steps of the writing process: draft, revise, edit/proofread, share.

Additional Lessons

Writing Skills Minilessons To provide differentiated support for writing skills, see pages T494–T499.

Extended Writing Lessons For a full set of lessons that support the writing process and writing in a specific genre, see pages T476–T487.

Self-Selected Writing

Children can explore different writing modes.

 Journal Writing

 Picture Spark

Planner

Customize your own lesson plans at
my.mheducation.com

Select from your Social Emotional Learning resources.

 LESSON 1

 LESSON 2

TEXT SET GOALS

- **I can read and understand texts.**
- **I can write about the texts I read.**
- **I know how the seasons are different.**

 90+ mins

Reading
Suggested Daily Time Includes Small Group

 SMALL GROUP OPTIONS
The designated lessons can be taught in small groups. To determine how to differentiate instruction for small groups, use Formative Assessment and Data Dashboard.

30+ mins

Writing
Suggested Daily Time

Reading

LESSON 1

Introduce the Concept, T246–T247
Build Knowledge: The Four Seasons

Listening Comprehension, T248–T253
Mama, Is It Summer Yet?

Word Work, T254–T257
Phonemic Awareness: Phoneme Isolation
Phonics/Spelling: Introduce /b/b, /l/l
Handwriting: Write *Bb, Ll*
High-Frequency Words: *is, little*

LESSON 2

Build the Concept, T260–T261
Phonological Awareness: Onsite Rime and Segmentation
Category Words: Seasons
Vocabulary Sentence Clues

Listening Comprehension, T262–T265
Mama, Is It Summer Yet?

Word Work, T266–T267
Phonemic Awareness: Phoneme Isolation
Phonics: Review *b* and *l*, Blend Words
High-Frequency Words: *is, little*

Shared Read, T268–T269
Read "Is It Hot?"

Writing

Modeled Writing, T258
Model Writing About the Literature Big Book
Grammar, T259
Singular and Plural Nouns

Interactive Writing, T270
Write About the Literature Big Book
Grammar, T271
Singular and Plural Nouns

Teacher-Led Instruction

 SMALL GROUP

Differentiated Reading
Leveled Readers
- *It Is Hot!,* T300–T301
- *Little Bear,* T308–T309
- *Ant and Grasshopper,* T314–T315

Differentiated Skills Practice, T302–T317
- **Approaching Level, T302–T307**
Phonological/Phonemic Awareness
  - Onset and Rime Segmentation, T302 [TIER 2]
  - Phoneme Isolation, T302 [TIER 2]
  - Phoneme Blending, T303
  - Phoneme Segmentation, T303

Phonics
- Sound-Spelling Review, T304 [TIER 2]
- Connect *b* to /b/ and *l* to /l/, T304 [TIER 2]
- Blend Words with /b/b and /l/l, T304
- Build Words with /b/b and /l/l, T305
- Reread the Decodable Reader, T305
- Sound/Spelling Fluency, T305
High-Frequency Words
- Reteach Words, T306 [TIER 2]
- Cumulative Review, T306
Oral Vocabulary Review Words, T307

Independent/Collaborative Work See pages T243K–T243L

Reading
Comprehension
- Realistic Fiction
- Visualize
- Events: Sequence

Word Work
Phonics
- /b/b, /l/l
High-Frequency Words
- *is, little*

Writing
Self-Selected Writing
Grammar
- Singular and Plural Nouns
Handwriting
- Upper and Lowercase *Bb, Ll*

ORAL VOCABULARY
weather, seasons, migrate, active, spot

 LESSON 3

 LESSON 4

 LESSON 5

Reading

Lesson 3

Build the Concept, T272
Oral Language

Listening Comprehension, T273
"A Tour of the Seasons"

Word Work, T274–T277
Phonemic Awareness: Phoneme Blending
Phonics: Review /b/b, /l/l; Blend Words; Spell Words
High-Frequency Words: *is, little*

Shared Read, T278–T279
Reread "Is It Hot?"

Lesson 4

Extend the Concept, T282–T283
Phonological Awareness: Onsite Rime and Segmentation
Category Words: Seasons
Vocabulary Sentence Clues

Paired Selection, T284–T287
"New Snow," "Rain Song," "Covers," excerpt from "Honey, I Love"

Word Work, T288–T289
Phonemic Awareness: Phoneme Blending
Phonics: Build and Read Words, Spell Words
High-Frequency Words: *is, little*

Research and Inquiry, T292–T293
A Season (Research)

Lesson 5

Word Work, T294–T295
Phonemic Awareness: Phoneme Segmentation
Phonics: Read Words, Spell Words
High-Frequency Words: *is, little*

Integrate Ideas, T298
Make Connections

Show Your Knowledge, T299

Writing

Lesson 3

Independent Writing, T280
Write About the Shared Read
Grammar, T281
Singular and Plural Nouns

Lesson 4

Independent Writing, T290
Write About the Shared Read
Grammar, T291
Singular and Plural Nouns

Lesson 5

Self-Selected Writing, T296
Grammar, T297
Singular and Plural Nouns

Comprehension
• Self-Selected Reading, T307
● **On Level, T310–T313**
Phonological/Phonemic Awareness
• Phoneme Isolation, T310
• Phoneme Blending, T310
• Phoneme Segmentation, T310
Phonics
• Review Phonics, T311
• Picture Sort, T311
• Blend Words with /b/b, /l/l, T312
• Reread the Decodable Reader, T312

High-Frequency Words
• Review Words, T313
Comprehension
• Self-Selected Reading, T313
● **Beyond Level, T316–T317**
Phonics
• Review, T316
High-Frequency Words
• Review, T316

Vocabulary
• Oral Vocabulary: Synonyms, T317
Comprehension
• Self-Selected Reading, T317

GIFTED and TALENTED

 ● **English Language Learners**
See ELL Small Group Guide, pp. 132–139

Content Area Connections

Content Area Reading
• Science, Social Studies, and the Arts
Research and Inquiry
• A Season (Research)

 ● **English Language Learners**
See ELL Small Group Guide, pp. 133, 135

Independent and Collaborative Work

As you meet with small groups, have the rest of the class complete activities and projects to practice and apply the skills they have been working on.

Student Choice and Student Voice

- Review the My Weekly Work blackline masters with children and identify the "Must Do" activities.
- Have children choose some additional activities that provide the practice they need.
- Remind children to reflect on their learning each day.

My Weekly Work BLMs

Reading

Text Options

Children can choose a **Center Activity Card** to use while they listen to a text or read independently.

Classroom Library
Read Aloud
A Kitten Tale
Genre: Fiction
Lexile: 590L

The Year at Maple Hill Farm
Genre: Informational Text
Lexile: 560L

Unit Bibliography
See the online bibliography. Children can select independent reading texts about how seasons are different.

Leveled Texts Online
 All **Leveled Readers** are provided in eBook format with audio support.
- **Differentiated Texts** provide English Language Learners with passages at different proficiency levels.

Literature Big Book e-Book
 Mama, Is It Summer Yet?
Genre: Realistic Fiction

Center Activity Cards

Visualize Card 1

Realistic Fiction Card 23

Sequence Card 11

Poetry: Rhyme Card 22

Digital Activities

Comprehension

Word Work

Center Activity Cards

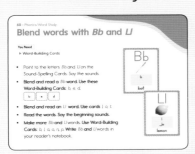

/b/b, /l/l Card 60

Word-Building Cards

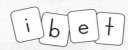

Practice Book BLMs

Phonological Awareness: pp. 241, 242–243, 244

Phonics: pp. 245–246, 248

Phonics/Spelling: p. 247

High-Frequency Words: p. 250

Category Words: p. 251

Take-Home Story: pp. 255–256

Decodable Readers

Unit 6, pp. 1–12

Digital Activities

Word Work — Phonemic Awareness, Phonics, High-Frequency Words

Writing

Center Activity Cards

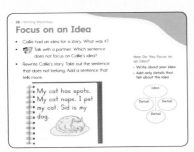

Focus on One Idea Card 38

Self-Selected Writing

- What do you know about the different seasons?
- Write about your favorite season and tell how it is different than other seasons.
- Draw and label a picture of one season.

Practice Book BLMs

Handwriting: p. 249
Grammar: pp. 252–254

Digital Activities

Grammar

Content Area Connections

Content Area Reading BLMs
- Additional texts related to Science, Social Studies, Health, and the Arts.

Research and Inquiry
- Complete Research a Season project

Progress Monitoring
Moving Toward Mastery

Practice Book

Reading/Writing Companion

Online Rubric

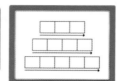

Response Board

Digital Activities

FORMATIVE ASSESSMENT

→ **STUDENT CHECK-IN**

✓ **CHECK FOR SUCCESS**

For ongoing formative assessment, use children's self-assessments at the end of each lesson along with your own observations.

Assessing skills along the way . . .

SKILLS	HOW ASSESSED
Phonological Awareness • Onset and Rime Segmentation	Practice Book
Phonemic Awareness • Phoneme Isolation • Phoneme Blending • Phoneme Segmentation	Practice Book, Response Board, Digital Activities
Phonics • /b/b, /l/l	Practice Book, Response Board, Digital Activities
High-Frequency Words • *is, little*	Practice Book, Response Board, Digital Activities
Category Words • Seasons	Practice Book
Grammar • Singular and Plural Nouns	Practice Book
Comprehension • Events: Sequence • Poetry: Rhyme	Reading/Writing Companion
Listening/Presenting/Research	Checklists

Making the Most of Assessment Results

Make data-based grouping decisions by using the following reports to verify assessment results. For additional support options for children, refer to the reteaching and enrichment opportunities.

ONLINE ASSESSMENT CENTER

- *Gradebook*

DATA DASHBOARD

- *Recommendations Report*
- *Activity Report*
- *Skills Report*
- *Progress Report*
- *Grade Card Report*

Reteaching Opportunities with Intervention Online PDFs

ASSESSED SKILLS	✓ CHECK FOR SUCCESS	RETEACH . . .
PHONOLOGICAL AND PHONEMIC AWARENESS	Can children blend and segment onset and rimes of spoken words? Can children isolate, blend, and segment phonemes? If not . . .	using lessons 38–43; 27–29, 62–71 in the **Phonemic Awareness PDF.**
PHONICS	Can children match /b/ and /l/ to the letters *b* and *l*? If not . . .	using lessons 27-28 in the **Phonics/Word Study PDF.**
HIGH-FREQUENCY WORDS	Can children recognize and read the high-frequency words? If not . . .	by using the **High-Frequency Word Cards** and asking children to read and spell the word. Point out any irregularities in sound-spellings.
COMPREHENSION	Can children identify sequence of events? Can children identify rhyme? If not . . .	using lessons 25–27 and 116 in the **Comprehension PDF.**
CATEGORY WORDS	Can children identify and sort season words? If not . . .	using lesson 18 in the **Vocabulary PDF.**

GIFTED and TALENTED

Enrichment Opportunities

Beyond Level small group lessons and resources include suggestions for additional activities in these areas to extend learning opportunities for gifted and talented children:

- *Leveled Reader*
- *Vocabulary*
- *Comprehension*
- *Leveled Reader Library Online*
- *Center Activity Cards*

Today's focus:

Learning to think critically to solve a problem or make decisions.

Super Grover 2.0: Lemonade Stand (5:15)   STORY

family time

You'll find the "Super Grover 2.0: Lemonade Stand" video and supporting activity in this week's School to Home family newsletter.

think it through

engage together

Let's Play: Super Eye Spy!

Play a guessing game to activate children's observational and deductive reasoning skills.

- Our super-powerful minds know how to make careful observations.
- Let's put these skills to work.
- I'll pick something in the classroom for you to guess. I'll give you clues to help you figure it out.
- *Collecting clues* is a super-skill.
- Here's the first clue: I super-spy with my eye something that is _____. Look all around! *Observing* is another super-skill.
- You guessed it! Describe your *reasoning*—or how you figured out the object from the clues.

explore together

Let's Watch: "Super Grover 2.0: Lemonade Stand"
Set a purpose for sharing today's story video.

- Some Arctic friends need Super Grover 2.0's help to solve a problem.
- During the video, I'll pause it, so we can think.
- We'll talk about the problem, what we know, and possible solutions.

(▶) **Play the video**

Let's Pause and Think: Will it melt?
Take pauses during the video to talk about Super Grover's ideas.

- What's the problem at the lemonade stand?
- Will shaking the lemonade solve the problem? Why or why not?
- Will the jackhammer? Why or why not?
- Let's brainstorm some possible solutions.

connect the learning

Let's Reflect: Problem-solving strategies.
Explore critical thinking strategies.

- Today we learned some thinking skills for solving problems.
- What skills did we use to play the Super Eye Spy guessing game?
- When the Arctic friends had a problem, what did we do that Super Grover *didn't do* to think of solutions?
- Let's remember these strategies when we need to come up with a plan or solve a problem.

THINKING SUPER-SKILLS

- Observe.
- Collect Clues.
- Pause and Think.

mindfulness moment
Candle Breaths
Controlling our breaths takes practice. *Let's sit quietly. Imagine there's a lighted candle in front of you. Take a deep breath in and slowly blow the air out, being careful not to blow out the candle flame.* **Repeat two times, then take a long breath in and blow the candle out.**

LOGIC & REASONING

LESSON 1

OBJECTIVES

Confirm understanding of a text read aloud or information presented orally or through other media by asking and answering questions about key details and requesting clarification if something is not understood.

Use words and phrases acquired through conversations, reading and being read to, and responding to texts.

Identify real-life connections between words and their use.

Follow agreed-upon rules for discussions (e.g., listening to others and taking turns speaking about the topics and texts under discussion).

ELA ACADEMIC LANGUAGE

• *seasons, question, clarify*

DIGITAL TOOLS

Watch Video

Visual Vocabulary Cards

LESSON FOCUS

READING
Introduce Essential Question
Read Literature Big Book
Mama, Is It Summer Yet?
• Introduce Genre: Realistic Fiction
• Introduce Strategy/Skill
Word Work
• Introduce /b/b, /l/l

WRITING
Writing/Grammar
• Shared Writing
• Introduce Grammar

Literature Big Book, pp. 3–33

MULTIMODAL

10 mins

Build Knowledge

 Essential Question

How are the seasons different?

Read the Essential Question aloud. Explain that we will learn about the seasons this week.

- **Video Routine** Play the Weekly Opener Video, "The Four Seasons" without sound and have partners narrate what they watch. Then replay the video with sound and have children listen.

- **Talk About the Video** Have partners share one thing they learned about the seasons.

Anchor Chart Create a Build Knowledge anchor chart and have volunteers share what they learned about the theme "The Four Seasons." Record their ideas on the chart.

Oral Vocabulary Words

Use the Define/Example/Ask routine on the print or digital **Visual Vocabulary Cards** to introduce the oral vocabulary words *weather* and *seasons.*

 Oral Vocabulary Routine

<u>Define</u>: **Weather** is what is happening outside, such as rain, snow, or hot or cold air.

<u>Example</u>: The weather today is cool and breezy.

<u>Ask</u>: What type of weather do you like most? Why?

<u>Define</u>: The **seasons** are the four parts of the year.

<u>Example</u>: Two of the seasons are fall and spring.

<u>Ask</u>: In which season does school start every year?

Visual Vocabulary Cards

Reading/Writing Companion, pp. 8–9

 ## Build Knowledge

Have children turn to pages 8-9 of their **Reading/Writing Companion.** Use the photo to guide a discussion about the seasons.

- **Talk** *How are the seasons different? What words tell about how the seasons are different?* List the words. Have children choose a word and think about how to illustrate it.

- **Draw and Write** Have children draw a picture that illustrates the word. Then have them write the word. Guide children on how to print letters that have not been taught yet.

Build Vocabulary

Have children share new words they learned about the seasons. Add words to a separate section of the Word Bank. Use the words during the week and encourage children to do the same.

 # English Language Learners

Use the following scaffolds with **Build Knowledge.**

Beginning

Help children describe the photo. Point to details, and model words such as *snow, sled, coats,* and *gloves* for children to say after you.

Intermediate

Guide children to use sentence frames as they describe the details: In winter, the kids play in the snow; sled down a hill; wear coats.

Advanced/Advanced High

Encourage partners to use complete sentences. Provide modeling.

 ## COLLABORATIVE CONVERSATIONS

Ask and Answer Questions As children engage in partner, small group, and whole group discussions, encourage them to:

- Ask questions to clarify ideas they do not understand.
- Ask questions about unfamiliar words.
- Ask for help getting information.
- Wait after asking a question to give others a chance to think.
- Answer questions with complete ideas, not one-word answers.

 ## NEWCOMERS

To help children develop oral language and build vocabulary, continue using **Newcomer Cards** 15-19 and the accompanying lessons in the **Newcomer Teacher's Guide.** For thematic connections, use **Newcomer Card** 9. For additional practice, have children complete the online **Newcomer Activities.**

MY GOALS ROUTINE

What I Know Now

Read Goals Read aloud the goals and the key on **Reading/Writing Companion** page 10.

Reflect Ask children to reflect on each goal and complete page 10 to show what they know now. Explain that they will complete page 11 at the end of the text set to show their progress.

MAMA, IS IT SUMMER YET?
Nikki McClure

Literature Big Book

OBJECTIVES

Recognize common types of texts.

With prompting and support, ask and answer questions about key details in a text.

With prompting and support, identify characters and major events in a story.

Actively engage in group reading activities with purpose and understanding.

ELA ACADEMIC LANGUAGE

• *visualize, sequence*

• Cognates: *visualizar, secuencia*

 DIFFERENTIATED READING

Celebratory Read You may wish to read the full selection aloud once with minimal stopping before reading with the prompts.

●● Approaching Level and English Language Learners After reading, have children listen to the selection to develop comprehension.

Read

 20 mins

Literature Big Book

Connect to Concept

Tell children that you will now read a story about a boy who is excited about summer. Ask: *What things happen that tell us summer is here?*

Genre: Realistic Fiction Tell children that the **Big Book** is realistic fiction. *What information do we know about realistic fiction?* (made-up story, events could happen in real life, characters are like real people) *Realistic fiction can also have characters who talk.*

 Anchor Chart Display the Realistic Fiction anchor chart and review the characteristics of the genre. *What information can we add to this chart?*

Visualize Remind children that they can use the words and pictures in the story to create pictures in their mind.

Events: Sequence Explain that an author tells the important events that happen in a story in a certain order or sequence. The words *beginning, middle,* and *end* tell the order.

Read the Selection

Concepts of Print Display the Big Book cover. Read the title aloud as children track the words from left to right with their finger. Point to the question mark. Remind children a question mark is used to ask a question.

Set Purpose *Let's read to find out what happens when summer is coming.*

Close Reading Routine

Read   DOK 1–2

• Identify key ideas and details.
• Take notes and retell.
• Use **ACT** prompts as needed.

Reread   DOK 2–3

• Analyze the text, craft, and structure.

Integrate   DOK 3–4

• Integrate knowledge and ideas.
• Make text-to-text connections.
• Complete the Show Your Knowledge task.
• Inspire action.

Pages 4–5

CONCEPTS OF PRINT

Remind children that sentences begin with a capital letter and end with a punctuation mark. After reading, ask: *What is the first letter of this sentence?* (capital *M*) *What is the punctuation mark?* (a question mark)

 Spotlight On Language

Page 4 *yet:* Explain that the word *yet* is used to ask if something has started or not. Model the word in questions, and help children respond. For example: *Has the school day started yet?* Yes, the school day has started. *Has lunchtime started yet?* No, lunch has not started yet.

Pages 6–7

REALISTIC FICTION DOK 2

Think Aloud I know that realistic fiction can have characters who talk. Mama is one of the characters in this story. On this page, Mama is talking to her son. She is saying it is not summer yet. These details tell me this story is realistic fiction.

Page 7 *swelling:* Clasp your hands together. Slowly open them to make a large circular shape. *When something is swelling, it is getting bigger.* Have children open their hands as they say *swelling.*

Pages 8–9

REALISTIC FICTION DOK 2

Which character is talking on this page? (the little boy) *Who is he talking to?* (his Mama) *How do you know?* (The words on the page show the little boy asking his Mama a question. The illustrations show the boy and his Mama.)

Page 9 *branch:* Point to the branches the little boy is carrying. Explain that branches are parts of a tree. *The branches are bare because it's winter. In summer, there will be leaves on them.*

 Access Complex Text

Use this ACT prompt when the complexity of the text makes it hard for children to understand the story.

Organization

This book is comprised of questions and answers. Point out that the child is asking Mama questions on the pages to the left. The pages on the right show Mama's answers. Explain that this book includes dialogue even though there are no quotation marks or other dialogue indicators.

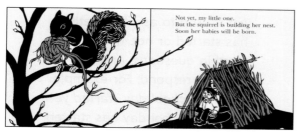

Pages 10–11

HIGH-FREQUENCY WORDS

Have children identify the high-frequency words *my* and *the*.

BUILD ORAL VOCABULARY

nest: animal home made of twigs and leaves

Page 11 *my little one:* Tell children that *my little one* is a special name that the mother calls her child. Ask children to list other names they know that show affection, such as *sweetie, honey,* or *dear.* Say the names aloud, and have children repeat.

Pages 12–13

PHONICS

Reread the sentence on page 12 and have children identify the words with the final /t/ sound. (it, yet) *What letter makes the /t/ sound?* (t)

Page 13 *watering can:* Point to the *watering can* the boy is holding. Ask children if they have seen one at home. Explain that a *watering can* is used for pouring water on plants so that they can grow.

Pages 14–15

EVENTS: SEQUENCE DOK 2

Think Aloud I know the events in a story are told in a certain order called sequence. First, I read the boy asks if it is summer. Then, the buds swell and the squirrel builds her nest. Now, the earth is soft. These details tell me the sequence and help me understand that summer is coming. You may wish to use the Events: Sequence graphic organizer as you continue reading the story.

BUILD ORAL VOCABULARY

sprout: begin to grow

Page 15 *sprout* and *root:* Draw a seed with *roots* growing down, a line to show the surface of the soil, and *sprouts* growing up out of the seed. Ask children to repeat the terms *sprout* and *root*. Point to each part as you say: *The seeds will root and sprout.* Have children make gestures up and down to represent *sprouts* and *roots*.

Pages 16–17

DETAILS DOK 1

How is the boy helping his mother? (The boy is helping his mother hammer a nail.) *How do you know?* I can see his hand on the hammer in the illustration.)

Page 1 *hammer:* Point to the *hammer* in the picture. Explain that a *hammer* is a tool. Explain that a tool can be used for building things, and for repairing things that are broken.

Pages 18–19

VISUALIZE DOK 2

Think Aloud The text tells about swallows singing. The lines behind the birds show that they are flying. I will close my eyes and picture the swallows flying through the air. I imagine they go in circles and fly quickly. This helps me understand what the swallows are doing.

BUILD ORAL VOCABULARY

blow: to move air

Pages 18–19 *swallow:* Tell children that *swallow* has more than one meaning. It can be an action (demonstrate) or a type of bird. Say the word, and have children repeat. *Let's count how many swallows are flying in the picture.* (seven)

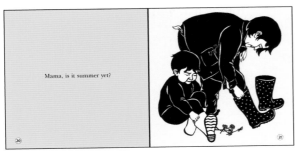

Pages 20–21

EVENTS: SEQUENCE DOK 2

What do you think the boy and his mother will do next? (I think they might be going near mud or water because the illustration shows them putting on rain boots.)

Page 21 *rain boots:* Point to the *rain boots* in the illustration. Explain that *rain boots* are special shoes that are made of material that keeps out the water.

Pages 22–23

VISUALIZE DOK 2

As you read the text, have children picture in their minds the little ducklings following their mother. Have volunteers share their responses. Then display the illustration as you reread the text.

BUILD ORAL VOCABULARY

ducklings: baby ducks

Page 23 *bold:* A person who grows *bold* becomes brave. When you are excited to try something new, you feel *bold.* Ask: *How can you tell when a duckling grows bold?* (It tries new things all by itself.)

Pages 24–25

REALISTIC FICTION DOK 1

Which character is talking? (the little boy) *Who is he talking to?* (his Mama) *What is he saying to his Mama?* (He is asking his Mama if it is summer yet.)

Page 25 *blanket:* Point to the illustration of the boy wrapped in a *blanket. The boy has a blanket to stay warm. Do you have a favorite blanket at home?*

 Spotlight On Language

Pages 26–27

EVENTS: SEQUENCE DOK 1

What happened after the ducklings followed the mother duck? (The trees are blossoming.) *What will happen after the trees blossom?* (Tiny apples will appear.)

Pages 26–27 *apples:* Show a photo of an *apple* to confirm meaning for children. Explain that *apples* grow on trees.

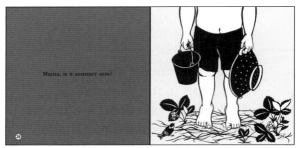

Pages 28–29

DETAILS DOK 2

What do you see in the illustration? (A boy that is wearing only shorts. He is barefoot. He is holding a pail and a strainer. The flowers are bloomed.) *Do you think it is summer now? Why or why not?*

Page 29 *pail:* Point to the picture of the *pail*. Explain that a *pail* is a small bucket used for carrying things like water, sand, or dirt.

Pages 30–31

VOCABULARY

Think Aloud When I see the word *honeybees,* I can see two words: *honey* and *bees.* I know that *honey* is a sweet, sticky liquid, and I know that *bees* are insects. *Honeybees* must be bees that make honey.

BUILD ORAL VOCABULARY

juicy: full of juice

Pages 30–31 *juicy:* Explain that berries and fruit are *juicy* when they have juice. *Berries can be so juicy that juice can drip down your chin when you eat them.* Ask children to name fruits that are *juicy.* (oranges, watermelon)

Pages 32–33

EVENTS: SEQUENCE DOK 1

What happens at the end of the story? (It is summer.) Explain to children that this is the last event in the story.

Pages 32–33 *bathing suit:* Point to the picture of the boy's Mama. Explain that a *bathing suit* is what we wear for swimming or playing in a pool.

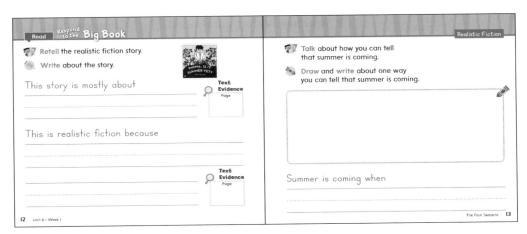

Reading/Writing Companion, pp. 12–13

Respond to the Text

Return to Purpose Remind children of their purpose for reading. Review what they learned about the signs of summer.

- **Retell** Have children open to page 12 of their **Reading/Writing Companion**. Guide them to retell the story. Have children use the **Retelling Cards** and the routine as needed.

- **Write** Have children write about the story on the lines provided on page 12. First ask them to write what the story is mostly about. Then have them write about how they know this story is realistic fiction. Remind them to find text evidence in the **Literature Big Book** to support their writing and to record the page numbers in the text evidence boxes. Share the Big Book with children, if needed.

- **Talk** Have children talk with a partner about the ways they know summer is coming. Encourage them to think about their own experiences when discussing with their partner.

- **Draw** and **Write** Then ask children to draw and write one way that they can tell summer is coming on page 13. Have children share their work.

Model Fluency

Remind children that exclamation points show strong feeling, such as excitement. Reread page 31 of *Mama, Is It Summer Yet?* emphasizing the expression used with exclamation points. Have children repeat the sentences with excitement and happiness in their voice.

Writing Fluency

To help children increase writing fluency, have them write as much as they can for four minutes. Tell them to write about what they learned about how the seasons change.

RETELLING ROUTINE

Tell children that they will use the Retelling Cards to retell the selection.

- Display Retelling Card 1. Based on children's needs use either the Modeled, Guided, or ELL retelling prompts on the back of the cards. The ELL prompts include support for children based on levels of language acquisition.

- Repeat with the rest of the cards, using the prompts as a guide. Encourage children to include details from the story and to tell the events in order.

- Discuss the story. Have children tell the events in order using words such as *beginning, middle* and *end*.

- Have children act out an event from the story with a partner.

Retelling Cards

⊘ STUDENT CHECK-IN

Have partners share an important detail from the story. Then have children reflect using the Check-In routine.

In a Flash: Sound-Spellings

Display the Sound-Spelling Card for *f*.

1. **Teacher:** What's the letter?   **Children:** f
2. **Teacher:** What's the sound?   **Children:** /f/
3. **Teacher:** What's the word?   **Children:** fire

Continue the routine for previously taught sounds.

LEARNING GOALS

- We can hear the sound /b/ in words.
- We can hear the sound /l/ in words.
- We can connect the sound /b/ to the letter *b*.
- We can connect the sound /l/ to the letter *l*.

OBJECTIVES

Isolate and pronounce the initial sounds in words.

Demonstrate basic knowledge of one-to-one letter-sound correspondences by producing the primary sound or many of the most frequent sounds for each consonant.

ELA ACADEMIC LANGUAGE

- connect, letter
- Cognates: conectar, letra

▶ TEACH IN SMALL GROUP

You may wish to teach the Word Work lesson in small groups.

ELL ENGLISH LANGUAGE LEARNERS

Phonemic Awareness, Guided Practice/Practice Encourage children to say /b/ several times. Point to a card, and ask children to name it. Help them self-correct by modeling pronunciation. Then help children identify the initial sound using a sentence frame. For example: Bike begins with the sound /b/. Repeat the routine with the Photo Cards for /l/.

---

5 mins MULTIMODAL

Phonemic Awareness

Phoneme Isolation

1 **Model** Display the **Photo Card** for *bat*. *Listen for the sound at the beginning of* bat. Bat *has the /b/ sound at the beginning. Say the sound with me: /b/.* Say *big, boy, bus* and have children repeat. Emphasize /b/. Repeat with /l/ using the *lemon* Photo Card and the words *lip, lamp, log*.

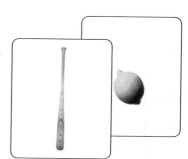

Photo Cards

♪ *Let's play a song. Listen for words with /b/ at the beginning.* Play "Play Ball," and have children listen for /b/. *Let's listen to the song again and tap the top of our heads when we hear words that begin with /b/.* Play or sing the letter song again, encouraging children to join in. Have children tap the tops of their heads when they hear a word that begins with /b/. Repeat with /l/ and "I Licked a Lemon."

2 **Guided Practice/Practice** Display and name the following Photo Cards: *bike, balloon, boy. Say each picture name with me. Tell me the sound at the beginning of the word.* Guide practice and provide corrective feedback as needed. Repeat with /l/ and the *ladder, lamp,* and *lock* Photo Cards. If children need additional practice identifying the /b/ or /l/ sounds, have them use **Practice Book** pages 242–243.

Articulation Support

Demonstrate how to say /b/. Put your lips together, and push a little air behind them. Let the air push through as you open your mouth. Your throat will vibrate, or hum. Put your hand on your throat to feel it. Say *bed, bat, big* and have children repeat. Emphasize /b/.

Demonstrate how to say /l/. Open your mouth. Put just the tip of your tongue on the roof of your mouth, just behind your teeth. Use your voice. Let the air pass by both sides of your tongue. Hold your hand in front of your mouth. Can you feel the air on both sides? Say *lid, lap, let* and have children repeat. Stretch /l/.

Phonics

Introduce /b/b, /l/l

1 Model Display the *bat* **Sound-Spelling Card**. *This is the* bat *card. The sound is /b/. The /b/ sound is spelled with the letter* b. *Say it with me: /b/. This is the sound at the beginning of the word* bat. *Listen: /b/, /b/, /b/,* bat.

Sound-Spelling Card

Display the song "Play Ball." (See **Spelling Song** online.) Sing the song with children. Point out that the word *ball* begins with the letter *b*. Model placing a self-stick note below the *b* in *ball*.

2 Guided Practice/Practice Read each line of the song. Stop after each line and ask children to place self-stick notes below words that begin with *B* or *b* and say the letter name and the sound it stands for.

Repeat Steps 1–2 with /l/l. If children need additional practice connecting letter *b* with the sound /b/ and letter *l* with the sound /l/, have them use **Practice Book** pages 245–246.

Play Ball!
You get the ball and I will get the bat.
You get the ball and I will get the bat.
You get the ball and I will get the bat.
Play ball! Play ball! Batter up!

I Licked a Lemon
I licked a lemon, and it had a sour taste.
I licked a lemon and I made a funny face.
I like lemon candy and I like lemonade,
and I like lemon cake and pie,
but a lemon I can't take!

ELL ENGLISH LANGUAGE LEARNERS

Phonics Transfers Use the chart on pages 10–13 in the **Language Transfers Handbook** to check for sound-spelling transfers.

CORRECTIVE FEEDBACK

Sound Error Model initial /b/. Say: *My turn. Bat /b/ /b/ /b/. Now it's your turn.* Have children say the words *bit* and *bad* and isolate the initial sound. Repeat for /l/l with the words *laugh* and *look*.

DIGITAL TOOLS

 **Phonemic Awareness** **Phonics**

 Phonics: Spelling Song

 **Phonics Video**

To differentiate instruction, use these results.

 **Phonics: Data-Generating**

 **Phonemic Awareness: pp. 242–243** **Phonics: pp. 245–246**

FORMATIVE ASSESSMENT

STUDENT CHECK-IN

Have partners name the letter that stands for /b/ and the letter that stands for /l/. Then have children reflect using the Check-In routine.

LESSON 1

LEARNING GOALS

- We can print the letters *b* and *l*.
- We can learn to read the words *is* and *little*.

OBJECTIVES

Print many upper- and lowercase letters.

Read common high-frequency words by sight.

ELA ACADEMIC LANGUAGE

- *uppercase, lowercase, around*

DIGITAL TOOLS

Handwriting

High-Frequency Words

To differentiate instruction, use these results.

High-Frequency Words: Data-Generating

MULTIMODAL LEARNING

Center Idea Have children use dried beans to make *Bb*. Ask them to trace the beans as they say /b/. Repeat with *Rr*.

Handwriting: p. 249

---

 5 mins

Handwriting: Write *Bb, Ll*

1 **Model** Say the handwriting cues below as you write and identify the uppercase and lowercase *Bb*. Trace the letters and say /b/.

Straight down. Go back to the top. Around and in, around and in.

Straight down. Go to the dotted line. Around all the way.

2 **Guided Practice**

- Say the cues together as children use their index finger to write *B* and *b* on the rug or a table as they say /b/.

3 **Practice**

- Distribute **Response Boards**. Have children write *B* and *b* on the Response Boards as they say /b/ each time they write the letter. Have them identify the uppercase and lowercase letters

- Observe children's pencil grip and paper position, and correct as necessary. Guide practice and provide corrective feedback.

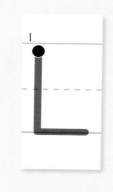

Straight down. Straight across the bottom line.

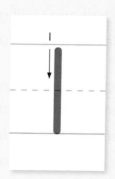

Straight down.

Repeat Steps 1–2 with *Ll.*

Daily Handwriting

Throughout the week, teach *Bb* and *Ll* using the Handwriting models. Then have children use **Practice Book** page 249.

In a Flash: High-Frequency Words

1. **Teacher:** Read the word.   **Children:** with
2. **Teacher:** Spell the word.   **Children:** w-i-t-h
3. **Teacher:** Write the word.   **Children write the word.**

Repeat routine with *he, are* and *my* from previous weeks.

5 mins

High-Frequency Words

MULTIMODAL

is	little

1 **Model** Display the **High-Frequency Word Cards** for *is* and *little*. Use the Read/Spell/Write routine to teach the words.

- **Read** Point to the word *is* and say the word. *This is the word* is. *Say it with me:* is. *My hat* is *yellow.*

- **Spell** *The word* is *is spelled i-s. Spell it with me.*

- **Write** *Let's write the word* is *on our* **Response Boards** *as we say each letter: i-s.*

- Point out that the letter *i* in *is* has the same /i/ sound as in the word *it* but the *s* in the word *is* has a /z/ sound.

- Have partners say sentences using the word.

COLLABORATE

Then display page 7 of the Big Book and read aloud the sentence: *Not yet, my little one.* Point to the high-frequency word *little*. Repeat the Read/Spell/Write routine with *little*. Point out that the /i/ and /t/ sounds in *little* are the same as in *it*.

2 **Guided Practice/Practice** Build sentences using **High-Frequency Word Cards, Photo Cards**, and teacher-made punctuation cards. Have children point to the high-frequency words *is* and *little*. Use these sentences. Guide practice and provide corrective feedback as needed.

The [ ] is little .

Is the [ ] little ?

ELL ENGLISH LANGUAGE LEARNERS

Use with **High-Frequency Words, Guided Practice/Practice** and the **High-Frequency Word Routine.**

Beginning
Tell children we can use *is* when we describe a person or thing. *What color is this book? This book* is *blue.*

Intermediate
Point to each card as you read the first sentence. Ask children to repeat. Ask a volunteer to point to *is*. Repeat with the second sentence.

Advanced/Advanced High
Challenge partners to create sentences using the words.

FORMATIVE ASSESSMENT

❯ STUDENT CHECK-IN

Handwriting Have children write *Bb* and *Ll*.

High-Frequency Words Have partners take turns pointing to and reading the words *is* and *little*.

Then have children reflect using the Check-In routine.

✓ CHECK FOR SUCCESS

Rubric Use your online rubric to record children's progress.

Can children isolate /b/ and /l/ and match them *Bb* and *Ll*?

Can children recognize and read the high-frequency words?

❯ Small Group Instruction

If No
- **Approaching** Reteach pp. T302–306
- **ELL** Develop pp. T302–306

If Yes
- **On** Review pp. T310–313
- **Beyond** Extend p. T316

LESSON 1

Literature Big Book

LEARNING GOALS

- We can write what we like to do in the summer.
- We can learn about words that name more than one person, place, or thing (plural nouns).

OBJECTIVES

Use a combination of drawing, dictating, and writing to compose opinion pieces in which they state an opinion or preference about the topic.

Continue a conversation through multiple exchanges.

Form regular plural nouns orally by adding /s/ or /es/.

ELA ACADEMIC LANGUAGE

- *season, summer, plural*
- Cognate: *plural*

COLLABORATIVE CONVERSATIONS

Turn and Talk Review this routine.

Child 1: *go swimming*

Child 2: *Can you say that in a complete sentence?*

Child 1: *I like to go swimming in the summer.*

Display the speech bubble, "Can you say that in a complete sentence?" Have partners use it to practice collaborating.

10 mins

Modeled Writing

Model Writing About the Literature Big Book

Build Oral Language Talk about what children learned from listening to the **Literature Big Book**. Review the seasons. Ask: *What season is this story about?* (summer) *What do you like to do in the summer?* Have partners use the Turn and Talk routine to talk about what they like to do in summer. When children are done, encourage them to share out what they talked about with their partner.

Model Writing a Sentence Write and display the following sentence: **I like to play in the park.** Then point out the following elements of writing using the Sample Teacher Talk.

- *This is the word* like. *I used the Word Bank to help me spell the word.* Like *is spelled with the letters* l-i-k-e. **HIGH-FREQUENCY WORDS**

- *I wrote the word* park. *I wrote the letter* p *at the beginning of the word because I hear the /p/ sound.* **PHONICS**

- *As I write my sentence, I will start on the left and move to the right.* **WRITING SKILL**

> What do you like to do in the summer?
>
> I like to play in the park.

Writing Practice

Turn to pages 14–15 of the **Reading/Writing Companion**. Say: *Now we are going to read a different sentence about summer.*

Analyze a Sentence Guide children to analyze the sentence using the prompts. Review the writing skill with children as necessary. Then have children write and analyze their own sentence.

Writing Practice

Write a Sentence

Talk about what the story tells about summer.

Listen to this sentence about summer.

> I like to swim in the summer.

Draw an arrow below the sentence from the first word to the last word.

Writing Skill
Remember: When you write, the words go from left to right.

14 Unit 6 · Week 1

Write a sentence about your favorite part of summer.

Draw an arrow below your sentence from the first word to the last word.

The Four Seasons 15

Reading/Writing Companion, pp. 14–15

Stephen Coburn/Shutterstock

Grammar

5 mins

Singular and Plural Nouns

1 Model Tell children that a singular noun names one person, place, or thing. Explain that some nouns name more than one person, place, or thing. These nouns are called plural nouns. We can make nouns plural by adding -s to the end.

The seed is small. (singular)   **The seeds are small.** (plural)

Read the sentences and underline the noun. Point out that the word *seed* names one thing. It is a singular noun. Point out that the word *seeds* names more than one thing. It is a plural noun.

2 Guided Practice Write these sentences and read them aloud. Guide children to identify the singular and plural nouns.

The leaf is green. (singular)   **The ducks are yellow.** (plural)
The birds are singing. (plural)   **The tree is tall.** (singular)

Continue guiding practice as necessary.

3 Practice Have children draw a picture of one or more animals. Have them label their drawing with a singular or plural noun.

Talk About It Have partners identify a noun on pages 26–27 of the **Big Book** (trees, apples) and generate sentences using those nouns.

Link to Writing Guide children to review the Shared Writing sentence and identify the noun *park* as a singular or plural noun.

English Language Learners

Use the following scaffolds with **Grammar, Guided Practice.**

Beginning

Review what nouns name. *Is a leaf a person, place, or thing?* (thing) *Does* leaf *name one thing or more than one thing? Leaf* names <u>one thing</u>. Repeat the routine with *birds*.

Intermediate

Help children identify the singular and plural nouns and tell what they name. <u>Leaf</u> names <u>one thing</u>. <u>Leaf</u> is a <u>singular</u> noun.

Advanced/Advanced High

Provide models to help children identify singular and plural nouns. Leaf names one thing. Ducks names more than one animal.

DIGITAL TOOLS

Grammar Activity

DIFFERENTIATED WRITING

● **English Language Learners** For more writing support, see the **ELL Small Group Guide,** p. 138.

FORMATIVE ASSESSMENT

◉ STUDENT CHECK-IN

Have partners share a plural noun they learned. Then have children reflect using the Check-In routine.

LEARNING GOALS

- We can say a word in two parts.
- We can use new words.
- We can learn words that tell about the seasons.
- We can use clues to find the meaning of a word.

OBJECTIVES

Segment onsets and rimes of single-syllable spoken words.

Use words and phrases acquired through conversations, reading and being read to, and responding to texts.

Identify new meanings for familiar words and apply them accurately.

Identify words about seasons.

Use context clues.

ELA ACADEMIC LANGUAGE

- *pattern*
- Cognate: *patrón*

DIGITAL TOOLS

Weekly Poem

Visual Vocabulary Cards

Category Words Activity

LESSON FOCUS

READING
Review Essential Question
Reread Literature Big Book
Mama, Is It Summer Yet?
- Study Genre/Skill

Read Shared Read
"Is It Hot?"
- Practice Strategy

Word Work
- Practice /b/b, /l/l

WRITING
Writing/Grammar
- Interactive Writing
- Practice Grammar

Literature Big Book, pp. 3–33

Reading/Writing Companion, pp. 20–27

---

 10 mins

Oral Language

MULTIMODAL

 Essential Question

How are the seasons different?

Remind children that this week we are learning about how the seasons are different. *What are the four seasons? What is your favorite season? Why? Let's read a poem about snowmen.* Read "Five Little Snowmen." As you read, have children hold up their five fingers and move one for each snowman. Then use the Build Knowledge anchor chart, the **Big Book,** and the **Weekly Poem** to guide children in discussing the Essential Question.

Phonological Awareness: Onset and Rime Segmentation

1 Model Tell children that you are going to say some words from the poem. Tell them that you will say the first sound and then the ending sounds in the words. Say the word *fifth*. Repeat the word, segmenting the onset and rime: /f/ /ifth/. Then segment the onset and rime in *years*, /y/ /îrz/.

2 Guided Practice/Practice Then say other words from the finger-play and have children segment the onset and rime in each one, such as: *five*, (/f/ /īv/); *day*, (/d/ /ā/); and *said*, (/s/ /ed/). Guide practice and provide corrective feedback as needed. If children need additional practice with onset and rime, have them use **Practice Book** page 241.

Review Oral Vocabulary Words

Use the Define/Example/Ask routine to review the oral vocabulary words *weather* and *seasons*. Prompt children to use the words in sentences.

Visual Vocabulary Cards

Category Words: Seasons

1 **Model** Use the **Big Book** *Mama, Is It Summer Yet?* to discuss season words. Explain that there are four seasons in a year: *winter, spring, summer, fall.* Display page 5. *What season is it? What clues help you know?* (It is winter. There are no leaves on the trees. I see mittens and a scarf.) Repeat with other illustrations in the book.

Read the following poem. Ask children to listen for season words.

Winter, spring, summer, fall. Which season is the best of all? Snow, rain, flowers, leaves. All four are great, I do believe.

Use a calendar to show when each season begins. Then have children share their favorite season and one thing they like to do in their favorite season.

2 **Guided Practice/Practice** Tell children that you will say some words. Have children sort words into the appropriate season.

rake	mittens	beach	planting seeds
flowers	pumpkin	sandals	snowballs

Vocabulary: Sentence Clues

1 **Model** Tell children that some words have more than one meaning. Use *Mama, Is It Summer Yet?* to model using sentence clues to determine the meaning of a multiple-meaning words and unfamiliar phrases.

Think Aloud I know the word *earth* has more than one meaning. In *Mama, Is It Summer Yet?* I can look for clues to understand what *earth* means here: *But the earth is soft. Soon the seeds will sprout and root.* I know that one meaning of *earth* is "the planet Earth." But the second sentence talks about seeds sprouting and rooting, so I know that *earth* means "soil" here.

2 **Guided Practice** Locate and discuss other multiple-meaning words in the book. Help children use clues from the sentences and illustrations to determine the meaning of the word.

*But the **swallows** are singing. Soon warmer winds will blow.*

3 **Practice** Discuss the different meanings of the word *seasons*. Model how to use *seasons* in different sentences to show the word's multiple meanings. Ask children which meaning of the word *seasons* would be used in *Mama, Is It Summer Yet?*

KIDS ON THE MOVE!

MULTIMODAL

Have children dramatize season-word sentences. As you say "We swim in summer," children should act out swimming in summer.

ELL ENGLISH LANGUAGE LEARNERS

Use the following scaffolds with **Context Clues: Sentence Clues, Guided Practice/ Practice**.

Beginning
Read aloud the sentence and point to *swallows* and *singing*. Have children repeat. *The swallows are singing. Birds sing.* Provide the sentence frame: Swallows are birds.

Intermediate
Review and demonstrate the verb *swallow*. Then point to *singing* in the text. Swallows *can be birds. Birds can sing.* Have children tell what *swallows* are in the sentence.

Advanced/Advanced High
Have children point to clues about the meaning of *swallows*. Then have them discuss the meaning with a partner.

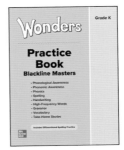

Phonological Awareness: p. 241

FORMATIVE ASSESSMENT

◯ STUDENT CHECK-IN

Oral Vocabulary Words Have partners say a sentence using a vocabulary word.

Category Words Have partners name a word that tells about a season.

Vocabulary Have partners explain how to figure out the meaning of a word.

Then have children reflect using the Check-in routine.

Literature Big Book

LEARNING GOALS

- We can tell what makes a story realistic fiction.
- We can identify sequence of events.

OBJECTIVES

Recognize common types of texts.

With prompting and support, identify characters and major events in a story.

ELA ACADEMIC LANGUAGE

- *sequence*
- Cognate: *secuencia*

Reread

10 mins

Literature Big Book

Genre: Realistic Fiction

1 **Model** Tell children that you will now reread the **Literature Big Book** *Mama, Is It Summer Yet?* Remind children that this story is realistic fiction.

 Anchor Chart Display and review the characteristics of realistic fiction that you have listed on the Realistic Fiction anchor chart. Add details as needed.

Think Aloud I know that the book *Mama, Is It Summer Yet?* is realistic fiction because it has characters who are like real people. The story also tells about things that could happen in real life. In *Mama, Is It Summer Yet?* the little boy and Mama are the main characters in the story. They talk to each other like a real mother and child. The little boy asks if it is summer yet and Mama responds with details about what is happening in the season.

2 **Guided Practice/Practice** Display and reread pages 8–9 of *Mama, Is It Summer Yet?* Ask: *Which main character is talking?* (The little boy.) *What is he saying?* (He is asking his Mama if it is summer yet.) Have children point out the little boy in the illustration. Now display and reread pages 10–11. *Which main character is talking?* (Mama) *What is she saying?* (It is not summer yet because the squirrel is building her nest.) Have children point out Mama in the illustration. Then ask: *What is happening on these pages that could happen in real life?* (The squirrel builds her nest.)

ELL English Language Learners

Genre: Realistic Fiction, Guided Practice/Practice Help children identify the characters in the illustrations. Read aloud page 8. *The boy is speaking. What does the boy call his mother?* ("Mama") Point out the sticks in the illustration. *What do the boy and his mother pick up?* (sticks) *Can this happen in real life?* (yes) Read aloud page 10. *What does the mother call her little boy?* ("my little one") Point out the squirrel in the illustration. *What does the boy watch with Mama?* (the squirrel) *Can this happen in real life?* (yes)

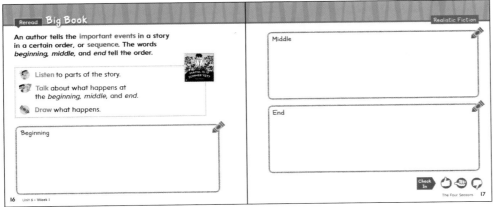

Reading/Writing Companion, pp. 16–17

Events: Sequence

1 **Model** Tell children that a story is made up of events. The events are told in the order that they happen. This is called sequence. We can talk about sequence using the words *beginning, middle,* and *end.*

 Anchor Chart Display the Main Story Elements: Events anchor chart. Ask: *What information about sequence should we add to the anchor chart?* (Events are told in sequence. We can use the words *beginning, middle,* and *end* to talk about the sequence.)

Think Aloud I know that events in a story are told in order. In this story each time the boy asks, "Mama, is it summer yet?" a new event happens. The story begins with the boy asking, "Mama, is it summer yet?" In the middle of the story, the author points out changes happening outside (buds swelling, squirrels building nests, seeds sprouting, swallows singing, ducklings following their mother, trees blooming) In the end of the story, we learn that it is summer. The author tells the events in order. This helps me understand the story.

2 **Guided Practice/Practice** Have children turn to pages 16–17 of the **Reading/Writing Companion**. Display and read pages 24–33 of *Mama, Is It Summer Yet?* Tell children to listen for the order of the events. Then have them describe important events in this part of the story by asking the following questions: *What happens in the beginning of the story?* (The boy asks, "Mama, is it summer yet?") *What happens in the middle of the story?* (Trees blossom.) *What happens in the end of the story?* (Summer arrives.) Guide children in completing pages 16–17 by drawing what happens in the *beginning, middle,* and *end.*

ENGLISH LANGUAGE LEARNERS

Events: Sequence, Guided Practice/ Practice Guide children to identify details in the pictures and text on pages 22–23, 26–27, and 30–31 to help them draw the events in sequence. Provide sentence frames to help children in preparing their drawings. First, the characters see the baby ducklings. Next, they see flowers blossom. Last, the characters eat juicy berries.

For additional support, see the **ELL Small Group Guide,** pp. 136–137.

FORMATIVE ASSESSMENT

⊙ STUDENT CHECK-IN

Skill Have partners share what makes the story realistic fiction.

Events Have children retell the order of events using the words *beginning, middle,* and *end.*

Then have children reflect on their learning using the Check-In routine.

✓ CHECK FOR SUCCESS

Can children identify characteristics of realistic fiction?

Can children identify sequence of events?

◇ **Small Group Instruction**

If No

● **Approaching** Reteach pp. T300–301

If Yes

● **On** Review pp. T308–309

● **Beyond** Extend pp. T314–315

LISTENING COMPREHENSION **T263**

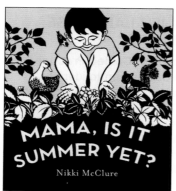

Literature Big Book

OBJECTIVES

With prompting and support, describe the relationship between illustrations and the story in which they appear.

With guidance and support from adults, explore word relationships and nuances in word meanings.

Analyze author's craft.

Analyze author and illustrator's purpose.

ELA ACADEMIC LANGUAGE

• *repeats, pattern*

Reread

10 mins Literature Big Book

Analyze the Text

Once children have reread *Mama, Is It Summer Yet?* to study the characteristics of the genre and practice the comprehension skill, guide them to analyze author's craft. Reread the passages specified below and use the scaffolded instruction in the prompts to help children answer the questions on pages 18-19 of the **Reading/Writing Companion**.

AUTHOR'S CRAFT DOK 3

Display and reread pages 4–5 of the **Big Book**. Talk about the author's use of the question "Mama, is it summer yet?" Ask: *Why do you think the author repeats the question?* (It's a way for the author to talk about the different signs of summer. It's a way for the author to show how badly the boy wants it to be summer. The question creates a repetitive pattern throughout the story.)

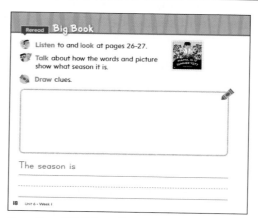

Reading/Writing Companion, p. 18

AUTHOR/ILLUSTRATOR'S PURPOSE DOK 2

Display and reread pages 26–27 of the Big Book. How does the author/ illustrator help you understand what season of the year it is? (The illustration shows Mama and the little boy dressed in short-sleeved shirts and lying on a blanket outside with no shoes. The author uses the words: "the trees are blossoming." These details tell me that it is spring.)

ELL English Language Learners

Author/Illustrator's Purpose Review how the temperature gets warmer in spring and how trees blossom. Point out how the characters are dressed differently earlier in the story. As children talk about how the illustrator shows spring, help them point to and say the clues.

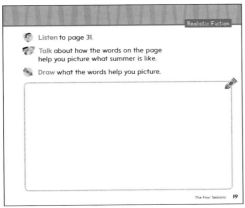

Reading/Writing Companion, p. 19

Listen to page 31.

Talk about how the words on the page help you picture what summer is like.

Draw what the words help you picture.

AUTHOR/ILLUSTRATOR'S PURPOSE DOK 2

Display and reread page 31 of the Big Book. *Which words does the author use to help you know what summer is like?* (The author uses words such as *honeybees, flowers, a warm sun,* and *juicy and sweet berries.*) *How does this help you visualize?* (The descriptive words help me create images in my mind.)

ⓔ️ Spotlight on Language

Author/Illustrator's Purpose Have children point to and say the words *honeybees, flowers, sun,* and *berries.* Then use the illustration and other visuals to review each word.

ORGANIZATION DOK 3

Why does the author have summer come at the end of the story? (The story's events are in sequence, or order. The story begins with winter and shows the signs of spring and, finally, the arrival of summer.) *How does the author let us know that summer is getting closer?* (The author uses words and illustrations to show us that spring is unfolding and summer is getting closer.)

Talk About It

Guide children to use their responses on the **Reading/Writing Companion** pages to answer the following question:

How does the author/illustrator help you understand that summer is coming?

If necessary, use the following sentence starters to focus the discussion: **In the beginning, the trees have _____. In the middle, the swallows are _____. In the end, the sun is _____.**

Integrate

Build Knowledge: Make Connections

Talk About the Text Have children discuss the seasons in the story. *What is something that happened in each season in the text?*

Add to the Anchor Chart Record any new ideas on the Build Knowledge Anchor Chart.

FORMATIVE ASSESSMENT

◉ STUDENT CHECK-IN

Have partners share something the author/illustrator do with the text and pictures to help understand the story. Then have children reflect using the Check-In routine.

LEARNING GOALS

- We can hear the sound /b/ at the end of a word.
- We can connect letters to sounds to read words.
- We can read *is* and *little*.

OBJECTIVES

Isolate and pronounce the initial and final sounds in three-phoneme words.

Demonstrate basic knowledge of one-to-one letter-sound correspondences by producing the primary sound or many of the most frequent sounds for each consonant.

Read common high-frequency words by sight.

ELA ACADEMIC LANGUAGE

- *beginning, end*

⊘ TEACH IN SMALL GROUP

You may wish to teach these lessons in small groups.

DIGITAL TOOLS

Word Work — Phonemic Awareness

To differentiate instruction for key skills, use these results.

Phonics: Data-Generating

High-Frequency Words: Data-Generating

In a Flash: Sound-Spellings

Display the Sound-Spelling Card for *b*.

1. **Teacher:** What's the letter?	**Children:** b	
2. **Teacher:** What's the sound?	**Children:** /b/	
3. **Teacher:** What's the word?	**Children:** bat	

Continue the routine with *l* and previously taught sounds.

 OPTIONAL 5 mins

Phonemic Awareness

Phoneme Isolation

1 **Model** Display the *bat* **Photo Card** and remind children of the /b/ sound heard at the beginning of *bat*. Have children say the sound /b/. Then display the *web* Photo Card. *The sound /b/ can also appear at the end of a word. Listen for the sound at the end of* web. Emphasize final /b/. *Say the sound with me: /b/.* Then say the following words and have children repeat: *job, cub, grab.*

2 **Practice** Say each of the following words and have children repeat. Have them say /b/ if they hear the sound at the end of the word. Guide children with the first word.

dab   bad   rub   big   tub   ball   crib

5 mins

Phonics

 MULTIMODAL

Review *b* and *l*

1 **Model** Display the *bat* **Sound-Spelling Card**. *This is the letter* b. *The letter* b *can stand for the /b/ sound heard at the beginning of the word* bat. *The letter* b *can also stand for the /b/ sound heard at the end of* web. Repeat for the initial sound/letter /l/ /l/ using the *lemon* Sound-Spelling Card.

2 **Guided Practice/Practice** Display the *bat* Sound-Spelling Card and point to the letter *Bb*. Have children say the letter name and sound with you. Then repeat using the *lemon* Sound-Spelling Card. Have children listen as you say some words. Ask them to write the letter *b* or the letter *l* on their **Response Boards** if the word begins with the sound /b/ or /l/. Guide practice and provide corrective feedback as needed.

ball   last   bus   boy   laugh   bike   bag
leaf   like   back   lock   book   lake   log

Blend Words

1 **Model** Place **Word-Building Cards** *b, e,* and *d* in a pocket chart. Point to the letter *b*. *This is the letter* b. *The letter* b *stands for /b/. Say /b/. This is the letter* e. *The letter* e *stands for /e/. Say /e/. This is the letter* d. *The letter* d *stands for /d/. Say /d/. Listen as I blend the three sounds together: /beeed/,* bed. *Let's blend the sounds to read the word.*

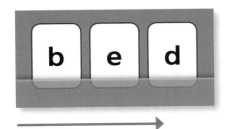

2 **Guided Practice/Practice** Change Word-Building Cards to *bet.* Point to the letter *b* and have children say /b/. Point to the letter *e* and have children say /e/. Point to the letter *t* and have children say /t/. Then move your hand from left to right under the word and have children blend and read the word *bet.* Repeat with *bat.* Repeat Steps 1–2 with *l* using the words *let, lit,* and *lot.* Guide practice and provide corrective feedback as needed.

OPTIONAL
5 mins

High-Frequency Words

MULTIMODAL

is	little

1 **Guided Practice** Display the **High-Frequency Word Cards** *is* and *little*. Use the Read/Spell/Write routine to teach the words. Ask children to write both words without looking at the word cards. Then have them self-correct by checking the High-Frequency Word Cards.

2 **Practice** Add high-frequency words *is* and *little* to the word bank.

• Have partners say sentences using the words.

Cumulative Review Review the high-frequency words *he, with, are, my, to, and, go, you,* and *do* by displaying each word and having children read it with automaticity.

• For additional practice with high-frequency words, use **Practice Book** page 250.

ELL **ENGLISH LANGUAGE LEARNERS**

High-Frequency Words, Practice
Provide sentence frames to help partners say sentences with *is* and *little*. Children can take turns gesturing and using the words in sentences: My shirt <u>is</u> blue. My pinky finger is <u>little</u>.

High-Frequency Words: p. 250

FORMATIVE ASSESSMENT

◆ STUDENT CHECK-IN

Phonics Have partners blend and read *bed* and *lit*.

High-Frequency Words Have partners take turns pointing to and reading *is* and *little*.

Then have children reflect using the Check-In routine.

⊘ CHECK FOR SUCCESS

Rubric Use your online rubric to record children's progress.

Can children isolate /b/ and /l/ and match them to the letters *Bb* and *Ll*?

Can children read and recognize the high-frequency words?

〉〉 Small Group Instruction

If No

● **Approaching** Reteach pp. T302–306

● **ELL** Develop pp. T302–306

If Yes

● **On** Review pp. T310–313

● **Beyond** Extend p. T316

LESSON 2

LEARNING GOALS

We can read and understand a text.

OBJECTIVES

Identify the front cover and title page of a book.

Know and apply grade-level phonics and word analysis skills in decoding words.

Demonstrate basic knowledge of one-to-one letter-sound correspondences by producing the primary sound or many of the most frequent sounds for each consonant.

Read common high-frequency words by sight.

With prompting and support, identify the main topic and retell key details of a text.

Read emergent-reader texts with purpose and understanding.

ELA ACADEMIC LANGUAGE

• *visualize, rhyme*

• Cognates: *visualizar, rimar*

 DIFFERENTIATED READING

● ● **English Language Learners** Have children listen to a summary of the selection, available in multiple languages.

Connect to Concept

As children read this selection, have them look for details to help them answer the Essential Question: *How are the seasons different?*

Foundational Skills

Book Handling Hold up the **Reading/Writing Companion** and point to the front cover of the book. Say: *This is the front cover of the book.* Then turn to page 20 and point to the title of the selection. Say: *This is the title.*

Concepts of Print Turn to page 21 and point to each sentence. *Each sentence begins with a capital letter and ends with a punctuation mark.* Ask: *What kind of punctuation mark is this?* (period) Invite volunteers to establish sentence boundaries by pointing first to the capital letter and then to the ending punctuation mark.

Phonics Have children review the letters *b* and *l* and their sounds.

High-Frequency Words Have children review the words *is* and *little.*

Read the Shared Read

Visualize Remind children that they can use the words on a page to make pictures in their mind of events in a story.

 Anchor Chart Display and review the Visualize anchor chart.

Choral Read Before reading, invite children to share any questions they have about the selection. Have children chorally read the story with you.

Read Read the selection and pause to ask the questions in the blue column. Explain that when a question asks them to circle something, they can circle the image, the words, or both.

Have children use the box on the right-hand pages to do the following:

• Draw a picture about the text or the photo.

• Draw something whose name includes the /b/ or /l/ sound.

• Write the letter *b* or *l.*

Reading/Writing Companion, pp. 20–21

SET PURPOSE

Have children read to find out what is hot.

HIGH-FREQUENCY WORDS

Tell children to circle the words *is* and *little.*

Reading/Writing Companion, pp. 22–23

PHONICS

Have children circle the photo that has the same beginning sound as the word *bed*. (bat)

Then tell them to underline the words with the same ending sound as *lab*. (Deb x2) *What letter makes the /b/ sound?*

Reading/Writing Companion, pp. 24–25

PHONICS

Have children circle the words that begin with the same sound as *lid*. (Let, Lin x2) *What letter makes the /l/ sound?*

RHYME

Tell children to underline the words that rhyme. (hop, top)

Reading/Writing Companion, pp. 26–27

COMPREHENSION

Tell children to circle what is on "top." (the red hat) Remind them to use clues to support their response.

Then have them retell the selection. Guide them to identify details about the topic: *seasons* as they retell.

Focus on Fluency: Accuracy

Model reading with accuracy for children. Remind them of the importance of recognizing high-frequency words as well as decoding words in the text correctly. Encourage children to practice reading for accuracy with a partner. Listen in and offer support and corrective feedback as needed.

Respond to the Text

Talk About It Have children talk about what they learned about the seasons from the text. Use this sentence starter to focus discussion. **I learned** _____. Help children cite text evidence to support their answers.

ENGLISH LANGUAGE LEARNERS

Use the following scaffolds with **Respond to the Text.**

Beginning
Point to the photos and say: *Summer is hot.* Have children point to the images and repeat: *Summer is* hot. *Winter is* not hot.

Intermediate
Provide sentence frames for children to describe the seasons: *Summer is* hot. *Winter is* not hot. *Snow is in* winter.

Advanced/Advanced High
Have partners talk about the seasons using complete sentences. Provide modeling. *Winter is cold. Snow is in winter. Summer is hot. Trees lose leaves in fall.*

FORMATIVE ASSESSMENT

⊙ STUDENT CHECK-IN

Have partners take turns sharing their retelling of the text with one another. Then have children reflect using the Check-In routine.

SHARED READ **T269**

LESSON 2

Literature Big Book

10 mins

Interactive Writing

Write About the Literature Big Book

Analyze the Prompt Tell children that today they will write a sentence about *Mama Is It Summer Yet?*: *Do you think the author did a good job of showing that summer is coming? Why or why not?* Have partners discuss the different ways they think the author shows that summer is coming.

Find Text Evidence Flip through the **Big Book**. Point out the things the author highlights on each page. For example, on pages 6–7, the buds are swelling and will soon be leaves. Help children to identify in which season that would happen and guide them to understand that by showing the signs of spring, the author is also letting us know that summer is coming.

Write a Response: Share the Pen Have children provide a response to the prompt and encourage them to share the pen to help you write a response. Alternatively, use the sentences on the anchor chart. Point out the following elements of writing using the Sample Teacher Talk below.

• *When we write a sentence, we start on the left and move to the right.* Ask a child to point to where *The* should be placed.   WRITING SKILL

• *Look at the Word Bank. Who can point to the word* are? *Let's spell it:* a-r-e. Write the word as children spell it.   HIGH-FREQUENCY WORDS

• *Say* buds. *Who can write the letters that stand for the sounds /b/ /u/ /d/ /s/?*   PHONICS

• *We are writing about the signs of summer. When we look for details, we must remember to think about summer.*   TRAIT: ORGANIZATION

> Do you think the author did a good job of showing that summer is coming? Why or why not?
>
> The author shows summer is coming by saying there are buds on the trees.

Writing Practice

Write Provide children with the following sentence starters and have them choose one to complete in their writer's notebook.

I think _____.   The author shows _____.

As children write, encourage them to:

• Use the Word Bank to help spell high-frequency words.

• Stretch the sounds they hear in words as they write.

• Write from left to right.

• Stay on the topic they are writing about: summer.

Stephen Coburn/Shutterstock

Grammar

5 mins

Singular and Plural Nouns

1 **Model** Remind children that nouns name people, places, animals, and things. We can add *-s* to the end of a noun to talk about more than one noun. Write and read this sentence aloud: **The store sells clocks**. Point to the word *store*. Say: *In this sentence,* store *is a singular noun because it is naming one thing*. Then point to the word *clocks*. Say: *In this sentence,* clocks *is a plural noun because it is naming more than one thing*. Underline the *-s* at the end of *clocks*.

2 **Guided Practice** Write and read aloud: **A man sells balloons**. Guide children to identify and underline the nouns in the sentence. (man, balloons) Then guide them to identify *man* as a singular noun and *balloons* as a plural noun. Invite a volunteer to circle the *-s* in balloons. Say: *The -s tells us that there is more than one balloon*. Continue guiding practice as necessary.

3 **Practice** Write and read aloud this sentence: **A girl sells red hats**. Have partners copy the sentence and underline the nouns. (girl, hats) Then have them tell which word names one thing and which word names more than one thing. Tell them to circle the *-s* that tells them the word is plural. If children need more practice with nouns, have them use **Practice Book** page 252.

Talk About It

Have partners identify an object in the classroom. Tell children to say the word that names only one of that object. Then ask children to say the word that names more than one.

English Language Learners

Grammar, Practice Sketch a simple hat on the board. Write the words *one hat*. Read the words holding up one finger. Have children echo-read and mimic the action. Add a second hat to your original sketch. Write *two hats*. Circle the *s* at the end of the word *hats*. Read *two hats* holding up two fingers. Have children repeat. To ensure children understand the *-s* ending means "more than one," draw a few more hats and say *more hats*. Display the practice sentence: *A girl sells red hats*. Circle *hats*. Draw an arrow pointing to the *-s* ending. *Is the girl selling one hat or more than one hat?* The girl is selling more than one hat. Repeat the routine with *girl*.

DIGITAL TOOLS

I see a fish.

Grammar Activity

DIFFERENTIATED WRITING

● **English Language Learners** For more writing support, see the **ELL Small Group Guide,** p. 138.

Grammar: p. 252

FORMATIVE ASSESSMENT

STUDENT CHECK-IN

Have partners share a plural noun they learned. Then have children reflect using the Check-In routine.

LEARNING GOALS

We can learn new words.

OBJECTIVES

Use words and phrases acquired through conversations, reading and being read to, and responding to texts.

Identify real-life connections between words and their use.

Develop oral vocabulary.

ELA ACADEMIC LANGUAGE

• *nonfiction, text*

• Cognates: *no ficción, texto*

DIGITAL TOOLS

Weekly Poem

Visual Vocabulary Cards

Interactive Read Aloud

FORMATIVE ASSESSMENT

○ STUDENT CHECK-IN

Have partners tell each other the meaning of one vocabulary word. Then have children reflect using the Check-in routine.

LESSON FOCUS

READING
Review Essential Question
Read Interactive Read Aloud
"A Tour of the Seasons"
• Practice Strategy
Word Work
• Practice /b/*b*, /l/*l*

Reread Shared Read
"Is It Hot?"
WRITING
Writing/Grammar
• Independent Writing
• Practice Grammar

Interactive Read-Aloud Cards

Reading/Writing Companion, pp. 20–27

---

5 mins

Oral Language

 Essential Question

How are the seasons different?

This week we are talking and learning about the seasons. How are the seasons different and what kinds of things do we do in each season? Then read the **Weekly Poem** together.

Oral Vocabulary Words

Remind children that on Lesson 1 we learned the vocabulary words *weather* and *season*. Ask: *What is the weather today? What are the four seasons? Be sure to use the words* weather *and* season *when responding to the questions.* Then use the Define/Example/Ask routine on the print or digital Visual Vocabulary Cards to introduce *migrate, active,* and *spot.*

Oral Vocabulary Routine

<u>Define</u>: To **migrate** means to move from one place to another, usually to a place that is warmer or colder.

<u>Example</u>: The birds migrate south to Florida every winter.

<u>Ask</u>: Why do many animals migrate to warmer places for the winter?

<u>Define</u>: An **active** person is someone who is busy and moves around a lot.

<u>Example</u>: The active child played with every toy in the room.

<u>Ask</u>: Are you more active when you're watching television or when you're outside? Why?

<u>Define</u>: When you **spot** something, you notice it or find it.

<u>Example</u>: It's easy to spot a giraffe in the zoo because it's so tall.

<u>Ask</u>: What can you spot in the night sky?

Visual Vocabulary Cards

Read the Interactive Read Aloud

Connect to Concept

Tell children they will listen to a nonfiction text. Remind children that we are learning about how the seasons are different. Use the print or digital **Interactive Read-Aloud Cards**. Read the title.

"A Tour of the Seasons"

Set Purpose Say: *Let's read to learn about each season.*

Oral Vocabulary Use the Oral Vocabulary prompts as you read the selection to provide more practice with the words in context.

Unfamiliar Words As you read "A Tour of the Seasons," ask children to listen for words they do not understand or for newly learned words they recognize and to think about what the words mean. Pause after Card 1 to model.

Teacher Think Aloud The park is *packed*. What does *packed* mean? The text says that children ride on sleds and friends build a snowman. I think *packed* must mean that there are a lot of people at the park.

Student Think Along After Card 3: I remember that we learned the word *delicious*. It means that something tastes very good. That makes sense because the text says you can smell *delicious* foods.

Build Knowledge: Make Connections

Talk About the Text Have partners describe their favorite seasons using evidence from the text.

Add to the Anchor Chart Record new ideas on the Build Knowledge anchor chart.

Add to the Word Bank Add new words children learned to a separate section of the Word Bank.

Compare Texts

Guide partners to connect "A Tour of the Seasons" with *Mama, Is it Summer Yet?* Discuss how both texts tell about the seasons. How are the texts different?

LESSON 3

LEARNING GOALS

- We can blend sounds to say words.
- We can blend and read words.

OBJECTIVES

Demonstrate understanding of spoken words, syllables, and sounds (phonemes).

Know and apply grade-level phonics and word analysis skills in decoding words

Demonstrate basic knowledge of one-to-one letter-sound correspondences by producing the primary sound or many of the most frequent sounds for each consonant.

Spell simple words phonetically, drawing on knowledge of sound-letter relationships.

Blend phonemes to form words.

ELA ACADEMIC LANGUAGE

- *blend, different*

 TEACH IN SMALL GROUP

You may wish to teach the Word Work lesson in small groups.

DIGITAL TOOLS

 **Phonemic Awareness**
Phonics

 Phonics: Spelling Song

---

5 mins MULTIMODAL

Phonemic Awareness

Phoneme Blending

1 **Model** Say: *Listen to the sounds in a word: /b/ /a/ /t/. I can blend those sounds to make the word: /baaat/, bat. Listen as I say more sounds and blend them to make words.* Model phoneme blending with the following.

/l/ /i/ /t/ lit   /t/ /u/ /b/ tub   /st/ /e/ /p/ step   /b /i/ /g/ big

2 **Guided Practice/Practice** Say: *Listen to the sounds in a different word: /sp/ /e/ /d/. Let's blend the sounds and say the word together: /sp/ /e/ /d/, /speeed/ sped.* Tell children to listen to the sounds in the following words, repeat the sounds, and then blend them to say the word. Guide practice and provide corrective feedback as needed.

/b/ /e/ /d/ bed	/l/ /i/ /t/ lit	/r/ /u/ /b/ rub
/b/ /e/ /l/ bell	/l/ /o/ /t/ lot	/b/ /e/ /t/ bet
/l/ /e/ /t/ let	/t/ /u/ /b/ tub	/l/ /ē / /f/ leaf

Review initial /b/ and /l/. Play and sing "Play Ball!" and "I Licked a Lemon." Have children clap when they hear initial /b/ or /l/. Demonstrate as you sing with children.

10 mins

Phonics

b l   MULTIMODAL

Review /b/b, /l/l

1 **Model** Display **Word-Building Card** b. *This is the letter* b. *The letter* b *stands for /b/, the sound you hear at the beginning of* bat *and at the end of* web. *Say the sound with me: /b/. I will write the letter* b *because* bat *has the /b/ sound in the beginning and* web *has the /b/ sound at the end.* Repeat with initial sound /l/l, the sound heard at the beginning of *lemon*.

2 **Guided Practice/Practice** Tell children that you will say some words that have /b/ or /l/ at the beginning. Have children say /b/ and write the letter *b* on their **Response Boards** when they hear /b/ at the beginning of the word. Have them say /l/ and write the letter *l* on their boards when they hear /l/ at the beginning of the word. Guide practice and provide corrective feedback as needed: *bed, lit, lid, band, Ben, log, lap, bug.*

Blend Words

1 **Model** Display Word-Building Cards b, e, t. *This is the letter* b. *It stands for /b/. This is the letter* e. *It stands for /e/. This is the letter* t. *It stands for /t/. Let's blend the three sounds together: /b/ /eee/ /t/, /beeet/. The word is* bet. Repeat with *bat, lad, lid.*

2 **Guided Practice/Practice** Write the following words. Have children read each word. Guide practice with the first word: *bit, rob, lip, let, tab, bad, led.* Write these sentences and prompt children to read the connected text, sounding out the decodable words: *Bob can bat and hit. Deb let him see the fat cat.*

Spell Words

Dictation Say the word *lip* and have children repeat. Ask children to say *lip* again, stretching the sounds. You may wish to have children use **Sound Boxes** before they write the word. Then write the word as you say the letter names and have children check their work. Repeat the routine for *lap, let, bet,* and *bat.* If children need additional practice with spelling, have them use **Practice Book** page 247.

EXTEND THE LESSON

Final Double Letters *ll*

Place the Word-Building Cards *b, e, l, l* in a pocket chart and model blending and reading the word. Point out that the two letters, *ll*, stand for one sound /l/. Have children blend and read the word *bell*. Continue with the word *tell*.

ⓔ ENGLISH LANGUAGE LEARNERS

Phonemic Awareness, Guided Practice/ Practice Say each sound in *sped*. Have children repeat. Then guide children to blend the sounds with you. Repeat with any words children struggle with.

CORRECTIVE FEEDBACK

Sound Error Model the sound that children missed when blending words, then have them repeat. For example, for the word *bet*, say: *My turn.* Tap under the letter *b* and ask: *Sound? What's the sound?* Return to the beginning of the word. *Let's start over.* Blend the word with children again.

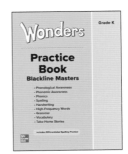

Phonics/Spelling: p. 247

FORMATIVE ASSESSMENT

❯ STUDENT CHECK-IN

Have partners read *bat* and *let*. Then have children reflect using the Check-In routine.

LESSON 3

LEARNING GOALS

- We can sort words that begin with the letter *b* or the letter *l*.
- We can read sentences with the words *is* and *little*.

OBJECTIVES

Demonstrate basic knowledge of one-to-one letter-sound correspondences by producing the primary sound or many of the most frequent sounds for each consonant.

Read common high-frequency words by sight.

Sort words by initial letter.

ELA ACADEMIC LANGUAGE

- *sort, beginning*

DIGITAL TOOLS

To differentiate instruction for key skills, use the results of this activity.

Phonics: Data-Generating

High-Frequency Words: Data-Generating

OPTIONAL 5 mins

Phonics

MULTIMODAL

Picture Sort

1 **Model** Remind children that the letter *b* can stand for /b/. Place the **Word-Building Card** *b* on the left side of a pocket chart. Continue the same routine for the letter *l*.

Hold up the **Photo Card** for *bat. Here is the picture for* bat. Bat *has the /b/ sound in the beginning. I will place* bat *under the letter* b *because the letter* b *stands for /b/.* Use the same routine for letter *l* and *lemon.*

Photo Cards

2 **Guided Practice/Practice** Have children sort the Photo Cards *boat, book, bus, leaf, light, lock.* Have them say the sound at the beginning of the word and tell which letter the Photo Card should be placed under. Guide practice and provide corrective feedback as needed.

Photo Cards

ELL English Language Learners

Phonics, Guided Practice/Practice Point to the boat, and have children say the /b/ sound in *boat.* Repeat with the *book* and *bus* cards. Repeat the routine, emphasizing the /l/ sound in *leaf, light,* and *lock.* Correct children's pronunciation as needed. Then, guide children to identify the initial sounds for the Photo Cards. *Is the beginning sound in* boat /b/ or /l/? (/b/) Use sentence frames to help children tell how they sorted the cards: Boat begins with the sound /b/. We place boat below the letter b.

High-Frequency Words

MULTIMODAL

| is | little |

1 **Guided Practice** Display the **High-Frequency Word Cards** *is, little*. Review the word using the Read/Spell/Write routine.

2 **Practice** Point to the High-Frequency Word Card *is* and have children read it. Repeat with the word *little* and previous weeks' words *he, with, are, my, to, and, go, you, do.*

Build Fluency

Word Automaticity Write the following sentences. Have children chorally read them as you track the print. Have them reread the sentences until they can read the words automatically and fluently.

Can Bob see the cat?
Ed can let the cat go.

Do you like a lot of ham?
I like to nap on the bed.

Read for Fluency Distribute **Practice Book** pages 255–256 and help children assemble their Take-Home Books. Chorally read the Take-Home Book. Have children reread the book to build automaticity.

BUILD YOUR WORD BANK

Use this lesson to teach additional high-frequency words.

1 **Model** Display the **Build Your Word Bank Cards** for *by, some,* and *brown* from the **Your Turn Practice Book High-Frequency Word Cards**. Use the Read/Spell/Write routine to teach each word.

- **Read** Point to the word *by* and say the word. *This is the word* by. *Say it with me:* by. *Rob sat* by *the fan.*
- **Spell** *The word* by *is spelled* b-y. *Spell it with me.*
- **Write** *Let's write the word* by *on our* **Response Boards** *as we spell it:* b-y. Point out that the letter *b* stands for /b/ as in *bat*.
  Repeat the Read/Spell/Write routine with: *some, brown.*

2 **Guided Practice** Display the **Build Your Word Bank Cards** for *by, some,* and *brown*. Point to each of the words and have children chorally read each word. Then have children take turns using the Build Your Word Bank words in a sentence. Guide practice and provide corrective feedback as needed.

ELL ENGLISH LANGUAGE LEARNERS

High-Frequency Words, Practice
Ask children to read aloud *is* and *little*. Then help them self-correct by modeling pronunciation. For additional practice, model simple sentences with the words for children to repeat. Then help children read aloud the previous weeks' words with you.

Take-Home Story: pp. 255–256

FORMATIVE ASSESSMENT

> STUDENT CHECK-IN

Phonics Have partners think of words that they would add to the word sort.

High-Frequency Words Have partners take turns reading a sentence from the Take-Home Book.

Then have children reflect using the Check-In routine.

✓ CHECK FOR SUCCESS

Rubric Use your online rubric to record children's progress.

Can children identify phonemes and sort words by initial sound/letter?

Can children read and recognize the high-frequency words?

>> Small Group Instruction

If No

● **Approaching** Reteach pp. T302–306

● **ELL** Develop pp. T302–306

If Yes

● **On** Review pp. T310–313

● **Beyond** Extend p. T316

LEARNING GOALS

We can read and understand a text.

OBJECTIVES

Identify the front cover, back cover, and title page of a book.

With prompting and support, describe the relationship between illustrations and the text in which they appear.

Demonstrate basic knowledge of one-to-one letter-sound correspondences by producing the primary sound or many of the most frequent sounds for each consonant.

Read common high-frequency words by sight.

Read emergent-reader texts with purpose and understanding.

ELA ACADEMIC LANGUAGE

• *punctuation*

• Cognate: *puntuación*

 10 mins

Reread "Is It Hot?"

Focus on Foundational Skills

Book Handling Demonstrate book handling. Hold up the **Reading/Writing Companion** and have volunteers come up and identify the front cover and the back cover of the book. Then turn to page 20 and have volunteers come up and point to the title of the selection.

Concepts of Print Reinforce sentence boundaries by pointing to page 21 and discussing each sentence. Have volunteers come up and point to the spaces between the words. Tell them to point to the first word in the sentence and the punctuation mark. Encourage children to say the first word and the capital letter, along with the name of the punctuation mark.

Focus on Comprehension

Reread Guide children to reread the story. Children should sound out the decodable words and read the high-frequency words with automaticity. Tell them to look for details that they did not notice in the first reading.

Have children use the box on the right-hand pages to do the following:

• Draw a picture about the text or the photo.

• Draw something whose name includes the /b/ or /l/ sound.

• Write the letter *b* or *l*.

Reading/Writing Companion, pp. 20–21

COMPREHENSION

What season do you think it is? Why do you think it is that season? Encourage children to use clues from the pictures to support their response.

Reading/Writing Companion, pp. 24–25

COMPREHENSION

What season do you think it is? Why do you think it is that season? Encourage children to use clues from the pictures to support their response.

Reading/Writing Companion, pp. 26–27

COMPREHENSION

What season do you think it is? Why do you think it is that season? Encourage children to use clues from the pictures to support their response. *Why do you think the author wrote this story?*

Focus on Fluency: Accuracy and Rate

Have partners practice reading the text "Is It Hot?" accurately. Encourage them to track the print as they sound out decodable words and read high-frequency words with automaticity. Remind children to pay attention to punctuation marks so they read sentences with the correct tone. Then have partners read the story again, this time focusing on rate—reading a bit more quickly and making the text sound more like speech.

Listen in: If children struggle with accuracy, have them start again at the beginning of the sentence and correct any errors. If they struggle with rate, model an appropriate rate as you read, and have them repeat.

 ## Build Knowledge: Make Connections

Talk About the Text Have partners discuss what they learned about the seasons from the text. Then have them choose two seasons and use the text and photographs to compare how they are different.

Write About the Text Have children add their ideas to their reader's notebook.

DECODABLE READERS

Have children read "Bob and Ben" (pp. 1–6) to practice decoding words in connected text.

Unit 6 Decodable Reader

ELL ENGLISH LANGUAGE LEARNERS

Comprehension Explain *top* on page 26. Pat the top of your head as you say the word aloud. Have children echo and mimic. Point to page 27. Explain that in this context *a bit* means "a small amount." *Is the temperature in the room a bit warm? Or is it a bit cool?*

FORMATIVE ASSESSMENT

STUDENT CHECK-IN

Have partners share something they learned from the text. Then have children reflect using the Check-In routine.

LESSON 3

LEARNING GOALS

- We can write about the texts we read.
- We can learn about words that name more than one thing (plural nouns).

OBJECTIVES

Use a combination of drawing, dictating, and writing to compose opinion pieces in which they state an opinion or preference about the topic or book.

Write a letter or letters for most consonant and short-vowel sounds.

Use frequently occurring nouns.

Form regular plural nouns orally by adding /s/ or /es/.

Write in response to a text.

ELA ACADEMIC LANGUAGE

- *singular, plural*
- Cognates: *singular, plural*

 TEACH IN SMALL GROUP

Choose from these options to enable all children to complete the writing activity:

- draw a picture
- complete sentence starters
- write a caption
- write one sentence

For differentiated support, see Writing Skills minilessons on pages T494-T499. These can be used throughout the year.

Independent Writing

5 mins

Write About the Shared Read

Analyze the Student Model Turn to pages 28-29 in the **Reading/ Writing Companion**. Read aloud the prompt: *Does the author do a good job of showing what winter is like? Why or why not?* Read aloud and guide children to analyze Anya's writing.

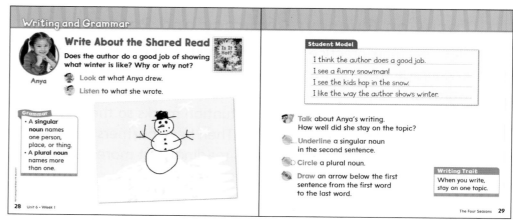

Reading/Writing Companion, pp. 28–29

 ## Write Your Response

Analyze the Prompt. Discuss the prompt on page 28 with children.

Find Text Evidence *Let's find clues on pages 16–17 to support our opinion. What do the photos show?* (flowers and a kitten) *What does the text say?* (It is a bit hot.)

Write a Response Have children use the text evidence to draw and write their response. Read aloud the writing checklist and have them check off the items as they include them in their draft.

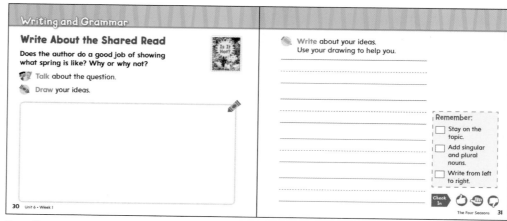

Reading/Writing Companion, pp. 30–31

Writing Support If needed, provide the sentence frames in the Quick Tip to help children share their opinion. **I think _____. I like _____.**

Grammar

OPTIONAL 5 mins

Singular and Plural Nouns

1 **Model** Remind children that nouns are naming words. Nouns name people, places, animals, and things. Write and read aloud: **I see the bushes**. Point out that *bushes* is a plural noun. Plural nouns name more than one thing. Underline the *-es* ending in *bushes*. Say: *Up until now, we have been adding* -s *to nouns to make them plural. To make some nouns plural, we need to add* -es. *We add* -es *to nouns that end in* s, x, z, ch, *or* sh. *The noun* wish *ends in* sh *so we add* -es *to the end of it to make it plural*. Write *wishes* on the board and underline the *-es*.

2 **Guided Practice/Practice** Display the *peach* and *tree* **Photo Cards**. Write and read this sentence aloud: **The peaches grow on a tree**. Guide children to identify the singular noun (tree) and the plural noun. (peaches) Invite a volunteer to underline the nouns. Then identify the plural ending *-es* and ask a volunteer to circle it. Continue to guide practice using the Photo Cards for *bus, mix, sandwich, six,* and *toothbrush*.

Display and name the Photo Cards fo *box, fox, inch, and peach*. Distribute the Photo Cards to small groups. Have groups add *-es* to each noun to make it plural and then say a sentence using the plural noun. Then have a volunteer from each group write the plural noun on the board and circle the *-es* ending.

Talk About It

Have children work with a partner to name things they eat. Ask them to say if the thing they eat is a singular noun or a plural noun.

English Language Learners

Independent Writing, Analyze the Student Model Have children finger point as they choral read the Student Model. Use the Actor/Action Routine to review the first and second sentences. Then guide children to identify singular and plural nouns in the second and third sentences. Have children trace with their fingers from left to right to show how Anya wrote her words. *What topic was Anya writing about?* (if the author did a good job showing what winter is like) *Do each of her sentences tell about this topic?* (yes)

For more writing support, refer to the **ELL Small Group Guide,** p. 139.

For more writing support, refer to the **ELL Small Group Guide,** p. 139.

DIGITAL TOOLS

Grammar Activity

FORMATIVE ASSESSMENT

▶ STUDENT CHECK-IN

Have partners share a plural noun they learned. Then have children reflect using the Check-In routine.

LESSON 4

LEARNING GOALS

- We can say a word in two parts.
- We can understand new words.
- We can use words that tell about the seasons.
- We can understand how to use clues to find the meaning of a word.

OBJECTIVES

Segment onsets and rimes of spoken words.

Use words and phrases acquired through conversations, reading and being read to, and responding to texts.

Determine or clarify the meaning of unknown and multiple-meaning words and phrases based on kindergarten reading and content.

Develop oral vocabulary.

Identify words about seasons.

ELA ACADEMIC LANGUAGE

- *clues*

DIGITAL TOOLS

Weekly Poem

Visual Vocabulary Cards

Category Words Activity

LESSON FOCUS

READING
Review Essential Question
Read/Reread Paired Selection
"New Snow"
"Rain Song"
"Covers"
"Honey, I Love"
Word Work
- Build words with /b/*b*, /l/*l*

WRITING
Writing/Grammar
- Independent Writing
- Practice Grammar
Research and Inquiry
- Create Presentation

Literature Big Book, pp. 34–40

(10 mins) MULTIMODAL

Oral Language

 Essential Question

How are the seasons different?

Have children discuss what they have learned about the seasons and how they are different. Add new ideas to the Build Knowledge anchor chart.

Phonological Awareness: Onset and Rime Segmentation

1 **Model** Remind children that a word can be divided into its beginning and ending sounds. Say: *The beginning sound in the word* day *is /d/. The ending sound in the word* day *is /ā/.*

2 **Guided Practice/Practice** Tell children that you will say other words from the finger-play, "Five Little Snowmen." Guide children to segment the following words and to say each word part aloud: *happy,* (/h/ /apē/); *little* (/l/ itēl/). Guide practice and provide corrective feedback as needed.

Review Oral Vocabulary Words

Use the Define/Example/Ask routine on print or digital **Visual Vocabulary Cards** to review the oral vocabulary words *weather, seasons, migrate, active,* and *spot.* Then have children use the words in sentences.

Visual Vocabulary Cards

Category Words: Seasons

1 **Explain/Model** Read aloud the following story. *Each time I say a season word, clap your hands.*

I play at the park all year. In winter, I like to build snow castles. In spring, the rain makes puddles. I like to jump over them. In summer, I like to sit in the shade to cool off. In fall, the trees lose their leaves. I like to slide into a pile of them!

Discuss what happens during each season. Encourage children to use season words in their responses.

2 **Guided Practice** Write the season words *winter, spring, summer,* and *fall* on the board. Next, display the **Photo Cards** *August, rake, green, October, under, fox, gate,* and *snow.* Have children name the season each Photo Card could show.

For additional practice use **Practice Book** page 251.

Vocabulary: Sentence Clues

1 **Model** Remind children to use clues found in the text and illustrations to find the meaning of unfamiliar words or phrases.

Teacher Think Aloud In *Mama, Is It Summer Yet?*, I'm unsure of the meaning of this sentence: *But the buds are swelling.* I know that buds are small bumps on plants that flowers or leaves grow from. The other sentences and the illustration on the page talk about spring. I know that buds start out tiny and get bigger in spring. That helps me understand that *swelling* means that buds are getting bigger during the spring.

2 **Guided Practice** Talk about the meaning of *unfold* in this sentence from *Mama, Is It Summer Yet?*: *Soon new leaves will unfold.* Ask children to name things that can be unfolded. (a piece of paper, a towel, a paper airplane) Reread the sentence and have children look at the illustration. Tell them to think about how buds grow into leaves. Ask them to picture how buds swell and *unfold* into leaves.

Use the following sentence to figure out the meaning of *sprout*: *Soon the seeds will* sprout *and root.* I know that roots are the part of a plant that grows under the ground. Have volunteers share what they think *sprout* means.

ENGLISH LANGUAGE LEARNERS

Vocabulary Strategy, Guided Practice/Practice Help children identify picture clues by showing how buds change throughout the story. Help them identify clues for *sprout* in sentences. Explain how *grow* is a clue for *sprout* in the sentence. *Trees began to grow, or sprout, leaves.*

KIDS ON THE MOVE! MULTIMODAL

Assign groups a season word. Then give simple directions using the season words. for children to act out: *In winter, shovel snow. In spring, plant some seeds.*

NEWCOMERS

Use the **Newcomer Online Visuals** to help children expand vocabulary and language about Food and Meals and Community (Unit 3). Use the Conversation Starters, Speech Balloons, and Games in the **Newcomer Teacher's Guide** to continue building vocabulary and developing oral and written language.

Category Words: p. 251

❯ STUDENT CHECK-IN

Oral Vocabulary Words Have partners tell why an *active* person might get tired.

Category Words Have partners describe a season.

Vocabulary Have partners tell how they can use clues to figure out the meaning of a word.

Then have children reflect using the Check-in routine.

Literature Big Book

OBJECTIVES

Recognize common types of texts.

Recognize and produce rhyming words.

With guidance and support from adults, explore word relationships and nuances in word meanings.

Actively engage in group reading activities with purpose and understanding.

Visualize to understand the language of a poem.

ELA ACADEMIC LANGUAGE

• poem, rhyme
• Cognates: poema, rima

Read

"New Snow," "Rain Song," "Covers," "Honey, I Love"

(10 mins)

Rhyme

1 **Explain/Model** Explain that you will be reading poems about the seasons. *Poems can have rhyme. Rhyme is when words have the same ending sounds. Rhyme is often found at the end of the line in a poem.*

Before reading the poems, use **Online Teaching Chart 22** to practice identifying rhyme. Read aloud the first two lines. Point to the words in yellow. Say: hen *and* ten *rhyme. They have the same ending sounds and end with the same letters.* Have a child point to *hen* and *ten. Where are they found in the line?* (at the end)

Online Teaching Chart 22

2 **Guided Practice/Practice** Read the rest of the poem. Ask: *What word rhymes with* pig? (jig) *What word rhymes with* Min? (spin) *What do you notice about the rhyming words* pig *and* jig? (They end with the same letters; -ig) *What do you notice about the rhyming words* Min *and* spin? (They end with the same letters; -in) Then have volunteers come up and point to the words and tell where they found.

Read the Paired Selection

Set Purpose *Let's read to find out more about the different seasons.*

Literature Big Book, pp. 34–35

RHYME DOK 2

Reread the second stanza. *What rhyming words do you hear?* (go, snow) *Where are they located?* (at the end of the line)

Literature Big Book, pp. 36–37

DETAILS DOK 2

The author uses colors to describe the rain in the different seasons. What color describes spring rain? (pink) *Why do you think the author chose that color for spring?* (It's the color of flowers.)

Literature Big Book, pp. 38-39

VISUALIZE DOK 2

Tell children to create pictures in their mind as you read the poem "Covers." Ask: *What do you picture in your mind when you hear the line, "Blankets cover me when I'm asleep"?* Have children share what they imagined and how they felt. Then display and reread the poem.

BUILD ORAL VOCABULARY

creep move very slowly

RHYME DOK 2

Reread the poem. Ask: *What rhyming words do you hear?* (cool, pool) *What do you notice about the rhyming words?* (they have the same ending sound /ool/ and end with the same letters -*ool*; they are at the end of the line)

Literature Big Book, p. 40

Return to Purpose

Remind children of their purpose for reading. (to read poems and learn more about the seasons) Prompt them to tell what new information they learned from the selection.

Retell

Help children use the illustrations to retell important details in the poems. Encourage them to use the vocabulary words they have been learning. You also may wish to invite children to retell the poems by sharing their favorite part(s) of the poem.

Close Reading Routine

Read DOK 1-2

• Identify key ideas and details.
• Take notes and retell.
• Use **A C T** prompts as needed.

Reread DOK 2-3

• Analyze the text, craft, and structure.

Integrate DOK 3-4

• Integrate knowledge and ideas.
• Make text-to-text connections.
• Complete the Show Your Knowledge task.
• Inspire action.

ELL SPOTLIGHT ON LANGUAGE

Pages 34-35 *sparkling:* Explain that things that are bright and shiny often *sparkle.* In the story, the snow is *sparkling* because the sunlight is shining on it. If possible, show something in the classroom that sparkles. Point to the object, and have children repeat *sparkles.*

Pages 36-37 *petals, whirl:* Point to the picture of the flower. Show how it has different parts. Point to the petals. Say the word, and prompt children to repeat. Model *whirling* in place. *Have you seen leaves whirl on the ground?*

Page 38-39 *glass:* Go to the window, and tap on the *glass* while saying *glass.* Have children say the word after you.

FORMATIVE ASSESSMENT

◐ STUDENT CHECK-IN

Have partners choose two words that rhyme from one of the poems. Then have children reflect using the Check-In routine.

LESSON
4

MAMA, IS IT SUMMER YET?
Nikki McClure

Literature Big Book

LEARNING GOALS

We can think about how an author uses a photo to share information.

OBJECTIVES

With guidance and support from adults, explore word relationships and nuances in word meanings.

Use words and phrases acquired through conversations, reading and being read to, and responding to texts.

Analyze the author's craft.

ELA ACADEMIC LANGUAGE

• *poem, rhyme*
• Cognates: *poema, rima*

Reread

(10 mins)

"New Snow," "Rain Song," "Covers," "Honey, I Love"

Analyze the Text

Reread "Honey, I Love." Use the prompts below to help children answer the questions on pages 32–33 in the **Reading/Writing Companion**.

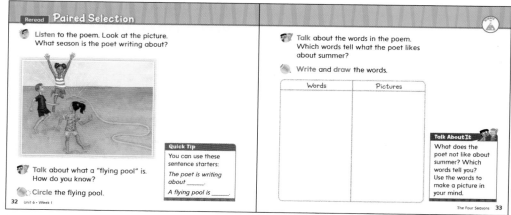

Reading/Writing Companion, pp. 32–33

AUTHOR'S CRAFT DOK 2

• Read page 40 of the **Big Book** aloud. *What is "Honey, I Love?"* (a poem) *How do you know?* (It has rhyming words) *What season is it about?* (summer) Have children tell how they know.

• Open to page 32 of the **Reading/Writing Companion**. *What are the children doing?* (cooling off under the sprinkler) The poem talks about a flying pool. Look closely at the pictures and think about the words. *What is a flying pool?* (a sprinkler) Tell children to circle the flying pool.

• Explain that a poet chooses words carefully so that readers can picture in their mind what the poet is describing. Reread the poem. *Which words tell what the poet likes about summer?* (turns the hose on, everybody jumps right in, water stings my stomach, feel so nice and cool, I love to feel a flying pool) Have children complete page 33. Say: *On the left side, write words from the poem. On the right side, draw what you see in your mind when you hear the words.*

Talk About It

Review "Honey, I Love." *Which words describe what the poet dislikes about summer?* (hot, icky, the sun sticks to my skin) Guide children to use the words to create a picture in their minds of a hot summer day. *What do you see in your mind? What does it feel like?* Invite children to describe what they see and tell how it helped them understand the poem.

Integrate

Build Knowledge: Make Connections

Talk About the Text Have children discuss how the rain is described in the poem "Rain Song." *How is the rain different in each season?*

Add to the Anchor Chart Record any new ideas on the Build Knowledge Anchor Chart.

Add to the Word Bank Record new words on the Word Bank.

English Language Learners

Use the following scaffolds with **Analyze the Text/Author's Craft.**

Beginning

Have children point to the sprinkler and water, and say each word after you. *In the picture, I see the children cool off. The children cool off in the water. What season is it? What is it like?* Provide sentence frames to help children respond: The season is summer. It is hot.

Intermediate

Guide children to identify details in the picture, such as the hose and sprinkler, or "flying pool," and the water. Help them answer questions using sentence frames. The season is summer. The kids cool off in the water. The water comes from the sprinkler. The author calls the sprinkler a flying pool.

Advanced/Advanced High

Have partners talk about how the picture helps them understand the poem. Provide modeling. *I see the flying pool. It is a hose and sprinkler. The water flies in the air. I see the children cool off in the water.*

CONNECT TO CONTENT

Seasonal Weather Circle

Create a circle with quadrants representing each season (winter, spring, summer, and fall). Have partners describe the weather that occurs in each season. Encourage them to think about how the weather is the same and how it is different as well as how it changes over season. Then as a class fill out the seasonal circle.

STEM

FORMATIVE ASSESSMENT

> **STUDENT CHECK-IN**

Have partners share something they learned from the photograph. Then have children reflect using the Check-In routine.

LISTENING COMPREHENSION **T287**

In a Flash: Sound-Spellings

Display the Sound-Spelling Card for *b*.
1. **Teacher:** What's the letter?   **Children:** b
2. **Teacher:** What's the sound?   **Children:** /b/
3. **Teacher:** What's the word?   **Children:** bat

Continue the routine for *l* and previously taught sounds.

LEARNING GOALS

- We can blend sounds to say words.
- We can build and spell words with the letters *b* and *l*.
- We can read sentences with the words *is* and *little*.

OBJECTIVES

Demonstrate understanding of spoken words, syllables, and sounds (phonemes).

Distinguish between similarly spelled words by identifying the sounds of the letters that differ.

Spell simple words phonetically, drawing on knowledge of sound-letter relationships.

Read common high-frequency words by sight.

Blend phonemes to form words.

ELA ACADEMIC LANGUAGE
- *blend, spell*

⊘ TEACH IN SMALL GROUP

You may wish to teach the Word Work lesson in small groups.

DIGITAL TOOLS

Word Work

Phonemic Awareness

Phonics

High-Frequency Words

Visual Vocabulary Cards

---

 5 mins

Phonemic Awareness

Phoneme Blending

1 Model Say: *Listen to the sounds in a word: /l/ /o/ /t/. I can blend those sounds to make the word: /lllooot/, lot. Listen as I say more sounds and blend them to make words.* Model phoneme blending with the following.

/b/ /i/ /t/ bit   /r/ /u/ /b/ rub   /b/ /a/ /d/ bad   /l/ /a/ /p/ lap

2 Guided Practice/Practice Say: *Listen to the sounds in a different word: /b/ /a/ /g/. Let's blend the sounds and say the word together: /b/ /a/ /g/, /baaag/ bag.* Tell children to listen to the sounds in words, repeat the sounds, and then blend them to say the word. Guide practice and provide corrective feedback as needed.

/b/ /e/ /t/ bet	/l/ /e/ /t/ let	/t/ /u/ /b/ tub
/b/ /e/ /d/ bed	/l/ /i/ /p/ lip	/b/ /e/ /l/ bell

If children need additional practice blending phonemes to form words, have them use **Practice Book** page 244.

 MULTIMODAL

 5 mins

Phonics

Build and Read Words

1 Guided Practice Provide children with **Word-Building Cards** *a–z.* Use the Word-Building Cards *b, i, n* to form the word *bin.* Have children use their word cards to build the word *bin.* Say: *I will change the letter* n *to* t *to make the word* bit. Read aloud the new word; then have children read it with you.

2 Practice Have children change *bit* to form the word *pit.* Have them tell which letters are the same and which letter is different and how the sound for the letter changes the word. Have them continue changing letters to form *spit, lit, let,* and *lot.* Then have children list the words and work with a partner to correct any errors they made when encoding.

If children need additional practice in identifying letters that differ in words, see Practice Book page 248.

Spell Words

Dictation Dictate each of the sounds for children to spell. Have them repeat the sound and then write the letter that stands for the sound.

/f/   /r/   /e/   /h/   /d/   /o/   /b/   /l/

Dictate the following words for children to spell: *bit, lid, bed, led, lap, lip, sob.* Model how to segment each word to scaffold the spelling.

When I say the word bit, *I hear three sounds: /b/ /i/ /t/. I know the letter* b *stands for /b/, the letter* i *stands for /i/, and the letter* t *stands for /t/. I will write the letters* b, i, t *to spell the word* bit.

When children finish, write the letters and words for them to self-correct.

High-Frequency Words

OPTIONAL 5 mins

MULTIMODAL

Practice Say the words *is* and *little* and have children write them. Then display the print or digital **Visual Vocabulary Cards** for *is* and *little*. Follow the Teacher Talk routine on the back.

Visual Vocabulary Cards

Build Fluency Build sentences in a pocket chart using **High-Frequency Word Cards** and **Photo Cards**. Use index cards to create punctuation cards for a period and a question mark. Have children chorally read the sentences as you track the print. Then have them identify the words *is* and *little*.

My apple *is little*.

Do you see the *little* ladybug?

The lemon *is* yellow.

| Is | the | 🐞 | little | ? |

Have partners say sentences using the words *is* and *little*.

Beach Ball Activity Write several high-frequency words on a beach ball with a permanent marker. Have children gently toss the ball to each other. Then have children read the words in the color facing them as they catch it. You may wish to have several beach balls to add more words the children learn throughout the year.

DECODABLE READERS

Have children read "Ben, Deb, Lin" (pp. 7–12).

Unit 6 Decodable Reader

Phonemic Awareness: p. 244
Phonics: p. 248

FORMATIVE ASSESSMENT

❯ STUDENT CHECK-IN

Phonics Have partners use Word-Building Cards to spell and read *bat* and *let*.

High-Frequency Words Have partners point to and read a sentence from the lesson.

Then have children reflect using the Check-In routine.

✓ CHECK FOR SUCCESS

Rubric Use your online rubric to record children's progress.

Can children blend words with /b/ and /l/ and match the sounds to *Bb* and *Ll*? Can children read and recognize high-frequency words?

❯ **Small Group Instruction**

If No
- **Approaching** Reteach pp. T302–306
- **ELL** Develop pp. T302–306

If Yes
- **On** Review pp. T310–313
- **Beyond** Extend p. T316

 Independent Writing
5 mins

Write About the Shared Read

 Revise

Reread the prompt about the selection "Is It Hot?" on page 30 of the **Reading/Writing Companion**: *Does the author do a good job of showing what spring is like? Why or why not?* Have children read their drafts to think about how they would revise their writing. Then have them check to see if they responded to the prompt by focusing on one idea, including singular and plural nouns, and writing from left to right.

Peer Review Have partners review each other's writing. Children should share what they like most about the writing, questions they have for the author, and additional ideas they think the author could include. Provide time for children to make revisions and add details to strengthen their writing.

Edit/Proofread

After children have revised their work, have them edit it carefully, checking for the following:

- A capital letter is used at the beginning of each sentence.
- Sentences tell a complete thought.

If children need additional practice with editing and proofreading, have them use **Practice Book** page 254.

 ### Write Final Draft

After children have edited their writing and finished their peer review, have them write their final draft in their writer's notebook. Tell children to write neatly so that others can read their writing, or guide them to explore a variety of digital tools they can use to publish their work.

Teacher Conference As children review their drafts, confer with them to provide guidance. Suggest places in their writing where they might add details or include singular and plural nouns.

 ### Share and Evaluate

After children have finalized their draft, have them work with a partner to practice presenting their writing to one another. Remind children to speak in complete sentences. If possible, record children as they share.

Have children add their work to their writing folder. Invite them to look at their previous writing and discuss with a partner how it has improved.

Grammar

5 mins

Singular and Plural Nouns

1 **Review** Remind children that singular nouns name one thing. Adding -s to most nouns makes the noun name more than one thing, or plural. To make a noun plural that ends in *s, x, z, ch,* or *sh,* add -es. Show the *bus* **Photo Card**. Write and read aloud: **I saw the bus.** Point out that *bus* names just one. Add -es and reread the sentence. Point out that *buses* names more than one.

2 **Guided Practice/Practice** Display the *pen* and *ox* Photo Cards. Write and read aloud: **The pens are new. Oxes are big.** Guide children to identify the plural nouns (pens, oxes). Have volunteers circle the *-s* and *-es.*

Display the Photo Cards for *bird, dog,* and *box.* Have partners copy and then change the nouns to plural (birds, dogs, boxes). Partners take turns saying a sentence with each of the plural nouns. If children need additional practice with singular and plural nouns, have them use **Practice Book** page 253.

Talk About It

Ask partners to point to and name one of the features on their face such as nose. Then ask them to say the noun that names more than one of that feature such as noses.

English Language Learners

Use with **Independent Writing, Edit/Proofread.**

Beginning
Help children use the Word Bank to check the spelling of high-frequency words. Write a sentence on the board. Circle the capital letter and the period. Children can refer to the example as they edit.

Intermediate
Ask questions to help children edit: *Did you begin each sentence with a capital letter? Did you end each sentence with a period?*

Advanced/Advanced High
Provide models for partners to use. *This sentence starts with a capital letter, but it does not have a period at the end. I will add a period to the end of this sentence.*

For small group support, see the **ELL Small Group Guide,** p. 139.

DIGITAL TOOLS

I see a fish.

Grammar Activity

Grammar: p. 253
Edit/Proofread: p. 254

FORMATIVE ASSESSMENT

❯ STUDENT CHECK-IN

Have partners share a plural noun they learned. Have children reflect using the Check-In routine.

LESSON 4

READING · RESEARCH AND INQUIRY

LEARNING GOALS

We can research about a season.

OBJECTIVES

With guidance and support from adults, recall information from experiences or gather information from provided sources to answer a question.

Add drawings or other visual displays to descriptions as desired to provide additional detail.

Produce and expand complete sentences in shared language activities.

Follow agreed-upon rules for discussions.

Participate in shared research and writing projects.

ELA ACADEMIC LANGUAGE
• *research, website*

COLLABORATIVE CONVERSATIONS

Add New Ideas As children engage in partner, small group, and whole class discussions, encourage them to:

• Stay on topic.

• Connect their own ideas to things their classmates have said.

• Connect their personal experiences or prior knowledge to the conversation.

Integrate

⏱ 10 mins

A Season

Model

Tell children that they will research about a season. Display pages 34–35 of the **Reading/Writing Companion**. Model completing each step in the research process.

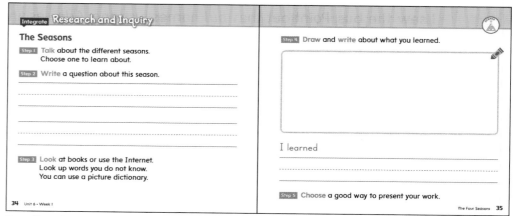

Reading/Writing Companion, pp. 34–35

STEP 1 Choose a Topic

First, I need to pick a season to research. I love the summer, so my topic to research will be summer.

STEP 2 Write Your Question

I need to decide what more I want to find out about summer. I would like to know what types of fruits and vegetables grow in the summer.

STEP 3 Find Information

To find the answer to my question, I need to do some research. I can research by looking at books in my classroom or at the library. I can also use websites on the Internet to find information.

STEP 4 Draw/Write What You Learned

I have learned more about what grows in the summer. I can draw a picture showing what grows. I will draw a corn field with corn stalks standing tall. I will write what I learned about corn *under the drawing.*

STEP 5 Choose a Way to Present Your Work

I am going to create a book that shows all types of fruits and vegetables that grow in the summer. I will add labels for each food item.

Apply

Have children turn to page 34 in their **Reading/Writing Companion**. Guide them through the steps of the research process. Help children select books that might help or suggest websites to find information.

Choose the Presentation Format

Have children turn to pages 34-35 in their Reading/Writing Companion to review their research, their drawings, and what they learned about their season. Tell them that today they are going to take the next step by creating their final presentation, which they will give in front of the class tomorrow. Work with children to select a good way to present their findings. Options may include drawing and labeling a picture, creating a poster, making a model or putting on a dramatic presentation.

Create the Presentation

Guide children to develop their presentation individually, in teams, or as a class. Remind them of the rules of working with others.

Gather Materials Gather together the materials children will need to create their finished product. Most of the materials should be available in the classroom or can be brought from home.

Make the Finished Product Once children have gathered the materials they need, provide time for them to create their finished product. You can dedicate an area in the classroom for project work and store all the materials there. Remind children that children will be presenting their work to their classmates the next day.

English Language Learners

Model, Step 3 Model how to look for information from books in the unit. Then guide children in the research process by showing them other books in the classroom that depict seasons and weather. You may also model how to use key words to look for pictures and other information on the Internet with an adult. Help children find details they can use in their writing or drawings to answer a research question.

⏵ TEACH IN SMALL GROUP

You may wish to have children create their presentation during Small Group time. Group children of varying abilities together, or group children together if they are doing similar projects.

CONNECT TO CONTENT

Seasons All Year Explain to children that seasons are cyclical, that they repeat in the same order each year. Tell the order of the seasons. Have children fold a piece of construction paper in half two times, creating four sections. Have them label the sections, *winter, spring, summer,* and *fall*. Tell them to draw a picture of something they wear or do in each season. Then add arrows to show the order of the seasons.

STEM

RESEARCH AND INQUIRY: SHARING FINAL PROJECTS

As children get ready to wrap up the week, have them share their Research and Inquiry projects. Then have children self-evaluate.

Prepare Have children gather any materials they need to present their Research and Inquiry project. Have partners practice their presentations.

Share Guide children to present their Research and Inquiry project. Encourage children to speak in complete sentences.

Evaluate Have children discuss and evaluate their own presentations. You may wish to have them complete the online Student Checklist.

FORMATIVE ASSESSMENT

⏵ STUDENT CHECK-IN

Have partners share one thing that is special about the season they researched. Then have children reflect using the Check-in routine.

LEARNING GOALS

- We can say and count each sound in a word.
- We can spell words with the letters *b* and *l*.
- We can spell the words *is* and *little*.

OBJECTIVES

Isolate and pronounce the initial, medial vowel, and final sounds (phonemes) in three-phoneme words.

Demonstrate basic knowledge of one-to-one letter-sound correspondences by producing the primary sound or many of the most frequent sounds for each consonant.

Spell simple words phonetically, drawing on knowledge of sound-letter relationships.

Read common high-frequency words by sight.

ELA ACADEMIC LANGUAGE

- *count, sounds*

TEACH IN SMALL GROUP

You may wish to teach this lesson in small groups.

DIGITAL TOOLS

Word Work

Phonemic Awareness

Visual Vocabulary Cards

LESSON FOCUS

READING
Wrap Up
Word Work
- Read Words
WRITING
Writing/Grammar
- Self-Selected Writing
- Review Grammar

Research and Inquiry
- Share and Evaluate Presentation
Text Connections
- Connect Essential Question to a painting
- Show Your Knowledge

Reading/Writing Companion, pp. 36–37

---

 5 mins

Phonemic Awareness

MULTIMODAL

Phoneme Segmentation

1 **Model** Use **Sound Boxes** and markers. *Listen to this word:* lip. *There are three sounds in* lip. *Say the sounds in* lip *with me: /l/ /i/ /p/. Let's place one marker for each sound in a Sound Box: /l/ /i/ /p/.* Repeat for *bet.*

2 **Guided Practice/Practice** Distribute Sound Boxes and markers. Have children say each sound in the word as they place a marker in a box. Then have them say the word and tell the number of sounds in the word. Guide practice and provide corrective feedback as needed.

bed /b/ /e/ /d/	bat /b/ /a/ /t/	fill /f/ /i/ /l/
lid /l/ /i/ /d/	led /l/ /e/ /d/	lot /l/ /o/ /t/

---

 5 mins

Phonics

MULTIMODAL

Read Words

1 **Guided Practice** Remind children that the letter *b* stands for /b/ and the letter *l* stands for /l/. Display **Word-Building Cards** *l, e, t.* Point to the letter l. *The letter* l *stands for /l/. Say /lll/. The letter* e *stands for /e/. Say /eee/. The letter* t *stands for /t/. Say /t/. Let's blend the sounds to make the word: /llleeet/,* let. *Now let's change the* l *to* b. Blend and read the word *bet* with children.

2 **Practice** Write these words and sentences for children to read:

lip	bat	led	cab	bed

I nap on my bed.   The cat sat on my lap.

Bob had a bat.   Ben and Deb like my pet cat.

Remove words from view before dictation.

In a Flash: Sound-Spellings

Display the Sound-Spelling Card for *b*.

1. **Teacher:** What's the letter?   **Children:** b
2. **Teacher:** What's the sound?   **Children:** /b/
3. **Teacher:** What's the word?   **Children:** bat

Continue the routine for *l* and previously taught sounds.

Spell Words

Dictation Dictate the following sounds for children to spell. As you say each sound, have children repeat it and then write the letter that stands for the sound.

/f/   /r/   /e/   /h/   /d/   /o/   /b/   /l/

Dictate the following words for children to spell. Model for children how to use **Sound Boxes** to segment each word to scaffold the spelling. *I will say a word. You will repeat the word, then think about how many sounds are in the word. Use your Sound Boxes to count the sounds. Then write one letter for each sound you hear.*

bat   led   lot   tab   let   bed

Then write the letters and words for children to self-correct.

(5 mins) High-Frequency Words

MULTIMODAL

1 **Review** Display the print or digital **Visual Vocabulary Cards** *is* and *little*. Have children Read/Spell/Write the words. Then choose a Partner Talk activity.

Visual Vocabulary Cards

Distribute one of the following **High-Frequency Word Cards** to children: *are, he, is, little, my, with*. Tell children that you will say some sentences. *When you hear a word that is on your card, stand and hold up your word card.*

He can go to the park.
Mary and John *are* going, too.
My sister can go to school.
Is your brother coming to play?
Mom says Jake can bring his *little* brother.
Can I go *with* you?

2 **Build Fluency: Word Automaticity** Display High-Frequency Word Cards *is, little, he, with, are,* and *my*. Point to each card, at random, and have children read as quickly as they can to build automaticity.

EXTEND THE LESSON

Final Double Letters *ll*
Use Word-Building Cards or write the word *hill*. Circle the *ll*. Point out that the two letters, *ll*, stand for one sound, */l/*. Blend and read the word and have children repeat. Continue with *fill, fell, bell, tell*.

(••) MULTIMODAL LEARNING

Color Coding After each dictation, reveal the secret color-coding-letter(s) for children to find on their **Response Boards**. Have them say the sound(s) as they trace each letter in color. Use one or two of the phonics skills of the week for color coding.

FORMATIVE ASSESSMENT

❯ STUDENT CHECK-IN

Phonics Have partners spell *lot* and *rib*.

High-Frequency Words Have partners spell the words *is* and *little*.

Then have children reflect using the Check-In routine.

✔ CHECK FOR SUCCESS

Rubric Use your online rubric to record children's progress.

Can children segment words into sounds and read words with /b/*b* and /l/*l*?

Can children read and recognize high-frequency words?

❯ Small Group Instruction

If No

- **Approaching** Reteach pp. T302–306
- **ELL** Develop pp. T302–306

If Yes

- **On** Review pp. T310–313
- **Beyond** Extend p. T316

LESSON 5

Self-Selected Writing

Talk About the Topic

Have children continue the conversation about seasons. Remind them of the Essential Question: *How are the seasons different?* Encourage them to share with a partner something they learned this week about the seasons.

Choose A Writing Activity

Tell children they will choose what type of writing to do today. They may choose to write about the seasons or about another topic that is important to them. Have them work in their writer's notebook. Encourage them to draw first as a way to get their ideas down on paper as well as to give more details to their writing. Children may choose from the following modes of writing:

 Journal Writing Remind children that a journal is a book in which they can draw and write about thoughts and ideas. They may wish to share their journal writing with others or keep it to themselves. Have children write in their journals about the season they chose or another topic that is important to them.

 Picture Spark Display a photograph or picture, showing the seasons. Remind children that pictures can often "spark" an idea for something to write about. Encourage children to look closely at the details in the picture and choose a detail to write about in their writer's notebook.

Use Digital Tools You may wish to explore different digital tools and have children publish their work.

Share Your Writing

 Invite volunteers to share their writing with the class or have partners share their writing with each other. Remind children to use the strategies below as they share out. After children share their work, you may wish to display it on a bulletin board or in a classroom writing area.

SPEAKING STRATEGIES	LISTENING STRATEGIES
✔ Wait until it is your turn to speak. ✔ Speak loud enough so that everyone can hear you.	✔ Listen actively and quietly. ✔ Wait until the speaker has finished to ask questions.

Grammar

10 mins

Singular and Plural Nouns

1 **Review** Remind children that plural nouns name more than one thing and can end in *-s* or *-es*. Hold up one pencil. In another hand, hold up three pencils. Say *pencil* or *pencils* as you hold up each hand.

2 **Guided Practice/Practice** Write and read aloud this sentence frame: **I have two _____.** Guide children to suggest nouns to complete the sentence. Repeat each noun, stressing the *-s* or *-es* ending, and then write the words on the boards. Have volunteers circle the plural endings.

Give partners an index card with a singular noun written on it, such as *girl, boy, car, dish, dress, glass,* or *hat.* Have children add *-s* or *-es* to make the word plural. On another index card, ask children to draw a picture of the plural noun. Circulate to help children with their writing and drawing and to offer corrective feedback as needed. Collect the cards. Have children work in small groups to play a game that involves matching nouns with their pictures.

English Language Learners

Self-Selected Writing, Choose a Writing Activity Present the writing activities, and tell the children that they will vote on one of the activities. Then, you will work on the writing as a group. Make sure to do the activity on chart paper as you will revise and publish it during small group time. Provide sentence frames and starters as you talk through the writing together. For example, if children have selected Picture Spark, show some images of seasons, and have children vote on which image they would like to write about. Then, talk about the picture. Possible sentence frames are: I like [season] because ___. During the [season], you can ___. The trees are ___ in the [season]. My favorite thing to do in the [season] is ___.

For small group support, see the **ELL Small Group Guide,** p. 139.

DIGITAL TOOLS

Grammar Activity

Presentation

TEACH IN SMALL GROUP

You may wish to review the grammar skill during Small Group time.

● **Approaching** Provide more opportunities for children to practice identifying nouns before they write sentences.

● ● **On-Level** and **Beyond** Children can do the Practice sections only.

● **ELL** Use the chart in the **Language Transfers Handbook** to identify grammatical forms that may cause difficulty.

FORMATIVE ASSESSMENT

STUDENT CHECK-IN

Have partners share which activity they chose and tell why. Then have children reflect using the Check-In routine.

LESSON 5

LEARNING GOALS

We can compare texts we have read.

OBJECTIVES

Confirm understanding of a text read aloud or information presented orally or through other media by asking and answering questions about key details and requesting clarification if something is not understood.

ELA ACADEMIC LANGUAGE

- *compare, experience*
- Cognates: *conectar, comparar*

Close Reading Routine

Read DOK 1–2

- Identify key ideas and details.
- Take notes and retell.
- Use **A C T** prompts as needed.

Reread DOK 2–3

- Analyze the text, craft, and structure.

Integrate DOK 3–4

- Integrate knowledge and ideas.
- Make text-to-text connections.
- Use the Integrate lesson.
- Complete the Show Your Knowledge task.

FORMATIVE ASSESSMENT

❯ STUDENT CHECK-IN

Have partners share what they learned from comparing texts.

Have children reflect using the Check-in routine.

Integrate

Make Connections

⏱ 10 mins

Connect to the Essential Question

Review the Essential Question. Turn to page 36 of the **Reading/Writing Companion.** Have children look at the painting. *What season do you see? How can you tell?*

Find Text Evidence Have children answer the following questions about this page and about the **Big Book**: *Is winter shown the same?* (no) *How is it shown differently?* (There is snow in the painting, but no snow in the book.) Use the Quick Tip box for support.

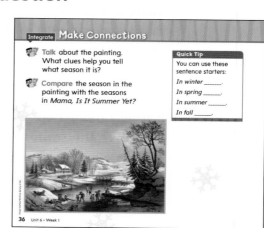

Reading/Writing Companion, p. 36

Record Ideas Guide partners to compare the season on page 36 of the Reading/Writing Companion with the seasons shown in *Mama, Is It Summer Yet? How are they alike? How are they different? How do they help you answer the Essential Question?* Help children use a Two-Tab Foldable® to record their ideas. Have children support their ideas with evidence from the painting and text.

Dinah Zike's
FOLDABLES
Study Organizer

Build Knowledge: Make Connections DOK 4

Talk About the Text Have partners compare the text with experiences from their own lives.

Add to the Anchor Chart Record any new ideas on the Build Knowledge anchor chart.

Integrate

Show Your Knowledge

15 mins

Write a Poem DOK 4

Display the texts for the week along with the Build Knowledge anchor chart and Word Bank. Turn to page 37 of the **Reading/Writing Companion** and guide children through the steps below.

1. Think Ask: *What did you learn about how the seasons are different?* Encourage partners to refer to their reader's notebook and the resources on display as they discuss their response.

2. Choose and Draw Have children choose a season to draw and write about. Have partners discuss the seasons that they chose. Then have children draw a detailed picture of the season.

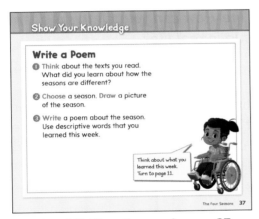

Reading/Writing Companion, p. 37

3. Write: Have children write a poem about the season. Encourage them to reference the Word Bank and use words they learned this week. Challenge them to use descriptive words.

Inspire Action

How do Seasons Affect Farms? Remind children that they learned about farms earlier in the year. Explain that farmers know what to plant and what to harvest depending on the season. Have partners discuss which season(s) they would plant and which season(s) they would harvest. This will vary by food and region.

Make a Class Poetry Book Bind the drawings and poems to make a class poetry book and make it available for children to share.

Choose Your Own Action Have children talk about the texts they read this week. *What do the texts inspire or make you want to do?*

LEARNING GOALS

LEARNING GOALS

We can show what we learned about how the seasons are different

OBJECTIVES

With guidance and support from adults, recall information from experiences or gather information from provided sources to answer a question.

Add drawings or other visual displays to descriptions as desired to provide additional detail.

Use words and phrases acquired through conversations, reading, and being read to, and responding to texts.

ELA ACADEMIC LANGUAGE

• *harvest, inspire*

DIGITAL TOOLS

To enhance the class discussion, use these additional components

Visual Vocabulary Cards

RUBRIC

Show Your Knowledge Rubric

ENGLISH LANGUAGE LEARNERS

Write Provide and model sentence frames for children to write a poem. For example: In spring, I see flowers bloom and leaves grow. Spring colors are pink and green. I love to play in puddles in the spring.

MY GOALS ROUTINE

Review Have children turn to page 11 of the **Reading/Writing Companion**. Read the goals aloud.

Reflect Have children think about the progress they've made toward the goals. Review the Key, if needed. Then have children complete page 11.

Lexile BR

OBJECTIVES

Recognize that spoken words are represented in written language by specific sequences of letters.

With prompting and support, identify characters, settings, and major events in a story.

Read emergent-reader texts with purpose and understanding.

ELA ACADEMIC LANGUAGE

• *fiction, sequence*
• Cognates: *ficción, secuencia*

● Approaching Level

Leveled Reader: *It Is Hot!*

Preview and Predict

Read the title and the names of the author and illustrator. Discuss the illustration on the cover. Ask: *What season do you think the illustration shows? How do you know?* Preview each illustration and identify the rebuses on each page. Ask: *What do you think this story is about?*

Review Genre: Fantasy

Remind children that this week they have been reading fiction. Tell them that now they will read a fantasy story. Say: *Fantasy is a kind of fiction in which things happen that could not happen in real life. How can you tell this is a fantasy story?* Say: *Can a dog actually drink from a cup in real life?*

Set Purpose

Remind children of the Essential Question: *How are the seasons different?* Help children set a purpose for reading: *Let's read to find out about all the seasons and how they are different from each other.* Review rebuses with children to help them name the words.

Foundational Skills

Model Concepts of Print Provide children with practice matching speech to print. As you read aloud slowly, ask children to try to match the words you say with the words on the page.

Review High-Frequency Words Point to the high-frequency word *is* on the second page of the story. Ask children to look through the rest of the book to find the word *is*.

Guided Comprehension

As children whisper-read *It Is Hot!*, monitor and provide guidance by offering support and corrective feedback as needed. Model visualizing and identifying the sequence of events where applicable.

Visualize

Remind children that as they read, they can make pictures in their minds of what is happening in the story.

Events: Sequence

Remind children that finding details in the text and the illustrations will help them to understand the story. Explain that, in this book, the illustrations provide details about the sequence of the seasons.

Think Aloud On pages 2 and 3, the pictures show it is spring. The words don't tell me that, but I see buds on the tree and tulips and daffodils. On page 4 it is summer. The text tells me that the beach is hot and I see that the woman in the picture has suntan lotion. What these key details tell me is that the book shows the order of the seasons.

Guide children to talk about how the picture details show the sequence of the seasons. Discuss that the seasons change in the same order as they are shown in the book: *spring, summer, fall,* and *winter.*

Respond to the Text

Have children respond to the text by discussing these questions:

- *What are some things that are hot?* (Possible answers: tea, soup, mug, beach, the dog, tub, corn)
- *What is the first season shown in the book?* (It is spring.)
- *Look at page 4. In what season are people at the hot beach?* (in the summer)
- *In what season do people sit by a warm fire?* (in the winter)

Retell Have children take turns retelling the story, using characters, the settings, and events. Help them make a personal connection. Ask: *What things do you do in different seasons?*

Focus on Fluency

Practice fluency with children. Remember that children need to read with accuracy first.

Once children have read the text with accuracy, have them read the story again, focusing on rate. Have them practice reading with partners. Provide corrective feedback as necessary.

Build Knowledge: Make Connections

- **Talk About the Texts** Have partners discuss the seasons.
- **Write About the Texts** Then have children add their ideas to their Build Knowledge page of their reader's notebook.

LITERACY ACTIVITIES

Have children complete the Collaborate and Write About It activities on the inside back cover of the book.

LITERATURE CIRCLES

Lead children in a literature circle using these questions to guide the discussion: *How are the seasons different from each other? What is your favorite season and why?*

LEVEL UP

IF Children read *It Is Hot!* Approaching Level with fluency and correctly answer the Respond to the Text questions,

THEN Tell children that they will read another story about how the seasons are different.

- Have children page through *Little Bear* On Level to preview the story and make connections to what they know about the seasons.
- Have children read the story, monitoring their comprehension and providing assistance as necessary.

●Approaching Level

Phonological/Phonemic Awareness

ONSET AND RIME SEGMENTATION

TIER 2

OBJECTIVES
Blend and segment onsets and rimes of single-syllable spoken words.

I Do To help children segment onset and rime, remind them that words are made up of parts. Say that *onset* refers to the beginning sound in a word and that *rime* refers to the rest of the sounds. Say the words *five, may,* and *nice* from "Five Little Snowmen." Have children repeat the words. Segment the words into their onset and rimes: /f/ /īv/; /m/ /ā /; /n/ /īs/.

We Do Say these words and guide children to segment the onset and rime of each word with you: stay, /st/ /ā/; away, /ə/ /wā /; cry, /cr/ /ī/.

You Do Say *day, men, snow, tray* and have children segment each word into its onset and rime. (/d/ /ā/; /m/ /en/; /sn/ /ō/; /tr/ /ā/)

PHONEME ISOLATION

TIER 2

OBJECTIVES
Isolate and pronounce the initial and final sounds in three-phoneme words.

I Do Display the *bat* **Photo Card**. *This is a bat. The first sound I hear in* bat *is /b/. Say the word and the beginning sound with me:* bat, /b/. Repeat the routine for initial /l/ using the *lemon* Photo Card.

We Do Display the *bike* Photo Card. *This is a bike. The first sound I hear in* bike *is /b/.* Have children repeat the word with you, emphasizing the initial sound. Then have children say the first sound with you: /b/. Repeat using the *butter* Photo Card. Repeat for /l/ using the *leaf* and *ladder* Photo Cards.

You Do Display the *boy* Photo Card. Have children name it and say the initial sound of the picture name. Repeat with the *boot* Photo Card. Repeat for /l/ using the *lightning* and *lock* Photo Cards.

Repeat the routine in *I Do* for final /b/ using the *web* Photo Card. In *We Do*, have children tell where they hear /b/ in *web*. (at the end) In *You Do*, have children say the following words and name the /b/ sound and its position in the words: *job, tab, big.*

PHONEME BLENDING

OBJECTIVES

Demonstrate understanding of spoken words, syllables, and sounds (phonemes).

Blend phonemes to make words.

I Do *Listen as I say the sounds in a word: /b/ /e/ /d/. Now I will blend the sounds to make a word: /beeed/,* bed. *I blended the sounds /b/ /e/ /d/ to make the word* bed. *Repeat with* big, tab.

We Do *Listen as I say the sounds in another word: /b/ /i/ /t/.* Have children repeat. *Let's blend the sounds and say the word together: /b/ /i/ /t/, /biiit/,* bit. *Repeat with* bib.

You Do Have children blend sounds to form words. Practice together: /b/ /a/ /t/, bat. Then have children practice blending the following sounds to say words: /b/ /e/ /t/, bet; /k/ /a/ /b/, cab; /d/ /a/ /b/, dab.

Repeat the routine for /l/ and the sounds in the words /l/ /a/ /b/, lab; /l/ /i/ /p/, lip; /l/ /e/ /d/, led.

You may wish to use a puppet, if one is available in the classroom, for the *I Do* and *We Do* parts of this lesson.

PHONEME SEGMENTATION

OBJECTIVES

Isolate and pronounce the initial, medial vowel, and final sounds in three-phoneme words.

I Do Use **Sound Boxes** and markers. *Listen as I say a word:* bid. *There are three sounds in* bid: */b/ /i/ /d/. I'll place a marker in one box for each sound.* Repeat for the word cab.

We Do Distribute Sound Boxes and markers. *Let's listen for the number of sounds in more words. Listen as I say a word:* bee. *Say the word with me:* bee. *Say the sounds with me: /b/ /ē/. Let's place a marker in one box for each sound. There are two sounds in* bee. *Repeat with* bet.

You Do Repeat the routine with the following words: bow, /b/ /ō/; bin, /b/ /i/ /n/; bag, /b/ /a/ /g/.

Repeat the routine for /l/ using the sounds in these words: lot, /l/ /o/ /t/; lie, /l/ /ī/; let, /l/ /e/ /t/; lab, /l/ /a/ /b/.

ELL You may wish to review phonological awareness, phonics, decoding, and fluency using this section. Use scaffolding methods as necessary to ensure children understand the meaning of the words. Refer to the **Language Transfers Handbook** for phonics elements that may not transfer in children's native languages.

●Approaching Level

Phonics

SOUND-SPELLING REVIEW

TIER 2

OBJECTIVES
Demonstrate basic knowledge of one-to-one letter-sound correspondences by producing the primary or many of the most frequent sounds for each consonant.

I Do Display **Word-Building Card** *r*. Say the letter name and the sound it stands for: *r, /r/*. Repeat for *f, e, h, d*.

We Do Display Word-Building Cards one at a time and together say the letter name and the sound that each letter stands for.

You Do Display Word-Building Cards one at a time and have children say the letter name and the sound that each letter stands for.

CONNECT *b* TO /b/ AND *l* TO /l/

TIER 2

OBJECTIVES
Demonstrate basic knowledge of one-to-one letter-sound correspondences by producing the primary or many of the most frequent sounds for each consonant.

I Do Display the *bat* **Sound-Spelling Card**. *The letter* b *stands for /b/ at the beginning of* bat. Repeat for final /b/ using the *web* Photo Card. *I'll write* b *when I hear /b/ at the beginning or end of these words:* bone, rib, crab.

We Do Beach *begins with /b/. Let's write* b. Guide children to write *b* when they hear a word that begins or ends with /b/: *best, song, bit, road, rub, tub, box.*

You Do Have children write *b* if a word begins or ends with /b/: *jab, far, scrub, ball*. Repeat for the initial /l/ *l* using the *lemon* Sound-Spelling Card and the words *library, home, look, last, race, friend, link.*

BLEND WORDS WITH /b/*b* AND /l/*l*

OBJECTIVES
Know and apply grade-level phonics and word analysis skills in decoding words.

Build words with *b* and *l*.

I Do Display Word-Building Cards *b, i, n. This is the letter* b. *It stands for /b/. This is the letter* i. *It stands for /i/. This is the letter* n. *It stands for /n/. Listen as I blend all three sounds: /biiinnn/,* bin. *The word is* bin.

We Do *Let's blend more sounds to make words. Let's blend: /taaab/,* tab.

You Do Distribute sets of Word-Building Cards with *b, e, a, i, o, d, l, p,* and *t*. Write: *bet, bad, Deb, bed*. Have children form the words and blend and read them. Repeat for /l/ using the words *lot, let, lip, lap, lid.*

BUILD WORDS WITH /b/b AND /l/l

OBJECTIVES

Know and apply grade-level phonics and word analysis skills in decoding words.

Build words with *b* and *l*.

I Do Display **Word-Building Cards** *b, i,* n. *These are letters* b, i, *and* n. *They stand for /b//i//n/. I will blend /b//i//n/ together: /biiinnn/,* bin. *The word is* bin.

We Do Distribute sets of Word-Building Cards with *b, i,* and *n.* Show how to make the word *bin.* Have children do the same. Replace *b* at the beginning of *in* with a *t* and have children do the same. *Let's blend /tiiinnn/,* tin. *Now we have read a new word,* tin.

You Do Distribute sets of Word-Building Cards with *b, e, a, i, o, d, l, p,* and *t.* Write: *bet, bad, Deb, bed.* Have children form the words and blend and read them. Repeat the routine for /l/l using the words *lot, let, lip, lap, lid.*

REREAD THE DECODABLE READER

OBJECTIVES

Know and apply grade-level phonics and word analysis skills in decoding words.

Read emergent-reader texts with purpose and understanding.

Unit 6 Decodable Reader

Focus on Foundational Skills

Review the high-frequency words *is* and *little* with children. Review the letter-sound correspondences /b/b and /l/l. Guide children to blend sounds to read *bet* and *lab.*

Read the Decodable Reader

Have children read "Bob and Ben" and "Ben, Deb, Lin." Have them point out the high-frequency words *is* and *little* as well as words with /b/ and /l/. If children struggle sounding out words, model blending.

Focus on Fluency

Have partners read "Bob and Ben" and "Ben, Deb, Lin." Guide them to focus on their accuracy. Children can give feedback on their accuracy to their partners. Then have them focus on reading with automaticity and at an appropriate rate. You may wish to have them reread "Is It Hot?" pp. 20-27 in the **Reading/Writing Companion.**

SOUND/SPELLING FLUENCY

Display the Word-Building Cards: *f, r, e, h, b,* and *l.* Have children chorally say each sound. Vary the pace.

●Approaching Level

High-Frequency Words

RETEACH WORDS

OBJECTIVES
Read common high-frequency words by sight.

I Do Display the **High-Frequency Word Card** *is* and use the Read/Spell/Write routine to reteach the high-frequency word *is*. Repeat for *little*.

We Do Write this sentence and read it aloud: *Fall is a beautiful season.* Have children point to the word *is* in the sentence. Distribute index cards with the word *is* written on them. Have children match their word card with the word *is* in the sentence. Use the same routine for *little* and the sentence: *The little bugs are cute.*

You Do Write the sentence frame **The little cat is in a _____** . Have children copy the sentence frame on their **Response Boards**. Then have partners work together to read and orally complete the frame by talking about where the little cat is hiding. Reteach previously introduced high-frequency words using the Read/Spell/Write routine.

CUMULATIVE REVIEW

OBJECTIVES
Read common high-frequency words by sight.

I Do Display the High-Frequency Word Cards *I, can, the, we, see, a, like, to, and, go, you, do, my, are, he, with, is,* and *little*. Use the Read/Spell/Write routine to review words. Have children practice reading the words until they can read them accurately and with automaticity. Use both sets of cards to create sentences, such as *I like to go and see. Can you go?*

We Do Use the High-Frequency Word Cards to create sentences such as: *Bob and I like to pet the red hen. Len can go with my Mom and Dad.* Have children identify the high-frequency words that are used in each sentence. Read the sentences together.

You Do Have partners use the High-Frequency Word Cards and **Word-Building Cards** to create short sentences. They can write using the Response Boards. Have partners take turns reading the sentences to each other.

Oral Vocabulary

REVIEW WORDS

OBJECTIVES

Use words and phrases acquired through conversations, reading and being read to, and responding to texts.

Identify real-life connections between words and their use.

I Do Use the Define/Example/Ask routine on the print or the digital **Visual Vocabulary Cards** to review *weather, seasons, migrate, active,* and *spot.*

We Do Ask questions to build understanding. *What should you wear in very cold weather? Which seasons are warm? Why do birds migrate in the winter? How can we be more active? Why are grasshoppers hard to spot in grass?*

You Do Have children complete these sentence frames:
**Our weather today is _____. My favorite season is _____.
Some animals migrate to _____. It is important to be active
because _____.**

Comprehension

SELF-SELECTED READING

OBJECTIVES

With prompting and support, identify characters, settings, and major events in a story.

Read emergent-reader texts with purpose and understanding.

Independent Reading

Help children select a fiction story for independent reading. Encourage them to read for twelve minutes. Remind children that an author tells the important events that happen in a story in a certain order, or sequence. The words *beginning, middle,* and *end* tell the order. Remind children that as they read, they can make pictures in their minds of what is happening in the story.

If children need more practice with concepts of print, have them use **Practice Book,** page 501.

After reading, guide children to participate in a group discussion about the story they read. In addition, children can choose activities from the **Reading Center Activity Cards** to help them apply skills to the text as they read. Offer assistance and guidance with self-selected assignments.

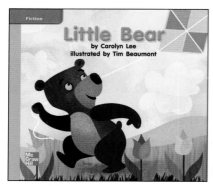

Lexile 300L

OBJECTIVES

Recognize that spoken words are represented in written language by specific sequences of letters.

With prompting and support, identify characters, settings, and major events in a story.

Read emergent-reader texts with purpose and understanding.

ELA ACADEMIC LANGUAGE

• *fantasy, comprehension, retelling*
• Cognates: *fantasía, comprensión*

●On Level

Leveled Reader: *Little Bear*

Preview and Predict

Read aloud the title and the names of the author and illustrator as children follow along in their books. Ask children what they think the story will be about. Preview each illustration and guide children to revise or confirm their predictions. Model the language pattern: *What does Little Bear like on this page? Yes, Little Bear likes a hat.*

Review Genre: Fantasy

Remind children that this week they have been reading fiction. Tell them that now they will read a fantasy story. Say: *Fantasy is a kind of fiction in which things happen that could not happen in real life. How can you tell this is a fantasy story?* (Possible answers: Animals do not fly kites. Animals do not wear hats and scarves.)

Set Purpose

Remind children of the Essential Question: *How are the seasons different?* Help children set a purpose for reading: *Let's read to find out the different things Little Bear does in different seasons.* Remind children to use the illustrations to help them understand the text.

Foundational Skills

Model Concepts of Print Turn to page 2 and point to the sentence. Say: *The sentence begins with a capital letter. Who can tell me what it ends with?* (a period) Provide children with more practice matching speech to print. As you read aloud, have children match the words you say with the words on the page.

Review High-Frequency Words Point out the word *little* on page 2. Have children look through the rest of the book and point to the word *little* on each page. Ask children to use this word in a sentence of their own.

Guided Comprehension

As children read *Little Bear*, monitor and provide guidance by offering support and corrective feedback as needed. Model visualizing and identifying the sequence of events where applicable.

Visualize

Remind children that, as they read, they can make pictures in their mind of what is happening in the story. This can help them understand what they read.

Events: Sequence

Remind children to look for details to find out more about the story. Explain that the details will tell them what the bear can do in different seasons and the order in which he does these things.

Think Aloud The pictures and text on pages 2 and 3 are about what Little Bear does. I can see from the details in the pictures that it's spring. I know tulips grow in spring and trees have new buds. Birds build their nests in spring, too. I wonder if the next pages will be about what Little Bear does in summer. I'll read to find out.

Guide children to use the pictures and text to find details that tell what Little Bear does and what season it is. Help them to see that the story follows the sequence of the seasons.

Respond to the Text

Have children respond to the text by discussing these questions:

- *What did Little Bear do in summer?* (Little Bear ate berries and smelled flowers.)

- *What details in the pictures tell you what season it is on pages 6 and 7?* (Bear's scarf, fall-colored leaves, and nuts tell me that it is fall.)

- *Why do we do different things in different seasons?* (Possible answer: Some things you can only do in certain weather, such as sledding.)

Retell Have children take turns retelling the story, using characters, the setting, and events. Help them make personal connections by asking: *What things do you like to do in each season?*

Focus on Fluency

Practice fluency with children. Remember that children need to read with accuracy first.

Once children have read the text with accuracy, have them read the story again, focusing on rate. Have them practice reading with partners. Provide corrective feedback as necessary.

Build Knowledge: Make Connections

- **Talk About the Texts** Have partners discuss the seasons.
- **Write About the Texts** Then have children add their ideas to their Build Knowledge page of their reader's notebook.

LITERACY ACTIVITIES

Have children complete the Collaborate and Write About It activities on the inside back cover of the book.

LITERATURE CIRCLES

Lead children in a literature circle using these questions to guide the discussion: *How many seasons are in one year? In what season does Little Bear go to sleep?*

LEVEL UP

IF Children read *Little Bear* On Level with fluency and correctly answer the Respond to the Text questions,

THEN Tell children that they will read another story about how the seasons are different.

- Have children page through *Ant and Grasshopper* Beyond Level as you talk about what we do to get ready for different seasons.

- Have children read the story, monitoring their comprehension and providing assistance as necessary.

●On Level

Phonological/Phonemic Awareness

PHONEME ISOLATION

OBJECTIVES
Isolate and pronounce the initial sounds in words.

I Do Display the *bat* **Photo Card**. *This is a* bat. *The first sound is /b/. Say it with me.* Repeat for final /b/ using the *web* Photo Card and with initial /l/ using the *lemon* Photo Card.

We Do Say *bit* and have children repeat. *What is the first sound?* (/b/) Say it together. Repeat for *bin, fit, set, bad.* Repeat for the final sound using *tub, lab, pin,* and /l/ using *lit, lap, bet, men.*

You Do Say *bed, bin, cot, let, fed, ham, lot* and have children tell the initial sound in each word. Repeat for the ending sound in *cab, pit, web, hop, tub.*

PHONEME BLENDING

OBJECTIVES
Demonstrate understanding of spoken words, syllables, and sounds (phonemes).

I Do *Listen as I say the sounds: /t/ /a/ /b/. Now I will blend the sounds to make a word: /taaab/,* tab. Repeat with *bad, led.*

We Do *I am going to say the sounds in a word. Listen: /l/ /a/ /p/.* Have children repeat. *Now let's blend the sounds and say the word: /lll/ /aaa/ /p/, /lllaaap/,* lap. Repeat with *bin* and *tub.*

You Do Say the following sounds. Ask children to blend the sounds and say the words: /l/ /o/ /t/, *lot;* /k/ /a/ /b/, *cab;* /b/ /e/ /d/, *bed;* /b/ /i/ /b/, *bib.*

PHONEME SEGMENTATION

OBJECTIVES
Isolate and pronounce the initial, medial vowel, and final sounds (phonemes) in three-phoneme words.

I Do Use **Sound Boxes** and markers. *Listen as I say* bat. *There are three sounds in* bat: /b/ /a/ /t/. *I'll place a marker in one box for each sound.* Repeat for *low.*

We Do Distribute Sound Boxes and markers. *Listen as I say* let: /l/ /e/ /t/. *There are three sounds in* let. *Place a marker in one box for each sound.* Repeat with *bin.*

You Do Use Sound Boxes and markers to repeat the practice with the words *lock, lie, by,* and *cab.*

Phonics

REVIEW PHONICS

OBJECTIVES

Demonstrate basic knowledge of one-to-one letter-sound correspondences by producing the primary sound or many of the most frequent sounds for each consonant.

I Do Display the *bat* **Sound-Spelling Card.** Say: *The letter* b *stands for the /b/ sound you hear at the beginning of* bat. Say *bat*, emphasizing the /b/. Repeat for initial /l/ using the *lemon* Sound-Spelling Card.

We Do Display the *ball, berries, boy, ladder, lamp,* and *leaf* **Photo Cards.** Have children say the name of each picture together with you. Then ask them to identify the words with /b/ at the beginning. Then have them identify the words with /l/ at the beginning.

You Do Write the words *bat, bed, bib, bit, let, lip, lab,* and *lit* and have children read each one. Provide corrective feedback as needed. Repeat, having children raise their hands if they hear /b/ at the beginning of a word. Repeat, having them raise their hands when they hear /b/ at the end of a word. Continue the routine, having children raise their hands when they hear /l/ at the beginning of a word.

PICTURE SORT

OBJECTIVES

Demonstrate basic knowledge of one-to-one letter-sound correspondences by producing the primary sound or many of the most frequent sounds for each consonant.

I Do Display **Word-Building Cards** *b* and *l* in a pocket chart. Then show the *bat* Photo Card. Say: */b/ /a/ /t/,* bat. *The sound at the beginning of* bat *is /b/. The letter* b *stands for /b/. I will put the* bat *Photo Card under the letter* b. Show the *lock* Photo Card. Say */l/ /o/ /k/,* lock. *The sound at the beginning is /l/. The letter* l *stands for /l/. I will put the* lock *Photo Card under the* l.

We Do Show the *bus* Photo Card and say *bus, /b/ /u/ /s/.* Have children repeat and say the sound they hear at the beginning of *bus.* Ask them if they should place the photo under the *b* or the *l.* (b)

You Do Continue the activity using the *box, leaf, light,* and *bike* Photo Cards. Have children say the picture name and the sounds in the name. Then have them place the card under the *b* or *l.*

●On Level

Phonics

BLEND WORDS WITH /b/*b*, /l/*l*

MULTIMODAL

OBJECTIVES

Know and apply grade-level phonics and word analysis skills in decoding words.

Build words with *b* and *l*.

I Do Display **Word-Building Cards** *l, i, t. This is the letter* l. *It stands for /l/. Say it with me: /lll/. This is the letter* i. *It stands for /i/. Say it with me: /iii/. This is the letter* t. *It stands for /t/. Say it with me: /t/. I'll blend the sounds together to read the word: /llliiit/,* lit. Repeat with initial /b/ with *bad* and *bit,* and final /b/ with *cab* and *rib.*

We Do Use Word-Building Cards to form the words *led* and *lab*. Guide children to blend the words sound by sound to read each word. Point out that the letter *l* is the same and the last two letters changed to *a* and *b* to make a new word.

You Do Write the following words and have children form and blend the words sound by sound to read each word: *bed, lid, bib,* and *lot.*

REREAD THE DECODABLE READER

OBJECTIVES

Know and apply grade-level phonics and word analysis skills in decoding words.

Read emergent-reader texts with purpose and understanding.

Unit 6 Decodable Reader

Focus on Foundational Skills

Review the high-frequency words *is* and *little* with children. Review the letter-sound correspondences /b/*b* and /l/*l*. Guide children to blend sounds to read *bet* and *lab*.

Read the Decodable Reader

Have children read "Bob and Ben" and "Ben, Deb, Lin." Ask them to identify the high-frequency words *is* and *little* as well as words with /b/ and /l/. If children struggle sounding out words, model blending.

Focus on Fluency

Have partners read "Bob and Ben" and "Ben, Deb, Lin." As children read, guide them to focus on their accuracy. Children can give feedback on their accuracy to their partners. Then have them focus on reading with automaticity and at an appropriate rate. You may wish to have them reread "Is It Hot?" on pages 20–27 of the **Reading/Writing Companion.**

High-Frequency Words

REVIEW WORDS

OBJECTIVES

Read common high-frequency words by sight.

I Do Display the **High-Frequency Word Card** *is* and use the Read/Spell/Write routine to review the word. Repeat for *little*.

We Do Write this sentence and read it aloud: *Fall is a beautiful season.* Point to the word *is* and have children read it. Chorally read the sentence. Have children frame and read the word *is* in the sentence. Repeat the routine with the word *little* and the sentence: *The little bugs are cute.*

You Do Say the word *is*. Ask children to close their eyes, picture the word, and write it as they see it. Have children self-correct. Repeat for *little*.

Reteach previously introduced high-frequency words, including the **Build Your Word Bank** high-frequency words, using the Read/Spell/Write routine.

Fluency Use the **Practice Book Word Cards** to review the previously introduced High-Frequency and Build Your Word Bank words. Point to the words. Have children practice reading the words until they can read accurately and with automaticity.

Comprehension

SELF-SELECTED READING

OBJECTIVES

With prompting and support, identify characters and settings in a story.

Read emergent-reader texts with purpose and understanding.

Independent Reading

Help children select an illustrated story for independent reading. Encourage them to read for twelve minutes. Guide children to transfer what they have learned this week as they read. Remind children that an author tells the important events that happen in a story in a certain order, or sequence. The words *beginning*, *middle*, and *end* tell the order. Remind children that as they read, they can make pictures in their minds of what is happening in the story.

After reading, guide children to participate in a group discussion about the story they read. In addition, children can choose activities from the **Reading Center Activity Cards** to help them apply skills to the text as they read. Offer assistance and guidance with self-selected assignments.

Lexile 280L

OBJECTIVES

Recognize common types of texts.

With prompting and support, identify characters, settings, and major events in a story.

With prompting and support, retell familiar stories, including key details.

Read emergent-reader texts with purpose and understanding.

ELA ACADEMIC LANGUAGE

• *sequence, details*

• Cognates: *secuencia, detalles*

●Beyond Level

Leveled Reader: *Ant and Grasshopper*

Preview and Predict

Ask children to point to the title and the names of the author and illustrator as you read them aloud. Ask children to describe what they see on the cover and to say what they think the book will be about. Ask: *Who do you think will be the characters in the story?*

Review Genre: Fantasy

Remind children that they have been reading fiction this week. Explain that now they will read fantasy, a kind of fiction in which things happen that could never happen in real life. Say: *How can you tell this story is fantasy?* (The ant and the grasshopper are wearing clothes. Ant has a garden and a house.)

Set Purpose

Remind children of the Essential Question: *How are the seasons different?* Say: *Let's read to find out how the seasons in this story are different and what the ant and the grasshopper do in each season.* Remind children to use the illustrations to help them understand the text.

Guided Comprehension

As children read *Ant and Grasshopper*, monitor and provide guidance by offering support and corrective feedback as needed. Model visualizing and identifying the sequence of events where applicable. Stop periodically to ask open-ended questions, such as, *What do you think will happen next?*

Visualize

Remind children that they will understand a story better if they visualize, or picture in their mind, what the characters are doing and feeling.

Events: Sequence

Remind children that finding details in the text and the illustrations will help them to understand the story. These details are usually given in the order that events happen in the story. Explain that, in this book, the illustrations and text provide details about what Ant and Grasshopper do each season.

Think Aloud When I read pages 2 and 3, I learn from details in the text and the illustrations that it is spring and Ant is planting a garden. I also see that Grasshopper is playing with his ball while Ant is working. I think pages 4 and 5 will show them in the summer.

As children read the rest of the book, point out the sequence of the seasons in the story. Guide them to look for details that tell them what Ant and Grasshopper do during the summer, fall, and winter. Have children point to evidence to support their statements.

Respond to the Text

Have children respond to the text by discussing these questions:

- Why do you think Ant is working so hard all summer and fall? (Ant is working to get ready for the long, cold winter when it will be hard to find food.)

- Why doesn't Grasshopper do any work to get ready for winter? (Possible answers: He is not thinking ahead; he is being foolish.)

- What happened after the leaves fell from the trees? (Ant picked his beans while Grasshopper played in the leaves.)

Retell Have children act out the story as they retell it, using characters, the setting, and events. Help them make a personal connection by asking: *What do you do to get ready for winter? How is what you do like or different from Ant?*

Focus on Fluency

Practice fluency with children. Remember that children need to read with accuracy first.

Once children have read the text with accuracy, have them read the story again, focusing on rate. Have them practice reading with partners. Provide corrective feedback as necessary.

Build Knowledge: Make Connections

- **Talk About the Texts** Have partners discuss the seasons.
- **Write About the Texts** Then have children add their ideas to their Build Knowledge page of their reader's notebook.

LITERACY ACTIVITIES

Have children complete the Collaborate and Write About It activities on the inside back cover of the book.

LITERATURE CIRCLES

Lead children in a literature circle using these questions to guide the discussion: *Who was better prepared for the winter season, Ant or Grasshopper? Why? Can you describe something you do to get prepared for winter?*

⭐ GIFTED AND TALENTED

Evaluate Have children think about what they can do in summer to get ready for winter. Invite them to work in small groups to brainstorm ideas together.

Extend Have children make a drawing to show how they can use the summer to get ready for the changes that come with the winter season.

●Beyond Level

Phonics

REVIEW

OBJECTIVES
Demonstrate basic knowledge of one-to-one letter-sound correspondences by producing the primary or many of the most frequent sounds for each consonant.

I Do Display the *bat* **Sound-Spelling Card.** Say: *The letter* b *stands for the /b/ sound you hear at the beginning of* bat. Say *bat*, emphasizing the */b/*. Repeat with the *lemon* Sound-Spelling Card.

We Do Display the *ball, berries, boy, ladder, lamp,* and *leaf* **Photo Cards.** Have children say the name of each picture together with you. Then ask children to share other words they know that begin with /b/ and /l/.

You Do Write the words *bat, bed, bib, bit, let, lip, lab,* and *lit.* Have partners read each word. Ask them to write the words on their **Response Boards,** underlining the letter in each word that stands for initial /b/ and /l/ and final /b/.

Fluency Have children reread "Is It Hot?" for fluency.

Innovate Have children create a new page for "Is It Hot?" by completing the sentence frame **We can _____ if it is not hot** and adding that an action the children in the story can do when the weather is not hot.

High-Frequency Words

REVIEW

OBJECTIVES
Read common high-frequency words by sight.

I Do Use the **Build Your Word Bank High-Frequency Word Cards** at the back of the **Practice Book** for *by, some,* and *brown.* Review the words using the Read/Spell/Write routine.

We Do Display the Practice Book High-Frequency Word Cards for *he, with, is,* and *little.* Have children help you create sentence frames using both sets of word cards.

You Do Have partners write sentences using the Build Your Word Bank High-Frequency words *by, some,* and *brown* on their Response Boards. Have them read their sentences.

Vocabulary

ORAL VOCABULARY: SYNONYMS

OBJECTIVES
With guidance and support from adults, explore word relationships and nuances in word meanings.

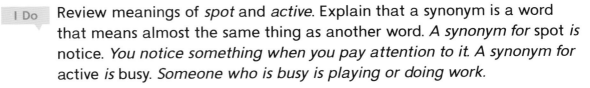

I Do Review meanings of *spot* and *active*. Explain that a synonym is a word that means almost the same thing as another word. *A synonym for* spot *is* notice. *You notice something when you pay attention to it. A synonym for* active *is* busy. *Someone who is busy is playing or doing work.*

We Do Write a few sentences together using the new words *notice* and *busy*. Read the sentences aloud.

You Do Have partners draw a picture and write a few sentences to tell about a trip to the market. Tell them to include the words *notice* and *busy* in their sentences. Ask them to share their pictures and sentences with the class.

GIFTED and TALENTED **Extend** Challenge children to use new words *notice* and *busy* to interview a partner about the seasons of the year. Then ask children to share two facts they learned about their partner and the seasons.

Comprehension

SELF-SELECTED READING

OBJECTIVES
With prompting and support, identify characters, settings, and major events in a story.

Read emergent-reader texts with purpose and understanding.

Independent Reading

Have children select an illustrated story for independent reading. Encourage them to read for twelve minutes. Guide children to transfer what they have learned this week as they read by identifying the sequence of events. Remind children that they will understand a story better if they visualize what the characters are doing and feeling.

After reading, guide children to participate in a group discussion about the story they read. In addition, children can choose activities from the **Reading Center Activity Cards** to help them apply skills to the text as they read. Offer assistance and guidance with self-selected assignments.

 Independent Study Challenge children to create a poster illustrating a fact about each season. Tell them to write sentences stating their opinion about one of this week's stories or poems.

Student Outcomes
✓ Tested in *Wonders* Assessments

FOUNDATIONAL SKILLS

Print Concepts
- Recognize that the first word in a sentence is capitalized
- Identify periods and exclamation points
- Identify parts of a book

Phonological Awareness
- Identify Rhyme
- ✓ Phoneme Isolation
- ✓ Phoneme Blending
- ✓ Phoneme Segmentation

Phonics and Word Analysis
- ✓ /k/k, ck

Fluency
- ✓ High-Frequency Words
  she   was

READING

Reading Literature
- ✓ Identify and describe the events in a story
- Retell familiar stories
- Actively engage in group reading activities

Reading Informational Text
- Describe the relationship between illustrations and the text
- Identify key details in a text
- Actively engage in group reading activities

COMMUNICATION

Writing
- Handwriting: *Kk*
- Use prompts to write about the text
- Respond to suggestions from peers and add details to strengthen writing

Speaking and Listening
- Present writing and research
- Engage in collaborative conversations
- Ask and answer questions to get information or to clarify something that is not understood

Conventions
- **Grammar:** Recognize proper nouns

Researching
- Recall or gather information to answer a question
- Conduct research about types of weather

Creating and Collaborating
- Add drawings and visual displays to descriptions
- Use digital tools to produce and publish writing

VOCABULARY

Academic Vocabulary
- Acquire and use grade-appropriate academic vocabulary

Vocabulary Strategy
- ✓ Identify and sort common words and objects into categories
- Distinguish shades of meaning among verbs

ELL Scaffolded supports for English Language Learners are embedded throughout the lessons, enabling children to communicate information, ideas, and concepts in English Language Arts and for social and instructional purposes within the school setting.

See the **ELL Small Group Guide** for additional support of the skills for the text set.

Wonders
ELL Small Group Guide

FORMATIVE ASSESSMENT

For assessment throughout the text set, use children's self-assessments and your observations.

Use the Data Dashboard to filter class, group, or individual student data to guide group placement decisions. It provides recommendations to enhance learning for gifted and talented children and offers extra support for children needing remediation.

DATA DASHBOARD

Develop Student Ownership

To build student ownership, children need to know what they are learning, why they are learning it, and determine how well they understood it.

Students Discuss Their Goals

TEXT SET GOALS

- I can read and understand texts.
- I can write about the texts I read.
- I know what happens in different kinds of weather.

Have children think about what they know and circle a hand in each row on **Reading/Writing Companion** page 40.

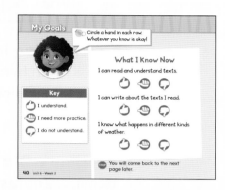

Students Monitor Their Learning

LEARNING GOALS

Specific learning goals identified in every lesson make clear what children will be learning and why. These smaller goals provide stepping stones to help children meet their Text Set Goals.

CHECK-IN ROUTINE

The Check-In Routine at the close of each lesson guides children to self-reflect on how well they understood each learning goal.

Review the lesson learning goal.
Reflect on the activity.
Self Assess by
- circling the hands in the **Reading/Writing Companion.**
- showing thumbs up, sideways, or down.

Share with your teacher.

Students Reflect on Their Progress

TEXT SET GOALS

After completing the Show Your Knowledge task for the text set, children reflect on their understanding of the Text Set Goals by circling a hand in each row on **Reading/Writing Companion** page 41.

Build Knowledge

Literature Big Book

Shared Read
Reading/Writing Companion p. 50

Paired Selection
Literature Big Book

Essential Question
What happens in different kinds of weather?

Video In windy weather, we can fly a kite. In warm weather, we can play on the beach. In the cool fall, we can rake fallen leaves. In cold weather, we can go ice skating.

Literature Big Book Animals on a hot, dry land sense rain is coming. Zebras see lightning flash. Baboons hear thunder boom. The rhino feels the rain. The lion tastes it. After the rain, grasses and fruits grow and leaves sprout.

Shared Read Kim and Nan go out to the bay. At first it is hot. Then the wind blows, clouds form, and it rains.

Interactive Read Aloud Thunder, Lightning, Rain, and Wind live in the sky together. Wind challenges Rain to see who is most powerful. Wind makes a tree sway, while a monkey clings to it. Rain is more powerful—her steady drops make the monkey leave the tree.

Paired Selection A dad shows his daughters clouds. Cirrus and cumulus clouds mean the weather will stay nice. Cumulonimbus clouds mean rain and storms are coming.

Photograph Children jump and play in a sprinkler in summer to cool off in the hot weather.

Differentiated Sources

Leveled Readers 🔊

🔴 Children and animals run quickly home to get out of the rain.

🔴🔴 A girl and her dog do different things in different seasons, such as throw snowballs in winter and jump in rain puddles in spring.

🔴 Kate and her dog, Tuck, wear appropriate clothes when they go out in each season, such as warm sweaters in fall and sunglasses in summer.

Build Knowledge Routine

After reading each text, ask children to document what facts and details that they learned to help answer the Essential Question of the text set.

 Talk about the source.

 Write about the source.

 Add to the class Anchor Chart

- Add to the Word Bank.

Show Your Knowledge

Write a Weather Forecast

Have children think about what they observe in different kinds of weather. Guide them to draw what they think the weather will be like tomorrow and write about their forecast. Encourage children to use vocabulary words they learned during the week in their forecast.

Social Emotional Learning

SESAME STREET

Emotional Functioning

Jealous (1:38)

SEL Focus: Observe children's developing abilities and need for individualized support as they identify and express a range of emotions.

Invite volunteers to share feeling faces for others to guess. Then begin the lesson titled "Feelings Detective," pp. T322–T323.

Family Time • Share the video and the activity in the **School to Home** newsletter.

Explore the Texts

Essential Question: What happens in different kinds of weather?

Literature Big Book	Literature Big Book	Interactive Read-Aloud	Reading/Writing Companion

Rain
Anchor Text
Fantasy

"Cloud Watch"
Paired Text
Informational Text

"The Battle of Wind and Rain"
Interactive Read Aloud
Folktale

"Kim and Nan"
Shared Read
pp. 50–57
Fiction

Qualitative

Meaning/Purpose: Moderate Complexity
Structure: Moderate Complexity
Language: Moderate Complexity
Knowledge Demands: Moderate Complexity

Meaning/Purpose: Low Complexity
Structure: Low Complexity
Language: Moderate Complexity
Knowledge Demands: Moderate Complexity

Meaning/Purpose: Moderate Complexity
Structure: Moderate Complexity
Language: Moderate Complexity
Knowledge Demands: Moderate Complexity

Meaning/Purpose: Low Complexity
Structure: Low Complexity
Language: Low Complexity
Knowledge Demands: Low Complexity

Quantitative

Lexile 360L

Lexile 270L

Lexile 530L

Lexile 120L

Reader and Task Considerations

Reader Background knowledge about the animals and weather in Africa will help with comprehension.

Reader In order to deepen comprehension, allow children to look closely at each type of cloud depicted.

Reader This selection has the potential to generate further discussion or encourage children to think of a different ending.

Reader Children will need to use their knowledge of sound-spelling correspondences and high-frequency words to read the text.

Task The questions for the Interactive Read Aloud are supported by teacher modeling. The tasks provide a variety of ways for students to build knowledge and vocabulary about the text set topic. The questions and tasks provided for the other texts are at various levels of complexity, ensuring that all students can interact with the text in meaningful ways.

Additional Read-Aloud Texts

Classroom Library
A Kitten Tale
Genre: Fiction
Lexile: 590L

The Year at Maple Hill Farm
Genre: Informational Text
Lexile: 560L

See Classroom Library Lessons.

Content Area Reading BLMs
Additional online texts related to grade-level Science, Social Studies, and Arts content.

Access Complex Text (ACT) boxes provide scaffolded instruction for seven different elements that may make the **Literature Big Book** complex.

A C T

Leveled Readers 🔊 (All Leveled Readers are provided in eBook format with audio support.)

Approaching
The Rain
Leveled Reader
Fiction

On
Weather Is Fun
Leveled Reader
Fiction

Beyond
Kate and Tuck
Leveled Reader
Fiction

ELL
Weather Is Fun
Leveled Reader
Fiction

Qualitative

Meaning/Purpose: Low Complexity
Structure: Low Complexity
Language: Low Complexity
Knowledge Demands: Low Complexity

Meaning/Purpose: Low Complexity
Structure: Low Complexity
Language: Low Complexity
Knowledge Demands: Low Complexity

Meaning/Purpose: Moderate Complexity
Structure: Low Complexity
Language: Moderate Complexity
Knowledge Demands: Low Complexity

Meaning/Purpose: Low Complexity
Structure: Low Complexity
Language: Low Complexity
Knowledge Demands: Low Complexity

Quantitative

Lexile BR

Lexile BR

Lexile 280L

Lexile BR

Reader and Task Considerations

Reader Children should be familiar with the topic of rain, but they may need extra support understanding why everyone is running.

Reader Children will need to have a basic understanding of the weather in each of the four seasons.

Reader Children need to have a basic understanding of the types of clothes that should be worn in different weather.

Reader Children will need to have a basic understanding of the weather in each of the four seasons.

Task The questions and tasks provided for the Leveled Readers are at various levels of complexity, ensuring that all students can interact with the text in meaningful ways.

Focus on Word Work

Build Foundational Skills with Multimodal Learning

MULTIMODAL

Photo Cards

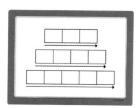
Response Board

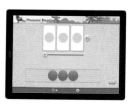
Phonemic Awareness Activities

Sound-Spelling Card

Word-Building Cards online

Phonics Practice Activities

Practice Book

Word-Building Cards online

Response Board

 she

 was

High-Frequency Word Cards

High-Frequency Word Activities

Visual Vocabulary Cards

Phonological/Phonemic Awareness

- Identify and produce rhyming words
- Isolate, blend, and segment phonemes

Phonics: /k/k, ck

- Introduce/review sound-spellings
- Blend/build words with sound-spellings
- Practice handwriting
- Decode and encode in connected texts

Spelling: /k/k, ck

- Spell words with /k/k, ck

High-Frequency Words

- Read/Spell/Write routine
- Optional: Build Your Word Bank

See Word Work, pages T332–T335, T344–T347, T352–T357, T366–T367, T372–T373.

Shared Read
Kim and Nan

Decodable Readers

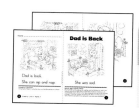
Take-Home Story

Apply Skills to Read

- Children apply foundational skills as they read decodable texts.
- Children practice fluency to develop word automaticity.

Letter Identification	Consonants	Short Vowels	Blends	Long Vowels

Explicit Systematic Instruction

Word Work instruction expands foundational skills to enable children to become proficient readers.

Daily Routine

- Use the In a Flash: Sound-Spelling routine and the In a Flash: High-Frequency Word routine to build fluency.
- Set Learning Goal.

Explicit Minilessons and Practice

Use daily instruction in both whole and small groups to model, practice, and apply key foundational skills. Opportunities include:

- Multimodal engagement.
- Corrective feedback.
- Supports for English Language Learners in each lesson.
- Peer collaboration.

Formative Assessment

Check-In

- Children reflect on their learning.
- Children show their progress by indicating thumbs down, thumbs sideways, or thumbs up in a Check-In routine.

Check for Success

- Teacher monitors children's achievement and differentiates for Small Group instruction.

Differentiated Instruction

To strengthen skills, provide targeted review and reteaching lessons and multimodal activities to meet children's diverse needs.

- **Approaching Level, ELL**
  - Includes Tier 2 TIER 2
- **On Level**
- **Beyond Level**
  - Includes Gifted and Talented ⭐GIFTED and TALENTED

OPTIONAL EXPRESS TRACK

Teachers can choose to introduce long vowel sound-spellings and/or additional high-frequency words.

- Build Your Word Bank

Independent Practice

Provide additional practice as needed. Have children work individually or with partners.

Center Activity Cards

Digital Activities

Word-Building Cards online

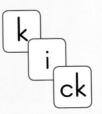

Decodable Readers

Practice Book

Inspire Early Writers

Build Writing Skills and Conventions

Practice Book

Handwriting Video

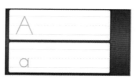

**Reading/Writing
Companion**

Write Letter *Kk*

- Learn to write the letters
- Practice writing

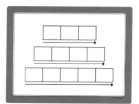

Response Board

Practice Book

**High-Frequency
Word Activities**

Write Words

- Write words with *Kk*
- Write high-frequency words

Reading/Writing Companion

Practice Book

Write Sentences

- Write sentences with high-frequency words
- Write sentences to respond to text

Follow Conventions

- Recognize proper nouns

Rain
Literature Big Book

Writing Fluency

To increase children's writing fluency, have them write as much as they can in response to the **Literature Big Book** for four minutes. Tell children to write about what they learned about rain.

For lessons, see pages T332–T337, T348–T349, T352–T355, T358–T359, T368–T369, T372–T375.

Write About Texts

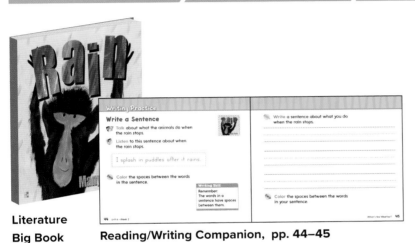

Literature Big Book

Reading/Writing Companion, pp. 44–45

Modeled Writing

Write about the **Literature Big Book** *Rain*

- Prompt: What do you like to do when it rains?

Interactive Writing

- Prompt: What did the animals enjoy doing after the rain?

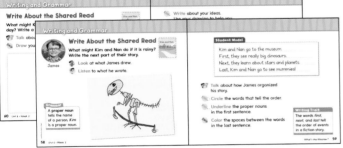

Reading/Writing Companion, pp. 58–61

Independent Writing

Write to the Shared Read "Kim and Nan"

- Prompt: What might Kim and Nan do another day? Write a story about their day.

- Have children follow the steps of the writing process: draft, revise, edit/proofread, share.

Additional Lessons

Writing Skills Minilessons To provide differentiated support for writing skills, see pages T494–T499.

Extended Writing Lessons For a full set of lessons that support the writing process and writing in a specific genre, see pages T476–T487.

Self-Selected Writing

Children can explore different writing modes.

Newspaper Article

Poem

Planner

Customize your own lesson plans at
my.mheducation.com

 **SESAME STREET**

Select from your Social Emotional Learning resources.

 LESSON 1

 LESSON 2

TEXT SET GOALS

- I can read and understand texts.
- I can write about the texts I read.
- I know what happens in different kinds of weather.

 90+ mins Reading Suggested Daily Time Includes Small Group

SMALL GROUP OPTIONS
The designated lessons can be taught in small groups. To determine how to differentiate instruction for small groups, use Formative Assessment and Data Dashboard.

 30+ mins Writing Suggested Daily Time

Reading

Lesson 1

Introduce the Concept, T324–T325
Build Knowledge: What's the Weather?

Listening Comprehension, T326–T331
Rain

Word Work, T332–T335
Phonemic Awareness: Phoneme Isolation
Phonics/Spelling: Introduce /k/k, ck
Handwriting: Write Kk
High-Frequency Words: *she, was*

Lesson 2

Build the Concept, T338–T339
Phonological Awareness: Identify Rhyme
Category Words: Weather Words
Vocabulary: Shades of Meaning

Listening Comprehension, T340–T343
Rain

Word Work, T344–T345
Phonemic Awareness: Phoneme Blending
Phonics: Review /k/k, ck, Blend Words
High-Frequency Words: *she, was*

Shared Read, T346–T347
Read "Kim and Nan"

Writing

Lesson 1

Modeled Writing, T336
Model Writing About the Literature Big Book
Grammar, T337
Proper Nouns

Lesson 2

Interactive Writing, T348
Write About the Literature Big Book
Grammar, T349
Proper Nouns

Teacher-Led Instruction

 SMALL GROUP

Differentiated Reading
Leveled Readers
- *The Rain,* T378–T379
- *Weather Is Fun,* T386–T387
- *Kate and Tuck,* T392–T393

Differentiated Skills Practice, T380–T395
Approaching Level, T380–T385
Phonological/Phonemic Awareness
- Recognize Rhyme, T380 🄦
- Phoneme Isolation, T380 🄦
- Phoneme Blending, T381
- Phoneme Segmentation, T381

Phonics
- Sound-Spelling Review, T382 🄦
- Connect k and ck to /k/, T382 🄦
- Blend Words with /k/k, ck, T382
- Reread the Decodable Reader, T383
- Sound/Spelling Fluency, T383
High-Frequency Words
- Reteach Words, T384 🄦
- Cumulative Review, T384
Oral Vocabulary
- Review Words, T385

Independent/Collaborative Work See pages T321I–T321J

Reading
Comprehension
- Fantasy
- Visualize
- Events: Sequence

Word Work
Phonics
- /k/k, ck
High-Frequency Words
- *she, was*

Writing
Self-Selected Writing
Grammar
- Proper Nouns
Handwriting
- Upper and Lowercase Kk

ORAL VOCABULARY

predict, temperature, drought, clever, storm

 LESSON 3

 LESSON 4

 LESSON 5

Reading

Build the Concept, T350
Oral Language

Listening Comprehension, T351
"The Battle of Wind and Rain"

Word Work, T352–T355
Phonemic Awareness: Phoneme Blending
Phonics: Review /k/k, ck; Blend Words; Spell Words
High-Frequency Words: *she, was*

Shared Read, T356–T357
Reread "Kim and Nan"

Extend the Concept, T360–T361
Phonological Awareness: Identify and Produce Rhyme
Category Words: Weather Words
Vocabulary: Shades of Meaning

Paired Selection, T362–T365
"Cloud Watch"

Word Work, T366–T367
Phonemic Awareness: Phoneme Segmentation
Phonics: Build and Read Words, Spell Words
High-Frequency Words: *she, was*

Research and Inquiry, T370–T371
Different Kinds of Weather (Research)

Word Work, T372–T373
Phonemic Awareness: Phoneme Segmentation
Phonics: Read Words, Spell Words
High-Frequency Words: *she, was*

Integrate Ideas, T376
Make Connections

Show Your Knowledge, T377

Writing

Independent Writing, T358
Write About the Shared Read
Grammar, T359
Proper Nouns

Independent Writing, T368
Write About the Shared Read
Grammar, T369
Proper Nouns

Self-Selected Writing, T374
Grammar, T375
Proper Nouns

Comprehension
• Self-Selected Reading, T385
● **On Level, T388–T391**
Phonological/Phonemic Awareness
• Phoneme Isolation, T388
• Phoneme Blending, T388
• Phoneme Segmentation, T388
Phonics
• Review Phonics, T389
• Picture Sort, T389
• Blend Words with /k/k, ck, T390
• Reread the Decodable Reader, T390

High-Frequency Words
• Review Words, T391
Comprehension
• Self-Selected Reading, T391
● **Beyond Level, T394–T395**
Phonics
• Review, T394
High-Frequency Words
• Review, T394

Vocabulary
• Oral Vocabulary: Synonyms, T395
Comprehension
• Self-Selected Reading, T395

⭐ GIFTED and TALENTED

 ● **English Language Learners**
See ELL Small Group Guide, pp. 140–147

Content Area Connections

Content Area Reading
• Science, Social Studies, and the Arts
Research and Inquiry
• Different Kinds of Weather (Research)

 ● **English Language Learners**
See ELL Small Group Guide, pp. 141, 143

WEEK 2

Independent and Collaborative Work

As you meet with small groups, have the rest of the class complete activities and projects to practice and apply the skills they have been working on.

Student Choice and Student Voice

- Review My Weekly Work blackline masters with children and identify the "Must Do" activities.
- Have children choose some additional activities that provide the practice they need.
- Remind children to reflect on their learning each day.

My Weekly Work BLMs

Reading

Text Options

Children can choose a **Center Activity Card** to use while they listen to a text or read independently.

Classroom Library Read Aloud
A Kitten Tale
Genre: Fiction
Lexile: 590L

The Year at Maple Hill Farm
Genre: Informational Text
Lexile: 560L

Unit Bibliography
See the online bibliography. Children can select independent reading texts about what happens in different kinds of weather.

Leveled Texts Online
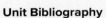 All **Leveled Readers** are provided in eBook format with audio support.
- **Differentiated Texts** provide English Language Learners with passages at different proficiency levels.

Literature Big Book e-Book
Rain
Genre: Fantasy

Center Activity Cards

Visualize Card 1

Fantasy Card 24

Sequence Card 11

Digital Activities

Comprehension

Word Work

Center Activity Cards

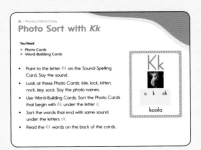

/k/ck Card 61

Word-Building Cards

Practice Book BLMs

Phonological Awareness: pp. 257, 258–259, 260

Phonics: pp. 261–262, 264

Phonics/Spelling: p. 263

High-Frequency Words: p. 266

Category Words: p. 267

Take-Home Story: pp. 271–272

Decodable Readers

Unit 6, pp. 13–24

Digital Activities

Word Work

Phonemic Awareness

Phonics

High-Frequency Words

Writing

Center Activity Cards

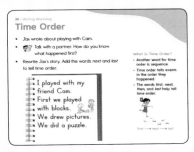

Time Order Card 39

Practice Book BLMs

Handwriting: p. 265

Grammar: pp. 268–270

Self-Selected Writing

- What kinds of weather do you know about?
- Write about what you wear in rainy weather.
- Draw and label a picture showing the weather where you live in winter.

Digital Activities

Grammar

Content Area Connections

Content Area Reading BLMs
- Additional texts related to Science, Social Studies, Health, and the Arts.

Research and Inquiry
- Complete Research the Weather project

Practice Book

Reading/Writing Companion

Online Rubric

Response Board

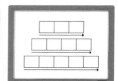

Digital Activities

FORMATIVE ASSESSMENT

❯ **STUDENT CHECK-IN**

✓ **CHECK FOR SUCCESS**

For ongoing formative assessment, use children's self-assessments at the end of each lesson along with your own observations.

Assessing skills along the way . . .

SKILLS	HOW ASSESSED
Phonological Awareness • Identify Rhyme	Practice Book
Phonemic Awareness • Phoneme Isolation • Phoneme Blending • Phoneme Segmentation	Practice Book, Response Board, Digital Activities
Phonics • /k/k, ck	Practice Book, Response Board, Digital Activities
High-Frequency Words • she, was	Practice Book, Response Board, Digital Activities
Category Words • Weather	Practice Book
Grammar • Proper Nouns	Practice Book
Comprehension • Events: Sequence • Text Feature: Speech Bubbles	Reading/Writing Companion
Listening/Presenting/Research	Checklists

Making the Most of Assessment Results

Make data-based grouping decisions by using the following reports to verify assessment results. For additional support options for children, refer to the reteaching and enrichment opportunities.

ONLINE ASSESSMENT CENTER
- *Gradebook*

DATA DASHBOARD
- *Recommendations Report*
- *Activity Report*
- *Skills Report*
- *Progress Report*
- *Grade Card Report*

Reteaching Opportunities with Intervention Online PDFs

ASSESSED SKILLS	✓ CHECK FOR SUCCESS	RETEACH . . .
PHONOLOGICAL AND PHONEMIC AWARENESS	Can children identify and produce rhyming words? Can children isolate, blend, and segment phonemes? If not . . .	using lessons 6–8 and 12–13; 27–29, and 62–71 in the **Phonemic Awareness PDF.**
PHONICS	Can children match /k/ to the letters *k, ck*? If not . . .	using lesson 29 in the **Phonics/Word Study PDF.**
HIGH-FREQUENCY WORDS	Can children recognize and read the high-frequency words? If not . . .	by using the **High-Frequency Word Cards** and asking children to read and spell the word. Point out any irregularities in sound-spellings.
COMPREHENSION	Can children identify sequence of events? Can children use text features including speech bubbles? If not . . .	using lessons 25–27 and 129 in the **Comprehension PDF.**
CATEGORY WORDS	Can children identify and sort weather words? If not . . .	using lesson 19 in the **Vocabulary PDF.**

GIFTED *and* TALENTED

Enrichment Opportunities

Beyond Level small group lessons and resources include suggestions for additional activities in these areas to extend learning opportunities for gifted and talented children:

- *Leveled Reader*
- *Vocabulary*
- *Comprehension*
- *Leveled Reader Library Online*
- *Center Activity Cards*

Today's focus:

Expressing and recognizing a range of emotions.

Jealous (1:38)   ANIMATION

Family Time
You'll find the "Jealous" video and supporting activity in this week's School to Home family newsletter.

feelings detectives

engage together

Let's Play: Mirror, Mirror
Engage children's observational skills.

- We have super detective tools. They're called our *senses*.
- We can learn a lot about how someone is feeling by observing closely.
- Let's play Mirror, Mirror with a partner. Stand up and face each other. One partner will be the leader and one will follow. Then we'll switch.
- The leader will use their face and body to show a feeling. The follower has to observe and copy as closely as possible. How closely can you mirror your partner?
- Nice mirroring!

explore together

Let's Watch: "Jealous"
Set a purpose for sharing today's animation video.

- Two robots are playing in the snow.
- The robots speak a robot language, but I bet you can figure out what they are feeling.
- Use your senses to watch and listen for clues.

  (▶) **Play the video**

Let's Figure It Out: We recognize feelings.
Explore how we can notice feelings in others and show empathy.

- How did the gray robot feel? Yes, when the gray robot saw the yellow robot's fancy snowman, he felt *jealous*. How could you tell the gray robot was feeling jealous?
- How did the yellow robot respond?
- The yellow robot wanted to help the gray robot feel better. He did it by sharing! Then how did the gray robot feel?

WHEN I FEEL...

- Excited, I wiggle.
- Angry, I frown.
- Joyful, I giggle.
- Disappointed, I sigh.
- Proud, I smile.

connect the learning

Let's Look for Clues: Feelings detectives.
Practice recognizing facial expressions and body language.

- Let's brainstorm a list of feelings (surprised, excited, proud, frustrated, disappointed, jealous).
- I'll act out different situations.
- See if you can guess how I'm feeling. Watch my facial expressions and body language for clues.
- What am I feeling? What clues helped you figure it out?
- How could you respond?

mindfulness moment
Scents & Smells!

Sensory experiences can help children bring their focus to the present moment. Make small scent containers, each filled with a distinct scent such as cinnamon, lavender, or lemon extract. Invite children to sniff and share how each scent makes them feel.

EMOTIONAL FUNCTIONING

LESSON 1

OBJECTIVES

Confirm understanding of a text read aloud or information presented orally or through other media by asking and answering questions about key details and requesting clarification if something is not understood.

Use words and phrases acquired through conversations, reading and being read to, and responding to texts.

Identify real-life connections between words and their use.

Follow agreed-upon rules for discussions (e.g., listening to others and taking turns speaking about the topics and texts under discussion).

ELA ACADEMIC LANGUAGE
• *weather, respect, opinion*
• Cognates: *respeto, opinión*

DIGITAL TOOLS

Watch Video

Visual Vocabulary Cards

LESSON FOCUS

READING
Introduce Essential Question
Read Literature Big Book
Rain
• Introduce Genre: Fantasy
• Introduce Strategy/Skill
Word Work
• Introduce /k/*k*

WRITING
Writing/Grammar
• Shared Writing
• Introduce Grammar

Literature Big Book, pp. 3–32

---

10 mins

Build Knowledge

MULTIMODAL

 Essential Question
What happens in different kinds of weather?

Read the Essential Question aloud. Explain that this week you will be learning about what happens in different kinds of weather. Have partners discuss the different kinds of weather they know about.

• **Video Routine** Play the Weekly Opener Video, "What's the Weather?" without sound and have partners narrate what they watch Then replay the video with sound and have children listen.

• **Talk About the Video** Have partners share one thing they learned about different kinds of weather.

 • **Anchor Chart** Create a Build Knowledge anchor chart and have volunteers share what they learned about the theme "What's the Weather?" Record their ideas on the chart.

Oral Vocabulary Words

Use the Define/Example/Ask routine on the print or digital **Visual Vocabulary Cards** to introduce the oral vocabulary words *predict* and *temperature*.

Oral Vocabulary Routine

<u>Define</u>: To **predict** is to guess what will happen in the future.

<u>Example</u>: I predict that you will enjoy that book.

Visual Vocabulary Cards

<u>Ask</u>: Who do you predict will win the race?

<u>Define</u>: The **temperature** tells how hot or cold something is.

<u>Example</u>: The outside temperature today is around 70 degrees.

<u>Ask</u>: Do you like warmer or colder temperatures? Why?

Reading/Writing Companion, pp. 38–39

 Build Knowledge

Have children turn to pages 38-39 of their **Reading/Writing Companion**. Use the photo to guide a discussion about the weather.

- **Talk** *What happens in different kinds of weather? What words tell about what happens in different kinds of weather?* List the words. Have children think about how to draw one of the words.

- **Draw** and **Write** Have children draw a picture that illustrates the word. Then have them write the word. Guide children on how to print letters that have not been taught yet.

Build Vocabulary

Have children share words about weather and add them to a separate section of the Word Bank. Use the words during the week and encourage children to do the same.

 # English Language Learners

Use the following scaffolds to help children with **Build Knowledge**.

Beginning

Point to the child in the photo. *It is raining. She has an umbrella.* Have children repeat. Repeat with other items in the photo.

Intermediate

Ask children to tell what they see in the photo. Provide sentence frames: I see a girl. It is raining. The girl is holding an umbrella.

Advanced/Advanced High

Encourage children to use complete sentences as they talk about the photo. Provide models: *The girl is standing in the rain. She is wearing a raincoat. She looks happy.*

COLLABORATIVE CONVERSATIONS

Be Open to All Ideas As children engage in partner and group discussions, have them do the following.

- Remember that all ideas and questions are important.
- Ask questions if you do not understand something.
- Ask questions if you do not understand a word.
- Respect other people's ideas and opinions.
- Share your opinions, even if they are different from those of other people.

ELL NEWCOMERS

To help children develop oral language and build vocabulary, use **Newcomer Cards** 20–24 and the accompanying lessons and in the **Newcomer Teacher's Guide**. For thematic connections, use **Newcomer Card** 9 (Weather). For additional practice, have children complete the online **Newcomer Activities**.

MY GOALS ROUTINE

What I Know Now

Read Goals Read aloud the goals and the key on **Reading/Writing Companion** page 40.

Reflect Ask children to reflect on each goal and complete page 40 to show what they know now. Explain that they will complete page 41 at the end of the text set to show their progress.

Literature Big Book

Read

Literature Big Book

Connect to Concept

Tell children that this story is about the rainy season in a hot and dry part of Africa. *How do you think the animals in this story feel about the rain?*

Genre: Fantasy Tell children that *Rain* is a fantasy. *Fantasy is a type of fiction. Things happen in a fantasy story that could not happen in real life. For example, animal characters in a fantasy can often talk.*

 Anchor Chart Create a Fantasy anchor chart. Write: *Fantasy is a made-up story with events that could not happen in real life. Fantasy stories often have animal characters that talk.*

Visualize Tell children that they can use the words and pictures in the story to form pictures in their mind as they read. Remind them that using this strategy can help them better understand what they read.

Events: Sequence Remind children that events in a story are usually told in a certain order, or sequence. Explain that we can use the words *beginning, middle,* and *end* to talk about the sequence of events.

Read the Selection

Concepts of Print Point to the quotation marks on page 6 of *Rain*. Say: *They show when a character is talking. Who is talking?* (a porcupine)

Set Purpose *Let's read to find out how the animals feel about the rain.*

Close Reading Routine

Read DOK 1–2

• Identify key ideas and details about different kinds of weather.
• Take notes and retell.
• Use **A C T** prompts as needed.

Reread DOK 2–3

• Analyze the text, craft, and structure.

Integrate DOK 3–4

• Integrate knowledge and ideas.
• Make text-to-text connections.
• Complete the Show Your Knowledge task.
• Inspire action.

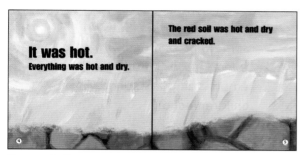

Pages 4–5

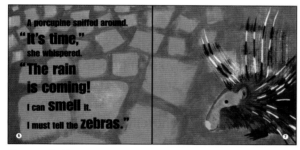

Pages 6–7

Pages 8–9

CONCEPTS OF PRINT

Remind children that sentences begin with a capital letter and end with a punctuation mark. Reread pages 4–5. *How many sentences are on the pages?* (three) *Which punctuation mark is at the end of each sentence?* (a period)

BUILD ORAL VOCABULARY

soil: dirt

cracked: broken

EVENTS: SEQUENCE DOK 2

Think Aloud I read earlier that it was hot and dry. Now I read that the rain is coming. This is the beginning of the story. This event happens in the first part of the story.

BUILD ORAL VOCABULARY

sniffed: smelled

VISUALIZE DOK 2

Think Aloud I read that lightning flashed and the rain is coming. In my mind I see a bright flash of lightning against a darkening sky. This helps me understand what the zebras in the story can see.

Page 5 *dry:* Explain that *dry* means "without water." When something is *dry*, it is not wet. Ask children to point to what is hot and dry in the picture.

Page 6 *It's time:* Explain that *it's time* means something is going to happen soon. *What do you do when I say, "It's time to clean up"?* (start cleaning up) Have children give other examples, using *it's time* in sentences. Check understanding that here it means the rain is coming soon.

Page 9 *baboons:* Explain that baboons are a type of monkey that lives in parts of Africa. Show children the baboons on the next page. Have them repeat the word.

A C T Access Complex Text

Use this ACT prompt when the complexity of the text makes it hard for children to understand the story.

Lack of Prior Knowledge

This book tells about the rainy season in a part of Africa.

Explain that some parts of the world have a rainy season and a dry season. These periods can last a long time, and they can be difficult for humans and animals alike. Guide children to understand that this book tells how the animals live before, during, and after the rainy season.

Pages 10–11

FANTASY DOK 2

Think Aloud I know that fantasy stories have events that could not happen in real life. On these pages the baboons cry, "The rain is coming!" I know that baboons cannot talk in real life. The fact that baboons are talking tells me that this story is a fantasy.

Page 10 *boomed:* Say: *If something* boomed, *it made a loud noise.* Say *boomed,* emphasizing the sound. Have children echo.

Pages 12–13

CONCEPTS OF PRINT

Remind children that quotation marks begin and end the words that a character says. Have children point out the quotation marks on these pages. Ask: *Which character is speaking?* (the rhino)

Page 12 *splashed:* Say: *When the raindrop hit the ground, it splashed.* Raise a fist and drop it toward the palm of your other hand. When you reach your palm, spread out your fingers to mimic a raindrop splashing. Have children repeat the gesture with you as you chorally reread the first sentence.

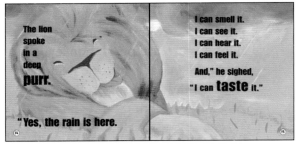

Pages 14–15

DETAILS DOK 1

How does the lion know that the rain has come? (He can smell it, see it, hear it, feel it, and taste it.) *What is the lion using to observe the rain?* (his five senses)

Page 14 *purr:* Tell children that cats purr, but *purr* can also mean "speak softly." Read aloud the lion's dialogue on pages 14–15 in a gentle way to show purring.

Pages 16–17

VISUALIZE DOK 2

Think Aloud Now I read that it rained and rained. I can see in my mind a rainstorm. I see puddles filling. Water is everywhere. This helps me understand how the weather in the story changed. It helps me see why such a big change is important to the animals.

Page 17 *gushed and gurgled:* Tell children to picture water that is flowing very fast. Explain that *gushed and gurgled* describe how fast-moving water looks and sounds.

Spotlight On Language

Pages 18–19

EVENTS: SEQUENCE DOK 1

What happened after it stopped raining? (Grasses grew. Trees sprouted leaves.)

BUILD ORAL VOCABULARY

sprout: grow

Page 18 *feathery:* Show children a picture of a feather. Say *feathery* aloud and have children repeat. Explain that birds have feathers. *If something is feathery, it looks or feels like a feather.*

Pages 20–21

PHONICS

Reread the sentence on page 20 and have children identify the words with the initial /l/ sound. (lion, leaves)

Page 20 *shade:* If the day is sunny, make a shadow by holding your hand over a table. *The dark place under my hand is the shade. Trees make shade outside.* Say *shade* and have children repeat.

Pages 22–23

VISUALIZE DOK 2

Think Aloud Before the rain, it was hot. The text says the mud is cool and soft. I can picture in my mind the rhino cooling off in the squishy mud. This helps me understand that the rain made the rhino feel happy.

BUILD ORAL VOCABULARY

squelchy: squishy and wet

Page 22 *squelchy:* Have children pretend they are walking in thick, sticky mud. *What kind of sound do you think it makes?* Have them vocalize different sounds. Explain that *squelchy* describes a sound something makes when it walks in mud.

Pages 24–25

EVENTS: SEQUENCE DOK 1

What do the baboons do after the rain stops? (They eat fresh fruit from the trees.)

Page 24 *juicy:* Explain that *juicy* means "full of juice." *Oranges are juicy.* Ask children to name other fruits that are juicy.

 Spotlight On Language

Pages 26–27

CONCEPTS OF PRINT

Reread page 27. Have children identify and read the first and last words of the sentence. (We, hole) Help them recognize that a comma is not end punctuation, but a period is.

Page 27 *refreshing:* Tell children that something that is refreshing makes you feel better and gives you energy. Point to the image on the page and say: *The zebras have a refreshing drink.* Have children repeat *refreshing.* Then ask children to name things that are refreshing to them.

Pages 28–29

PHONICS

Reread page 29 and have children identify the words with the final sound /n/. (rain, porcupine, again, when)

Page 29 *whisper:* Say in a whisper, Whispering *means "talking very, very softly." How softly can you whisper?* Have children practice whispering.

Pages 30–31

HIGH-FREQUENCY WORDS

Have children identify and read the word *the* in two places on page 30.

Page 30 *plain:* Tell children that one meaning of *plain* is "flat land." Have them tell you a word that describes the opposite of a plain. (mountain, hill)

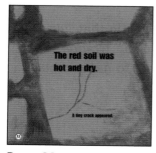

Page 32

EVENTS: SEQUENCE DOK 1

What happens at the end of the story? (Cracks appear in the dry soil. It is dry and hot again.)

Page 32 *soil:* Remind children that soil is dirt that plants can grow in. If there are plants in the classroom, use them to have children show their understanding of *soil.*

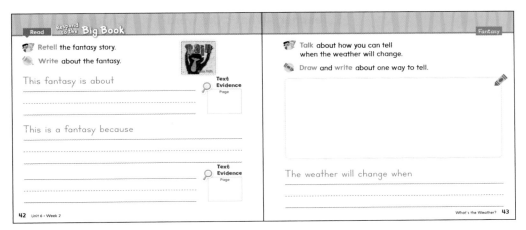

Reading/Writing Companion, pp. 42-43

Respond to the Text

Return to Purpose Remind children of their purpose for reading. Review what children have learned about rain and how the animals feel about it.

- **Retell** Direct children to page 42 of the **Reading/Writing Companion.** Have them retell the story using the **Retelling Cards** and the routine.

- **Write** Have children complete the sentence telling what the story is about. Model for them how to find text evidence to support their response and how to record the page number in the text evidence box. Share the **Big Book** with children to give them a chance to look at the pages. Then have children write the page number in the text evidence box. Repeat this routine as children complete the page. For the second sentence starter, have children tell how they know this story is a fantasy. (The animals talk.)

- **Talk** Have children talk with a partner about how they can tell that the weather is about to change. (Possible responses: The sky gets dark. It gets windy. There is thunder and lightning.)

- **Draw** and **Write** Turn to page 43 and have children draw and write about one way they can tell that the weather is changing.

Model Fluency

Reread page 29 of *Rain*. Explain that when you read what characters say, you try to speak as the character would. Point out the word *whispered* in the second line. Tell children this is a clue to how the porcupine sounds. Read the page in a whispering voice. Have children repeat and mimic.

Writing Fluency

To help children increase writing fluency, have them write as much as they can for four minutes. Tell them to write about what they learned about rain. *Why is rain important?*

RETELLING ROUTINE

Have children use the **Retelling Cards** to retell the story.

- Display Retelling Card 1. Based on children's needs, use either the Modeled, Guided, or ELL retelling prompts. The ELL prompts provide support for children based on levels of language acquisition. Repeat with the rest of the cards, using the prompts as a guide. Remind children to include important details from the story.

- Discuss the story. After retelling, have children tell how the animals feel about the rain.

- Have partners act out one or more events from the story.

Retelling Cards

FORMATIVE ASSESSMENT

▶ STUDENT CHECK-IN

Have partners tell one another an important detail from the story. Then have children reflect on their learning using the Check-In routine.

In a Flash: Sound-Spellings

Display the Sound-Spelling Card for *b*.

1. **Teacher:** What's the letter?　　**Children:** b
2. **Teacher:** What's the sound?　　**Children:** /b/
3. **Teacher:** What's the word?　　**Children:** bat

Continue the routine for previously taught sounds.

LEARNING GOALS

- **We can hear the sound /k/ in words.**
- **We can connect the sound /k/ to the letters *k* and *ck*.**

OBJECTIVES

Isolate and pronounce the initial sounds in words.

Demonstrate basic knowledge of one-to-one letter-sound correspondences by producing the primary sound or many of the most frequent sounds for each consonant.

ELA ACADEMIC LANGUAGE

- *beginning, end, spelled*

▶ TEACH IN SMALL GROUP

You may wish to teach the Word Work lesson in small groups.

ELL ENGLISH LANGUAGE LEARNERS

Phonemic Awareness, Guided Practice/Practice
Encourage children to say /k/ several times. Point to a card and ask children to name it. Help them self-correct by modeling pronunciation. Then help children identify the initial sound, using a sentence frame. For example: The word king begins with the sound /k/.

Phonemic Awareness:
pp. 258–259
Phonics: pp. 261–262

Phonemic Awareness

MULTIMODAL

Phoneme Isolation

1 **Model** Display the **Photo Card** for koala. *Listen for the sound at the beginning of* koala. Koala *has the /k/ sound at the beginning.* Say *key, king, kite* and have children repeat. Emphasize initial /k/. Repeat the instruction with final /k/. Use the *lock* Photo Card and the words *lick, pack,* and *rock.* Emphasize final /k/.

Photo Card

🎵 *Let's play a song. Listen for words with /k/ at the beginning.* Play "Koala" and have children listen for /k/. *Let's listen to the song again and clap our hands when we hear a word that begin with /k/.* Play or sing the letter song again, encouraging children to join in. Have children clap when they hear a word that begins with /k/.

2 **Guided Practice/Practice** Display and name the following Photo Cards: *king, kitten, kite. Say each picture name with me. Tell me the sound at the beginning of the word.* Guide practice with the first word. Repeat with words that end with the /k/ sound spelled *ck* and the *lock, sock, rock* Photo Cards. If children need additional practice identifying the initial and final /k/ sound, use **Practice Book** pages 258–259.

Articulation Support

Demonstrate the way to say /k/. Open your mouth. Put your tongue on the top of your mouth, toward the back. Let a puff of air out as you lower your tongue. Hold your hand up to your mouth. Do you feel the puff of air? Then have children say these words: *kangaroo, kid, key.* Emphasize initial /k/ when you say the word. Then have children repeat.

Phonics
10 mins

MULTIMODAL

Introduce /k/k, ck

1 Model Display the *koala* **Sound-Spelling Card**. *This is the* koala *card. The sound is /k/. The /k/ sound can be spelled with the letter* k. *Say it with me: /k/. This is the sound at the beginning of the word* koala. *Listen: /k/, /k/, /k/,* koala. Repeat this instruction with the ending sound /k/ spelled *ck,* using the *lock* **Photo Card**.

Sound-Spelling Card

Display the song "Koala." (See **Spelling Song** online.) Read or sing the song with children. Reread the title and point out that the word *Koala* begins with the letter *k*. Model placing a self-stick note below the *K* in *koala*.

2 Guided Practice/Practice Read each line of the song. Stop after each line. Ask children to place a self-stick note below words that begin with *K* or *k* and say the letter name and the sound it stands for. If children need additional practice connecting letters *k* or *ck* with the sound /k/, use **Practice Book** pages 261–262.

Corrective Feedback

Sound Error Model the sound /k/ in the initial position; then have children repeat the sound. *My turn. Key /k/ /k/ /k/. Now it's your turn.* Have children say the words *kit* and *kiss,* isolating the initial sound. Repeat with words that end with /k/ spelled *ck,* such as *back* and *sick.*

Koala

Koala, koala, as happy as can be.

Koala, koala, won't you come and dance with me?

Koala, koala, sitting high up in the tree,

Koala, koala, munching eucalyptus leaves.

ENGLISH LANGUAGE LEARNERS
ELL

Phonics Transfers Use the chart on pages 10–13 in the **Language Transfers Handbook** to check for sound-spelling transfers from a child's native language into English. You can use the Sound-Spelling Cards to support teaching transferable and nontransferable skills.

DIGITAL TOOLS

Word Work — **Phonemic Awareness Phonics**

Phonics: Spelling Song

Phonics Video

Phonics: Data-Generating

FORMATIVE ASSESSMENT

○ STUDENT CHECK-IN

Have partners name the letter(s) that stands for /k/. Then have children reflect using the Check-In routine.

Handwriting: p. 265

Handwriting: Write *Kk*

5 mins

MULTIMODAL

1 **Model** Say the handwriting cues below as you write and then identify the upper- and lowercase forms of *Kk*. Then trace the letters as you say /k/.

Straight down. Go back to the top. Slant in, slant out.

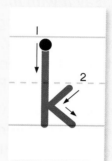

Straight down. Slant in, slant out.

2 **Guided Practice**

- Say the cues together as children trace both forms of the letter with their index finger. Have children identify the upper- and lowercase forms of the letter.

- Have children use their index finger to write *K* and *k* on the rug or a table as they say /k/ multiple times.

3 **Practice**

- Distribute **Response Boards**. Have children write *K* and *k* on their Response Boards as they say /k/ each time they write the letter.

- Observe children's pencil grip and paper position and correct as necessary. Guide practice and provide corrective feedback.

Repeat steps 1–3 to review writing *c*. Then have children spell and print *ck*.

Center Idea Have children use pencils or wooden sticks to make capital K. Emphasize the three lines used to form the letter. Then have children to pretend to kick a ball as they say /k/.

Daily Handwriting

Throughout the week, teach upper- and lowercase letters *Kk,* using the Handwriting models. At the end of the week, have children use **Practice Book** page 265 to practice handwriting using appropriate directionality.

In a Flash: High-Frequency Words   little

1. **Teacher:** Read the word.   **Children:** little
2. **Teacher:** Spell the word.   **Children:** l-i-t-t-l-e
3. **Teacher:** Write the word.   **Children write the word.**

Repeat routine with *is, he,* and *with* from previous weeks.

High-Frequency Words

MULTIMODAL

5 mins

she	was

1 Model Display the **High-Frequency Word Card** for *was*. Use the Read/Spell/Write routine to teach the word.

- **Read** Point to the word *was* and say the word. *This is the word* was. *Say it with me:* was. I was happy.

- **Spell** *The word* was *is spelled* w-a-s. *Spell it with me.*

- **Write** *Let's write the word* was *on our **Response Boards** as we say each letter:* w-a-s. Guide children on how to form and print the letter *w*.

- Point out that the letter *a* in *was* has a different sound from the /a/ sound in *nap*. Explain that the letter *s* has a /z/ sound as in *is*.

- Have partners say sentences using the word.

Display the **High-Frequency Word Card** for *she*. Use the Read/Spell/Write routine to teach the word. Explain that the letter *e* has a different sound from the /e/ sound in *pet*. Point out that the letter *s* has a different sound from the /s/ in *sit* and that the letter *h* has a different sound from the /h/ in *hop*.

2 Guided Practice/Practice Build sentences using **High-Frequency Word Cards, Photo Cards,** and teacher-made punctuation cards. Have children point to the high-frequency words *she* and *was*. Use these sentences. Guide practice and provide corrective feedback as needed.

She can go to the farm.

Was she with the baby?

She was the little girl.

ELL ENGLISH LANGUAGE LEARNERS

Use with **High-Frequency Words, Guided Practice/Practice** and the **High-Frequency Word Routine.**

Beginning
We can use she *to talk about a girl or woman.* Point to a female student. *What is she wearing?* She is wearing <u>shoes</u>.

Intermediate
Point to each card as you read the first sentence. Ask children to repeat. Ask a volunteer to point to *she*. Repeat with the second sentence.

Advanced/Advanced High
Challenge partners to create sentences using the words.

FORMATIVE ASSESSMENT

▶ STUDENT CHECK-IN

Handwriting Have children print *Kk*.

High-Frequency Words Have partners take turns pointing to and reading the words *she* and *was*.

Then have children reflect using the Check-In routine.

✓ CHECK FOR SUCCESS

Rubric Use your online rubric to record children's progress.

Can children isolate /k/ and match it with *Kk* and *ck*?

Can children recognize and read the high-frequency words?

▶ Small Group Instruction

If No

● **Approaching** Reteach pp. T380–384

● **ELL** Develop pp. T380–384

If Yes

● **On** Review pp. T388–390

● **Beyond** Extend p. T394

LESSON 1

Literature Big Book

- We can write what we do when the rain stops.
- We can learn about words that are names of people and places (proper nouns).

OBJECTIVES

Demonstrate command of the conventions of standard English capitalization, punctuation, and spelling when writing.

Follow agreed-upon rules for discussions.

Continue a conversation through multiple exchanges.

Identify proper nouns.

ELA ACADEMIC LANGUAGE

- *sentence, proper noun, exact*

COLLABORATIVE CONVERSATIONS

Turn and Talk Review this routine.

Child 2: *play when it rains*

Child 1: *Can you say that in a complete sentence?*

Child 2: *I play inside when it rains.*

Display the speech bubble, "Can you say that in a complete sentence?" Have partners use it to practice collaborating.

10 mins

Modeled Writing

Model Writing About the Literature Big Book

Build Oral Language Discuss what children learned from listening to the **Literature Big Book**. Review what the animals did when it rained. Ask: *What do you like to do when it rains?* Have partners use the Turn and Talk routine to discuss what they do when it rains. When children are done, encourage them to share what they talked about with their partner.

Model Writing a Sentence Write and display the following sentence: **I like to step in puddles**. Then point out the following elements of writing using the Sample Teacher Talk.

- *I wrote the word* like. *I used the Word Bank to help me spell the word.* Like *is spelled* l-i-k-e. HIGH-FREQUENCY WORDS

- *I wrote the word* step. *I heard the /st/ sounds at the beginning of* step *so I wrote the letters* st *at the beginning.* PHONICS

- *I know that a sentence is made up of words that have spaces between them.* Point to the spaces between the words. *I put spaces between my words.* WRITING SKILL

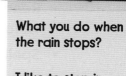

What you do when the rain stops?

I like to step in puddles.

Writing Practice

Turn to pages 44-45 of the **Reading/Writing Companion**. Say: *Now we are going to read a sentence about what animals do after it rains.*

Analyze a Sentence Guide children to analyze the sentence, using the prompts. Review the writing skill as necessary. Then have children write and analyze their own sentence.

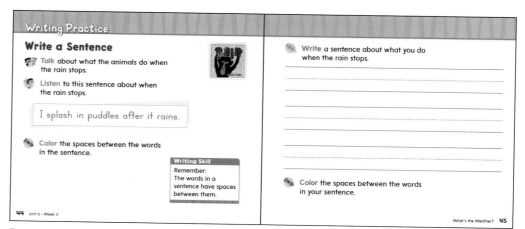

Reading/Writing Companion, pp. 44–45

Grammar

5 mins

Proper Nouns

1 **Model** Remind children that a noun names a person, place, or thing. Explain that the exact name of a person, place, or thing is called a proper noun. Write the following sentences and read them aloud: **Mila plays basketball every Sunday in May.** Underline and read *Mila, Sunday,* and *May.* Say: *These tell exact names. They are proper nouns. Proper nouns begin with a capital letter.*

2 **Guided Practice** Write this sentence and read it aloud: **Jay hopes the Toy Treasures store will open in March.** Work with children to identify the proper nouns. Then ask them to name other proper nouns, such as their name, their birthday month, and the name of their school. Write children's examples. Invite volunteers to underline the initial capital letters.

3 **Practice** Write and read aloud the following sentence: **Leo visits Tye Park on Fridays.** Have partners copy the sentence and work together to circle the proper nouns.

Talk About It Have partners work together to identify proper nouns they use every day, such as friend's names and city names.

Link to Writing Guide children to add a proper noun, such as the name of a friend or the name of a street, to their sentence.

ELL English Language Learners

Use the following scaffolds with **Grammar, Guided Practice.**

Beginning

Reread the first sentence. *Who is the person?* The person is <u>Mila</u>. Point out that *Mila* is a specific or exact person. Reread the second sentence. *What is the place?* The place is <u>Summer Street</u>. Again, point out that *Summer Street* names an exact street.

Intermediate

Provide a sentence frame to prompt children to use proper nouns: The name of our school is _____. My name is _____.

Advanced/Advanced High

Encourage children to use complete sentences as they identify proper nouns. Model as needed. Mila *tells the name of a person.* Mila *is a proper noun.*

DIGITAL TOOLS

Grammar Activity

DIFFERENTIATED WRITING

● **English Language Learners** For more writing support, see the **ELL Small Group Guide** p. 146.

FORMATIVE ASSESSMENT

❯ STUDENT CHECK-IN

Have partners share a proper noun they learned. Have children reflect using the Check-In routine.

LESSON 2

LEARNING GOALS

- We can tell if words rhyme.
- We can use new words.
- We can learn words that tell about the weather.
- We can learn about words that mean almost the same thing.

OBJECTIVES

Recognize rhyming words.

Use words and phrases acquired through conversations, reading and being read to, and responding to texts.

Distinguish shades of meaning among verbs describing the same general action by acting out the meanings.

Identify weather words.

ELA ACADEMIC LANGUAGE

- *sort, categories, similar*
- Cognate: *categoría*

DIGITAL TOOLS

Weekly Song

Visual Vocabulary Cards

Category Words Activity

LESSON FOCUS

READING
Review Essential Question
Reread Literature Big Book
Rain
- Study Genre/Skill
Word Work
- Practice /k/*k*

Read Shared Read
"Kim and Nan"
- Practice Strategy
WRITING
Writing/Grammar
- Interactive Writing
- Practice Grammar

Literature Big Book, pp. 3–32

Reading/Writing Companion, pp. 50–57

---

10 mins

Oral Language

MULTIMODAL

Essential Question

What happens in different kinds of weather?

Remind children that this week we are learning about what happens in different kinds of weather. *Let's sing a song about rain.* Sing "Rain, Rain, Go Away." As you sing, wiggle your fingers to look like rain each time you sing he word *rain*. Have children join in. Then use the Build Knowledge anchor chart, the **Big Book,** and the **Weekly Song** to guide children in discussing the Essential Question.

Phonological Awareness: Identify and Produce Rhyme

 1 Model Point out that the words *away* and *day* rhyme. Remind children that words that rhyme have the same ending sounds. Say: *Another word that rhymes with* away *and* day *is* stay. *All the words have the /ā/ sound at the end.*

2 Guided Practice/Practice Say the following word pairs and have children tell if the words rhyme: *car, far; joy, toy; rain, pan; go, slow; want, sing; day, door; up, cup.* For each rhyming pair, have children name another rhyming word. Guide practice and provide corrective feedback as needed. If children need more practice identifying and producing rhyming words, have them use **Practice Book** page 257.

Review Oral Vocabulary Words

Use the Define/Example/Ask routine to review the oral vocabulary words *predict* and *temperature.* Prompt children to use the words in sentences.

Visual Vocabulary Cards

Category Words: Weather Words

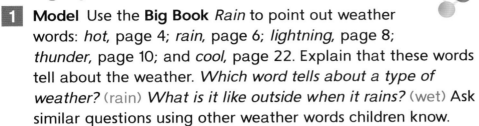

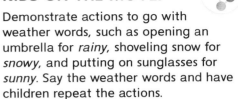

1 **Model** Use the **Big Book** *Rain* to point out weather words: *hot*, page 4; *rain*, page 6; *lightning*, page 8; *thunder*, page 10; and *cool*, page 22. Explain that these words tell about the weather. *Which word tells about a type of weather?* (rain) *What is it like outside when it rains?* (wet) Ask similar questions using other weather words children know.

Recite or sing the song "Rain, Rain, Go Away." Then ask children to identify the weather word.

Rain, rain, go away.

Come again some other day.

Rain, rain, go away.

Little children want to play.

Discuss other kinds of weather that might make it hard to play outside, such as windy, snowy, and cold weather.

2 **Guided Practice/Practice** Write the weather words *snowy, sunny, hot, icy, cold, warm*. Read each word. Have children sort the words into the categories *Winter* and *Summer*. Then have children draw and label a picture to illustrate one of the words.

Vocabulary: Shades of Meaning

1 **Model** Explain to children that words with similar meanings can have small but important differences in meaning. Use *Rain* to model how to identify the shades of meaning between verbs.

Think Aloud In *Rain*, I see the verb *whispered* in this sentence: *"It's time," she whispered.* The verb *whispered* names one way to say something. The verb *said* names another way: *"The rain is coming!" said the zebras.* Both *whispered* and *said* are verbs that name different ways to speak.

2 **Guided Practice** Work with children to find more examples of verbs that name ways to say things.

"The rain is coming!" *cried* **the baboons.**

"We can't hear the rain now," *shouted* **the baboons, "but we can eat fresh, juicy fruit from the trees."**

3 **Practice** Have children find more examples of verbs that name how to say things. (sighed, purred) Have children whisper, say, cry, shout, sigh, and purr a sentence, such as *The rain is coming.* Discuss the differences in meaning among these verbs.

KIDS ON THE MOVE!

Demonstrate actions to go with weather words, such as opening an umbrella for *rainy*, shoveling snow for *snowy*, and putting on sunglasses for *sunny*. Say the weather words and have children repeat the actions.

ELL ENGLISH LANGUAGE LEARNERS

Use the following with **Category Words, Guided Practice/Practice.**

Beginning
Review *rainy, gloomy, cloudy, windy, snowy,* and *sunny*. Have children choose a word and draw a picture to represent it.

Intermediate
Review weather words. Have children choose two or three words and draw a picture that represents them. Have children label their pictures.

Advanced/Advanced High
Have partners discuss the weather, encouraging them to use the words they've learned. *What is the weather like today? What was the weather yesterday? What might it be tomorrow?*

Phonological Awareness: p. 257

STUDENT CHECK-IN

Oral Vocabulary Words Have partners say a sentence using a vocabulary word.

Category Words Have partners name a word that tells about the weather.

Vocabulary Have partners tell the difference in the meanings of *whispered* and *said*.

Then have children reflect using the Check-In routine.

LESSON 2

Literature Big Book

Reread

 10 mins

Literature Big Book

Genre: Fantasy

1 **Model** Tell children that you will now reread the **Literature Big Book** *Rain.* Remind children that this story is a fantasy.

Anchor Chart Display and review the characteristics of fantasy that you have listed on the Fantasy anchor chart. Add details as needed.

Think Aloud I know that the book *Rain* is a fantasy because things happen in this story that could not happen in real life. For example, the animal characters talk and act like people. They talk to each other about the rain and pass on the news that the rain is coming. That is not the way animals act in real life.

2 **Guided Practice/Practice** Display and reread pages 6–7. Ask: *What does the porcupine do on these pages that real porcupines cannot do?* (The porcupine talks. She says she must tell the zebras as if she can really talk to the zebras.)

 # English Language Learners

Genre: Fantasy: Guided Practice/Practice Use sentence frames as needed to help children discuss how this is an example of a fantasy text. Point to the porcupine. *What is this?* That is <u>a porcupine</u>. *What is it doing?* The porcupine is <u>whispering</u>. *Do porcupines really whisper?* (no) *Who does the porcupine want to talk to?* The porcupine wants to talk to <u>the zebras</u>. Turn to pages 8–9 and ask children to point to the zebra. *Can porcupines really talk to zebras?* (no) *Can animals talk like people?* (no) *Is this a real story or a made-up story?* (a made-up story) Remind children that in a fantasy, things occur that can't happen in real life.

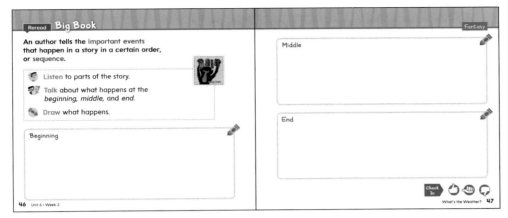

Reading/Writing Companion, pp. 46-47

Events: Sequence

1 **Model** Remind children that an author tells the important events in a story in a certain order, or sequence. We can use the words *beginning*, *middle*, and *end* to talk about sequence. Model, using the Think Aloud below.

 Anchor Chart Display and review the Main Story Elements: Events anchor chart, adding details about sequence as needed.

Think Aloud I know this story is about animals in a hot and dry part of Africa, waiting for the rainy season. I can tell the events in order. In the beginning, the animals sense that the rain is coming and tell one another. Then, in the middle, the rain comes, and the animals use their senses to enjoy the effects of the rain. In the end of the story, the author shows the land getting hot and dry all over again. Thinking about the sequence helps me understand the story better.

2 **Guided Practice/Practice** Direct children to pages 46-47 of the **Reading/Writing Companion**. Have them listen as you read pages 6-15 of *Rain*. Then have children describe the sequence of events by asking the following questions: *What happens in the beginning of the story?* (The animals sense that the rain is coming, and they tell one another.) Read pages 18-27 aloud and ask: *What happens in the middle of the story?* (The rain stops, and the animals eat, drink, and cool off.) Then read pages 30-32 aloud and ask: *What happens at the end of the story?* (It is hot again, and everything is drying out.) Review with children what happens in the beginning, middle, and end of the story. Then have them draw and write about it in the boxes provided.

ENGLISH LANGUAGE LEARNERS

Events: Sequence: Guided Practice/Practice Ask children guiding questions to help them determine the sequence of events in the story. Focus their attention on pages 6–15. *The animals feel the rain is coming. They tell each other it is coming. What happens first?* First, the animals feel the rain is coming. Repeat with the remaining events in the story. Provide sentence frames, as needed, to help children discuss the sequence: Next, _____. Then _____. Last _____.

For additional support, see the **ELL Small Group Guide** pp. 144-145.

FORMATIVE ASSESSMENT

❯ STUDENT CHECK-IN

Genre Have partners tell one another what makes the story a fantasy.

Events: Select a section of the story and have children identify the sequence of events.

Then have children reflect on their learning using the Check-In routine.

✔ CHECK FOR SUCCESS

Can children identify the characteristics of fantasy?

Can children identify sequence?

❯❯ Small Group Instruction

If No

● **Approaching** Reteach pp. T378-379

If Yes

● **On** Review pp. T386-387

● **Beyond** Extend pp. T392-393

Literature Big Book

Reread

Literature Big Book

Analyze the Text

Once children have reread *Rain* to study the characteristics of the genre and practice the comprehension skill, guide them to analyze author's craft. Reread the passages specified below and use the scaffolded instruction in the prompts to help children answer the questions on pages 48–49 of the **Reading/Writing Companion**.

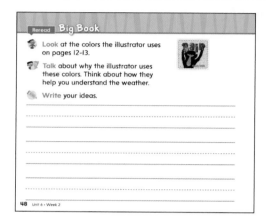

Reading/Writing Companion, p. 48

AUTHOR'S/ILLUSTRATOR'S CRAFT DOK 3

Display and reread pages 12–13 of *Rain. How do the colors help you understand the weather in this part of the story?* Have partners discuss. (Possible responses: The colors red and yellow show that it is hot and dry. The cloudy blue and gray in the sky show that a rainstorm is coming.) Have children write their ideas.

LEARNING GOALS

We can name the choices an author made when writing a story.

OBJECTIVES

With prompting and support, describe the relationship between illustrations and the story in which they appear.

With guidance and support from adults, explore word relationships and nuances in word meanings.

Analyze author's/illustrator's craft.

ELA ACADEMIC LANGUAGE

• compare, imagine
• Cognates: *comparar, imaginar*

English Language Learners

Author's Craft Help children name the colors. Guide them to make and label their own drawings with colors that show hot and cool.

ORGANIZATION DOK 1

Display and reread pages 6–15 of the Big Book. Say: *The author tells the story of the changing weather by having the animals use their five senses. Which animal is the first to sense that the rain is coming?* (the porcupine) *Which animal uses all five senses to determine that the rain had arrived?* (the lion)

USE ILLUSTRATIONS DOK 2

Compare pages 12–13 with pages 18–19 of the Big Book. Ask: *How do the illustrations show that the rain has changed the land?* (On pages 12–13, the reds and yellows show that the land is hot and dry. The tree is bare and brown. On pages 18–19, the different shades of green show that everything is fresh and alive. The flowers are blooming, and the trees are sprouting leaves.)

Reading/Writing Companion, p. 49

AUTHOR'S CRAFT DOK 2

Display and reread pages 16–17 of the **Big Book**. Ask: *Which words sound like the actions they name?* (gushed, gurgled) *What do the words* gushed *and* gurgled *help you imagine about the rain?* (that it rained so much that streams of water flowed everywhere) Have children write the words and complete the sentence starter.

(ELL) Spotlight on Language

Author's Craft As you read through pages 16–17, encourage children to imitate the sounds the river makes. Ask: *What does* gurgling *sound like? What about* gushing?

AUTHOR'S/ILLUSTRATOR'S CRAFT DOK 2

Display and reread page 32. *Why do you think the author made this page completely red?* (to show that the soil is hot and dry again)

Talk About It

Guide children to use their responses on the **Reading/Writing Companion** pages to answer the following question:

How does the author/illustrator help you understand how the rain changes the land?

If necessary, use the following sentence starters to focus the discussion:

At first the ground is _____. Then the rain comes, and the land is _____. The animals are _____. _____ and _____ grow.

Integrate

📋 Build Knowledge: Make Connections

Talk About the Text Have partners discuss what they learned about rain from the story. *What happens to the animals when it rains? What happens to their environment when it rains?*

Add to the Anchor Chart Record any new ideas on the Build Knowledge Anchor Chart.

FORMATIVE ASSESSMENT

❯ STUDENT CHECK-IN

Have children share something that the author/illustrator does with the text and pictures to help them understand the story. Then have children reflect on their learning using the Check-In routine.

In a Flash: Sound-Spellings

Display the Sound-Spelling Card for *k*.

1. **Teacher:** What's the letter?   **Children:** k
2. **Teacher:** What's the sound?   **Children:** /k/
3. **Teacher:** What's the word?   **Children:** koala

Continue the routine for previously taught sounds.

LEARNING GOALS

- We can blend sounds to say words.
- We can connect letters to sounds to read words.
- We can read *she* and *was*.

OBJECTIVES

Demonstrate understanding of spoken words, syllables, and sounds (phonemes).

Demonstrate basic knowledge of one-to-one letter-sound correspondences by producing the primary sound or many of the most frequent sounds for each consonant.

Read common high-frequency words by sight.

Blend phonemes to form words.

ELA ACADEMIC LANGUAGE

- *blending, different*

ⓓ TEACH IN SMALL GROUP

You may wish to teach the Word Work lesson in small groups.

DIGITAL TOOLS

Word Work

Phonemic Awareness

To differentiate instruction for key skills, use the results of this activity.

Phonics: Data-Generating

High-Frequency Words: Data Generating

OPTIONAL 5 mins

Phonemic Awareness

Phoneme Blending

1 **Model** Say: *I am going to say sounds in a word: /k/ /i/ /t/. I can blend those sounds to make the word: /kiiit/, kit. Listen as I say the sounds and blend them to make words.* Model phoneme blending with the following.

/k/ /i/ /s/ kiss   **/k/ /i/ /d/ kid**   **/k/ /ē/ /p/ keep**

2 **Guided Practice/Practice** Say: *Listen to the sounds in a different word: /k/ /ā/ /l/. Let's blend the sounds and say the word together: /k/ /ā/ /l/, /kāāāl/ kale.* Tell children to listen to the sounds in each word below, repeat the sounds, and then blend them to say the word. Guide practice and provide corrective feedback as needed.

/k/ /i/ /k/ kick   **/k/ /ē/ key**   **/k/ /e/ /n/ Ken**   **/k/ /ī/ /t/ kite**

Repeat instruction with words ending with /k/ spelled *ck*, such as *lock, sick,* and *pack.*

5 mins

Phonics

MULTIMODAL

Review /k/*k, ck*

1 **Model** Display the *koala* **Sound-Spelling Card**. *This is the letter* k. *The letter* k *can stand for the sound /k/ as in the word* koala. Repeat for final /k/ spelled *ck* using the sock **Photo Card**.

2 **Guided Practice/Practice** Display the *koala* Sound-Spelling Card and point to the letter *Kk*. Have children say the letter name and sound with you. Review /k/*ck* with the *sock* Photo Card. Have children listen as you say some words. Ask them to write the letter *k* on their **Response Boards** if the word begins with /k/ or ends with /k/ spelled *ck*. Do the first two words with children. Emphasize /k/.

keep	**lock**	**king**	**key**
nest	**door**	**kite**	**sick**

Blend Words

1 **Model** Place **Word-Building Cards** *k, i, t* in a pocket chart. Point to *k*. *This is the letter* k. *The letter* k *stands for /k/. Say /k/. This is the letter* i. *The letter* i *stands for /i/. Say /i/. This is the letter* t. *The letter* t *stands for /t/. Listen as I blend the sounds together: /kiiit/. Blend the sounds with me to read the word.*

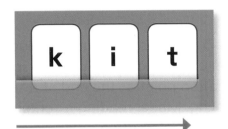

2 **Guided Practice/Practice** Change the Word-Building Cards to *kid*. Point to the letter *k* and have children say /k/. Point to the letter *i* and have children say /i/. Point to the letter *d* and have children say /d/. Then move your hand from left to right under the word and have children blend and read the word, *kid*. Repeat Steps 1–2 with these words from the *-ock* word family: *rock, sock, lock*. Guide practice and provide corrective feedback.

OPTIONAL
5 mins

High-Frequency Words

 MULTIMODAL

| she | was |

1 **Guided Practice** Display the **High-Frequency Word Cards** *she* and *was*. Then ask children to write the words without looking at the word cards. If needed, guide children on how to form the letter *w* because it has not been taught yet. Then have children self-correct by checking the High-Frequency Word Cards.

2 **Practice** Add *she* and *was* to the cumulative Word Bank.

- Have partners say sentences using the words.

Cumulative Review Review high-frequency words *little, is, with, he, are, my, to, and, go, you,* and *do* by displaying each word and having children read it with automaticity.

- For additional practice with high-frequency words, see **Practice Book** page 266.

ELL ENGLISH LANGUAGE LEARNERS

High-Frequency Words, Practice Help children say *she* and *was* after you. Provide sentence frames and modeling to help children create sentences. *She was in the classroom.*

High-Frequency Words: p. 266

FORMATIVE ASSESSMENT

⊘ STUDENT CHECK-IN

Phonics Have partners blend and read *lock*.

High-Frequency Words Have partners take turns pointing to and reading *she* and *was*.

Then have children reflect using the Check-In routine.

✓ CHECK FOR SUCCESS

Rubric Use your online rubric to record children's progress.

Can children isolate /k/ and match it to the letters *Kk* and *ck*?

Can children read and recognize the high-frequency words?

⊘ Small Group Instruction

If No

● **Approaching** Reteach pp. T380–384

● **ELL** Develop pp. T380–384

If Yes

● **On** Review pp. T388–390

● **Beyond** Extend p. T394

Read "Kim and Nan"

⏱ 10 mins

Connect to Concept

As children read, have them look for details that help them answer the Essential Question: *What happens in different kinds of weather?*

Foundational Skills

Concepts of Print Turn to page 51 and read the first sentence, tracking the print with your finger to help children develop print-to-speech match. Remind children that an exclamation point at the end of a sentence tells us to read the sentence with feeling. Model reading a sentence ending in a period and then one ending in an exclamation point. Have volunteers point to the periods and exclamation points throughout the story.

Phonics Have children review the letter *k* and the /k/ sound.

High-Frequency Words Have children review the words *she* and *was*.

Read the Shared Read

Visualize Remind children that they can use the words and the illustrations in the story to form pictures in their mind. Point out that doing this as they read will deepen their understanding of the story.

Anchor Chart Display and review the Visualize anchor chart. Remind children to stop from time to time as they read to make pictures of story events in their mind.

Choral Read Before reading, invite children to ask questions about what they are about to read. Then have them chorally read the story with you.

Read Tell children that now they will read the story, and you will pause to ask them the questions in the blue column.

Have children use the box on the right-hand pages to do the following:

• Draw a picture about the text or the art.

• Draw something or someone whose name begins or ends with /k/.

• Write the letter *k*.

Reading/Writing Companion, pp. 50–51

SET PURPOSE

Have children read to find out about Kim and Nan.

HIGH-FREQUENCY WORDS

Have children underline and read the words *She* and *was*.

Reading/Writing Companion, pp. 52–53

Reading/Writing Companion, pp. 54–55

Reading/Writing Companion, pp. 56–57

Focus on Fluency: Accuracy

Model reading with accuracy. Remind children of the importance of recognizing high-frequency words and decoding other words in the text correctly. Encourage them to practice reading for accuracy with a partner. Listen in and offer support and corrective feedback.

Respond to the Text

Talk About It Have children talk about what they learned about Kim and Nan and what they like to do. Use this sentence starter to focus the discussion. **Kim and Nan like to_____.** Help children cite text evidence to support their answers.

CONCEPTS OF PRINT

As children read, have them point to the spaces between words in each sentence.

COMPREHENSION

Have children circle the word and picture of the character who sat on the little rock. (Kim)

COMPREHENSION

Have children circle the red sack on page 54.

COMPREHENSION

How do Nan and Kim feel on page 55? (cold) *How do you know?* (Wind is blowing their hair. Nan's arms are crossed. The text says it was not hot.)

VISUALIZE

Picture in your mind what Kim is thinking on page 57. Share what you visualized.

COMPREHENSION

Have children use the text and illustrations to retell the events in the story in order.

ELL ENGLISH LANGUAGE LEARNERS

Use the following scaffolds with **Respond to the Text.**

Beginning
Point to the sun on page 52. *The weather is hot.* Have children point to the image and repeat. *What is the weather?* The weather is hot. Repeat the routine, using *windy* on page 55 and *raining* on page 56.

Intermediate
Point to page 52. *What is the weather?* Give sentence frames to help children respond. The weather is sunny and hot. Repeat with other pages in the story, having children generate words to describe the weather.

Advanced/Advanced High
Encourage children to use complete sentences as they discuss with a partner. Have children point to the images as they discuss weather.

FORMATIVE ASSESSMENT

⊙ STUDENT CHECK-IN

Have partners take turns sharing their retelling of the story with one another. Then have children reflect on their learning using the Check-In routine.

Literature Big Book

OBJECTIVES

Use a combination of drawing, dictating, and writing to compose informative/explanatory texts in which they name what they are writing about and supply some information about the topic.

Write a letter or letters for most consonant and short-vowel sounds (phonemes).

Demonstrate command of the conventions of standard English grammar and usage when writing or speaking.

Capitalize proper nouns.

ELA ACADEMIC LANGUAGE

• text, proper nouns, exact

• Cognate: texto

 **COLLABORATIVE CONVERSATIONS**

Circulate as partners talk about the prompt. Notice who is using incomplete sentences.

---

 10 mins # Interactive Writing

Write About the Literature Big Book

 Analyze the Prompt Tell children that today they will write about the **Literature Big Book**, *Rain*. Ask: *What did the animals enjoy doing after the rain?* Turn to pages 20–21. Have children turn and talk about what the animals like to do after it rains.

Find Text Evidence Reread pages 20–21. Have children identify what the lion does after it rains. (The lion enjoys the shade of the leaves.) Encourage children to use the text and pictures to continue identifying what the animals enjoy doing after it rains.

Write a Response: Share the Pen Have children provide a response to the prompt and encourage them to share the pen to help you write a response. Alternatively, use the sentence on the anchor chart. Then point out the following elements of writing, using the Sample Teacher Talk.

• *We can look at the Word Bank to help us spell the word* the. *Who can point to the word* the? *Let's spell it:* t-h-e. Have a volunteer(s) write *the*. **HIGH-FREQUENCY WORDS**

• Say *lion. What is the first sound we hear? /l/ I know that the letter* l *stands for the /l/ sound. That helps us know* lion *begins with* l. Invite a volunteer to come up and write *lion*. **PHONICS**

• *When we write, we leave spaces between the words.* Ask a child to model placing their finger between words. **WRITING SKILL**

• *When we write, we tell events in sequence, or the order in which they happened. We are writing about what happens after the rain.* **TRAIT: ORGANIZATION**

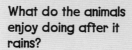

What do the animals enjoy doing after it rains?

After the rain, the lion enjoyed the shade of the leaves.

 ## Writing Practice

Write Provide children with the following sentence starters and have them complete them in their writer's notebook.

The baboons ate _____.   **The zebras _____.**

As children write, encourage them to:

• Use the Word Bank to help spell high-frequency words.

• Identify phonics skills. Stretch the sounds they hear in words as they write.

• Remember to leave a space between words.

• Tell events in sequence, which is the order of how the events happened.

Grammar

5 mins

Proper Nouns

1 **Model** Remind children that exact names are called proper nouns and that they begin with a capital letter. Point out that each child's name is a proper noun and give an example from the class. Say: *This is a girl. Her name is Sofia. The word* girl *is a noun.* Sofia *is a proper noun because it is this person's exact name.* Repeat using the name of your school, the month, and the day of the week.

2 **Guided Practice** Display the illustration on pages 18–19 of the **Big Book**. *This looks like a park.* Write *park* on the board. *The word* park *is not a proper noun because it is not an exact name. It could be any park.* Guide children to think of an exact name for the park and write it on the board. Point out the difference in capitalization. Continue guiding practice with other place names, such as *street* and *library*.

3 **Practice** Have partners write and read aloud: **"We can't see the rain now," said the zebras**. Have partners work together to find the nouns in the sentence. (rain, zebras) *Are* rain *and* zebras *proper nouns?* (No, they do not name something specific.) Then have them give one of the zebras a name. Ask: *Is the zebra's name a proper noun?* (yes) Help children write their name for a zebra, reminding them to use a capital letter. If children need additional practice with proper nouns, have them use Practice Book page 268 or online activities.

Talk About It

Have partners work together to generate sentences with proper nouns. You may wish to have them use these sentence frames:
My friend's name is _____. The name of my city/town is _____.

English Language Learners

Grammar, Practice Help children identify the nouns in the sentence. *Does* rain *name a person, place or thing?* (yes) Rain *is a noun. Does* said *name a person, place, or thing?* (no) Said *is not a noun.* Repeat the routine with *zebras. Should* rain *have a capital letter?* (no) *Why not?* Have children respond: Rain is not a proper noun. Guide partners to give a zebra a name. Help them write the name, pointing out the capital letter.

DIGITAL TOOLS

Grammar Activity

DIFFERENTIATED WRITING

● **English Language Learners** For more writing support, see the **ELL Small Group Guide** p. 146.

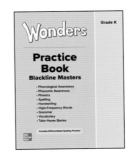

Grammar: p. 286

FORMATIVE ASSESSMENT

STUDENT CHECK-IN

Have partners share a proper noun they learned. Have children reflect using the Check-In routine.

LESSON 3

LEARNING GOALS

We can learn new words.

OBJECTIVES

Use words and phrases acquired through conversations, reading and being read to, and responding to texts.

Identify real-life connections between words and their use.

Develop oral vocabulary.

ELA ACADEMIC LANGUAGE

• *folktale, important*
• Cognate: *importante*

DIGITAL TOOLS

Weekly Song

Visual Vocabulary Cards

Interactive Read Aloud

FORMATIVE ASSESSMENT

❯ STUDENT CHECK-IN

Have partners tell each other the meaning of one vocabulary word. Then have children reflect using the Check-In routine.

LESSON FOCUS

READING
Review Essential Question
Read Interactive Read Aloud
"The Battle of Wind and Rain"
• Practice Strategy
Word Work
• Practice /k/*k* and /k/*ck*

Reread Shared Read
"Kim and Nan"
WRITING
Writing/Grammar
• Independent Writing
• Practice Grammar

Interactive Read-Aloud Cards

Reading/Writing Companion, pp. 50–57

Oral Language

(5 mins)

MULTIMODAL

 Essential Question
What happens in different kinds of weather?

This week we are learning about different kinds of weather. Have children discuss what they have learned about weather. Then sing the **Weekly Song** together.

Oral Vocabulary Words

Remind children that in Lesson 1 they learned the vocabulary words *predict* and *temperature*. Ask: *What can you predict? How does knowing the temperature help us get dressed?* Then use the Define/Example/ Ask routine on the print or digital **Visual Vocabulary Cards** to introduce *drought, clever,* and *storm.*

Oral Vocabulary Routine

<u>Define</u>: A **drought** is a long period of time with no rain.

<u>Example</u>: The drought caused the dirt to dry up and crack.

<u>Ask</u>: Why do people wish for rain during a drought?

<u>Define</u>: If you have a **clever** idea, you have a smart idea.

<u>Example</u>: The clever bird played with the ball.

<u>Ask</u>: What clever idea have you had recently? Explain.

<u>Define</u>: During a **storm**, there are strong winds, heavy rain, or snow.

<u>Example</u>: After the rain storm, there were large puddles in the street.

<u>Ask</u>: What would a town look like after a snow storm?

Visual Vocabulary Cards

Read the Interactive Read Aloud

Connect to Concept

Explain that we will hear a folktale. A folktale is a made-up story told by people long ago. Remind children that we are learning about what happens in different kinds of weather. Use the print or digital **Interactive Read-Aloud Cards**. Read the title.

"The Battle of Wind and Rain"

Set Purpose *Let's read to find out what happens in a contest between the wind and the rain.*

Oral Vocabulary Use the Oral Vocabulary prompts as you read the selection to provide more practice with the words in context.

Unfamiliar Words As you read "The Battle of Wind and Rain," ask children to listen for words they do not understand and to think about what the words might mean. Pause after Card 1 to model.

Teacher Think Aloud *"We're trying to sleep" groaned Thunder.* What is *groaned*? I know that a groan is a sound someone makes when they are upset. I know that *-ed* at the end of a word means that the action happened in the past. *Groaned* must mean that Thunder was upset when he told Wind that they wanted to sleep.

Student Think Along After Card 3: The text said Wind was gasping for breath. What is *gasping*? It said that Wind blew and blew. Then it said that Wind gave up and that he couldn't do it. *Gasping* must be when you breathe fast after working hard.

Build Knowledge: Make Connections

Talk About the Text Have partners share why Rain won the battle. *Do you think wind or rain is more powerful? Why?*

Add to the Anchor Chart Record new ideas on the Build Knowledge anchor chart.

Add to the Word Bank Add new words children learned to a separate section of the Word Bank.

Compare Texts

Guide partners to connect "The Battle of Wind and Rain" with the **Big Book**, *Rain.* Discuss how the rain is represented in each story.

We can listen actively to understand the folktale.

OBJECTIVES

Ask and answer questions about unknown words in a text.

Determine or clarify the meaning of unknown and multiple-meaning words and phrases based on kindergarten reading and content.

With prompting and support, compare and contrast the adventures and experiences of characters in familiar stories.

 SPOTLIGHT ON LANGUAGE

Card 1 *snore*: Explain that a snore is a sound some people make when they sleep. *Have you ever heard someone snore? What does a snore sound like?* Make a snoring sound and have children repeat.

For additional support, see the **ELL Small Group Guide** pp. 142–143.

FORMATIVE ASSESSMENT

◯ STUDENT CHECK-IN

Have partners share the reason why Rain agreed to the contest. Then have children reflect using the Check-In routine.

LESSON 3

Display the Sound-Spelling Card for *k*.

1. **Teacher:** What's the letter?   **Children:** k
2. **Teacher:** What's the sound?   **Children:** /k/
3. **Teacher:** What's the word?   **Children:** koala

Continue the routine for previously taught sounds.

LEARNING GOALS

- We can blend sounds to say words.
- We can blend and read words.

OBJECTIVES

Demonstrate understanding of spoken words, syllables, and sounds (phonemes).

Know and apply grade-level phonics and word analysis skills in decoding words.

Demonstrate basic knowledge of one-to-one letter-sound correspondences by producing the primary sound or many of the most frequent sounds for each consonant.

Spell simple words phonetically, drawing on knowledge of sound-letter relationships.

Blend phonemes to form words.

ELA ACADEMIC LANGUAGE
- *blend, different*

 TEACH IN SMALL GROUP

You may wish to teach the Word Work lesson in small groups.

DIGITAL TOOLS

Word Work

Phonemic Awareness

Phonics

Phonics: Spelling Song

⏱ 5 mins Phonemic Awareness

 MULTIMODAL

Phoneme Blending

1 **Model** Say: *Listen to the sounds in a word: /l/ /o/ /k/. I can blend those sounds to make the word: /llloook/, lock. Listen as I say more sounds and blend them to make words.* Model phoneme blending.

/k/ /i/ /d/ kid   /h/ /a/ /t/ hat   /sp/ /i/ /l/ spill

2 **Guided Practice/Practice** Say: *Listen to the sounds in a different word: /k/ /e/ /n/. Let's blend the sounds and say the word together: /k/ /e/ /n/, /keeennn/ Ken.* Tell children to listen to the sounds in each word below, repeat the sounds, and then blend them to say the word. Guide practice and provide corrective feedback as needed.

/k/ /i/ /i/ kit   /k/ /i/ /k/ kick   /b/ /a/ /k/ back

/l/ /o/ /k/ lock   /k/ /i/ /d/ kid   /k/ /ē/ /p/ keep

 Review initial /k/. Play and sing "Koala." Have children clap when they hear initial /k/. Demonstrate as you sing with children.

⏱ 20 mins Phonics

 MULTIMODAL

Review /k/ *k, ck*

1 **Model** Display **Word-Building Card** for *kick*. Point to *ck*. *These letters are* c *and* k. *Together, they stand for one sound: /k/. When /k/ is at the end of a word, we use* ck *to spell it, as in* kick. *Say /k/. Listen as I say the word* kick. *I will write the letters* c *and* k *because* kick *has the /k/ sound at the end.* Review initial /k/*k* using the same word.

2 **Guided Practice/Practice** Tell children that you will say words with /k/ either at the beginning or at the end. Have children say /k/ and write *k* on their **Response Boards** when they hear /k/ at the beginning of the word and write *ck* when they hear /k/ at the end. Guide practice and provide corrective feedback.

pick	kid	truck	Rick	koala
kitten	track	pack	kiss	kite

Blend Words

1 **Model** Display **Word-Building Cards** *s, i, c, k. This is the letter* s. *It stands for /s/. This is the letter* i. *It stands for /i/. These are the letters* ck. *When these letters are at the end of a word, they stand for /k/. Let's blend the three sounds together: /sssiiik/. The word is* sick. Continue with the following words: *lick, kick, kit.*

2 **Guided Practice/Practice** Write the following words: *sick, tack, kin, kid.* Have children read each word. Guide practice with the first word. Write these sentences and prompt children to read the connected text, sounding out the decodable words: *I am sick in bed. Did Ken pack the map? I see the red rock.*

Spell Words

Dictation Say the word *Kim* and have children repeat. Ask children to say the name *Kim* again, stretching the sounds. You may wish to have children use **Sound Boxes** before they write the word. Then write the word as you say the letter names and have children check their work. Repeat the routine for *kit, tick, tack,* and *rock.* If children need additional spelling practice, use **Practice Book** page 263.

ENGLISH LANGUAGE LEARNERS

Use the following scaffolds with **Phonemic Awareness, Guided Practice/ Practice.**

Beginning

Help children pronounce each sound in words such as *kit, kid,* and *lock.* Blend the sounds in each word with children.

Intermediate

Provide support for children who have difficulty repeating each sound in a word. Then guide children to blend the sounds with you.

Advanced/Advanced High

Encourage children to practice the skill with words they find difficult. Help them self-correct by modeling pronunciation.

CORRECTIVE FEEDBACK

Sound Error Model the sound that children missed when blending words, then have them repeat. For example, for the word *lick,* tap under the letters *ck* and ask: *What's the sound?* Return to the beginning of the word. *Let's start over.* Blend the word with children again. Repeat with words that have /k/ at the beginning of the word.

Phonics/Spelling: p. 263

STUDENT CHECK-IN

Have partners read *rock* and *kick.* Then have children reflect using the Check-In routine.

LESSON 3

- We can sort words that begin or end with /k/.
- We can read sentences with the words *she* and *was*.

OBJECTIVES

Demonstrate basic knowledge of one-to-one letter-sound correspondences by producing the primary sound or many of the most frequent sounds for each consonant.

Read common high-frequency words by sight.

Sort words by initial or final phonemes.

ELA ACADEMIC LANGUAGE

- *sort, spell*

DIGITAL TOOLS

Phonics Activity

To differentiate instruction for key skills, use the results of this activity.

Phonics: Data-Generating

High-Frequency Words: Data-Generating

OPTIONAL 5 mins

MULTIMODAL

Phonics

Picture Sort

1 **Model** Remind children that the letter *k* can stand for /k/. Place the **Word-Building Card** *k* on the left side of a pocket chart.

Hold up the **Photo Card** for *koala. Here is the picture for* koala. Koala *has the /k/ sound at the beginning. I will place* koala *under the letter* k *because the letter* k *stands for /k/.*

Repeat for final /k/ spelled *ck*. Place Word-Building Cards *ck* on the right side of the pocket chart. Use the Photo Card for *lock*.

Photo Cards

2 **Guided Practice/Practice** Have children sort the Photo Cards *kangaroo, king, kite, kitten, rock, sock.* Have them identify /k/ at the beginning or at the end of the word and tell if the photo card should be placed under *k* or *ck*. Guide practice and provide corrective feedback as needed.

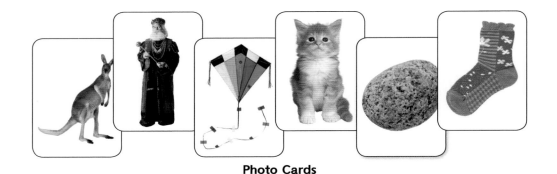

Photo Cards

ELL English Language Learners

Phonics, Guided Practice/Practice Confirm children's understanding that *ck* stands for /k/ in certain words. Say the words with children and help them identify /k/ as the initial or final sound in each. *Is /k/ at the beginning or end of the word* king? (beginning) Use sentence frames to help children tell how they sorted the cards: King begins with the sound /k/. We place king below the letter k.

High-Frequency Words

1 **Guided Practice** Display the **High-Frequency Word Cards** *she* and *was*. Review the words using the Read/Spell/Write routine.

2 **Practice** Point to the High-Frequency Word Cards *she* and *was* and have children read them. Repeat with previous weeks' words *little, is, with, he, are, my, to, and, go, you, do*.

Build Fluency

Word Automaticity Write the following sentences. Have children chorally read them as you track the print. Have them reread the sentences until they can read the words automatically and fluently.

She was sad.

Was the cat on the bed?

Was Bill on the cot?

She can go with you and Kim.

Read for Fluency Distribute **Practice Book** pages 271–272 and help children assemble their Take-Home Books. Chorally read the Take-Home Book with children. Then have children reread the book to review high-frequency words and to build automaticity.

BUILD YOUR WORD BANK

You may wish to use this lesson and the Read/Spell/Write routine to teach additional high-frequency words.

1 **Model** Display the **Build Your Word Bank Cards** for *now, way,* and *under* from the **Practice Book High-Frequency Word Cards**. Use the Read/Spell/Write routine to teach each word.

- **Read** Point to the word *now* and say the word. *This is the word* now. *Say it with me:* now. *I can play* now.
- **Spell** *The word* now *is spelled* n-o-w. *Spell it with me.*
- **Write** *Let's write the word* now *on our* **Response Boards** *as we spell it:* n-o-w.

  Repeat the Read/Spell/Write routine with *way* and *under*.

2 **Guided Practice** Display the Build Your Word Bank Cards for *now, way,* and *under*. Point to each word and have children chorally read it. Then have children take turns using the Build Your Word Bank words in a sentence. Guide practice and provide corrective feedback as needed.

ELL ENGLISH LANGUAGE LEARNERS

High-Frequency Words, Practice Review the correct pronunciation of *she*. Then help children read the word aloud. Give corrective feedback. For additional practice, model simple sentences with the word and have children repeat after you. Repeat with *was*.

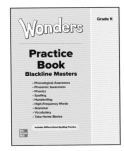

Take-Home Story: pp. 271–272

FORMATIVE ASSESSMENT

❯ STUDENT CHECK-IN

Phonics Have partners think of words that they would add to the word sort.

High-Frequency Words Have partners take turns reading a sentence from the Take-Home Book.

Then have children reflect using the Check-In routine.

✔ CHECK FOR SUCCESS

Rubric Use your online rubric to record progress. Can children identify phonemes and sort words by initial /k/*k* and final /k/*ck*? Can they read the high-frequency words?

❯ Small Group Instruction

If No
- **Approaching** Reteach pp. T380–384
- **ELL** Develop pp. T380–384

If Yes
- **On** Review pp. T388–390
- **Beyond** Extend p. T394

LEARNING GOALS

We can read and understand a story.

OBJECTIVES

Identify the front cover, back cover, and title page of a book.

Demonstrate basic knowledge of one-to-one letter-sound correspondences by producing the primary sound or many of the most frequent sounds for each consonant.

Read common high-frequency words by sight.

Read emergent-reader texts with purpose and understanding.

ELA ACADEMIC LANGUAGE

• *capital letter, punctuation*

• Cognate: *puntuación*

---

10 mins # Reread "Kim and Nan"

Focus on Foundational Skills

Book Handling Demonstrate book handling. Hold up the **Reading/Writing Companion** and point to the front cover. Say: *This is the front cover of the book.* Point to the back cover. *This is the back cover.* Model turning the pages of the book.

Concepts of Print Turn to page 51. Remind children that a sentence begins with a capital letter and ends with a punctuation mark. Point to and read the second sentence. Say: *The word* She *has a capital* S *because it begins the sentence. There is a period at the end of this sentence.* Invite a volunteer to come up and point to the capital letter and the period.

Focus on Comprehension

Reread Guide children to reread the story. Children should sound out the decodable words and read the high-frequency words with automaticity. Encourage them to look for details that they did not notice the first time they read the story.

Encourage children to use the box on the right-hand pages to:

• Draw a picture about the text or the art.

• Draw something or someone whose name begins or ends with /k/.

• Write the letter *k*.

Reading/Writing Companion, pp. 50–51

COMPREHENSION

Who is this story about? (Kim and Nan) *Which character is Kim?* (Kim is the little girl.)

Reading/Writing Companion, pp. 52–53

COMPREHENSION

Where do Kim and Nan go? (to the beach) *Why is Kim wearing a hat?* (to protect her from the sun) *What does Kim do to cool off?* (She drinks lemonade.)

Reading/Writing Companion, pp. 54–55

Reading/Writing Companion, pp. 56–57

COMPREHENSION

What is in Kim's red sack? (food for the birds) *On page 55, how do you know Nan is cold?* (She is folding her arms. The wind is blowing her hair.) *Why do you think it got cold?* (The sun went behind the clouds.)

COMPREHENSION

Why are Nan and Kim running? (It is raining.) *On page 57, what do you think Kim is thinking about?* (Possible response: Her next trip with Nan.)

Focus on Fluency: Accuracy and Rate

Have partners practice reading the story "Kim and Nan" accurately. Encourage them to track the print as they sound out decodable words and read high-frequency words with automaticity. Remind children to pay attention to punctuation marks so that they read senentces with the correct tone. Then have partners read the story again, this time focusing on rate—reading a bit more quickly and making the text sound more like speech.

Listen in: If children struggle with accuracy, have them start again at the beginning of a sentence and correct any errors. If they struggle with rate, model an appropriate rate and have them repeat.

 ## Build Knowledge: Make Connections

Talk About the Text Have partners discuss the different types of weather in the story. *What are some things that Kim and Nan do in the different kinds of weather? What else could they do?*

Write About the Text Have children add their ideas to their reader's notebook.

DECODABLE READERS

Have children read "Pack It, Kim" (pages 13–18) to practice decoding words in connected text.

Unit 6 Decodable Reader

ELL ENGLISH LANGUAGE LEARNERS

Comprehension Point to Kim's pack on page 52. Say *pack* aloud and have children repeat. Pack *has more than one meaning. Here,* pack *is another word for* backpack. Have children point to Kim's pack. Say: Pack *can also mean "put things into a bag or box."* Then use gestures or objects that are available in the classroom to demonstrate the verb *pack.*

⊙ STUDENT CHECK-IN

Have partners share something they learned from the story. Then have children reflect on their learning using the Check-In routine.

LEARNING GOALS

- We can write about the texts we read.
- We can learn about words that tell the exact names of people, places, and things (proper nouns).

OBJECTIVES

Use a combination of drawing, dictating, and writing to narrate a single event or several loosely linked events, tell about the events in the order in which they occurred.

Understand that words are separated by spaces in print.

Write in response to a text.

Capitalize proper nouns.

ELA ACADEMIC LANGUAGE

- *proper noun, exact*

▶ TEACH IN SMALL GROUP

Choose from these options to enable all children to complete the writing activity:

- draw a picture
- complete sentence starters
- write a caption
- write one sentence

For differentiated support, see Writing Skills minilessons on pages T494–T499. These can be used throughout the year.

Independent Writing

5 mins

Write About the Shared Read

Analyze the Student Model Turn to pages 58–59 of the **Reading/Writing Companion**. Read the prompt: *What might Kim and Nan do if it is rainy? Write the next part of their story*. Read aloud and guide children to analyze James' writing.

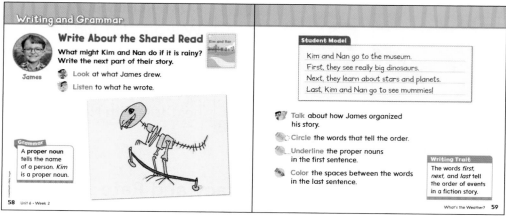

Reading/Writing Companion, pp. 58–59

Write Your Response

Analyze the Prompt. Discuss the prompt on page 58 with children.

Find Text Evidence *Let's look on pages 48–49 to get ideas for our story. What are Kim and Nan doing?* (getting lemonade at the beach) *What might they do on another day?* (go to the park)

Write a Response Have children use the text evidence to draw and write their response. Read the writing checklist aloud and have children check off the items as they include them in their draft.

Reading/Writing Companion, pp. 60–61

Writing Support If needed, provide sentence frames: **First, Kim and Nan go to _____. Next, they _____. Last, Kim and Nan _____.**

Grammar

Proper Nouns

1 **Review** Remind children that exact names begin with a capital letter and are called proper nouns. Write and read aloud the words *boy, school,* and *month.* Explain that these words are not proper nouns. Below each word, write a corresponding proper noun (the name of a boy in the class, the name of the school, and the month). Explain that these words are proper nouns because they name a particular boy, school, and month.

2 **Guided Practice/Practice** Write the following sentence frames and read them aloud: _____ **is in our class. We go to** _____ **together**. Guide children to complete the sentences with you by naming a child in the class and the name of your school. Write the completed sentences, circling the capital letters in the proper nouns.

Have partners work together to complete this sentence frame about each other: **This is** _____ **[name], whose birthday is in** _____. Have them circle the capital letters in the proper nouns.

Talk About It

Have partners work together to generate sentences with proper nouns. Challenge them to identify the letters that should be capitalized in each word.

English Language Learners

Independent Writing, Analyze the Student Model Have children point as they choral read the Student Model. Use the Actor/Action Routine to review the first two sentences. Then guide children to identify the proper nouns. *Clap when you hear a proper noun.* Then review the organization of the story. *How did James organize his story?* Have children respond: James put the events in order. Help children identify the words that tell the order of events. Then have them point to the spaces between the words.

For additional support, refer to the **ELL Small Group Guide** p. 147.

DIGITAL TOOLS

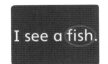

Grammar Activity

FORMATIVE ASSESSMENT

STUDENT CHECK-IN

Have partners share a proper noun they learned. Have children reflect using the Check-In routine.

LESSON 4

LEARNING GOALS

- We can tell if words rhyme.
- We can understand new words.
- We can use words that tell about the weather.
- We can tell about words that mean almost the same thing.

OBJECTIVES

Recognize and produce rhyming words.

Use words and phrases acquired through conversations, reading and being read to, and responding to texts.

Distinguish shades of meaning among verbs describing the same general action by acting out the meanings.

Develop oral vocabulary.

Identify weather words.

ELA ACADEMIC LANGUAGE

- *similar, differences*

DIGITAL TOOLS

Weekly Song

Visual Vocabulary Cards

Category Words Activity

LESSON FOCUS

READING
Review Essential Question
Read/Reread Paired Selection
"Cloud Watch"
Word Work
- Build words with *k, ck*

WRITING
Writing/Grammar
- Independent Writing
- Practice Grammar
Research and Inquiry
- Create Presentation

Literature Big Book, pp. 33–36

---

10 mins

Oral Language

MULTIMODAL

? Essential Question

What happens in different kinds of weather?

Have children discuss what they have learned about different types of weather. Add new ideas to the Build Knowledge anchor chart.

Phonological Awareness: Identify and Produce Rhyme

1 **Model** Point out the rhyming words *away* and *day* in the song "Rain, Rain, Go Away." Say: *Words that rhyme have the same ending sound. Listen:* away, day. *I can say more words that have the same ending sound:* play, say, may, ray.

2 **Guided Practice/Practice** Ask children to listen as you say different word pairs and raise their hand if the words rhyme. Pause between word pairs: *rake/rip; late/wait; seat/some; tip/hip; pan/man.* For each rhyming pair, ask children to name another rhyming word. Guide practice and provide corrective feedback as needed.

Review Oral Vocabulary Words

Use the Define/Example/Ask routine on the print or digital **Visual Vocabulary Cards** to review the words *predict, temperature, storm, clever,* and *drought.* Then prompt children to use the words in sentences.

Visual Vocabulary Cards

Category Words: Weather Words

1 **Explain/Model** Write the following sentence frames. Have children provide a weather word to complete each sentence.

When it rains, we say it is _____. (rainy)

When the sun shines, we say it is _____. (sunny)

When the sky is full of clouds, we say it is _____. (cloudy)

When the wind blows, we say it is _____. (windy)

Discuss each weather word. *What do you do when it is rainy? What does a tree look like on a windy day?*

2 **Guided Practice** Display **Photo Cards** for *October, lightning, quilt, fan, sky, snow, under,* and *kite*. Work with children to make up sentences using Photo Cards and weather words. (Possible response: I use a quilt when it is cold outside.) For additional practice with weather words use **Practice Book** page 267.

Vocabulary: Shades of Meaning

1 **Model** Remind children that words with similar meanings can have small but important differences.

Think Aloud In *Rain,* we read the sentence *It rained until every river gushed and gurgled.* The verbs *gushed* and *gurgled* name two ways the river moved and sounded. *Gushed* tells that the water moved fast, while *gurgled* tells that the water made a bubbling noise.

2 **Guided Practice/Practice** Help children find similar word pairs in *Rain,* such as *sniffed* and *smell, grew* and *sprout.* Have children take turns inserting the pairs of words into the same sentence. Then have them act out the words. Discuss how each word describes the same action in a slightly different way.

English Language Learners

Use the following scaffolds with **Category Words, Guided Practice.**

Say the words on the cards and have children repeat them, pointing to the named image. Then help children create sentences. Use sentence frames and modeling as needed: When it is windy, I can fly a kite/lay under a quilt. When it is hot, I can use a fan. Adjust sentence frames to children's proficiency levels.

KIDS ON THE MOVE!

Play "Simon Says," giving directions that include weather words. For example: *Simon says: Open an umbrella on a rainy day. Simon says: Put on sunglasses on a sunny day.*

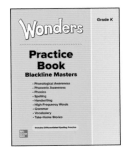

Category Words: p. 267

ELL NEWCOMERS

Use the **Newcomer Online Visuals** and their accompanying prompts to help children expand vocabulary and language about Weather (Unit 1, 9a-f). Use the Conversation Starters, Speech Balloons, and Games in the **Newcomer Teacher's Guide** to continue building vocabulary and developing oral and written language.

FORMATIVE ASSESSMENT

❯ STUDENT CHECK-IN

Oral Vocabulary Words Have partners predict what will happen at school tomorrow.

Category Words Have partners use weather words to tell about their favorite kind of weather.

Vocabulary Strategy Have partners use their hands to demonstrate *little* and *tiny* to show the difference in meaning.

Then have children reflect using the Check-In routine.

Literature Big Book

We can use speech bubbles to learn new information.

OBJECTIVES

Recognize common types of texts.

With prompting and support, retell key details of a text.

Actively engage in group reading activities with purpose and understanding.

Visualize to help with comprehension.

Use speech bubbles to gather information.

ELA ACADEMIC LANGUAGE

• *speech bubbles*

 **SPOTLIGHT ON LANGUAGE**

Page 33 *predict*: Point to the term *predict*. Say: Predict *means "to guess what will happen."* Ask children to predict what the weather will be like today. Provide a sentence frame to help them make their prediction: I predict that it will be <u>sunny</u>. If children are able, ask them to tell why they made their prediction.

 Read

🕐 10 mins

"Cloud Watch"

Text Feature: Speech Bubbles

1 **Explain/Model** Tell children that you will read a nonfiction text about the way clouds look in different types of weather. Explain that the text uses speech bubbles. Speech bubbles contain the exact words a character says. Display page 33 of the **Big Book** and point to the speech bubble on the left. *This is a speech bubble. It tells me what the girl in the picture is saying. I know it is the girl's words because the speech bubble points to her.* Read the speech bubble aloud.

2 **Guided Practice/Practice** Point to the speech bubble on the right. Ask: *Who is saying the words in this speech bubble?* (the dad) Read the speech bubble aloud. *What is the dad telling the girls about?* (the clouds and the weather) Flip through the rest of the text and have a volunteer point to the character who is saying the words in each speech bubble.

Read the Paired Selection

Display the Big Book. Read the title and look at the photo. *What do you predict this book will be about?* Write and display children's predictions.

Set Purpose *Let's read to find out more about clouds and the weather.*

 Read

Literature Big Book, p. 33

VISUALIZE DOK 2

The text says the clouds look like feathers. Close your eyes and think about feathers. What do feathers look like? (a line with other thin lines coming from the sides) *How did you imagine the clouds looked?* (Possible responses: long, skinny, soft, feathery)

Literature Big Book, pp. 34–35

TEXT FEATURE: SPEECH BUBBLES DOK 1

Think Aloud We read the speech bubbles from left to right. On page 35, the first one points to the younger girl. She is worried about Socks, the cat. The second one points to the dad. He is talking about the clouds. The third one points to the older girl. She sees Socks go inside.

Literature Big Book, p. 36

ASK AND ANSWER QUESTIONS DOK 2

The text asks: Can you predict the weather by looking at each cloud? What is your answer? (Yes, the clouds' shapes tell about the kinds of weather to expect.)

Return to Purpose

Read children's predictions. Ask: *Were the predictions correct?* Remind children of their purpose for reading. (to learn more about clouds and the weather) Prompt them to tell what new information they learned from the selection.

Retell

Help children use the pictures and the text to retell important details in the selection. Encourage them to use the vocabulary words they have been learning this week.

Close Reading Routine

Read DOK 1–2

- Identify key ideas and details about different kinds of weather.
- Take notes and retell.
- Use **A C T** prompts as needed.

Reread DOK 2–3

- Analyze the text, craft, and structure.

Integrate DOK 3–4

- Integrate knowledge and ideas.
- Make text-to-text connections.
- Complete the Show Your Knowledge task.
- Inspire action.

FORMATIVE ASSESSMENT

⊘ STUDENT CHECK-IN

Have partners share one thing they learned from a speech bubble. Then have children reflect on their learning using the Check-In routine.

LESSON 4

Literature Big Book

LEARNING GOALS

We can think about how an author uses photos to share information about a text.

OBJECTIVES

With prompting and support, describe the relationship between illustrations and the text in which they appear.

With guidance and support from adults, explore word relationships and nuances in word meanings.

Use words and phrases acquired through conversations, reading and being read to, and responding to texts.

Analyze the author's craft.

ELA ACADEMIC LANGUAGE
• speech bubbles, labels

Reread

"Cloud Watch"

10 mins

Analyze the Text

After children read and retell "Cloud Watch," reread it with them. Use the instructions in the prompts below to help children answer the questions on pages 62–63 in the **Reading/Writing Companion**.

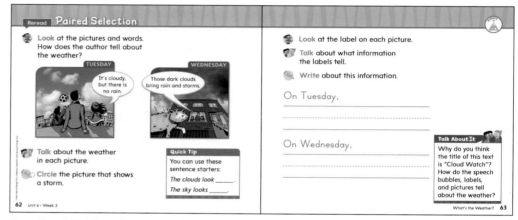

Reading/Writing Companion, pp. 62–63

AUTHOR'S CRAFT DOK 2

• Have children look at the pictures and words on page 62. Ask: *How does the author tell about the weather?* (The author uses pictures and words in speech bubbles. There are also labels.)

• Read the label in the corner of each picture. *What do the labels tell us?* (which day the event is happening) Read page 62 aloud. *What does the speech bubble tell us about Tuesday's weather?* (cloudy, but no rain) *What does the speech bubble tell us about Wednesday's weather?* (Dark clouds bring rain and storms.) *Who is speaking on Wednesday?* (the dad) Have children circle the picture/day that shows a storm. (Wednesday)

• Have children turn to page 63 and complete the sentence starters.

Talk About It

Review page 36 of the **Big Book** with children. *What is this text about?* (different types of clouds) *Why do you think it is called "Cloud Watch"?* (because it tells how clouds help us predict the weather) *How do the speech bubbles, labels, and pictures help us understand the weather in this text?* (The speech bubbles tell what the characters are saying about the weather. The labels tell us about the days of the week. The pictures show us what the clouds look like and how they are different.)

Integrate

 ### Build Knowledge: Make Connections

Talk About the Text Have children discuss what they learned about clouds and weather from the text. *How did the clouds change with the different kinds of weather?*

Add to the Anchor Chart Record any new ideas on the Build Knowledge Anchor Chart.

Add to the Word Bank Record new words on the Word Bank.

ELL English Language Learners

Use the following scaffolds to help children with **Analyze the Text: Author's Craft**

Beginning
Point to the speech bubbles on page 58. *This is a speech bubble. It tells us that someone is talking.* Read it aloud and then ask: *Who is talking?* The girl is talking.

Intermediate
Point to the speech bubbles on page 58 and read them aloud. Ask children to identify who is speaking in each one. Provide sentence frames to help them respond: The girl is talking. *What does she say?* It is cloudy.

Advanced/Advanced High
Point to each speech bubble and ask children to identify who is speaking. Ask additional questions to help children consider how the author uses labels. *What tells you what day it is?* (the labels) Have children point to the labels for Tuesday and Wednesday.

 CONNECT TO CONTENT

Weather Report Review the three kinds of clouds, what they look like, and what kind of weather each brings. (cirrus, feathery, nice weather; cumulus, puffy, cloudy but no rain; cumulonimbus, dark, rain and storms) Have partners look out the window and discuss the clouds they see. Ask: *What kind of weather do you predict?* Have children cite text evidence to support their answers.

STEM

 **FORMATIVE ASSESSMENT**

❯ STUDENT CHECK-IN
Have partners share something they learned from the selection. Then have children reflect on their learning using the Check-In routine.

In a Flash: Sound-Spellings

Display the Sound-Spelling Card for *s*.

1. **Teacher:** What's the letter?	**Children:** s
2. **Teacher:** What's the sound?	**Children:** /s/
3. **Teacher:** What's the word?	**Children:** sun

Continue the routine for previously taught sounds.

LEARNING GOALS

- We can say and count each sound in a word.
- We can build and spell words with *k* and *ck*.
- We can read sentences with the words *she* and *was*.

OBJECTIVES

Isolate and pronounce the initial, medial vowel, and final sounds (phonemes) in three-phoneme words.

Distinguish between similarly spelled words by identifying the sounds of the letters that differ.

Spell simple words phonetically, drawing on knowledge of sound-letter relationships.

Read common high-frequency words by sight.

ELA ACADEMIC LANGUAGE

- *same, different*

▷ TEACH IN SMALL GROUP

You may wish to teach the Word Work lesson in small groups.

DIGITAL TOOLS

Word Work

Phonemic Awareness

Phonics

High-Frequency Words

Visual Vocabulary Cards

---

5 mins — ## Phonemic Awareness

MULTIMODAL

Phoneme Segmentation

1 **Model** Use the **Sound Boxes** and markers. Say: *Listen as I say a word:* kiss. *Say the sounds in* kiss *with me:* /k/ /i/ /s/. *I'll place a marker in a box for each sound:* /k/ /i/ /s/. *There are three sounds in* kiss. Repeat for *luck*.

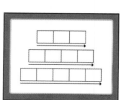

Sound Boxes

2 **Guided Practice/Practice** Distribute Sound Boxes and markers. Have children say each sound in the word as they place a marker in a box. Then have them say the word and tell the number of sounds in the word. Guide children with the first word.

keep /k/ /ē/ /p/	dock /d/ /o/ /k/	Kim /k/ /i/ /m/
key /k/ /ē/	kit /k/ /i/ /t/	sick /s/ /i/ /k/

If children need additional practice segmenting words into phonemes, have them use **Practice Book** page 260.

---

5 mins — ## Phonics

Build and Read Words

Provide children with **Word Building Cards** a–z. Have children put the letters in alphabetical order as quickly as possible.

1 **Guided Practice** Use the **Word-Building Cards** *k, i, t* to form the word *kit*. Have children use their word cards to build the word *kit*. Then say: *I will change the letter* t *in* kit *to* ck *to make the word* kick. Read the new word aloud; then have children read it with you.

2 **Practice** Have children change *kick* to form the word *kiss*. Have them tell which letters are the same and which letters are different and how the word changes. Have them continue changing letters to form *kit, lit, lick,* and *sick*. Then have children list the words and work with a partner to correct any errors they made when encoding.

If children need additional practice building words, have them use **Practice Book** page 264.

Spell Words

Dictation Dictate each of these sounds: /b/, /l/, /f/, /r/, /i/, /t/, /k/. Have children repeat the sound and then write the letter that stands for the sound.

Dictate the following words for children to spell: *kit, kid, sick, back,* and *snack.* Model how to segment each word to scaffold the spelling.

When I say the word kit, *I hear three sounds:* /k/ /i/ /t/. *I know the letter* k *stands for* /k/, *the letter* i *stands for* /i/, *and the letter* t *stands for* /t/. *I will write the letters* k, i, t *to spell* kit. Write the letters and words for children to self-correct.

High-Frequency Words

Practice Say *she* and *was* and have children write them. Then display the print or digital **Visual Vocabulary Cards** for *she* and *was.* Follow the Teacher Talk routine on the back.

Visual Vocabulary Cards

Build Fluency Build sentences in a pocket chart using **High-Frequency Word Cards** and **Photo Cards.** Use index cards to create punctuation cards for a period and a question mark. Have children chorally read the sentences as you track the print. Then have them identify the words *she* and *was.*

She can see the balloon.   **Was she with you?**

The kitten was with you.

The [image] was little .

Have partners say sentences using the words *she* and *was.*

High-Frequency Word Hopscotch Activity Use the High-Frequency Word Cards or index cards to create a hopscotch course. Have children toss a marker and hop to the word, saying each word along the way. You may wish to create a hopscotch course with chalk outside as weather permits.

DECODABLE READERS

Have children read "Kick It, Nick!" (pages 19–24).

Unit 6 Decodable Reader

Phonemic Awareness: p. 260
Phonics: p. 264

❯ STUDENT CHECK-IN

Phonics Have partners use Word-Building Cards to spell and read *kid* and *deck.*

High-Frequency Words Have partners read a sentence from the lesson.

Then have children reflect using the Check-In routine.

✓ CHECK FOR SUCCESS

Rubric Use your online rubric to record children's progress.

Can children blend words with /k/ and match it with *Kk* and *ck*?

Can children read and recognize high-frequency words?

❯ Small Group Instruction

If No
- **Approaching** Reteach pp. T380–384
- **ELL** Develop pp. T380–384

If Yes
- **On** Review pp. T388–390
- **Beyond** Extend p. T394

- We can revise our writing.
- We can learn about words that are names of people and places (proper nouns).

OBJECTIVES

With guidance and support from adults, respond to questions and suggestions from peers and add details to strengthen writing as needed.

Capitalize the first word in a sentence.

Produce and expand complete sentences in shared language activities.

Demonstrate command of the conventions of standard English capitalization, punctuation, and spelling when writing.

Capitalize proper nouns.

ELA ACADEMIC LANGUAGE

- *revise, edit, proper noun, exact*
- Cognates: *revisar, editar*

 Independent Writing

5 mins

Write About the Shared Read

 Revise

Reread the prompt about "Kim and Nan" on page 60 of the **Reading/ Writing Companion**: *What might Kim and Nan do on another day?* Have children read their drafts to think about how they would revise their writing. Then have them check to see if they responded to the prompt by telling events in order, using proper nouns, and leaving a space between words.

Peer Review Have partners review each other's writing. Children should share what they like most, questions they have for the author, and additional ideas they think the author could include. Provide time for children to make revisions and add details to strengthen their writing.

Edit/Proofread

After children have revised their work, have them edit the work carefully, checking for the following:

- Use a capital letter at the beginning of each sentence.
- Make sure your sentences tell a complete thought.

If children need additional practice with editing and proofreading, have them use **Practice Book** page 270.

 Write Final Draft

After children have edited their writing and finished their peer review, have them write their final draft in their writer's notebook. Tell children to write neatly so that others can read their writing or guide them to explore a variety of digital tools they can use to publish their work.

Teacher Conference As children review their drafts, confer with them to provide guidance. Suggest places in their writing where they might add details or a proper noun.

 Share and Evaluate

After children have finalized their draft, have them work with a partner to practice presenting their writing. Remind children to speak in complete sentences. If possible, record children as they share so that they can see themselves presenting or you can use the recording as a topic of discussion during a teacher conference.

Have children add their work to their writing folder. Invite them to look at their previous writing and discuss with a partner how it has improved.

Grammar

5 mins

Proper Nouns

1 **Review** Remind children that exact names are called proper nouns and begin with a capital letter. Display the October **Photo Card**. Say: *The word* month *is a noun. The word* October *is a proper noun because it is the name of a specific month.* Write *month* and *October*. Underline the capital letter in *October*.

2 **Guided Practice/Practice** Display the *dog* Photo Card. Guide children to help you complete the sentence frames: **A _____ is a kind of animal. _____ is the name of a pet.** Write *dog* in the first blank and a dog's name in the second blank. Point out that the name is a proper noun and begins with a capital letter. Repeat with the *rabbit* Photo Card.

Display the *boy, girl, cowboy,* and *doctor* Photo Cards. Have partners choose a card to complete this sentence: **A _____ is a person.** Have them make up a name for the person and use it to complete a second sentence frame: **Her name is _____. His name is _____.** Remind children to capitalize the proper noun. If children need additional practice with proper nouns, have them use **Practice Book** page 269 or online activities.

Talk About It

Have partners create sentences with proper nouns. Then have them identify the proper nouns they used. Provide modeling if necessary.

English Language Learners

Use the following scaffolds with **Independent Writing, Revise**.

Beginning
Review *first, next,* and *last*. If necessary, help children add these words to their sentences and capitalize proper nouns.

Intermediate
Help children check that they have written events in correct order. *Did you use words to tell which event happened first, next, and last?*

Advanced/Advanced High
Challenge children to identify the words they used to show the order of events. Then have them circle proper nouns they used and check for capital letters.

For additional support, see the **ELL Small Group Guide** p. 147.

DIGITAL TOOLS

Grammar Activity

Grammar: p. 269
Edit/Proofread: p. 270

FORMATIVE ASSESSMENT

STUDENT CHECK-IN
Have partners share a proper noun they learned. Have children reflect using the Check-In routine.

LESSON 4

 10 mins

Different Kinds of Weather

LEARNING GOALS

We can research about a kind of weather.

OBJECTIVES

With guidance and support from adults, recall information from experiences or gather information from provided sources to answer a question.

Add drawings or other visual displays to descriptions as desired to provide additional detail.

Produce and expand complete sentences in shared language activities.

Follow agreed-upon rules for discussions.

Participate in shared research and writing projects.

ELA ACADEMIC LANGUAGE

• *temperature*

COLLABORATIVE CONVERSATIONS

Listen Carefully As children engage in partner and group discussions, encourage them to do the following:

• Look at the person who is speaking.

• Listen to what the speaker is saying.

• Respect others by not interrupting them.

• Repeat classmates' ideas to check understanding.

Model

Tell children that they will research about a kind of weather. Display pages 64–65 of the **Reading/Writing Companion**. Model completing each step in the research process.

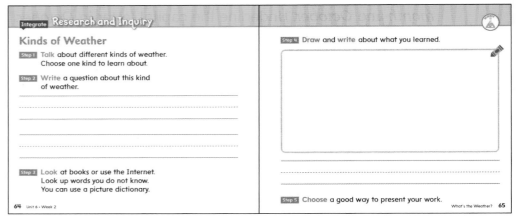

Reading/Writing Companion, pp. 64–65

STEP 1 Choose a Topic

First, I need to think about a type of weather I would like to learn more about. Winter is my favorite season, so I am going to research snow.

STEP 2 Write Your Question

I need to decide what I want to learn about snow. I would like to know what temperature it has to be outside for it to snow.

STEP 3 Find Information

To find the answer to my question, I'll do research by looking in books. I can also use weather websites on the Internet to find information.

STEP 4 Draw and Write What You Learned

I can draw a picture showing what I learned. I will also include a picture of a thermometer to show the temperature it needs to be for it to snow.

STEP 5 Choose a Way to Present Your Work

I will create a poster showing things people can do when it snows.

Apply

Have children turn to page 64 in their **Reading/Writing Companion**. Guide them through the steps of the research process.

Choose the Presentation Format

Have children turn to pages 64-65 in their **Reading/Writing Companion** to review their research, their drawing, and what they learned about a type of weather. Tell them that today they are going to take the next step by creating their finished product, which they will present the next day. Help children select an appropriate mode of delivery for their presentation. Options may include drawing and labeling a picture, creating a poster, making a model, or putting on a dramatic presentation.

Create the Presentation

Guide children to develop their presentation individually, in teams, or as a class. Remind them of the rules of working with others.

Gather Materials Gather the materials children will need to create their finished product. Most of the materials should be available in the classroom or can be brought from home.

Make the Finished Product Once children have the materials they need, provide time for them to create their finished product. You can dedicate an area in the classroom for project work and store all the materials there. Remind children that they will present their work to their classmates the next day.

English Language Learners

Apply, Step 4 Model drawing a picture of snow as described in Model, Step 4. Check understanding of *rain, snow, wind,* and *sunny*. Then work with children to help them identify the elements to include in their picture. For example, *I will draw rain. I will draw a person with an umbrella standing in the rain.* Allow children to work together to talk about weather and what they will draw. Monitor children as they work, prompting them with questions and sentence frames as needed.

 TEACH IN SMALL GROUP

You may wish to have children create their presentation during Small Group time. Group children of varying abilities or those doing similar projects.

 CONNECT TO CONTENT

What's the Forecast? Explain that a meteorologist is a weather scientist. Meteorologists study the weather closely. They use special tools to help them predict the weather. Have children watch a weather report on television. Encourage them to pay close attention to the different tools the meteorologist uses in the report. Ask: *What do the different tools do?* **STEM**

RESEARCH AND INQUIRY: SHARING FINAL PROJECTS

As children get ready to wrap up the week, have them share their Research and Inquiry project. Then have them self-evaluate.

Prepare Have children gather any materials they need to present their Research and Inquiry project. Have partners practice their presentations.

Share Guide children to present their Research and Inquiry project. Encourage children to speak in complete sentences.

Evaluate Have children discuss and evaluate their own presentation. You may wish to have them complete the online Student Checklist.

FORMATIVE ASSESSMENT

STUDENT CHECK-IN

Have partners share one thing about the weather they researched. Have children reflect using the Check-In routine.

LESSON 5

LEARNING GOALS

- We can say and count each sound in a word.
- We can spell words with the letters *k* and *ck*.
- We can spell the words *she* and *was*.

OBJECTIVES

Isolate and pronounce the initial, medial vowel, and final sounds (phonemes) in three-phoneme words.

Demonstrate basic knowledge of one-to-one letter-sound correspondences by producing the primary sound or many of the most frequent sounds for each consonant.

Spell simple words phonetically, drawing on knowledge of sound-letter relationships.

Read common high-frequency words by sight.

ELA ACADEMIC LANGUAGE

- *count, sounds*

 **TEACH IN SMALL GROUP**

You may wish to teach this lesson in small groups.

DIGITAL TOOLS

 Word Work — Phonemic Awareness

 Visual Vocabulary Cards

 Phonics: Spelling Song

LESSON FOCUS

READING
Wrap Up
Word Work
- Read Words

Writing/Grammar
- Self-Selected Writing
- Review Grammar

WRITING
Research and Inquiry
- Share and Evaluate Presentation

Text Connections
- Connect Essential Question to a photo
- Show Your Knowledge

Reading/Writing Companion pp. 66–67

---

 5 mins

Phonemic Awareness

 MULTIMODAL

Phoneme Segmentation

1 **Model** Use the **Sound Boxes** and markers. Say: *Listen to this word:* kit. *There are three sounds in* kit. *Listen to the sounds in* kit: /k/ /i/ /t/. *I'll place one marker for each sound in the Sound Box:* /k/ /i/ /t/. Repeat for the three sounds in *pick*.

2 **Guided Practice/Practice** Distribute Sound Boxes and markers. Have children say each sound in the word as they place a marker in a box. Then have them say the word and tell the number of sounds in the word. Guide practice and provide corrective feedback as needed.

Ken, /k/ /e/ /n/	sock, /s/ /o/ /k/	Dan, /d/ /a/ /n/
key, /k/ /ē/	keep, /k/ /ē/ /p/	kite, /k/ /ī/ /t/

---

 5 mins

Phonics

 MULTIMODAL

Read Words

1 **Guided Practice** Remind children that the letter *k* and the letters *ck* together stand for /k/. Display **Word-Building Cards** *p, a, c, k*. Point to the letter *p*. *The letter* p *stands for* /p/. *Say* /p/. *The letter* a *stands for* /a/. *Say* /aaa/. *The letters* ck *together stand for* /k/. *Say* /k/. *Let's blend the letters to make the word:* /paaak/ pack. *Now let's change* p *to* b. Blend *back* with children. Repeat with *kid*.

2 **Practice** Write these words and sentences for children to read: *pick, peck, kid, Ken; Mack is at the dock.; Ken is sick in bed.; Can you sit on the deck?* Remove words from view before dictation.

♪ Review initial /k/k. Have children write *k* on their **Response Boards**. Play and sing "Koala." Have them hold up and show *k* on their board when they hear initial /k/. Demonstrate as you sing with children.

In a Flash: Sound-Spellings

Display the Sound-Spelling Card for *k*.

1. **Teacher:** What's the letter?   **Children:** k
2. **Teacher:** What's the sound?   **Children:** /k/
3. **Teacher:** What's the word?   **Children:** koala

Continue the routine for previously taught sounds.

Spell Words

MULTIMODAL

Dictation Dictate the following sounds. Say each sound, have children repeat it, and then write the letter that stands for it.

/b/   /l/   /f/   /r/   /e/   /h/   /k/

Dictate the following words. Model how to use **Sound Boxes** to segment each word. *I will say a word. You will repeat the word and then think about how many sounds are in it. Use your Sound Boxes to count the sounds. Write a letter or letters for each sound.*

sack   kit   dock   Kim   pick   back   stack

Then write the letters and words for children to self-correct.

High-Frequency Words

MULTIMODAL

⏱ 5 mins

1 **Review** Display the print or digital **Visual Vocabulary Cards** *she* and *was*. Read the sentences and have children point to *she* and *was*. Have children Read/Spell/Write the words. Choose a Partner Talk Activity.

Visual Vocabulary Cards

Distribute **High-Frequency Word Cards**:
she, was, little, is, he, are, my. Tell children that you will say sentences. *When you hear a word that is on your card, stand and hold up your card.*

My umbrella *is* blue.	*He* has big yellow rain boots.
The dog is *with* me.	*She* was afraid of the storm.
I *was* late for school.	A *little* ray of sun shone.

2 **Build Fluency: Word Automaticity** Display High-Frequency Word Cards *little, is, with, he, she, was.* Point to each card and have children read as quickly as they can to build automaticity.

⦿ MULTIMODAL LEARNING

Color Coding After each dictation, reveal the secret color-coding-letter(s) for children to find on their response board. Have them say the sound(s) as they trace each letter in color. Use one or two of the phonics skills of the week for color coding.

ⓔ ENGLISH LANGUAGE LEARNERS

High-Frequency Words, Review Guide children to differentiate between /s/ and /sh/. Demonstrate the correct mouth and tongue position for each sound. Then model saying each sound and have children repeat. Have children practice saying these sentences: *She has a dog named Sandy. She was here today.*

FORMATIVE ASSESSMENT

❯ STUDENT CHECK-IN

Phonics Have partners spell *lock* and *kick*.

High-Frequency Words Have partners spell the words *she* and *was*.

Then have children reflect using the Check-In routine.

✓ CHECK FOR SUCCESS

Rubric Use your online rubric to record children's progress.

Can children read and decode words with /k/k, ck? Can children read and recognize high-frequency words?

❱ Small Group Instruction

If No

● **Approaching** Reteach pp. T454–458

● **ELL** Develop pp. T454–458

If Yes

● **On** Review pp. T462–464

● **Beyond** Extend p. T468

LEARNING GOALS

- We can choose a writing activity and share it.
- We can learn about words that are names of people and places (proper nouns).

OBJECTIVES

With guidance and support from adults, explore a variety of digital tools to produce and publish writing, including in collaboration with peers.

Speak audibly and express thoughts, feelings, and ideas clearly.

Ask and answer questions in order to seek help, get information, or clarify something that is not understood.

Demonstrate command of the conventions of standard English capitalization, punctuation, and spelling when writing.

Capitalize proper nouns.

ELA ACADEMIC LANGUAGE

- *article, poem, proper noun, exact*
- Cognate: *poema*

⏵ DIFFERENTIATED WRITING

You may wish to conference with children to provide additional support for the writing activities below:

- Newspaper Article: Have partners ask and answer *What? Where?* and *When?* questions about their weather event before writing.

- Poem: Have children write the name of their type of weather. Then provide sentence frames for each sense: **See _____, Hear _____, Smell _____, Feel _____.**

Self-Selected Writing

5 mins

Talk About the Topic

Have children continue the conversation about weather. Remind them of the Essential Question: *What happens in different kinds of weather?* Encourage them to share with a partner something they learned this week about different kinds of weather.

Choose a Writing Activity

Tell children they will choose what type of writing to do. They may choose to write about weather or about a different topic. Have them work in their writer's notebook. Encourage them to draw first to get their ideas down on paper. Children may choose from the following modes of writing:

Newspaper Article Explain that a newspaper article gives information about a real event. Display examples of age-appropriate newspaper articles. Have children recall a recent weather event. Tell them they can write and illustrate an article to inform people about *when* it happened, *where* it happened, and *what* happened, making sure to tell events in order.

Poem Explain that a sensory poem is a poem that uses our senses to describe something. Show a model sensory poem: *Thunderstorm / Smell rain / Feel wind / See clouds / Hear thunder.* Guide children to think of a kind of weather they want to describe and the things they see, hear, feel, and smell during that kind of weather.

Use Digital Tools You may wish to work with children to explore a variety of digital tools to produce or publish their work.

Share Your Writing

Invite volunteers to share their writing with the class or have partners share. Remind children to use the strategies below as they share. After children share, you may wish to display their work on a bulletin board or in a classroom writing area.

SPEAKING STRATEGIES	LISTENING STRATEGIES
✓ Wait until it is your turn to speak.	✓ Listen actively and quietly.
✓ Answer listeners' questions in complete sentences.	✓ Ask a question if you did not understand something.

Grammar

Proper Nouns

1 **Review** Remind children that exact names are called proper nouns and that they begin with a capital letter. Say: *I want to write,* Suma will have a party in May at Splash Water Park. *I know* Suma *is an exact name, so I will start with a capital* S. Repeat with the other proper nouns as you write the sentence.

2 **Guided Practice/Practice** Write these sentence frames: **My name is ____. I was born in ____. I live in ____.** Guide volunteers to complete the sentences with their name, the month they were born, and the town where they live. Read the completed sentences. Have volunteers circle the capital letters in the proper nouns.

Display the sentences below and read them aloud. Prompt children to reread them with you chorally. Have children work with a partner to identify the proper nouns.

Goose Toy Store always has a big sale in June.
Bradley, Joy, and Ming walk to school.
Mr. Gonzalez teaches at Oak Avenue School.

English Language Learners

Self-Selected Writing, Choose a Writing Activity Present the writing activities. Tell children that they will vote to select one of the activities and then you will work on the writing as a group. Make sure to do the activity on chart paper as you will revise and publish it during small group time. Provide sentence frames and starters as you talk through the writing together. For example, if children have selected writing a newspaper article about a weather event, then ask *when/where/what* questions about the event. Possible sentence frames are: On [date], there was a ____ in ____. There was so much ____ that ____. Everyone was ____. Schools had to ____.

For additional support, see the **ELL Small Group Guide** p. 147.

DIGITAL TOOLS

Grammar Activity

⊳ TEACH IN SMALL GROUP

You may wish to review the grammar skill during Small Group time.

● **Approaching** Provide more opportunities for children to practice identifying proper nouns before they write sentences.

●● **On-Level** and **Beyond** Children can do the Practice sections only.

● **ELL** Use the chart in the **Language Transfers Handbook** to identify grammatical structures that may cause difficulty.

FORMATIVE ASSESSMENT

⊗ STUDENT CHECK-IN

Have partners share which activity they chose and tell why. Have children reflect using the Check-In routine.

LESSON 5

We can compare texts we have read.

OBJECTIVES

Confirm understanding of a text read aloud or information presented orally or through other media by asking and answering questions about key details and requesting clarification if something is not understood.

ELA ACADEMIC LANGUAGE

• *compare, experience*
• Cognate: *comparar*

Close Reading Routine

Read   DOK 1–2

• Identify key ideas and details.
• Take notes and retell.
• Use (A)(C)(T) prompts as needed.

Reread   DOK 2–3

• Analyze the text, craft, and structure.

Integrate   DOK 3–4

• Integrate knowledge and ideas.
• Make text-to-text connections.
• Use the Integrate lesson.
• Complete the Show Your Knowledge task.

❯ STUDENT CHECK-IN

Have partners share what they learned from comparing texts.

Have children reflect using the Check-In routine.

Integrate

⏱ 10 mins

Make Connections

Connect to the Essential Question

COLLABORATE

Review the Essential Question. Turn to page 66 of the **Reading/Writing Companion**. Have children look at the photo. What clues tell them about the weather?

Reading/Writing Companion, p. 66

Find Text Evidence Have children answer the following questions about this page and about the **Big Book**: *How is the weather the same?* (It's hot.) *How is it different?* (It rains in the book.) Use the Quick Tip box for support.

Record Ideas Guide partners to compare the photo on page 66 of the Reading/Writing Companion with the story *Rain. How are they alike? How are they different? How do they help you answer the Essential Question?* Help children use a Two-Tab Foldable® to record their ideas. Have them support their ideas with evidence from the photo and story.

Dinah Zike's
FOLDABLES
Study Organizer

Build Knowledge: Make Connections DOK 4

Talk About the Text Have partners compare the text with experiences from their own lives.

Add to the Anchor Chart Record any new ideas on the Build Knowledge anchor chart.

Integrate

Show Your Knowledge

15 mins

Write a Weather Forecast DOK 4

Display the texts for the week, along with the Build Knowledge anchor chart and Word Bank. Turn to page 67 of the **Reading/ Writing Companion** and guide children through the steps below.

1. Think Ask: *What did you learn about what happens in different kinds of weather?* Encourage partners to refer to their reader's notebook and the resources on display as they discuss their response.

2. Draw Guide children to discuss what the weather has been like this week. Have them predict what the weather will be like tomorrow and create a drawing that reflects their prediction.

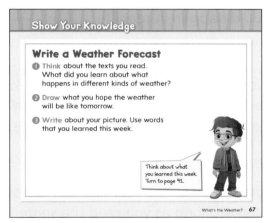

Reading/Writing Companion, p. 67

3. Write Tell children to write the weather word that matches their prediction on their drawing. Encourage them to reference the Word Bank and use words they learned this week. Collect the drawings and post them on a "Weather Forecast" bulletin board.

Inspire Action

Weather Reporter Invite children to pretend to be weather reporters by announcing upcoming weather on the "Weather Forecast" bulletin. Encourage audience members to ask questions.

Weather Forecast Ask: *How can we learn what the weather is supposed to be like tomorrow?* Show children actual weather reports and interviews and discuss what they noticed.

Choose Your Own Action Have children talk about the texts they read this week. *What do the texts inspire or make you want to do?*

Lexile BR

OBJECTIVES

Recognize that spoken words are represented in written language by specific sequences of letters.

With prompting and support, identify characters, settings, and major events in a story.

Read emergent-reader texts with purpose and understanding.

With prompting and support, retell familiar stories, including key details.

ELA ACADEMIC LANGUAGE

• *fiction, characters, illustrations*
• Cognates: *ficción, ilustraciones*

● Approaching Level

Leveled Reader *The Rain*

Preview and Predict

Read the title and the names of the author and illustrator as children follow along in their copies of the book. Ask children to tell what they see on the cover and what they think the story will be about. Preview the illustrations throughout the book and ask children to describe what they see. Ask: *What kind of weather is it? How do you think the children feel?*

Review Genre: Fiction

Explain to children that they have read fantasy this week and now they will read fiction. Remind them that in fiction the characters, events, and settings are made up. Unlike fantasy, events in fiction could happen in real life.

Set Purpose

Remind children of the Essential Question: *What happens in different kinds of weather?* Help children set a purpose for reading: *Let's read to find out what happens when it rains.* Review rebuses to help children name the words.

Foundational Skills

Model Concepts of Print Have children point to the first and last words in the sentence on page 2. Have them follow along as you read the sentence. Ask children to try and match the words you say with the words on the page.

Review High-Frequency Words Point to the high-frequency word *was* on each page of the story. Then ask children to say the word *was* aloud each time they see it on a new page.

Guided Comprehension

As children read *The Rain*, monitor and provide guidance by offering support and corrective feedback as needed. Model visualizing and identifying the sequence of events where applicable.

Visualize

Remind children that as they read, they can make pictures in their mind of what is happening in the story.

Events: Sequence

Remind children that finding details in a story will help them understand what is happening and the order of the events. Explain that, in this book, the illustrations provide details about the sequence of the story.

Think Aloud As I read pages 2 and 3, I see that the rain starts out as a few drops on page 2. On page 3, there are more drops. The text tells me that the dog and the chick are fast. I will keep reading to see what happens next.

Point out that the rain keeps getting harder and that it is a detail shown in the illustrations. Guide children to talk about which animals run from the rain first. Explain that each page shows another detail about the rainstorm.

Respond to the Text

Have children respond to the text by discussing these questions:

- *What happens as the rain comes closer and gets heavier?* (The dog, chick, mouse, girl, boy, and duck run to get away from the rain.)

- *Which animal runs from the rain first? Next?* (first the dog and then the chick)

- *What happens at the end of the story?* (It is raining hard.)

Retell Have children take turns retelling the story, including characters, setting, and events. Help them make a personal connection by asking: *Have you ever been caught in the rain? What happened?*

Focus on Fluency

Practice fluency with children. Remember that children need to read with accuracy first.

Once children have read the text with accuracy, have them read the story again, focusing on rate. Have them practice reading with partners. Provide corrective feedback as necessary.

Build Knowledge: Make Connections

- **Talk About the Texts** Have partners discuss different kinds of weather.
- **Write About the Texts** Then have children add their ideas to the Build Knowledge page of their Reader's Notebook.

LITERACY ACTIVITIES

Have children complete the Collaborate and Write About It activities on the inside back cover of the book.

LITERATURE CIRCLES

Lead children in a literature circle, using these questions to guide the discussion: *Who ran away from the rain in the story? Do you run when it is raining? Why or why not?*

LEVEL UP

IF Children read *The Rain* Approaching Level with fluency and correctly answer the Respond to the Text questions,

THEN Tell children that they will read another story about what happens in different kinds of weather.

- Have children page through *Weather Is Fun* On Level and make connections to what they know about things we do in different weather.

- Have children read the story, monitoring their comprehension and providing assistance as necessary.

●Approaching Level

Phonological/Phonemic Awareness

RECOGNIZE RHYME

OBJECTIVES
Recognize rhyming words.

I Do Remind children that words that rhyme have the same ending sounds. Tell them that in "Rain, Rain, Go Away," the words *away* and *day* rhyme. Say the words and have children repeat them with you. *The word* say *also rhymes with* away *and* day. *Say the words with me:* away, day, say.

We Do Say the following word pairs and guide children to say whether the words rhyme: *bake, lake; sand, Sam; jump, thump; vest, pest; skin, skip.*

You Do *I'll say some word pairs. Give a thumbs up if the words rhyme:* fish, dish; Tim, tip; tug, ton; hall, fall; patch, scratch; wrong, strong.

PHONEME ISOLATION

OBJECTIVES
Isolate and pronounce the initial sounds (phonemes) in words.

I Do Display the *koala* **Photo Card**. *This is a* koala. *The first sound in* koala *is /k/. Say the word and the beginning sound with me:* koala, /k/.

We Do Display the *kitten* Photo Card. *This is a* kitten. Have children say the name. *What is the first sound in* kitten? Say /k/ together. Repeat with the *key* Photo Card.

You Do Display and name the *king* Photo Card. Have children name it and say the initial sound. Repeat with the *kite* Photo Card.

Repeat the routine for final /k/ spelled *ck* using the *rock* Photo Card in *I Do* and the Photo Cards for *lock* and *sock* in the rest of the lesson.

> **ELL** You may wish to review phonological awareness, phonics, decoding, and fluency using this section. Use scaffolding methods as necessary to ensure children understand the meaning of the words. Refer to the **Language Transfers Handbook** for phonics elements that may not transfer in children's native languages.

PHONEME BLENDING

OBJECTIVES

Demonstrate understanding of spoken words, syllables, and sounds (phonemes).

Blend phonemes to make words.

I Do *Listen as I say the sounds in a word: /k/ /ī/ /t/. I will blend the sounds to make a word: /kīīīt/, kite. I blended the sounds /k/ /ī/ /t/ to make the word kite. Repeat with kit.*

We Do *Listen as I say the sounds in a word: /k/ /i/ /m/. Have children repeat. Now let's blend the sounds and say the word together: /kiiimmm/, Kim. Repeat with kid.*

You Do Say the following sounds. Ask children to blend the sounds and say the words: /k/ /ē/ /p/, /kēēēp/, keep; /k/ /i/ /s/, /kiiisss/, kiss.

Repeat the routine for final /k/ spelled ck using these words: tack, /t/ /a/ /k/; sick, /s/ /i/ /k/; deck, /d/ /e/ /k/.

You may wish to use a puppet, if one is available, for the *I Do* and *We Do* parts of this lesson.

PHONEME SEGMENTATION

OBJECTIVES

Isolate and pronounce the initial, medial vowel, and final sounds in three-phoneme words.

I Do Use **Sound Boxes** and markers. *Listen as I say a word:* kit. *There are three sounds in* kit: /k/ /i/ /t/. *I'll place a marker in one box for each sound.* Repeat for the word keep.

We Do Distribute Sound Boxes and markers. *Let's listen for the number of sounds in more words. Listen as I say a word:* key. *Say the word with me:* key. *Say the sounds with me:* /k/ /ē/. *Let's place a marker in one box for each sound. There are two sounds in* key. Repeat with kin.

You Do Repeat the practice with the following words: kiss, /k/ /i/ /s/; kite, /k/ /ī/ /t/; Ken, /k/ /e/ /n/.

Repeat the routine for final /k/ spelled ck, using the sounds in these words: lick, /l/ /i/ /k/; sack, /s/ /a/ /k/; peck, /p/ /e/ /k/; tuck, /t/ /u/ /k/.

● Approaching Level

Phonics

SOUND-SPELLING REVIEW

OBJECTIVES
Demonstrate basic knowledge of one-to-one letter-sound correspondences by producing the primary sound or many of the most frequent sounds for each consonant.

> **I Do** Display **Word-Building Card** *l*. Say the letter name and the sound it stands for: *l, /l/*. Repeat for *b, f, r, e, h*.

> **We Do** Display Word-Building Cards one at a time and together say the letter name and the sound that the letter stands for.

> **You Do** Display Word-Building Cards one at a time and have children say the letter name and the sound that the letter stands for.

CONNECT *k* AND *ck* TO /k/

OBJECTIVES
Demonstrate basic knowledge of one-to-one letter-sound correspondences by producing the primary sound or many of the most frequent sounds for each consonant.

> **I Do** Display the *koala* **Sound-Spelling Card**. *The letter* k *stands for /k/ at the beginning of* koala. *What is this letter? What sound does it stand for? I will write* k *when I hear /k/ in these words:* kangaroo, lion, Ken, flash, kazoo.

> **We Do** *The word* keep *begins with /k/. Let's write* k. Guide children to write *k* when they hear a word that begins with /k/: *leaf, kept, kitten, fudge, Kansas.*

> **You Do** Have children write *k* if a word begins with /k/: *fish, kettle, kind, rope, king.*
>
> Repeat the routine for final /k/ spelled *ck*. Use the *lock* Sound-Spelling Card and the words *hack, ham, base, black, pack, page, stack, stove, brick, band.*

BLEND WORDS WITH /k/ *k, ck*

OBJECTIVES
Know and apply grade-level phonics and word analysis skills in decoding words.

Build words with *k* and *ck*.

> **I Do** Display **Word-Building Cards** *k, i, n*. *This is the letter* k. *It stands for /k/. This is the letter* i. *It stands for /i/. This is the letter* n. *It stands for /n/. Listen as I blend all three sounds: /kiiinnn/,* kin. *The word is* kin.

> **We Do** *Let's blend more sounds to make words.* Make *Kim. Let's blend: /kiiimmm/,* Kim. Have children blend to read the word. Repeat with *kit: /k/ /iii/ /t/, kit.*

> **You Do** Distribute sets of Word-Building Cards with *k, c, e, i, d, n,* and *t*. Write: *Ken, kid, kit*. Have children form each word and then blend and read it.
>
> Repeat the routine for final /k/ spelled *ck*, reminding children to use two letters, *c* and *k*, to make words. Use the words *back, sack, deck, lick.*

REREAD THE DECODABLE READER

OBJECTIVES

Know and apply grade-level phonics and word analysis skills in decoding words.

Read words in context.

Unit 6 Decodable Reader

Focus on Foundational Skills

Review the high-frequency words *she* and *was* with children. Review the letter-sound correspondences /k/k and /k/ck. Guide children to blend sounds to read *kit* and *back*.

Read the Decodable Reader

Have children read "Pack It, Kim" and "Kick It, Nick!" Have them point out the high-frequency words *she* and *was* as well as words with /k/ spelled *k* or *ck*. If children struggle sounding out words, model blending.

Focus on Fluency

Have partners read "Pack It, Kim" and "Kick It, Nick!" Guide them to focus on their accuracy. Children can give feedback on their accuracy to their partners. Then have them focus on reading with automaticity and at an appropriate rate. You may wish to have them reread "Kim and Nan" (pp. 50–57) in the **Reading/Writing Companion**.

SOUND/SPELLING FLUENCY

Display the following Word-Building Cards: *k, b, l, f, r, e,* and *h*. Have children chorally say each sound. Repeat and vary the pace.

●Approaching Level

High-Frequency Words

RETEACH WORDS

OBJECTIVES
Read common high-frequency words by sight.

I Do Display **High-Frequency Word Card** *she* and use the Read/Spell/Write routine to reteach the word. Repeat for *was*.

We Do Write this sentence and read it aloud: **She can kick the ball.** Have children point to the word *she*. Use the same routine for *was* and the sentence: **Monday was a hot day!**

You Do Write the sentence frame **She was at the _____.** Have children copy the sentence frame on their **Response Boards**. Then have partners work together to read and orally complete the frame by talking about places where someone might be. Reteach previously introduced high-frequency words, using the Read/Spell/Write routine.

CUMULATIVE REVIEW

OBJECTIVES
Read common high-frequency words by sight.

I Do Display the High-Frequency Word Cards *I, can, the, we, see, a, like, to, and, go, you, do, my, are, he, with, is,* and *little*. Use the Read/Spell/Write routine to review words. Have children practice reading the words until they can read them accurately and with automaticity. Write sentences such as: **Do you see my little cap? Ben and Ron are with Pop.**

We Do Chorally read the sentences. Then guide children to create a sentence as a class using the high-frequency words. Have children identify the high-frequency words in each sentence. Read the sentences together.

You Do Have partners use the High-Frequency Word Cards and **Word-Building Cards** to create short sentences. Remind them to refer to the High-Frequency Word Cards as needed. Then have them write the words on their **Response Boards**. Have partners take turns reading the sentences to each other.

Oral Vocabulary

REVIEW WORDS

OBJECTIVES

Use words and phrases acquired through conversations, reading and being read to, and responding to texts.

Identify real-life connections between words and their use.

I Do Use the Define/Example/Ask routine on the print or digital **Visual Vocabulary Cards** to review *predict, temperature, storm, clever,* and *drought.*

We Do Ask questions to build understanding. *What do you predict will happen during a storm? What is the temperature of an ice cube? What kinds of noises do you hear during a storm? What is a clever idea you once had? Why don't farmers like a drought?*

You Do Have children complete these sentence frames:

In winter, I predict the weather will _____. During the storm, I _____.
I had a clever idea when _____. A drought is bad because _____.
The temperature in the summer feels _____.

Comprehension

SELF-SELECTED READING

OBJECTIVES

With prompting and support, identify characters, settings, and major events in a story.

Read emergent-reader texts with purpose and understanding.

Independent Reading

Help children select an illustrated fiction story for independent reading. Encourage them to read for twelve minutes. Remind children that an author tells the important events that happen in a story in a certain order, or sequence. Remind children that as they read, they can make pictures in their mind of what is happening in the story.

If children need more practice with concepts of print, have them use **Practice Book** page 507.

After reading, guide children to participate in a group discussion about the story they read. In addition, children can choose activities from the Reading **Center Activity Cards** to help them apply skills to the text as they read. Offer assistance and guidance with self-selected assignments.

Lexile BR

OBJECTIVES

Recognize that spoken words are represented in written language by specific sequences of letters.

With prompting and support, identify characters, settings, and major events in a story.

Read emergent-reader texts with purpose and understanding.

ELA ACADEMIC LANGUAGE

• *purpose, sequence, punctuation mark*

• Cognate: *secuencia*

●On Level

Leveled Reader *Weather Is Fun*

Preview and Predict

Read the title and the names of the author and illustrator as children follow along in their copy of the book. Discuss the cover illustration and ask children to predict what the book might be about. Preview each illustration and allow children to confirm or revise their predictions about the book.

Review Genre: Fiction

Remind children that, like fantasy, fiction tells stories about made-up characters and events. Explain that the difference is the events in a fantasy story could not happen in real life, but the events in fiction could. Say: *Look at the pictures in this story. Do the things that happen in this story look like they could happen in real life?*

Set Purpose

Remind children of the Essential Question: *What happens in different kinds of weather?* Help children set a purpose for reading: *Let's read to find out what people can do in different kinds of weather.* Remind children to use the illustrations to help them understand the text.

Foundational Skills

Model Concepts of Print Turn to pages 2 and 3. Ask children to point to the first and last word in each sentence. Review that the first word in a sentence starts with an uppercase letter and the last word is followed by a punctuation mark. Provide children with more practice matching speech to print. As you read aloud, have children match the words you say with the words on the page.

Review High-Frequency Words Point out the word *was* on page 2. Have children point to *was* on each page.

Guided Comprehension

As children read *Weather Is Fun*, monitor and provide guidance by offering support and corrective feedback as needed. Model visualizing and identifying the sequence of events where applicable.

Visualize

Remind children that, as they read, they can make pictures in their mind of what is happening in the story to better understand it.

Events: Sequence

Remind children that they should look for details in the text and in the illustrations to help them understand the story.

Think Aloud On page 2, I learn from the details in the text and the illustration that it is winter and the girl is throwing snowballs. On page 3, I don't see any snow and the girl is not wearing a coat. I think it is now spring. I will keep reading to see what happens next.

As children read, guide them to pay attention to what the girl does in each season.

Respond to the Text

Have children respond to the text by discussing these questions:

- In what weather do we throw snowballs? (in the snowy winter)
- What does the girl do in the rain? (She jumps in puddles.)
- What happens after the girl swings? (She sleeps in a tent.)
- What happens at the end of the story? (The girl kicks leaves.)

Retell Have partners take turns retelling and acting out the story for each other. Remind children to include characters, setting, and events. Help them make personal connections by asking: *What kind of weather do you think is fun? Why?*

Focus on Fluency

Practice fluency with children. Remember that children need to read with accuracy first.

Once children have read the text with accuracy, have them read the story again, focusing on rate. Have children practice reading in pairs. Provide corrective feedback as necessary.

Build Knowledge: Make Connections

- **Talk About the Texts** Have partners discuss different kinds of weather.
- **Write About the Texts** Then have children add their ideas to the Build Knowledge page of their Reader's Notebook.

LITERACY ACTIVITIES

Have children complete the Collaborate and Write About It activities on the inside back cover of the book.

LITERATURE CIRCLES

Lead children in a literature circle using these questions to guide the discussion: *What is the last season shown in the story, when the girl is kicking leaves? What is one thing you like to do during your favorite season?*

LEVEL UP

IF Children read *Weather is Fun* On Level with fluency and correctly answer the Respond to the Text questions,

THEN Tell children that they will read another story about what happens in different kinds of weather.

- Have children page through *Kate and Tuck* Beyond Level as you talk about what we wear in different kinds of weather.
- Have children read the story, monitoring their comprehension and providing assistance as necessary.

●On Level

Phonological/Phonemic Awareness

PHONEME ISOLATION

OBJECTIVES
Isolate and pronounce the initial sounds in words.

| I Do | Display the *koala* **Photo Card**. *This is a* koala. *The first sound is /k/. Say it with me.* Repeat for final /k/ using the *lock* Photo Card. |

We Do Say *kite* and have children repeat it. *What is the first sound in* kite? (/k/) Say the sound together. Continue with *keen, fin,* and *lab*. Ask children which word begins with /k/. Repeat for final /k/ using the words *flock, frown, far,* and *stick*.

You Do Say *led, kin, rat, bet, lit, Ken, kiss* and have children tell the initial sound in each word. Repeat, using the words *train, trick, wick, miss, ran*.

PHONEME BLENDING

OBJECTIVES
Demonstrate understanding of spoken words, syllables, and sounds (phonemes).

I Do *Listen as I say the sounds in a word: /k/ /i/ /t/. Now I will blend the sounds to make the word: /kiiit/,* kit. Repeat for final /k/ with *pick*.

We Do *I am going to say the sounds in a word. Listen: /k/ /i/ /m/.* Have children repeat. *Now let's blend the sounds and say the word: /k/ /iii/ /mmm/, /kiiimmm/,* Kim. Repeat with *kin, kiss, tack, sick*.

You Do Say the following sounds. Ask children to blend the sounds and say the words: /k/ /i/ /n/, *kin;* /k/ /i/ /d/, *kid;* /p/ /a/ /k/, *pack;* /d/ /o/ /k/, *dock.*

PHONEME SEGMENTATION

OBJECTIVES
Isolate and pronounce the initial, medial vowel, and final sounds in three-phoneme words.

I Do Use **Sound Boxes** and markers. *Listen to the sounds in* kick. *There are three sounds: /k/ /i/ /k/. I'll place a marker in one box for each sound.* Repeat for *keep.*

We Do Distribute Sound Boxes and markers. *Listen as I say:* key, /k/ /ē/. *Let's place a marker in one box for each sound. There are two sounds in* key. Repeat for *rock, kite,* and *sock.*

You Do Repeat the practice with the words *lick, back, kit, mock, Kim.*

Phonics

REVIEW PHONICS

OBJECTIVES

Demonstrate basic knowledge of one-to-one letter-sound correspondences by producing the primary sound or many of the most frequent sounds for each consonant.

I Do Display the *koala* **Sound-Spelling Card**. Say: *The letter* k *stands for the /k/ sound you hear at the beginning of* koala. Say *koala*, emphasizing the /k/.

We Do Display the *king, kite,* and *key* **Photo Cards**. Have children name each picture. Repeat each name, emphasizing initial /k/. Repeat using the *lock, rock,* and *sock* Photo Cards, emphasizing final /k/ spelled *ck*. Then have children identify words with /k/ in the beginning. Repeat, using words with /k/ at the end.

You Do Write the words *kit, Kim, kid, kick, rock, back, deck,* and *lock* and have children read each one. Provide corrective feedback as needed. Repeat, having children raise their hand when they hear /k/ at the beginning of a word. Repeat, having them raise their hand when they hear /k/ at the end of a word.

PICTURE SORT

OBJECTIVES

Demonstrate basic knowledge of one-to-one letter-sound correspondences by producing the primary sound or many of the most frequent sounds for each consonant.

I Do Display **Word-Building Cards** *k* and *b* in a pocket chart. Then show the *kite* Photo Card. Say /k/ /ī/ /t/, kite. *The sound at the beginning is /k/. The letter* k *stands for /k/. I will put the* kite *under the letter* k. Show the *bus* Photo Card. Say /b/ /u/ /s/, bus. *The sound at the beginning is /b/. The letter* b *stands for /b/. I will put the* bus *under the* b.

We Do Show the *bat* Photo Card and say *bat,* /b/ /a/ /t/. Have children repeat and tell the sound they hear at the beginning of *bat*. Ask them if they should place the photo under the *k* or the *b*. (b)

You Do Continue the activity using *box, key, boat,* and *king* Photo Cards. Have children say the picture name and the sounds in the name. Then have them place the card under the *k* or *b*.

Change the Word-Building Cards to *ck* and *n*. Repeat the routine for final /k/ spelled *ck* and final /n/ *n*. Use the Photo Cards *lock, sock, rock, pen, fan, man*.

●On Level

Phonics

BLEND WORDS WITH /k/ck, k

OBJECTIVES

Know and apply grade-level phonics and word analysis skills in decoding words.

Build words with *ck* and *k*.

I Do Display **Word-Building Cards** l, i, c, k. *This is the letter* l. *It stands for /l/. Say it with me: /lll/. This is the letter* i. *It stands for /i/. Say it with me: /iii/. These are the letters* c *and* k. *Together they stand for /k/ at the end of a word. Say the sound with me: /k/. I'll blend the sounds together to read the word: /llliiik/,* lick. Repeat the routine, using the word *kid.*

We Do Use Word-Building Cards to form the words *pick* and *kit*. Guide children to blend each word sound by sound and then say the word. Discuss how changing the letters in the word makes a new word.

You Do Write the following words. Have children form and blend each one sound by sound to read each word: *Kim, deck, kick, tack.*

REREAD THE DECODABLE READER

OBJECTIVES

Know and apply grade-level phonics and word analysis skills in decoding words.

Read emergent-reader texts with purpose and understanding.

Unit 6 Decodable Reader

Focus on Foundational Skills

Review the high-frequency words *she* and *was* with children. Review the letter-sound correspondences /k/*k* and /k/*ck*. Guide children to blend sounds to read *kit* and *back*.

Read the Decodable Reader

Have children read "Pack It, Kim" and "Kick It, Nick!" Ask them to identify the high-frequency words *she* and *was* as well as words with /k/ spelled *k* or *ck*. If children struggle sounding out words, model blending.

Focus on Fluency

Have partners read "Pack It, Kim" and "Kick It, Nick!" As children read, guide them to focus on their accuracy. Children can give feedback on their accuracy to their partners. Then have them focus on reading with automaticity and at an appropriate rate. You may wish to have them reread "Kim and Nan" (pages 50–57) in the **Reading/Writing Companion**.

High-Frequency Words

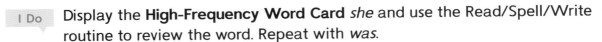

REVIEW WORDS

OBJECTIVES

Read common high-frequency words by sight.

I Do Display the **High-Frequency Word Card** *she* and use the Read/Spell/Write routine to review the word. Repeat with *was*.

We Do Write this sentence and read it aloud: **She can kick the ball**. Point to the word *she* and have children read it. Then chorally read the sentence. Have children frame and read the word *she* in the sentence. Repeat with the sentence **Monday was a hot day!** and the word *was*.

You Do Say the word *she*. Ask children to close their eyes, picture the word, and write it as they see it. Have children self-correct. Repeat the routine for *was*.

Reteach previously introduced high-frequency words, including the **Build Your Word Bank** high-frequency words, using the Read/Spell/Write routine.

Fluency Use the **Practice Book Word Cards** to review the previously introduced High-Frequency and Build Your Word Bank words. Have children practice reading them until they can read accurately and with automaticity.

Comprehension

SELF-SELECTED READING

OBJECTIVES

With prompting and support, identify characters and settings in a story.

Read emergent-reader texts with purpose and understanding.

Independent Reading

Help children select an illustrated story for independent reading. Encourage them to read for twelve minutes. Guide them to transfer what they have learned this week as they read. Remind them that an author tells the important events that happen in a story in a certain order, or sequence. Also remind them that, as they read, they can make pictures in their mind of what is happening in the story to better understand it.

After reading, guide children to participate in a group discussion about the story they read. In addition, children can choose activities from the Reading **Center Activity Cards** to help them apply skills to the text as they read. Offer assistance and guidance with self-selected assignments.

Lexile 280L

OBJECTIVES

Recognize common types of texts.

With prompting and support, identify characters, settings, and major events in a story.

With prompting and support, retell familiar stories, including key details.

Read emergent-reader texts with purpose and understanding.

ELA ACADEMIC LANGUAGE
- *predict, retell*
- Cognate: *predecir*

●Beyond Level

Leveled Reader *Kate and Tuck*

Preview and Predict

Ask children to point to the title and the name of the author on the cover of their book as you read them aloud. Ask children to use the cover illustration to try to identify the characters of Kate and Tuck. Ask: *Who do you think is Kate? Which one do you think is Tuck?* Invite children to look through the illustrations and predict what they think the story will be about.

Review Genre: Fiction

Remind children that fiction books are made-up stories with characters and events. Explain that unlike a fantasy story, the events in some fiction stories could happen in real life. Ask: *Do you think the things that happen in this story could happen in real life?*

Set Purpose

Remind children of the Essential Question: *What happens in different kinds of weather?* Help children set a purpose for reading. Say: *Let's read to find out what Kate and Tuck do in different kinds of weather.* Remind children to use the illustrations to help them understand the text.

Guided Comprehension

As children read *Kate and Tuck*, monitor and provide guidance by offering support and corrective feedback as needed. Model visualizing and identifying the sequence of events where applicable. Point out quotation marks to children. Ask: *How can you tell when a character is talking in a fiction story?*

Visualize

Remind children that they will understand a story better if they try to picture in their mind what the characters are doing.

Events: Sequence

Remind children that finding details in the text and the illustrations will help them better understand the story. Explain that, in this book, the illustrations provide details about the weather and the sequence of the seasons.

Think Aloud On page 2, the story says that it was a cool fall day. I learn from the text and the illustration that Kate and Tuck are wearing sweaters to keep warm. On page 3, there is a new character, Mack. So, first Kate and Tuck put on sweaters and then they play in the leaves with Mack. I will keep reading to see what happens next.

Guide children to look for details about what Kate and Tuck do and wear next. Discuss how the weather changes when the seasons change.

Respond to the Text

Have children respond to the text by discussing these questions:

- *What does Kate wear on a cold winter day?* (She wears mittens, boots, and a scarf.)
- *What do Kate and Tuck do after they are dressed warmly for winter?* (They play with Mack in the snow.)
- *Why must we dress differently in different kinds of weather?* (We have to keep our bodies warm or cool or protected from the weather.)

Retell Have children take turns retelling the story, including characters, setting, and events. Help them make a personal connection by asking: *What do you wear in different types of weather?*

Focus on Fluency

Practice fluency with children. Remember that children need to read with accuracy first.

Once children have read the text with accuracy, have them read the story again, focusing on rate. Have them practice with partners. Provide corrective feedback as necessary.

Build Knowledge: Make Connections

- **Talk About the Texts** Have partners discuss different kinds of weather.
- **Write About the Texts** Then have children add their ideas to the Build Knowledge page of their Reader's Notebook.

LITERACY ACTIVITIES

Have children complete the Collaborate and Write About It activities on the inside back cover of the book.

LITERATURE CIRCLES

Lead children in a literature circle, using these questions to guide the discussion: *What is the order of the four seasons, starting with winter? Can you describe, using full sentences, something Kate and Tuck do together in the story?*

⭐ GIFTED AND TALENTED

Evaluate Have children think about what they wear in different weather. First, have them name different kinds of weather and then decide what clothing would be best for that type of weather.

Extend Have children make a poster and draw what people should wear in each type of weather.

Beyond Level

Phonics

REVIEW

OBJECTIVES
Demonstrate basic knowledge of one-to-one letter-sound correspondences by producing the primary or many of the most frequent sounds for each consonant.

I Do Display the *koala* **Sound-Spelling Card**. Say: *The letter* k *stands for the /k/ sound you hear at the beginning of* koala. Say *koala*, emphasizing the /k/. Repeat for final /k/ spelled *ck* using the *lock* **Photo Card**.

We Do Display the *king, kite,* and *key* Photo Cards. Have children name each picture with you. Repeat the name, emphasizing initial /k/. Repeat using the *lock, rock,* and *sock* Photo Cards, emphasizing final /k/ spelled *ck*. Then ask children to share other words they know that begin with /k/ spelled *k*. Repeat for words that end with /k/ spelled *ck*.

You Do Write the words *kit, Kim, kid, kick, rock, back, deck,* and *lock*. Have partners read each decodable word. Ask them to write the words on their **Response Boards**, underlining the letters in each word that stand for initial or final /k/.

Fluency Have children reread "Kim and Nan" for fluency.

Innovate Have children create a new page for "Kim and Nan" by completing the sentence frame: **Kim and Nan go to the _____.** Have them name places that Kim and Nan can go.

High-Frequency Words

REVIEW

OBJECTIVES
Read common high-frequency words by sight.

I Do Use the **Build Your Word Bank High-Frequency Word Cards** at the end of the **Practice Book** for *now, way,* and *under*. Introduce the words, using the Read/Spell/Write routine.

We Do Display the **Practice Book High-Frequency Word Cards** for *see, and, a, little, I, like, the,* and *my*. Have children help you create sentence frames using both sets of word cards.

You Do Have partners write sentences using the Build Your Word Bank High-Frequency words *now, way,* and *under* on their Response Boards. Have them read their sentences.

Vocabulary

ORAL VOCABULARY: SYNONYMS

OBJECTIVES

With guidance and support from adults, explore word relationships and nuances in word meanings.

I Do Review meanings of the oral vocabulary words *predict* and *temperature*. Explain that a synonym is a word that means almost the same thing as another word. *A synonym for* predict *is* guess. *We guess when we decide what will probably happen.* I can guess what will happen next by looking at the pictures. *A synonym for* drought *is* dryness. *Dryness happens when there is no water for a long time.* The dryness caused the plants to droop.

We Do Write a few sentences together, using the new words *guess* and *dryness*. Read the sentences aloud.

You Do Have partners write a weather report. Have them include the words *guess* and *dryness* in their report. Ask them to report the weather to the group.

★ GIFTED and TALENTED Extend Have children choose which type of weather is their favorite. Then have partners take turns interviewing each other. Encourage children to guess why the type of weather their partner named is their favorite.

Comprehension

SELF-SELECTED READING

OBJECTIVES

With prompting and support, identify characters, settings, and major events in a story.

Read emergent-reader texts with purpose and understanding.

Independent Reading

Have children select an illustrated story for independent reading. Encourage them to read for twelve minutes. Guide children to transfer what they have learned this week by identifying the sequence of events. Remind them that they will understand a story better if they try to picture in their mind what the characters are doing.

After reading, guide children to participate in a group discussion about the story they read. In addition, children can choose activities from the Reading **Center Activity Cards** to help them apply skills to the text as they read. Offer assistance and guidance with self-selected assignments.

★ GIFTED and TALENTED Independent Study Have children write a few sentences giving an opinion about a text they read this week. Ask them to create a book cover illustrating what they wrote.

Student Outcomes
✓ Tested in *Wonders* Assessments

FOUNDATIONAL SKILLS

Print Concepts
- Locate a printed word on a page
- Recognize that the first word in a sentence is capitalized
- Identify parts of a book

Phonological Awareness
- Identify Alliteration
- Phoneme Identity
- ✓ Phoneme Blending
- ✓ Phoneme Addition

Phonics and Word Analysis
- l-blends: *bl, cl, fl, sl*

Fluency
- ✓ High-Frequency Words

  are   he   is   little   my   she   was   with

READING

Reading Literature
- ✓ Identify and describe the events in a story
- ✓ Identify and explain descriptive words in a text
- Retell familiar stories
- Actively engage in group reading activities

Reading Informational Text
- Describe the relationship between illustrations and the text
- Identify key details in a text
- Actively engage in group reading activities

COMMUNICATION

Writing
- Handwriting: Sentences with *h, e, f, r, b, l, k, ck*
- Use prompts to write about the text
- Respond to suggestions from peers and add details to strengthen writing

Speaking and Listening
- Present writing and research
- Engage in collaborative conversations
- Ask and answer questions to get information or to clarify something that is not understood

Conventions
- **Grammar:** Recognize singular and plural nouns

Researching
- Recall or gather information to answer a question
- Conduct research about how to stay safe in bad weather

Creating and Collaborating
- Add drawings and visual displays to descriptions
- Use digital tools to produce and publish writing

VOCABULARY

Academic Vocabulary
- Acquire and use grade-appropriate academic vocabulary

Vocabulary Strategy
- Identify and sort common words and objects into categories
- Understand and use question words

ELL Scaffolded supports for English Language Learners are embedded throughout the lessons, enabling students to communicate information, ideas, and concepts in English Language Arts and for social and instructional purposes within the school setting.

See the **ELL Small Group Guide** for additional support of the skills for the text set.

FORMATIVE ASSESSMENT

For assessment throughout the text set, use students' self-assessments and your observations.

Use the Data Dashboard to filter class, group, or individual student data to guide group placement decisions. It provides recommendations to enhance learning for gifted and talented children and offers extra support for children needing remediation.

DATA DASHBOARD

Develop Student Ownership

To build student ownership, children need to know what they are learning, why they are learning it, and determine how well they understood it.

Students Discuss Their Goals

TEXT SET GOALS

- I can read and understand texts.
- I can write about the texts I read.
- I know how to stay safe in bad weather.

Have children think about what they know and circle a hand in each row on **Reading/Writing Companion** page 70.

EXTENDED WRITING GOALS

- I can write a realistic fiction story.

See **Reading/Writing Companion** page 98.

Students Monitor Their Learning

LEARNING GOALS

Specific learning goals identified in every lesson make clear what children will be learning and why. These smaller goals provide stepping stones to help children meet their Text Set Goals.

CHECK-IN ROUTINE

The Check In Routine at the close of each lesson guides children to self-reflect on how well they understood each learning goal.

Review the lesson learning goal.
Reflect on the activity.
Self Assess by
- circling the hands in the **Reading/Writing Companion**.
- showing thumbs up, sideways, or down.

Share with your teacher.

Students Reflect on Their Progress

TEXT SET GOALS

After completing the Show Your Knowledge task for the text set, children reflect on their understanding of the Text Set Goals by circling a hand in each row on **Reading/Writing Companion** page 71.

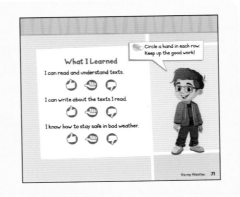

EXTENDED WRITING GOALS

After children complete the evaluation of their writing, they reflect on their ability to write a fiction story by completing **Reading/Writing Companion** page 107.

WEEK 3 Build Knowledge

Literature Big Book

Shared Read
Reading/Writing Companion p. 80

Paired Selection
Literature Big Book

Essential Question
How can you stay safe in bad weather?

Video When there is lightning and thunder, we can stay safe inside. In a blizzard, we can watch safely from inside. Adults shovel the sidewalks so people can walk safely.

Literature Big Book A little girl is worried about an approaching storm. Her mother brings her inside where it's safe and warm. They cuddle and watch the storm.

Shared Read Two mice, Mack and Ben, come inside during a rainstorm. They wait inside, a little sad and scared, until the storm passes.

Interactive Read Aloud A playful wind plays a trick by mixing up all the shop signs in a market. The shop owners stay safe while the wind blows by closing their windows, bringing their goods inside, and having candles ready if needed.

Paired Selection In a blizzard, schools and stores close, and we stay inside. In a hurricane, we follow grown-ups' directions. During thunderstorms we stay away from trees and go inside. We should know our phone number and address and have a safety kit.

Photograph A family stays warm and safe together inside by the fireplace.

Differentiated Sources

Leveled Readers 🔊

🔵 A girl and her mother bundle up and shovel snow. Then they warm up by the fireplace.

🔵⚫ A woman prepares for a storm by getting water, blankets, games, and flashlights. Friends come over and enjoy these together.

🔵 Before a storm, a family brings everything from outside in. They have flashlights in case the lights go out. They stay safe inside.

Build Knowledge Routine

After reading each text, ask children to document what facts and details that they learned to help answer the Essential Question of the text set.

 Talk about the source.

 Write about the source.

 Add to the class Anchor Chart

• Add to the Word Bank.

Show Your Knowledge

Make a Weather Safety Book

Have children think about ways they can stay safe during bad weather. Guide them to make a page of a weather safety book by drawing how to stay safe in one kind of bad weather and writing about their picture. Encourage children to use vocabulary words they learned during the week.

Social Emotional Learning

SESAME STREET

Flexible Thinking

SEL Focus: Encourage and expand children's flexible thinking by asking open-ended questions.

Talk together about the meaning of the word *flexible*. Then launch the lesson titled "Different Ideas," pp. T400–T401.

Car Experiment (2:06)

Family Time • Share the video and the activity in the **School to Home** newsletter.

Explore the Texts

Essential Question: How can you stay safe in bad weather?

Literature Big Book	Literature Big Book	Interactive Read-Aloud	Reading/Writing Companion

Waiting Out the Storm Anchor Text Realistic Fiction	**"Be Safe in Bad Weather"** Paired Text Informational Text	**"The Storm that Shook the Signs"** Interactive Read Aloud Fairy Tale	**"Mack and Ben"** Shared Read pp. 80–87 Fiction

Qualitative

Meaning/Purpose: High Complexity **Structure:** Moderate Complexity **Language:** Moderate Complexity **Knowledge Demands:** Low Complexity	**Meaning/Purpose:** Low Complexity **Structure:** Moderate Complexity **Language:** Moderate Complexity **Knowledge Demands:** Low Complexity	**Meaning/Purpose:** Moderate Complexity **Structure:** Low Complexity **Language:** Moderate Complexity **Knowledge Demands:** Moderate Complexity	**Meaning/Purpose:** Moderate Complexity **Structure:** Low Complexity **Language:** Low Complexity **Knowledge Demands:** Low Complexity

Quantitative

Lexile 490L	Lexile 480L	Lexile 660L	Lexile 250L

Reader and Task Considerations

Reader The reader will understand the purpose and likely relate to the girl's feelings.	**Reader** Reassurance from adults may help children who respond to extreme weather with feelings of fear or anxiety.	**Reader** This text has the potential to lead to a social-emotional conversation on how to adapt to unexpected changes.	**Reader** Children will need to use their knowledge of sound-spelling correspondences and high-frequency words to read the text.

Task The questions for the Interactive Read Aloud are supported by teacher modeling. The tasks provide a variety of ways for students to build knowledge and vocabulary about the text set topic. The questions and tasks provided for the other texts are at various levels of complexity, ensuring that all students can interact with the text in meaningful ways.

Additional Read-Aloud Texts

Content Area Reading BLMs

Additional online texts related to grade-level Science, Social Studies, and Arts content.

Access Complex Text (ACT) boxes provide scaffolded instruction for seven different elements that may make the **Literature Big Book** complex.

Leveled Readers (All Leveled Readers are provided in eBook format with audio support.)

Approaching	On	Beyond	ELL
Bad Weather	***Getting Ready***	***The Storm***	***Getting Ready***
Leveled Reader	Leveled Reader	Leveled Reader	Leveled Reader
Fiction	Fiction	Fiction	Fiction

Qualitative

Meaning/Purpose: Low Complexity	**Meaning/Purpose:** Moderate Complexity	**Meaning/Purpose:** Low Complexity	**Meaning/Purpose:** Moderate Complexity
Structure: Low Complexity	**Structure:** Low Complexity	**Structure:** Low Complexity	**Structure:** Low Complexity
Language: Low Complexity	**Language:** Low Complexity	**Language:** Moderate Complexity	**Language:** Low Complexity
Knowledge Demands: Low Complexity	**Knowledge Demands:** Moderate Complexity	**Knowledge Demands:** Low Complexity	**Knowledge Demands:** Moderate Complexity

Quantitative

Lexile BR	Lexile 30L	Lexile 170L	Lexile BR

Reader and Task Considerations

Reader Children who live in warmer climates may need extra support to understand snow storms.	**Reader** Children should be familiar with the objects mentioned in the text, but they may need extra support to understand what the character is getting ready for.	**Reader** Reassurance from adults may help children who respond to storms with feelings of fear or anxiety.	**Reader** Children should be familiar with the objects mentioned in the text, but they may need extra support to understand what the character is getting ready for.

Task The questions and tasks provided for the Leveled Readers are at various levels of complexity, ensuring that all students can interact with the text in meaningful ways.

Focus on Word Work

Build Foundational Skills with Multimodal Learning MULTIMODAL

Photo Cards

Response Board

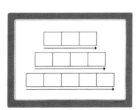
Phonemic Awareness Activities

Word-Building Cards online

Phonics Practice Activities

Practice Book

Word-Building Cards online

Response Board

High-Frequency Word Cards

High-Frequency Word Activities

Visual Vocabulary Cards

Phonological/Phonemic Awareness

- Identify alliteration
- Identify, add, and blend phonemes

Phonics: *l*-blends

- Introduce/review sound-spellings
- Blend/build words with sound-spellings
- Practice handwriting
- Decode and encode in connected texts

Spelling: *l*-blends

- Spell words with *l*-blends

High-Frequency Words

- Read/Spell/Write routine
- Optional: Build Your Word Bank

See Word Work, pages T410–T413, T422–T425, T430–T435, T444–T445, T450–T451.

Shared Read

Decodable Readers

Take-Home Story

Apply Skills to Read

- Children apply foundational skills as they read decodable texts.
- Children practice fluency to develop word automaticity.

Explicit Systematic Instruction

Word Work instruction expands foundational skills to enable children to become proficient readers.

Daily Routine

- Use the In a Flash: Sound-Spelling routine and the In a Flash: High-Frequency Word routine to build fluency.
- Set Learning Goal.

Explicit Minilessons and Practice

Use daily instruction in both whole and small groups to model, practice, and apply key foundational skills. Opportunities include:

- Multimodal engagement.
- Corrective feedback.
- Supports for English Language Learners in each lesson.
- Peer collaboration.

Formative Assessment

Check-In

- Children reflect on their learning.
- Children show their progress by indicating thumbs down, thumbs sideways, or thumbs up in a Check-In routine.

Check for Success

- Teacher monitors children's achievement and differentiates for Small Group instruction.

Differentiated Instruction

To strengthen skills, provide targeted review and reteaching lessons and multimodal activities to meet children's diverse needs.

● ● **Approaching Level, ELL**
- Includes Tier 2 ②

● **On Level**

● **Beyond Level**
- Includes Gifted and Talented GIFTED and TALENTED

OPTIONAL EXPRESS TRACK

Teachers can choose to introduce long vowel sound-spellings and/or additional high-frequency words.

- Build Your Word Bank

Independent Practice

Provide additional practice as needed. Have children work individually or with partners.

Center Activity Cards

Digital Activities

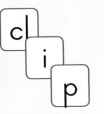

Word-Building Cards online

Decodable Readers

Practice Book

Inspire Early Writers

WEEK 3

Build Writing Skills and Conventions

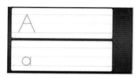

Handwriting Video

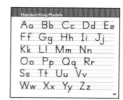

Reading/Writing Companion

Write l-blends *bl, cl, fl, sl*

- Learn to write the letters
- Practice writing

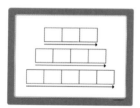

Response Board

Practice Book

High-Frequency Word Activities

Write Words

- Write words with *l*-blends *bl, cl, fl, sl*
- Write high-frequency words

Reading/Writing Companion

Practice Book

Write Sentences

- Write sentences with high-frequency words
- Write sentences to respond to text

Follow Conventions

- Recognize singular and plural nouns

Waiting Out the Storm
Literature Big Book

Writing Fluency

To increase children's writing fluency, have them write as much as they can in response to the **Literature Big Book** for four minutes. Tell children to write about what they learned about staying safe in a storm.

For lessons, see pages T410–T415, T426–T427, T430–T433, T436–T437, T446–T447, T450–T453.

Write About Texts

WRITING ROUTINE

Analyze the Prompt ▶ Find Text Evidence ▶ Write to the Prompt

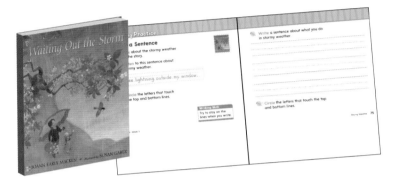

Literature Big Book

Reading/Writing Companion, pp. 74–75

Modeled Writing

Write about the **Literature Big Book** *Waiting Out the Storm*

- Prompt: What do you like to do when it rains?

Interactive Writing

- Prompt: What can the girl and her mother do when the storm stops? Write the next part of the story.

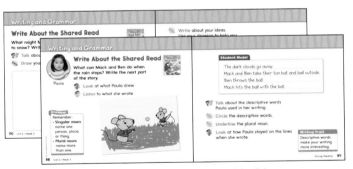

Reading/Writing Companion, pp. 88–91

Independent Writing

Write to the Shared Read "Mack and Ben"

- Prompt: What might Mack and Ben do it if starts to snow? Write a story.

- Have children follow the steps of the writing process: draft, revise, edit/proofread, share.

Additional Lessons

Writing Skills Minilessons To provide differentiated support for writing skills, see pages T494–T499.

Extended Writing Lessons For a full set of lessons that support the writing process and writing in a specific genre, see pages T476–T487.

Self-Selected Writing

Children can explore different writing modes.

Journal Writing

Book Review

Planner

Customize your own lesson plans at
my.mheducation.com

Select from your Social Emotional
Learning resources.

LESSON 1 LESSON 2

TEXT SET GOALS

- I can read and understand texts.
- I can write about the texts I read.
- I know how to stay safe in bad weather.

90+ mins

Reading
Suggested Daily Time
Includes Small Group

SMALL GROUP OPTIONS
The designated lessons can be taught in small groups. To determine how to differentiate instruction for small groups, use Formative Assessment and Data Dashboard.

30+ mins

Writing
Suggested Daily Time

EXTENDED WRITING GOALS

I can write a realistic fiction story.

Reading

Introduce the Concept, T402–T403
Build Knowledge: Stormy Weather

Listening Comprehension, T404–T409
Waiting Out the Storm

Word Work, T410–T413
Phonemic Awareness: Phoneme Identity Review
/e/e, /h/h, /f/f, /r/r, /b/b, /l/l, /k/k
Phonics/Spelling: *l*-Blends
Handwriting: Write Sentences with *h, e, f, r, b, l, k, ck*
High-Frequency Words: *are, he, is, little, my, she, was, with*

Build the Concept, T416–T417
Phonological Awareness: Identify Alliteration
Category Words: Question Words
Vocabulary: Question Words

Listening Comprehension, T418–T421
Waiting Out the Storm

Word Work, T422–T423
Phonemic Awareness: Phoneme Blending
Phonics: Review *l*-Blends, Blend Words
High-Frequency Words: *are, he, is, little, my, she, was, with*

Shared Read, T424–T425
Read "Mack and Ben"

Writing

Modeled Writing, T414
Model Writing About the Literature Big Book
Grammar, T415
Singular and Plural Nouns

Extended Writing: Realistic Fiction
Expert Model, T476–T477
Writing Lesson Bank, T486–T487, T494–T499

Interactive Writing, T426
Write About the Literature Big Book
Grammar, T427
Singular and Plural Nouns

Extended Writing: Realistic Fiction
Plan: Choose Your Topic, T478–T479
Writing Lesson Bank, T486–T487, T494–T499

Teacher-Led Instruction

Differentiated Reading
Leveled Readers
- *Bad Weather,* T456–T457
- *Getting Ready,* T464–T465
- *The Storm,* T470–T471

Differentiated Skills Practice, T458–T473

Approaching Level, T458–T463
Phonological/Phonemic Awareness
- Recognize Alliteration, T458 **2**
- Phoneme Identity, T458 **2**
- Phoneme Blending, T459
- Phoneme Addition, T459

Phonics
- Sound-Spelling Review, T460 **2**
- Connect to *l*-Blends, T460 **2**
- Blend Words with *l*-Blends, T460
- Build Words with *l*-Blends, T461
- Reread the Decodable Reader, T461
- Sound/Spelling Fluency, T461
High-Frequency Words
- Reteach Words, T462 **2**
- Cumulative Review, T462 **2**
Oral Vocabulary
- Review Words, T463

SMALL GROUP

Independent/Collaborative Work See pages T399I–T399J

Reading
Comprehension
- Realistic Fiction
- Visualize
- Events: Sequence

Word Work
Phonics
- *l*-Blends
High-Frequency Words
- *are, he, is, little, my, she, was, with*

Writing
Self-Selected Writing
Extended Writing: Realistic Fiction
Grammar
- Singular and Plural Nouns
Handwriting
- Sentences with *h, e, f, r, b, l, k, ck*

ORAL VOCABULARY
safe, prepare, notice, celebration, enough

 LESSON 3

 LESSON 4

 LESSON 5

Reading

Build the Concept, T428
Oral Language

Listening Comprehension, T429
"The Storm that Shook the Signs"

Word Work, T430–T433
Phonemic Awareness: Phoneme Blending
Phonics: Review *l*-Blends, Blend Words, Spell Words
High-Frequency Words: *are, he, is, little, my, she, was, with*

Shared Read, T434–T435
Reread "Mack and Ben"

Extend the Concept, T438–T439
Phonological Awareness: Identify Alliteration
Category Words: Question Words
Vocabulary: Question Words

Paired Selection, T440–T443
"Be Safe in Bad Weather"

Word Work, T444–T445
Phonemic Awareness: Phoneme Addition
Phonics: Build and Read Words
High-Frequency Words: *are, he, is, little, my, she, was, with*

Research and Inquiry, T448–T449
Stormy Weather (Research)

Word Work, T450–T451
Phonemic Awareness: Phoneme Addition
Phonics: Read Words, Spell Words
High-Frequency Words: *are, he, is, little, my, she, was, with*

Integrate Ideas, T454
Make Connections

Show Your Knowledge, T455

Writing

Independent Writing, T436
Write About the Shared Read
Grammar, T437
Singular and Plural Nouns

Extended Writing: Realistic Fiction
Draft, T480–T481
Writing Lesson Bank, T486–T487, T494–T499

Independent Writing, T446
Write About the Shared Read
Grammar, T447
Singular and Plural Nouns

Extended Writing: Realistic Fiction
Revise and Edit, T482–T483
Writing Lesson Bank, T486–T487, T494–T499

Self-Selected Writing, T452
Grammar, T453
Singular and Plural Nouns

Extended Writing: Realistic Fiction
Publish, Present, and Evaluate, T484–T485
Writing Lesson Bank, T486–T487, T494–T499

Comprehension
• Self-Selected Reading, T463
● **On Level, T466–T469**
Phonological/Phonemic Awareness
• Phoneme Identity, T466
• Phoneme Blending, T466
• Phoneme Addition, T466
Phonics
• Review Phonics, T467
• Picture Sort, T467
• Blend Words with *l*-Blends, T468
• Reread the Decodable Reader, T468

High-Frequency Words
• Review Words, T469
Comprehension
• Self-Selected Reading, T469
● **Beyond Level, T472–T473**
Phonics
• Review, T472
High-Frequency Words
• Review, T472

Vocabulary
• Oral Vocabulary: Synonyms, T473
Comprehension
• Self-Selected Reading, T473

 English Language Learners
See ELL Small Group Guide, pp. 148–155

Content Area Connections
Content Area Reading
• Science, Social Studies, and the Arts
Research and Inquiry
• Stormy Weather (Research)

 ● **English Language Learners**
See ELL Small Group Guide, pp. 149, 151

WEEK 3

Independent and Collaborative Work

As you meet with small groups, have the rest of the class complete activities and projects to practice and apply the skills they have been working on.

Student Choice and Student Voice

- Review My Weekly Work with children and identify the "Must Do" activities.
- Have children choose some additional activities that provide the practice they need.
- Remind children to reflect on their learning each day.

My Weekly Work BLMs

Reading

Text Options

Children can choose a **Center Activity Card** to use while they listen to a text or read independently.

Classroom Library Read Aloud
A Kitten Tale
Genre: Fiction
Lexile: 590L

The Year at Maple Hill Farm
Genre: Informational Text
Lexile: 560L

Unit Bibliography
See the online bibliography. Children can select independent reading texts about how we can stay safe in bad weather.

Leveled Texts Online
 All **Leveled Readers** are provided in eBook format with audio support.
- **Differentiated Texts** provide English Language Learners with passages at different proficiency levels.

Literature Big Book e-Book
Waiting Out the Storm
 **Genre:** Realistic Fiction

Center Activity Cards

Visualize Card 1

Realistic Fiction Card 23

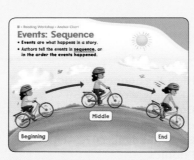

Sequence Card 11

Digital Activities

Comprehension

Word Work

Center Activity Cards

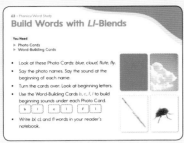

Ll-blends Card 63

Word-Building Cards

Practice Book BLMs

Phonological Awareness: p. 273
Phonics Review: pp. 274–276
Phonics: p. 277
Phonics/Spelling: p. 278
High-Frequency Words: p. 279
Category Words: p. 280
Category Words Review: p. 281
Take-Home Story: pp. 285–286

Decodable Readers

Unit 6, pp. 25-36

Digital Activities

Phonemic Awareness
Phonics
High-Frequency Words

Writing

Center Activity Cards

Descriptive Words Card 41

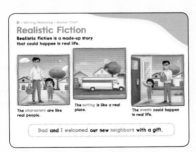

Realistic Fiction Card 31

Practice Book BLMs

Grammar: pp. 282–284

Self-Selected Writing

- What do you know about staying safe in bad weather?
- Write about a time when you had to find a safe place in bad weather.
- Draw and label a picture of a person or family doing something to stay safe during a storm.

Digital Activities

Grammar

Content Area Connections

Content Area Reading BLMs
- Additional texts related to Science, Social Studies, Health, and the Arts.

Research and Inquiry
- Complete Stormy Weather project

Progress Monitoring
Moving Toward Mastery

Practice Book

Reading/Writing Companion

Online Rubric

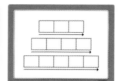

Response Board

Digital Activities

FORMATIVE ASSESSMENT

- ➤ STUDENT CHECK-IN
- ✔ CHECK FOR SUCCESS

For ongoing formative assessment, use children's self-assessments at the end of each lesson along with your own observations.

Assessing skills along the way . . .

SKILLS	HOW ASSESSED
Phonological Awareness • Identify Alliteration	Practice Book
Phonemic Awareness • Phoneme Identity • Phoneme Blending • Phoneme Addition	Practice Book, Response Board, Digital Activities
Phonics • l-blends: *bl, cl, fl, sl*	Practice Book, Response Board, Digital Activities
High-Frequency Words • *are, he, is, little, my, she, was, with*	Practice Book, Response Board, Digital Activities
Category Words • Question Words	Practice Book
Grammar • Singular and Plural Nouns	Practice Book
Comprehension • Events: Sequence • Text Feature: Directions	Reading/Writing Companion
Listening/Presenting/Research	Checklists

Making the Most of Assessment Results

Make data-based grouping decisions by using the following reports to verify assessment results. For additional support options for children, refer to the reteaching and enrichment opportunities.

ONLINE ASSESSMENT CENTER
- *Gradebook*

DATA DASHBOARD
- *Recommendations Report*
- *Activity Report*
- *Skills Report*
- *Progress Report*
- *Grade Card Report*

TIER 2 Reteaching Opportunities with Intervention Online PDFs

ASSESSED SKILLS	✓ CHECK FOR SUCCESS	RETEACH . . .
PHONOLOGICAL AND PHONEMIC AWARENESS	Can children identify and produce alliterative words? Can children identify, blend, and add phonemes? If not . . .	using lessons 18–19; 16–17, 62–66, and 98–99 in the **Phonemic Awareness PDF.**
PHONICS	Can children match the letters to the sounds /bl/*bl*, /kl/*cl*, /fl/*fl*, /sl/*sl*? If not . . .	using lessons 21 and 23–29 in the **Phonics/Word Study PDF.**
HIGH-FREQUENCY WORDS	Can children recognize and read the high-frequency words? If not . . .	by using the **High-Frequency Word Cards** and asking children to read and spell the word. Point out any irregularities in sound-spellings.
COMPREHENSION	Can children identify sequence of events? Can children use text features including directions? If not . . .	using lessons 25–27 and 138 in the **Comprehension PDF.**
CATEGORY WORDS	Can children identify and sort question words? If not . . .	using lesson 20 in the **Vocabulary PDF.**

GIFTED and TALENTED

Enrichment Opportunities

Beyond Level small group lessons and resources include suggestions for additional activities in these areas to extend learning opportunities for gifted and talented children:

- *Leveled Reader*
- *Vocabulary*
- *Comprehension*
- *Leveled Reader Library Online*
- *Center Activity Cards*

Today's focus:

Demonstrating flexibility in thinking and behavior.

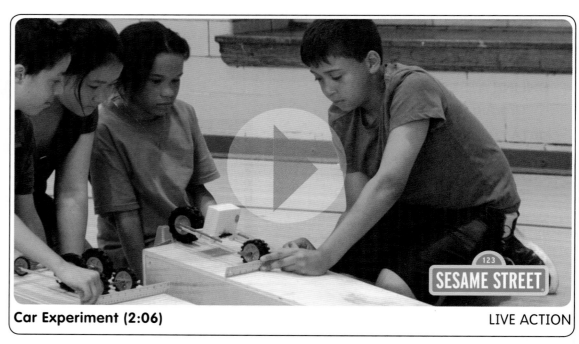

Car Experiment (2:06) LIVE ACTION

different ideas

family time
You'll find the "Car Experiment" video and supporting activity in this week's School to Home family newsletter.

engage together

Let's Play: What else can this do?
Model flexible thinking by brainstorming different ways to play with a ball.

- We are a classroom of creative and *flexible thinkers*!
- Let's give our brains a kiss! Now, let's put our brains to work.
- How many ways can we play with this small ball?
- Let's think of ten different ideas.
- I'll get us started. We can juggle the ball like this.
- Who would like to share another idea?
- Wow, we came up with a lot of creative ideas!

explore together

Let's Watch: "Car Experiment"

Set a purpose for sharing today's live action video.

- Murray challenges his friends to design a car that can go far.
- As you watch, notice that each friend comes up with a different idea.
- Let's see how the challenge turns out.

(▷) **Play the video**

Let's Think: Try, try again.

Analyze the importance of trial and error.

- Murray's friends all tried different ideas.
- Let's identify some of the ideas they came up with. What worked best?
- Sometimes finding the *just right* solution means trying many different ideas.
- If one plan doesn't work, that's ok. It helps us learn what to do differently next time!

> **TRIAL AND ERROR IS...**
>
> ...trying out different ideas to solve a problem.

connect the learning

Let's Experiment: Think like an engineer.

Give children an opportunity to practice their flexible thinking.

- The children in the videos worked as *engineers*.
- Engineers solve problems. They want to know *how* and *why* things work.
- Let's think like engineers. How can we build a structure out of paper that can support our ball?
- Turn to your partner to come up with a plan. What shape should the structure be?
- We'll chart our different ideas to try later today or during the week.

mindfulness moment
Superhero Pose

Help children feel more confident and in control with a simple posture change. *Let's take a wide stance, feet apart, like a superhero. Place our hands on our hips and lift our chests. Let's hold this pose for a moment and breathe. We're flexible and confident thinkers!*

FLEXIBLE THINKING

OBJECTIVES

Confirm understanding of a text read aloud or information presented orally or through other media by asking and answering questions about key details and requesting clarification if something is not understood.

Use words and phrases acquired through conversations, reading and being read to, and responding to texts.

Identify real-life connections between words and their use.

Follow agreed-upon rules for discussions (e.g., listening to others and taking turns speaking about the topics and texts under discussion).

ELA ACADEMIC LANGUAGE

• *weather, details*
• Cognate: *detalles*

DIGITAL TOOLS

Watch Video

Visual Vocabulary Cards

LESSON FOCUS

READING
Introduce Essential Question
Read Literature Big Book
Waiting Out the Storm
• Introduce Genre: Realistic Fiction
• Introduce Strategy/Skill
Word Work
• Introduce *l*-Blends
• Review /e/e, /h/h, /f/f

WRITING
Writing/Grammar
• Shared Writing
• Introduce Grammar

Literature Big Book, pp. 3–27

---

10 mins

Build Knowledge

MULTIMODAL

 ## Essential Question

How can you stay safe in bad weather?

Read the Essential Question. Explain that this week we will learn how to stay safe in bad weather. Have children turn to a partner and discuss what they know about staying safe in bad weather.

• **Video Routine** Play the Weekly Opener Video, "Stormy Weather" without sound and have partners narrate what they watch. Then replay the video with sound and have children listen.

• **Talk About the Video** Have partners share one thing they learned about how stay safe in bad weather.

 • **Anchor Chart** Create a Build Knowledge anchor chart and have volunteers share what they learned about the theme "Stormy Weather." Record their ideas on the chart.

Oral Vocabulary Words

Use the Define/Example/Ask routine on the print or digital **Visual Vocabulary Cards** to introduce the oral vocabulary words *safe* and *prepare*.

 ### Oral Vocabulary Routine

Define: When you are **safe**, you are not in danger.

Example: I feel safe when I am with my family.

Visual Vocabulary Cards

Ask: What helps you feel safe? Why?

Define: When you **prepare**, you get ready for something.

Example: A runner can prepare for a race by stretching.

Ask: How do you prepare for school?

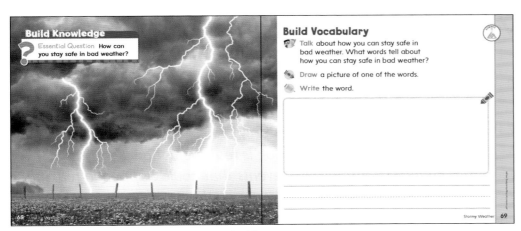

Reading/Writing Companion, pp. 68–69

 ## Build Knowledge

Turn to pages 68–69 of the **Reading/Writing Companion**. Use the photo to guide a discussion about staying safe in bad weather.

- **Talk** *How can you stay safe in bad weather? What words tell about how you can stay safe in bad weather?* List the words. Have children choose one word and think about how to illustrate it.

- **Draw** and **Write** Have children draw a picture that illustrates the word. Then have them write the word. Guide children on how to print letters that have not been taught yet.

Build Vocabulary

Have children share new words they learned about staying safe in bad weather. Add words to a separate section of the Word Bank. Use the words during the week and encourage children to do the same.

 # English Language Learners

Use the following scaffolds with **Build Knowledge.**

Beginning

Point to the lightning. *This is lightning.* Have children repeat. Repeat with *rainstorm* and *clouds*.

Intermediate

Help children describe the photo. There is a <u>rainstorm</u>. The <u>lightning</u> is bright. The clouds are <u>dark</u>.

Advanced/Advanced High

What do you see? Is this bad weather? What could you do to stay safe? It is <u>bad weather</u>. You can <u>stay safe by going inside</u>.

 ## COLLABORATIVE CONVERSATIONS

Provide Details As children engage in partner, small group, and whole group discussions, encourage them to:

- Give details to express their thoughts, feelings and ideas clearly.
- Use details to describe people, places, things, and events.
- Give details when asking about things they do not understand.

 ## NEWCOMERS

To help children develop oral language and build vocabulary, continue using **Newcomer Cards** 20-24 and the accompanying lessons in the **Newcomer Teacher's Guide**. For thematic connections, use Newcomer Card 9. For additional practice, have children complete the online **Newcomer Activities**.

MY GOALS ROUTINE

What I Know Now

Read Goals Read aloud the goals and the key on **Reading/Writing Companion** page 70.

Reflect Ask children to reflect on each goal and complete page 70 to show what they know now. Explain that they will complete page 71 at the end of the text set to show their progress.

LESSON 1

Literature Big Book

Read

Waiting Out the Storm

Connect to Concept

Tell children that you will read a story about a mother and daughter and how they notice that a storm is coming.

Genre: Realistic Fiction Say: *This book is realistic fiction. Realistic fiction has characters, settings, and events that could happen in real life. Characters in realistic fiction act like real people.*

 Anchor Chart Display the Realistic Fiction anchor chart. Add: *Characters in realistic fiction are like real people.*

Visualize Encourage children to use the words and images to form pictures in their mind about the events in the story.

Events: Sequence Remind children that events in a story are often told in order, or sequence. Explain that we can use the words *beginning, middle,* and *end* to talk about the order of story events.

Read the Selection

Concepts of Print Display and read aloud page 7 of the **Literature Big Book**. Remind children that sentences are complete thoughts. Point out the beginning and ending of each sentence.

Set Purpose *Let's read to find out how a mother and daughter stay safe during a storm.*

Close Reading Routine

Read   DOK 1–2

• Identify key ideas and details.
• Take notes and retell.
• Use **A C T** prompts as needed.

Reread   DOK 2–3

• Analyze the text, craft, and structure.

Integrate   DOK 3–4

• Integrate knowledge and ideas and make text-to-text connections.
• Use the Integrate lesson.
• Complete the Show Your Knowledge task.
• Inspire action.

ELL Spotlight On Language

Pages 4–5

CONCEPTS OF PRINT

Remind children that groups of words make up a sentence. A sentence is a complete thought. Point out the spaces between the words and the question marks.

BUILD ORAL VOCABULARY

buttercup: a flower and a term of endearment

Page 5 *buttercup:* Say, *A buttercup is a pretty yellow flower that grows in fields. It is also the special name the mother calls her daughter.* Have children share special names their families have for them.

Pages 6–7

EVENTS: SEQUENCE DOK 1

What's happens in the beginning of the story that lets the girl and her mom know that a storm is coming? (The wind whistles.)

Page 7 *whistle:* Say, *A whistle is a sound that air makes when it blows through something, like trees or a chimney.* Show how children can make a whistling sound, too. Demonstrate, and have children practice whistling.

Pages 8–9

VISUALIZE DOK 2

Think Aloud On page 8, it says that the raindrops come when the wind calls. The text makes me imagine that the raindrops are excited. It says they are skipping and leaping and laughing out loud. I imagine the drops of rain happy and dancing.

BUILD ORAL VOCABULARY

tumble: fall or roll

Page 8 *burst:* Say, *Imagine a balloon filled with too much air. When the balloon pops, it bursts.* Have children make the sound of a balloon bursting.

 Access Complex Text

Use this ACT prompt when the complexity of the text makes it hard for children to understand the selection.

Sentence Structure

Complex sentence structures throughout a text may impede understanding of the text as a whole.

- *Waiting Out the Storm* includes dialogue printed in italics and regular font. The story does not include quotation marks or other dialogue indicators.
- Guide children to understand that the words printed in ordinary letters are what the girl says. The words printed in italics, or slanted letters, are what the mother says.

LESSON 1

 Spotlight On Language

Pages 10–11

EVENTS: SEQUENCE DOK 2

Where are the girl and her mom going? (They are going into the house.) *Why?* (They want to get out of the rain.)

Page 11 *what's:* Explain that *what's* is a contraction of two words: *what is.* Reread the sentence from the story replacing *what's* with *what is.* Point out that *what's* and *what is* have the same meaning. Have children repeat the line from the story with the contraction and then with *what is.*

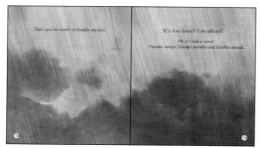

Pages 12–13

REALISTIC FICTION DOK 2

Think Aloud I know that realistic fiction is a made-up story with characters that act like real people. In the story, the girl is afraid because the thunder is loud. The girl is acting like a real little girl by being afraid of the thunder.

BUILD ORAL VOCABULARY

stumbles: acts in a clumsy way

bumbles: acts in a clumsy way

Pages 12–13 *rumble, stomps:* Tell children that *rumbles* and *stomps* are sounds. Have children tap their hands on their desks to make a *rumble.* Then have them *stomp* their feet to make stomping sounds. *What is another sound that thunder can make?* (boom, crack)

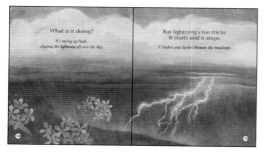

Pages 14–15

DETAILS DOK 1

I read that the lightning flashes and dashes. Look at the illustration. What does the illustration tell you about the lightning? (Possible response: It is bright and it makes crooked lines.)

BUILD ORAL VOCABULARY

dashes: moves quickly

Page 15 *tricky:* Say, If something is tricky, it is sneaky or clever. The lightning is tricky because it flashes quickly. You never know where lightning will strike.

Spotlight On Language

Pages 16–17

VISUALIZE DOK 2

Think Aloud I read that the ducks like to paddle all day. I can see their feet in the pictures. I close my eyes and make a picture in my mind of the ducks' feet moving quickly under the water. They are swimming and happy. This helps me to understand what ducks do in the rain.

Page 16 *fret:* Say, *To fret* means "to worry." Ask children what the girl frets about. (the turtles being outside in the storm) Then have them talk to a partner about something that makes them fret. Provide a sentence frame: I fret when _____.

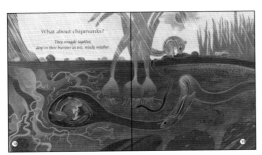

Pages 18–19

VOCABULARY

Reread the second sentence. *What do you think a* burrow *is? Use the illustration and other clues to help you.* (a hole dug deep in the ground) Remind children to ask and answer questions about other unfamiliar words in the story.

BUILD ORAL VOCABULARY

snuggle: hug or cuddle

Page 18 *burrows:* Say the word *burrows,* and have children repeat. Have children point to the word and then find the burrow in the illustration. *A burrow is under the ground. The chipmunks live in this burrow. What is another word we could use for* burrow? (home)

Pages 20–21

PHONICS

Reread page 20 and have children identify the words with the initial /b/ and initial /l/ sounds. (birds, beneath, little)

Page 20 *There, there:* Tell children that *there, there* is another way to say "don't worry." *The mother bird is telling her little chicks not to worry about the storm.*

 Spotlight On Language

Pages 22–23

HIGH-FREQUENCY WORDS

Have children identify the high-frequency words *with, like, see, you,* and *go*.

Page 22 *comfy:* Tell children that *comfy* is short for *comfortable*. *Comfy* is the feeling you get sitting in a soft chair or being in bed under the covers. *What things make you feel comfy?*

Pages 24–25

REALISTIC FICTION DOK 2

Do you think this part of the story could happen in real life? (yes) *Why?* (The girl and her mother go in the house when the storm comes. In real life, people would go to some place safe and dry to get out of the storm.)

Page 25 *wait out:* Explain that when you *wait out* something, you wait until it is finished. *The mother and daughter will wait until the storm is finished. Then, they will go outside.*

Pages 26–27

EVENTS: SEQUENCE DOK 2

What are the girl and her mom doing at the end of the story? (watching the rain through the window) *How do the girl and her mother feel?* (safe and happy) *How do you know?* (Possible response: They are smiling in the picture.)

Page 26 *snuggling:* Say, *We like to snuggle things that are soft and warm, like kittens and puppies.* What do you like to *snuggle?* Provide a sentence frame: I like to snuggle <u>my pet</u>.

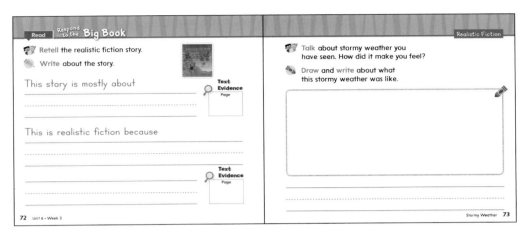

Reading/Writing Companion, pp. 72–73

Respond to the Text

Return to Purpose Remind children of their purpose for reading. Review what they learned about what happens in a storm.

- **Retell** Have children turn to page 72 of the **Reading/Writing Companion**. Guide them to retell the selection in order. Have children use the **Retelling Cards** and the routine as needed.

- **Write** Have children write what the story is about. Model for them how to find text evidence in the **Literature Big Book** to support their response and how to record the page number in the text evidence box. You may wish to share the Big Book with each table or group of children to give them an opportunity to look closely at the pages. Repeat this routine with the second sentence starter by having children tell what makes this a realistic fiction story.

- **Talk** Have partners talk about stormy weather that they have seen. Encourage them to tell how the stormy weather they saw made them feel.

- **Draw** and **Write** Then have children draw and write about the stormy weather they saw. Encourage them to include any signs that let them know the weather was coming. Have children write a descriptive sentence about what it was like.

Model Fluency

Turn to page 16 of the Big Book. Remind children that the different styles of letters show that two people are speaking. Change your voice as your read the dialogue. Then have partners each take a role and repeat what the girl and the mother say to each other. Continue with other pages in the book.

Writing Fluency

To help children increase writing fluency, you may wish to have them write as much as they can for four minutes. Tell them to write about what they learned about staying safe in a storm.

RETELLING ROUTINE

Tell children that they will use the **Retelling Cards** to retell the selection in order.

- Display Retelling Card 1. Based on children's needs, use either the Modeled, Guided, or ELL retelling prompts. The ELL prompts contain support for children based on levels of language acquisition. Repeat with the rest of the cards, using the prompts as a guide. Encourage children to include important details from the story.

- Choose an event in the story and explain what it tells about the weather in a storm. Offer support as needed.

- Invite children to choose a favorite part of the story and act it out.

Retelling Cards

FORMATIVE ASSESSMENT

❯ STUDENT CHECK-IN

Have partners tell each other an important detail from the story. Then have children reflect using the Check-In routine.

In a Flash: Sound-Spellings

Display the Sound-Spelling Card for *k*.

1. **Teacher:** What's the letter?   **Children:** k
2. **Teacher:** What's the sound?   **Children:** /k/
3. **Teacher:** What's the word?   **Children:** koala

Continue the routine for previously taught sounds.

LEARNING GOALS

- We can name the first sound in a group of words.
- We can connect the sounds /cl/, /bl/, /fl/, /sl/ to the letters *cl, bl, fl, sl*.

OBJECTIVES

Isolate and pronounce the initial sounds (phonemes) in words.

Demonstrate basic knowledge of one-to-one letter-sound correspondences by producing the primary sound or many of the most frequent sounds for each consonant.

Associate the short sounds with common spellings (graphemes) for the five major vowels.

ELA ACADEMIC LANGUAGE

- *same, spelled, vowel*

▶ TEACH IN SMALL GROUP

You may wish to teach the Word Work lesson in small groups.

ELL ENGLISH LANGUAGE LEARNERS

Phonemic Awareness, Guided Practice/Practice Encourage children to repeat the phonemes /f/, /h/, /e/, /d/ and /n/. Help children say the names in each set of cards. Give corrective feedback by modeling pronunciation. Then help them identify the initial sound in each set using: <u>Fire, fish</u> and <u>fork</u> begin with the sound <u>/f/</u>.

Phonics: pp. 274–276
Phonics: p. 277

⏱ 5 mins Phonemic Awareness

Phoneme Identity

1 **Model** Display the **Photo Cards** for egg, elevator, and exit. Say: *I will say three picture names:* egg, elevator, exit. *Say the names with me:* egg, elevator, exit. *What sound is the same in* egg, elevator, exit? *Yes, the first sound, /e/, is the same.* Repeat the instruction with Photo Cards *football, five, farm* (to review initial /f/); *hand, helicopter, hippo* (to review initial /h/); and *jet, gem, net* (to review /e/ in the medial position).

Photo Card

2 **Guided Practice/Practice** Show children sets of the Photo Cards. Name the pictures with children and have them say the first sound of the words in each set. Guide practice and provide corrective feedback.

fire, fish, fork	hat, hair, hippo
envelope, egg, elevator	football, fox, fan
hay, hook, horse	exit, elbow, egg
deer, dog, door	nest, nut, nose

Articulation Support

If children need additional support, refer to Articulation Support in Unit 5: page T14 for /h/; T92 for /e/; T170 for /f/ and /r/. Refer to Unit 6: page T254 for /b/ and /l/, and T332 for /k/.

⏱ 10 mins Phonics

MULTIMODAL

Introduce *l*-Blends

1 **Model** Display the *cloud* Photo Card. Point to the letters *c* and *l* on the back of the card. Say: *This is the* cloud *Photo Card. The first two sounds in* cloud *are /kl/. They are spelled with the letters* c *and* l. *Say the sounds with me: /kl/.* Repeat for these *l*-blends: /bl/ (*blue* Photo Card), /fl/ (*flute* Photo Card), and /sl/.

Photo Card

2 **Guided Practice/Practice** Guide practice connecting *c* and *l* to /kl/ by writing the letters. Say: *Now do it with me. Say /kl/ as I write* c *and* l. *Now write* c *and* l *on your* **Response Boards** *and say /kl/ as you write the letters.* Repeat for the *l*-blends /bl/ *bl*, /fl/ *fl*, and /sl/ *sl*. Use **Practice Book** page 277 for additional practice with initial consonant *l*-blends sound-spellings.

Review /e/*e*, /h/*h*, /f/*f*, /r/*r*, /b/*b*, /l/*l*, /k/*k*

1 **Model** Display the *Egg* **Sound-Spelling Card**. *This is the letter* e. *The letter* e *can stand for the sound /e/ as at the beginning of the word* egg *or in the middle of the word* gem. Remind children that the letter *e* is a vowel. Repeat for /h/*h*, /f/*f*, /r/*r*, /b/*b*, /l/*l*, and /k/*k* with the *hippo, fire, rose, bat, lemon,* and *koala* Sound-Spelling Cards.

2 **Guided Practice/Practice** Have children listen as you say some words. Ask them to write the letter *e* on their Response Boards and say the sound it stands for. If children need additional practice reviewing sound-spellings, have them use Practice Book pages 274–276.

exit   dig   end   road   ever   echo   tip   empty

Repeat for /h/*h* and /f/*f*.

help	pack	hit	home	nose	hill	hand
face	fox	make	five	fish	cow	foot

Repeat for /r/*r*, /b/*b*, /l/*l*, and /k/*k*.

key	light	big	king	rake	ball	keep
lamp	bus	kiss	rock	road	leaf	bite

Corrective Feedback

Sound Error Model the sound /h/ in the initial position, then have children repeat the sound. Say: *My turn. Hit. /h/ /h/ /h/. Now it's your turn.* Have children say the words *hot* and *hat* and isolate the initial sound. Repeat for /f/ with the words *fan, foot, fed;* initial /e/ with the words *egg, elf;* and medial /e/ with *pen, bed.*

LESSON 1

5 mins

Handwriting: Write Sentences with *h, e, f, r, b, l, k, ck*

MULTIMODAL

1 **Guided Practice** Review handwriting and letter sound correspondence with the letters *h, e, f, r, b, l, k, ck*.

- Write the following sentence. *Rick and Kim had fed the cat.* Read the sentence with children and track the print.

- *I hear the /r/ sound in the word* Rick. *I know that the letter* r *stands for /r/. I will underline the letter* r *because it stands for /r/. Which words have the sound /k/?* (Rick, Kim) *Which letter(s) stands for /k/?* Underline the letter *k* at the beginning of *Kim* and *ck* at the end of *Rick*. Continue asking children which word has the sound /h/ and which letter stands for the sound (had, *h*); /f/ (fed, *f*) and /e/ (fed, *e*). Underline the letters that stand for the sounds and read the words with children.

2 **Practice**

- Write the following sentence for children to copy: *Ben let Rob pack the hat.* Give them ample time to write the sentence. Chorally read the sentence.

- Ask children to identify which words have the sound /b/. (Ben, Rob) Have them underline the letter that stands for the sound (*b*) and read the words. Ask children to identify words with the following sounds and to underline the letter that stands for the sound: /l/ (let, *l*); /e/ (Ben, let *e*); /r/ (Rob, *r*); /k/ (pack, *ck*); and /h/ (hat, *h*).

- Have children check that the words in their sentences are separated by spaces. Remind them that all sentences begin with a capital letter and have end punctuation. Have them correct as needed.

- **Multisensory Activity** Write the following on a sentence strip in advance: *Deb and Pam fed the red clam.* Trace the sentence with glue and cover with a textured surface, such as sand or beans. After it dries, have children trace the words with their finger as they say the words aloud. Then have them write the sentence.

Daily Handwriting

Throughout the week, review writing words and sentences using appropriate directionality with *h, e, k, f, r, b, l, ck*.

In a Flash: High-Frequency Words

she

1. **Teacher:** Read the word.   **Children:** she
2. **Teacher:** Spell the word.   **Children:** s-h-e
3. **Teacher:** Write the word.   **Children write the word.**

Repeat routine with previously taught words.

High-Frequency Words

MULTIMODAL

are	he	is
little	my	she
was	with	

1 **Model** Display the **High-Frequency Word Card** *my* to review the word using the Read/Spell/Write routine.

- **Read** Point to the word *my* and say the word. *This is the word* my. *Say it with me:* my. *I like to ride my bicycle.*

- **Spell** *The word* my *is spelled* m-y. *Spell it with me.*

- **Write** *Let's write* my *on your* **Response Boards** *as we say each letter:* m-y. Guide children on how to form and print letters that have not been taught yet.

Repeat the routine with *are, he, is, little, she, was,* and *with.*

2 **Guided Practice/Practice** Build sentences using High-Frequency Word Cards, **Photo Cards**, and teacher-prepared punctuation cards. Have children point to the high-frequency words *are, he, is, little, my, she, was, with.* Use these sentences. Guide practice and provide corrective feedback as needed.

***She was with** the queen.*   ***Are** you **little**?*

***He** can see a **little** barn.*

Is	my		little	?

ELL ENGLISH LANGUAGE LEARNERS

Use with **High-Frequency Words, Guided Practice/Practice** and the **High-Frequency Word Routine.**

Beginning
Stand next to a child and say: *I am with _____.* Repeat with another child. Have partners complete the sentence frame.

Intermediate
Point out the question mark in the second sentence. Model reading the sentence correctly. Have children repeat.

Advanced/Advanced High
Challenge partners to create sentences using the words.

FORMATIVE ASSESSMENT

⊘ STUDENT CHECK-IN

Handwriting Have children print *Hh, Ee, Ff, Rr, Bb, Ll, Kk, ck.*

High-Frequency Words Have partners take turns pointing to and reading the words *are, he, is, little, my, she, was, with.*

Then have children reflect using the Check-In routine.

✓ CHECK FOR SUCCESS

Rubric Use your online rubric to record children's progress.

Can children match /e/, /h/, /f/ to *Ee, Hh,* and *Ff?*

Can children recognize and read the high-frequency words?

≫ Small Group Instruction

If No
- **Approaching** Reteach pp. T458–T462
- **ELL** Develop pp. T458–T462

If Yes
- **On** Review pp. T466–T468
- **Beyond** Extend pp. T472

LESSON
1

Literature Big Book

OBJECTIVES

Demonstrate command of the conventions of standard English capitalization, punctuation, and spelling when writing.

Continue a conversation through multiple exchanges.

Form regular plural nouns orally by adding /s/ or /es/.

ELA ACADEMIC LANGUAGE

• line, noun, plural
• Cognates: línea, plural

 COLLABORATIVE CONVERSATIONS

Turn and Talk Review this routine.

Child 1: *Play inside.*

Child 2: *Can you say that in a complete sentence?*

Child 1: *I play inside when it rains.*

Display the speech bubble, "Can you say that in a complete sentence?" Have partners use it to practice collaborating.

Modeled Writing
10 mins

Model Writing About the Literature Big Book

 Build Oral Language Talk about what children learned from listening to the **Literature Big Book**. Review what the people and animals do during the storm. Ask: *What do you like to do when it rains?* Have children share their response with the class. Model restating children's ideas as complete sentences. Have partners use the Turn and Talk routine to talk about something they do when it rains. Encourage them to share out one thing they talked about with their partner.

Model Writing a Sentence Write and display this sentence: **I like to read a book when it rains**. Then point out the following elements of writing using the Sample Teacher Talk.

• *This is the word* book. *I wrote the letter* k *at the end of* book *because I heard the /k/ sound at the end of the word.* Phonics

• *This is the word* to. *I used the Word Bank to help me spell the word.* To *is spelled with the letters:* t-o. High-Frequency Word

• *As I wrote my sentence, I stayed on the lines.* Writing Skill

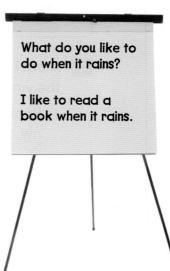

What do you like to do when it rains?

I like to read a book when it rains.

Writing Practice

Turn to pages 74-75 of the **Reading/Writing Companion**. Say: *Now we are going to read a different sentence about what someone does in stormy weather.*

Analyze a Sentence Guide children to analyze the sentence using the prompts. Review the writing skill with children as necessary. Then have children write and analyze their own sentence.

Writing Practice

Write a Sentence

Talk about the stormy weather in the story.

Listen to this sentence about stormy weather.

I see lightning outside my window.

Circle the letters that touch the top and bottom lines.

Writing Skill
Try to stay on the lines when you write.

74 Unit 6 · Week 3

Write a sentence about what you do in stormy weather.

Circle the letters that touch the top and bottom lines.

Stormy Weather 75

Reading/Writing Companion, pp. 74-75

Grammar

5 mins

Singular and Plural Nouns

1 **Model** Remind children that nouns are naming words. Review that singular nouns name one person, place, animal, or thing. Plural nouns name more than one. Point out that plural nouns often end in *-s* or *-es*. Explain that we add *-s* to most words to make them plural: *boy/boys, car/cars, day/days.* Write the following letters/blends on the board as you say their sounds aloud: *-s, -ss, -sh, -ch, -x, -z.* Explain to children that they should add *-es* to words with these endings to make them plural: *dish/dishes, mess/messes, lunch/lunches, ax/axes.*

2 **Guided Practice** Write and read aloud: *box, clock, dress, bush,* and *tree.* Ask: *What endings will make these words tell about more than one thing?* Guide children to identify the correct endings using the examples you provided during the model. (*-es* for *box, dress,* and *bush; -s* for *clock* and *tree*)

3 **Practice** Give children a list of the following nouns: *fox, sock, glass, wish,* and *bee.* Have partners determine whether to add *-s* or *-es* to make the noun plural using the list of endings that require *-es* written on the board.

Talk About It Have partners work together to generate sentences with singular and plural nouns such as: *dishes, sink,* and *nights.*

Link to Writing Guide children to review the Shared Writing sentences and identify any plural nouns they may have used.

English Language Learners

Use the following scaffolds with **Grammar, Practice.**

Beginning

Show pictures with labels for *sock/socks* and *glass/glasses.* Have children point to the *-s* or *-es* endings as they say each word.

Intermediate

Draw a T-chart on the board with *-s* and *-es* column headings. Beneath *-es,* write the letters/blends that cause that ending. Help children sort the nouns into the correct columns.

Advanced/Advanced High

Have partners make the nouns plural by using the T-chart.

DIGITAL TOOLS

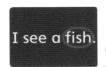

Grammar Activity

DIFFERENTIATED WRITING

● **English Language Learners** For more writing support, see the **ELL Small Group Guide,** p. 154.

FORMATIVE ASSESSMENT

STUDENT CHECK-IN

Have partners share a plural noun they learned. Have children reflect using the Check-In routine.

LEARNING GOALS

- We can tell if words begin with the same sound.
- We can use new words.
- We can learn about words that ask questions.
- We can put words into groups.

OBJECTIVES

Isolate and pronounce the initial sounds (phonemes) in words.

Use words and phrases acquired through conversations, reading and being read to, and responding to texts.

With guidance and support from adults, explore word relationships and nuances in word meanings.

Understand and use question words (interrogatives). (e.g., who, what, where, when, why, how).

ELA ACADEMIC LANGUAGE

- *categories*
- Cognate: *categorías*

DIGITAL TOOLS

Weekly Poem

Visual Vocabulary Cards

Category Words Activity

LESSON FOCUS

READING
Review Essential Question
Reread Literature Big Book
Waiting Out the Storm
- Study Genre/Skill
Read Shared Read
"Mack and Ben"
- Practice Strategy

Word Work
- Review *l*-Blends
- Blend Words with *l*-Blends
WRITING
Writing/Grammar
- Interactive Writing
- Practice Grammar

Literature Big Book, pp. 3–27

Reading/Writing Companion, pp. 80–87

---

10 mins

Oral Language

MULTIMODAL

? Essential Question

How can you stay safe in bad weather?

Remind children that we are learning about weather. Say: *Think about the weather in the story,* Waiting Out the Storm. *What type of weather was it? How did the girl and her mom stay safe from the weather? Let's read a poem about weather.* Read "Whether the Weather." Then use the Build Knowledge anchor chart, the **Big Book,** and the **Weekly Poem** to guide children in discussing the Essential Question.

Phonological Awareness: Identify Alliteration

1 **Model** Tell children that some words begin with the same sounds. Say *whatever* and *weather* from the poem and point out that both start with the /w/ sound. Give another example of a group of words that begin with the same initial sound: *nap, nest, nickel. These words all begin with the sound /n/.*

2 **Guided Practice/Practice** Say the following word sets, have children repeat, and then have them raise their hands if the words in the set begin with the same sound: *happy hairy hippo; big book; wet floor; lost little lamb.* Guide practice and provide corrective feedback as needed. If children need additional practice recognizing alliteration, have them use **Practice Book** page 273.

Review Oral Vocabulary Words

Use the Define/Example/Ask routine to review the oral vocabulary words *prepare* and *safe.* Prompt children to use the words in sentences.

Visual Vocabulary Cards

Category Words: Question Words

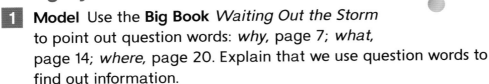

1 **Model** Use the **Big Book** *Waiting Out the Storm* to point out question words: *why,* page 7; *what,* page 14; *where,* page 20. Explain that we use question words to find out information.

Sing the following verses from "Mary Had a Little Lamb."

**Mary had a little lamb whose fleece was white as snow.
And everywhere that Mary went, the lamb was sure to go.
It followed her to school one day, which was against the rules.
It made the children laugh and play, to see a lamb at school.**

Use question words to ask children about the nursery rhyme. *Who is the song about?* (Mary) *What did she have?* (a lamb)

2 **Guided Practice/Practice** Say the words below. Have children raise their hands when they hear a question word.

who	word	talk	where
what	teacher	why	time

Vocabulary: Question Words

1 **Model** Explain that words that have something in common can be grouped into categories. Use *Waiting Out the Storm* to model how words can be grouped into categories.

Think Aloud In *Waiting Out the Storm*, the little girl asks many questions. We can group all of the question words together because they are similar and show how the girl is trying to gather information. The words *why, what, how, where,* and *who* are words that fit into a category called question words.

2 **Guided Practice** Help children locate words in the book that fall into different kinds of categories, such as *question words* and *weather words*. Make a list of the words in each category.

3 **Practice** Work with children to ask questions about preparing for storms, using each of the question words. Discuss and answer the questions.

KIDS ON THE MOVE!

Have children stand side by side. Children should take one step forward when they hear a sentence with a question word. Have children take one step backward if the sentence does not have a question word.

Phonological Awareness: p. 273

ELL ENGLISH LANGUAGE LEARNERS

Use with **Category Words, Practice.**

Beginning
Help children ask questions using *what.* Model and have them repeat: *What do you need?* Help them respond: I need a rain coat.

Intermediate
Help children ask questions using *what* and *where.* Model and have them repeat: *Where do you go?* I go inside.

Advanced/Advanced High
Help children ask and answer questions using *what, where,* and *who.* Provide a model: *Who do you ask for help?* I ask my mother.

FORMATIVE ASSESSMENT

● STUDENT CHECK-IN

Oral Vocabulary Words Have partners share one way to stay *safe.*

Category Words Have partners name a word that asks a question.

Vocabulary Have partners name a word that they grouped with question words.

Then have children reflect using the Check-In routine.

Literature Big Book

LEARNING GOALS

- **We can tell what makes a story realistic fiction.**
- **We can identify the sequence of events.**

OBJECTIVES

Recognize common types of texts.

With prompting and support, identify characters, settings, and major events in a story.

ELA ACADEMIC LANGUAGE

- *realistic fiction, events*
- Cognates: *ficción realista, eventos*

Reread

Literature Big Book

Genre: Realistic Fiction

1 **Model** Tell children that you will now reread the **Literature Big Book** *Waiting Out the Storm*. Remind them that this story is realistic fiction.

 Anchor Chart Display and review the characteristics of realistic fiction that you have listed on the Realistic Fiction anchor chart. Add details as needed.

Think Aloud I know that the book *Waiting Out the Storm* is realistic fiction because it is a made-up story about events that could happen in real life. The characters in the story act like real people. The story is about a rainstorm, which is a real-life event. The characters react to the storm like people would in real life. The girl and her mom go in the house to get out of the rainstorm. I would also want to stay dry and safe in a rainstorm. Just like the characters in the story, I would go inside to get out of the rainstorm.

2 **Guided Practice/Practice** Explain to children that the story tells about animals that are found in real life and how they react to the storm. Reread pages 16–21 of *Waiting Out the Storm* and point out the animals. Turn to pages 16–17 and ask: *What animals do you see?* (turtles and ducks) *How do the ducks respond to the storm?* (They paddle in the water.) Turn to pages 18–19. Ask: *What animal do you see?* (chipmunks) *What do the chipmunks to do in the storm?* (snuggle together in their burrow) Turn to pages 20–21 Ask: *Where do the birds go in the storm?* (beneath mama's wings) *What is happening on these pages that could happen in real life?* (The animals in the story all respond to the storm the way animals in real life would.)

ELL English Language Learners

Genre: Realistic Fiction, Guided Practice Guide children to contribute to the discussion by using the illustrations. For example, for pages 16–17, ask: *What animals do you see?* Provide a sentence frame: I see <u>turtles</u> and <u>ducks</u>. *Do you think this could really happen? What else in this story could really happen?* Have children point to the illustrations. Help children tell what the animals or the girl and mother are doing.

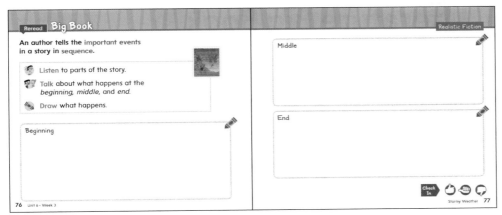

Reading/Writing Companion, pp. 76-77

Events: Sequence

1 **Model** Remind children that a story is made up of different events. The author tells the story in the order that the events happen. Words such as *beginning, middle* and *end* can help us talk about the events in a story.

Anchor Chart Display the Main Story Elements: Events anchor chart. Encourage children to identify new information about sequence to add to the anchor chart.

Think Aloud This story is about a girl and her mother and how they stay safe in a rainstorm. In the beginning of the story, there are signs that that a storm is coming. In the middle of the story, the author shares how the animals react to the storm. At the end of the story, the girl and her mother go in the house to stay safe from the storm. I use the words *beginning, middle* and *end* to think about the order of events or sequence. These words help me share the most important parts of the story.

2 **Guided Practice/Practice** Turn to pages 76-77 of the **Reading/ Writing Companion**. Ask children to listen as you reread pages 4–15 of *Waiting Out the Storm. What happens in the begining of the story that let the girl and her mother know a storm is coming?* (wind whistles; raindrops dance; thunder rumbles) Read pages 16–21. *What happens in the middle of the story?* (turtles sit on a rock; ducks paddle in the water; chipmunks snuggle in their burrow; birds hide beneath their mother's wings) Finally read pages 22–27. *What happens at the end of the story?* (The girl and her mother go in the house to be safe and warm.) Pause between the different parts of the story to give children time to choose and draw one event that happens in the *beginning, middle,* and *end.*

ELL ENGLISH LANGUAGE LEARNERS

Events: Sequence: Guided Practice/ Practice Give children sentence frames to help them discuss the events sequence. Pages 4–15: *What happens first in the story?* The girl and her mother hear the storm coming. Pages 16–21: *What happens next in the story?* Have children point to the animals. Help them name the different animals and describe what they are doing. Provide a sentence frame: The girl learns what animals do when a storm comes. Pages 22–27: Have children point to what the girl and mother are doing. Help them describe what is happening. The girl and her mother go into the house.

For additional support, see the **ELL Small Group Guide**, pp. 152-153.

FORMATIVE ASSESSMENT

❯ STUDENT CHECK-IN

Genre Have partners share what makes the story realistic fiction.

Events Have children identify the sequence of the story using the words *beginning, middle,* and *end.*

Then have children reflect on their learning using the Check-In routine.

✓ CHECK FOR SUCCESS

Can children identify characteristics of realistic fiction?

Can children identify sequence?

❯❯ **Small Group Instruction**

If No

● **Approaching** Reteach pp. T456–T457

If Yes

● **On** Review pp. T464–465

● **Beyond** Extend pp. T470-471

Literature Big Book

LEARNING GOALS

We can name the choices the author made when writing a story.

OBJECTIVES

With guidance and support from adults, explore word relationships and nuances in word meanings.

With prompting and support, describe the relationship between illustrations and the story in which they appear.

Analyze author's/illustrator's craft.

ELA ACADEMIC LANGUAGE

• *illustrations, italic*

• Cognate: *ilustraciones*

Reread

10 mins

Literature Big Book

Analyze the Text

Once children have reread *Waiting Out the Storm* to study the characteristics of the genre and practice the comprehension skill, guide them to analyze author's craft. Reread the passages specified below and use the scaffolded instruction in the prompts to help children answer the questions on pages 78-79 of the **Reading/Writing Companion**.

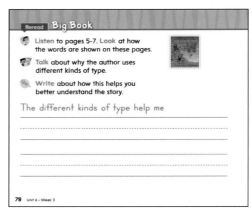

Reread Big Book

- Listen to pages 5-7. Look at how the words are shown on these pages.
- Talk about why the author uses different kinds of type.
- Write about how this helps you better understand the story.

The different kinds of type help me

_____

_____

_____

_____

78 Unit 6 • Week 3

Reading/Writing Companion, p. 78

AUTHOR'S/ILLUSTRATOR'S CRAFT DOK 3

Display and reread pages 5–7 of the **Big Book**. Notice the text. The author uses regular type for the child's words and italics for the mother's words. Ask: *What can you learn about the story from the way the text is written?* (The girl's words are larger and in the form of questions. The mother's words are italic and help to visualize what is happening.)

English Language Learners

Author's Craft Explain that the italics are the slanted words on the page. Ask children to point to them on each page. Ask: *Who is speaking here? How do you know?*

WORD CHOICE DOK 2

Display and reread pages 6–7 of the Big Book. Explain to children that the mother describes the wind and rain as if they are people to keep the girl from being afraid of the storm. Ask: *What words describe what the wind does?* (whistles; calls the raindrops to play) *What do these words tell you about the wind and the rain?* (Possible response: It makes them sound like friends.)

AUTHOR'S CRAFT DOK 2

Display and reread page 8 of the Big Book. *What words does the author use to help you visualize how the raindrops act when the wind calls?* (skipping, leaping, laughing, spin, tumble, bounce, dance) *If the raindrops do these things, how do you think they feel when the wind calls?* (happy)

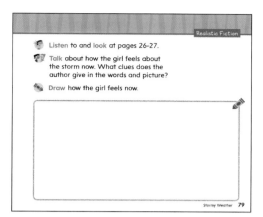

Reading/Writing Companion, p. 79

AUTHOR/ILLUSTRATOR'S CRAFT DOK 2

Display and reread pages 26–27 of the **Big Book**. Look closely at the illustration and talk about how the little girl feels about the storm now that she is in the house. *How does the illustration help you know how the girl feels?* (The girl is snuggling with her mother and watching the rain. I think she feels safe and happy to be in the house.)

Spotlight on Language

Author's/Illustrator's Craft Look at pages 24–25 and help children describe what they see. Ask: *What is the mother doing? What is the girl doing? How does the girl feel? How do you know?* Give children sentence frames to help them answer as needed.

WORD CHOICE DOK 2

Display pages 26–27 of the Big Book. *What do you think the word* snuggling *means?* (warm and comfortable) *Who is snuggling in the pictures?* (The rabbits and the girl and her mom.)

Talk About It

Guide children to use their responses on the **Reading/Writing Companion** pages to answer the following question:
How does the girl feel about the storm?
If necessary, use the following sentence starters to focus the discussion:
The girl hears the _____ and she is _____. The girl sees the _____ and she is _____. The girl feels safe when _____.

Integrate

Build Knowledge: Make Connections

Talk About the Text Have partners discuss the weather in the story. *What do the girl and her mom do to stay safe in a thunderstorm? What other ways can they be safe during a thunderstorm?*

Add to the Anchor Chart Record any new ideas on the Build Knowledge Anchor Chart.

MAKE INFERENCES

Remind children that when we make an inference, we use clues in the story to figure out something the author does not say.

Think Aloud. On pages 14–15, the author uses rhyming words to describe the lightning. The rhyming words help the mother describe the lightning to the daughter in a way that is fun. The author shows that the mother is trying to make the girl be less afraid.

FORMATIVE ASSESSMENT

⊘ STUDENT CHECK-IN

Have partners share something that the author/illustrator does with the text and images to help you understand the story. Then have children reflect using the Check-In routine.

Display the **Word-Building Card** for *bl*.
1. **Teacher:** What's the letter? **Children:** bl
2. **Teacher:** What's the sound? **Children:** /bl/

Continue the routine for previously taught sounds.

LEARNING GOALS

- We can blend sounds to say words.
- We can connect letters to sounds to read words.
- We can read high-frequency words.

OBJECTIVES

Demonstrate understanding of spoken words, syllables, and sounds (phonemes).

Demonstrate basic knowledge of one-to-one letter-sound correspondences by producing the primary sound or many of the most frequent sounds for each consonant.

Read common high-frequency words by sight.

Review *l*-blends.

ELA ACADEMIC LANGUAGE

- *high-frequency word*

⊙ TEACH IN SMALL GROUP

You may wish to teach Word Work in small groups.

DIGITAL TOOLS

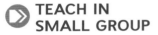

Word Work

Phonemic Awareness

Phonics: Spelling Song

To differentiate instruction for key skills, use the results of these activities.

Phonics: Data-Generating

High-Frequency Words: Data-Generating

OPTIONAL 5 mins

Phonemic Awareness

Phoneme Blending

1 **Model** Say: *Listen to the sounds in a word: /b/ /e/ /t/. I can blend those sounds to make a word: /beeet/ bet. When I blend the sounds together, it makes the word* bet. Model phoneme blending with the following:

/k/ /i/ /k/   /h/ /o/ /p/   /n/ /e/ /t/   /f/ /i/ /l/

2 **Guided Practice/Practice** *Listen to the sounds in a different word: /s/ /t/ /i/ /k/. Let's blend the sounds and say the word together: /s/ /t/ /i/ /k/, /stiiik/ stick.* Tell children to listen to the sounds in words, repeat the sounds, and then blend them to say the word. Guide practice and provide corrective feedback as needed.

/l/ /e/ /s/, less   /k/ /i/ /t/, kit   /f/ /a/ /n/, fan

/r/ /e/ /d/, red   /s/ /n/ /a/ /k/, snack   /s/ /p/ /e/ /k/, speck

5 mins

Phonics

MULTIMODAL

Review *l*-Blends

1 **Model** Display **Word-Building Cards** *c, l.* Review the sounds /kl/ spelled *cl* using the word *click*. Repeat for additional *l*-blends /bl/, /fl/, and /sl/, using Word-Building Cards to review the letter sound correspondences for each blend.

2 **Guided Practice/Practice** Have children listen as you say some words. Ask them to write the letters *cl, bl, fl,* or *sl* that stand for the beginning *l*-blend sound they hear in each word on their **Response Boards.** Guide practice and provide corrective feedback as needed.

fly   club   slide   blue   close   slip

sleep   blend   clown   flow   blocks   clock

🎵 Review /h/*h* from Lesson 1. Have children write *h* on their Response Boards. Play "There's a Hippo in the House." Have children show their Response Boards when they hear /h/. Repeat for /f/*f* using "Let's Build a Fire."

Blend Words

1 **Model** Place **Word-Building Cards** *b, l, o,* and *t* in a pocket chart. Point to *b* and *l. These are the letters* b *and* l*. They stand for /bl/. Say /bl/. Listen as I blend the sounds: /bl/. This is the letter* o*. The letter* o *stands for /o/. Say /o/. This is the letter* t*. The letter* t *stands for /t/. Say /t/. Listen as I blend the four sounds together: /blooot/.* Continue by modeling how to blend the words *clap, flip,* and *sled.*

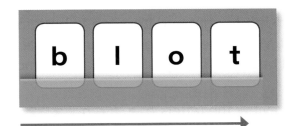

2 **Guided Practice/Practice** Change the Word-Building Cards to *s, l, i, p.* Point to the letters *s* and *l* and have children say /sl/. Point to the letter *i* and have children say /i/. Point to the letter *p* and have children say /p/. Then move your hand from left to right under the word and have children blend and read the word, *slip.* Repeat with the words *clip, flip,* and *block.*

OPTIONAL 5 mins

 MULTIMODAL

High-Frequency Words

1 **Guided Practice** Display the **High-Frequency Word Card** *are.* Use the Read/Spell/Write routine to review the word. Then ask children to write the word without looking at the word card. If needed, guide children on how to form letters that have not been taught yet. Then have children self-correct by checking the High-Frequency Word Card.

2 **Practice** Review the current words in the word bank.

• Have partners say sentences using the word.

Repeat with the other high-frequency words.

Cumulative Review Review the high-frequency words *to, and, go, you, do* and *with* by displaying each word and having children read it with automaticity.

For additional practice with high-frequency words, have them use **Practice Book** page 279.

 ENGLISH LANGUAGE LEARNERS

High-Frequency Words, Practice
Display the Word Card and provide sentence frames for children to practice using *are.* For example: *We _____ in school. [Name] and [Name] _____ friends.* Repeat with the other high-frequency words.

High-Frequency Words: p. 279

FORMATIVE ASSESSMENT

❯ STUDENT CHECK-IN

Phonics Have partners blend and read *flip.*

High-Frequency Words Have partners take turns pointing to and reading *are, he, is, little, my, she, was* with.

Then have children reflect using the Check-In routine.

✓ CHECK FOR SUCCESS

Rubric Use your online rubric to record children's progress.

Can children blend and read words with *l*-blends?

Can children read and recognize the high-frequency words?

❯ Small Group Instruction

If No

● **Approaching** Reteach pp. T458–T462

● **ELL** Develop pp. T458–T462

If Yes

● **On** Review pp. T466–T468

● **Beyond** Extend p. T472

LESSON **2**

Read "Mack and Ben"

10 mins

LEARNING GOALS

We can read and understand a story.

OBJECTIVES

Follow words from left to right, top to bottom, and page by page.

Know and apply grade-level phonics and word analysis skills in decoding words.

Demonstrate basic knowledge of one-to-one letter-sound correspondences by producing the primary sound or many of the most frequent sounds for each consonant.

Read common high-frequency words by sight.

Read emergent-reader texts with purpose and understanding.

ELA ACADEMIC LANGUAGE

• *sentence, visualize*

• Cognate: *visualizar*

DIFFERENTIATED READING

● **English Language Learners**
Have children listen to a summary of the selection, available in multiple languages.

Connect to Concept

As children read this story, have them look for details that will help them answer the Essential Question: *How can you stay safe in bad weather?*

Foundational Skills

Concepts of Print Turn to page 81 of the **Reading/Writing Companion** and model reading from left to right and from top to bottom, using your finger to track the print. When I read, I start on the left side of the page and move to the right. I begin at the top of the page and move to the bottom.

Phonics Have children review the letters *h, e, f, r, b, l, k, ck,* and the sounds they stand for. Have children review the *l*-Blends *bl, cl, fl,* and *sl.*

High-Frequency Words Have children review the words *are, she, is, little, my, was,* and *with.*

Read the Shared Read

Visualize Remind children that they can use the words and the illustrations in a story to form pictures in their minds of what is happening.

 Anchor Chart Display and review the Visualize anchor chart. Tell children they will be using this strategy with the story they are about to read.

Choral Read Have children preview the illustrations. Invite them to share any questions they have. Have children chorally read the story with you.

Read Tell children that now they will read the story, and you will pause to ask them the questions in the blue column. Remind children to use the pictures to help them when understanding breaks down.

Have children use the box on the right-hand pages to:

• Draw a picture about the text or the art.

• Draw something whose name includes the /h/, /f/, /r/, /b/, /l/, or /k/ sounds or *bl, cl, fl* and *sl* blends.

• Write the letters *h, e, f, r, b, l, k, ck* and the blends *bl, cl, fl, sl.*

Reading/Writing Companion, pp. 80–81

SET PURPOSE

Have children read to find out about Mack and Ben.

PHONICS

Tell children to circle the word that begins with the same sounds as *sled.* (slip)

Reading/Writing Companion, pp. 82–83

Reading/Writing Companion, pp. 84–85

Reading/Writing Companion, pp. 86–87

Focus on Fluency: Accuracy

Model reading with accuracy for children. Remind them of the importance of recognizing high-frequency words as well as decoding words in the text correctly. Encourage children to practice reading for accuracy with a partner. Listen in, offer support, and give corrective feedback.

Respond to the Text

Talk About It Have partners discuss what Mack and Ben did while waiting for the rain to stop. Use the sentence starter to focus the discussion. **Mack and Ben _____.** Help children cite text evidence to support their answers.

VISUALIZE

Have children visualize what Mack is thinking. (Children's ideas should reflect that Mack is sad about the weather.)

PHONICS

Have children underline words that begin with the same sound as *he*. (hot, hot, ham)

PHONICS

Have children circle a picture whose name begins with the same sounds as *clip*. (clock)

PHONICS

Tell children to underline words that end with the same sounds as *rock*. (clock, tick, tock, Mack, Mack, kick)

HIGH-FREQUENCY WORDS

Have children circle and read the high-frequency word *are*.

COMPREHENSION

Have children use the setting to retell the story. Encourage them to reference the pictures and words as needed.

ENGLISH LANGUAGE LEARNERS

Use the scaffolds with **Respond to the Text.**

Beginning

Point to illustrations on pages 81 and 82. *Mack runs with Ben. They run home. They stay inside.* Have children repeat. Help children complete a shortened sentence frame: You should stay inside.

Intermediate

Encourage children to tell about the story. Provide sentence frames: The characters run home. Mack and Ben stay inside. They wait for the storm to end.

Advanced/Advanced High

Have partners talk about what happens in the story and use the details to complete the sentence frame. Provide modeling. *I learned that when a storm comes you should stay inside.*

❯ STUDENT CHECK-IN

Have partners take turns sharing their retelling of the story with one another. Then have children reflect using the Check-In routine.

Waiting Out the Storm

J0ANN EARLY MACKEN · Illustrated by SUSAN GABER

Literature Big Book

LEARNING GOALS

- We can write what the girl and her mother can do when the storm stops.
- We can learn about words that name more than one person, place, or thing (plural nouns).

OBJECTIVES

Use a combination of drawing, dictating, and writing to narrate a single event or several loosely linked events.

Write a letter or letters for most consonant and short-vowel sounds (phonemes).

Use frequently occurring nouns.

Form regular plural nouns orally by adding /s/ or /es/.

Write in response to a text.

ELA ACADEMIC LANGUAGE

- *describe, plural*
- Cognates: *describir, plural*

 COLLABORATIVE CONVERSATIONS

Circulate as partners talk about the prompt. Notice who is speaking in incomplete sentences. Remind them to use the speech bubble.

 Interactive Writing · 10 mins

Write About the Literature Big Book

 Analyze the Prompt Tell children that today they will write about the Literature Big Book, *Waiting Out the Storm*. Ask: *What can the girl and her mother do when the storm stops? Write the next part of the story.* Turn to page 27. Have children turn and talk about the different things the girl and her mother could do once the storm stops.

Find Text Evidence Turn to pages 26–27. Ask: *What are the girl and the mother doing?* (snuggling and looking out the window) *What do they see?* (flowers, leaves, and tree branches) Encourage children to make predictions about what the mother and the girl might do after the storm.

Write a Response: Share the Pen Have children provide a response to the prompt and encourage them to share the pen to help you write a response. Alternatively, use the sentence on the anchor chart. Point out the following elements of writing using the Sample Teacher Talk below.

- *Look at the Word Bank. Who can point to the word* go? *Let's spell it:* g-o. Write the word as children dictate it to you.   HIGH-FREQUENCY WORDS

- *Say* flowers. *What are the first sounds we hear? /fl/ What letters stand for that sound?* Have a volunteer write the word *flowers*.   PHONICS

- *When we write, we make sure to stay on the lines.* Have volunteers circle the letters that touch the top and bottom lines.   WRITING SKILL

- *When we write, we use words to describe. In our sentence, the word* pretty *describes the flowers.*   TRAIT: WORD CHOICE

> What can the girl and her mother do when the storm stops? Write the next part of the story.
>
> They can go outside to smell the pretty flowers.

 ### Writing Practice

Write Provide children with the following sentence frames and have them complete them in their writer's notebook.

Mama, can we _____?   **Buttercup, I would love to _____.**

As children write, encourage them to:

- Use the Word Bank to help spell high-frequency words.
- Stretch the sounds they hear in words as they write.
- Stay on the lines as they write.
- Use descriptive words in their writing.

Grammar

5 mins

Singular and Plural Nouns

1 Model Remind children that nouns are naming words. Review that singular nouns name one person, place, animal, or thing. Plural nouns name more than one. Remind children that they should add -s to most words to make them plural, *girl/girls*, and add -es to words with these endings:-s, -ss, -sh, -ch, -x, and -z. For example: *bus/bus*es. Show pictures of the birds in the **Big Book** and circle the ending in the plural noun *birds*.

2 Guided Practice Point to the flowers, branches, umbrella, basket, squirrels, and birds in the Big Book. Ask children to name these things as you write the words on the board. Guide them to identify which words name one thing and which name more than one thing. Then guide volunteers to circle the ending in each plural noun. Provide guidance as needed.

3 Practice Have children create sentences using things shown in the Big Book. For example: *The squirrels play in the branches.* Write children's sentences on the board as they dictate. Have partners draw a picture for one of the sentences. Have them write the sentence and then circle the ending in each plural noun. Ask partners to share their work with the class. If children need additional practice with plural nouns, have them use **Practice Book** page 282 or online activities.

Talk About It

Give partners **Photo Cards** that show singular nouns. Have them say the word shown and then make the word plural. Challenge children to identify if the plural ending is -s or -es.

English Language Learners

Grammar, Practice Help children describe their drawings and create sentences that include plural nouns. Point out the usages of -s or -es. For example, if the drawing shows a squirrel, indicate one squirrel and say *squirrel*. Then indicate more than one squirrel and say *squirrels*. Have children repeat each word. Repeat the routine with *branch/branches*.

Speakers of Cantonese, Hmong, Korean, Vietnamese, Arabic, and Spanish may have difficulty remembering to use the plural marker -s.

DIGITAL TOOLS

Grammar Activity

DIFFERENTIATED WRITING

● **English Language Learners** For more writing support, see the **ELL Small Group Guide**, p. 154.

Grammar: p. 282

FORMATIVE ASSESSMENT

STUDENT CHECK-IN

Have partners share a plural noun they learned. Have children reflect using the Check-In routine.

LESSON 3

LEARNING GOALS

We can learn new words.

OBJECTIVES

Use words and phrases acquired through conversations, reading and being read to, and responding to texts.

Identify real-life connections between words and their use.

Develop oral vocabulary.

ELA ACADEMIC LANGUAGE

• *text*
• Cognate: *texto*

DIGITAL TOOLS

Weekly Poem

Visual Vocabulary Cards

Interactive Read Aloud

FORMATIVE ASSESSMENT

❯ STUDENT CHECK-IN

Have partners tell each other the meaning of one vocabulary word. Then have children reflect using the Check-In routine.

LESSON FOCUS

READING
Review Essential Question
Read Interactive Read Aloud
"The Storm that Shook the Signs"
• Practice Strategy
Word Work
• Review /-Blends

Reread Shared Read
"Mack and Ben"
WRITING
Writing/Grammar
• Independent Writing
• Practice Grammar

Interactive Read-Aloud Cards

Reading/Writing Companion, pp. 50–57

5 mins · # Oral Language

MULTIMODAL

? Essential Question

How can you stay safe in bad weather?

 This week we are talking and learning about how to stay safe in bad weather. What are some examples of bad weather? What can we do to stay safe? Read the **Weekly Poem** together.

Oral Vocabulary Words

Remind children that on Lesson 1 we learned the vocabulary words *safe* and *prepare*. *Why do we need to stay safe? How can we prepare for bad weather?* Use the Define/Example/Ask routine on the print or digital **Visual Vocabulary Cards** to introduce *notice*, *celebration*, and *enough*.

Oral Vocabulary Routine

Define: When you **notice** something, you see it clearly.

Example: I notice the stripes on a zebra.

Ask: What do you notice when a storm is coming?

Define: A **celebration** is a special activity in honor of a person or an event.

Example: We had a big celebration for 100 days in school.

Ask: If you could have a celebration, what would it be for? Why?

Define: When something is **enough**, it is all that is needed.

Example: We brought enough snacks for everyone to share.

Ask: How many pencils would be enough for everyone in our class to have one?

Visual Vocabulary Cards

Read the Interactive Read Aloud

Connect to Concept

Tell children that they will listen to a fairy tale. Explain that a fairy tale is a made-up story from long ago. Remind children that this week we are learning about how to stay safe in bad weather. Use the print or digital **Interactive Read-Aloud Cards**.

"The Storm that Shook the Signs"

Set Purpose *Let's find out what happens when a storm comes to a small town.*

Oral Vocabulary Use the Oral Vocabulary prompts as you read the story to provide more practice with the words in context.

Unfamiliar Words As you read "The Storm that Shook the Signs," ask children to listen for words they do not understand and to think about what the words mean. Pause after Card 1 to model.

Teacher Think Aloud What is a *tailor*? The text says that the signs on the shops showed what was sold or made there. The *tailor* had a shirt on the sign. A *tailor* must be someone that sews clothes.

Student Think Along After Card 2: "The baker *peered* through his window at the big sign outside his bakery." What does *peered* mean? I've never heard that word before. I think *peered* must be another word for looked because it says he *peered* out a window.

Build Knowledge: Make Connections

Talk About the Text Have partners share an important detail about how a shop owner stayed safe in stormy weather.

Add to the Anchor Chart Record new ideas on the Build Knowledge anchor chart.

Add to the Word Bank Add new words children learned to a separate section of the Word Bank.

Compare Texts

Guide partners to connect "The Storms that Shook the Signs" with the **Big Book,** *Waiting Out the Storm?* Discuss what happened to show a storm was coming.

We can listen actively to understand what happens to the signs on shops after a storm.

OBJECTIVES

Ask and answer questions about unknown words in a text.

Determine or clarify the meaning of unknown and multiple-meaning words and phrases based on *kindergarten reading and content.*

With prompting and support, compare and contrast the adventures and experiences of characters in familiar stories.

ENGLISH LANGUAGE LEARNERS

Card 1 Explain that signs show information. Point out the shop owners' signs. Explain that they show information about what people are selling. Have children find the fish seller's sign. *What does the fish seller have to sell?* (fresh fish) Repeat with the shoemaker's sign. Help children say the words on the signs.

For additional support, see the **ELL Small Group Guide**, pp. 150–151.

⊙ STUDENT CHECK-IN

Have partners share what happened after the shop owners saw the mixed-up signs. Then have children reflect using the Check-In routine.

READING · WORD WORK

In a Flash: Sound-Spellings

| bl |

Display the Sound-Spelling Card for *bl*.
1. Teacher: What's the letter?   Children: bl
2. Teacher: What's the sound?   Children: /bl/
Continue the routine for previously taught sounds.

LEARNING GOALS

• We can blend sounds to say words.
• We can blend and read words.

OBJECTIVES

Demonstrate understanding of spoken words, syllables, and sounds (phonemes).

Know and apply grade-level phonics and word analysis skills in decoding words.

Demonstrate basic knowledge of one-to-one letter-sound correspondences by producing the primary sound or many of the most frequent sounds for each consonant.

Associate the long sounds with the common spellings (graphemes) for the five major vowels.

Spell simple words phonetically, drawing on knowledge of sound-letter relationships.

Review *l*-blends.

ELA ACADEMIC LANGUAGE
• *blend, pattern*

 TEACH IN SMALL GROUP

You may wish to teach the Word Work lesson in small groups.

DIGITAL TOOLS

 Phonemic Awareness
Phonics

 Phonics: Spelling Song

 5 mins

Phonemic Awareness

 MULTIMODAL

Phoneme Blending

1 **Model** Say: *Listen to the sounds in a word: /m/ /e/ /t/. I can blend those sounds to make the word: /mmmeeet/, met. Listen as I say more sounds and blend them to make words.* Repeat, blending the sounds /b/ /a/ /k/ to form the word *back*.

2 **Guided Practice/Practice** Say: *Listen to the sounds in a different word: /k/ /i/ /k/. Let's blend the sounds and say the word together: /k/ /i/ /k/, /kiiik/ kick.* Tell children to listen to the sounds in words, repeat the sounds, and then blend them to say the word. Guide practice and provide corrective feedback as needed.

/r/ /i/ /d/ rid	/s/ /o/ /k/ sock	/k/ /i/ /s/ kiss
/s/ /t/ /a/ /k/ stack	/h/ /i/ /p/ hip	/h/ /e/ /d/ head
/e/ /l/ /k/ elk	/f/ /a/ /s/ /t/ fast	/r/ /ī/ /d/ ride
/b/ /o/ /ks/ box	/l/ /u/ /k/ luck	/k/ /i/ /d/ kid

🎵 Review initial /r/ and /b/. Play and sing "A Rose." Have children clap when they hear initial /r/. Repeat for /b/ using "Play Ball." Demonstrate as you sing with children.

 10 mins

Phonics

| cl |

Review *l*-Blends

1 **Model** Display the **Word-Building Card** *cl. These are the letters* c, l. *Together, the letters* c *and* l *stand for /kl/, the sounds at that the beginning of* cloud. *Say the sounds with me: /kl/. I will write the letters* c *and* l *because* cloud *starts with the /kl/ sounds.* Repeat for *l*-blends /bl/, /fl/, and /sl/, using Word-Building Cards *bl, fl,* and *sl*.

2 **Guided Practice/Practice** Have children practice connecting the letters and sounds. Point to the Word-Building Cards and the letters *c, l.* Ask: *What are these letters?* (c, l) *What sounds do they stand for?* (/kl/) Repeat the routine for *l*-blends /bl/, /fl/, and /sl/. Guide practice and provide corrective feedback as needed.

T430 UNIT 6 WEEK 3

Blend Words

1 **Model** Display **Word-Building Cards** *c, l, i, p. These are the letters* c *and* l. *They stand for /kl/. This is the letter* i. *It stands for /i/. This is the letter* p. *It stands for /p/. Listen as I blend the sounds: /klIIiiip/.* Repeat with *black, flat,* and *slip.*

2 Then write: *Tom can pet the black cat. The red hen can peck.* Prompt children to read the connected text, sounding out the decodable words. Provide corrective feedback.

Spell Words

Dictation Say the word *pack* and have children repeat. Ask children to say *pack* again, stretching the sounds. Write the word as you say the letter names. Have children read the word and say the letter names. Then say the words: *rack, sack, back,* and *stack* and have children write them. Point out the *ack* sound-spelling pattern. For more spelling practice, use **Practice Book** page 278.

LONG VOWEL EXPRESS TRACK »»»

Introduce /ī/i_e

You may wish to use this lesson to teach long vowel *i* earlier in the year, prior to its introduction in Unit 9.

1 **Model** Remind children that the letter *i* can stand for the short and long sounds as in *pin* and *pine.* Say: *Today we're going to learn one of the spellings for the /ī/ sound.* Hold up the *five* **Sound-Spelling Card** as you point to the *i_e* spelling. Point out that *i* and *e* act as a team to make the long *i* sound /ī/. Use **Word-Building Cards** or write *bit. Bit has the sound /i/. Let's add an* e *to the end. The new word is* bite. *Listen as I say the word:* bite. *Repeat with* hid *and* hide.

2 **Guided Practice/Practice** Use Word-Building Cards or have children write *pin.* Read the word; then make *pine.* Repeat with: d*im*/d*ime*, r*ip*/r*ipe*, T*im*/t*ime*, r*id*/r*ide*, f*in*/f*ine*, k*it*/k*ite*.

Review Have children review short and long a by saying these word pairs: *cap/cape; fat/fate, hat/hate, rat/rate.*

Long Vowel Express Decodable Reader: Have children read "A Ripe Lime" to practice decoding words in connected text.

Use with **Phonemic Awareness, Guided Practice/Practice.**

Beginning
Help children pronounce each sound in *rid, luck,* and *head.* Blend the sounds in each word, and have children repeat.

Intermediate
Model blending the sounds in each word. Provide support for children who have difficulty repeating each sound. Guide children to blend the words with you.

Advanced/Advanced High
Encourage children to practice blending the words they find more difficult. Help them self-correct by modeling pronunciation.

CORRECTIVE FEEDBACK

Sound Error Model the sound that children missed when blending words, then have them repeat. For example, for the word *clip,* say: *My turn.* Tap under the letters *cl* and ask: *Sound? What's the sound?* Return to the beginning of the word. *Let's start over.* Blend the word with children again.

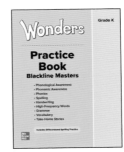

Phonics/Spelling: p. 278

FORMATIVE ASSESSMENT

❯ STUDENT CHECK-IN

Have partners read *clip* and *black.* Then have children reflect using the Check-In routine.

LESSON 3

LEARNING GOALS

- We can sort words that begin with different letters.
- We can read sentences with high-frequency words.

OBJECTIVES

Demonstrate basic knowledge of one-to-one letter-sound correspondences by producing the primary sound or many of the most frequent sounds for each consonant.

Read common high-frequency words by sight.

Sort words by initial letter.

ACADEMIC LANGUAGE

- sort, high-frequency

DIGITAL TOOLS

To differentiate instruction for key skills, use the results of this activity.

Phonics: Data-Generating

High-Frequency Words: Data-Generating

OPTIONAL
5 mins

Phonics

MULTIMODAL

Picture Sort

1 **Model** Remind children that the letter *r* can stand for /r/. Place the **Word-Building Card** *r* on the left side of a pocket chart. Continue the same routine for the letters *k* and *h*.

Hold up the **Photo Card** for *rabbit. Here is the picture for* rabbit. Rabbit *has the /r/ sound at the beginning. Listen, /rrrabit/. I will place* rabbit *under the letter* r *because the letter* r *stands for /r/.* Use the same routine for *hat* and *kite.*

Photo Cards

2 **Guided Practice/Practice** Have children sort the Photo Cards *rope, hair, key, hook, kangaroo, rake, ring, hand.* Have them say the sound at the beginning of the word and tell which letter the Photo Card should be placed under.

Repeat the routine for /b/b, /l/l, /f/f using the following photo cards: *banana, boat, boot, bowl, feet, fish, five, fork, lamp, ladder, ladybug, leaf.* Guide practice and provide corrective feedback as needed.

Photo Cards

English Language Learners

Phonics, Guided Practice/Practice Confirm children's understanding that *r, h,* and *k* stand for /r/, /k/, and /h/. Guide children to identify the initial sounds for the Photo Cards. *Is the beginning sound in* rope *the sound /k/, /h/ or /r/?* (/r/) Use sentence frames to help children tell how they sorted the cards: Rope begins with the sound /r/. We place rope below the letter r.

5 mins

High-Frequency Words

 MULTIMODAL

1 **Guided Practice** Display the **High-Frequency Word Cards** *are, he, is, little, my, she, was,* and *with.* Review each word using the Read/Spell/Write routine.

2 **Practice** Point to the High-Frequency Word Card *are* and have children read it. Repeat with words *he, is, little, my, she, was* and *with.*

Build Fluency

Word Automaticity Write the following sentences. Have children chorally read them as you track the print. Have them reread the sentences until they can read the words automatically and fluently.

She can go with Matt.   **My cat is little.**

Dan and Kim are with me.   **Did he see my pet?**

Read for Fluency Distribute **Practice Book** pages 285–286 and help children assemble their Take-Home Books. Chorally read the Take-Home Book. Then have children reread to build automaticity.

BUILD YOUR WORD BANK

You can use this lesson to teach more high-frequency words.

1 **Model** Display the **Build Your Word Bank Cards** for *than, his, three, when, which, soon, many, them, eat, by, some, brown, now, way, under* from the **Practice Book High-Frequency Word Cards.** Use the Read/Spell/Write routine to review each word.

- **Read** Point to the word *than* and say the word. *This is the word* than. Say it with me: than. *I wrote more* than *Nat.*

- **Spell** *The word* than *is spelled t-h-a-n. Spell it with me.*

- **Write** *Let's write* than *on our Response Boards as we say the letters to spell the word: t-h-a-n.*

Repeat Read/Spell/Write routine with *his, three, when, which, soon, many, them, eat, by, some, brown, now, way, under.*

2 **Guided Practice** Display the Build Your Word Bank Cards for *than, his, when, which, many, them, by, some, now,* and *way.* Point to each of the words and have children chorally read each word. Then have children take turns using the Build Your Word Bank words in a sentence. Guide practice and provide feedback.

ELL ENGLISH LANGUAGE LEARNERS

High-Frequency Words, Practice Review correct pronunciation of *are* and *have.* Have children read the words aloud with you. Model the words *he, is, little, my, she, was,* and *with* in phrases or short sentences for children to repeat.

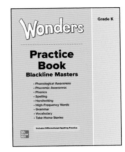

Take-Home Story: pp. 285–286

FORMATIVE ASSESSMENT

❯ STUDENT CHECK-IN

Phonics Have partners think of words that they would add to the word sort.

High-Frequency Words Have partners take turns reading a sentence from the Take-Home Book.

Then have children reflect using the Check-In routine.

✓ CHECK FOR SUCCESS

Rubric Use your online rubric to record children's progress.

Can children sort words by initial sound/letter?

Can children read and recognize the high-frequency words?

❯❯ **Small Group Instruction**

If No

🔴 **Approaching** Reteach pp. T458–462

⚫ **ELL** Develop pp. T458–462

If Yes

🔵 **On** Review pp. T466–468

🔵 **Beyond** Extend p. T472

LESSON 3

LEARNING GOALS

We can read and understand a story.

OBJECTIVES

Identify the front cover, back cover, and title page of a book.

Demonstrate basic knowledge of one-to-one letter-sound correspondences by producing the primary sound or many of the most frequent sounds for each consonant.

Read common high-frequency words by sight.

Read emergent-reader texts with purpose and understanding.

ELA ACADEMIC LANGUAGE

- *reread, details*
- Cognate: *detalles*

Reread "Mack and Ben"

Focus on Foundational Skills

Book Handling Demonstrate book handling. Hold up the **Reading/Writing Companion** and point to the front cover. Say: *This is the front cover of the book.* Point to the back cover. *This is the back cover.* Model turning the pages of the book.

Concepts of Print As you read the story, point out sentence boundaries. Review the fact that the first word in each sentence begins with a capital letter and ends with a punctuation mark. Display pages 60–61 of the Reading/Writing Companion. Invite volunteers to come up and point to the capital letter that begins the first word in each sentence.

Focus on Comprehension

Reread Have children reread the story. Tell them to sound out the decodable words and read the high-frequency words with automaticity. Guide them to look for details that they did not notice in the first reading.

You may wish to have children use the box on the right-hand pages to do the following:

- Draw a picture about the text or the art.
- Draw something whose name includes the /h/, /f/, /r/, /b/, /l/, or /k/ sounds or *bl, cl, fl,* and *sl* blends.
- Write the letters *h, e, f, r, b, l, k, ck* and the blends *bl, cl, fl, sl.*

Reading/Writing Companion, pp. 80–81

COMPREHENSION

Who are the main characters in the story? (Mack and Ben)

Reading/Writing Companion, pp. 82–83

COMPREHENSION

Why is Mack sad? (He is probably unhappy that it is raining and he can't play outside.) *Why does Ben hide?* (He is afraid of the storm.)

Reading/Writing Companion, pp. 84–85

Reading/Writing Companion, pp. 86–87

COMPREHENSION

What are Mack and Ben doing on page 84? (sitting; drinking) *What do you think Mack would rather be doing?* (playing baseball or soccer.)

COMPREHENSION

What does the author mean by "Mack and Ben are back!"? (Possible response: They are back outside because the storm is over.)

DECODABLE READERS

Have children read "Rock Ken" (pages 25–30) to practice decoding words in connected text.

Unit 6 Decodable Reader

ENGLISH LANGUAGE LEARNERS

Comprehension Point to the picture on page 76. Explain that *a bit* means "a small amount." Mack was *a bit* sad means Mack was not very sad, but he was a little sad. Ask children why they think Mack was *a bit* sad. Ask them to point to a clue in the picture.

Have children point to the clock in the illustration on page 78. Explain that *tick tock* is a sound a *clock* makes. Imitate the sound, and have children copy you.

Focus on Fluency: Accuracy and Rate

Have partners practice reading the story "Mack and Ben" accurately. Encourage them to track the print as they sound out decodable words and read high-freqency words with automaticity. Remind children to pay attention to punctuation marks so they read sentences with the correct tone. Then have partners read the story again this time focusing on rate—reading a bit more quickly and making the text sound more like speech.

Listen in: If children struggle with accuracy, have them start again at the beginning of the sentence, and correct any errors they make. If they struggle with rate, model an appropriate rate and then have them repeat.

Build Knowledge: Make Connections

Talk About the Text Have partners discuss the weather in the story. *How did Mack and Ben stay safe in bad weather?*

Write About the Text Have children add their ideas to the reader's notebook.

FORMATIVE ASSESSMENT

❯ STUDENT CHECK-IN

Have partners share something they learned from the story. Then have children reflect using the Check-In routine.

LEARNING GOALS

- We can write about the texts we read.
- We can learn about words that name more than one thing (plural nouns).

OBJECTIVES

Use a combination of drawing, dictating, and writing to narrate a single event or several loosely linked events and tell about the events in the order in which they occurred.

Write a letter or letters for most consonant and short-vowel sounds.

Use frequently occurring nouns.

Form regular plural nouns orally by adding /s/ or /es/.

Write in response to a text.

ELA ACADEMIC LANGUAGE

- singular, plural
- Cognates: singular, plural

TEACH IN SMALL GROUP

Choose from these options to enable all children to complete the writing activity:

- draw a picture
- complete sentence starters
- write a caption
- write one sentence

For differentiated support, see Writing Skills minilessons on pages T494-T499. These can be used throughout the year.

Independent Writing

⏱ 5 mins

Write About the Shared Read

Analyze the Student Model Turn to pages 88-89 of the **Reading/Writing Companion**. Read the prompt aloud: *What can Mack and Ben do when the rain stops? Write the next part of the story.* Read aloud and guide children to analyze Paula's writing.

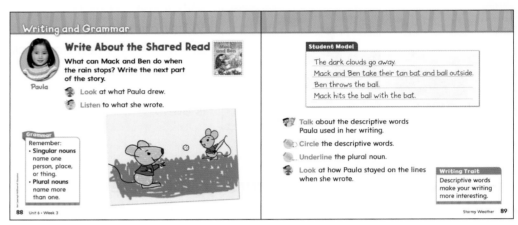

Reading/Writing Companion, pp. 88–89

Write Your Response

Analyze the Prompt Discuss the prompt on page 88 with children.

Find Text Evidence *Let's look on pages 48–49 to get ideas for our story. What do Mack and Ben like to do?* (play outside) *What might they do if it starts to snow?* (Answers will vary.)

Write a Response Have children use the text evidence to draw and write their response. Read aloud the writing checklist and have them check off the items as they include them in their draft.

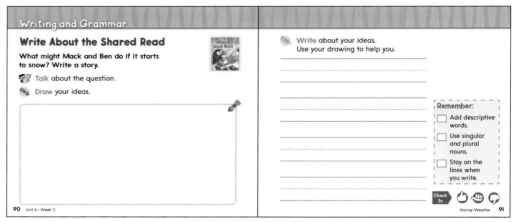

Reading/Writing Companion, pp. 90–91

Writing Support If needed, provide the sentence frames in the Quick Tip: **Mack and Ben like to _____. Mack and Ben _____ in the snow.**

Grammar

OPTIONAL 5 mins

DIGITAL TOOLS

Grammar
Activity

Singular and Plural Nouns

1 **Review** Review that singular nouns name one person, place, animal, or thing, and plural nouns name more than one person, place, animal or thing. Remind children that they should add -s to most words to make them plural. Now write the following letters/blends on the board as you say their sounds aloud: -s, -ss, -sh, -ch, -x, and -z. Remind children that they should add -es to words with these ending sounds. Display the *apple* and *peach* **Photo Cards**. Write the words *apple* and *peach*. Model adding -s to *apple* and -es to *peach* to make both words plural.

2 **Guided Practice/Practice** Display the *bike* and *box* Photo Cards. Have children write both words. Guide them to make both nouns plural. Guide them to add -s to *bike* and read it aloud, *bikes*. Then point to the *x* at the end of *box*. Prompt children to add -es to the end of *box* to make it plural, *boxes*.

Give partners one of the following sets of Photo Cards: *ant, bus; inch, key; watch, banana; lamp, ax; fox, rabbit;* and *toothbrush, shirt*. Have partners work together to change each word into a plural noun. Circulate and provide assistance as needed.

Talk About It

Have partners generate sentences with plural nouns about the weather, such as: *I feel raindrops. We need our umbrellas.*

English Language Learners

Independent Writing, Analyze the Student Model Have children finger point as they choral read the Student Model. Use the Actor/Action routine to review the second and third sentences. Then guide children to identify singular and plural nouns in the first two sentences. *Clap once if you hear a singular noun. Clap twice if you hear a plural noun.* Guide children to identify descriptive details. *What word tells more about the clouds?* (dark) *What word tells more about the bat?* (tan) *Paula stayed on the lines when she wrote her sentences.* Have children trace Paula's sentences with their finger as they say: Paula stayed on the lines.

For additional support, see the **ELL Small Group Guide,** p. 155.

FORMATIVE ASSESSMENT

> STUDENT CHECK-IN

Have partners share a plural noun they learned. Then have children reflect using the Check-In routine.

LESSON 4

LEARNING GOALS

- We can tell if words begin with the same sound.
- We can understand new words.
- We can use words that ask questions.
- We can put words into groups.

OBJECTIVES

Demonstrate understanding of spoken words, syllables, and sounds (phonemes).

Use words and phrases acquired through conversations, reading and being read to, and responding to texts.

Understand and use question words (interrogatives).

Develop oral vocabulary.

Recognize alliterative words.

ELA ACADEMIC LANGUAGE

- *repeat, categories, similar, related*
- Cognates: *repetir, categorías*

DIGITAL TOOLS

Weekly Poem

Visual Vocabulary Cards

Category Words Activity

LESSON FOCUS

READING
Review Essential Question
Read/Reread Paired Selection
"Be Safe in Bad Weather"
• Review Strategy/Skill
Word Work
• Build Words

WRITING
Writing/Grammar
• Independent Writing
• Review Grammar
Research and Inquiry
• Create Presentation

Literature Big Book, pp. 32–38

Oral Language *MULTIMODAL*

10 mins

? Essential Question

How can you stay safe in bad weather?

Have children discuss what they have learned about how to stay safe in bad weather. Add new ideas to the Build Knowledge anchor chart.

Phonological Awareness: Identify Alliteration

1 **Model** Remind children that some words, such as *whatever* and *weather*, begin with the same sounds. Say the following and have children repeat: *Peter piper picked a peck of pickled peppers.* Say: *I hear the same sound at the beginning of most of these words. I hear the sound /p/ repeat.*

2 **Guided Practice/Practice** Say the following phrases, have children repeat, and then have them raise their hands if the words in the set begin with the same sound: *goodness gracious; big boy; handy dandy; last laugh, oh no.* Guide practice and provide corrective feedback as needed.

Review Oral Vocabulary Words

Use the Define/Example/Ask routine on print or digital **Visual Vocabulary Cards** to review the oral vocabulary words *safe, prepare, enough, celebration,* and *notice.* Then have children use the words in sentences.

Visual Vocabulary Cards

Category Words: Question Words

1 **Model** Remind children that *who, what, why, when, where* and *how* are question words. *Listen to this story. Raise your hands when you hear a question word.* Read the story aloud.

"We are going on a field trip!" Mr. Garcia told the class.

"**Where** are we going?" Julia asked.

"We are going to the museum," Mr. Garcia answered.

"**What** will we see?" Michael asked.

"We will see fossils," said Mr. Garcia

"**How** will we get there?" Raven wanted to know.

"We will take a bus," replied Mr. Garcia.

"**When** are we going?" Maggie asked.

"Tomorrow!" Mr. Garcia said.

2 **Guided Practice** Place the following **Photo Cards** facedown: *door, elbow, envelope, farm, gate, gorilla, helicopter, juggle, nest*. Have children choose a Photo Card. Ask them to make up questions about the picture. For example: **What is the gorilla thinking? How do you juggle?**

For additional practice use **Practice Book** pages 280–281.

Vocabulary: Question Words

1 **Model** Explain that grouping words into categories helps us notice how they are similar or related.

Think Aloud When we want to find out more about something, we ask questions. To ask good questions, we first need to think of question words. *How, where, why, who, what,* and *when* are all words that fit into the word category of "question words." We can use these words to ask good questions.

2 **Guided Practice/Practice** Write and display a list of question words. Ask volunteers to use the question words to ask questions about the illustrations or unfamiliar words in *Waiting Out the Storm.* Encourage other children to answer the questions.

KIDS ON THE MOVE!

Assign each corner of the classroom a question word. Then assign each child with a question word. Gather all children in the middle of the classroom. Tell children on your command to move to the corner that represents the question word that they have. Repeat the activity a few times, giving children a different question word each time.

Category Words: pp. 280–281

ELL ENGLISH LANGUAGE LEARNERS

Category Words, Guided Practice Provide sentence frames to help children ask questions about the Photo Cards. For example: What is in the nest/envelope? Where is the helicopter/gorilla going? Who lives on a farm? Challenge children to think of a *who* or *what* question for the *door* Photo Card.

ELL NEWCOMERS

Continue to use the **Newcomer Online Visuals** and their accompanying prompts to help children expand vocabulary and language about Weather (Unit 1, 9a-f). Use the Conversation Starters, Speech Balloons, and Games in the **Newcomer Teacher's Guide** to continue building vocabulary and developing oral and written language.

FORMATIVE ASSESSMENT

❯ STUDENT CHECK-IN

Oral Vocabulary Words Have partners tell how they *prepare* for school.

Category Words Have partners ask a question.

Vocabulary Have partners ask a question beginning with *why.*

Then have children reflect using the Check-In routine.

Literature Big Book

OBJECTIVES

Recognize common types of texts.

With prompting and support, identify the main topic and retell key details of a text.

With prompting and support, describe the relationship between illustrations and the text in which they appear.

Visualize to help with comprehension.

Use directions to gather information.

ELA ACADEMIC LANGUAGE

• *visualize, directions*

• Cognate: *visualizar*

 Read

"Be Safe in Bad Weather"

Text Feature: Directions

1 **Explain/Model** Tell children that they are going to listen to a nonfiction text about staying safe in different types of weather. Display page 28 of the **Big Book**. Explain that this selection provides different types of directions. *Directions tell us what we need to do. In this selection, the directions tell us how to stay safe.*

Display **Online Teaching Chart 15**. Read the title aloud. Explain to children that the directions tell us how to plant seeds. Point to the numbers. Tell children that sometimes directions have numbers and need to be followed in number order. Sometimes directions do not have numbers but they still need to be followed. Point to the first two directions and read them aloud. Say: *I will follow these directions to plant a seed. First, I will pack dirt in a pot. Then I will poke holes in the dirt.*

Online Teaching Chart 15

2 **Guided Practice/Practice** Point out the remaining directions and read them aloud. Ask: *What are the next set of directions I need to follow?* (Drop in the seeds; Pack down the dirt; Water the seeds.) *What do the directions tell us?* (how to plant seeds) *Why is it important to follow these directions in order?* (So the seeds can grow into plants and flowers.)

Read the Paired Selection

Display the Big Book. Read the title and look at the photo. *What do you predict this text will be about?* Write and display children's predictions. **Set Purpose** *Let's read to find out how to stay safe in bad weather.*

Literature Big Book, pp. 28–29

VISUALIZE DOK 2

Read page 29 of the Big Book. Have children create a mental image of a blizzard as you read the text. *What did the blizzard look like? How did it feel? What did you do?* Then reread the text as you display the photograph.

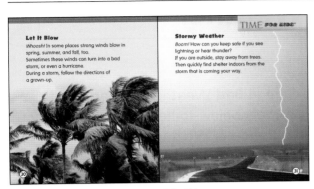

Literature Big Book, pp. 30–31

DETAILS DOK 1

Look at the photograph on page 31. *What things in the picture tell you that there is a storm coming?* (Possible responses: the dark sky and the lightning)

Literature Big Book, p. 32

TEXT FEATURE: DIRECTIONS DOK 2

Display and read page 32. *What are some things the author recommends learning as a way to stay safe?* (know your phone number; street address; name of the state and town you live in) *Point to the yellow box. Why does the author use a list to show the safety kit?* (The list helps to keep track of what is in the kit and what is needed. The checkmarks show that everything is included.)

Return to Purpose

Read children's predictions. Ask: *Were the predictions correct?* Remind children of their purpose for reading. (to learn ways to stay safe in bad weather) Prompt them to tell what new information they learned from the selection.

Retell

Help children use the photographs and text to retell important details of the selection in order. Remind them to include directions when retelling. Encourage them to use the vocabulary words they have been learning.

Close Reading Routine

Read DOK 1-2

- Identify key ideas and details.
- Take notes and retell.
- Use prompts as needed.

Reread DOK 2–3

- Analyze the text, craft, and structure.

Integrate DOK 3–4

- Integrate knowledge and ideas.
- Make text-to-text connections.
- Complete the Show Your Knowledge task.
- Inspire action.

ELL SPOTLIGHT ON LANGUAGE

Pages 30–31 *whoosh, boom:* Point to the word *whoosh.* Say: Whoosh *sounds like a blowing wind.* Say the word, emphasizing the wind sound, and have children repeat with swaying arm movements. Then have children look at the photo on page 31. *What do you think* boom *sounds like?* (thunder) Have children clap their hands and say *boom!*

FORMATIVE ASSESSMENT

❯ STUDENT CHECK-IN

Have partners share one thing they learned from directions. Then have children reflect using the Check-In routine.

Literature Big Book

We can think about how the author uses photos to share information about a text.

OBJECTIVES

With prompting and support, describe the relationship between illustrations and the story in which they appear.

Use words and phrases acquired through conversations, reading and being read to, and responding to texts.

Analyze the author's craft.

ELA ACADEMIC LANGUAGE

• *directions, checklist*

Reread

"Be Safe in Bad Weather"

Analyze the Text

After children read and retell "Be Safe in Bad Weather" reread it with them. Use the instructions in the prompts below to help children answer the questions on pages 92-93 in the **Reading/Writing Companion**.

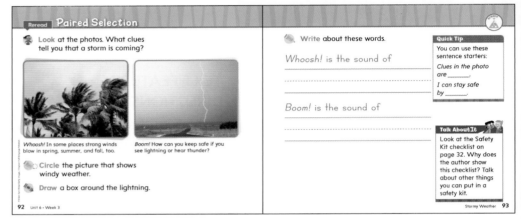

Reading/Writing Companion, pp. 92–93

AUTHOR'S CRAFT DOK 2

• Look at the photographs on page 92 of the Reading/Writing Companion. Ask: *What clues in the photos show that a storm is coming?* (dark clouds, lightning, and trees being blown.) *What words does the author use to tell that a storm is coming?* (whoosh, strong winds, boom, lightning, and thunder) Have children circle the picture that shows windy weather and draw a box around the lightning.

• Then have children turn to page 93. Ask: *What makes the sound whoosh?* (the wind) *What makes the sound boom?* (thunder) Guide children to complete the sentence starters with their responses.

Talk About It

Review the Safety Kit checklist on page 32 of the **Big Book**. Say: *Why does the author show this checklist?* (to help us prepare for and stay safe in bad weather) Then have children turn to a partner and discuss what other things they would put in a safety kit. Encourage children to think about information they already know and have learned about staying safe in bad weather. Have volunteers share their responses. Remind them to use vocabulary words they have learned so far.

Integrate

Build Knowledge: Make Connections

Talk About the Text Have children discuss the different types of weather in the text. *What are some ways you can stay safe in each type of weather?*

Add to the Anchor Chart Record any new ideas on the Build Knowledge Anchor Chart.

Add to the Word Bank Record any new ideas on the Word Bank.

ELL English Language Learners

Use the following scaffolds to help children with **Analyze the Text, Author's Craft.**

Beginning

Help children point to and name clues that a storm is coming in the photos on page 68. Provide sentence frames: I see blowing trees. The sky is dark. I see lightning.

Intermediate

Have children point to and describe what they see in each photo. The wind is blowing the trees. The sky is gray and full of clouds. There is lightning in the sky. These photos show that a storm is coming. Help children circle the words that tell about the bad weather.

Advanced/Advanced High

Ask children to point to the photographs and describe what they see using full sentences. Provide a model: I see trees bending in the wind. Confirm children's ideas, and revise for form. When you repeat their sentences, correct any grammar or pronunciation errors. Then have partners work together to circle the words that tell about the bad weather.

CONNECT TO CONTENT

Stormy Weather Review with children the different kinds of bad weather they learned about in "Be Safe in Bad Weather." (blizzards, wind storms, hurricanes) Then have children identify other types of weather they know. (sunny, rain) Post all ideas on the board. Then write the the words *Winter, Spring, Summer,* and *Fall* on chart paper. Call out the different types of weather children have identified and have volunteers come up and point to the season when they think they would see this type of weather. **STEM**

FORMATIVE ASSESSMENT

❯ STUDENT CHECK-IN

Have partners share something they learned from the photographs. Then have children reflect using the Check-In routine.

LESSON 4

Display the Word-Building Card for *bl*.

1. **Teacher:** What's the letter?   **Children:** bl
2. **Teacher:** What's the sound?   **Children:** /bl/

Continue the routine for previously taught sounds.

LEARNING GOALS

- **We can add a sound to words to make new words.**
- **We can build and spell words.**
- **We can read sentences with high-frequency words.**

OBJECTIVES

Add individual sounds in simple, one-syllable words to make new words.

Distinguish between similarly spelled words by identifying the sounds of the letters that differ.

Associate the long sounds with the common spellings (graphemes) for the five major vowels.

Read common high-frequency words by sight.

ELA ACADEMIC LANGUAGE

- *add, high-frequency*

▷ TEACH IN SMALL GROUP

You may wish to teach the Word Work lesson in small groups.

DIGITAL TOOLS

Word Work

Phonemic Awareness

Phonics

High-Frequency Words

Visual Vocabulary Cards

 5 mins

Phonemic Awareness

Phoneme Addition

1 **Model** Say: *Listen as I say a word:* all. *When I add* /f/ *to the beginning of* all, *I make the word* fall. Fall *is the word I make when I add* /f/ *to the beginning of* all. *Repeat: Add* /f/ *to* ill *to make* fill.

2 **Guided Practice/Practice** Have children add initial phonemes to words to make new words. Guide practice and provide corrective feedback as needed.

What word do you have if you add /l/ *to the beginning of* it? (lit)

What word do you have if you add /f/ *to the beginning of* Ed? (fed)

What word do you have if you add /h/ *to the beginning of* am? (ham)

What word do you have if you add /t/ *to the beginning of* rain? (train)

What word do you have if you add /b/ *to the beginning of* in? (bin)

What word do you have if you add /s/ *to the beginning of* nap? (snap)

 5 mins

Phonics

MULTIMODAL

Build and Read Words

Provide children with Word **Building Cards** *a–z*. Have children put the letters in alphabetic order as quickly as possible.

1 **Guided Practice** Use the **Word-Building Cards** *s, i, p* to form the word *sip*. Have children use their word cards to build the word *sip*. Then say: *I will add the letter* l *to make the word* slip. Add *l* after the *s* in *sip*, and read aloud the word *slip*. Point to the letters *sl* and remind children that these letters together make the sounds /sl/. Ask children to read the word with you.

2 **Practice** Have children continue changing letters using Word-Building Cards to form and read the words *lip, flip, clip, click, slick,* and *block*. Once children have finished using the word cards to build each word, have them write each word in the list on a sheet of paper. Children can work with a partner to correct any errors they make when encoding.

LONG VOWEL
EXPRESS TRACK ▶▶▶

You may wish to teach long vowel *i* early, prior to presenting it in Unit 9.

1 Model Display the *five* **Sound-Spelling Card**. Point to the i_e spelling. Remind children that the letters *i* and *e* act as a team to stand for the long i sound /ī/ in *ice*. Place **Word Building Cards** *h, i, d, e* in a pocket chart. *The letter* h *stands for /h/. These are the letters* i *and* e. *They stand for the long* i *sound* /ī/. *The letter stands for /d/. Listen:* /hhhīīīd/, /hīd/.

2 Guided Practice/Practice Write the word *kite.* Point to the letter *k* and have children say the sound. Point to the letters *i* and *e* and have children say the long *i* sound. Point to the letter *t* and have children say the sound. Have children read *kite.* Repeat with: *life, like, fine, bite, lime, hike, ride, side, nine, bike.*

Review Have children review blending words with long *a* using the words *made, tape, cape, late, name.*

Long Vowel Express Decodable Reader: Have children read "Ride, Hike, Hide" to practice decoding words in connected text.

OPTIONAL 5 mins

MULTIMODAL

High-Frequency Words

Practice Say the word *are* and have children write it. Then display the **Visual Vocabulary Card** *are.* Follow the Teacher Talk routine on the back. Repeat with *he, is, little, my, she, was,* and *with.*

Build Fluency Build sentences in a pocket chart using **High-Frequency Word Cards** and **Photo Cards**. Use index cards to create a period and a question mark. Have children read the sentences and identify the words *are, he, is, little, my, she, was, with.*

> **He can go to my farm. Is she with you?**
>
> **The plates are blue. She was with the little dog.**

Have partners say sentences using the words.

Word Mat Activity Tape several High-Frequency Word Cards to a wall or large sheet. Have children take turns tossing a soft ball and say the word the ball hits. You may also use a fly swatter or pointer, have the child tap the word and say it. This can be done as a small group or center activity.

DECODABLE READERS

Have children read "Flip, Flop, Flip!" (page 31-36) to practice decoding words in connected text.

Unit 6 Decodable Reader

FORMATIVE ASSESSMENT

❯ STUDENT CHECK-IN

Phonics Have partners use Word-Building Cards to spell and read *block.*

High-Frequency Words Have partners point to and read a sentence from the lesson.

Then have children reflect using the Check-In routine.

✓ CHECK FOR SUCCESS

Rubric Use your online rubric to record children's progress.

Can children add phonemes to make new words and blend and read words with *l*-blends?

Can children read and recognize high-frequency words?

❯ **Small Group Instruction**

If No

● **Approaching** Reteach pp. T458–462

● **ELL** Develop pp. T458–462

If Yes

● **On** Review pp. T466–468

● **Beyond** Extend p. T472.

LESSON 4

Independent Writing

OBJECTIVES

With guidance and support from adults, respond to questions and suggestions from peers and add details to strengthen writing as needed.

Capitalize the first word in a sentence.

Produce and expand complete sentences in shared language activities.

Use frequently occurring nouns.

Form regular plural nouns by adding /s/ or /es/.

ELA ACADEMIC LANGUAGE

- *revise, edit, plural noun*
- Cognates: *revisar, editar*

Write About the Shared Read

Revise

Reread the prompt about "Mack and Ben" on page 90 of the **Reading/Writing Companion**: *What might Mack and Ben do if it starts to snow? Write a story*. Have children read their drafts to think about how they would revise their writing. Then have them check to see if they responded to the prompt by staying on the lines as they wrote, including descriptive words, and using singular and plural nouns in their writing.

Peer Review Have partners review each other's writing. Children should share what they like most about the writing, questions they have for the author, and additional ideas they think the author could include. Provide time for children to make revisions.

Edit/Proofread

After children have revised their work, have them edit their work carefully, checking for the following:

- Use a capital letter at the beginning of each sentence.
- Make sure your sentence(s) tells a complete thought.

If children need additional practice with editing and proofreading, have them use **Practice Book** page 284.

Write Final Draft

After children have edited their writing and finished their peer review, have them write their final draft in their writer's notebook. Tell children to write neatly so that others can read their writing, or guide them to explore a variety of digital tools they can use to publish their work.

Teacher Conference As children review their drafts, confer with them to provide guidance. Suggest places in their writing where they might add descriptive words or include plural nouns.

Share and Evaluate

After children have finalized their draft, have them work with a partner to practice presenting their writing to one another. Remind children to speak in complete sentences. If possible, record children as they share so that they can see themselves presenting, or you can use as a topic of discussion for a teacher conference.

Have children add their work to their writing folder. Invite children to look at their previous writing and discuss with a partner how it has improved.

Grammar

5 mins

DIGITAL TOOLS

Grammar Activity

Singular and Plural Nouns

1 **Review** Remind children that plural nouns name more than one person, place, animal, or thing and end in *-s* or *-es*. *Add -s to most nouns to make them plural. Add -es to nouns that end with the letters -s, -ss, -sh, -ch, -x, or -z to make them plural.*

Display the *car* **Photo Card**. Write and read aloud: *The cars are red.* Circle the *s* in *cars*. Explain: *The -s lets us know that the word* cars *is plural. There is more than one car.*

2 **Guided Practice/Practice** Display the *lemon* Photo Card. Write the following sentences and read them aloud: **I put two lemons on a plate. I put a lemon on a plate.** Guide children to draw a picture for each sentence. Then guide them to label each drawing with the words *one lemon* or *two lemons*.

Show the *shirt* Photo Card. Have children work in pairs to create sentences with *shirt* in both singular and plural forms. If needed, provide these sentence frames: **I have one _____. I have two _____.** Then have children draw a picture for each sentence. If children need additional practice with plural nouns, have them use **Practice Book,** page 283 or online activities.

Grammar: p. 283
Edit/Proofread: p. 284

Talk About It

Have partners work together to generate sentences with plural nouns about the things they do at home when the weather is bad.

English Language Learners

Use the following scaffolds with **Independent Writing, Revise.**

Beginning

Brainstorm descriptive words that could be added to children's stories. Help them add descriptive words to their stories.

Intermediate

Ask questions to help children add descriptive words, such as: *What words could describe this? How might the snow have felt?*

Advanced/Advanced High

Have partners brainstorm descriptive words and suggest where their partner could add them to their story. Provide guidance as needed.

For additional support, see the **ELL Small Group Guide,** p. 155.

FORMATIVE ASSESSMENT

❯ STUDENT CHECK-IN

Have partners share a plural noun they learned. Then have children reflect using the Check-In routine.

LEARNING GOALS

We can research how to stay safe in bad weather.

OBJECTIVES

Participate in shared research and writing projects.

With guidance and support from adults, recall information from experiences or gather information from provided sources to answer a question.

Add drawings or other visual displays to descriptions as desired to provide additional detail.

Produce and expand complete sentences in shared language activities.

Follow agreed-upon rules for discussions.

ELA ACADEMIC LANGUAGE
• *picture dictionary*

COLLABORATIVE CONVERSATIONS

Listen Carefully As children engage in partner, small group, and whole class discussions, encourage them to do the following:

• Look at the person who is speaking.

• Listen to what the speaker is saying.

• Respect others by not interrupting them.

• Repeat classmates' ideas to check understanding.

Integrate

Stormy Weather

⏱ 10 mins

Model

Tell children that they will research how to stay safe in bad weather. Display pages 94-95 of the **Reading/Writing Companion**. Model completing each step in the research process.

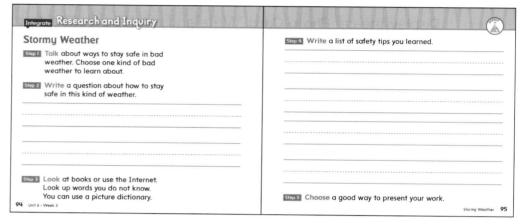

Reading/Writing Companion, pp. 94–95

STEP 1 Choose a Topic

The kind of bad weather I choose to learn more about is hurricanes.

STEP 2 Write Your Question

My question will be: How can we stay safe during a hurricane?

STEP 3 Find Information

I can do research by looking at books or using the Internet. I can look up words I do not know in a picture dictionary.

STEP 4 Write What You Learned

Now that I have done my research, I can write down what I have learned. I can make a list of tips about how to stay safe in a hurricane.

STEP 5 Choose a Way to Present Your Work

I will create a page for a class book about staying safe in bad weather.

Apply

Have children turn to page 94 in their Reading/Writing Companion. Remind them that they are doing formal research. Have them choose a topic about staying safe in bad weather, write a question to guide their research, and look up words they do not know in a picture dictionary. Circulate and provide guidance as needed.

Choose the Presentation Format

Have children turn to pages 94-95 in their **Reading/Writing Companion** to review their research, their list of safety tips, and what they learned about staying safe in bad weather. Tell them that today they are going to take the next step by creating their final presentation, which they will give in front of the class tomorrow. Work with children to select a good way to present their findings. Options may include drawing and labeling a picture, creating a poster, making a model or putting on a dramatic presentation.

Create the Presentation

Guide children to develop their presentation individually, in teams, or as a class. Remind them of the rules of working with others.

Gather Materials Gather together the materials children will need to create their finished product. Most of the materials should be available in the classroom or can be brought from home.

Make the Finished Product Once children have gathered the materials they need, provide time for them to create their finished product. You can dedicate an area in the classroom for project work and store all the materials there. Explain that children will be presenting their work to their classmates the next day.

English Language Learners

Apply, Step 2 Help children in writing a research question. Give them sentence starters to complete as they look for more information: How do I stay safe during _____? When/Where does it _____ the most? What should I do when _____? Give children examples of how to complete the sentences. Have children share their questions with a partner.

TEACH IN SMALL GROUP

You may wish to have children create their presentation during Small Group time. Group children of varying abilities together, or group children together if they are doing similar projects.

CONNECT TO CONTENT

Observing Weather Changes Tell children that scientists study patterns in the weather to help them understand it. Track the weather with the class for a week. Have children choose one of these words to describe the weather: *sunny, cloudy, rainy, windy, snowy, stormy.* Record their findings on a chart. At the end of the week, have children talk about what they learned. **STEM**

RESEARCH AND INQUIRY: SHARING FINAL PROJECTS

As children get ready to wrap up the week, have them share their Research and Inquiry projects. Then have children self-evaluate.

Prepare Have children gather any materials they need to present their Research and Inquiry projects. Have partners practice their presentations.

Share Guide children to present their Research and Inquiry projects. Encourage children to speak in complete sentences.

Evaluate Have children discuss and evaluate their own presentations. You may wish to have them complete the online Student Checklist.

FORMATIVE ASSESSMENT

STUDENT CHECK-IN

Have partners share what type of weather they researched. Have children reflect using the Check-In routine.

LESSON 5

OBJECTIVES

Add individual sounds in simple, one-syllable words to make new words.

Demonstrate basic knowledge of one-to-one letter-sound correspondences by producing the primary sound or many of the most frequent sounds for each consonant.

Spell simple words phonetically, drawing on knowledge of sound-letter relationships.

Associate the long sounds with the common spellings (graphemes) for the five major vowels.

Read common high-frequency words by sight.

Read words with *l*-blends.

ELA ACADEMIC LANGUAGE

- *high-frequency*

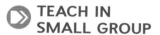

TEACH IN SMALL GROUP

You may wish to teach this lesson in small groups.

DIGITAL TOOLS

Word Work

Phonemic Awareness

Visual Vocabulary Cards

LESSON FOCUS

READING
Wrap Up
Word Work
- Read Words

WRITING
Writing/Grammar
- Self-Selected Writing
- Review Grammar

Research and Inquiry
- Share and Evaluate Presentation

Text Connections
- Connect Essential Question to a photograph
- Show Your Knowledge

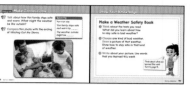

Reading/Writing Companion, pp. 96–97

---

5 mins — # Phonemic Awareness

Phoneme Addition

1 **Model** Say: *Let's add sounds to the beginning of words to make new words. Listen:* at. *Say the word:* at. *Let's add /b/ to the beginning of* at. *What is the word when you add /b/ to the beginning of* at? (bat)

2 **Guided Practice/Practice** Have children add initial sounds to words to form new words. Guide practice and provide corrective feedback.

Say *ick.* Add /t/ to the beginning of *ick.* What's the new word? (tick)
Say *tick.* Add /s/ to the beginning of *tick.* What's the word? (stick)
Say *lap.* Add /k/ to the beginning of *lap.* What's the word? (clap)
Say *lap.* Add /f/ to the beginning of *lap.* What's the word? (flap)

---

5 mins — # Phonics

 MULTIMODAL

Read Words

1 **Guided Practice** Display **Word-Building Cards** *f, l, a, t.* Point to the letters *f* and *l. The letters f and l stand for /fl/. This is the letter* a. *It stands for /a/. This is the letter* t. *It stands for /t/. Let's blend the sounds to make the word: /flaaat/ flat.* Change *fl* to *sl* to form *slat* and blend and read with children. Repeat the process, building word pairs *slam* and *clam* and *lock* and *block* to read with children.

2 **Practice** Write these words and sentences for children to read: *had, fed, red, sled, slid, clap, flat, clock, block; Ed ran with him; Is my black cat sick?; Rick can nap on a bed.* Guide practice and provide corrective feedback. Remove words from view before dictation.

Spell Words

Dictation Dictate the sounds /h/, /e/, /f/, /r/, /b/, /l/, /bl/, /fl/, /kl/, /sl/ for children to spell. Then dictate the words *lap, slap, kit, fed, fled, hop, rip, deck.* Model for children how to segment each word. Write the words for children to self-correct.

In a Flash: Sound-Spellings

bl

Display the Word-Building Card for *bl*.

1. **Teacher:** What's the letter?   **Children:** bl
2. **Teacher:** What's the sound?   **Children:** /bl/

Continue the routine for previously taught sounds.

LONG VOWEL
EXPRESS TRACK >>>

Dictation

You may wish to use this lesson to teach long vowel *i* earlier in the year, prior to its introduction in Unit 9.

Model for children how to segment each word to scaffold spelling. *When I say the word* kite, *I hear three sounds: /k/ /ī/ /t/. I know the letter* k *stands for the /k/ sound. I also know that the letters* i_e *stand for /ī/ and the letter* t *stands for /t/. I will write the letters* k, i, t, e *to spell the word* kite.

Dictate these sounds for the children to spell. Have them repeat the sound and write the appropriate letter(s). Remind children to write both letters that act together to stand for the /i/ sound: /t/ /f/ /k/ /l/ /i/ /ī/ /n/ /m/ /v/. Dictate the following words for children to spell: *five, time, nine, line, kite.*

Review: Repeat the dictation routine for long a using the following words: *make, take, name, cake, tape.*

High-Frequency Words

MULTIMODAL

⏱ 5 mins

1 **Review** Display the print or digital **Visual Vocabulary Cards** *are, he, is, little, my, she, was,* and *with*. Have children Read/Spell/Write the words.

Distribute one of the following **High-Frequency Word Cards** to children: *are, he, is, little, my, she, was, with*. Tell children that you will say some sentences. *When you hear the word that is on your card, stand and hold up your word card.*

There *are* clouds in the sky.   *He* has a blue umbrella.
What color *is* your umbrella?   *She* has a yellow one.
My umbrella *is* green with stripes.   It *was* quite a storm.

2 **Build Fluency: Word Automaticity** Display High-Frequency Word Cards *are, he, is, little, my, she, was,* and *with*. Point to each card, at random, and have children read as quickly as they can to build automaticity.

MULTIMODAL LEARNING

Color Coding After each dictation, reveal the secret color-coding letter(s) for children to find on their response boards. Have them say the sound(s) as they trace each letter in color. Use one or two of the phonics skills of the week for color coding.

FORMATIVE ASSESSMENT

❯ STUDENT CHECK-IN

Phonics Have partners spell *flat*.

High-Frequency Words Have partners spell two of the high-frequency words.

Then have children reflect using the Check-In routine.

✔ CHECK FOR SUCCESS

Rubric Use your online rubric to record children's progress.

Can children read and decode words with /b/b, /d/d, /h/h, /e/e, /f/f, /i/i, /k/k, ck, /l/l, /r/r, /t/t and *l*-blends?

Can children read and recognize high-frequency words?

❯❯ **Small Group Instruction**

If No

● **Approaching** Reteach pp. T458–T462

● **ELL** Develop pp. T458–T462

If Yes

● **On** Review pp. T466–T468

● **Beyond** Extend pp. T472

LESSON 5

- We can choose a writing activity and share it.
- We can learn about words that name more than one thing (plural nouns).

OBJECTIVES

Use words and phrases acquired through conversations, reading and being read to, and responding to texts.

With guidance and support from adults, explore a variety of digital tools to produce and publish writing, including in collaboration with peers.

Speak audibly and express thoughts, feelings, and ideas clearly.

Produce and expand complete sentences in shared language activities.

Use frequently occurring nouns.

Form regular plural nouns by adding /s/ or /es/.

ELA ACADEMIC LANGUAGE

- *journal, book review, plural*

DIFFERENTIATED WRITING

For children who need guidance with Self-Selected Writing, you may wish to:

- Journal Writing: Ask children questions to write and draw answers about in their journals: *Where should you go during a storm? How will this help to keep you safe?*

- Book Review: Provide sentence frames for children to use: **I liked the book _____. It was a good book because _____.**

⏱ 5 mins   Self-Selected Writing

Talk About the Topic

Have children continue the conversation about weather. Remind children of the Essential Question: *How can you stay safe in bad weather?* Encourage them to share with a partner something they learned this week about staying safe in bad weather.

Choose A Writing Activity

Tell children they will choose what type of writing to do today. They may choose to write about staying safe in bad weather or a different topic that is important to them. Have them work in their writer's notebook. Encourage them to draw first as a way to get their ideas down on paper. Children may choose from the following modes of writing:

 Journal Writing Remind children that a journal is a book in which they can write and draw their thoughts about whatever they wish. Have children write and draw in their journals about a time they stayed safe during bad weather or a different topic of their choice.

 Book Review Explain that a book review gives an opinion about a book. Have children write their about one of the texts they read this week about bad weather or another book of their choice from the classroom library. Their book review should tell whether they liked or disliked the book or selection and why. Model as necessary. Tell children to add drawings to their writing.

Use Digital Tools You may wish to explore different digital tools and have children publish their work.

Share Your Writing

 Invite volunteers to share their writing with the class or have partners share their writing with each other. Remind children to use the strategies below as they share out. After children share their work, you may wish to display it on a bulletin board or in a classroom writing area.

SPEAKING STRATEGIES	LISTENING STRATEGIES
✓ Wait until it is your turn to speak. ✓ Speak loudly and clearly.	✓ Listen actively to the speaker. ✓ Ask questions to understand information.

Grammar

10 mins

Singular and Plural Nouns

1 **Review** Review that singular nouns name one person, place, animal, or thing, and plural nouns name more than one. Remind children to add *-s* to most words to make them plural and *-es* to words that end with the following letters/blends: *-s, -ss, -sh, -ch, -x,* or *-z.*

2 **Guided Practice/Practice** Draw single and multiple objects, such as a chair, tables, pens, or a pencil on separate index cards. Hold up the cards one at a time and have children say with you the name of the object or objects in each card. Guide them to identify whether it is a singular or plural noun. Have children help you sort the cards into two piles—one for singular nouns and the other for plural nouns. Guide practice as needed.

Have children work in groups to draw single and multiple objects. Circulate among the groups, having children tell you the names of the objects they are drawing. Then ask children to sort their drawings according to whether they represent singular nouns or plural nouns. Provide corrective feedback.

English Language Learners

Self-Selected Writing, Choose a Writing Activity Present the writing activities, and tell the children that they will vote on one of the activities. Then, you will work on the writing as a group. Make sure to do the activity on chart paper as you will revise and publish it during small group time. Provide sentence frames and starters as you talk through the writing together. For example, if children have selected writing in their journals, model writing a journal entry. Tell children they will be able to write their own journal entry in small group. Possible sentence frames are: Last ___, there was a bad ___. The ___ was ___, so I decided to ___. During that day, I ___. It was ___!

For additional support, see the **ELL Small Group Guide,** p. 155.

DIGITAL TOOLS

Grammar Activity

⊙ TEACH IN SMALL GROUP

You may wish to review the grammar skill during Small Group time.

● **Approaching** Provide more opportunities for children to practice identifying singular and plural nouns before they write sentences.

●● **On Level** and **Beyond** Children can do the Practice sections only.

● **ELL** Use the chart in the **Language Transfers Handbook** to identify grammatical forms that may cause difficulty.

FORMATIVE ASSESSMENT

⊙ STUDENT CHECK-IN

Have partners share which activity they chose and tell why. Then have children reflect using the Check-In routine.

LEARNING GOALS

We can compare texts we have read.

OBJECTIVES

Confirm understanding of a text read aloud or information presented orally or through other media by asking and answering questions about key details and requesting clarification if something is not understood.

ELA ACADEMIC LANGUAGE

• *compare, experience*
• Cognate: *comparar*

Close Reading Routine

Read DOK 1-2

• Identify key ideas and details.
• Take notes and retell.
• Use Ⓐ Ⓒ Ⓣ prompts as needed.

Reread DOK 2–3

• Analyze the text, craft, and structure.

Integrate DOK 3–4

• Integrate knowledge and ideas.
• Make text-to-text connections.
• Use the Integrate lesson.
• Complete the Show Your Knowledge task.

FORMATIVE ASSESSMENT

❯ STUDENT CHECK-IN

Have partners share what they learned from comparing texts.

Have children reflect using the Check-In routine.

Integrate

⏱ 10 mins Make Connections

MULTIMODAL

Connect to the Essential Question

Review the Essential Question. Turn to page 96 of the **Reading/Writing Companion**. Have children look at the photo. What do they think the weather outside is like?

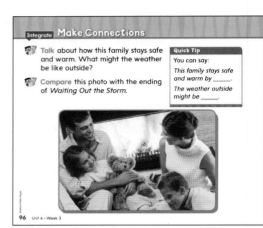
Reading/Writing Companion, p. 96

Find Text Evidence Have children answer the following questions about this page and page 27 of the **Big Book**: *How are the scenes the same?* (A parent and child are snuggling.) *How are they different?* (In the book, the parent and child look out the window at the rain.) Use the Quick Tip box for support.

Record Ideas Guide partners to compare the picture on page 96 of the Reading/Writing Companion with the picture on page 27 of the selection *Waiting Out the Storm. How are the pictures alike? How are they different? How do they help you answer the Essential Question?* Help children use a Two-Tab Foldable® to record their ideas. Have children support their ideas with evidence from the pictures and the text.

Dinah Zike's
FOLDABLES
Study Organizer

Build Knowledge: Make Connections DOK 4

Talk About the Text Have partners compare the text with experiences from their own lives.

Add to the Anchor Chart Record any new ideas on the Build Knowledge anchor chart.

Integrate

Show Your Knowledge

15 mins

Make a Weather Safety Book DOK 4

Display the texts for the week along with the Build Knowledge anchor chart and Word Bank. Turn to page 97 of the **Reading/Writing Companion** and guide children through the steps below.

1. Think Ask: *What did you learn about how to stay safe in bad weather?* Encourage partners to refer to their reader's notebook and the resources on display as they discuss their response.

2. Choose and Draw Tell children that you will make a class book together. Guide them to choose one kind of bad weather and draw a picture of it. Have children turn the paper over. On the blank side, have children draw another picture showing how to stay safe in that kind of weather.

Reading/Writing Companion, p. 97

3. Write Encourage children to refer to the Word Bank as they label or write a sentence on their pictures. Bind the drawings to make a class book and make it available for children to share.

Inspire Action

Make a Storm Invite children to rub their hands together to make wind noises. Ask: *What other noises are in a storm? How can we make them? What will help us stay safe? How can we make those noises?* Encourage children to use new weather and safety words.

Read and Act Out the Weather Read the class weather book aloud. Invite children to act out the weather and then how to stay safe in each kind of weather.

Choose Your Own Action Have children talk about the texts they read this week. *What do the texts inspire or make you want to do?*

LEARNING GOALS

We can show what we learned about how to stay safe in bad weather.

OBJECTIVES

With guidance and support from adults, recall information from experiences or gather information from provided sources to answer a question.

Add drawings or other visual displays to descriptions as desired to provide additional detail.

Use words and phrases acquired through conversations, reading, and being read to, and responding to texts.

Describe familiar people, places, things, and events and, with prompting and support, provide additional detail.

ELA ACADEMIC LANGUAGE

• *inspire*

ENGLISH LANGUAGE LEARNERS

Show Your Knowledge, Write Provide and model sentence frames or starters to write about how to stay safe in the bad weather. For example, When _____, you should _____. If it _____, then _____. Go to _____ if _____.

DIGITAL TOOLS

To enhance the class discussion, use these additional components.

Visual Vocabulary Cards

Show Your Knowledge Rubric

MY GOALS ROUTINE

Review Goal Have children turn to page 71 of the **Reading/Writing Companion**. Read the goals aloud.

Reflect Have children think about the progress they've made toward the goals. Review the Key, if needed. Then have children complete page 71.

Lexile BR

OBJECTIVES

Recognize that spoken words are represented in written language by specific sequences of letters.

With prompting and support, identify characters, settings, and major events in a story.

Read emergent-reader texts with purpose and understanding.

ELA ACADEMIC LANGUAGE

• *realistic fiction, prediction, characters*

• Cognates: *ficción realista, predicción*

●Approaching Level

Leveled Reader: *Bad Weather*

Preview and Predict

Read aloud the title and the names of the author and illustrator as children follow along in their books. Ask: *What kind of weather is bad weather? What do you think will happen in bad weather?* Preview each illustration and guide children to revise or confirm their predictions. Model the language pattern: *What does the woman get here? Yes, she gets her coat.*

Review Genre: Realistic Fiction

Remind children that realistic fiction stories are made up, but they are about things that could happen in real life. Say: *Characters in realistic fiction are like real people. The things that happen to them are just like things that happen to you and me.* Ask: *Who are the characters in this story?* (a girl and her mother)

Set Purpose

Remind children of the Essential Question: *How can you stay safe in bad weather?* Help children set a purpose for reading: *Let's find out how the characters stay safe in bad weather.* Review rebuses with children to help them name the words.

Foundational Skills

Model Concepts of Print Remind children that a sentence begins with a capital letter and ends with a punctuation mark. Provide children with more practice matching speech to print. As you read aloud, have children match the words you say with the words on the page.

Review High-Frequency Words Point to the high-frequency word *she* on each page of the story. Then ask children to say the word *she* aloud each time they point to it on a new page.

Guided Comprehension

As children read *Bad Weather*, monitor and provide guidance by offering support and corrective feedback as needed. Model visualizing and identifying the sequence of events where applicable.

Visualize

Remind children that, as they read, they can use information from the story and illustrations to make pictures in their minds of what is happening.

Events: Sequence

Remind children that finding details in a story will help them understand what is happening in that story. Explain that, in this book, the text and illustrations provide details about the sequence of the story.

Think Aloud The pictures in this story tell me what the characters are doing. They tell me the important ideas the author wants me to know. On page 2, I see the woman putting on a coat to go outside in the snow. This shows me how she is getting ready for cold weather.

Guide children to find more details in the pictures and text. Discuss what details the illustrations add to the text.

Respond to the Text

Have children respond to the text by discussing these questions:

- *What kind of weather are the mother and girl getting ready for?* (for snowy weather)

- *What do they do to get ready for the weather?* (They put on coats, hats, boots, and scarves. They get a shovel, hot drink, and flashlight.)

- *Why do the girl and her mother need the flashlight?* (The power has gone out.)

Retell Have children take turns retelling the story, using characters, the setting, and events. Then ask: *How do you get ready for different kinds of weather?*

Focus on Fluency

Practice fluency with children. Remember that children need to read with accuracy first.

Once children have read the text with accuracy, have them read the story again, focusing on rate. Have them practice reading with partners. Provide corrective feedback as necessary.

Build Knowledge: Make Connections

- **Talk About the Texts** Have partners discuss how to prepare for different kinds of weather.

- **Write About the Texts** Then have children add their ideas to their Build Knowledge page of their reader's notebook.

LITERACY ACTIVITIES

Have children complete the Collaborate and Write About It activities on the inside back cover of the book.

LITERATURE CIRCLES

Lead children in a literature circle using these questions to guide the discussion: *What should you do in bad weather? Why? What is your favorite thing to do when it is snowing?*

LEVEL UP

IF Children read *Bad Weather* Approaching Level with fluency and correctly answer the Respond to the Text questions,

THEN Tell children that they will read another story about how to stay safe in bad weather.

- Have children page through *Getting Ready* On Level and help children make connections to getting ready for a snowstorm.

- Have children read the story, monitoring their comprehension and providing assistance as necessary.

●Approaching Level

Phonological/Phonemic Awareness

RECOGNIZE ALLITERATION

TIER 2

OBJECTIVES
Recognize and produce rhyming words.

I Do Reread the line *Whether the weather be fine* from the poem "Whether the Weather." Point out that the words *whether* and *weather* sound almost the same at the beginning. Repeat these two words, exaggerating the initial sounds. Have children echo you.

We Do Say *Peter Piper picked a peck of pickled peppers* and have children repeat. Guide them to figure out which sound is the same at the beginning of most of the words. (/p/)

You Do Tell children that you will say some words. Have them repeat the words and tell if the words begin with the same sounds and, if so, which sound is the same: *huge happy hippo; five fast foxes; big buzzing bee; cute little duck; sing silly songs.*

PHONEME IDENTITY

TIER 2

OBJECTIVES
Isolate and pronounce the initial, medial, and final sounds in words.

I Do Display the *rose, rabbit,* and *rock* **Photo Cards**. Say the picture names and have children repeat them with you. Ask: *What sound is the same in* rose, rabbit, *and* rock? *Yes, the first sound, /r/, is the same.* Repeat with the *pen, net,* and *jet* Photo Cards to review the medial /e/ sound.

We Do Show and name the following sets of Photo Cards. Have children repeat. Guide them to identify the sound that is the same in each set:

elbow, exit, egg	five, fork, farm	kitten, kite, king
bird, boat, boot	leaf, lamp, light	hair, hay, house

You Do Show the sets of Photo Cards again. Have children name each picture in a set and then say the sound that is the same in the set.

PHONEME BLENDING

OBJECTIVES

Demonstrate understanding of spoken words, syllables, and sounds (phonemes).

Blend phonemes to make words.

I Do *Listen as I say the sounds in a word: /f/ /i/ /b/. Now I will blend the sounds together to make a word: /fffiiib/, fib. I blended the sounds /f/ /i/ /b/ to make the word fib.* Repeat with *hen, lap.*

We Do *Listen as I say the sounds in a word.* Have children repeat. *Now let's blend the sounds and say the word together: /r/ /o/ /k/, /rrroook/, rock.* Repeat with *kin.*

You Do Say the following sounds. Ask children to blend the sounds and say the words:

/l/ /e/ /d/   /r/ /a/ /k/   /h/ /o/ /p/   /f/ /i/ /n/   /b/ /e/ /t/

You may wish to use a puppet, if one is available in the classroom, for the *I Do* and *We Do* parts of this lesson.

PHONEME ADDITION

OBJECTIVES

Add or substitute individual sounds (phonemes) in simple, one-syllable words to make new words.

I Do *Listen as I say a word: it. Now I will add /l/ to the beginning of it. Say: lit. By adding /l/ to it, I made a new word: lit.* Repeat the routine, adding /f/ and /h/ to *it.*

We Do Say *Ed,* then add /l/ to make *led.* Have children repeat the new word. Then guide children to add sounds to *Ed* to make the words *bed, fed, sled,* and *red.*

You Do Say *in* and the sound /f/. Ask children to add the sound /f/ to *in* to make *fin.* Repeat, having them add sounds /b/ and /k/ to *in* to make *bin* and *kin.*

You may wish to use a puppet, if one is available, for the *I Do* and *We Do* parts of this lesson.

ELL You may wish to review phonological awareness, phonics, decoding, and fluency using this section. Use scaffolding methods as necessary to ensure children understand the meaning of the words. Refer to the **Language Transfers Handbook** for phonics elements that may not transfer in children's native languages.

● Approaching Level

Phonics

SOUND-SPELLING REVIEW

OBJECTIVES
Demonstrate basic knowledge of one-to-one letter-sound correspondences by producing the primary sound or many of the most frequent sounds for each consonant.

I Do Display **Word-Building Cards** one at a time. Say the letter name and its sound. For example: Letter *r*, /r/. Repeat for *b, e, f, h, l, c, k* and *bl, cl, fl, sl.*

We Do Display Word-Building Cards one at a time and together say the letter name and the sound that each letter stands for.

You Do Display Word-Building Cards one at a time and have children say the letter name and the sound that each letter stands for.

CONNECT TO *l*-BLENDS

OBJECTIVES
Demonstrate basic knowledge of one-to-one letter-sound correspondences by producing the primary sound or many of the most frequent sounds for each consonant.

I Do Display Word-Building Cards *c* and *l*. *These are lowercase* c *and* l. *When the letters appear together at the beginning of a word, we say the sounds together:* /kl/. *I'm going to trace the letters as I say* /kl/. Trace the letters while saying /kl/. Repeat for the blends *bl, fl,* and *sl.*

We Do *The word* clay *begins with* /kl/. *Let's write* c *and* l *on our* **Response Boards.** Continue with *blot, flow,* and *slide.* Guide children to write the initial letters that stand for the initial sounds they hear in each word.

You Do Say *lip, clip, slid* and have children write the letters for the initial sounds.

BLEND WORDS WITH *l*-BLENDS

MULTIMODAL

OBJECTIVES
Know and apply grade-level phonics and word analysis skills in decoding words.

Build words with *l*-blends.

I Do Display Word-Building Cards *l, a, p. This is the letter* l. *It stands for* /l/. *This is* a. *It stands for* /a/. *This is* p. *It stands for* /p/. *Listen as I blend the sounds together to make* /lllaaap/, lap. Repeat for *clap,* placing *c* in front of the word to make a new word. Explain that we say the /kl/ sounds together.

We Do *Now let's blend more sounds to make words.* Make the word *lid. Let's blend* /l/ /i/ /d/, /llliiid/, lid. Have children blend to read the word. Repeat with the word *slid. Let's blend* /sl/ /i/ /d/, /sliiid/, slid.

You Do Distribute sets of Word-Building Cards. Write: *sip, slip, flip, block.* Have children form the words and then blend and read them.

BUILD WORDS WITH *l*-BLENDS

OBJECTIVES

Know and apply grade-level phonics and word analysis skills in decoding words.

Build words with *l*-blends.

I Do Display **Word-Building Cards** *l, a, p. This is the letter* l. *It stands for /l/. This is the letter* a. *It stands for /a/. This is the letter* p. *It stands for /p/. Listen as I blend the three sounds together to make the word: /lllaaap/* lap. Repeat for *clap*, placing *c* in front of the word to make a new word. Explain that we say the /kl/ sounds together.

We Do *Now let's blend more sounds to make words.* Make the word *lid. Let's blend /l/ /i/ /d/, /llliiid/,* lid. Have children blend to read the word. Repeat with the word *slid. Let's blend /sl/ /i/ /d/, /sliiid/,* slid.

You Do Distribute sets of Word-Building Cards. Write: *sip, slip, flip, block.* Have children form the words and then blend and read them.

REREAD THE DECODABLE READER

OBJECTIVES

Know and apply grade-level phonics and word analysis skills in decoding words.

Read words in context.

Unit 6 Decodable Reader

Focus on Foundational Skills

Review the high-frequency words *are, he, is, little, my, she, was,* and *with* with children. Review the *l*-blends /kl/, /bl/, /fl/, and /sl/. Guide children to blend sounds to read *clam* and *slip.*

Read the Decodable Reader

Have children read "Rock Ken" and "Flip, Flop, Flip!" Have them point out the high-frequency words as well as words with *l*-blends and other previously learned sound-spellings. If children struggle sounding out words, model blending.

Focus on Fluency

Have partners read "Rock Ken" and "Flip, Flop, Flip!" As children read, guide them to focus on their accuracy. Then have them focus on reading with automaticity and at an appropriate rate. You may wish to have them reread "Mack and Ben" (pages 80–87) in the **Reading/Writing Companion**.

SOUND/SPELLING FLUENCY

Display the following Word-Building Cards: *e, h, f, r, b, l, k, bl, cl, fl,* and *sl.* Have children chorally say each sound. Repeat and vary the pace.

● Approaching Level

High-Frequency Words

RETEACH WORDS

OBJECTIVES
Read common high-frequency words by sight.

I Do Display **High-Frequency Word Cards** *my, are, he, with, is, little, she,* and *was.* Use the Read/Spell/Write routine to reteach the high-frequency words.

We Do Continue to display the High-Frequency Word Cards and read aloud each word with children. Then write this sentence and read it aloud together: *My friend Nick was with me.* One at a time show the High-Frequency Word Cards for *my, are, he, with, is, little, she,* and *was.* Have children say the word on the card. Ask them whether the word is in the sentence. If they say yes, have them touch and say the word in the sentence. Use the same routine for the sentences: *She and I are drawing. He is a little dog.*

You Do Write the sentence frame: **She is on the dock with my little _____.** Have children copy the sentence frame on their **Response Boards**. Then have partners work together to read and orally complete the frame by talking about what or who might be on the dock.

CUMULATIVE REVIEW

OBJECTIVES
Read common high-frequency words by sight.

I Do Display the High-Frequency Word Cards *I, can, the, we, see, a, like, to, and, go, you, do, my, are, he, with, is, little, she,* and *was.* Use the Read/Spell/Write routine to review words. Have children practice reading the words until they can read them accurately and with automaticity.

We Do Use the High-Frequency Word Cards to create sentences, such as *Do you see a rip in the little red sack? He and I are with my mom and pop.* Have children identify the high-frequency words that are used in each sentence. Read the sentences together.

You Do Have children create sentences with a partner. Remind them to refer to the High-Frequency Word Cards as needed. Then have them write the words on their Response Boards. Have partners take turns reading the sentences to each other.

Oral Vocabulary

REVIEW WORDS

OBJECTIVES

Use words and phrases acquired through conversations, reading and being read to, and responding to texts.

Identify real-life connections between words and their use.

| I Do | Use the Define/Example/Ask routine on the print or digital **Visual Vocabulary Cards** to review *safe, prepare, notice, celebration,* and *enough.* |

| We Do | Ask questions to build understanding. *Why do you feel safe inside when it is dark outside? How can you prepare dinner? Do you notice anything different in our classroom? What can people do to make a celebration special? How many mittens would be enough for both of your hands?* |

| You Do | Have children complete these sentence frames: |

A cat feels safe when _____.   **A fish will notice food if you** _____.

I prepare for school by _____.   **We have a big celebration for** _____.

Comprehension

SELF-SELECTED READING

OBJECTIVES

With prompting and support, identify major events in a story.

With prompting and support, ask and answer questions about key details in a text.

Read emergent-reader texts with purpose and understanding.

Independent Reading

Help children select a realistic fiction for independent reading. Encourage them to read for ten minutes. Remind children that the important events in a story are often told in a certain order, or sequence. Review with children that readers ask themselves questions before, during, and after they read and look for answers in the photographs and the text.

If children need practice with concepts of print, use **Practice Book** page 507.

After reading, guide children to participate in a group discussion about the selection they read. In addition, children can choose activities from the Reading **Center Activity Cards** to help them apply skills to the text as they read. Offer assistance and guidance with self-selected assignments.

Lexile 30L

OBJECTIVES

Recognize that spoken words are represented in written language by specific sequences of letters.

With prompting and support, identify characters, settings, and major events in a story.

Read emergent-reader texts with purpose and understanding.

ELA ACADEMIC LANGUAGE
• *predict, sequence, sentence*
• Cognates: *predecir, secuencia*

●On Level

Leveled Reader: *Getting Ready*

Preview and Predict

Read the title and the names of the author and illustrator. Have children talk about what they see on the cover. Preview the illustrations and allow children to predict what the book is about. Ask: *What kind of weather do you see in the pictures? Why would the woman be getting ready for the snow?*

Review Genre: Realistic Fiction

Remind children that realistic fiction stories are made up, but they are about things that could happen in real life. Ask: *Who is the main character in this story? How can you tell?* (The woman is the main character. She is in all the pictures.)

Set Purpose

Remind children of the Essential Question: *How can you stay safe in bad weather?* Help children set a purpose for reading: *Let's find out how people can stay safe in bad weather.* Remind children to use the illustrations to help them understand the text.

Foundational Skills

Model Concepts of Print Discuss with children what makes up a sentence. Point to the uppercase letter at the beginning of the first word in a sentence. Then point to the period at the end of the sentence. Provide children with more practice matching speech to print. As you read aloud, have children match the words you say with the words on the page.

Review High-Frequency Words Point out the word *she* on page 2. Have children find and read the word *she* on each page of the book.

Guided Comprehension

As children read *Getting Ready*, monitor comprehension and provide guidance by offering support and corrective feedback to help them make adjustments as needed. Model visualizing and identifying the sequence of events where applicable.

Visualize

Remind children that, as they read, they can make pictures in their minds of what is happening in the story to better understand it. They can use information from the text and illustrations to visualize what is happening.

Events: Sequence

Remind children that they should look for details in the text and pictures to help them understand the story. Explain that details in a story often show how the events happened in a certain order.

Think Aloud As I read, I think about what's happening in the story. I use the pictures to see what the woman is doing. She is getting things to help her during a snowstorm that is coming. On page 8, I see that there is snow coming down. All of the things she carries in the pictures show me what she needs to get ready for the storm.

Guide children to choose other pages to analyze the details. Discuss why the woman might need each of the items during a storm.

Respond to the Text

Have children respond to the text by discussing these questions:

- *What does the woman need to get ready for the snowstorm?* (She needs water, snacks, wood, blankets, flashlights, games, and friends.)
- *What does the woman get out of the closet?* (blankets)
- *Who does the woman spend time with during the storm?* (friends)
- *Why does she need the flashlights?* (the power may go out)

Retell Have children take turns retelling the story, using characters, the setting, and events. Help them make personal connections. Ask: *What do you think is an important thing to do to get ready for a snowstorm?*

Focus on Fluency

Practice fluency with children. Remember that children need to read with accuracy first.

Once children have read the text with accuracy, have them read the story again, focusing on rate. Have children practice reading in pairs. Provide corrective feedback as necessary.

Build Knowledge: Make Connections

- **Talk About the Texts** Have partners discuss how to prepare for different kinds of weather.
- **Write About the Texts** Then have children add their ideas to their Build Knowledge page of their reader's notebook.

LITERACY ACTIVITIES

Have children complete the Collaborate and Write About It activities on the inside back cover of the book.

LITERATURE CIRCLES

Lead children in a literature circle using these questions to guide the discussion: *Why do you think the power may go out in the story? How would you and your family get ready for a snowstorm?*

LEVEL UP

IF Children read *Getting Ready* On Level with fluency and correctly answer the Respond to the Text questions,

THEN Tell children that they will read another story about staying safe in bad weather.

- Have children page through *The Storm* Beyond Level as you talk about what people do to get ready for a windy rainstorm.
- Have children read the story, monitoring their comprehension and providing assistance as necessary.

●On Level

Phonological/Phonemic Awareness

PHONEME IDENTITY

OBJECTIVES

Isolate and pronounce the initial sounds in words.

I Do Display and name the *horse, hand,* and *hippo* **Photo Cards**. Have children repeat the names with you. Ask them to identify the sound that is the same in *horse, hand,* and *hippo.*

We Do Show the following sets of Photo Cards. Name the pictures with children and guide them to say the sound that is the same in each set: *rake, rope, ring; farm, five, football; egg, exit, elbow.*

You Do Show these Photo Cards. Have children name each picture and say the sound the words begin with: *key, king, koala; boil, bear, bowl; ladder, leaf, lock.*

PHONEME BLENDING

OBJECTIVES

Demonstrate understanding of spoken words, syllables, and sounds (phonemes).

I Do Place *pen, hat, fan, net, lock, rock,* and *bat* Photo Cards facedown. Choose a card, but do not show it to children. *These are the sounds in the word: /h/ /a/ /t/. I will blend the sounds: /haaat/,* hat. *The word is* hat. Show the picture.

We Do Choose another Photo Card and say the sounds in the name. Together say the sounds and blend them to say the word. Then show the picture.

You Do Choose other Photo Cards. For each card, say the sounds of the picture name and have children blend the sounds to say the word.

PHONEME ADDITION

OBJECTIVES

Add or substitute individual sounds (phonemes) in simple, one-syllable words to make new words.

I Do *I can add a sound to a word to make a new word. When I add /h/ to the beginning of* am, *it makes* ham. Repeat with *am* and /r/.

We Do *Say the sound /f/ together with me: /f/. Let's add /f/ to* an: fan. *Say the new word with me:* fan. Repeat with *it* and /l/.

You Do Say *it* and the sound /k/. Have children add the sound to make *kit.* Repeat, having them add the sounds /b/, /l/, /f/, and /h/ to make new words.

Phonics

REVIEW PHONICS

OBJECTIVES

Demonstrate basic knowledge of one-to-one letter-sound correspondences by producing the primary sound or many of the most frequent sounds for each consonant.

I Do Display **Word-Building Cards** *c* and *l*. *When the letters* c *and* l *appear together at the beginning of a word, we say the sounds together:* /kl/. *Say* cloud, *emphasizing* /kl/. Repeat for *l*-blends /bl/, /fl/, and /sl/.

We Do Display a picture of a slide and the *cloud, blue,* and *fly* **Photo Cards**. Have children say the name of each picture together with you. Then ask them to identify the words that begin with /sl/, /kl/, /bl/, and /fl/.

You Do Write the words *lip, slip, lock, block, lap, clap,* and *flap*. Have children read each word. Repeat to practice fluency. Provide corrective feedback as needed.

PICTURE SORT

OBJECTIVES

Associate the long and short sounds with the common spellings (graphemes) for the five major vowels.

I Do Display Word-Building Cards *e* and *o* in a pocket chart. Then show the *web* Photo Card. Say /w/ /e/ /b/, web. *The sound in the middle is* /e/. *The letter* e *stands for* /e/. *I will put the* web *Photo Card under the letter* e. Show the *fox* Photo Card. Say /f/ /o/ /ks/, fox. *The sound in the middle is* /o/. *The letter* o *stands for* /o/. *I will put the* fox *Photo Card under the* o.

We Do Show the *mop* Photo Card. *Listen:* mop, /m/ /o/ /p/. *Say it with me:* mop, /m/ /o/ /p/. *What sound is in the middle?* (/o/) *Where do I place this Photo Card?* (under *o*) Continue with the *gem* Photo Card.

You Do Continue the activity using Photo Cards for *box, rock, lock, net, jet,* and *pen*. Have children say the picture name and the sounds in the name. Then have them place the card under the *e* or *o*.

● On Level

Phonics

BLEND WORDS WITH *l*-BLENDS

OBJECTIVES

Know and apply grade-level phonics and word analysis skills in decoding words.

Build words with *l*-blends.

I Do Display **Word-Building Cards** *c, l, a, p. These are the letters* c *and* l. *Together, the letters stand for* /kl/. *This is the letter* a. *It stands for* /a/. *This is the letter* p. *It stands for* /p/. *Listen as I blend the sounds together to make the word:* /klaaap/, clap.

We Do Use Word-Building Cards to form the words *lid, slid, sip, slip, flip,* and *black.* Guide children to blend the words sound by sound to read each word.

You Do Distribute sets of Word-Building Cards. Write each of the following words. Have children form the word and then blend and read the word: *lock, clock, block, flock,* and *slick.*

REREAD THE DECODABLE READER

OBJECTIVES

Know and apply grade-level phonics and word analysis skills in decoding words.

Read emergent-reader texts with purpose and understanding.

Unit 6 Decodable Reader

Focus on Foundational Skills

Review the high-frequency words *are, he, is, little, my, she, was,* and *with* with children. Review the *l*-blends /kl/, /bl/, /fl/, and /sl/. Guide children to blend sounds to read *clam* and *slip.*

Read the Decodable Reader

Have children read "Rock Ken" and "Flip, Flop, Flip!" Point out the high-frequency words as well as words with *l*-blends and other previously learned sound-spellings. If children struggle sounding out words, model blending.

Focus on Fluency

Have partners read "Rock Ken" and "Flip, Flop, Flip!" As children read, guide them to focus on their accuracy. Children can give feedback on their accuracy to their partners. Then have them focus on reading with automaticity and at an appropriate rate. You may wish to have them reread "Mack and Ben" (pages 80–87) in the **Reading/Writing Companion.**

High-Frequency Words

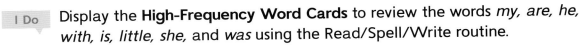

REVIEW WORDS

OBJECTIVES
Read common high-frequency words by sight.

I Do Display the **High-Frequency Word Cards** to review the words *my, are, he, with, is, little, she,* and *was* using the Read/Spell/Write routine.

We Do Write sentences: **My friend Nick was with me. She and I are drawing. He is a little dog.** Point to *My, was, with, She, are, He, is,* and *little* in the sentences. Have children read each word. Then chorally read the sentences. Have children frame and read each high-frequency word in the sentences.

You Do Display the High-Frequency Word Cards and have children read aloud each word. Say the word *little*. Have children close their eyes, picture the word, and write it as they see it. Have children self-correct. Repeat for *my, are, he, with, is, she,* and *was.*

Fluency Use the **Practice Book Word Cards** to review the previously introduced High-Frequency and **Build Your Word Bank** words. Have children practice reading the words until they can read accurately and with automaticity.

Comprehension

SELF-SELECTED READING

OBJECTIVES
With prompting and support, identify major events in a story.

With prompting and support, ask and answer questions about key details in a text.

Read emergent-reader texts with purpose and understanding.

Independent Reading

Help children select a realistic fiction for independent reading. Encourage them to read for ten minutes. Guide children to transfer what they have learned this week as they read. Remind children that the important events in a story are often told in a certain order, or sequence. Review with children that as they read, they can ask questions about things they do not understand and look for answers in the text and photographs.

After reading, guide children to participate in a group discussion about the selection they read. In addition, children can choose activities from the Reading **Center Activity Cards** to help them apply skills to the text as they read. Offer assistance and guidance with self-selected assignments.

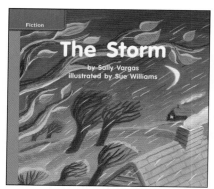

Lexile 170L

OBJECTIVES

Recognize common types of texts.

With prompting and support, identify characters, settings, and major events in a story.

With prompting and support, retell familiar stories, including key details.

Read emergent-reader texts with purpose and understanding.

ELA ACADEMIC LANGUAGE

• *author, illustrator, visualize*

• Cognates: *autor, ilustrador, visualizar*

●Beyond Level

Leveled Reader: *The Storm*

Preview and Predict

Ask children to point to the title and the names of the author and illustrator as you read them aloud. Ask children to discuss what they see in the cover illustration. Ask: *What kind of weather do you see?* Invite children to look through the illustrations and predict what they think the story will be about.

Review Genre: Realistic Fiction

Ask children if they think this book is a realistic fiction or nonfiction book and ask them to explain why. Confirm that nonfiction books give facts and realistic fiction books are made up stories, but they are about things that could really happen. Explain that we can understand what any kind of fiction story is about by thinking about what the characters say and do. Ask: *How can you tell when a character is talking in a fiction story?* Point out quotation marks to children.

Set Purpose

Remind children of the Essential Question: *How can you stay safe in bad weather?* Help children set a purpose for reading. Say: *Let's read to find out what this family does to get ready for a big rainstorm.* Remind children to use the illustrations to help them understand the text.

Guided Comprehension

As children read *The Storm,* monitor and provide guidance by offering support and corrective feedback as needed. Model visualizing and identifying the sequence of events where applicable. Remind children to pause when they come to words that are unfamiliar. Prompt them to sound out words using what they know about letter-sound relationships and to use picture clues to confirm they understand what they are reading.

Visualize

Remind children that, as they read, they can use information from the text and illustrations to visualize or make pictures in their mind of what is happening in the story.

Events: Sequence

Remind children that they can find details in a story from the words on the page and from the illustrations. These details are usually given in the order that events happen in the story. Sometimes the illustrations give information that is not in the text.

Think Aloud When I look at the picture on page 3, I see the girl and her mom carrying things from the yard inside the house. I know that they are getting ready for a storm. I can see from this picture that they are doing hard work. Mom says that the things will be safe inside.

Guide children to find details throughout the story, identifying information in the illustrations and text that tells how the characters are staying safe, how they are preparing for the storm, and the sequence of the events.

Respond to the Text

Have children respond to the text by discussing these questions:

- *What things do the family put away before the storm?* (the table, the bat, the ball, and the bike)

- *Why would the family need flashlights and candles in a storm?* (They would need them to have light if the power goes out.)

- *On page 7, it says that the wind bent the trees. What might the wind have done to the toys outside?* (It would have blown them away, and they might have hit something.)

- *Why is it important to get ready for a storm before it comes?* (so we can be safe when the storm comes)

Retell Have children take turns retelling the story, using characters, the setting, and events. Help them make a personal connection by asking: *Have you ever gotten ready for a storm? What did you do?*

Focus on Fluency

Practice fluency with children. Remember that children need to read with accuracy first.

Once children have read the text with accuracy, have them read the story again, focusing on rate. Have them practice reading with partners. Provide corrective feedback as necessary.

Build Knowledge: Make Connections

- **Talk About the Texts** Have partners discuss how to prepare for different kinds of weather.

- **Write About the Texts** Then have children add their ideas to their Build Knowledge page of their reader's notebook.

LITERACY ACTIVITIES

Have children complete the Collaborate and Write About It activities on the inside back cover of the book.

LITERATURE CIRCLES

Lead children in a literature circle using these questions to guide the discussion: *What things would you need to bring inside your house if a storm is coming? Can you describe, using full sentences, how these things are similar or different than those in the story?*

⭐ GIFTED AND TALENTED

Evaluate Have children think about different kinds of weather that people should get ready for ahead of time. Have them work in small groups and help them make a list of their ideas.

Extend Have children make a drawing of each type of weather and label it.

Beyond Level

Phonics

REVIEW

OBJECTIVES

Demonstrate basic knowledge of one-to-one letter-sound correspondences by producing the primary or many of the most frequent sounds for each consonant.

I Do Display **Word-Building Cards** *c* and *l*. *When the letters* c *and* l *appear together at the beginning of a word, we say the sounds together:* /kl/. Say *cloud,* emphasizing /kl/. Repeat for *l*-blends /bl/, /fl/, and /sl/.

We Do Display a picture of a slide and the *cloud, blue,* and *fly* **Photo Cards**. Have children say the name of each picture. Repeat the names, emphasizing the beginning consonant blend. Then ask children to share other words they know that begin with the same sounds as any of the picture names.

You Do Write the words *lip, slip, lock, block, lap, clap,* and *flap*. Have partners read each word. Ask them to write the words on their **Response Boards**, underlining the letter or letters that make the beginning sound or *l*-blend. Provide corrective feedback as needed.

Fluency Have children reread the story "Mack and Ben" for fluency.

Innovate Have children create a new page for "Mack and Ben" using the sentence frame **Mack hid in my _____.** to name another place that the frightened dog might hide during the bad weather.

High-Frequency Words

REVIEW

OBJECTIVES

Read common high-frequency words by sight.

I Do Use the **Build Your Word Bank High-Frequency Word Cards** at the back of the **Practice Book** for *than, his, three, when, which, soon, many, them, eat, by, some, brown, now, way,* and *under*. Review the words using the Read/Spell/Write routine.

We Do Display the Practice Book High-Frequency Word Cards for *my, are, with, is, little, she,* and *was*. Have children help you create sentence frames using both sets of word cards.

You Do Have partners write sentences using the Build Your Word Bank High-Frequency words on their Response Boards. Have them read their sentences.

Vocabulary

ORAL VOCABULARY: SYNONYMS

OBJECTIVES

With guidance and support from adults, explore word relationships and nuances in word meanings.

I Do Review the meanings of the oral vocabulary words *safe* and *celebration*. Explain that a synonym is a word that means almost the same thing as another word. *A synonym for* safe *is* protected. *To be protected is to be kept away from harm.* Coats and gloves protect us from the cold air. *A synonym for* celebration *is* party. *A party* is a group of people having a good time. My family went to the party for our town's new playground.

We Do Write a few sentences together using the new words *safe* and *celebration*. Read the sentences aloud.

You Do Have partners write a short poem about an animal family. Tell them to include the words *safe* and *celebration*. Explain that the poem doesn't need to rhyme. Have children share their poems with the class.

 Extend Have children plan and act out short plays about staying safe in bad weather. Encourage children to use synonyms, *protected* and *party*, in their skits.

Comprehension

SELF-SELECTED READING

OBJECTIVES

With prompting and support, identify major events in a story.

With prompting and support, ask and answer questions about key details in a text.

Read emergent-reader texts with purpose and understanding.

Independent Reading

Help children select a realistic fiction for independent reading. Encourage them to read for ten minutes. Guide children to transfer what they have learned this week as they read by identifying the sequence of events. Remind children that readers ask questions as they read to help understand the text.

After reading, guide children to participate in a group discussion about the selection they read. In addition, children can choose activities from the Reading **Center Activity Cards** to help them apply skills to the text as they read. Offer assistance and guidance with self-selected assignments.

GIFTED and TALENTED Have children write a letter to the girl in *Waiting Out the Storm* telling her how to stay safe and create an illustration to go with the letter.

Extended Writing
Realistic Fiction

Writing

Extended Writing Goal

- I can write a realistic fiction story.

Children will engage in the writing process to write a realistic fiction story over the course of one week. Explicit writing instruction and flexible minilessons are provided to support children in their writing development. Children apply writing skills during Independent writing time.

Suggested Pacing

	Lesson 1	Lesson 2	Lesson 3	Lesson 4	Lesson 5
Week 3	Expert and Student Models	Plan	Draft	Revise and Edit	Publish, Present, and Evaluate

Writing Process Lessons

Study Expert and Student Models

Waiting Out the Storm **Literature Big Book**, pp. 4–5

- Analyze the Expert Model

Reading/Writing Companion, pp. 98–99

- Analyze the Student Model
- Discuss features of realistic fiction

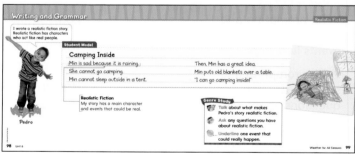

Plan the Realistic Fiction Story

Reading/Writing Companion, pp. 100–101

- Brainstorm ideas for a realistic fiction story
- Plan, draw, and write ideas

Draft the Realistic Fiction Story

Reading/Writing Companion, pp. 102–103

- Discuss Expert and Student Models
- Draft a realistic fiction story

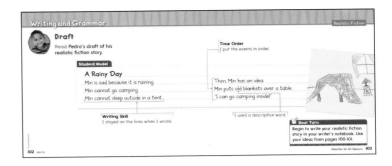

Revise and Edit

Reading/Writing Companion, pp. 104–105

- Discuss Student Model
- Revise the draft and edit for mistakes

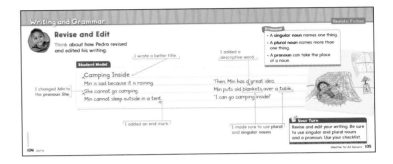

Publish, Present and Evaluate

Reading/Writing Companion, pp. 106–107

- Prepare the final draft
- Share and evaluate writing

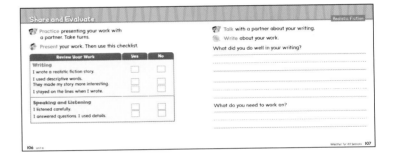

Flexible Minilessons

Choose from the following minilessons to focus on areas where your children need support.

Realistic Fiction Minilessons

For more support with writing a realistic fiction Story, use these minilessons:
- Focus on One Idea, T486
- Realistic Characters, Setting, and Events, T486
- Sequence of Events, T487
- Descriptive Details, T487

Developmental Writing Support

For more support with planning your writing conferences and small group instruction, see the Student Models, pp. T488–T493.

Writing Skills Minilesson Bank

Use these flexible minilessons on pages T494–T499 to differentiate instruction and develop critical writing skills.

- Left-to-Right Progression
- Letters and Words
- Stretch Sounds
- Use Word Bank
- Spaces Between Words
- Words in a Sentence

- Sentence Capitalization
- End Punctuation
- Return Sweep
- Write on the Lines
- Top-to-Bottom Progression

LESSON
1

LEARNING GOALS

We can name what makes a text realistic fiction.

OBJECTIVES

Use a combination of drawing, dictating, and writing to narrate a single event or several loosely linked events, tell about the events in the order in which they occurred, and provide a reaction to what happened.

Recognize common types of texts.

Analyze an expert model of realistic fiction.

ELA ACADEMIC LANGUAGE

• *realistic fiction, character*

• Cognate: *ficción realista*

Expert Model

15 mins

Features of Realistic Fiction

Remind children that they have read realistic fiction in Units 5 and 6. Ask: *Can you name any of the realistic fiction stories we have read so far?* (My Garden, Mama, Is It Summer Yet?, Waiting Out the Storm) *We will soon begin to write our own realistic fiction story! First, let's review what we know about realistic fiction.*

Anchor Chart Display the realistic fiction anchor chart. Say: *Realistic fiction has characters, a setting, and events. Characters in realistic fiction are like real people, and the events could happen in real life.* Add ideas to the chart as necessary.

Analyze the Expert Model

Talk About It Display the Unit 6 **Literature Big Book** *Waiting Out the Storm*. Explain that you will read part of the text. Ask children to listen for clues that tell them that the story is realistic fiction.

Mama?

Yes, buttercup?

What's that I hear?

Ask: *Who are the main characters?* (Mama and Buttercup) *What are they doing that real people would do?* Have children turn and talk to a partner to discuss their ideas. (Possible response: They are talking to each other the way that a real mother and daughter might.)

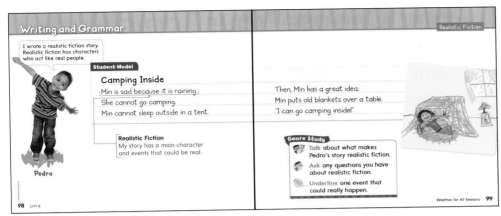

Reading/Writing Companion, pp. 98-99

Analyze the Student Model

Direct children to pages 98-99 in the **Reading/Writing Companion**. Read the speech bubble, the student model, and the call-out aloud. Help children find clues showing that the text is realistic fiction.

Genre Have children complete the Genre activity on page 99.

- **Talk** Have partners talk about what makes Pedro's writing realistic fiction. (It has a character and events that could be real.)

- **Circle** Have children circle who the story is about. (Min)

- **Underline** Have children underline one story event. (Children should underline the first, fourth, or fifth sentence of the story.)

Your Turn

Ask children to draw and label a picture of a made-up character doing something that a real person would do.

English Language Learners

Use these scaffolds with **Analyze the Student Model**.

Beginning

Point to and read the first sentence of the student model. *Who is the story about?* The story is about Min. Min is sad.

Intermediate

Help children reread the sentences on pp. 98-99. Use sentence frames to help them talk about who the story is about and one event in the story: The story is about Min. Min puts blankets over a table.

Advanced/Advanced High

Have children use complete sentences to talk about how they know the student model is realistic fiction.

ELL NEWCOMERS

To help children develop their writing, display some of the **Newcomer Cards** and online **Weekly Opener Build Background Images** for Units 1–5. Help children identify what they see with a partner. Provide sentence frames: What do you see? I see a girl. Have children point to the image as they ask and answer. Then help them write words, phrases, or sentences in their notebooks according to their ability.

FORMATIVE ASSESSMENT

❯ STUDENT CHECK-IN

Have partners share one thing that makes a text realistic fiction. Then have children reflect using the Check-In routine.

LEARNING GOALS

We can choose a topic to write about.

OBJECTIVES

Use a combination of drawing, dictating, and writing to narrate a single event or several loosely linked events, tell about the events in the order in which they occurred, and provide a reaction to what happened.

Choose a topic for writing.

ELA ACADEMIC LANGUAGE

• *plan, topic*

• Cognate: *plan*

Plan: Choose Your Topic

15 mins

Brainstorm

Talk About It Before children begin writing, have them practice telling about a made-up character in a story. Have partners tell each other about a favorite story character who does things that could happen in real life. Model telling some of the details that happen in *Waiting Out the Storm*:

Think Aloud Buttercup asks her mama questions about the weather and the animals. Her mother answers her questions. She helps her feel safe.

As partners tell each other about a realistic story character they know about, circulate and listen in.

Review the Student Model Tell children that they will plan and write a realistic fiction story. Explain that the first step in writing realistic fiction is choosing a topic. *Before Pedro wrote his story, his class brainstormed and drew pictures to generate ideas. This helped Pedro think of the idea for his story.* Write examples of ideas and characters Pedro might have listed:

• A dad takes his son to baseball practice.

• A little girl wants to go camping, but it is raining.

• A teacher takes a trip to the library with her class.

Point out that after brainstorming, Pedro chose the idea he liked best. *Pedro decided to write a story about a little girl who wants to go camping.*

Now lead a class discussion about characters and events that could be real to help children generate ideas for writing.

Choose Your Topic

Have children turn to page 100 in the **Reading/Writing Companion**. Invite children to discuss their topic ideas. Read aloud the text in the Quick Tip box to help guide children's discussions. Then instruct children to choose their favorite story idea and draw it in the space provided.

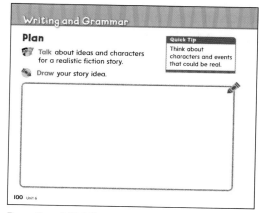

Reading/Writing Companion, p. 100

Write Your Ideas

Explain that Pedro continued planning his realistic fiction story by writing his character's name and writing about one event that happens in the story. Share Pedro's plan with children:

- **My character's name is Min.**
- **Min puts blankets over a table. She makes a pretend tent.**

Read the prompts on page 101 of the **Reading/Writing Companion** aloud. Guide children to write their character's name. Then ask: *What is one thing that this character does?* Have children write about one event that happens to this character. Explain that they will include this event in their story.

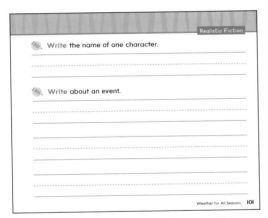

Reading/Writing Companion, p. 101

English Language Learners

To help children begin work on their stories, use these scaffolds with **Choose Your Topic**.

Beginning

Point to the Quick Tip box and read it aloud again. *Think about a fun character who could be real and you want to write about.* A fun character who could be real is _____.

Intermediate

Help children talk about fun, realistic events and characters. A fun character who could be real is _____. A fun event that could be real is _____.

Advanced/Advanced High

Help partners add ideas and characters to their realistic fiction story idea. Another fun, realistic idea could be to add _____.

FORMATIVE ASSESSMENT

⊙ STUDENT CHECK-IN

Have partners share the topic for their writing. Then have children reflect using the Check-In routine.

OBJECTIVES

Use a combination of drawing, dictating, and writing to narrate a single event or several loosely linked events, tell about the events in the order in which they occurred, and provide a reaction to what happened.

ELA ACADEMIC LANGUAGE

· *draft, plot, time order, event, organization*

· Cognate: *organización*

 TEACH IN SMALL GROUP

See pages T486-T487 for additional minilessons that support writing Realistic Fiction that includes:

· focusing on a topic

· including facts

· adding details

For differentiated support, see Writing Skills minilessons on pages T494-T499. These can be used throughout the year.

Draft

10 mins

Analyze the Expert Model

Genre Review the characteristics of realistic fiction with children. Ask a volunteer to tell one way that he or she knows that *Waiting Out the Storm* is a realistic fiction story.

 Writer's Craft: Organization Explain that writers organize their ideas so that the story makes sense to the readers. Read this text from *Waiting Out the Storm* aloud:

Mama?

Yes, buttercup?

What's that I hear?

That's just the rumble of thunder, my dear.

Explain that there are two people speaking here, having a conversation. Point out that this is how the author organizes the story. She tells what happens using the words that the mother and daughter say to each other.

Analyze the Student Model

 Have children turn to pages 102-103 of the **Reading/Writing Companion.** Say: *We're going to take another look at Pedro's writing.*

· **Realistic Fiction: Time Order** Pedro wrote the events of his realistic fiction story in time order, or the order in which the events happen. Invite volunteers to identify the time order on pages 102-103.

· **Writing Skill:** Pedro stays on the lines when he writes.

· **Writer's Craft: Organization** Reread the first three sentences of Pedro's writing. Point out that Pedro explains why Min is sad and cannot go camping. His writing is organized in a way that makes sense.

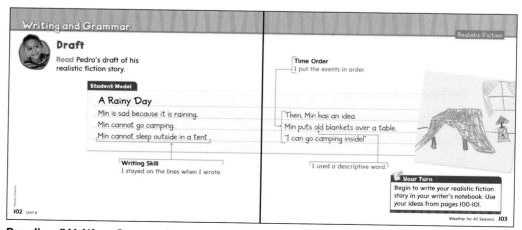

Reading/Writing Companion, pp. 102-103

Draft

Tell children that now they will start writing their own realistic fiction story. Explain that they are going to use the work they did on the Plan pages to write a first draft of their story. Model writing a short realistic fiction story using a Think Aloud such as the following:

Think Aloud The topic of my realistic fiction story will be a farmer taking care of her animals. The character and events will be made-up but could be real. I will make sure to organize my events in time order so that the story makes sense to the reader.

Write the beginning of your realistic fiction story and read it aloud.

Farmer Meg has a big farm.

Meg raises cows.

One cow, named Aria, wanders beyond the fence.

Meg wakes up one morning and can't find Aria.

Have children tell what they noticed about your writing. Ask: *How can you tell my writing is a realistic fiction story? What is the order of events? How did I organize my ideas?*

  Your Turn Have children use the work they did on pages 100-101 to write their drafts in their writer's notebook. Remind them that realistic fiction stories are written in time order so that the order of events is clear to the reader. Encourage children to write about characters that could be real and events that could really happen.

English Language Learners

Use these scaffolds with **Analyze the Student Model, Realistic Fiction: Time Order.**

Beginning

Read the student model aloud. Help children describe the order of events. At first, Min is <u>sad</u>. Then Min has an <u>idea</u>.

Intermediate

Use sentence frames to help children talk about the order of events: At first, Min is sad. <u>Then</u> Min has an idea! The word <u>then</u> shows the <u>order</u> of events.

Advanced/Advanced High

Have children describe the events in time order using *at first* and *then*. Then have them talk about the events they will use in their realistic fiction draft.

FORMATIVE ASSESSMENT

STUDENT CHECK-IN

Have partners read their drafts to each other. Then have children reflect using the Check-In routine.

LESSON 4

- **We can revise and edit our draft.**

OBJECTIVES

Use a combination of drawing, dictating, and writing to narrate a single event or several loosely linked events, tell about the events in the order in which they occurred, and provide a reaction to what happened.

With guidance and support from adults, respond to questions and suggestions from peers and add details to strengthen writing as needed.

Demonstrate command of the conventions of standard English grammar and usage when writing or speaking.

ELA ACADEMIC LANGUAGE

- *revise, edit*
- Cognates: *revisar, editar*

DIGITAL TOOLS

Writer's Checklist

Peer Conferencing

15 mins

Revise and Edit

Analyze the Student Model

Direct children to pages 104-105 in the **Reading/Writing Companion** to see how Pedro revised his writing. Say: *Pedro wrote a better title for his story. He also added a detail to make his writing more interesting. When we revise our writing, we think about how to make it better.*

Then point out what Pedro did to edit his work. *In the second sentence, Pedro changed* Min *to the pronoun* She. *Then he added an end mark to the next sentence. Pedro checked that he used plural and singular nouns correctly. We edit our writing to make it clearer.*

Your Turn Explain to children that they will now revise and edit their draft.

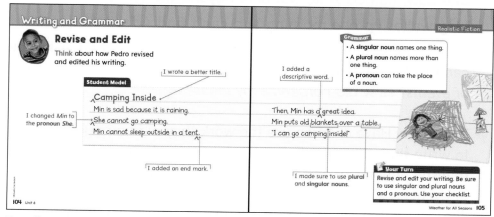

Reading/Writing Companion, pp. 104-105

Revise

Tell children that when they revise, they can add details or rewrite sentences. Ask children the following questions:

- Could your title be better?
- Did you tell what happened in the order it happened?
- Do you need to add details?

Have children use the Writer's Checklist as they revise their work.

COLLABORATE

Peer Review Review the rules for peer conferencing and/or show children the Peer Conferencing video. Then have partners exchange drafts. Have children check to see that each other's story includes the following:

- realistic events, in the order that they happened
- interesting details

Children should take notes about what they liked most, questions they have for the author, and ideas they think the author could include. Have partners share their ideas. Provide time for children to make revisions.

Edit and Proofread

Explain that now children will edit and proofread their work. To edit, they add, change, or delete words and correct errors in grammar. To proofread, they read carefully to find and correct errors in spelling and punctuation. Have children check their work for the following:

- All my sentences have end marks.
- Singular and plural nouns are used correctly.
- Subjective pronouns are used correctly.

Tell children to use the Writer's Checklist as they edit and proofread.

Peer Edit Have partners exchange drafts and review them for the issues listed above. Encourage partners to discuss errors. While pairs are peer editing, you can meet with children individually for teacher conferencing. Follow the steps in the Teacher Conferences box.

Final Draft

Your Turn After children have edited and proofread their writing and finished their peer edits, have them write their final draft in their writer's notebook. Tell children to write neatly so that others can read their writing, or guide them to explore a variety of digital tools they can use to produce and publish their writing.

English Language Learners

To help children revise their stories, use these scaffolds with **Revise.**

Beginning

Help children write a better title. Ask: *Does your title tell the reader what they are going to read about?* Help children add a detail to their title to make it better. *What is your story about? What is a detail in the story you can add to the title?*

Intermediate

Help children add a detail about their character or an event in their story. Provide sentence frames: [Name of character/Event] is _____. I can add that _____.

Advanced/Advanced High

Encourage children to add a detail to one of the events in their story or to their character. Have partners help to suggest details to add to each other's stories.

TEACHER CONFERENCES

Step 1
Talk about the strengths of the writing.

The character you wrote about seems real even though she is made up.

Step 2
Focus on the writer's craft.

You organized your ideas in a way that makes sense.

Step 3
Make concrete suggestions for revision.

Maybe you could give your story a catchier title to get readers interested.

TEACH IN SMALL GROUP

You may wish to work with a small group of children who need support with the following:

- features of realistic fiction
- telling the events in order
- using singular and plural nouns correctly
- using pronouns correctly

FORMATIVE ASSESSMENT

STUDENT CHECK-IN

Have partners share one way they revised or edited their draft. Then have children reflect using the Check-In routine.

WRITING · REALISTIC FICTION

LEARNING GOALS

- **We can present and evaluate our realistic fiction.**

OBJECTIVES

Use a combination of drawing, dictating, and writing to narrate a single event or several loosely linked events, tell about the events in the order in which they occurred, and provide a reaction to what happened.

Produce and expand complete sentences in shared language activities.

Demonstrate command of the conventions of standard English grammar and usage when writing or speaking.

Speak audibly and express thoughts, feelings, and ideas clearly.

Confirm understanding of a text read aloud or information presented orally or through other media by asking and answering questions about key details and requesting clarification if something is not understood.

ELA ACADEMIC LANGUAGE

- *share*

DIGITAL TOOLS

How to Give Presentations

---

10 mins

Publish, Present, and Evaluate

Publish

Have children review their final drafts and make any last-minute changes. Guide them to use digital tools to prepare their work for presentation.

Prepare to Share Have children turn to page 106 in the **Reading/Writing Companion**. Have them work in pairs to practice their presentation. Remind them to take turns speaking and listening.

Speaking and Listening Review the Speaking and Listening skills.

- Remind children to use more formal language for their presentations. As needed, model speaking clearly at an appropriate pace, using formal language.

- Tell children to listen carefully to what each speaker says.

- Encourage listeners to ask questions and guide speakers to provide details when answering.

Allow children five minutes to rehearse their presentation. Remind them to use the appropriate voice and tone as they rehearse.

Present

Before children begin presenting, you may wish to show the How to Give Presentations video. Remind children that not only will they take on the role of presenter, but they will also be a part of the audience for their classmates' presentations. Remind children to be respectful of their classmates. Allow time after the presentations for children to ask questions and give comments.

Share and Evaluate

Practice presenting your work with a partner. Take turns.

Present your work. Then use this checklist.

Review Your Work	Yes	No
Writing		
I wrote a realistic fiction story.	☐	☐
I used descriptive words. They made my story more interesting.	☐	☐
I stayed on the lines when I wrote.	☐	☐
Speaking and Listening		
I listened carefully.	☐	☐
I answered questions. I used details.	☐	☐

Realistic Fiction

Talk with a partner about your writing.

Write about your work.

What did you do well in your writing?

_____
_____
_____
_____

What do you need to work on?

_____
_____
_____

106 Unit 6

Weather for All Seasons 107

Reading/Writing Companion, pp. 106–107

Evaluate

Have children discuss and evaluate their presentations. Then have them record their self-evaluations on page 107 of the **Reading/Writing Companion.**

Use the Writing Rubric for Realistic Fiction online to evaluate children's writing.

Ask children to select one finished piece of writing, as well as a revision to include in their writing folder. Invite them to look at their previous writing and discuss with a partner how it has improved.

Publish children's work by hanging it on a bulletin board or placing it in the classroom library for other children to read.

English Language Learners

Use the following scaffolds to help children practice expressing their ideas during **Publish/Prepare to Share.**

Beginning

Help children prepare to read their realistic fiction stories aloud. First, read the text aloud to model appropriate pronunciation. Then, allow children to practice reading the text aloud, clarifying appropriate pronunciation, rate, and rhythm as needed.

Intermediate

Have children practice presenting in pairs. Have them each read aloud their realistic fictional stories to their partner, monitoring their reading and modeling appropriate pronunciation, rate, and rhythm as needed. Encourage repeat readings to promote automaticity.

Advanced/Advanced High

Have children practice sharing their realistic fiction stories with a partner. Have them take turns reading aloud their own text, then have them swap. Encourage repeat readings to promote automaticity. Provide guidance on pronunciation, rate, and rhythm as needed.

FORMATIVE ASSESSMENT

◉ STUDENT CHECK-IN

Have partners share one part of their presentation they did well. Then have children reflect using the Check-In routine.

Writing Minilessons

FOCUS ON AN IDEA

OBJECTIVES

Use a combination of drawing, dictating, and writing to narrate a single event or several loosely linked events, tell about the events in the order in which they occurred, and provide a reaction to what happened.

I Do Display the **Literature Big Book** *Waiting Out the Storm*. Explain that this is realistic fiction. The author wrote a story about characters and events that could happen in real life. Read aloud pages 5–7. Then point out what Buttercup and Mama talk about: how the sound of the wind tells that a storm is coming. Begin a discussion about the author's idea for the story. Make sure children understand that the author focused on one idea.

We Do Read pages 7–8. Ask partners to talk about how Mama tells about what the raindrops do during a storm. Repeat the routine with pages 11–13, having partners discuss the details about thunder.

With children, brainstorm ideas they could write a realistic fiction story about. Write and display their ideas. Have them choose the idea they like best. Then ask them to talk about two events for the idea they chose. Provide sentence frames as needed: *My topic is _____.*

You Do Have children write sentences about their topic independently. Encourage them to write about two events. Provide guidance to make sure their sentences focus on their idea. Have volunteers share their writing.

REALISTIC CHARACTERS, SETTING, AND EVENTS

OBJECTIVES

Use a combination of drawing, dictating, and writing to narrate a single event or several loosely linked events, tell about the events in the order in which they occurred, and provide a reaction to what happened.

I Do Begin a discussion of realistic characters, setting, and events. Explain that realistic fiction has characters, settings, and events that could be real. Display pages 4–5 of the **Literature Big Book** *Waiting Out the Storm*. Say: *The illustrations of grass, trees, and flowers show a setting that is like a real place.* Then point to the two characters in the illustration and explain that the characters look and act realistic.

We Do Display and read pages 10–11. Have partners discuss what makes the characters, setting, and the event on these pages realistic. Repeat the routine for pages 22–23.

Ask children to think of something that could happen in real life, such as a swimming lesson or going to the library. Guide partners to turn the idea into an idea for a story by talking about the realistic characters, settings, and events that would be in the story. Provide sentence frames as necessary.

You Do Have children write sentences about their story independently. Provide guidance as necessary to make sure the characters, setting, and events are realistic. Invite volunteers to share their writing.

EVENTS TOLD IN TIME ORDER

OBJECTIVES

Use a combination of drawing, dictating, and writing to narrate a single event or several loosely linked events, tell about the events in the order in which they occurred, and provide a reaction to what happened.

I Do Begin a discussion about the events told in time order in the **Literature Big Book** *Waiting Out the Storm*. Explain that the author of this book tells the events in the order they happened. This helps readers understand what is happening. Tell children that when we tell story events in time order, we can use the words *first, next,* and *last*. Read pages 5–7 and then pages 8–9. Have children think about the order of events for these pages. Then restate the events using time order words, such as: *First, Buttercup and her mom hear the wind blowing. Next, the raindrops come.*

We Do Display pages 22–23 and read page 22 aloud. Point out that this is at the end of the story. Prompt partners to talk about what happens last.

Give children a story idea, such as a celebration. Have children think of what might happen at a celebration. Write and display the words *first, next,* and *last,* and ask partners to use them to tell the events of the celebration in order.

You Do Have children independently write their story-event sentences in order. Encourage them to use time order words. Provide guidance as necessary, and have volunteers share their writing.

DESCRIPTIVE DETAILS

OBJECTIVES

Use a combination of drawing, dictating, and writing to narrate a single event or several loosely linked events, tell about the events in the order in which they occurred, and provide a reaction to what happened.

I Do Begin a discussion about descriptive details in the **Literature Big Book** *Waiting Out the Storm*. Explain that Mama's answers to Buttercup's questions contain descriptive details about the storm. They help readers see, hear, touch, smell, or taste what is happening. Display page 8. Before reading, explain that "They" refers to the "raindrops" Mama mentions on the previous page. After reading, point to and identify the descriptive details "burst from a cloud" and "skipping and leaping." Ask: *What other details does Mama give to describe raindrops?*

We Do Read aloud page 18. Have partners find the descriptive details Mama gives about chipmunks.

Ask children to think of a place or event they might describe, such as the street they live on. Ask questions to guide them to describe it, such as *What can you see there?* and *What can you hear?* Provide sentence frames as necessary: *My street has _____. On my street, I can hear _____.*

You Do Have children write their sentences with descriptive details independently. Provide guidance as necessary, and have volunteers share their writing.

Developmental Writing
Plan Writing Instruction

UNITS 1-10

AUTHOR INSIGHT

"Children's early writing efforts reveal what they're noticing and holding onto in their efforts to express their own words and sentences on paper. Parents and teachers may fear that young children will perseverate in these early writing "errors"— the misformed letters, ill-spelled words, and sloppy formatting— but research shows (e.g., Campbell, 2019) that growth in early writing is substantial, highly variable, and rapid. As experience with reading increases and instruction in printing and spelling are provided, those short-lived errors fade away without a trace."

—Dr. Timothy Shanahan

Courtesy of Timothy Shanahan

Writing in Kindergarten

Overview

Children in Kindergarten begin the year drawing and learning how to write letters. By the end of the year, they will have learned how to write cohesive sentences. They respond to the texts they are reading and they learn to write informative, narrative, and opinion texts as well. In *Wonders,* children write every day.

As they progress, children learn basic Writing Skills, such as writing from left-to-right and leaving spaces between words. They are also taught to apply Grammar skills and Writing Traits to help them shape and organize their ideas into recognizable pieces of writing. They learn how to write complete sentences and begin to think about how their sentences can come together to tell a story.

In this section you will see ten Student Models of writing that show a progression of writing abilities across the year. Use the models to informally assess how children are progressing with their writing development and guide their growth. Meet with children regularly to discuss their growth and writing goals. Use this routine when you meet with children.

Supporting Emergent Writers

1. Identify Strengths

Choose a piece of student writing. Think about the writing skills and traits previously-taught.

- What does the writer know about writing?
- What does he or she do well?

Share your observations with the child.

2. Choose an Area for Improvement

Think about what instruction the child would benefit from. Identify a Next Step writing skill to focus on.

3. Next Steps

Share the Next Step goal with the child. You may meet individually with a child or choose to have a small group minilesson with children that have the same instructional needs. You can choose from the following minilessons to focus on:

- Writing Skill Lesson Bank
- Writing Trait Lesson Bank

In addition, see the Instructional Routines Handbook for more information on supporting children in writing about texts, the Writing Process, and Grammar skills.

Choose an Area for Improvement Refer to the **Language Transfers Handbook** to determine what transfer errors in speaking and writing in standard English children might need help with.

Writing Model 1

Name_____

Dictation: My dog

Student Model 1   Copyright © McGraw Hill. Permission is granted to reproduce for classroom use.

STRENGTHS

• Dictation is connected to the picture

NEXT STEPS

• Add details to the picture
• Add words to the image

Writing Model 2

Name_____

Dictation: I got a dog.

Student Model 2   Copyright © McGraw Hill. Permission is granted to reproduce for classroom use.

STRENGTHS

• Included letters
• Picture is connected to dictation

NEXT STEPS

• Add a label to the picture
• Add details to the writing

DEVELOPMENTAL WRITING: What to Look For

HANDWRITING

As you review children's writing, look for signs that they need some support with their fine motor development. Notice when children are:

• Writing too lightly.
• Using write-on lines incorrectly.
• Gripping the pencil incorrectly.

See the Handwriting lessons for additional support.

Developmental Writing

Writing Model 3

Name_____

P G

I G T A B N D G.

Dictation: I got a brown dog.

Student Model 3

Copyright © McGraw Hill. Permission is granted to reproduce for classroom use.

STRENGTHS

• Included a label in picture
• Included a detail in writing

NEXT STEPS

• Add spaces between words
• Stretch sounds to write words

Writing Model 4

Name_____

i hvA bon

Pupe

Dictation: I have a brown puppy.

Student Model 4

Copyright © McGraw Hill. Permission is granted to reproduce for classroom use.

STRENGTHS

• Put spaces between words
• Included upper and lowercase letters

NEXT STEPS

• Include capital letters and end punctuation
• Use Word Bank to spell words

DEVELOPMENTAL WRITING: What to Look For

SPELLING

Review children's spelling and notice if children need additional support with:

• Spelling Word Bank words correctly.
• Stretching sounds to spell words.

See the weekly Spell Words lessons and the Writing Skill Lesson Bank to help children with spelling. Throughout kindergarten, it is common for children to misspell irregular and multisyllabic words. Provide additional support and guidance as necessary.

Writing Model 5

Name_____

I have a bran pupeGus.

Dictation: I have a brown puppy Gus.

Student Model 5   Copyright © McGraw Hill. Permission is granted to reproduce for classroom use.

STRENGTHS
- Included a capital letter and end punctuation
- Used Word Bank to spell words

NEXT STEPS
- Print words neatly and use correct letter formation
- Use proper spacing between letters and words

Writing Model 6

Name_____

I have a pupe and he is bron and he is Gus.

Student Model 6   Copyright © McGraw Hill. Permission is granted to reproduce for classroom use.

STRENGTHS
- Printed words neatly with correct letter formation
- Used proper spacing

NEXT STEPS
- Write a complete sentence
- Add details to the story

DEVELOPMENTAL WRITING: What to Look For

SENTENCES

Review children's writing in terms of sentence composition. Notice if they:

- Write complete sentences.
- Begin each sentence with a capital letter.
- Use correct end punctuation.
- Use proper subject-verb agreement.

For additional support with writing sentences, see the Grammar lessons and the Writing Skill Lesson Bank.

Developmental Writing

Writing Model 7

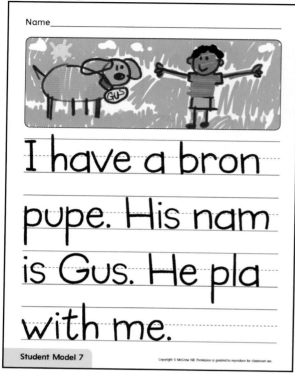

Name_____

I have a bron pupe. His nam is Gus. He pla with me.

Student Model 7   Copyright © McGraw Hill. Permission is granted to reproduce for classroom use.

STRENGTHS

- Wrote complete sentences
- Added details to the story

NEXT STEPS

- Use correct subject-verb agreement
- Add ideas to the story

Writing Model 8

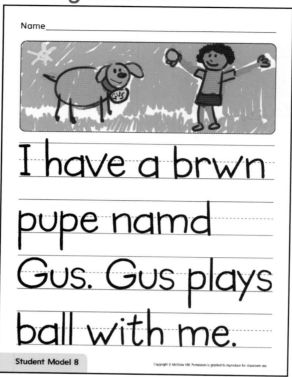

Name_____

I have a brwn pupe namd Gus. Gus plays ball with me.

Student Model 8   Copyright © McGraw Hill. Permission is granted to reproduce for classroom use.

STRENGTHS

- Used correct subject-verb agreement
- Added ideas to the story

NEXT STEPS

- Add a title
- Vary beginning of sentences

DEVELOPMENTAL WRITING: What to Look For

As children master writing sentences and begin to write different types of sentences, notice whether they need support with:

- When to write a telling sentence and when to write an asking sentence.
- Capitalization of the pronoun *I*.
- Capitalization of proper nouns.
- Use of correct sentence capitalization and end punctuation.

For additional support, see the Writing and Conventions lessons, the Writing Skill Lesson Bank, and the Writing Trait Lesson Bank.

Writing Model 9

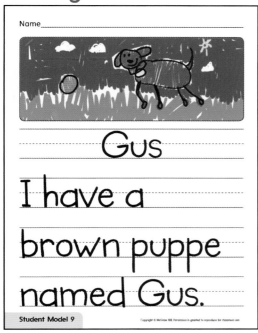

Name_____

Gus

I have a
brown puppe
named Gus.

Student Model 9   Copyright © McGraw Hill. Permission is granted to reproduce for classroom use.

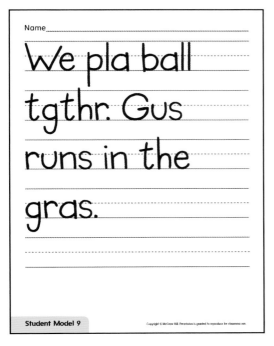

Name_____

We pla ball
tgthr. Gus
runs in the
gras.

Student Model 9   Copyright © McGraw Hill. Permission is granted to reproduce for classroom use.

Writing Model 10

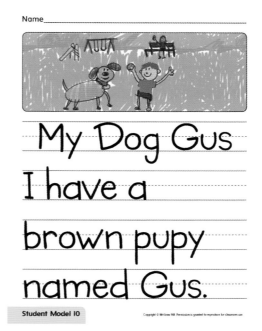

Name_____

My Dog Gus

I have a
brown pupy
named Gus.

Student Model 10   Copyright © McGraw Hill. Permission is granted to reproduce for classroom use.

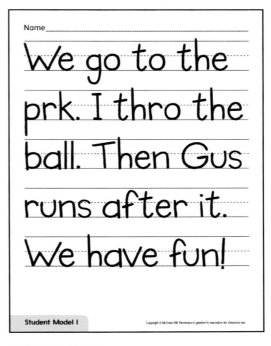

Name_____

We go to the
prk. I thro the
ball. Then Gus
runs after it.
We have fun!

Student Model I   Copyright © McGraw Hill. Permission is granted to reproduce for classroom use.

STRENGTHS
- Added a title
- Varied the beginning of sentences

NEXT STEPS
- Put events in order
- Use connecting words

STRENGTHS
- Put events in order
- Added a connecting word

Writing Skills

LEFT-TO-RIGHT PROGRESSION

OBJECTIVES

Follow words from left to right, top to bottom, and page by page.

Write from left-to-right.

I Do Display the **Literature Big Book** *What About Bear?* to discuss the skill of left-to-right progression. Read aloud page 12 as you track the words with your finger. Explain that the author started writing the sentence on the left and moved to the right as she wrote each word. Review left and right with children as necessary.

We Do Show page 16, and have a child point to where the author started writing. Have a volunteer track words from left to right with their finger as you read the text on the page aloud. Repeat the routine with page 24.

Guide children to think of games they like to play. Have children share some of their favorite games. Provide sentence frames as necessary, such as: *I like to play _____.*

You Do Have children write a sentence about their favorite games independently. Remind them to start writing on the left side of their papers and move to the right. Provide guidance as necessary. Have children share their writing.

WORDS ARE MADE UP OF LETTERS

OBJECTIVES

Recognize that spoken words are represented in written language by specific sequences of letters.

I Do Display the **Literature Big Book** *Senses at the Seashore.* Turn to page 6, and begin a discussion about distinguishing letters from words by saying: *I know that each word is made up of letters.* Point to the word *See,* and say: *I see three letters in the word* See. Explain that the author wrote the three letters in this word: *S, e, e.* She also wrote three letters in the word *the.* Then ask: *How many letters are in the word that comes after* the? Restate the answer that there are four letters in the word *blue.*

We Do Point to page 7. Point to the word *Hear,* and ask a child how many letters are in the word. (four) Repeat the routine for the words *the, waves,* and *crash.* (three, five, five) Explain to children that when they write a word in a sentence, they should write all of the letters that make up the word.

Give children a place as a topic, such as a park or a place to eat. Guide them to think about what they see, hear, smell, or taste at that place. Provide sentence frames as necessary, such as *See the _____. Smell the _____.*

You Do Have children write independently in response to the prompt. Provide guidance as needed. Remind children to think about the letters that make up each word they write. Encourage them to share their writing.

STRETCH SOUNDS TO WRITE WORDS

OBJECTIVES

Write a letter or letters for most consonant and short-vowel sounds (phonemes).

Write words by stretching the sounds in words.

I Do Display the **Literature Big Book** *The Handiest Things in the World* or another book the class is reading. Turn to page 4, and point to the word *hand*. Model stretching the sounds in the word by saying: *To read or write this word, I can stretch the sounds at the beginning, in the middle, and at the end: /hhhaaannnddd/.* Explain that stretching the sounds in a word helps writers write the letters for the sounds they hear. Ask children to practice reading and stretching the sounds in *hand.*

We Do Turn to page 10, and point to the word *wet.* Have partners stretch the sounds as they say and write the word. wwweeet Repeat the routine with the words *flap* on page 22 and *push* on page 23.

Have children brainstorm ways to help out. Record them on the board. Guide partners to talk about how they help others. Provide guidance and sentence frames as needed.

You Do Have children independently write their sentence about helping. Remind children to sound out words they wish to write by stretching the sounds in the words. Have children share their writing.

USE THE WORD BANK

OBJECTIVES

Read common high-frequency words by sight.

Use the Word Bank to spell and write words.

I Do Display the **Literature Big Book** *Shapes All Around.* Turn to page 5, and read until you reach the word *see.* Model finding *see* in the Word Bank. Tell children: *We can use the Word Bank to help us spell and write words.* Read and point to the word *the* in the Word Bank. Say each letter in the word, and have children repeat. Then model writing the word.

We Do Read page 6 aloud. Have partners take turns pointing to words that are in the Word Bank. (the, we, can) Ask a volunteer to point to the Word Bank as you spell each word. Have children orally repeat each spelling and then write each word by copying it from the Word Bank.

Then guide children to discuss shapes they can see in your classroom. Provide guidance and sentence frames as needed, such as *I _____ see a square.* or *I can _____ a circle.*

You Do Have children write their sentences independently. Provide guidance as necessary, noting if children use the Word Bank to help them write words. Then invite children to share their writing.

Writing Skills

SPACES BETWEEN WORDS

OBJECTIVES

Demonstrate understanding of the organization and basic features of print.

Understand that words are separated by spaces in print.

I Do Use the **Literature Big Book** *I Love Bugs* to reinforce putting spaces between words. Turn to page 9, and point to each word as you read the sentence aloud. Tell children that when the author wrote, she left spaces between words. Point to each space between the words and then count the words. Tell children there are eleven words in the sentence.

We Do Point to the sentence on page 10. Have a child point to the spaces between words in the first three lines of text. Then have partners browse other books looking at the spaces between words. Have them count the words in the sentences they find.

Tell children to write a sentence telling about the kind of dog or bird they love: *I love* _____. Encourage them to use descriptive words, just like the author of *I Love Bugs*. Tell children they can place their pencil after each word to help them leave spaces.

You Do Have children write their sentence independently. Remind them to leave spaces between words as they write their sentence. Provide guidance as necessary, and have children share their writing.

SENTENCES ARE MADE UP OF WORDS

OBJECTIVES

Demonstrate understanding of the organization and basic features of print.

Count the number of words in sentences.

I Do Display page 26 of the **Literature Big Book** *How Do Dinosaurs Go to School?* Point to each word as you read the first sentence aloud. Explain that a sentence is made up of a group of words that means something. Sentences can have different numbers of words. Count the number of words in the first sentence. Make sure children understand there are six words in the sentence. Repeat the routine for the second sentence.

We Do Turn to page 30, and say each word in the sentence. Then have children count the words. (ten) Explain that all of the words that make up the sentence give the sentence its meaning.

Have partners talk about what the dinosaurs in the story do at school. Then have children think about what they do at school. Tell children to use words to write a sentence about one thing they do at school. Provide the sentence frame: *At school I* _____.

You Do Have children write their sentence independently. Provide guidance as necessary. Remind them to write all of the words that make up their sentence. Encourage children to share their writing.

SENTENCE CAPITALIZATION

OBJECTIVES

Demonstrate command of the conventions of standard English capitalization, punctuation, and spelling when writing.

Capitalize the first word in a sentence and the pronoun *I*.

I Do Use the **Literature Big Book** paired selection "Sounds Are Everywhere" to discuss sentence capitalization. Display page 34, and read the first sentence aloud. Have a child point to the first word. Then point to the first letter of *Where*. Explain that it is a capital letter. Reinforce that writers begin the first word of a sentence with a capital letter. This tells the reader that a new sentence is beginning.

We Do Continue with the next sentence on page 34, and read it aloud. Have a child point to the capital letter at the beginning of the sentence. Have another child identify the capital letter and the word. Repeat the routine with the remaining sentences on pages 35–36.

Have partners talk about sounds they can make, such as clapping or whistling. Provide the following sentence frame: *One sound I can make is* _____. Point out that the word *I* is capitalized even when it does not begin a sentence.

You Do Have children write their sentence independently. Remind them to begin their sentence with a capital letter. Ask volunteers to share their writing.

END PUNCTUATION

OBJECTIVES

Demonstrate command of the conventions of standard English capitalization, punctuation, and spelling when writing.

Recognize and name end punctuation.

I Do Display and read aloud page 5 of the **Literature Big Book** *Please Take Me for a Walk*. Ask a child to point to the last word in the sentence. Then point to the period. Say: *The author ended the sentence with an end mark. This end mark is called a period.*

We Do Read the sentence on page 9 aloud. Have a child point to the end mark and say what it is called. Repeat with page 10. Turn to page 26. Ask: *Do you see an end mark?* Explain that there is no end mark because the sentence has not ended. Read the words aloud, and then turn the page to read the rest of the sentence. Have children tell where the end mark is.

Tell partners to imagine they are a pet, such as a cat or a bird. Have them talk about what they would want and need, using the pattern: *Please* _____. *I need to* _____. Provide examples as necessary.

You Do Have children write their sentence independently. Remind children to put a period at the end of each sentence. Provide guidance as necessary, and have volunteers share their writing.

Writing Skills

RETURN SWEEP

OBJECTIVES
Follow words from left to right, top to bottom, and page by page.

I Do Display page 32 of the **Literature Big Book** paired selection "Workers and Their Tools" to discuss the skill of return sweep. Track the words with your finger as you read the page aloud. Ask: *When the author was writing, what did the author do at the end of the line?* Have partners turn and talk. Then have volunteers share their thinking. Note what children understand about a return sweep.

We Do Remind children that when we come to the end of a line, we continue writing at the beginning of the next line. Have a child point to where the first line continues on page 34. Have a different child track the print as you read the page aloud. Repeat the routine with page 35.

Have partners discuss some workers and their tools that they know about. Provide sentence frames: *A _____ is one kind of worker. One tool a _____ uses is a _____.* Provide examples and vocabulary as necessary.

You Do Have children use the prompts to write their sentences independently. Provide guidance as necessary to make sure they do return sweeps correctly. Ask volunteers to share their writing.

STAY ON THE LINES WHEN WRITING

OBJECTIVES
Demonstrate understanding of the organization and basic features of print.

Write on the lines.

I Do Display page 6 of the **Literature Big Book** *Waiting Out the Storm*. To reinforce staying on the lines when writing, write the sentence from the page on writing lines. Say: *As I wrote, I made sure to stay on the lines.* Ask a child to circle the letters that touch the top line. (*l, l, h, d, d*) Have another child circle in a different color the letters that touch the bottom line. (*y, p*) You can use the technique with any book the class is reading.

We Do Display page 15, and point to the second sentence: "It starts and it stops." Tell children to make sure to stay on the lines as they write the sentence on lined paper. Then have them identify the letters that touch the top line (*l, d*) and the letter that touches the bottom line. (*p*)

Talk about sounds we hear during a storm. Tell children they will write a sentence that tells what they hear during a storm. Provide a sentence frame: *I hear _____ in a storm.*

You Do Have children write their sentence independently. Remind them to stay on the lines when they write their sentence. Provide guidance as necessary. Then encourage volunteers to share their writing.

LEFT-TO-RIGHT AND TOP-TO-BOTTOM PROGRESSION

OBJECTIVES

Follow words from left to right, top to bottom, and page by page.

I Do Display page 8 in the **Literature Big Book** *Bringing Down the Moon*. Have children point with their left hand to the beginning of the text. Have them point with their right hand to where the first line of text ends. Point to each word as you read the first line of text aloud. Ask: *Did the author start writing on the top of the page or the bottom? Did the author move left or right as he wrote?* Make sure children understand that the author wrote left-to-right and top-to-bottom.

We Do Read aloud page 12, and have children track the print. Tell children that we move left to right and top to bottom to read. Explain that authors do the same when they write. Repeat the routine on pages 14 and 15.

Have partners discuss all the things in the sky that we can see. Guide them to think about what those objects look like from the ground. Provide the sentence frames: *I can see _____ in the sky. It looks like _____.*

You Do Have children write their sentences independently. Remind children to begin on the top left side of their paper and write each word moving to the right. Provide guidance as necessary. Then have volunteers share their writing.

UNITS 5-6

Student Outcomes

READING

Reading Informational Text
- Identify the main topic and details in a text
- Retell key details of a text
- Actively engage in group reading activities.

COMMUNICATION

Writing

Opinion Writing
- Using a combination of drawing, dictating, and/or writing, express opinions about a topic or text with at least one supporting reason.

Writing
- Use a combination of drawing, dictating and writing to supply factual information about a topic.

Speaking and Listening
- Participate in collaborative conversations about kindergarten topics and texts
- Describe familiar people, places, things, and events.

Researching
- Recall information to answer a question

Creating and Collaborating
- Add drawings and visual displays to descriptions.

VOCABULARY

Academic Vocabulary
- Acquire and use grade-appropriate academic vocabulary

ELL Scaffolded supports for English Language Learners are embedded throughout the lessons, enabling children to communicate information, ideas, and concepts in English Language Arts and for social and instructional purposes within the school setting.

Planner

	LESSON 1	**LESSON 2**	**LESSON 3**
60+ mins Reading/Writing **Suggested Daily Time**	**Reading/Writing**		
LESSON GOALS • I can listen actively to understand a social studies text. **SMALL GROUP OPTIONS** The designated lessons can be taught in small groups. To determine how to differentiate instruction for small groups, use Formative Assessment and Data Dashboard.	⟩ **Reading Digitally, T502–T503** Read "Changes with the Wind" **TIME KiDS** ⟩ **Connect to Content: Social Studies, T504–T505** Read "A Farm Year" **Choose Your Own Book, T508**	**Connect to Content: Social Studies, T506–T507** Make a Seasons Poster **Wrap Up the Unit, T509** Connect to the Big Idea	**Think About Your Learning, T510** **Wrap Up Units 5 and 6, T511** **Summative Assessment and Next Steps, T512–T514**

Extend, Connect, and Assess

Extend

Reading Digitally
"Changes with the Wind"
Genre: Online Article

Choose Your Own Book
Reading/Writing Companion, p. 112

Connect

Social Studies

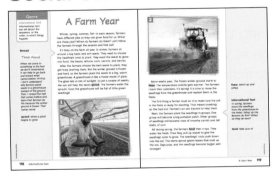

Genre Read-Aloud, pp. 118–121

"A Farm Year"

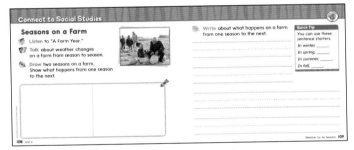

Reading/Writing Companion, pp. 108–109

Respond to the Text

Assess

Unit Assessments

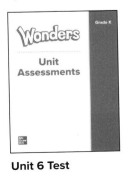

Unit 6 Test

Unit 6 Test Online

Fluency

EVALUATE STUDENT PROGRESS

Use the *Wonders* online assessment reports to evaluate children's progress and help you make decisions about small-group instruction and assignments.

Self-Assess Have children complete Reflect on Your Learning and note any areas where they need improvement.

OBJECTIVES

With prompting and support, identify the main topic and retell key details of a text.

With guidance and support from adults, recall information from experiences or gather information from provided sources to answer a question.

With guidance and support from adults, explore a variety of digital tools to produce and publish writing, including in collaboration with peers.

Read and interact with digital texts online.

ELA ACADEMIC LANGUAGE

• *hyperlinks, Internet*
• Cognate: *Internet*

▶ DIFFERENTIATED READING

◐ ● **Approaching Level** and **ELL** Read the text aloud to children. Have partners work together to complete the graphic organizer.

● ● **On Level** and **Beyond Level** Have partners read the text and access the interactive features independently, as they are able. Complete the Reread activities during Small Group.

TIME for KiDS

Changes with the Wind

Before Reading

Preview Explain to children that the Internet connects computers all around the world. Go to the online article "Changes with the Wind" and tell children that the article is digital—it is on a website. Point to the scroll bar and arrows. Model how to scroll through the article. Point out interactive features, such as the **hyperlinks**. Then point out the genre and the text features, such as headings and captions. Tell children that you will read the article together first and then you will show them how to use the interactive features.

Close Reading Online

Read

Take Notes Read the article aloud, including the headings and the captions. Model taking notes, using the online **Word Web Graphic Organizer**. Identify the main topic of the article. In the center of the web, write the following and read it aloud: *Winds in Different Seasons*. Then reread each section and have children retell a detail about a wind effect in each season to add to the web. Make sure children understand domain-specific terms, such as *blizzard, hurricane,* and *electricity*.

Access Interactive Features Model how to access the interactive elements by clicking on each feature. Discuss what each feature adds to the text.

Retell Review the main topic and details with children. Model using the information to begin retelling "Changes with the Wind." Then encourage children to continue retelling the rest of the selection.

Reread

Craft and Structure Tell children you will reread parts of the article to help them answer these questions:

• *How does the author organize the information?* (by season)

• *What is the last section in the article about?* (how people use wind)

Integrate

Make Connections

Text Connections Have children compare what they learned about different types of weather in "Changes with the Wind" with what they learned about weather in other texts they read in this unit.

Research Online

Choose a Topic Tell children that online texts may include hyperlinks. Explain that hyperlinks help you go from the web page you are on to another screen or video that tells more about the topic. Model how to use a hyperlink by clicking on the one labeled "windmills." Discuss the information on the screen the hyperlink takes you to.

Cyber Safety Explain to children that it is important to be careful when they are online. Make sure they understand the following rules:

- Go only to websites that adults have told you are okay to visit.
- Never give out personal information when you are online. Personal information includes your name, photograph, home address, email address, telephone number, school name, school address, names of family members, and passwords.

Inspire Action

Weather in Different Seasons Remind children that we can expect different weather during different seasons. Point to photographs of different seasons in the online article. Explain that weather changes day by day, but the seasons usually follow a pattern, depending on where you live. Help children identify information in this article to answer the following questions:

- *What kind of wind might blow in the winter?*
- *What kind of storm might the winds bring in autumn?*

ELL ENGLISH LANGUAGE LEARNERS

Reread/Craft and Structure
Point out the section headings. Reread the headings and have children identify the name of the season in each. (winter, spring, summer, autumn) *How does the author organize the information?* The author tells about the <u>wind</u> in each <u>season</u>.

FORMATIVE ASSESSMENT

❯ STUDENT CHECK-IN

Have partners share what they learned about wind from the online article. Have children reflect using the Check-In routine.

OBJECTIVES

Actively engage in group reading activities with purpose and understanding.

Use words and phrases acquired through conversations, reading and being read to, and responding to texts.

With prompting and support, ask and answer questions about unknown words in a text.

Participate in collaborative conversations with diverse partners about *kindergarten topics and texts* with peers and adults in small and larger groups.

ELA ACADEMIC LANGUAGE
- *weather, affect*
- Cognate: *afectar*

DIGITAL TOOLS

Genre Read-Aloud

DIFFERENTIATED READING

● ● **Approaching Level** and **English Language Learners** After reading, have children listen to the selection to develop comprehension.

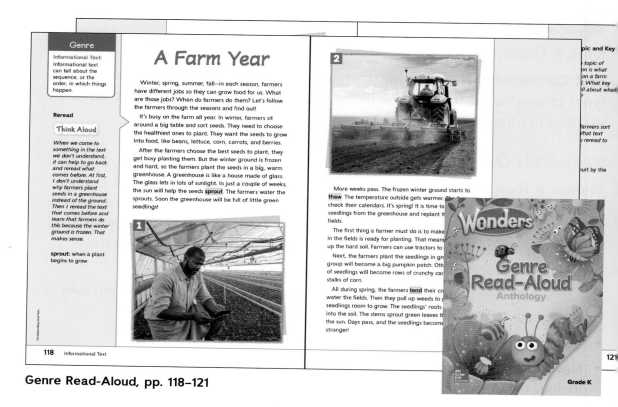

Genre Read-Aloud, pp. 118–121

Read Aloud: "A Farm Year"

Build Knowledge Talk about the Big Idea question: *How do weather and seasons affect us?* Encourage children to think about what they have learned from the selections and share what they learned about how weather and seasons affect us. Then explain you will read a selection about how weather affects farms and the jobs farmers do.

Set Purpose *Let's read to find out how the weather and seasons affect farms and farmers. Listen for the different kinds of jobs farmers do in different seasons.*

Read the Selection

Read "A Farm Year." Pause to ask children what farmers do in each of the different seasons. You may wish to use the prompts from the **Genre Read-Aloud**.

Oral Vocabulary As needed, define the words below from the selection.

- **sprout:** when a plant begins to grow
- **thaw:** warm up and soften
- **tend:** take care of
- **freeze:** hurt by the cold

Connect to Science

Seasons on a Farm

👧 Listen to "A Farm Year."

👦 Talk about weather changes on a farm from season to season.

✏️ Draw two seasons on a farm. Show what happens from one season to the next.

108 Unit 6

 Write about what happens on a farm from one season to the next.

Quick Tip

You can use these sentence starters:

In winter, _____.

In spring, _____.

In summer, _____.

In fall, _____.

Weather for All Seasons 109

Reading/Writing Companion, pp. 108–109

Respond to the Text

Tell children that they will now draw and write in response to the selection by doing the following:

Turn and Talk Have children turn and talk with a partner to discuss how weather changes on a farm from season to season. What different jobs do farmers do in each season? How does the weather affect how things grow on the farm? Encourage children to use the oral vocabulary words: *sprout, thaw, tend,* and *freeze.*

Draw Have children complete page 108 of the **Reading/Writing Companion**. Ask them to think about how the changing weather of each season changes what happens on a farm. The subject of the drawing can be from the selection or children can draw their own ideas of how seasons affect a farm. Encourage children to add details to their drawing.

Write Have children talk with a partner about how weather affects the farm from one season to the next. Ask: *How do seasons change what farmers do?* (Farmers' jobs change with each season. They choose seeds in the cold winter, plant in the spring, tend their crops in the warm summer, and pick crops in the fall before they freeze.) *How do the seasons affect when plants grow?* (Plants grow in the spring, summer, and fall when the weather is warm enough. They can't grow in the winter when the ground is frozen.) Then have children complete page 109 of the **Reading/Writing Companion**. Encourage them to use the Quick Tip box to get started.

ELL ENGLISH LANGUAGE LEARNERS

Respond to the Text, Write To help children complete page 109, say: *We are going to write about how the weather changes what happens on the farm from one season to the next season. That means we are going to tell what happens on a farm at different times of the year when the weather is warm and when the weather is cold.* Use the photographs in "A Farm Year" to review seasons and what happens on the farm during each one. Have children complete the sentence orally before writing: From one season to the next, farmers do different jobs as the weather changes.

FORMATIVE ASSESSMENT

◉ STUDENT CHECK-IN

Have partners share important ideas from the text about how the weather can affect farms. Have children reflect using the Check-In routine.

Make a Seasons Poster

Discuss Have a discussion about the weather in different seasons. Explain that the seasons are different in other parts of the country. Ask: *How does the weather affect what you do in each season?* Write the names of the four seasons on the board and list things children say they do in each season.

Explain and Model Tell children they will make a poster about how the weather affects something they do in one of the seasons. They will begin by drawing a picture of themselves doing something in the season they pick. Encourage them to add details to their drawing to show what season it

Spring

I play in puddles.

is. Sketch a quick picture of a person on a beach with a big sun overhead. Ask children what season they think it is. Label the poster: *Summer*. Then ask what additional details you could add to the drawing to show how the weather affects you in the summer.

Talk About It Have partners discuss their ideas about what season they want to draw. Then have them gather the materials they will need to do the activity.

What to Do

Read aloud the steps for doing the activity on **Reading/Writing Companion** page 110.

STEP 1 **Draw** Have children turn to page 111 and draw a picture of themselves in a particular season.

STEP 2 **Add** Have children look at their drawings and think about details they could add to make them better. Ask: *How can you improve your drawing? What details could you add to make your drawing clearer or more interesting?* Encourage children to improve their drawing by adding important details.

STEP 3 **Label** Ask: *What season does your drawing show?* Have children add a label naming the season they chose.

STEP 4 **Write** Have children talk with a partner about their drawing. Ask:

• *What does your drawing show?*

• *What details show how the season affects what you do?*

Have children write a sentence about what they do in this season on the bottom of page 111. Have children share their poster with the class.

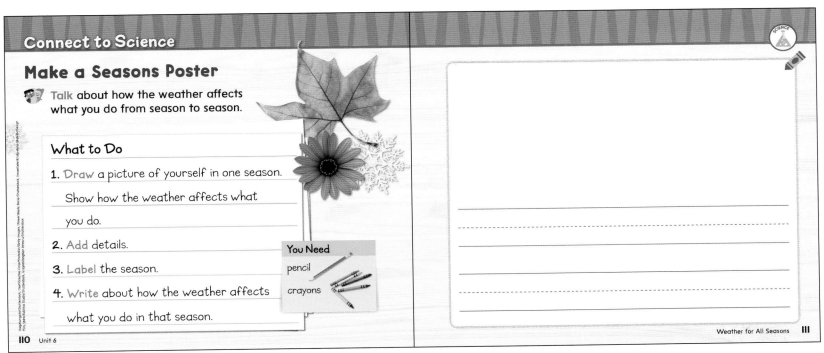

Reading/Writing Companion, pp. 110–111

 # English Language Learners

Use the following scaffolds with **What to Do, Write.**

Beginning

What does your drawing show? Have children respond: My drawing shows me in spring. *Point to details in your drawing that show the season. What details did you add?* I added rain boots. Provide a sentence frame to help children write a sentence on the bottom of page 111: I wear rain boots when it rains.

Intermediate

Encourage partners to use sentence frames to ask and answer questions, such as: What season did you draw? The season I drew is spring. What kind of weather does this season have? The weather is rainy. What do you do in this season? In spring, I wear rain boots. Provide a sentence frame to complete their caption as needed.

Advanced/Advanced High

After partners ask and answer questions to discuss their posters, challenge children to create their own sentence to describe or explain their work. Provide a model: *I drew a picture of myself in spring, wearing rain boots and carrying an umbrella. My sentence could be: I wear rain boots when it rains.* Have children say their sentence orally before writing. Provide vocabulary and spelling support as needed.

FORMATIVE ASSESSMENT

◯ STUDENT CHECK-IN

Have children share the season they illustrated on their poster. Have children reflect using the Check-In routine.

LEARNING GOALS

We can choose a book to read and share our opinions about it.

OBJECTIVES

Use a combination of drawing, dictating, and writing to compose opinion pieces in which they tell a reader the name of the book they are writing about and state an opinion or preference about the book.

Choose a book to read.

TEACHER CONFERENCES

Step 1

Help children identify a topic of interest.

What is your favorite thing to do at school? Would you like to learn more about it?

Step 2

Help children identify a book that is appropriate for them by previewing the pictures and text.

Can you read most of those words? If so, this will be a great choice.

FORMATIVE ASSESSMENT

❯ STUDENT CHECK-IN

Have children share their favorite part about the book. Have children reflect using the Check-In routine.

Extend Your Learning

Choose Your Own Book

Minutes I Read

🖉. Write the title of the book.

✎ Tell a partner why you want to read it. Then read the book.

🖉. Write your opinion of the book.

112   Unit 6

Reading/Writing Companion, p. 112

Choose Your Own Book

Explain Tell children that choosing books they like is one of the pleasures of being a reader. Set up a specific time each day for children to choose their own reading materials.

Write Once children have chosen a book to read, have them read the title and preview the book. Point out key words and ideas to help them identify why they want to read it. Then have them turn to page 112 of the **Reading/Writing Companion**. Guide them to write the title of the book they chose on the line.

Tell Have partners trade information about a book they would like to read. Be sure that each student tells the other why they'd like to read the book they chose. Then provide time for children to read for 12 minutes or longer during class. Encourage them to read a little longer the next time they read at school or at home.

Write After children have finished reading their book of choice, have them turn back to page 112. Guide them to fill in the number of minutes they read in the box. Then have them write their opinion of the book expressing what they like or dislike about it. Remind children that an opinion is a thought or feeling about a topic. Tell them their opinion about the book should include whether they like or dislike the book and at least one reason that supports their opinion.

he Big Idea: *How do weather nd seasons affect us?*

onnect to the Big Idea

xt to Text Display the **Literature Big Books** *Mama, Is It Summer Yet?* d *Rain.* Tell children that you will compare the selections, using a Two-Tab dable®. Say: *The Two-Tab Foldable® will help us record and organize our ormation.* Explain that you will compare the way the books tell about how eather and the seasons affect us.

 a class, create a Two-Tab Foldable® out of ster board. On the left flap, write *Mama, Is It mmer Yet?* On the right flap, write *Rain.*

Dinah Zike's
FOLDABLES®
Study Organizer

splay the story *Mama Is It Summer?* Remind ildren that each time the boy asked, "Mama, it summer yet?" the author taught us a little ore about the signs of summer. Help children call some of the details from the story. Say: *One sign I remember is that the eds began to sprout.* Write that on the Two-Tab Foldable®. As a class, discuss her signs of summer. Say: *Who remembers some of the other signs of summer m the story?* (Possible responses: squirrel building a nest, swallows singing, cklings, trees blossoming, etc.)

peat the process for the story *Rain.* Ask: *How did the animals five senses tell em rain was coming?* (Possible responses: the porcupine smelled it, zebra saw htning, the baboons heard the thunder, etc.) List their responses on the right side flap of the Two-Tab Foldable®.

lp children understand that the weather and the seasons can impact many ings.

Collaborative Conversations Have children turn and talk with a partner about their favorite season or type of weather.

esent Ideas and Synthesize Information When children have finished their nversations, have volunteers share their ideas with the class. As children share, lp them make connections to the Unit 6 Big Idea. Lead a class discussion and t children's ideas on the board.

ilding Knowledge Have children continue to build knowledge about the it 6 Big Idea. Display classroom and library resources and give children time explore and find more information about the Big Idea. If time permits, have lunteers share something new they learned.

LEARNING GOALS

We can make connections across texts to gain information.

OBJECTIVES

With prompting and support, identify basic similarities in and differences between two texts on the same topic.

Participate in collaborative conversations with diverse partners about *kindergarten topics and texts* with peers and adults in small and larger groups.

Follow agreed-upon rules for discussions.

FORMATIVE ASSESSMENT

⊘ **STUDENT CHECK-IN**

Have children reflect on how well they compared information across texts. Have children reflect using the Check-In routine.

LEARNING GOALS

We can reflect on our learning.

___

OBJECTIVES

Follow agreed-upon rules for discussions (e.g., listening to others and taking turns speaking about the topics and texts under discussion).

Reflect on and record skills learned in the unit.

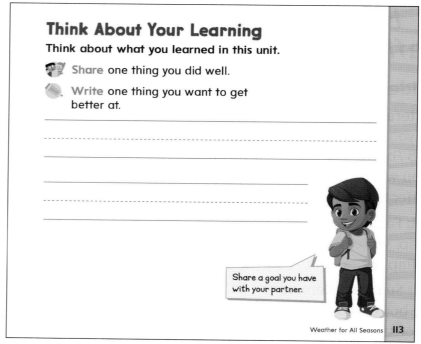

Reading/Writing Companion, p. 113

What Did You Learn?

Guide children in thinking about and discussing some of the skills, concepts, and content they learned during this unit. You may also have them recall how they rated themselves in the **Reading/Writing Companion.**

Have children turn to page 113 in the Reading/Writing Companion.

- Have children turn to a partner and share something they think they did well in this unit.

- After partners have finished sharing, have children look at the pencil icon. Tell them to fill in the set of blank lines by writing one thing they want to get better at as the year continues.

Review Activities

Review the skills and concepts taught in Units 5 and 6. Children can reflect on and discuss what they have learned, preparing them for Unit Assessment.

Comprehension

Use the Main Story Elements: Events anchor chart to guide discussion about the texts from Units 5 and 6. Have children describe some of the important events in the stories. Then discuss other texts using the Character, the Setting, and the Topic and Details anchor charts.

Oral Vocabulary

Use the Define/Example/Ask routine with the **Visual Vocabulary Cards** to review ten oral vocabulary words children learned in Units 5 and 6. As you review each word, prompt children to turn to a partner and use the word in a sentence.

Foundational Skills

Use the **Reading/Writing Companion** to review the high-frequency words and the phonics skills from Units 5 and 6.

- High-Frequency Words: *my, are, with, he, is, little, she, was*
- Phonics: /h/h; /e/e; /f/f; /r/r; /b/b; /l/l; /k/k, ck; *l*-blends

Ask for volunteers to read each page of "Mack and Ben" in the Reading/Writing Companion. As children read, stop periodically to have them identify the high-frequency words and words with the phonics elements. Have children draw and label a word that begins with a sound from these units.

Category Words

Divide the class into six groups and assign each group a category from Units 5 and 6.

- Unit 5: Size Words, Tree Parts, Food Words
- Unit 6: Seasons, Weather Words, Question Words

Have each group identify words that belong in their category. Then have each group share their list with the rest of the class. Invite volunteers to add other words that belong in the category.

OBJECTIVES

With prompting and support, identify characters and major events in a story.

With prompting and support, identify the main topic and retell key details of a text.

Use words and phrases acquired through conversations, reading and being read to, and responding to texts.

Read common high-frequency words by sight.

Demonstrate basic knowledge of one-to-one letter-sound correspondences by producing the primary sound or many of the most frequent sounds for each consonant.

Associate the short sounds with the common spellings (graphemes) for the five major vowels.

Summative Assessment

UNIT 6

After every three weeks of instruction, *Wonders* assesses foundational skills taught in the unit. After every six weeks of instruction, *Wonders* provides a more comprehensive assessment of comprehension skills, foundational skills, high-frequency words, and category words.

Online Assessment Center

Unit 6 Tested Skills

COMPREHENSION	HIGH-FREQUENCY WORDS	PHONOLOGICAL/ PHONEMIC AWARENESS	PHONICS	CATEGORY WORDS
• Character, Setting, Events • Events: Sequence • Topic and Details	• *are* • *he* • *is* • *little* • *my* • *she* • *was* • *with*	• Phoneme Isolation • Phoneme Blending • Phoneme Segmentation • Phoneme Addition	• /b/b (initial/final) • /l/l (initial) • /k/k (initial) • /k/ck (final)	• Food Words • Weather Words

Additional Assessment Options

Fluency
Access fluency using the Letter Naming Fluency (LNF), Phoneme Segmentation Fluency (PSF), and Sight Word Fluency (SWF) assessments in **Fluency Assessment**.

ELL Assessment
Assess English Language Learner proficiency and track children's progress using the **English Language Development Assessment**. This resource provides unit assessments and rubrics to evaluate children's progress in the areas of listening and reading comprehension, vocabulary, grammar, speaking, and writing. These assessments can also be used to determine the language proficiency levels for subsequent set of instructions.

Making the Most of Assessment Results

Make data-based grouping decisions by using the following reports to verify assessment results. For additional support options for children, refer to the reteaching and enrichment opportunities.

ONLINE ASSESSMENT CENTER
- *Gradebook*

DATA DASHBOARD
- *Recommendations Report*
- *Activity Report*
- *Skills Report*
- *Progress Report*
- *Grade Card Report*

TIER 2

Reteaching Opportunities with Intervention Online PDFs

IF CHILDREN ANSWER . . .	THEN RETEACH . . .
0-3 **comprehension** items correctly	tested skills using the **Comprehension PDF**
0-1 **high-frequency words** items correctly	tested skills using Section 3 of the **Fluency PDF**
0-3 **phonological/phonemic awareness** items correctly	tested skills using the **Phonemic Awareness PDF**
0-3 **phonics** items correctly	tested skills using the **Phonics/Word Study PDF** and Sections 2 and 4 of the **Fluency PDF**
0-1 **category words** items correctly	tested skills using the **Vocabulary PDF**

GIFTED and TALENTED

Enrichment Opportunities

Beyond Level small group lessons include suggestions for additional activities in the following areas to extend learning opportunities for gifted and talented children:

- *Leveled Readers*
- *Vocabulary*
- *Comprehension*

- *Leveled Reader Library Online*
- *Center Activity Cards*

UNIT 6

Next Steps

NEXT STEPS FOR YOUR CHILDREN'S PROGRESS . . .

Interpret the data you have collected from multiple sources throughout this unit, including formal and informal assessments.

Data Dashboard

Who — Regrouping Decisions

- Check children's progress against your interpretation of the data. Consider whether children are ready to Level Up or accelerate.
- Use the English Learner Benchmark Assessment to determine how English language learners are progressing.

What — Target Instruction

- Decide whether to review and reinforce particular skills or concepts or whether you need to reteach them.
- Target instruction to meet children's strengths/needs.
- Use Data Dashboard recommendations to help determine which lessons to provide to different groups of children.

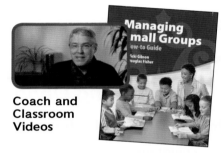

Coach and Classroom Videos

Methodology

How — Modify Instruction

- Vary materials and/or instructional strategies.
- Address children's social and emotional development.
- Provide children with opportunities for self-reflection and self-assessment.

AUTHOR INSIGHT

The many essential decisions that educators make to help every student succeed should be informed by multiple sources of information, including daily observations of each student's performance, along with progress checks provided by progress monitoring and unit assessments.
— Dr. Jan Hasbrouck

Roger Pelissier

PROFESSIONAL DEVELOPMENT

NEXT STEPS FOR YOU . . .

As you prepare your children to move on to the next unit, don't forget to take advantage of the many opportunities available online for self-evaluation and professional development.

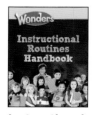

Instructional Routines

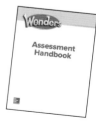

Manage Assessments

Program Author Whitepapers

Research Base

Contents

Program Information

Additional Digital Resources

my.mheducation.com

- Unit Bibliography

- Word Lists

- More Resources

Scope and Sequence

	Big Books	Shared Read	Read Alouds	Vocabulary
Week 1 **We Are Special** **Essential Question:** How is everyone special?	**Animals in the Park: An ABC Book** **Big Book of Rhymes:** "Jack and Jill" "Mary Wore Her Red Dress" "Wee Willie Winkie" "Little Miss Muffet" "Humpty Dumpty"	"I Am Special" **Genre:** Fiction "Look at Me!" **Genre:** Informational Text	**Interactive Read Aloud:** **"The Ugly Duckling"** **Genre:** Fairy Tale **Teacher's Edition:** "The Three Sisters" **Genre:** Folktale	**Category Words:** Names
Week 2 **My Family and Me** **Essential Question:** Who is in your family?	**Animals in the Park: An ABC Book** **Big Book of Rhymes:** "Twinkle, Twinkle, Little Star" "1, 2, Buckle My Shoe" "Mix a Pancake" "Chook, Chook, Chook" "1, 2, 3, 4, 5"	"Family Fun!" **Genre:** Fiction "Fun Together!" **Genre:** Fiction	**Interactive Read Aloud:** "Mama Mouse and El Gato" **Genre:** Fable **Teacher's Edition:** "Teddy's Week" **Genre:** Fiction	**Category Words:** Numbers
Week 3 **I Can!** **Essential Question:** What can you do?	**Animals in the Park: An ABC Book** **Big Book of Rhymes:** "Sing a Song of Sixpence" "Pat-a-Cake" "Hickory, Dickory, Dock" "Hey, Diddle, Diddle" "As I Was Going to St. Ives"	"At School" **Genre:** Fiction "What Can I Do?" **Genre:** Informational Text	**Interactive Read Aloud:** "Kindergartners Can!" **Genre:** Informational Text **Teacher's Edition:** "We Can Help" **Genre:** Folktale	**Category Words:** Days of the Week

Comprehension	Print Concepts	Phonological Awareness	Phonics	High-Frequency Words	Writing	Weekly Project
Details	Parts of a Book Book Handling Reading from Left to Right	Sentence Segmentation Identify Rhyme	**Letter Recognition:** *Aa, Bb, Cc, Dd, Ee, Ff, Gg, Hh*	*I*	**Write About the Text**	**Project:** I Am Special!
Details	Parts of a Book Distinguish Letters from Words Reading from Left to Right	Sentence Segmentation Identify Rhyme	**Letter Recognition:** *Ii, Jj, Kk, Ll, Mm, Nn, Oo, Pp, Qq, Rr*	*can*	**Write About the Text**	**Project:** My Family and Me
Details	Parts of a Book Distinguish Letters from Words Space Between Words	Recognize Syllables Blend Syllables	**Letter Recognition:** *Ss, Tt, Uu, Vv, Ww, Xx, Yy, Zz*	*I, can*	**Write About the Text**	**Project:** I Can!

Scope and Sequence

Unit 1: Take a New Step **The Big Idea:** What can we learn when we try new things?	Literature Big Book	Shared Read	Interactive Read Aloud	Leveled Readers	Vocabulary
Week 1 **Make New Friends** **Essential Question:** How can we get along with new friends? **Genre Focus:** Fiction	**Anchor Text:** *What About Bear?* **Genre:** Fiction **Paired Selection:** "How to Be a Friend" **Genre:** Informational Text	"I Can" **Lexile:** BR "Can I?" **Lexile:** BR	"The Lion and the Mouse" **Genre:** Fable	**Genre:** Fiction ⬤ *The Tree House* **Lexile:** BR ⬤ *The Mouse and The Moose* **Lexile:** BR ⬤ *The Mouse and The Moose* **Lexile:** BR ⬤ *Come and Play!* **Lexile:** 90L	**Oral Vocabulary Words:** *friend* *problem* *grasped* *escape* *rescue* **Category Words:** Feeling Words
Week 2 **Get Up and Go!** **Essential Question:** How do baby animals move? **Genre Focus:** Fiction	**Anchor Text:** *Pouch!* **Genre:** Fiction **Paired Selection:** "Baby Animals on the Move!" **Genre:** Informational Text	"We Can!" **Lexile:** BR "I Can, We Can" **Lexile:** BR	"The Tortoise and the Hare" **Genre:** Fable	**Genre:** Fiction ⬤ *Hop!* **Lexile:** BR ⬤ *We Hop!* **Lexile:** BR ⬤ *We Hop!* **Lexile:** BR ⬤ *We Can Move!* **Lexile:** 140L	**Oral Vocabulary Words:** *adventure* *movement* *exhausted* *excited* *arrived* **Category Words:** Family Words
Week 3 **Use Your Senses** **Essential Question:** How can your senses help you learn? **Genre Focus:** Informational Text: Nonfiction	**Anchor Text:** *Senses at the Seashore* **Genre:** Informational Text **Paired Selection:** "I Smell Springtime," "Taste of Purple," "Rain" **Genre:** Poetry	"Sam Can See" **Lexile:** BR "I Can See" **Lexile:** BR	"A Feast of the Senses" **Genre:** Informational Text	**Genre:** Informational Text ⬤ *The Beach* **Lexile:** BR ⬤ *At School* **Lexile:** BR ⬤ *At School* **Lexile:** BR ⬤ *See It Grow!* **Lexile:** BR	**Oral Vocabulary Words:** *explore* *senses* *feast* *finished* *kneads* **Category Words:** Sensory Words

Comprehension	Print Concepts	Phonological/ Phonemic Awareness	Phonics/Spelling/ Handwriting	High- Frequency Words	Writing and Grammar	Research and Inquiry
Ask and Answer Questions Main Story Elements: Character Photographs	Left-to-Right Tracking Hold Book Right Side Up	**Phonological Awareness:** Onset and Rime Blending **Phonemic Awareness:** Phoneme Isolation, Phoneme Identity, Phoneme Categorization	**Phonics:** /m/m (initial/final) **Spelling:** Words with *m*; *the* **Handwriting:** Upper and Lowercase *Mm* **Decodable Readers:** "I Can" "Can I?"	*the* **Build Your Word Bank:** *out*	**Write About the Text:** Expository **Writing Skill:** Left-to-Right Progression **Writing Trait:** Details **Grammar:** Naming Words (Nouns)	**Project:** How to Be a Good Friend
Ask and Answer Questions Main Story Elements: Character Labels	Parts of a Book Left to Right, Top to Bottom Tracking	**Phonological Awareness:** Identify Rhyme **Phonemic Awareness:** Phoneme Isolation, Phoneme Blending, Phoneme Identity	**Phonics:** /a/a (initial/medial) **Consonant Review:** /m/m **Spelling:** Words with *a; we* **Handwriting:** Upper and Lowercase *Aa* **Decodable Readers:** "I Am" "We Can"	*we* **Build Your Word Bank:** *down*	**Write About the Text:** Expository **Writing Skill:** Left-to-Right Progression **Writing Trait:** Details **Grammar:** Naming Words (Nouns)	**Project:** How Baby Animals Move
Ask and Answer Questions Topic and Details Sensory Words	Parts of a Book Left to Right, Top to Bottom Tracking	**Phonological Awareness:** Onset and Rime Blending **Phonemic Awareness:** Phoneme Isolation, Phoneme Blending, Phoneme Categorization	**Phonics:** /s/s (initial) **Consonant/Vowel Review:** /a/a, /m/m **Spelling:** Words with *s; see* **Handwriting:** Upper and Lowercase *Ss* **Decodable Readers:** "Sam Can See" "Sam"	*see* **Build Your Word Bank:** *will, jump*	**Write About the Text:** Opinion **Writing Skill:** Words Are Made up of Letters **Writing Trait:** Details **Grammar:** Naming Words (Nouns)	**Project:** The Senses

Scope and Sequence

Unit 2: Let's Explore The Big Idea: What can you find out when you explore?	Literature Big Book	Shared Read	Interactive Read Aloud	Leveled Readers	Vocabulary
Week 1 **Tools We Use** **Essential Question:** How do tools help us to explore? **Genre Focus:** Informational Text: Nonfiction	**Anchor Text:** *The Handiest Things in the World* **Genre:** Informational Text **Paired Selection:** "Discover with Tools" **Genre:** Informational Text	"Pam Can See" **Lexile:** BR "We Can See!" **Lexile:** BR	"Timimoto" **Genre:** Folktale	**Genre:** Informational Text ● *We Need Tools* **Lexile:** BR ● *A Trip* **Lexile:** BR ● *A Trip* **Lexile:** BR ● *What Can You See?* **Lexile:** 90L	**Oral Vocabulary Words:** *tools* *discover* *defeated* *fetch* *rumble* **Category Words:** Color Words
Week 2 **Shapes All Around Us** **Essential Question:** What shapes do you see around you? **Genre Focus:** Informational Text: Nonfiction	**Anchor Text:** *Shapes All Around* **Genre:** Informational Text **Paired Selection:** "Find the Shapes" **Genre:** Informational Text	"We Like Tam!" **Lexile:** BR "I Like Sam" **Lexile:** BR	"Kites in Flight" **Genre:** Informational Text	**Genre:** Informational Text ● *Shapes!* **Lexile:** BR ● *Play with Shapes!* **Lexile:** BR ● *Play with Shapes!* **Lexile:** BR ● *Use a Shape!* **Lexile:** 140L	**Oral Vocabulary Words:** *materials* *nature* *decoration* *games* *world* **Category Words:** Shape Words
Week 3 **World of Bugs** **Essential Question:** What kind of bugs do you know about? **Genre Focus:** Poetry	**Anchor Text:** *I Love Bugs!* **Genre:** Poetry **Paired Selection:** "Bugs All Around" **Genre:** Informational Text	"Pat" **Lexile:** BR "Tap! Tap! Tap!" **Lexile:** BR	"From Caterpillar to Butterfly" **Genre:** Informational Text	**Genre:** Fiction ● *We Like Bugs!* **Lexile:** BR ● *The Bugs Run* **Lexile:** BR ● *The Bugs Run* **Lexile:** BR ● *I See a Bug!* **Lexile:** BR	**Oral Vocabulary Words:** *curious* *observe* *attaches* *process* *slender* **Category Words:** Texture Words

Units 1 and 2	Connect to Content: Science	Extend Your Learning
Extend, Connect, and Assess	**Genre Read-Aloud** "Look and Learn" **Activities** Learn About Tools Observe with Tools	**Choose Your Own Book**

Comprehension	Print Concepts	Phonological/ Phonemic Awareness	Phonics/Spelling/ Handwriting	High-Frequency Words	Writing and Grammar	Research and Inquiry
Ask and Answer Questions Topic and Details Headings	Left to Right, Top to Bottom Tracking Locate Printed Word	**Phonological Awareness:** Identify Alliteration **Phonemic Awareness:** Phoneme Isolation, Phoneme Blending, Phoneme Categorization	**Phonics:** /p/p (initial/final) **Consonant/Vowel Review:** /a/a, /m/m, /s/s **Spelling:** Words with p; we **Handwriting:** Upper and Lowercase Pp **Decodable Readers:** "A Sap Map" "Pam Can See"	we **Build Your Word Bank:** there, our	**Write About the Text:** Opinion **Writing Skill:** Stretch Sounds to Write Words **Writing Trait:** Details **Grammar:** Action Words (Verbs: Present Tense)	**Project:** Tools for Exploring
Ask and Answer Questions Topic and Details Bold Print	Locate Printed Word Distinguish Letters from Words Parts of a Book Left to Right, Top to Bottom Tracking	**Phonological Awareness:** Onset and Rime Blending **Phonemic Awareness:** Phoneme Isolation, Phoneme Blending, Phoneme Identity	**Phonics:** /t/t (initial/final) **Consonant/Vowel Review:** /a/a, /m/m, /s/s **Spelling:** Words with t; like **Handwriting:** Upper and Lowercase Tt **Decodable Readers:** "Tap the Mat" "I Am Pat"	like **Build Your Word Bank:** two, well	**Write About the Text:** Expository **Writing Skill:** Use Word Bank **Writing Trait:** Details **Extended Writing:** Expository Text: Nonfiction **Grammar:** Action Words (Verbs: Present Tense)	**Project:** Shapes Survey
Ask and Answer Questions Poetry: Rhyme Captions	Distinguish Letters from Words Left to Right, Top to Bottom Tracking Parts of a Book	**Phonological Awareness:** Count and Segment Syllables **Phonemic Awareness:** Phoneme Segmentation, Phoneme Blending **Long Vowel Awareness:** Long a	**Phonics:** Review /m/m, a/a, /s/s, /p/p, /t/t **Spelling Pattern:** at pattern; the, a, see, we, like **Handwriting:** Write Sentences with Mm, Aa, Ss, Pp, Tt **Decodable Readers:** "We See Tam"	the a see we like **Build Your Word Bank:** for, out, down, will, jump, there, our, two, well	**Write About the Text:** Opinion **Writing Skill:** Spaces Between Words **Writing Trait:** Descriptive Details **Grammar:** Action Words (Verbs: Present Tense)	**Project:** Bugs

Scope and Sequence

Unit 3: Going Places **The Big Idea:** What can you learn by going to different places?	Literature Big Book	Shared Read	Interactive Read Aloud	Leveled Readers	Vocabulary
Week 1 **Rules to Go By** **Essential Question:** What rules do we follow in different places? **Genre Focus:** Fiction	**Anchor Text:** *How Do Dinosaurs Go to School?* **Genre:** Fiction: Fantasy **Paired Selection:** "Be Safe!" **Genre:** Informational Text	"Can I Pat It?" **Lexile:** BR "Tim Can Tip It" **Lexile:** 300L	"The Boy Who Cried Wolf" **Genre:** Fable	**Genre:** Fantasy ● *We Run* **Lexile:** BR ● *Go, Nat!* **Lexile:** BR ● *Go, Nat!* **Lexile:** BR ● *The Birdhouse* **Lexile:** BR	**Oral Vocabulary Words:** *rules* *cooperate* *guard* *prank* *responsible* **Category Words:** Action Words
Week 2 **Sounds Around Us** **Essential Question:** What are the different sounds we hear? **Genre Focus:** Fiction	**Anchor Text:** *Clang! Clang! Beep! Beep! Listen to the City* **Genre:** Fiction **Paired Selection:** "Sounds Are Everywhere!" **Genre:** Informational Text	"Nat and Tip" **Lexile:** 250L "Tim and Nan" **Lexile:** 250L	"The Turtle and the Flute" **Genre:** Tale	**Genre:** Fiction ● *City Sounds* **Lexile:** BR ● *Farm Sounds* **Lexile:** 280L ● *Farm Sounds* **Lexile:** BR ● *A Noisy Night* **Lexile:** 190L	**Oral Vocabulary Words:** *listen* *volume* *chat* *exclaimed* *familiar* **Category Words:** Sound Words
Week 3 **The Places We Go** **Essential Question:** What places do you go to during the week? **Genre Focus:** Fiction	**Anchor Text:** *Please Take Me for a Walk* **Genre:** Fiction **Paired Selection:** "A Neighborhood" **Genre:** Informational Text	"We Go to See Nan" **Lexile:** 140L "Can We Go?" **Lexile:** 60L	"Field Trips" **Genre:** Informational Text	**Genre:** Fiction ● *We Can Go* **Lexile:** BR ● *Going by Cab* **Lexile:** 160L ● *Going by Cab* **Lexile:** BR ● *Cal's Busy Week* **Lexile:** 110L	**Oral Vocabulary Words:** *local* *routine* *neighborhood* *volunteer* *intelligent* **Category Words:** Sequence Words

Comprehension	Print Concepts	Phonological/ Phonemic Awareness	Phonics/Spelling/ Handwriting	High-Frequency Words	Writing and Grammar	Research and Inquiry
Visualize Main Story Elements: Character Lists	Left to Right, Top to Bottom Tracking Locate Printed Word	**Phonological Awareness:** Identify Rhyme **Phonemic Awareness:** Phoneme Isolation, Phoneme Blending, Phoneme Categorization	**Phonics:** /i/*i* (medial) **Consonant/Vowel Review:** /a/*a*, /m/*m*, /p/*p*, /s/*s*, /t/*t* **Extend the Lesson:** Final Double Letters: *ss, tt* **Spelling:** Words with *i; to* **Handwriting:** Upper and Lowercase *Ii* **Decodable Readers:** "Tim Can Sit" "We Like It"	*to* **Build Your Word Bank:** *her, one, say*	**Write About the Text:** Narrative **Writing Skill:** Sentences Are Made up of Words **Writing Trait:** Descriptive Details **Grammar:** Sentences	**Project:** Rules for Safety
Visualize Main Story Elements: Setting Captions	Locate Printed Word Left to Right, Top to Bottom Tracking Parts of a Book	**Phonological Awareness:** Onset and Rime Blending **Phonemic Awareness:** Phoneme Isolation, Phoneme Blending, Phoneme Categorization	**Phonics:** /n/*n* **Consonant/Vowel Review:** /a/*a*, /m/*m*, /p/*p*, /s/*s*, /t/*t* **Spelling:** Words with *n; and* **Handwriting:** Upper and Lowercase *Nn* **Decodable Readers:** "Nat and Nan" "Nan and Nat See"	*and* **Build Your Word Bank:** *then, new, saw*	**Write About the Text:** Expository **Writing Skill:** Sentence Capitalization **Writing Trait:** Descriptive Details **Grammar:** Sentences	**Project:** Experiment with Sounds
Visualize Main Story Elements: Character Map	Left to Right, Top to Bottom Tracking Parts of a Book	**Phonological Awareness:** Count and Segment Syllables **Phonemic Awareness:** Phoneme Isolation, Phoneme Blending, Phoneme Identity, Phoneme Segmentation **Long Vowel Awareness:** Long *i*	**Phonics:** /k/*c* **Consonant/Vowel Review:** /a/*a*, /m/*m*, /p/*p*, /s/*s*, /t/*t* **Spelling Pattern:** *an* pattern **Handwriting:** Upper and Lowercase *Cc* **Decodable Readers:** "Cam Cat" "See the Cat"	*go* **Build Your Word Bank:** *could, place, white*	**Write About the Text:** Expository **Writing Skill:** End Punctuation **Writing Trait:** Descriptive Details **Grammar:** Sentences	**Project:** School Places Interview

Scope and Sequence

Unit 4: Around the Neighborhood	Literature Big Book	Shared Read	Interactive Read Aloud	Leveled Readers	Vocabulary
The Big Idea: What do you know about the people and the places in your neighborhood?					
Week 1 **Time for Work** **Essential Question:** What do people use to do their jobs? **Genre Focus:** Informational Text: Nonfiction	**Anchor Text:** *Whose Shoes? A Shoe for Every Job* **Genre:** Informational Text **Paired Selection:** "Workers and Their Tools" **Genre:** Informational Text	"Tom on Top!" **Lexile:** 70L	"Little Juan and the Cooking Pot" **Genre:** Tale	**Genre:** Informational Text ● *You Cook* **Lexile:** BR ● *On the Job* **Lexile:** BR ● *On the Job* **Lexile:** BR ● *The Neighborhood* **Lexile:** 120L	**Oral Vocabulary Words:** *equipment uniform utensils expect remained* **Category Words:** Jobs
Week 2 **Meet Your Neighbors** **Essential Question:** Who are your neighbors? **Genre Focus:** Realistic Fiction	**Anchor Text:** *What Can You Do with a Paleta?* **Genre:** Realistic Fiction **Paired Selection:** "My Great Neighborhood!" **Genre:** Personal Narrative	"Sid" **Lexile:** 340L	"Cultural Festivals" **Genre:** Informational Text	**Genre:** Fiction ● *My Neighbors* **Lexile:** BR ● *Neighborhood Party* **Lexile:** 100L ● *Neighborhood Party* **Lexile:** BR ● *Parade Day* **Lexile:** 100L	**Oral Vocabulary Words:** *appreciate cultures prefer proud tradition* **Category Words:** Food Words
Week 3 **Pitch In** **Essential Question:** How can people help to make your community better? **Genre Focus:** Informational Text: Nonfiction	**Anchor Text:** *Roadwork* **Genre:** Informational Text **Paired Selection:** "A Community Garden" **Genre:** Informational Text	"I Can, You Can!" **Lexile:** 180L	"The Bundle of Sticks" **Genre:** Fable	**Genre:** Informational Text ● *We Clean!* **Lexile:** BR ● *Can You Fix It?* **Lexile:** 60L ● *Can You Fix It?* **Lexile:** BR ● *Helping Mom* **Lexile:** 290L	**Oral Vocabulary Words:** *community improve confused harvest quarrel* **Category Words:** Position Words

Units 3 and 4	Connect to Content: Social Studies	Extend Your Learning
Extend, Connect, and Assess	**Genre Read-Aloud** "Firefighters Help Out" **Activities** Find Out About Firefighters Make a Job Poster	**Choose Your Own Book**

Comprehension	Print Concepts	Phonological/ Phonemic Awareness	Phonics/Spelling/ Handwriting	High-Frequency Words	Writing and Grammar	Research and Inquiry
Ask and Answer Questions Topic and Details Labels	Parts of a Book Match Speech to Print	**Phonological Awareness:** Onset and Rime Segmentation **Phonemic Awareness:** Phoneme Isolation, Blending, and Categorization	**Phonics:** /o/o (initial/medial) **Consonant/Vowel Review:** /a/a, /k/c, /l/l, /m/m, /n/n, /p/p, /s/s, /t/t **Spelling:** Words with o; you **Handwriting:** Upper and Lowercase Oo **Decodable Readers:** "Tom Can" "Mom and Nan"	you **Build Your Word Bank:** all, that, four	**Write About the Text:** Expository **Writing Skill:** Return Sweep **Writing Trait:** Supporting Details **Grammar:** Describing Words (Adjectives)	**Project:** Workers and Their Tools
Ask and Answer Questions Main Story Elements: Character, Setting Illustrations	Parts of a Book Match Speech to Print	**Phonological Awareness:** Sentence Segmentation **Phonemic Awareness:** Phoneme Isolation, Blending, and Segmentation **Long Vowel Awareness:** Long o	**Phonics:** /d/d (initial/final) **Consonant/Vowel Review:** /a/a, /k/c, /l/l, /m/m, /n/n, /p/p, /s/s, /t/t **Spelling:** Words with d; do **Handwriting:** Upper and Lowercase Dd **Decodable Readers:** "Did Dan?" "Did Sid See Don?"	do **Build Your Word Bank:** day, long, blue	**Write About the Text:** Expository **Writing Skill:** Stretch Sounds to Write Words **Writing Trait:** Supporting Details **Extended Writing:** Personal Narrative **Grammar:** Describing Words (Adjectives)	**Project:** Neighbors Interview
Ask and Answer Questions Details: Time Order Captions	Capitalization Left to Right, Top to Bottom Tracking Parts of a Book	**Phonological Awareness:** Identify Rhyme **Phonemic Awareness:** Phoneme Identity, Blending, and Segmentation	**Phonics:** Review /i/i, n/n, /k/c, /o/o, /d/d; s-Blends **Consonant/Vowel Review:** /a/a, /k/c, /l/l, /m/m, /n/n, /p/p, /s/s, /t/t **Long Vowel Express (optional):** Long a (a_e) **Spelling Pattern:** ot pattern **Handwriting:** Write Sentences with i, n, c, o, d **Decodable Readers:** "Tip It"; "Stop the Top!"	and do go to you **Build Your Word Bank:** her, one, say, then, new, saw, could, place, white, all, that, four, day, long, blue	**Write About the Text:** Expository **Writing Skill:** Use Word Bank **Writing Trait:** Focus on One Idea **Grammar:** Describing Words (Adjectives)	**Project:** Interview About School

Scope and Sequence

Unit 5: Wonders of Nature The Big Idea: What kinds of things can you find growing in nature?	Literature Big Book	Shared Read	Interactive Read Aloud	Leveled Readers	Vocabulary
Week 1 **How Does Your Garden Grow?** **Essential Question:** What do living things need to grow? **Genre Focus:** Realistic Fiction	**Anchor Text:** *My Garden* **Genre:** Realistic Fiction **Paired Selection:** "Tommy," "Maytime Magic," "The Seed," "Garden" **Genre:** Poetry	"Hop Can Hop!" **Lexile:** 110L	"Growing Plants" **Genre:** Informational Text	**Genre:** Fiction ● *My Garden* **Lexile:** BR ● *My Garden Grows* **Lexile:** 100L ● *My Garden Grows* **Lexile:** BR ● *The Mystery Seeds* **Lexile:** 240L	**Oral Vocabulary Words:** *require* *plant* *harmful* *soak* *crowd* **Category Words:** Size Words Plurals with -s
Week 2 **Trees** **Essential Question:** How do living things change as they grow? **Genre Focus:** Informational Text: Nonfiction	**Anchor Text:** *A Grand Old Tree* **Genre:** Informational Text **Paired Selection:** "From a Seed to a Tree" **Genre:** Informational Text	"Ed and Ned" **Lexile:** 230L	"The Pine Tree" **Genre:** Fairy Tale	**Genre:** Informational Text ● *The Tree* **Lexile:** BR ● *Many Trees* **Lexile:** 70L ● *Many Trees* **Lexile:** BR ● *Our Apple Tree* **Lexile:** 250L	**Oral Vocabulary Words:** *develop* *amazing* *content* *enormous* *imagine* **Category Words:** Tree Parts Inflectional Ending -ed
Week 3 **Fresh from the Farm** **Essential Question:** What kinds of things grow on a farm? **Genre Focus:** Informational Text: Nonfiction	**Anchor Text:** *An Orange in January* **Genre:** Informational Text **Paired Selection:** "Farmers' Market" **Genre:** Informational Text	"Ron With Red" **Lexile:** 170L	"Farms Around the World" **Genre:** Informational Text	**Genre:** Informational Text ● *The Farmer* **Lexile:** BR ● *Let's Make a Salad!* **Lexile:** BR ● *Let's Make a Salad!* **Lexile:** BR ● *Farm Fresh Finn* **Lexile:** 260L	**Oral Vocabulary Words:** *fresh* *delicious* *beneath* *raise* *special* **Category Words:** Food Words Sentence Clues

Comprehension	Print Concepts	Phonological/ Phonemic Awareness	Phonics/Spelling/ Handwriting	High-Frequency Words	Writing and Grammar	Research and Inquiry
Reread Main Story Elements: Character, Setting, Events Rhyme and Repetition	Locate Printed Word Parts of a Book	**Phonological Awareness:** Count and Blend Syllables **Phonemic Awareness:** Phoneme Isolation, Phoneme Blending, Phoneme Categorization	**Phonics:** /h/h (initial) **Consonant/Vowel Review:** /a/a, /k/c, /d/d, /l/l, /m/m, /n/n, /o/o, /p/p, /s/s, /t/t **Extend the Lesson:** Final /z/s **Spelling:** Words with h; *my* **Handwriting:** Upper and Lowercase *Hh* **Decodable Readers:** "Hap Hid the Ham" "Hip Hop"	*my* **Build Your Word Bank:** *than, his, three*	**Write About the Text:** Opinion **Writing Skill:** End Punctuation **Writing Trait:** Focus on One Idea **Grammar:** Pronouns (Subjective)	**Project:** Parts of a Plant
Reread Topic and Details Diagram	Left to Right, Top to Bottom Tracking; Return Sweep Parts of a Book	**Phonological Awareness:** Onset and Rime Blending **Phonemic Awareness:** Phoneme Isolation, Phoneme Blending, Phoneme Segmentation	**Phonics:** /e/e (initial/medial) **Consonant/Vowel Review:** /a/a, /k/c, /d/d, /h/h, /l/l, /m/m, /n/n, /o/o, /p/p, /s/s, /t/t **Spelling:** Words with /e/e; *are* **Handwriting:** Upper and Lowercase *Ee* **Decodable Readers:** "Ed and Ted Can Go" "Not a Pet"	*are* **Build Your Word Bank:** *when, which, soon*	**Write About the Text:** Opinion **Writing Skill:** Return Sweep **Writing Trait:** Words That Connect Ideas **Grammar:** Pronouns (Subjective)	**Project:** How Trees Grow
Reread Topic and Details Lists	Parts of a Book Match Speech to Print	**Phonological Awareness:** Identify Rhyme **Phonemic Awareness:** Phoneme Isolation, Phoneme Blending, Phoneme Addition **Long Vowel Awareness:** Long e: ee	**Phonics:** /f/f (initial/final), /r/r (initial) **Consonant/Vowel Review:** /a/a, /k/c, /d/d, /e/e, /h/h, /l/l, /m/m, /n/n, /o/o, /p/p, /s/s, /t/t **Spelling Pattern:** *en* pattern **Handwriting:** Upper and Lowercase *Ff* and *Rr* **Decodable Readers:** "Ron Ram" "Red and Ron"	*with* *he* **Build Your Word Bank:** *many, them, eat*	**Write About the Text:** Expository **Writing Skill:** Stretch Sounds to Write Words **Writing Trait:** Sequence **Grammar:** Pronouns (Subjective)	**Project:** Plants on a Farm

Scope and Sequence

Unit 6: Weather for All Seasons The Big Idea: How do weather and seasons affect us?	Literature Big Book	Shared Read	Interactive Read Aloud	Leveled Readers	Vocabulary
Week 1 **The Four Seasons** **Essential Question:** How are the seasons different? **Genre Focus:** Realistic Fiction	**Anchor Text:** *Mama, Is It Summer Yet?* **Genre:** Realistic Fiction **Paired Selection:** "New Snow," "Rain Song," "Covers," excerpt from "Honey I Love" **Genre:** Poetry	"Is It Hot?" **Lexile:** 200L	"A Tour of the Seasons" **Genre:** Informational Text	**Genre:** Fiction ● *It Is Hot!* **Lexile:** BR ● *Little Bear* **Lexile:** 300L ● *Little Bear* **Lexile:** 300L ● *Ant and Grasshopper* **Lexile:** 280L	**Oral Vocabulary Words:** weather seasons migrate active spot **Category Words:** Seasons Sentence Clues
Week 2 **What's the Weather?** **Essential Question:** What happens in different kinds of weather? **Genre Focus:** Fantasy	**Anchor Text:** *Rain* **Genre:** Fantasy **Paired Selection:** "Cloud Watch" **Genre:** Informational Text	"Kim and Nan" **Lexile:** 120L	"The Battle of Wind and Rain" **Genre:** Tale	**Genre:** Fiction ● *The Rain* **Lexile:** BR ● *Weather Is Fun* **Lexile:** BR ● *Weather Is Fun* **Lexile:** BR ● *Kate and Tuck* **Lexile:** 280L	**Oral Vocabulary Words:** predict temperature drought clever storm **Category Words:** Weather Words Shades of Meaning
Week 3 **Stormy Weather** **Essential Question:** How can you stay safe in bad weather? **Genre Focus:** Realistic Fiction	**Anchor Text:** *Waiting Out the Storm* **Genre:** Realistic Fiction **Paired Selection:** "Be Safe in Bad Weather" **Genre:** Informational Text	"Mack and Ben" **Lexile:** 210L	"The Storm that Shook the Signs" **Genre:** Fairy Tale	**Genre:** Realistic Fiction ● *Bad Weather* **Lexile:** BR ● *Getting Ready* **Lexile:** 30L ● *Getting Ready* **Lexile:** BR ● *The Storm* **Lexile:** 170L	**Oral Vocabulary Words:** safe prepare notice celebration enough **Category Words:** Question Words

Units 5 and 6	Reading Digitally	Connect to Content: Social Studies	Extend Your Learning
Extend, Connect, and Assess	"Changes with the Wind" **Genre:** Online Article	**Genre Read-Aloud** "A Farm Year" **Activities** Seasons on a Farm Make a Seasons Poster	**Choose Your Own Book**

Comprehension	Print Concepts	Phonological/ Phonemic Awareness	Phonics/Spelling/Handwriting	High- Frequency Words	Writing and Grammar	Research and Inquiry
Visualize Events: Sequence Rhyme	Left to Right, Top to Bottom Tracking Parts of a Book	**Phonological Awareness:** Onset and Rime Segmentation **Phonemic Awareness:** Phoneme Isolation, Blending, and Segmentation	**Phonics:** /b/*b* (initial/final), /l/*l* (initial) **Consonant/Vowel Review:** /a/*a*, /k/*c*, /d/*d*, /e/*e*, /f/*f*, /h/*h*, /l/*l*, /m/*m*, /n/*n*, /o/*o*, /p/*p*, /r/*r*, /s/*s*, /t/*t* **Extend the Lesson:** Final double letters: *l* **Spelling:** Words with *b, l; is, little* **Handwriting:** Upper and Lowercase *Bb, Ll* **Decodable Readers:** "Bob and Ben"; "Ben, Deb, Lin"	*is* *little* **Build Your Word Bank:** *by, some, brown*	**Write About the Text:** Opinion **Writing Skill:** Left-to-Right Progression **Writing Trait:** Focus on One Idea **Grammar:** Nouns (Singular and Plural)	**Project:** The Seasons
Visualize Events: Sequence Speech Bubbles	Capitalization Periods and Exclamation Marks Parts of a Book	**Phonological Awareness:** Identify Rhyme **Phonemic Awareness:** Phoneme Isolation, Blending, and Segmentation	**Phonics:** /k/*k* (initial), /k/*ck* (final) **Consonant/Vowel Review:** /a/*a*, /b/*b*, /k/*c*, /d/*d*, /e/*e*, /f/*f*, /h/*h*, /i/*i*, /l/*l*, /m/*m*, /n/*n*, /o/*o*, /p/*p*, /r/*r*, /s/*s*, /t/*t* **Spelling:** Words with *k, ck; she, was* **Handwriting:** Upper and Lowercase *Kk* **Decodable Readers:** "Pack It, Kim"; "Kick It, Nick!"	*she* *was* **Build Your Word Bank:** *now, way, under*	**Write About the Text:** Narrative **Writing Skill:** Spaces Between Words **Writing Trait:** Sequence **Grammar:** Proper Nouns	**Project:** Kinds of Weather
Visualize Events: Sequence Directions	Locate Printed Word Capitalization Parts of a Book	**Phonological Awareness:** Identify Alliteration **Phonemic Awareness:** Phoneme Identity, Blending, and Addition	**Phonics:** Review /h/*h*, /e/*e*, /f/*f*, /r/*r*, /b/*b*, /l/*l*, /k/*k*, /k/*ck*; *l*-Blends **Consonant/Vowel Review:** /a/*a*, /b/*b*, /k/*c*, /k/*ck*, /d/*d*, /e/*e*, /f/*f*, /h/*h*, /i/*i*, /l/*l*, /m/*m*, /n/*n*, /o/*o*, /p/*p*, /r/*r*, /s/*s*, /t/*t* **Long Vowel Express (optional):** Long *i (i_e)* **Spelling Pattern:** *ack* pattern **Handwriting:** Write Sentences with *h, e, f, r, b, l, k, ck*; *l*-Blends **Decodable Readers:** "Rock Ken"; "Flip, Flop, Flip!"	*are* *he* *is* *little* *my* *she* *was* *with* **Build Your Word Bank:** *than, his, three, eat, when, now, which, soon, many, them, by, some, brown, way, under*	**Write About the Text:** Narrative **Writing Skill:** Write on the Lines **Writing Trait:** Descriptive Words **Extended Writing:** Realistic Fiction **Grammar:** Nouns (Singular and Plural)	**Project:** Stormy Weather

Scope and Sequence

Unit 7: The Animal Kingdom **The Big Idea:** What are different kinds of animals?	Literature Big Book	Shared Read	Interactive Read Aloud	Leveled Readers	Vocabulary
Week 1 **Baby Animals** **Essential Question:** How are some animals alike and how are they different? **Genre Focus:** Informational Text: Nonfiction	**Anchor Text:** *ZooBorns!* **Genre:** Informational Text **Paired Selection:** "Mischievous Goat," "Over in the Meadow," "Kitty Caught a Caterpillar" **Genre:** Poetry	"A Pup and a Cub" **Lexile:** 110L	"Baby Farm Animals" **Genre:** Informational Text	**Genre:** Informational Text ● *Two Cubs* **Lexile:** 10L ● *Animal Bodies* **Lexile:** 80L ● *Animal Bodies* **Lexile:** 80L ● *Two Kinds of Bears* **Lexile:** 420L	**Oral Vocabulary Words:** *appearance* *behavior* *exercise* *wander* *plenty* **Category Words:** Animal Parts Compound Words
Week 2 **Pet Pals** **Essential Question:** How do you take care of different kinds of pets? **Genre Focus:** Realistic Fiction	**Anchor Text:** *The Birthday Pet* **Genre:** Realistic Fiction **Paired Selection:** "Lola and Bella" **Genre:** Personal Narrative	"I Hug Gus!" **Lexile:** 300L	"The Family Pet" **Genre:** Informational Text	**Genre:** Fiction ● *My Cats* **Lexile:** BR ● *Their Pets* **Lexile:** 270L ● *Their Pets* **Lexile:** BR ● *Will's Pet* **Lexile:** 190L	**Oral Vocabulary Words:** *responsibility* *train* *depend* *compared* *social* **Category Words:** Pets Prepositions
Week 3 **Animal Habitats** **Essential Question:** Where do animals live? **Genre Focus:** Fantasy	**Anchor Text:** *Bear Snores On* **Genre:** Fantasy **Paired Selection:** "Animal Homes" **Genre:** Informational Text	"A Vet in a Van" **Lexile:** 250L	**"Aunt Nancy"** **Genre:** Tale	**Genre:** Fantasy ● *We Want Water* **Lexile:** 110L ● *A New Home* **Lexile:** 50L ● *A New Home* **Lexile:** 300L ● *Bird's New Home* **Lexile:** 190L	**Oral Vocabulary Words:** *habitat* *wild* *complain* *join* *stubborn* **Category Words:** Animal Homes Shades of Meaning

Comprehension	Print Concepts	Phonological/ Phonemic Awareness	Phonics/Spelling/ Handwriting	High-Frequency Words	Writing and Grammar	Research and Inquiry
Reread Fact and Opinion Alliteration	Locate Printed Word Parts of a Book	**Phonological Awareness:** Onset and Rime Blending **Phonemic Awareness:** Phoneme Isolation, Phoneme Blending, Phoneme Deletion	**Phonics:** /u/u (initial/medial) **Consonant/Vowel Review:** /a/a, /b/b, /k/c, /k/ck, /k/k, d/d, /e/e, /f/f, /h/h, /i/i, /l/l, /m/m, /n/n, /o/o, /p/p, /r/r, /s/s, /t/t **Spelling:** Words with u; for, have **Handwriting:** Upper and Lowercase Uu **Decodable Readers:** "Sun Fun" "Pup and Cub"	*for* *have* **Build Your Word Bank:** *from, how, pretty*	**Write About the Text:** Expository **Writing Skill:** Sentence Capitalization **Writing Trait:** Descriptive Words **Grammar:** Verbs (Present Tense)	**Project:** Animal Features
Make and Confirm Predictions Events: Problem and Solution Narrator	Left to Right, Top to Bottom Tracking Exclamation Point Parts of a Book	**Phonological Awareness:** Identify and Produce Rhyming Words **Phonemic Awareness:** Phoneme Isolation, Phoneme Blending, Phoneme Substitution	**Phonics:** /g/g (initial/final), /w/w (initial) **Consonant/Vowel Review:** /a/a, /b/b, /k/c, /k/ck, /k/k, /d/d, /e/e, /f/f, /h/h, /i/i, /l/l, /m/m, /n/n, /o/o, /p/p, /r/r, /s/s, /t/t, /u/u **Spelling:** Words with g, w; of, they **Handwriting:** Upper and Lowercase Gg, Ww **Decodable Readers:** "Wet Gus" "See a Bug?"	*of* *they* **Build Your Word Bank:** *water, these, yellow*	**Write About the Text:** Narrative **Writing Skill:** Left-to-Right Progression **Writing Trait:** Descriptive Words **Grammar:** Verbs (Past Tense)	**Project:** Caring for a Pet
Make and Confirm Predictions Events: Cause and Effect Glossary	Distinguish Letters from Words Parts of a Book	**Phonological Awareness:** Onset and Rime Segmentation **Phonemic Awareness:** Phoneme Isolation, Phoneme Blending, Phoneme Substitution **Long Vowel Awareness:** Long u: u_e	**Phonics:** /ks/x (final), /v/v (initial) **Consonant/Vowel Review:** /a/a, /b/b, /k/c, /k/ck, /k/k, /d/d, /e/e, /f/f, /g/g, /h/h, /i/i, /l/l, /m/m, /n/n, /o/o, /p/p, /r/r, /s/s, /t/t, /u/u, /w/w **Spelling Pattern:** et pattern **Handwriting:** Upper and Lowercase Vv, Xx **Decodable Readers:** "Rex the Vet" "Fox Had a Big Box"	*said* *want* **Build Your Word Bank:** *people, work, funny*	**Write About the Text:** Opinion **Writing Skill:** Use Word Bank **Writing Trait:** Descriptive Words **Grammar:** Verbs (Future Tense)	**Project:** Animal Habitats

Scope and Sequence

Unit 8: From Here to There **The Big Idea:** Where can you go that is far and near?	Literature Big Book	Shared Read	Interactive Read Aloud	Leveled Readers	Vocabulary
Week 1 **On the Move** **Essential Question:** What can help you go from here to there? **Genre Focus:** Realistic Fiction	**Anchor Text:** *When Daddy's Truck Picks Me Up* **Genre:** Realistic Fiction **Paired Selection:** "From Here to There" **Genre:** Informational Text	"Dad Got a Job" **Lexile:** 190L	"The King of the Winds" **Genre:** Tale	**Genre:** Fiction ● *I Go Places* **Lexile:** BR ● *Run, Quinn!* **Lexile:** BR ● *Run, Quinn!* **Lexile:** 70L ● *Going to Gran's House* **Lexile:** 190L	**Oral Vocabulary Words:** *transportation* *vehicle* *journey* *fierce* *wide* **Category Words:** Vehicles Context Clues
Week 2 **My U.S.A.** **Essential Question:** What do you know about our country? **Genre Focus:** Informational Text: Nonfiction	**Anchor Text:** *Ana Goes to Washington, D.C.* **Genre:** Informational Text **Paired Selection:** "See Our Country" **Genre:** Informational Text	"Pack a Bag!" **Lexile:** 160L	"The Best of the West" **Genre:** Informational Text	**Genre:** Informational Text ● *See This!* **Lexile:** BR ● *Places to See* **Lexile:** BR ● *Places to See* **Lexile:** BR ● *My Trip to Yellowstone* **Lexile:** 370L	**Oral Vocabulary Words:** *country* *travel* *careful* *purpose* *connect* **Category Words:** Location Words Synonyms
Week 3 **Look to the Sky** **Essential Question:** What do you see in the sky? **Genre Focus:** Fantasy	**Anchor Text:** *Bringing Down the Moon* **Genre:** Fantasy **Paired Selection:** "Day and Night Sky" **Genre:** Informational Text	"Up, Up, Up!" **Lexile:** 90L	"A View from the Moon" **Genre:** Informational Text	**Genre:** Fiction ● *Going Up* **Lexile:** 100L ● *In the Clouds* **Lexile:** 50L ● *In the Clouds* **Lexile:** BR ● *How Sun and Moon Found Home* **Lexile:** 300L	**Oral Vocabulary Words:** *distance* *recognize* *space* *challenge* *surface* **Category Words:** Opposites Similes

Units 7 and 8	Reading Digitally	Connect to Content: Social Studies	Extend Your Learning
Extend, Connect, and Assess	"The Way We Go to School" **Genre:** Online Article	**Genre Read-Aloud** "Our Country Celebrates!" **Activities** Time to Celebrate! Make a Holiday Postcard	**Choose Your Own Book**

Comprehension	Print Concepts	Phonological/ Phonemic Awareness	Phonics/Spelling/ Handwriting	High- Frequency Words	Writing and Grammar	Research and Inquiry
Make and Confirm Predictions Main Story Elements: Character, Setting, Events Headings	Left to Right, Top to Bottom Tracking Capitalization Parts of a Book	**Phonological Awareness:** Syllable Addition **Phonemic Awareness:** Phoneme Isolation, Blending, and Segmentation	**Phonics:** /j/j, /kw/qu **Consonant/Vowel Review:** /a/a, /b/b, /k/c, /k/ck, /k/k, /d/d, /e/e, /f/f, /g/g, /h/h, /i/i, /l/l, /m/m, /n/n, /o/o, /p/p, /r/r, /s/s, /t/t, /u/u, /v/v, /w/w, /ks/x **Spelling:** Words with j, qu; here, me **Handwriting:** Upper and Lowercase Jj, Qq **Decodable Readers:** "Get It Quick"; "Jen Is Quick!"	here me **Build Your Word Bank:** about, may, away	**Write About the Text:** Expository **Writing Skill:** End Punctuation **Writing Trait:** Use Complete Sentences **Grammar:** Sentences (with Prepositions)	**Project:** Kinds of Vehicles
Reread Fact and Opinion Captions	Quotation Marks Sentence Boundaries Parts of a Book	**Phonological Awareness:** Identify and Produce Rhyming Words **Phonemic Awareness:** Phoneme Isolation, Blending, and Substitution	**Phonics:** /y/y, /z/z **Consonant/Vowel Review:** /a/a, /b/b, /k/c, /k/ck, /k/k, /d/d, /e/e, /f/f, /g/g, /h/h, /i/i, /j/j, /l/l, /m/m, /n/n, /o/o, /p/p, /kw/qu, /r/r, /s/s, /t/t, /u/u, /v/v, /w/w, /ks/x **Spelling:** Words with y, z; this, what **Handwriting:** Upper and Lowercase Yy, Zz **Decodable Readers:** "Yes, Zack Can Go!"; "Rex, Kim, and Zig"	this what **Build Your Word Bank:** or, each, please	**Write About the Text:** Expository **Writing Skill:** End Punctuation **Writing Trait:** Sentence Length **Grammar:** Sentences (with Prepositions)	**Project:** An Important American
Make and Confirm Predictions Events: Problem and Solution Headings	Quotation Marks Left to Right, Top to Bottom Tracking Parts of a Book	**Phonological Awareness:** Syllable Deletion **Phonemic Awareness:** Phoneme Identity, Categorization, and Addition	**Phonics:** Review /u/u, /g/g, /w/w, /ks/x, /v/v, /j/j, /kw/qu, /y/y, /z/z; r-Blends **Consonant/Vowel Review:** /a/a, /b/b, /k/c, /k/ck, /k/k, /d/d, /e/e, /f/f, /g/g, /h/h, /i/i, /j/j, /l/l, /m/m, /n/n, /o/o, /p/p, /kw/qu, /r/r, /s/s, /t/t, /u/u, /v/v, /w/w, /ks/x, /y/y, /z/z **Long Vowel Express (optional):** Long o (o_e) **Spelling Pattern:** it pattern **Handwriting:** u, g, w, x, v, j, qu, z; r-Blends **Decodable Readers:** "Zig-Zag Jet Can Zip"; "A Big Trip for Gram"	for have they of said want here me this what **Build Your Word Bank:** from, how, pretty, water, these, yellow, people, work, funny, about, may, away, or, each, please	**Write About the Text:** Expository **Writing Skill:** Left-to-Right and Top-to-Bottom Progression **Writing Trait:** Use Complete Sentences **Extended Writing:** Fantasy **Grammar:** Sentences (with Prepositions)	**Project:** Objects in the Sky

Scope and Sequence

Unit 9: How Things Change The Big Idea: How do things change?	Literature Big Book	Shared Read	Interactive Read Aloud	Leveled Readers	Vocabulary
Week 1 **Growing Up** **Essential Question:** How can you help out at home? **Genre Focus:** Realistic Fiction	**Anchor Text:** *Peter's Chair* **Genre:** Realistic Fiction **Paired Selection:** "Mom's Helpers" **Genre:** Drama	"Jake and Dale Help!" **Lexile:** 300L	"Helping Out at Home" **Genre:** Informational Text	**Genre:** Fiction ● *Let Me Help You* **Lexile:** 90L ● *How Can Jane Help?* **Lexile:** 140L ● *How Can Jane Help?* **Lexile:** 180L ● *I Used to Help Too* **Lexile:** 240L	**Oral Vocabulary Words:** chores contribute member organize accomplish **Category Words:** Household Furniture Prefixes and Suffixes
Week 2 **Good Citizens** **Essential Question:** What do good citizens do? **Genre Focus:** Fantasy	**Anchor Text:** *Hen Hears Gossip* **Genre:** Fantasy **Paired Selection:** "Team Up to Clean Up" **Genre:** Informational Text	"We Can Play" **Lexile:** 220L	"The Little Red Hen" **Genre:** Fable	**Genre:** Fantasy ● *Mike Helps Out* **Lexile:** BR ● *Clive and His Friend* **Lexile:** 60L ● *Clive and His Friend* **Lexile:** 110L ● *Farmer White's Best Friend* **Lexile:** 460L	**Oral Vocabulary Words:** citizen respect tidy necessary hauled **Category Words:** Farm Animals Question Words
Week 3 **Our Natural Resources** **Essential Question:** How can things in nature be used to make new things? **Genre Focus:** Informational Text: Nonfiction	**Anchor Text:** *Bread Comes to Life* **Genre:** Informational Text **Paired Selection:** "Nature Artists" **Genre:** Informational Text	"Look! A Home!" **Lexile:** 170L	"Nature's Art Fair" **Genre:** Drama	**Genre:** Informational Text ● *Look Where It Is From* **Lexile:** 40L ● *What's for Breakfast?* **Lexile:** 110L ● *What's for Breakfast?* **Lexile:** 30L ● *Nature at the Craft Fair* **Lexile:** 410L	**Oral Vocabulary Words:** natural resources create designs weave knowledge **Category Words:** Foods Made from Grain Sentence Clues

Comprehension	Print Concepts	Phonological/ Phonemic Awareness	Phonics/Spelling/ Handwriting	High-Frequency Words	Writing and Grammar	Research and Inquiry
Ask and Answer Questions Events: Sequence Format of a Play	Left to Right, Top to Bottom Tracking; Return Sweep Locate Printed Word Parts of a Book	**Phonological Awareness:** Syllable Segmentation **Phonemic Awareness:** Phoneme Identity, Phoneme Blending, Phoneme Deletion	**Phonics:** Long *a*: *a_e* **Consonant/Vowel Review:** /a/*a*, /b/*b*, /k/*c*, /k/*ck*, /k/*k*, /d/*d*, /e/*e*, /f/*f*, /g/*g*, /h/*h*, /i/*i*, /j/*j*, /l/*l*, /m/*m*, /n/*n*, /o/*o*, /p/*p*, /kw/*qu*, /r/*r*, /s/*s*, /t/*t*, /u/*u*, /v/*v*, /w/*w*, /ks/*x*, /y/*y*, /z/*z* **Extend the Lesson:** Digraph *sh* **Spelling:** Words with Long *a*: *a_e*; *help, too* **Handwriting:** Write Sentences with *a_e* Words **Decodable Readers:** "Jake Made Cake" "We Help Make It!"	*help* *too* **Build Your Word Bank:** *other, into, more*	**Write About the Text:** Expository **Writing Skill:** Stay on the Lines **Writing Trait:** Words That Connect Ideas **Grammar:** Adjectives	**Project:** Helping Out at Home
Reread Events: Cause and Effect Captions	Left to Right, Top to Bottom Tracking Capitalization Parts of a Book	**Phonological Awareness:** Identify and Produce Rhyming Words **Phonemic Awareness:** Phoneme Identity, Phoneme Blending, Phoneme Deletion	**Phonics:** Long *i*: *i_e* **Consonant/Vowel Review:** /a/*a*, /b/*b*, /k/*c*, /k/*ck*, /k/*k*, /d/*d*, /e/*e*, /f/*f*, /g/*g*, /h/*h*, /i/*i*, /j/*j*, /l/*l*, /m/*m*, /n/*n*, /o/*o*, /p/*p*, /kw/*qu*, /r/*r*, /s/*s*, /t/*t*, /u/*u*, /v/*v*, /w/*w*, /ks/*x*, /y/*y*, /z/*z* **Extend the Lesson:** Digraph *ch* **Spelling:** Words with Long *i*: *i_e*; *has, play* **Handwriting:** Write Sentences with *i_e* Words **Decodable Readers:** "Lake Time Fun" "Pike Lane"	*has* *play* **Build Your Word Bank:** *find, over, were*	**Write About the Text:** Expository **Writing Skill:** Sentence Capitalization **Writing Trait:** Sequence **Grammar:** Adjectives (Including Articles)	**Project:** Being a Good Citizen
Reread Details: Time Order Photographs	Distinguish Letters from Words Parts of a Book	**Phonological Awareness:** Segment and Blend Syllables **Phonemic Awareness:** Phoneme Identity, Phoneme Blending, Phoneme Substitution	**Phonics:** Long *o*: *o_e* **Consonant/Vowel Review:** /a/*a*, /b/*b*, /k/*c*, /k/*ck*, /k/*k*, /d/*d*, /e/*e*, /f/*f*, /g/*g*, /h/*h*, /i/*i*, /j/*j*, /l/*l*, /m/*m*, /n/*n*, /o/*o*, /p/*p*, /kw/*qu*, /r/*r*, /s/*s*, /t/*t*, /u/*u*, /v/*v*, /w/*w*, /ks/*x*, /y/*y*, /z/*z* **Spelling Pattern:** *oke* pattern **Handwriting:** Write Sentences with *o_e* Words **Decodable Readers:** "Jo Made It at Home" "Joke Note"	*where* *look* **Build Your Word Bank:** *know, would, write*	**Write About the Text:** Expository **Writing Skill:** End Punctuation **Writing Trait:** Focus on One Idea **Grammar:** Adjectives	**Project:** Products from Trees

Scope and Sequence

Unit 10: Thinking Outside the Box **The Big Idea:** How can new ideas help us?	Literature Big Book	Shared Read	Interactive Read Aloud	Leveled Readers	Vocabulary
Week 1 **Problem Solvers** **Essential Question:** What can happen when we work together? **Genre Focus:** Fantasy	**Anchor Text:** *What's the Big Idea, Molly?* **Genre:** Fantasy **Paired Selection:** "Better Together" **Genre:** Opinion Text	"A Good Time for Luke!" **Lexile:** 270L	"The Elves and the Shoemaker" **Genre:** Fairy Tale	**Genre:** Fantasy ● *Animal Band* **Lexile:** BR ● *We Want Honey* **Lexile:** 180L ● *We Want Honey* **Lexile:** 90L ○ *A Good Idea* **Lexile:** 290L	**Oral Vocabulary Words:** *decide* *opinion* *ragged* *marvel* *grateful* **Category Words:** Directions Sentence Clues
Week 2 **Sort It Out** **Essential Question:** In what ways are things alike? How are they different? **Genre Focus:** Poetry	**Anchor Text:** *All Kinds of Families!* **Genre:** Poetry **Paired Selection:** "Good for You" **Genre:** Opinion Text	"We Come on Time!" **Lexile:** 270L	"The Perfect Color" **Genre:** Informational Text	**Genre:** Fiction ● *My Box* **Lexile:** BR ● *Let's Make a Band* **Lexile:** 250L ● *Let's Make a Band* **Lexile:** 30L ○ *Going Camping* **Lexile:** 300L	**Oral Vocabulary Words:** *sort* *similar* *perfect* *endless* *experiment* **Category Words:** Opposites Antonyms
Week 3 **Protect Our Earth** **Essential Question:** What ideas can you suggest to protect the environment? **Genre Focus:** Informational Text: Nonfiction	**Anchor Text:** *Panda Kindergarten* **Genre:** Informational Text **Paired Selection:** "Save Big Blue!" **Genre:** Informational Text	"Who Can Help?" **Lexile:** 360L	"Protect the Environment" **Genre:** Informational Text	**Genre:** Informational Text ● *Help Clean Up* **Lexile:** 90L ● *Let's Save Earth* **Lexile:** 160L ● *Let's Save Earth* **Lexile:** 110L ○ *Babysitters for Seals* **Lexile:** 300L	**Oral Vocabulary Words:** *environment* *protect* *recycle* *wisely* *encourage* **Category Words:** Names of Baby Animals Suffixes

Units 9 and 10	Reading Digitally	Connect to Content: Science	Extend Your Learning
Extend, Connect, and Assess	"What's Next?" **Genre:** Online Article	**Genre Read-Aloud** "Little and Big" and "Buttons" **Activities** Ways to Sort Observe and Sort	**Choose Your Own Book**

Comprehension	Print Concepts	Phonological/ Phonemic Awareness	Phonics/Spelling/ Handwriting	High-Frequency Words	Writing and Grammar	Research and Inquiry
Make and Confirm Predictions Events: Sequence Photographs	Left to Right, Top to Bottom Tracking; Return Sweep Parts of a Book	**Phonological Awareness:** Syllable Segmentation **Phonemic Awareness:** Phoneme Identity, Blending, and Substitution	**Phonics:** Long *u*: *u_e* **Consonant/Vowel Review:** /a/a, /b/b, /k/c, /k/ck, /k/k, /d/d, /e/e, /f/f, /g/g, /h/h, /i/i, /j/j, /l/l, /m/m, /n/n, /o/o, /p/p, /kw/qu, /r/r, /s/s, /t/t, /u/u, /v/v, /w/w, /ks/x, /y/y, /z/z **Spelling:** Words with Long *u*: *u_e; good, who* **Handwriting:** Write *u_e* Words **Decodable Readers:** "Tube Race"; "The Sad Duke"	*good* *who* **Build Your Word Bank:** *part, only, words*	**Write About the Text:** Expository **Writing Skill:** Left-to-Right and Top-to-Bottom Progression **Writing Trait:** Descriptive Words **Grammar:** Pronouns	**Project:** Working Together Interview
Ask and Answer Questions Poetry: Rhyme Labels	Left to Right, Top to Bottom Tracking; Return Sweep Parts of a Book	**Phonological Awareness:** Syllable Substitution **Phonemic Awareness:** Phoneme Identity, Blending, and Substitution	**Phonics:** Long *e*: *e, ee, e_e* **Consonant/Vowel Review:** /a/a, /b/b, /k/c, /k/ck, /k/k, /d/d, /e/e, /f/f, /g/g, /h/h, /i/i, /j/j, /l/l, /m/m, /n/n, /o/o, /p/p, /kw/qu, /r/r, /s/s, /t/t, /u/u, /v/v, /w/w, /ks/x, /y/y, /z/z **Extend the Lesson:** Digraph *th* **Spelling Pattern:** Words with Long *e*: *e, ee, e_e; come, does* **Handwriting:** Write Words with *e, ee, e_e* **Decodable Readers:** "Pete and Eve"; "Pete Can Fix It"	*come* *does* **Build Your Word Bank:** *first, sound, their*	**Write About the Text:** Expository **Writing Skill:** Stretch Sounds to Write Words **Writing Trait:** Sentence Length **Grammar:** Pronouns	**Project:** Name Sort
Reread Topic and Details Captions	Left to Right, Top to Bottom Tracking; Return Sweep Parts of a Book Distinguish Letters from Words	**Phonological Awareness:** Identify Alliteration **Phonemic Awareness:** Phoneme Segmentation, Blending, and Substitution	**Phonics:** Long *a, i, o, u, e*; Final Blends **Consonant/Vowel Review:** /a/a, /b/b, /k/c, /k/ck, /k/k, /d/d, /e/e, /f/f, /g/g, /h/h, /i/i, /j/j, /l/l, /m/m, /n/n, /o/o, /p/p, /kw/qu, /r/r, /s/s, /t/t, /u/u, /v/v, /w/w, /ks/x, /y/y, /z/z **Spelling Pattern:** *eep* pattern **Handwriting:** Write Sentences with Long *a, i, o, u, e* **Decodable Readers:** "We Can Save!"; "We Can Use It!"	*help* *too* *play* *has* *where* *look* *who* *good* *come* *does* **Build Your Word Bank:** *other, into, more, find, over, were, know, would, write, part, only, words, first, sound, their*	**Write About the Text:** Expository **Writing Skill:** Use Word Bank **Writing Trait:** Descriptive Words **Extended Writing:** Opinion Writing **Grammar:** Pronouns	**Project:** Protecting Our Planet

Social Emotional Development

Emotional Self Regulation
Manages feelings, emotions, and words with decreasing support from adults

» As the child collaborates with a partner, the child uses appropriate words calmly when disagreeing. »

Behavioral Self Regulation
Manages actions, behaviors, and words with decreasing support from adults

»   »

Rules and Routines
Follows classroom rules and routines with increasing independence

Transitioning from one activity to the next, the child follows established routines, such as putting away materials, without disrupting the class. »

Working Memory
Maintains and manipulates distinct pieces of information over short periods of time

»   »   »

Focus Attention
Maintains focus and sustains attention with minimal adult supports

» During Center Time, the child stays focused on the activity assigned and is able to stop working on the activity when it is time to move on to a different task.

Relationships and Prosocial Behaviors
Engages in and maintains positive relationships and interactions with familiar adults and children

»

Social Problem Solving
Uses basic problem solving skills to resolve conflicts with other children

»   »

Self Awareness
Recognizes self as a unique individual as well as belonging to a family, community, or other groups; expresses confidence in own skills

»

Creativity
Expresses creativity in thinking and communication

»

Initiative
Demonstrates initiative and independence

» When working independently, the child understands when to ask for help and gets the help needed. »

Task Persistence
Sets reasonable goals and persists to complete the task

»

Logic and Reasoning
Thinks critically to effectively solve a problem or make a decision

»

Planning and Problem Solving
Uses planning and problem solving strategies to achieve goals

»   »

Flexible Thinking
Demonstrates flexibility in thinking and behavior

»

Throughout the grades, students continue to progress in each aspect of their social emotional growth. See the Social Emotional Development checklists for each grade span to monitor students' progress.

GRADE 2 GRADE 3 GRADE 4 GRADE 5

During class discussions, the child can wait until called upon to provide a response, without shouting out.

When responding to a text, the child can identify text evidence from notes previously recorded.

The child willingly works with any other child in the class on partner or group activities that are assigned.

When working on a project in a small group, the child negotiates roles and cooperates with others to complete the task.

In class discussion, the child is not fearful of sharing a unique perspective while respecting the opinions of others.

The child finds a creative way to gather information needed for a writing assignment.

When assigned to read a difficult text, the child applies routines or strategies learned to complete the reading.

Through logic and reasoning, the child is able to figure out how the author's choices of words and structures affect the communication of ideas.

When working on a long-term research project, the student can think through how to complete the different parts of the assignment over a period of time.

As the child struggles with an activity, he or she can determine a different way to complete the activity successfully.

(t) Radius Images/Image Source; (b) Patrick Foto/Shutterstock

Text Complexity Rubric

In *Wonders*, children are asked to read or listen to a range of texts within a text set to build knowledge. The various texts include:

- Literature Big Books
- Shared Reads
- Paired Selections
- Leveled Readers

Understanding the various factors that contribute to the complexity of a text, as well as considering what each child brings to the text, will help you determine the appropriate levels of scaffolds for children. Quantitative measures, such as Lexile scores, are only one element of text complexity. Understanding qualitative factors and reader and task considerations is also important to fully evaluate the complexity of a text.

At the beginning of each text set in the *Wonders* Teacher's Edition, information on the three components of text complexity for the texts is provided.

Qualitative

The qualitative features of a text relate to its content or meaning. They include meaning/purpose, structure, language, and knowledge demands.

Low Complexity	Moderate Complexity	High Complexity
Meaning/Purpose The text has a single layer of meaning explicitly stated. The author's purpose or central idea of the text is immediately obvious and clear.	**Meaning/Purpose** The text has a blend of explicit and implicit details, few uses of multiple meanings, and isolated instances of metaphor. The author's purpose may not be explicitly stated but is readily inferred from a reading of the text.	**Meaning/Purpose** The text has multiple levels of meaning and there may be intentional ambiguity. The author's purpose may not be clear and/or is subject to interpretation.
Structure The text is organized in a straightforward manner, with explicit transitions to guide the reader.	**Structure** The text is largely organized in a straightforward manner, but may contain isolated incidences of shifts in time/place, focus, or pacing.	**Structure** The text is organized in a way that initially obscures meaning and has the reader build to an understanding.
Language The language of the text is literal, although there may be some rhetorical devices.	**Language** Figurative language is used to build on what has already been stated plainly in the text.	**Language** Figurative language is used throughout the text; multiple interpretations may be possible.
Knowledge Demands The text does not require extensive knowledge of the topic.	**Knowledge Demands** The text requires some knowledge of the topic.	**Knowledge Demands** The text requires significant knowledge of the topic.

Quantitative

Wonders provides the Lexile score for each text in the text set.

Low Complexity	Moderate Complexity	High Complexity
Lexile Score Text is below or at the lower end of the grade-level band according to a quantitative reading measure.	**Lexile Score** Text is in the midrange of the grade-level band according to a quantitative reading measure.	**Lexile Score** Text is at the higher end of or above the grade-level band according to a quantitative reading measure.

Reader and Task Considerations

This component of text complexity considers the motivation, knowledge, and experiences a child brings to the text. Task considerations take into account the complexity generated by the tasks children are asked to complete and the questions they are expected to answer.

In *Wonders*, children are asked to interact with the texts in many different ways. Texts such as the Shared Reads and Anchor Texts are read over multiple days and include tasks that increase in difficulty. The complexity level provided for each text considers the highest-level tasks students are asked to complete with the texts.

Low Complexity	Moderate Complexity	High Complexity
Reader The text is well within the student's developmental level of understanding and does not require extensive background knowledge.	**Reader** The text is within the student's developmental level of understanding, but some levels of meaning may be impeded by lack of prior exposure.	**Reader** The text is at the upper boundary of the student's developmental level of understanding and will require that the student has background knowledge of the topic.

Task

The questions and tasks provided for all texts are at various levels of compexity, ensuring that all students can interact with the text in meaningful ways.

Index

A

T367, T379, T387, T393, T420, T445, T457, T465, T471, **9:** T37, T61, T69, T75, T115, T139, T148, T153, T193, T205, T217, T225, T231, **10:** T256, T268, T276, T279, T290, T291, T297, T303, T307, T311, T314, T315, T317, T346, T354, T357, T368, T369, T375, T381, T389, T393, T395, T412, T424, T432, T435, T446, T453, T459, T467, T471, T473

choral reading, 1: T28, S34, S64, T76, S94, T116, T139, T151, T158, T201, T214, T221, **2:** T280, T302, T362, T384, T444, **3:** T28, T50, T110, T132, T192, T214, **4:** T358, **5:** T28, T106, T184, **6:** T268, T346, T424, **7:** T28, T37, T49, T73, T115, T143, T151, T184, T193, T205, T229, **8:** T268, T277, T289, T346, T355, T424, T433, T469, **9:** T14, T26, T34, T37, T48, T49, T55, T65, T73, T115, T127, T143, T151, T193, T205, T211, T221, T229, **10:** T270, T279, T307, T315, T348, T357, T385, T393, T435, T463, T471

echo reading, 2: T265, T347, T393, T429, T445, T453, T457

expression, 1: T203, T229, T237, **5:** T195, **7:** T69, T75, T147, T153, T225, T231, **8:** T309, T312, T315, T331, T387, T390, T393, T409, T461, T465, T468, T471, **10:** T255, T385, T392, T395, T463, T470

in connected text, 1: T111, T233, **2:** T321, T403, T485, **3:** T151, T233, **5:** T65, T143, T221, **6:** T305, T383, T461, **7:** T65, T143, T221, **8:** T305, T383, T461, **9:** T65, T143, T221, **10:** T307, T385, T463

intonation, 1: T147, T155, T229, T237, **7:** T65, T72, T143, T150, T221, T228, **8:** T305, T383, **9:** T65, T72, T143, T150

modeling fluent reading, 1: T13, T29, T51, T95, T133, T177, **2:** T265, T275, T347, T429, T438–T439, **3:** T13, T23, T51, T95, T111, T177, T181, T186, T193, **4:** T265, T343, T421, T469, T477, T483, **5:** T13, T61, T69, T91, T139, T169, **6:** T253, T331, T409, **7:** T13, T29, T39, T91, T107, T117, T169, T185, T195, **8:** T253, T269, T279, T331, T342, T347, T357, T409, T425, T435, **9:** T13, T29, T39, T91, T107, T117, T169, T185, T195, **10:** T255, T271, T281, T333, T349, T359, T411, T427

partner reading. *See* **Fluency: rereading for.**

phrasing, 2: T265

rate, 1: T39, T59, T121, T158, T177, T203, T223, T240, **2:** T291, T311, T373, T393, T455, T475, **3:** T39, T59, T121, T141, T223, **4:** T291, T369, T447, **5:** T39, T117, T195, **6:** T269, T279, T357, T435, **7:** T39, T117, T195, **8:** T279, T357, T435, **9:** T39, T117, T195, **10:** T281, T359, T437

reading aloud, 1: T65, T73, T79, T133, T147, T155, T161, T193, T237, **3:** T16

reading for, 1: T37, T65, T73, T79, T119, T147, T155, T161, T215, T243, **2:** T303, T371, T445, T467, **3:** T29, T37, T65, T119, T201, T215, **6:** T277, T355, T383, T390, T394, T433, T461, T468, **7:** T37, T115, T193, T221,

T228, **8:** T277, T312, T355, T383, T390, T433, T461, T468, **9:** T37, T115, T228, T233, **10:** T279, T357, T385, T392, T435, T463, T470

read with purpose and understanding. *See* **Shared read.**

rereading for, 1: T39, T59, T70, T141, T152, T203, T223, T234, T241, **2:** T291, T311, T322, T329, T373, T393, T404, T429, T455, T475, T486, T493, **3:** T39, T59, T70, T77, T121, T141, T152, T159, T203, T222–T223, T234, T241, **6:** T316, T331, T355, T394, T433, T472, **7:** T37, T76, T115, T154, T193, T232, **8:** T265, T277, T316, T331, T355, T394, T409, T420, T433, T434, T472, **9:** T13, T37, T76, T115, T154, T228, T232, **10:** T255, T279, T318, T333, T357, T396, T411, T435

sound/spelling, 1: T59, T69, T96, T108, T130, T139, T151, T178, T190, T198, T212, T221, T233, **2:** T266–T267, T278, T286, T300, T309, T321, T348, T360, T368, T382, T391, T403, T430, T442, T450, T464, T473, T484–T485, **3:** T24, T26, T34, T48, T57, T69, T96, T108, T116, T130, T139, T151, T178, T190, T198, T212, T220, **4:** T266, T278, T286, T301, T307, T317, T344, T356, T364, T378, T385, T395, T422, T434, T442, T456, T463, T473, T480, **5:** T14, T26, T34, T48, T55, T65, T92, T104, T112, T126, T133, T143, T170, T182, T190, T204, T211, T221, **6:** T254, T266, T274, T288, T295, T332, T344, T352, T366, T373, T383, T410, T422, T430, T444, T451, T461, **7:** T26, T34, T48, T55, T65, T104, T112, T126, T133, T143, T182, T190, T204, T211, T221, **8:** T254, T266, T274, T288, T295, T305, T332, T344, T352, T366, T373, T383, T410, T422, T430, T435, T451, T461, **9:** T14, T26, T34, T48, T55, T65, T92, T104, T112, T126, T133, T143, T170, T182, T190, T204, T211, T221, **10:** T256, T268, T276, T290, T297, T307, T346, T354, T368, T375, T385, T412, T424, T432, T446, T453, T463

track print, 1: T37, T49, T119, T131, T201, T214, **2:** T302, T454

word automaticity, 1: S27, S57, T57, S87, T119, T139, T201, T221, **2:** T289, T309, T371, **3:** T57, T119, T139, T201, **4:** T289, T367, T445, **5:** T37, T55, T115, T133, T193, **6:** T277, T295, T355, T373, T433, T451, **7:** T37, T55, T115, T133, T193, T211, **8:** T277, T295, T355, T373, T433, T451, **9:** T37, T55, T115, T133, T193, T211, **10:** T279, T297, T357, T375, T435, T453

writing, 2: T347, T429, **3:** T13, T177, **4:** T265, T421, **5:** T91, T169, **6:** T331, T409, **7:** T13, T91, T169, **8:** T253, T331, T409, **9:** T91, T169, **10:** T255, T333, T411. *See also* **Approaching Level Options: fluency; Beyond Level Options: fluency; On Level Options: fluency.**

Format of a play. *See* **Comprehension: format of a play.**

Foundational skills. *See* **Fluency; High-frequency words; Phonemic awareness; Phonics/Word analysis; Phonological awareness; Print concepts.**

G

Genre

literature/fiction/prose and poetry

fable, 1: T33, S48, S55, S85, T115, **3:** T33, **4:** T441, **9:** T111

fairy tale, 1: S18, S25, **5:** T111, **6:** T429, **10:** T275

fantasy, 6: T308, T314, T326–T331, T340–T343, T377, **7:** T164–T169, T178–T181, T187, T197, T209, T216, T224, T230, **8:** T404–T408, T418, T456, T470, T478–487, T586–T587, **9:** T86–T91, T100–T103, T102, T138, T146, T152, **10:** T248–T254, T264–T267, T302, T310, T316

fiction, 1: T8, T22, S60, T64–T65, T72, T78, S90, T90, T104, T146, T154, T160, **2:** T480, T488, T494, **3:** T8, T8–T13, T18, T20, T22, T64, T72, T78, T90–T95, T94, T104, T146, T154, T160, T172, T186, T227–T228, T236, **5:** T60, T68, T74, **8:** T327, T340, **9:** T60, T68, T74

folktale/folklore, 1: S30, **2:** T285, **3:** T115, **4:** T285, **6:** T351, **7:** T189

myth, 8: T273

personal narrative, 4: T374–T375, T488–T499, **7:** T122

play, 9: T44–T45, T46, T59, T189

poetry, 1: T20, S26, T42, S56, S86, T144, T170, T206–T211, **2:** T424, T424–T429, T438, **6:** T284–T286, T299, **7:** T44–T45, T46–T47, **10:** T328–T332, T329, T332, T342–T345, T344

realistic fiction, 4: T338, T352, T390, T398, T404, **5:** T8, T22–T25, T60, T230, **6:** T248–T253, T259, T262–T265, T300, T308, T378, T386, T392, T404–T409, T418–T421, T455, T456, T464, T470, **7:** T86–T91, T100–T103, T137, T138, T146, T152, **8:** T248–T253, T252, T262–T265, T263, T264, T299, T300, T308, T314, T464, T465, **9:** T8–T12, T22–T25, T23, T60, T68, T74, **10:** T380, T388, T394

nonfiction

expository text, 2: T500–T501

informational text, 1: S78, T172, T186, T205, T219, T227, T228, T236, T242, **2:** T260–T265, T274, T315–T316, T324, T330, T344, T356–T359, T398, T408, T412, **3:** T242, **4:** T260–T265, T274, T312, T320, T326, T416–T421, T430, T468, T476, T482, **5:** T86–T91, T100, T138, T146, T152, T164–T169, T178, T216,

Key 1 = Unit 1

M

Main story elements. *See* Comprehension: main story elements.

Media Literacy, 8: T292–T293

Mental images, creating. *See* Comprehension strategies: visualize.

Mentor text. *See* Expert models.

Monitor comprehension: reread. *See* Comprehension strategies: reread.

Multimodal learning, 1: T16, T57, T98, T139, T180, T220, 2: T268, T309, T391, T432, T473, 3: T57, T139, T221, 4: T307, T385, T424, T463, 5: T16, T55, T94, T133, T172, T211, T256, 6: T295, T334, T373, 7: T16, T55, T94, T133, T172, T211, 8: T256, T295, T334, T373, T451, 9: T16, T54, T94, T133, T172, T211, 10: T258, T297, T336, T451

Music

chants. *See* Songs, rhymes, chants.

Music/Fine Arts activities, 1: T14–T15, T34–T35, T38, T88, T96–T97, T103, T116, T124, T148, T178–T179, 2: T267, T286, T349, T368, T422, T431, 3: T14–T15, T25, T34, T97, T102–T103, T116, T124, T138, T178–T179, T184, T196, T198, T220, 4: T267, T405, 5: T15, T93, 6: T255, T324, T333, 7: T6, T171, 8: T246, T254–T255, T324, T332–T333, T338, 9: T14–T15, T34, T84, T92–T93, T98, T110, T120, T170–T171, T200–T203, T230–T231, 10: T246, T256–T257, T329, T334–T335, T353, T378

N

Narrative text. *See* Writing genre: narrative.

Narrator. *See* Comprehension: narrator.

Notes, taking, 6: T356, 7: T18, T96, T174

Nursery Rhymes

chants. *See* Songs, rhymes, chants.

O

On Level Options

comprehension, 1: T72, T77, T159, T241, 2: T324–T325, T329, T411, T488–T489, T493, 3: T77, T159, T241, 4: T325, T403, T481, 5: T73, T151, T229, 6: T313, T391, T469, 7: T73, T151, T229, 8: T313, T391, T469, 9: T73, T151, T229, 10: T315, T393, T471

fluency, 1: T73, T155, T237, T241, 2: T325, T329, T489, 3: T77, T241, 5: T72, T150, T228, 6: T312, T390, T468, 7: T72, T150, T228, 8: T309, T312, T387, T390, T465, T468, 9: T69, T72, T147, T150, T225,

T228, 10: T311, T314, T389, T392, T467, T470

high-frequency words, 1: T76–T77, T158–T159, T240–T241, 2: T324, T328, T410–T411, T492–T493, 3: T76, T158–T159, T240–T241, 4: T325, T403, T481, 5: T73, T151, T229, 6: T313, T394, T469, 7: T73, T151, T229, 8: T313, T391, T469, 9: T73, T151, T229, 10: T315, T393, T471

Leveled Reader lessons, 1: T72–T73, T154–T155, T236–T237, 2: T324–T325, T406–T407, T488–T489, 3: T72–T73, T154–T155, T236–T237, 4: T320–T321, T398–T399, T476–T477, 5: T68–T69, T146–T147, T224–T225, 6: T308–T309, T386–T387, T464–T465, 7: T68–T69, T146–T147, T224–T225, 8: T308–T309, T386–T387, T464–T465, 9: T68–T69, T146–T147, T224–T225, 10: T310–T311, T388–T389, T466–T467

phonemic awareness, 1: T74, T156, T238, 2: T326, T408, T490, 3: T74, T156, T238, 4: T322, T400, T478, 5: T70, T148, T226, 6: T310, T388, T466, 7: T70, T148, T226, 8: T310, T388, T466, 9: T70, T148, T226, 10: T312, T390, T468

phonics, 1: T75–T76, T157–T158, T239–T240, 2: T327–T328, T409–T410, T491–T492, 3: T75–T76, T157–T158, T239–T240, 4: T323–T324, T401–T402, T479, T481, 5: T71, T148–T149, T226–T227, 6: T311–T312, T389–T390, T467–T468, 7: T71–T72, T149–T150, T227–T228, 8: T311–T312, T389–T390, T467–T468, 9: T71–T72, T149–T150, T227–T228, 10: T313–T314, T391–T392, T469–T470

self-selected reading, 1: T77, T159, T241, 2: T329, T411, T493, 3: T77, T159, T241, 4: T325, T403, T481, 5: T73, T151, T229, 6: T313, T391, T469, 7: T73, T151, T229, 8: T313, T391, T469, 9: T73, T151, T229, 10: T315, T393, T471

Online instructions. *See* Digital learning.

Oral grammar. *See* Grammar.

Oral language, 1: S16–S17, T18, T20–T21, S24, S27–S28, T32, S38, T42–T43, S46–S47, S54, S57–S58, S68, S76–S77, S84, S87–S88, S98, T102–T103, T114, T124–T125, T184–T185, T196, T206–T207, 2: T270, T272–T273, T284, T354–T355, T366, T376–T377, T436–T437, T448, T458–T459, 3: T18, T20–T21, T32, T42–T43, T102–T103, T114, T124–T125, T184–T185, T196, T206–T207, 4: T272–T273, T284, T294–T295, T348, T350–T351, T362, T372–T373, T428–T429, T440, T450–T451, T475, 5: T20–T21, T32, T42–T43, T98–T99, T110, T120–T121, T176–T177, T188, T198–T199, 6: T260–T261, T272, T282–T283, T338–T339, T350, T360–T361, T416–T417, T428, T438–T439, 7: T20–T21, T32, T42–T43, T98–T99, T110, T120–T121, T176–T177, T188, T198–T199, 8: T260–T261, T272–T273, T282–T283, T338–T339, T350–T351, T360–T361, T416–T417, T428–T429, T438–T439, 9: T20–T21, T32, T42–T43, T98–T99, T110, T120–T121, T176–T177,

T188, T198–T199, 10: T262–T263, T274, T284–T285, T340–T341, T352, T362–T363, T418–T419, T430, T440–T441. *See also* Vocabulary: oral vocabulary.

Oral presentations, 1: S31, T55, S61, S91, T137, T219, 2: T389, T471, 3: T55, T137, T219, 4: T305, T308, T386, T460–T461, 5: T56, T134, T208–T209, 6: T293, T296, T371, T374, T449, T452, 7: T53, T56, T131, T134, T209, T212, 8: T293, T296, T371, T374, T449, T452, 9: T53, T56, T131, T134, T209, T212, 10: T295, T298, T373, T376, T451, T454

multimedia, 1: T55, T137, T219, 2: T307, T389–T390, T471, 3: T55, T137, T219, 4: T305, T383, T461, 5: T53, T131, T209, 6: T293, T371, T449, 7: T53, T131, T209, 8: T293, T371, T449, 9: T53, T131, T209, 10: T295, T373, T451

Oral vocabulary. *See* Vocabulary: oral vocabulary.

P

Paired selections

"Animal Homes," 7: T200–T203

"Baby Animals on the Move!" 1: T126–T127

"Be Safe," 3: T44–T37

"Be Safe in Bad Weather," 6: T440–T443

"Better Together," 10: T286–T289

"Bugs All Around," 2: T460–T463

"Cloud Watch," 6: T362–T365

"Community Garden, A," 4: T452–T453, T454–T455

"Covers," 6: T284–T285

"Day and Night Sky," 8: T440–T443

"Discover with Tools," 2: T296–T299

"Farmers Markets," 5: T200–T203

"Find the Shapes," 2: T378

"From a Seed to a Tree," 5: T122–T123, T124

"From Here to There," 8: T284–T287

"Good for You," 10: T364–T367

"Honey, I Love," 6: T284–T285

"How to Be a Friend," 1: T44–T45

"I Smell Springtime," 1: T208–T209

"Kitty Caught a Caterpillar," 7: T44–T45

"Mischievous Goat," 7: T44–T45

"Mom's Helpers," 9: T44–T47

"My Great Neighborhood," 4: T374–T375

"Nature Artists," 9: T200–T203

"Neighborhood, A," 3: T208–T211

"New Snow," 6: T284–T285

"Over in the Meadow," 7: T44–T45

"Rain Song," 6: T284–T285

"Save Big Blue!" 10: T442–T445

"Seed, The," 5: T46–T47

"See Our Country," 8: T362–T365

R

Key 1 = Unit 1

W